LSAT®

2007 Edition

Comprehensive Program

With 3 Real LSAT Practice Tests

Other Kaplan Books on Law School Admissions

LSAT 2007 Edition Premier Program

Get into Law School: A Strategic Approach

LSAT 180

LSAT Logic Games Workbook

LSAT®

2007 Edition

Comprehensive Program

WITH 3 REAL LSAT PRACTICE TESTS

The Staff of Kaplan Test Prep and Admissions

KAPLAN PUBLISHING

New York • Chicago

Contributing Editors: Ben Baron, Steven Marietti
Editorial Director: Jennifer Farthing
Editor: Eileen McDonnell
Production Artist: Jan Gladish
Cover Designer: Carly Schnur

Published by Kaplan Publishing, a division of Kaplan, Inc.
888 Seventh Ave.
New York, NY 10106

Materials used in this book were adapted from the following sources:
Dr. Ed Newman and Bob Verini, "The Kaplan Advantage™ Stress Management System" Copyright 1996, Kaplan, Inc.
Martin V. Melosi, "Hazardous Waste and Environmental Liability: An Historical Perspective," *Houston Law Review*, Volume 25: 741, 1988. Reprinted by permission.
Wendy S. Zeligson, "Pool Coverage, Press Access, and Presidential Debates: What's Wrong with This Picture?" *Cardozo Law Review*, Vol. 9, 1988. Reprinted by permission.
Dan W. Brock and Allen E. Buchanan, "The Profit Motive in Medicine," *Journal of Medicine and Philosophy*, Vol. 12, 1987. Reprinted by permission.
Fred Anderson, "The Republic Reborn by Steven Watts," *American Historical Review*, vol. 94, no. 2 (April 1989), p. 516. Reprinted by permission.
Judith Olans Brown, Phyllis Tropper Baumann, and Elaine Miller Melnick, "Equal Pay for Jobs of Comparable Worth: An Analysis of the Rhetoric," *Harvard Civil Rights & Civil Liberties Review*, No. 1, Winter 1986. Reprinted by permission; copyright 1988 by the President and Fellows of Harvard College.
Ward & Trent, et al, *The Cambridge History of English and American Literature.* New York: G.P. Putnam's Sons, 1907–21.
National Cancer Institute, "Molecular Test Can Predict Both the Risk of Breast Cancer Recurrence and Who Will Benefit From Chemotherapy." Posted 12/10/2004. www.cancer.gov/newscenter.
Reynolds, Anne, "Nazi Looted Art: The Holocaust Records Preservation Project, Part 1." Prologue Magazine, Fall 2002, Vol. 34, No. 3. Viewed 24 December, 2004. U.S. National Archives and Records Administration at www.archives.gov/publications.
Wollstonecraft, Mary, *A Vindication of the Rights of Woman*. Printed at Boston, by Peter Edes for Thomas and Andrews, Faust's statue, no. 45, Newbury-street, 1792.

Printed in the United States of America

June 2006
10 9 8 7 6 5 4 3 2 1

ISBN-13: 978-1-4195-4190-2
ISBN-10: 1-4195-4190-0

Kaplan Publishing books are available at special quantity discounts to use for sales promotions, employee premiums, or educational purposes. Please call our Special Sales Department to order or for more information at 800-621-9621, ext. 4444, e-mail kaplanpubsales@kaplan.com, or write to Kaplan Publishing, 30 South Wacker Drive, Suite 2500, Chicago, IL 60606-7481.

Table of Contents

How to Use the LSAT Comprehensive Program

Are you ready for a totally unique test prep experience?

The LSAT team at Kaplan understands what you are going through. First, you're facing perhaps the single most important test of your career. Second, you're struggling to balance your normal activities—social life, school, or even work—with LSAT prep. And finally, you need options about when to study, where to study, and most of all—*how to study*.

That's why you need the LSAT Comprehensive Program with real LSAT practice tests. It's *your* program—flexible and customizable. *You* control the variety and amount of study that best suits your skills and objectives. Since you learn best by varying study and practice methods, we made the Program interactive, with both book and online resources. And since the most test-like practice is the best practice, we offer three actual LSAT practice tests with Kaplan's detailed explanations!

To get you started, we put a Diagnostic Quiz and several essay prompts online so you can get used to moving between book and computer—and making the most of your Comprehensive Program components. Need to practice but can't take your book or computer with you? You can download the one-page study sheet of key strategies for study on the go.

Kaplan is the world leader in test prep. In this interactive program, the main techniques and approaches from Kaplan's classroom and tutoring programs are distilled in a clear, easy-to-grasp format. Here's the plan, step-by-step.

STEP 1: REGISTER YOUR PROGRAM ONLINE

To register, have your book in front of you. You will be prompted for the serial number on the lower left corner of the inside back cover. Go to:

kaptest.com/LSATbooksonline

Registration is important because:

1. It gives you access, through your online syllabus, to all the LSAT Comprehensive Program components that are not included between the covers of this book, such as your Diagnostic Quiz, essay writing practice, and links to Kaplan's best LSAT information.

2. It protects your Comprehensive Program so that your practice content remains exclusive to you.

3. It gives you access to important LSAT information and developments, along with any updates and additions to this book.

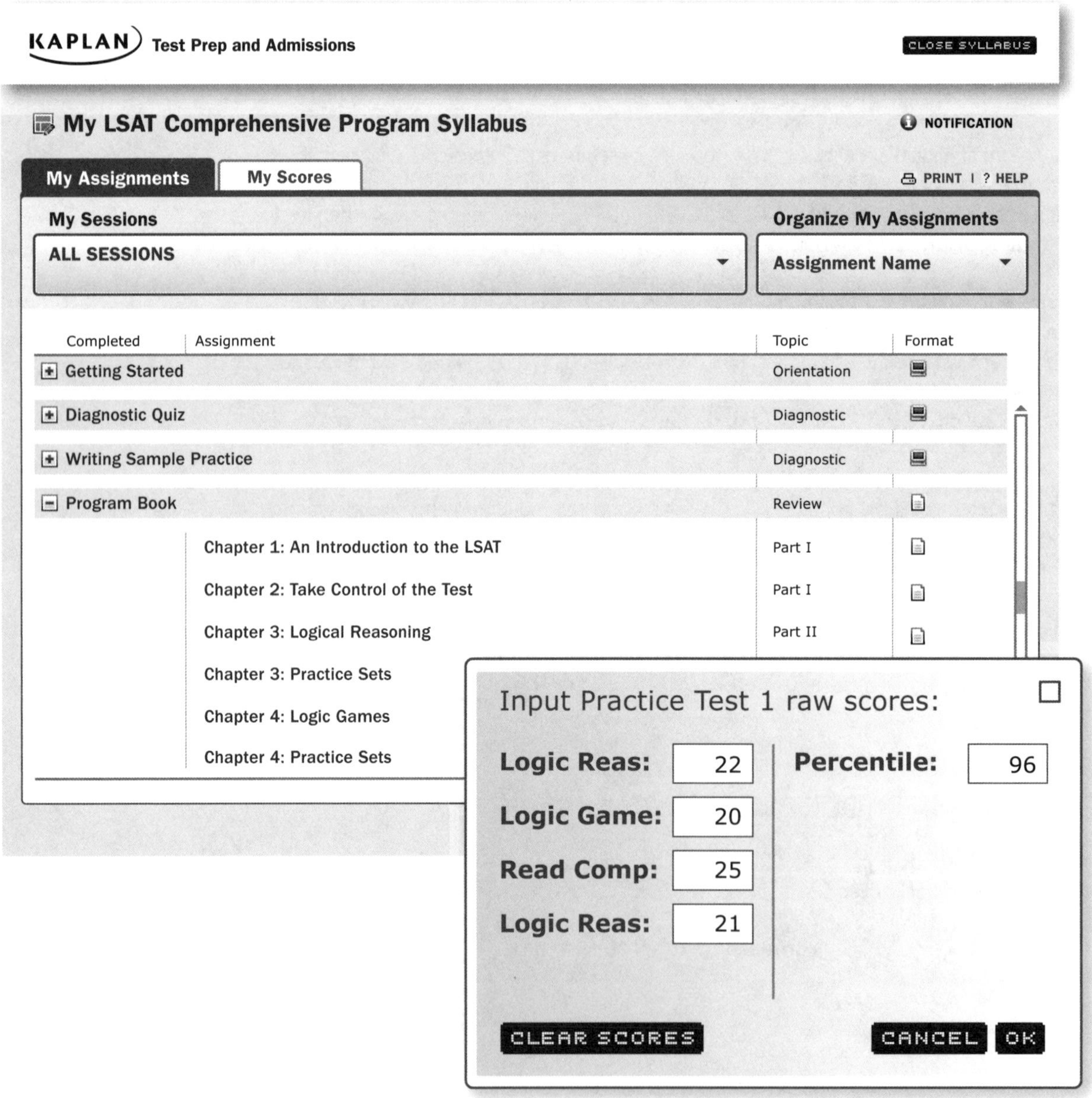

KAPLAN Test Prep and Admissions
CLOSE SYLLABUS
My LSAT Comprehensive Program Syllabus
NOTIFICATION
My Assignments
My Scores
PRINT | ? HELP
My Sessions
ALL SESSIONS
Organize My Assignments
Assignment Name

Completed	Assignment	Topic	Format
Getting Started		Orientation	
Diagnostic Quiz		Diagnostic	
Writing Sample Practice		Diagnostic	
Program Book		Review	
	Chapter 1: An Introduction to the LSAT	Part I	
	Chapter 2: Take Control of the Test	Part I	
	Chapter 3: Logical Reasoning	Part II	
	Chapter 3: Practice Sets		
	Chapter 4: Logic Games		
	Chapter 4: Practice Sets		

Input Practice Test 1 raw scores:
Logic Reas: 22
Logic Game: 20
Read Comp: 25
Logic Reas: 21
Percentile: 96
CLEAR SCORES
CANCEL
OK

Once you have registered, you may access your online syllabus whenever you want to. It lists all Comprehensive Program elements—Diagnostic Quiz, book chapters, three real LSAT tests, practice sets, downloadable study sheet, and more!

STEP 2: TAKE THE ONLINE DIAGNOSTIC QUIZ

The Diagnostic Quiz will help you to assess your strengths and weaknesses—information that will enable you to focus and customize your study time.

1. This half-length LSAT provides you with samples of the questions in each test section, allowing you to accurately gauge what you know and what you need to work on.

2. Review the explanation for each question to better understand where you went wrong and to target your practice time to specific question types or concepts.

STEP 3: TRY AN ONLINE WRITING SAMPLE PROMPT

Your online companion includes prompts similar to those you will see on test day.

1. Choose a prompt, and allow yourself 35 minutes to write your essay.

2. When you are finished, compare it to the model response provided.

How did you do? There are a total of 6 essay prompts to practice with over the course of your test prep so you can track your improvement.

STEP 4: IDENTIFY YOUR STRENGTHS AND WEAKNESSES

Check your answers to the Diagnostic Quiz, noting how many questions you got right and how many you got wrong. Look for patterns. Did you ace the Logical Reasoning assumption questions? Did Reading Comp inference questions trip you up?

Don't limit your initial review to the questions you got wrong. Read all of the explanations—even those for questions you got right—to reinforce key concepts, sharpen your skills, and learn strategies that can speed your work.

STEP 5: CUSTOMIZE YOUR STUDY PLAN USING THE ONLINE SYLLABUS

Based on your performance on the Diagnostic Quiz (and the amount of time you have available to study), use the online syllabus to select the lessons, practice sets, and other tools that will constitute your customized study plan.

The best study plan will adapt to your individual needs and should:

- Start with a review of content weaknesses and include quizzes on weaker topics to boost skills and understanding.
- Devote time to reinforcing content strengths through lesson reviews and practice sets.
- Use full-length practice tests as milestones.
- To maximize their benefit, use one or more of the three real LSAT practice tests as your last practice before test day.

1. Think about the topics on which you need to focus. Go back to the syllabus to help you find those concepts, so you can chart your personalized study plan. Plan to read those lessons and take the practice sets in the book.

2. As time permits, go back to the question types that you aced so you can keep that material sharp.

3. Plan time to go online and practice with the remaining Writing Sample prompts, even if writing is your best subject.

4. There are three real LSAT full-length practice tests in this Comprehensive Program; don't save them all for the final weeks.

STEP 6: REVIEW, REINFORCE, AND BUILD SKILLS

Once you've made your plan, follow through. Targeted LSAT study is a sure way to perform well on the test. You will maximize your study time by focusing on those areas you need to cover most.

1. Read the lessons you identified in the book, take the practice sets, and read the answer explanations. Chart your improvement by recording quiz and practice set scores in your online syllabus.

2. Take time to practice the Writing Sample. Understanding its requirements and practicing periodically will help you deliver the right paragraphs on test day.

3. As soon as you get comfortable with the LSAT question types and Kaplan strategies, take a full-length real LSAT practice test. Test yourself periodically and chart your progress on the syllabus. If your strengths and weaknesses change, adjust your plan appropriately.

ABOUT THIS PROGRAM BOOK

In addition to the online syllabus, this book has a detailed Table of Contents: if you're away from a computer, you will still be able to navigate the LSAT Comprehensive Program.

- The characteristics of a standardized test can be used to your advantage. The "Take Control of the Test" chapter offers section management techniques and advice about which questions to answer and which to guess on.
- Part Two offers specific methods, strategies, and practice problems for every type of LSAT question you're likely to see in Logical Reasoning, Logic Games, Reading Comprehension, and the Writing Sample.
- The material in this book is up-to-date at the time of publication, but the LSAC may institute changes in the test or the registration process. Be sure to read the materials you receive from LSAC carefully. Any important late-breaking developments—or changes or corrections to anything in this book—can be found posted on the online syllabus.

Throughout the book, we've added icons to keep your program helpful and flexible.

Icon Key

 **READ MORE** – Suggestions for additional study materials

 **GO ONLINE** – More information and practice online

 **KAPLAN STRATEGY** – Proven strategies to master the LSAT

KAPLAN **EXCLUSIVE** – Methods to score higher on the LSAT

EXCLUSIVE: "GETTING INTO LAW SCHOOL" SECTION

Your LSAT performance is very important, but a host of other parts of your application can make or break your candidacy. So, to give you the very best odds, you'll find expert advice to lead you through the application process before and beyond the LSAT: an overview of the application process and a plan to make your application as strong as it can be. Checklists and schedules are included to keep you on track.

HOW DID WE DO?

When you've finished studying and taken your LSAT, remember to go back to the online companion and fill out the survey for us. We want to know how you did on the test and how we did at preparing you.

Thanks, and Good Luck!

| PART ONE |

The LSAT

Chapter 1: **An Introduction to the LSAT**

The LSAT is probably unlike any other test you've taken in your academic career. Most tests you've encountered in high school and college have been content-based—that is, they required you to recall and be conversant with a certain body of facts, formulas, theorems, or other acquired knowledge.

But the LSAT is a skills-based test. It doesn't ask you to repeat memorized facts or to apply learned formulas to specific problems. In fact, all you'll be asked to do on the LSAT is think—thoroughly, quickly, and strategically. There's no required content to study!

Sound too good to be true? Well, before you get the idea that you can skate into the most important test of your life without preparing, let's clarify the very important distinction between study and preparation.

ABOUT THE LSAT

The LSAT is designed to test the critical reading, data management, and analytical thinking skills that have been deemed necessary (by the governing bodies of law schools themselves) for success in the first year of law school.

These are skills that you already possess to some extent. But what you probably haven't yet acquired is the know-how to use these skills to your best advantage in the context of a standardized, skills-based test, requiring careful time management.

The LSAT is also an endurance test—175 minutes of multiple-choice testing, plus a 35-minute writing sample. Add in the administrative details at both ends of the test, and a 10- to 15-minute break midway through, and you can count on being in the test room for at least $4\frac{1}{2}$ hours.

It's a grueling experience, and if you can't approach it with confidence and rigor, you'll quickly lose your composure. That's why it's so important to take control of the test, just as you've been taking control of the rest of your application process.

Study vs. Preparation

And that's where test preparation comes in. While you can't technically study for a standardized, skills-based test like the LSAT, you can and must prepare for it.

The Kaplan LSAT program will teach you to tailor your existing skills to the very idiosyncratic tasks required by the LSAT, and how to use your critical reading skills most effectively to unlock dense but highly structured arguments and passages. Similarly, while you've probably developed plenty of sound, logical ways to analyze problems in everyday life, the Kaplan program will teach you to apply those deductive and analytical skills to the unusual demands of Logical Reasoning and Logic Games.

The LSAT Question Types

The LSAT consists of five multiple-choice sections: two Logical Reasoning sections, one Logic Games section, one Reading Comprehension section, and one unscored "experimental" section that will look exactly like one of the other multiple-choice sections.

At the end of the test, there will be a Writing Sample section in which you'll have to write a short essay. Here's how the sections break down:

Section	Number of Questions	Minutes
Logical Reasoning	24–26	35
Logical Reasoning	24–26	35
Logic Games	22–24	35
Reading Comprehension	26–28	35
"Experimental"	22–28	35
Writing Sample	n/a	35

The five multiple-choice sections can appear in any order, but the Writing Sample comes last. A 10- or 15-minute break will come between the third and fourth sections of the test.

Each question type is covered in its own chapter. You'll be answering roughly 125 multiple-choice questions (101 of which are scored) over the course of three intense hours. That's an average of just a little over a minute per question, not counting the time required to read passages and set up games. Clearly, you're going to have to move fast. But don't let yourself get careless. Taking control of the LSAT means increasing the speed only to the extent you can do so without sacrificing accuracy. Good time management involves maximizing the use of each second of your time by working strategically—for example, skipping questions and passages that slow you down and coming back to them if you have time, and determining which questions you can answer and which you should guess on. There are questions in the test designed solely to see whether you will get bogged down in them, and questions that may be especially challenging to you personally. No one question is worth more than any other, so over-commitment to any one question can be fatal.

First, just familiarize yourself with the kinds of questions asked on each section.

Logical Reasoning

What It Is: Each of the two scored Logical Reasoning sections consists of 24–26 questions based on short passages called *stimuli*. Most stimuli involve an **argument**—a conclusion based on evidence. You need to understand the stimulus argument to answer the one or two questions based on it. Many, perhaps most, Logical Reasoning stimuli aren't full arguments; they're a series of facts from which you must make logical deductions. Although you don't need to know the technical terms of formal logic, you do need the critical reasoning skills that enable you to analyze a stimulus and make judgments accordingly.

Why It's on the Test: Law schools want to see whether you can understand, analyze, evaluate, and manipulate arguments, and draw reliable conclusions—as every law student and attorney must. This question type makes up half of your LSAT score, so you know that the law schools value these skills.

What It's Like: Here are the directions to the section, along with a sample question:

> **Directions:** This test consists of questions that ask you to analyze the logic of statements or short paragraphs. You are to choose as the answer to each question the one choice you consider best on the basis of your common-sense evaluation of the statement and its assumptions. Although a question may seem to have more than one acceptable answer, there is only one best answer, and it is the one that does not entail making any illogical, extraneous, or conflicting assumptions about the question.

1. A study of twenty overweight men revealed that each man experienced significant weight loss after adding SlimDown, an artificial food supplement, to his daily diet. For three months, each man consumed one SlimDown portion every morning after exercising, and then followed his normal diet for the rest of the day. Clearly, anyone who consumes one portion of SlimDown every day for at least three months will lose weight and will look and feel his or her best.

   Which one of the following is an assumption on which the argument depends?

   (A) The men in the study will gain back the weight they lost if they discontinue the SlimDown program.

   (B) No other dietary supplement will have the same effect on overweight men.

   (C) The daily exercise regimen was not responsible for the effects noted in the study.

   (D) Women will not experience similar weight reductions if they adhere to the SlimDown program for three months.

   (E) Overweight men will achieve only partial weight loss if they do not remain on the SlimDown program for a full three months.

Choice (C) is correct.

READ MORE

When you finish this program, there's more practice on the tougher questions, games, and passages in Kaplan's *LSAT 180*.

Logic Games

What It Is: There are 22–24 questions in the Logic Games (a.k.a. Analytical Reasoning) section, based on four games with 5–7 questions each. They require an ability to reason clearly and deductively from a given set of rules or restrictions, all under tight time restrictions. Games are highly susceptible to systematic technique and the proper use of scratchwork.

Why It's on the Test: The section tests your command of detail, your formal deductive abilities, your understanding of how rules limit and order behavior (which is the very definition of law itself), and your ability to cope with many pieces of data simultaneously to solve problems.

What It's Like: What follows are directions to the Logic Games section with a short sample game and two questions:

Directions: Each group of questions is based on a set of conditions. You may wish to draw a rough sketch to help you answer some of the questions. Choose the best answer for each question and fill in the corresponding space on your answer sheet.

Questions 2–3

Five workers—Mona, Patrick, Renatta, Saffie, and Will—are scheduled to clean apartments on five days of a single week, Monday through Friday. There are three cleaning shifts available each day—a morning shift, an afternoon shift, and an evening shift. No more than one worker cleans on any given shift. Each worker works exactly two cleaning shifts during the week, but no one works more than one cleaning shift in a single day.

Exactly two workers clean on each day of the week.
Mona and Will clean on the same days of the week.
Patrick does not clean on any afternoon or evening shifts during the week.
Will does not clean on any morning or afternoon shifts during the week.
Mona cleans on two consecutive days of the week.
Saffie's second cleaning shift of the week occurs on an earlier day of the week than Mona's first cleaning shift

2. Which one of the following must be true?
   (A) Saffie cleans on Tuesday afternoon.
   (B) Patrick cleans on Monday morning.
   (C) Will cleans on Thursday evening.
   (D) Renatta cleans on Friday afternoon.
   (E) Mona cleans on Tuesday morning.

3. If Will does not clean on Friday, which one of the following could be false?
   (A) Renatta cleans on Friday.
   (B) Saffie cleans on Tuesday.
   (C) Mona cleans on Wednesday.
   (D) Saffie cleans on Monday.
   (E) Patrick cleans on Tuesday.

For question 2, the answer is (C); for 3 it's (E). You'll see an explanation for this game in the Logic Games chapter.

Reading Comprehension

What It Is: The Reading Comp section consists of four passages, each 450–550 words long, with 5–8 questions per passage. The topics are chosen from the areas of social sciences, humanities, natural sciences, and law.

Why It's on the Test: The purpose of the section is to see whether you can quickly get the gist of long, difficult prose—just as you'll have to do in law school and in your law career.

What It's Like: Here are the directions and an excerpt from a sample passage.

> **Directions:** Each selection in this test is followed by several questions. After reading the selection, choose the best response to each question and mark it on your answer sheet. Your replies are to be based on what is *stated* or *implied* in the selection.

It has been suggested that post–World War II concepts of environmental liability, as they pertain to hazardous waste, grew out of issues regarding municipal refuse collection and disposal and industrial waste disposal in the period 1880–1940. To a great degree, the remedies available to Americans for dealing with the burgeoning hazardous waste problem were characteristic of the judicial, legislative, and regulatory tools used to confront a whole range of problems in the industrial age. At the same time, these remedies were operating in an era in which the problem of hazardous waste had yet to be recognized. It is understandable that an assessment of liability was narrowly drawn and most often restricted to a clearly identified violator in a specific act of infringement of the property rights of someone else. Legislation, for the most part, focused narrowly on clear threats to the public health and dealt with problems of industrial pollution meekly if at all.

4. The author's primary purpose is to discuss
   (A) contrasts in the legislative approaches to environmental liability before and after World War II
   (B) legislative trends which have been instrumental in the reduction of environmental hazardous wastes
   (C) the historical and legislative context in which to view post–World War II hazardous waste problems
   (D) early patterns of industrial abuse and pollution of the American environment
   (E) the growth of an activist tradition in American jurisprudence

The answer is (C). Of course, actual passages will be longer and will have as few as 5 or as many as 8 questions. We'll show you how to approach this passage and its questions in the Reading Comp chapter.

The Experimental Section

The experimental (unscored) section allows LSAC to try out questions for use on future tests. This section will look just like one of the others—Logical Reasoning, Logic Games, or Reading Comp—so don't try to figure out which section is experimental and cruise through that section. That's an extremely risky proposition. Just do as well as you can on every section.

 KAPLAN STRATEGY

Know the test sections, their relative value, and what they test.

Logical Reasoning

- Accounts for 50 percent of your score.
- Tests ability to understand, evaluate, and manipulate arguments.

Logic Games

- Accounts for just under 25 percent of your score.
- Tests logic, ability to organize and manipulate data, and attention to detail.

Reading Comp

- Accounts for just over 25 percent of your score
- Tests ability to quickly break down dense material, identifying structure and reasoning.

The Writing Sample

What It Is: The Writing Sample comes at the end of your LSAT day. You'll have 35 minutes to either write an argument or analyze one, depending on the prompt you're given.

Why It's on the Test: The writing sample shows law schools whether you can argue for a position while breaking down the argument of an opponent, or whether you can understand and explain why some else's argument is or isn't convincing. This essay isn't graded but is sent to law schools along with your LSAT score.

What It's Like: Here's one type of sample topic:

> The Daily Tribune, a metropolitan newspaper, is considering two candidates for promotion to business editor. Write an argument for one candidate over the other with the following considerations in mind:
>
> - The editor must train new writers and assign stories.
> - The editor must be able to edit and rewrite stories under daily deadline pressure.
>
> Laura received a B.A. in English from a large university. She was managing editor of her college newspaper and served as a summer intern at her hometown daily paper. Laura started working at the Tribune right out of college and spent three years at the city desk covering the city economy. Eight years ago the paper formed its business section and Laura became part of the new department. After several years covering state business, Laura began writing on the national economy. Three years ago, Laura was named senior business and finance editor on the national business staff; she is also responsible for supervising seven writers.
>
> Palmer attended an elite private college where he earned both a B.S. in business administration and an M.A. in journalism. After receiving his journalism degree, Palmer worked for three years on a monthly business magazine. He won a prestigious national award for a series of articles on the impact of monetary policy on multinational corporations. Palmer came to the Tribune three years ago to fill the newly created position of international business writer. He was the only member of the international staff for two years and wrote on almost a daily basis. He now supervises a staff of four writers. Last year, Palmer developed a bi-monthly business supplement for the Tribune that has proved highly popular and has helped increase the paper's circulation.

Topics are chosen and set up so that there can be no right or wrong answer, but there can be good and bad responses. You'll see one possible response to this topic in the Writing Sample chapter.

HOW THE LSAT IS SCORED

You'll receive one score for the LSAT ranging between 120 and 180 (no separate scores for Logical Reasoning, Logic Games, and Reading Comprehension). Here's how it's calculated.

There are roughly 101 scored multiple-choice questions on each exam:

- About 52 from the two Logical Reasoning sections
- About 22 from the Logic Games section
- About 27 from the Reading Comprehension section

Your **raw score**, the number of questions that you answer correctly, will be multiplied by a complicated scoring formula (different for each test, to accommodate differences in difficulty level) to yield the **scaled score**—the one that will fall somewhere in that 120–180 range—which is reported to the schools.

Because the test is graded on a largely preset curve, the scaled score will always correspond to a certain percentile, which will also be given on your score report. A score of 160, for instance, corresponds roughly to the 80th percentile, meaning that 80 percent of test takers scored at or below your level. The percentile figure is important because it allows law schools to see where you fall in the pool of applicants.

All scored questions are worth the same amount—one raw point—and there's no penalty for guessing. That means that you should always fill in an answer for every question, whether you get to that question or not.

What's a "Good" LSAT Score?

Of course, what you consider a good LSAT score depends on your own expectations and goals, but here are a few interesting statistics:

KAPLAN EXCLUSIVE

Never let time run out on any section without filling in an answer for every question.

If you got about half of all of the scored questions right (a raw score of roughly 50), you would earn a scaled score of roughly 147, putting you in about the 30th percentile—not a great performance. But on the LSAT, a little improvement goes a long way. In fact, getting only one additional question right every ten minutes would give you a raw score of about 64, pushing you into the 60th percentile—a huge improvement.

SAMPLE PERCENTILES

Percentile	Approx. Scaled Score (Range 120–180)	Approx. Raw Score
99th percentile	174	~94 correct out of 101
95th percentile	168	~88 correct out of 101
90th percentile	164	~82 correct out of 101
80th percentile	160	~76 correct out of 101
75th percentile	157	~71 correct out of 101
50th percentile	152	~61 correct out of 101

Note: Exact percentile-to-scaled-score relationships vary from test to test.

So you don't have to be perfect to do well. On most LSATs, you can get as many as 28 wrong and still remain in the 80th percentile or as many as 20 wrong and still be in the 90th percentile. Most students who score 180 get a handful of questions wrong.

Although many factors play a role in admissions decisions, the LSAT score is usually one of the most important. And—generally speaking—being average won't cut it. The median LSAT score is somewhere around 152. And if you're aiming for the top, you've got to do even better. The median LSAT scores accepted by the best law schools in the country, such as Yale, Stanford, and Columbia, range from the high 160s to the low 170s. That translates to a percentile figure of 95 and up.

In the next chapter you'll start to learn how to approach—and master—the test in a general way. As you'll see, knowing specific strategies for each type of question is only part of your task. To really do your best, you have to approach the entire test in the proper spirit, and the proactive, take-control kind of thinking it inspires—the LSAT mindset.

LSAT Checklist

BEFORE THE TEST

Get the *LSAT/LSDAS Registration and Information Book.*

- ☐ It's available at most colleges and law schools; you can also get a copy at www.LSAC.org or order it by phone at (215) 968-1001.

Choose a test date.

- ☐ June is best (that is, 14–15 months before your anticipated law school entrance date), October second best (see chapter 8).

Complete your LSAT/LSDAS Registration.

- ☐ You can register online, by mail, or by phone.
- ☐ Make sure you list a first- and second-choice test center. If you register online, you can confirm test center availability in real time.
- ☐ If you register by mail, don't forget to sign the form and include payment.
- ☐ Download the free PrepTest and order additional practice tests.

Receive your LSAT admission ticket.

- ☐ If you register online, you can print out your ticket immediately (and can reprint it if it is lost).
- ☐ Be sure you have your ticket before the late registration date.
- ☐ Check it for accuracy; correct any errors promptly.

Create a test-prep calendar to ensure that you're ready by the day of the test.

- ☐ If you skipped it, go back and read "How to Use the LSAT Comprehensive Program."
- ☐ On a calendar, block out the weeks you have to prepare for the test.
- ☐ Based on your strengths and weaknesses, establish a detailed plan of study. Don't forget to include some days off for stress control.
- ☐ Reevaluate your strengths and weaknesses from time to time and revise the plan accordingly.

Check out your test center.

- ☐ Know the kind of desk you'll be working on and whether the room is likely to be hot or cold.
- ☐ Know the directions to the building and room where you'll be tested.
- ☐ Use Kaplan's exclusive "Test Center Rater" at *www.kaptest.com/testsites* for information from former test takers about desk space, noise, levels, proctors, and more..

THE DAY OF THE TEST

- ☐ Make sure you have your LSAT admission ticket and acceptable ID.
- ☐ Make sure you have your LSAT Survival Kit (see chapter 7).

Chapter 2: **Take Control of the Test**

To do your best on the LSAT, keep in mind that it's like no other test you've taken. If you took a test in college and got a quarter of the questions wrong, you'd probably receive a pretty low grade. But on the LSAT, you can get a quarter of the questions wrong and still score higher than the 80th percentile. The test is geared so that only those who exercise strong time-management skills are able to finish every section.

What does this mean for you? Just as you shouldn't let one bad game or passage ruin an entire section, you shouldn't let what you consider a below-par performance on one section ruin your performance on the rest of the test.

If you feel you've done poorly on a section, it could be the experimental. And even if it's not, chances are it's just a difficult section—a factor that will already be figured into the scoring curve. Remain calm; do your best on each section and, once a section is over, forget about it and move on. Losing a few extra points won't do you in, but losing your head will.

KAPLAN EXCLUSIVE

Never, ever, try to guess which section is experimental. Handle each section as if it counts.

LSAT MINDSET

The Strategy and Practice chapters will arm you with the tools you need to do well on the LSAT. But you must wield those tools in the right spirit. This involves taking a certain stance toward the entire test.

The Right Attitude

Those who approach the LSAT as an obstacle and rail against the necessity of taking it don't fare as well as those who see the LSAT as an opportunity to show off the reading and reasoning skills that law schools are looking for—to distinguish themselves from the rest of the applicant pack.

With that in mind:

- Look at the LSAT as a challenge, but try not to obsess over it; you certainly don't want to psyche yourself out of the game.
- Remember that the LSAT is important, but this one test will not single-handedly determine the outcome of your life.

- Try to have fun with the test. Learning how to match your wits against the test makers can be very satisfying, and the skills you'll acquire will benefit you in law school and in your career.
- Remember that, when you've trained with Kaplan, you're more prepared than most people. You have the tools you need and the know-how to use those tools.

Confidence

Confidence feeds on itself, and unfortunately, so does self-doubt. Confidence in your ability leads to quick, sure answers and a sense of wellbeing that translates into more points. If you lack confidence, you end up reading sentences and answer choices two, three, or four times, until you confuse yourself and get off-track. This leads to timing difficulties that perpetuate the downward spiral, causing anxiety and a tendency to rush.

If you subscribe to the LSAT mindset, however, you'll gear all of your practice toward taking control of the test. When you've achieved that goal—armed with the principles, techniques, strategies, and methods in this book—you'll be ready to face the LSAT with confidence.

Stamina

The LSAT is a grueling experience, and some test takers simply run out of gas before it's over. To avoid this, take full-length practice tests in the weeks before the test. That way, five sections plus a writing sample will seem like a breeze (well, maybe not a breeze, but at least not a hurricane). On the other hand, don't just rush from one practice test right into another. Learn what you can from your review of each test; then work on your weaknesses and build your strengths before tackling another full-length test.

Get as much test practice as possible. Order PrepTests from LSAC to use as your final practice tests.

In addition to the practice tests included in the Kaplan Program, you can buy PrepTests published by LSAC. The available PrepTests are listed in the *LSAT Registration and Information Book*. Send away for them early, since they can take several weeks for delivery. You can also download a single free PrepTest from the LSAC website.

TEST EXPERTISE

It's one thing to answer a Logical Reasoning question correctly, and quite another to answer 25 of them correctly in 35 minutes. Time pressure affects virtually every test taker. So when you're comfortable with the content of the test, your next challenge will be to manage your time.

On most tests you take in school, you wouldn't dream of not taking at least a try at every one of the questions. If a question seems particularly difficult, you spend significantly more time on it, since you'll probably earn more points for correctly answering a hard question.

Not so on the LSAT. Every LSAT question, no matter how hard, is worth a single point. And since there are so many questions to do in so little time, it's foolish to spend three minutes getting a point for a hard question and then not have time to get a couple of quick points from two easy questions later in the section.

Given this combination—limited time, all questions equal in weight—you've got to develop a way of handling the test sections to make sure you get as many points as you can, as quickly and easily as you can. Here are the principles that will help you do that:

Answer Questions in the Order That's Best for You

One of the most valuable strategies to help you finish sections in time is to recognize and deal first with the questions, games, and passages that are easier and more familiar to you. Temporarily skip those that promise to be difficult and time consuming—come back to them at the end, and if you run out of time, you're much better off not getting to questions you may have had difficulty with, rather than missing easier ones. (Since there's no wrong-answer penalty, always fill in an answer to every question on the test, whether you get to it or not.)

Come back and re-read this section occasionally, to be sure you don't overlook any strategies.

Remember, LSAT questions, games, and passages are not presented in order of difficulty; in fact, the test makers scatter easy and difficult questions throughout the section, in effect rewarding those who get to the end. If you find sequencing games particularly easy, seek out the sequencing game on the Logic Games section and do it first.

Know That There Will Be Difficult Questions

It's imperative that you remain calm and composed while working through a section. Don't be rattled by one hard logic game, logical reasoning question, or reading passage. Part of the job of a top-notch test taker is to recognize those tough questions, games, and passages and leave them for last, making sure to pick up all of the quicker, easier points before investing time where the payoff is questionable. Expect to find at least one difficult passage or game on every section; you won't be the only one to have trouble with it. The test is curved to take the tough material into account. Understand that part of the test maker's goal is to reward those who keep their composure.

Control Time Instead of Letting Time Control You

The last thing you want is to have time called on a section before you've gotten to half the questions. It's essential, therefore, that you pace yourself. Don't spend exactly one-and-one-quarter minutes on every Logical Reasoning question. But you should have a sense of the average time you have to do each question, so you know when you're exceeding the limit and should start to move faster.

Keeping track of time is also important for guessing. It pays to leave time at the end to guess on any questions you couldn't answer. For instance, let's say you never get a chance to do the last logic game in the section. If you leave the grids for those questions blank, you'll get no points for that entire game. If, on the other hand, you give yourself a little time at the end to fill in a guess for each of those questions, you'll have a very good chance of getting lucky on one or two questions.

Grid In Answers Efficiently

You not only have to pick the right answers, you also have to mark those right answers on the answer grid in an efficient and accurate way. It sounds simple, but it's extremely important: Don't make mistakes filling out your answer grid! When time is short, it's easy to get confused going back and forth between your test book and your grid. Here are a few methods of avoiding mistakes:

1. **Always Circle Answers You Choose:** Circle the correct answers in your test booklet, but don't transfer the answers to the grid right away. That wastes too much time. Circling your answers in the test book will also make it easier to check your grid against your book.

2. **Grid About Five Answers at Once:** Transfer your answers after every five questions, or at the end of each Reading Comp passage or Logic Game, or at the end of a two-page spread in your test booklet (find the method that works best for you). You won't keep breaking your concentration to mark the grid, so you'll save time and improve accuracy.

3. **Always Circle Questions You Skip:** Put a big circle in your test book around the number of any question you skip (or circle the whole question). When you go back, it will be easy to locate them. And if you accidentally skip a box on the grid, you can more easily check your grid against your book to see where you went wrong.

4. **Save Time at the End for a Final Grid Check:** Take time at the end of every section to check your grid. Make sure you've got an oval filled in for each question in the section. Remember, a blank grid has no chance of earning a point.

KAPLAN STRATEGY

To meet the LSAT's stringent time demands, cultivate:

- **A sense of timing**
- **A system that enables you to skip around without getting confused**
- **An ability to assess the difficulty level of a question, passage, or game**

SECTION MANAGEMENT

Logical Reasoning

Time Per Question

Tackling 24–26 questions in 35 minutes works out to roughly a minute and a quarter per question. Keep in mind that this is only an average; there are bound to be questions that take more or less time. It's okay if the occasional question takes you two minutes, if you're able to balance it out with a question that takes 45 seconds.

Remember, too, that every question is worth one point, so don't get hung up on any one question. No single point on this section is worth three minutes of your valuable time. And if a question is that hard, there's a good chance that you may get it wrong anyway and have nothing to show for that extra time.

Managing the Section

What kind of Logical Reasoning questions should you skip? You'll develop your own answer to this question as you learn your strengths and weaknesses. Skip questions containing stimuli that are indecipherable to you after a quick reading. Questions containing extra-long stimulus arguments may be good to skip initially as well, especially if you're running out of time. But don't automatically be intimidated by the sheer length of a stimulus; often, the long ones are uncomplicated and easy to understand.

As you'll see in chapter 3, the Kaplan Method is to read the question stem first; you may be able to single out questions to postpone based solely on question type. If a question involves finding a principle that lends credence to an argument, and you know that principle questions are a problem for you, then that's a good question to postpone.

A good stimulus to tackle early is one that comes with two questions attached. There are usually anywhere from two to four double-question stimuli on each Logical Reasoning section. Working through these, as opposed to single question arguments, saves a little time, as you can potentially rack up two points for reading only one stimulus.

> **KAPLAN EXCLUSIVE**
>
> **If you decide to skip a question you've already spent some time on, be sure to cross out answers you already know are wrong.**

Logic Games

Time Per Game

Four games in 35 minutes means roughly eight and a half minutes per game. Remember, just as in Logical Reasoning, this is an average—games that are harder or have more questions should take a little more time than others.

Managing the Section

First, and most important, preview the section. Literally flip through the pages, having a glance at each game in order to decide which games look the easiest and most familiar to you. Previewing is not foolproof; a game that looks fairly straightforward at first glance can turn out to be challenging. However, if you look for game-type familiarity, concrete rules, and straightforward actions, and attack those games first, your efficiency will improve.

The goal is to tackle the games in order of difficulty, from easiest to hardest. But if you achieve nothing more than saving the hardest game for last, the strategy is a winner.

The best way to know which games may be difficult is to be familiar with the game types discussed in chapter 4, and to have a sense of which types you're strongest in.

A game that doesn't look familiar at all could be an oddball game—a good candidate to postpone. But don't necessarily be scared off by games with a lot of rules; sometimes, this works to your advantage. If you're given numerous rules that are clear and concrete, your set-up will be more complete and the questions will be easier to answer. By the same token, a game with few rules, especially if they're conditional rules, may take little time to set up but also give you little to work with. When it comes to rules, quality is more important than quantity.

If you have several Logic Games to practice on, you may wish to build gradually to the point where you're ready to take full-length sections. First attempt one game in 8–9 minutes. Next, try two games in 16–18 minutes. When you're ready to move on, try three games in 24–27 minutes, until finally you can reliably handle a full four-game section in 35 minutes.

Finally, remember the way the test makers test efficiency. They're crafty—they'll sometimes throw an intentionally time-consuming question at the end of a game, possibly one involving a rule change that requires you to backtrack and set the game up all over again. When this happens, they may not be testing who's smart enough to get the right answer, but rather who's clever enough to skip the troublesome question in order to devote precious time to the next game, with a possible payoff of six or seven new points.

Reading Comprehension

Time per Passage

Reading Comp is similar in structure to the Logic Games section: four passages in 35 minutes means about eight and a half minutes per passage. But don't apply this timing too rigidly; denser passages and those with more questions should take a little more time than others. Kaplan's Reading Comp strategies and techniques will help you to get through each passage as quickly as possible, but here are a few additional points about tackling a full section.

Managing the Section

It may seem more difficult at first to choose which Reading Comprehension passages to attack first, but as you become familiar with the passage types and with reading for structure, you'll know what to look for: clear topic, scope, and purpose and a clear passage structure. And if you start working your way through a passage and find that you've made a mistake, you're not chained to it—move on to a different passage as soon as you recognize the difficulties. As in Logic Games, the goal is to save the most difficult for last, so if you can't get a handle on the passage's structure, move on.

Quite often, you'll encounter Reading Comp passages that contain technical details or difficult concepts, only to find that few if any questions deal with the part of the passage that's so dense. Just as in the Logic Games, the test makers aren't necessarily testing who's smart enough to understand that passage; they may want to see who's clever enough to skim past those details. Chapter 5 prepares you for the Reading Comp section.

MANAGING STRESS

Some test stress is normal and good; it's a motivation to study and the adrenaline that gets pumped into your bloodstream helps you stay alert and think more clearly. But high stress levels can make it difficult to concentrate, and you can't work under stress for prolonged periods without exhausting yourself. Practice using techniques to get stress under control, and learn which of them will work best for you during the test.

KAPLAN EXCLUSIVE

Never practice for more than about 3 hours at a stretch; take breaks and come back refreshed.

Take Control

Research shows that if you don't have a sense of control over what's happening in your life, you can easily end up feeling helpless and hopeless. Try to identify the sources of the stress you feel. Which of these can you do something about?

Set Realistic Goals

Facing your problem areas give you some distinct advantages. What do you want to accomplish in the time remaining? Make a list of realistic goals. You can't help feeling more confident when you know you're actively improving your chances of earning a higher test score.

Focus on Your Strengths

Make a list of your strengths that will help you do well on the test. Recognizing your own strengths is like having reserves of solid gold. You'll be able to draw on your reserves as you need them. And every time you recognize a new area of strength, solve a challenging problem, or score well on a practice test, you'll increase your reserves.

Imagine Yourself Succeeding

Close your eyes and imagine yourself in a relaxing situation. Breathe easily and naturally, and think of a real-life situation in which you scored well on a test or did well on an assignment. Focus on this success. Now turn your thoughts to the LSAT, and keep your thoughts and feelings in line with that successful experience. Don't make comparisons between them; just imagine yourself taking the upcoming test with the same feelings of confidence and relaxed control.

Exercise

Whether it is jogging, biking, yoga, or a pickup basketball game, physical exercise stimulates your mind and body and improves your ability to think and concentrate. A surprising number of students fall out of the habit of regular exercise, ironically because they're spending so much time prepping for exams.

Eat Well

Good nutrition helps you focus and think clearly. Eat plenty of fruits and vegetables, low-fat protein such as fish, skinless poultry, beans, and legumes, and whole grains such as brown rice, whole wheat bread, and pastas. Don't eat a lot of sugar, high-fat snacks, or salty foods.

Keep Breathing

Conscious attention to breathing is an excellent way to manage stress. Most of the people who get into trouble during tests take shallow breaths: They breathe using only their upper chests and shoulder muscles and may even hold their breath for long periods of time. Breathe deeply in a slow, relaxed manner.

Stretch

If you find yourself getting spaced out or burned out as you're studying for or taking the test, stop for a brief moment and stretch. Stretching will help to refresh you and refocus your thoughts.

Avoid Drugs

Using drugs (prescription or recreational) specifically to prepare for and take a big test is self-defeating. Mild stimulants like coffee or cola can sometimes help as you study because they keep you alert. But too much of them can lead to agitation, restlessness, and insomnia.

SUMMARY

- LSAT questions are not presented in order of difficulty; answer them in any order that seems effective.
- There is no penalty for wrong answers; always guess if you can't answer a question.
- All questions are worth the same amount; don't spend excessive time on one of them.
- In Logical Reasoning, spend an average of 12 minutes on each block of 10 questions, save for last any question types that give you trouble, and look for the double-questions to get more points for your minutes.
- In Logic Games, preview the section for the most familiar games, spend an average of $8^1/_2$ minutes per game, and save for last any rule-change questions or others that are especially time-consuming for you.
- In Reading Comp, skip passages that are slowing you down too much, and spend an average of $8^1/_2$ minutes per passage.
- Practice stress-management throughout your preparation to maximize your effectiveness.

| PART TWO |

Strategies and Practice

Chapter 3: **Logical Reasoning**

- **The 6 basic principles of Logical Reasoning**
- **Formal Logic in Logical Reasoning**
- **The 9 Logical Reasoning question types and their strategies**
- **Kaplan's 4-Step Method for Logical Reasoning**

The fact that Logical Reasoning makes up half of your LSAT score is actually good news because you already have most of the skills you need for the section. In fact, we all do. But the LSAT tests your ability to use those skills thoroughly, quickly, and strategically.

THE 6 BASIC PRINCIPLES OF LOGICAL REASONING

GO ONLINE

Your downloadable study sheet summarizes these principles, strategies, and methods.

On the LSAT, in law school, and in your law career, you'll need the ability to understand complex reasoning. It's not enough to sense whether an argument is strong or weak; you'll need to analyze precisely why it is so. This involves an even more fundamental skill—the ability to isolate and identify the various components of any given argument. Assumption, Strengthen, Weaken, and Flaw questions, which make up about half of the Logical Reasoning sections, call on these skills. (Other Logical Reasoning question types, such as Paradox and Parallel Reasoning questions, draw on other skills and plans of attack specific to those question types, which will be discussed later.)

Understand the Structure of Arguments

Success in Logical Reasoning depends on the ability to break an argument down into its core components.

In Logical Reasoning, the word **argument** doesn't mean a conversation in which two or more people are shouting at one another. It means any piece of text in which an author puts forth a set of ideas and a point of view and attempts to support them.

Most LSAT Logical Reasoning stimuli—and all arguments—involve two parts:

- The **conclusion** (the point that the author is trying to make)
- The **evidence** (the support that the author offers for the conclusion)

Success on this section hinges on your ability to identify these parts of the argument. There is no general rule about where conclusion and evidence appear in the argument—the conclusion could be the first sentence, followed by the evidence; or it could be the last sentence, with the evidence preceding it; or it could be any sentence in between.

 GO ONLINE

As you read through the basic principles, consider how each might have improved your Diagnostic Quiz performance.

Keywords

Use structural signals or keywords when attempting to isolate evidence and conclusion. Words in the stimulus such as *because, for*, and *since* usually indicate evidence is about to follow, while words such as *therefore, hence, thus,* and *consequently* usually signal a conclusion. Keywords are also important in recognizing formal logic concepts like *if/then* statements and in distinguishing what is *necessary* from what is *sufficient.*

Single Sentence Test

Consider the following short stimulus:

> The Brookdale Public Library will require extensive physical rehabilitation to meet the new building codes passed by the town council. For one thing, the electrical system is inadequate, causing the lights to flicker sporadically. Furthermore, there are too few emergency exits, and even those are poorly marked and sometimes locked.

Suppose that the author of this argument were allowed only one sentence to convey her meaning. Do you think that she would waste her lone opportunity on the statement: "The electrical system at the Brookdale Public Library is inadequate, causing the lights to flicker sporadically"? Would she walk away satisfied that she got her main point across? Probably not. Given a single opportunity, she would have to state the first sentence: "The Brookdale Public Library will require extensive physical rehabilitation. . . . " This is her conclusion. If you pressed her for her reasons for making this statement, she would then cite the electrical and structural problems with the building.

But does that mean that the statement, "The electrical system at the Brookdale Public Library is inadequate" can't be a conclusion? No; it's not the conclusion for this particular argument. Every statement must be evaluated in the context of the stimulus. For the sake of argument (no pun intended), see what a stimulus would look like in which the statement above serves as the conclusion:

> The electrical wiring at the Brookdale Public Library was installed over forty years ago and appears to be corroded in some places (evidence). An electrician, upon inspection of the system, found a few frayed wires as well as some blown fuses (evidence). Clearly, the electrical system at the Brookdale Public Library is inadequate (conclusion).

The explanations of the Practice Tests in this book discuss the structure of of the Logical Reasoning arguments contained there; read them carefully, even for the questions you get right.

READ MORE

To keep improving, re-read these principles from time to time. Which are you using effectively? Which are you overlooking?

Paraphrase the Author's Point

As you read the stimulus, restate the author's argument in your own words. Frequently, authors in Logical Reasoning (and in Reading Comp) say pretty simple things in complex ways. In the library argument, for instance, you probably don't want to deal with the full complexity of the author's stated conclusion:

> The Brookdale Public Library will require extensive physical rehabilitation to meet the new building codes just passed by the town council.

Instead, carry a simpler form of the point in your mind, something like:

> The library needs fixing up to meet new codes.

You can concentrate on only a certain amount of information at one time. Restating the argument in your own words will not only help you get the author's point in the first place, but it'll also help you hold on to it until you've found the correct answer.

Judge the Argument's Persuasiveness

You must read actively, not passively, on the LSAT. Active readers question whether the author's argument seems valid. Since many of the questions deal with finding flaws in the author's reasoning, it's imperative to read with a very critical eye.

How persuasive is the argument in the library stimulus? Well, it's pretty strong, since the evidence certainly seems to indicate that certain aspects of the library's structure need repair. But without more evidence about what the new building codes are like, you can't say for sure that the conclusion of this argument is valid. So this is a strong argument, but not an airtight one.

Don't allow yourself to fall into the bad habits of the passive reader—reading solely for the purpose of getting through the stimulus. Those who read this way invariably find themselves having to read the stimuli twice or even three times. Then they wonder why they run out time on the section. Read the stimuli right the first time—with a critical eye.

Answer the Question Being Asked

It's disheartening when you fully understand the author's argument and then lose the point by supplying an answer to a question that wasn't asked. For example, when you're asked for an inference supported by the argument, it does you no good to jump on the choice that paraphrases the author's stated conclusion. Likewise, if you're asked for an assumption, don't be fooled into selecting a choice that looks vaguely like a piece of the author's stated evidence.

When asked why they chose a particular wrong choice, students sometimes respond by saying such things as, "Well, it's true, isn't it?" and "Look, it says so right there," pointing to the stimulus. Well, that's simply not good enough. The question stem doesn't ask, "Which one of the following looks vaguely familiar to you?" It asks for something very specific. It's your job to follow the test makers' line of reasoning to the credited response.

Also, be on the lookout for "reversers"—words such as *not* and *except,* which are easy to miss, but entirely change what you're looking for among the choices.

Remember the Scope of the Argument

One of the most important Logical Reasoning skills, particularly when you're at the point of actually selecting one of the five choices, is the ability to focus in on the scope of the argument. The majority of wrong choices on this section are what the test makers call **distracters** (tempting wrong answers) because they are "outside the scope." In everyday language, that simply means that these choices contain elements that go beyond the context of the stimulus.

Some common examples of scope problems are choices that are too narrow, too broad, or literally have nothing to do with the author's points. To illustrate this, look again at the question above:

> The author's argument depends on which of the following assumptions about the new building codes?

Say one of the choices reads as follows:

> (A) The new building codes are far too stringent.

Knowing the scope of the argument would help you to eliminate this very quickly. That argument is just a claim about what the new codes will require—that the library be rehabilitated. It's not an argument about whether the requirements of the new codes are good, or justifiable, or ridiculously strict. That kind of value judgment is outside the scope of this argument.

Recognizing scope problems is a great way to eliminate dozens of wrong answers quickly. Pay special attention to the scope issues discussed in practice set and Practice Test explanations.

Eliminate Wrong Choices First If You Have to Guess

One or more of the wrong answer choices on any question will fall into patterns that, with practice, you'll quickly recognize. Any wrong choice you can eliminate improves your chance of choosing the correct answer. On Logical Reasoning questions, common wrong answer types are:

- **Outside Scope:** As you just saw, these are very common.
- **Extreme:** Unless the language of the argument is extreme, choices using words like *always, never, none, all,* and *every* are most likely wrong.
- **Distortion:** Some choices use language or ideas from the stimulus, but misapply them conspicuously; you can eliminate those.
- **$^1/_2$ Right, $^1/_2$ Wrong:** Some choices join a correct statement with an incorrect one; don't be hasty and choose your answer without reading the entire choice.

- **180:** Choices that are exactly the opposite of the correct one are common, especially on questions that ask for exceptions or on strengthen/weaken questions.
- **Irrelevant Comparison:** These often involve statistical evidence that compares apples and oranges: e.g., a statistic about all of a school's students in one statement may be compared to a statistic about freshman students in another.

 KAPLAN STRATEGY

Kaplan's principles for success in Logical Reasoning are:

- **Understand the structure of arguments.**
- **Paraphrase the author's point.**
- **Judge the argument's persuasiveness.**
- **Answer the question being asked.**
- **Remember the scope of the argument.**
- **Eliminate wrong choices first if you have to guess.**

FORMAL LOGIC IN LOGICAL REASONING

The manner in which formal logic is tested on the LSAT has evolved. Gone (at least for now) are the days when the test makers would line up formal *if/then* and *all/some/none* statements and ask you what *can, must,* or *cannot* be true on the basis of them. Nowadays, the test makers bury formal statements in the context of a casual argument, asking for one or more inferences that can be drawn. You may not easily recognize formal logic when you see it, and questions of this nature are fewer in number than in the past. But formal logic is tested in Logic Games as well, so it's best to get a solid handle on it.

Look at an example:

> Ian will go to the movies only when his wife is out of town. He'll go to a matinee alone, but will see a movie at night only if accompanied by Ezra and Mabel.

This simple stimulus looks like any other casual argument in Logical Reasoning, but in fact, it's made up of a couple of formal logic statements, each fraught with its own implications. Formal logic statements resemble rules in Logic Games. Be on the lookout for Logical Reasoning stimuli that contain sentences that can be boiled down to such hard and fast rules, and apply the following principles of formal logic to help you arrive at the correct answer.

The Contrapositive

The **contrapositive** of any *if/then* statement is formed by reversing and negating the terms. The general model goes like this:

Original: If X, then Y.

Contrapositive: If not Y, then not X.

KAPLAN EXCLUSIVE

Formal Logic is usually tested in the context of causal arguments that hinge on the differences between what is *sufficient* and what is *necessary*.

For any *if/then* statement (or any statement that can be translated into *if/then* form) the contrapositive will be equally valid. This is a nice shortcut to employ when faced with formal logic. Consider the following strict formal logic statement:

If the building has vacancies, then the sales office will be open.

To form the contrapositive, reverse and negate the terms:

If the sales office is NOT open, then the building does NOT have vacancies.

This would be a valid inference based on the original statement. The contrapositive, while quite a fancy term, is nothing more than everyday common sense. Now apply the contrapositive to the first sentence of the earlier example. Here's the original:

Ian will go to the movies only when his wife is out of town.

You can translate this statement into an *if/then* statement without changing its original meaning:

If Ian goes to the movies, then his wife must be out of town.

If that statement is true, what statement must also be true? Its contrapositive, of course:

If Ian's wife is not out of town, then Ian does not go to the movies.

One caveat: wrong answers often result from either forgetting to switch around the terms before negating them, or negating only one of the terms. For instance, if Ian doesn't go to the movies, you can't infer anything about whether his wife is in or out of town. Similarly, if Ian's wife is out of town, you can't tell for sure whether Ian goes to the movies or not.

If one part of the formal logic statement contains a compound phrase, then both parts of the phrase must be taken into account. For example, take the other part of the stimulus above:

Ian will see a movie at night only if accompanied by Ezra and Mabel.

- **Translation:** If Ian sees a movie at night, then he's accompanied by Ezra and Mabel.
- **Contrapositive:** If Ian is not with Ezra and Mabel, then he does not see a movie at night.
- **Correct Interpretation:** If either Ezra or Mabel is missing, then Ian can't go to a night movie.

Finally, if one part of a formal logic statement is already in the negative, the same rules that apply to math apply to forming the contrapositive: negating a negative yields a positive.

If the sun is shining, then Samantha does not wear green.

- **Contrapositive:** If Samantha is wearing green (if she's not not wearing green), then the sun is not shining.

Necessary Versus Sufficient Conditions

For success in formal logic, it's crucial that you distinguish clearly between necessary and sufficient conditions. Here are examples of each:

- **Sufficient:** If I yell loudly at my cat Adrian, he will run away.
- **Necessary:** The TV will work only if it is plugged in.

My yelling loudly is a sufficient condition for Adrian to run away. It's all I need to do to get the cat to run; it's sufficient. But it's not necessary. My cat might run if I throw water at him, even if I don't yell loudly.

The TV's being plugged in, on the other hand, is a necessary condition for it to work. My TV won't work without it, so it's necessary. But it's not sufficient. Other conditions must apply for the TV to work (for example, the electricity to the house must be on).

You must be clear on what kinds of deductions you can and can't make based on statements of necessary and sufficient conditions. For instance, sufficient conditions are usually signaled by an *if/then* statement, which means that the contrapositive can be used.

- If I yell loudly at my cat Adrian, he will run away.

Given that the above statement is true, which one of the following statements must also be true?

- **Not Valid:** If I don't yell loudly at my cat Adrian, he will not run away.
- **Not Valid:** If my cat Adrian has run away, then I yelled loudly at him.
- **Valid:** If my cat Adrian has not run away, then I did not yell loudly at him.

The third statement, the contrapositive, is the only one of the three that's inferable from the original. My yelling loudly is sufficient to make Adrian run away, but it's not necessary; it'll do the trick, but it's not the only possible thing that will make him head for the hills. If I squirt him with a water gun, he'll also run away. This is why the first two statements are not inferable from the original statement.

Necessary conditions, on the other hand, are usually signaled by the keyword *only*:

- The TV will work only if it is plugged in.

If that statement is true, which of the following statements must also be true?

- **Not Valid:** If my TV is plugged in, it will work.
- **Not Valid:** If my TV is not working, then it must not be plugged in.
- **Valid:** If my TV is working, then it must be plugged in.
- **Valid:** If my TV is not plugged in, then it won't work.

True, the TV won't work without plugging it in, but plugging it in is not a guarantee that the TV will work. Maybe the picture tube is broken or my electricity is out. So the first two statements above are not inferable from the original statement, while the last two are.

THE 9 CRUCIAL LOGICAL REASONING QUESTION TYPES

Now that you're familiar with the basic principles of Logical Reasoning, look at the most common types of questions you'll be asked. Of the types discussed below, the first three predominate on most Logical Reasoning sections, but become familiar with the others as well.

 GO ONLINE

As you read through the question types, think about which you had trouble with on your Diagnostic Quiz. Learn your strengths and weaknesses.

Assumption Questions

An **assumption** bridges the gap between an argument's stated evidence and conclusion. It's a piece of support that isn't explicitly stated but that is required for the conclusion to be valid. Whenever you find that a central term appears only in the conclusion, there's one or more assumptions at work.

When the question stem specifically asks for a *necessary* assumption, you can use the **Denial Test**. Simply negate the statement and see if the argument falls apart. If it does, that is the correct assumption. If, on the other hand, the argument is unaffected, the choice is wrong. Consider this simple stimulus:

> Allyson plays volleyball for Central High School. Therefore, Allyson must be more than 6 feet tall.

Based on the keyword *Therefore*, you should recognize the second sentence as the conclusion, and the first sentence as the evidence. But is the argument complete? No; the piece that's missing—the unstated link between the evidence and conclusion—is the assumption. You could probably predict this one pretty easily:

> All volleyball players for Central High School are more than 6 feet tall.

To test whether this really is an assumption necessary to the argument, apply the Denial Test by negating it. What if it's not true that all volleyball players for Central High School are more than 6 feet tall? Can you still logically conclude that Allyson must be taller than 6 feet? No, you can't. Sure, it's possible that she is, but just as possible that she's not. By denying the statement, then, the argument falls to pieces; it's simply no longer valid. And that's our conclusive proof that the statement is a necessary assumption of this argument.

You can often predict the answer to an Assumption question. In more difficult Assumption questions, the answers may not be as obvious. When the question stem asks for a necessary component of the argument, you can use the Denial Test to verify your prediction, or to test answer choices. However, don't forget that the Denial Test only works when the question stem is looking for a necessary element—not all Assumption questions can be attacked this way.

Sample Stems

Here are some of the ways that Assumption questions are worded:

- Upon which one of the following assumptions does the author rely?
- Which one of the following, if added to the passage, will make the conclusion logical?
- The validity of the argument depends on which one of the following?

Strengthen or Weaken Questions

Determining an argument's necessary assumption, as you've just seen, is required to answer assumption questions. But it also is often necessary for another common question type—Strengthen and Weaken questions.

One way to weaken an argument is to break down a central piece of evidence. Another way is to attack the validity of any assumption the author is making. The answer to many Strengthen questions provides additional support by affirming the truth of an assumption or by presenting more persuasive evidence.

Consider the stimulus used before, but look at it in the context of these other question types:

> Allyson plays volleyball for Central High School. Therefore, Allyson must be more than 6 feet tall.

The assumption holding this argument together was that all volleyball players for Central High School are more than 6 feet tall. So, if the question asked you to weaken the argument, the answer might attack that assumption:

> Which one of the following, if true, would most weaken the argument?

Answer: Not all volleyball players at Central High School are more than 6 feet tall. But what about strengthening the argument? Again, the key may be a necessary assumption:

> Which one of the following, if true, would most strengthen the argument?

Answer: All volleyball players at Central High School are more than 6 feet tall. Here, by making explicit the author's central assumption, you've ve in effect bolstered the argument.

Weaken questions tend to be more common on the LSAT than Strengthen questions. But here are a few concepts that apply to both question types:

- Weakening an argument is not the same thing as disproving it, and strengthening is not the same as proving the conclusion true. A strengthener tips the scale towards the validity of the conclusion, while a weakener tips the scale in the other direction.
- The wording of these questions often takes the form "Which one of the following, if true, would most [weaken/strengthen] the argument?" The *if true* part means that you have to accept the truth of the choice right off the bat, no matter how unlikely it may sound to you.
- Don't be careless. Wrong answer choices in these questions often have exactly the opposite of the desired effect. That is, if you're asked to strengthen an argument, it's quite likely that one or more of the wrong choices will contain information that actually weakens it.

Sample Stems

The stems associated with these two question types are usually self-explanatory. Here are some alternate forms you can expect to see on the test:

Weaken:

- Which one of the following, if true, would most seriously damage the argument above?
- Which one of the following, if true, casts the most doubt on the argument above?

Strengthen:

- Which one of the following, if true, would provide the most support for the conclusion in the argument above?
- The argument above would be more persuasive if which one of the following were found to be true?

Flaw Questions

This question type asks you to recognize what's wrong with an argument. There are two basic types.

In the **general** type, the correct choice will critique the reasoning by pointing out a classic fallacy (e.g., "The argument attacks the source of an opinion, rather than the opinion itself"). In this case, the flaw falls into a general, well-defined category.

In the **specific** type, the correct answer will attack a specific piece of the argument's reasoning. An example of this would be: "It cannot be concluded that the number of male turtles has increased simply because the percentage of turtles that are male has increased." Notice that the subject of this statement isn't turtles; it's the author's faulty reasoning about turtles. The most common specific flaws in Logical Reasoning are unwarranted assumptions, ignored alternative possibilities, and scope shifts.

In each case, the required skill is the ability to identify the structure of the author's argument—and where the argument goes wrong. Use your practice to become familiar with each of these types.

Inference Questions

Another of the most common question types in Logical Reasoning is the Inference question. Drawing an **inference** is a matter of considering one or more statements as evidence and then drawing a conclusion from them. (This same concept, also known as **deduction**, is central to Logic Games, as well.)

Sometimes the inference is very close to the author's main point. Other times, it deals with a less central point. A valid inference is something that must be true if the statements in the passage are true—an extension of the argument rather than a necessary part of it.

For instance, take a somewhat expanded version of the volleyball team argument:

> Allyson plays volleyball for Central High School, despite the team's rule against participation by nonstudents. Therefore, Allyson must be over 6 feet tall.

Inference: Allyson is not a student at Central High School. If Allyson plays volleyball *despite* the team's rule against participation by nonstudents, she must not be a student. Otherwise, she wouldn't be playing despite the rule; she'd be playing in accordance with the rule. But note that this inference is not an essential assumption of the argument, since the conclusion about Allyson's height doesn't depend on it.

So be careful; unlike an assumption, an inference need not have anything to do with the author's stated conclusion.

Sample Stems

Inference questions probably have the most varied wording of all the Logical Reasoning question stems. Some question stems denote inference fairly obviously. Others are more subtle, and still others may even look like other question types entirely. Here's a sample of the various forms that Inference questions can take:

- Which one of the following is implied by the argument above?
- The author suggests that . . .
- If all the statements above are true, which one of the following must also be true?
- The author of the passage would most likely agree with which one of the following?
- The passage provides the most support for which one of the following?
- Which of the following is probably the conclusion towards which the author is moving?

KAPLAN EXCLUSIVE

Understanding argument structure is key in Flaw, Method of Argument, and Parallel Reasoning questions.

Method of Argument Questions

Method of Argument questions ask you to demonstrate an understanding of how an author's argument is put together. Unlike Flaw questions, Method of Argument questions don't always involve faulty logic. The key skill—once again—involves being able to analyze the structure of an argument.

There are two types of Method of Argument questions. The **general** type deals with classic argument structures, such as, "arguing from a small sample to a larger group," or "inferring a causal relationship from a correlation." The **specific** type gives you a description of the argument in much more specific terms. An example of this might read, "The author presents the case of his mother in order to show that not all astronauts are men."

The questions you should ask yourself in order to determine the author's method of argument are: What is the evidence? What is the conclusion? How does the author link the evidence and conclusion together?

Parallel Reasoning Questions

Parallel Reasoning questions require you to identify the choice that contains the argument most similar to that in the stimulus. To do this, you need to grasp the distinction between an argument's form and its content.

"A causal relationship concluded from a correlation" is a form—a type—of reasoning. Arguments with this form can contain virtually any content. Your task is to abstract the argument's form, with as little content as possible, and then locate the choice that uses the same form. Don't let yourself be drawn to a choice based on its subject matter. A stimulus about music may have an answer choice that also involves music, but that doesn't mean that the reasoning in the two arguments is similar.

A good approach to these questions is to see first if the argument can be symbolized algebraically, using X's and Y's. Take the following example:

> All cows eat grass. This animal eats grass. Therefore, it must be a cow.

This (flawed) argument can be symbolized in the following way:

> All X do Y. This does Y. Therefore, this must be an X.

If the stimulus can be symbolized this way, your job will be to search for the choice that can be symbolized in the same way. Your answer might look something like this:

> Every politician (all X) tells lies (does Y). Stegner is lying (this does Y). So he must be a politician (therefore, this must be an X).

Notice that the wording doesn't have to match exactly ("all X" means "every X"), and that the subject matter doesn't have to match in the least. What's important is the parallel structure.

KAPLAN EXCLUSIVE

The right choice in a Parallel Reasoning question mimics the structure, not the content, of the stimulus.

Sometimes, though, an argument's reasoning isn't amenable to symbolization. In such a case, see if you can put a label on the type of argument being used, such as "Arguing from a Part to a Whole," or "Circular Reasoning" (evidence and conclusion are identical). Naming the argument will often help eliminate two or three choices that don't even come close to this general form.

As long as you can summarize the argument's form without including content, you're well on your way to finding the parallel argument among the choices.

Here are a few general tips on parallel reasoning:

- All elements of the original argument must be present in its parallel. For example, if the original argument made a generalization to a specific case, a second argument, no matter how similar in structure otherwise, cannot be parallel unless it makes a comparable generalization.
- Stay away from answer choices written about the same subject matter as the original. This is an old trick of the test makers.
- To be logically parallel it isn't necessary that all logical elements be in the same sequence, as long as all elements of the first argument exist in the second.

Paradox Questions

A paradox exists when an argument contains two or more seemingly inconsistent statements. You'll know you're dealing with a paradoxical situation if the argument ends with what seems to be a bizarre contradiction. In a typical Paradox question, you'll be asked either to find the choice that "explains the paradoxical result" or "resolves the apparent discrepancy." The correct answer will reconcile the seemingly inconsistent statements while allowing them all to still be true.

Take the following question:

> Fifty-seven percent of the registered voters in this district claimed to support the Democratic candidate, and yet the Republican candidate won the election with 55 percent of the vote.
>
> Which of the following would resolve the apparent discrepancy above?

The stimulus seems paradoxical since the Republican won the election, even though more registered voters preferred the Democrat. But do all registered voters vote? No. So a correct answer for this question might read something like this:

> Because of an intensive get-out-the-vote effort in traditionally Republican neighborhoods, a disproportionate number of registered Republicans actually voted in the election.

This statement reconciles the seemingly contradictory elements of the argument by showing that the group of registered voters is not identical to the group of people who actually voted in the election.

KAPLAN EXCLUSIVE

The correct choice in a Paradox question will often involve realizing that two groups presented as identical are actually different.

Here are a few tips for handling this question type:

- Before attempting to resolve it, make sure you have a good grasp of what the paradox is.
- Resolving paradoxes is often a matter of recognizing that the things being compared aren't really comparable. Read critically to note these subtle distinctions.
- In Paradox questions, avoid choices that merely amplify points already raised in the argument.

Principle Questions

Principle questions—the closest question type to the actual practice of law—involve fitting a specific situation into a global generality (or, occasionally, vice versa). Usually, you'll be given an argument and asked to find the principle that seems to justify the author's reasoning. For example, suppose that an author's evidence leads to this conclusion in the final sentence of the stimulus:

> Therefore, Marvin should provide a home for his ailing grandmother until she gets back on her feet.

The question stem might read: "The author's position most closely conforms to which one of the following principles?" In other words, what principle best accounts for or justifies the author's position? The answer could sound like this:

> If a close relative is in need, one should always do one's best to help that person, regardless of personal inconvenience.

On the other hand, the question stem might read: "Which one of the following principles would justify Marvin's refusal to follow the author's recommendation?" In this case, the answer may be something like this:

> No person should be obligated to provide support for another person, even if that other person is a close relative.

Notice the general nature of both principles. Whereas they don't specifically mention Marvin or his grandmother, or the exact conditions of the stimulus per se, the general situation (helping a relative in need) is addressed in both.

The correct answer to Principle questions is usually the one that expresses the key concepts and contains the key terms that the other choices leave out. Be extremely wary of choices that are outside scope. Most of the wrong choices contain principles that sound very formal and look good on the page by themselves, but that don't address the author's main concern.

Point at Issue Questions

A relatively new question type, these always involve a stimulus with two or more expressed opinions, and your task is to identify the issue on which they take differing positions. To see where two arguments differ, separately compare their conclusions and their evidence. The trick is to stay within the scope of both speakers' arguments; the point at issue can't be something that one speaker raises, but the other doesn't address at all. The correct answer will describe a point addressed by both speakers and about which the speakers hold conflicting views.

Sample Stems

The stems associated with these questions are usually self-explanatory. Here are a couple of examples:

- A and B disagree over which of the following
- The point at issue between A and B is

Now that you've learned the basic Logical Reasoning principles and have been exposed to the full range of question types, it's time to learn how to orchestrate all of that knowledge into a systematic approach to Logical Reasoning.

KAPLAN'S 4-STEP METHOD FOR LOGICAL REASONING

1. Read the Question Stem First.

Preview the stem so that you know exactly what you're looking for in the stimulus. For example, say the question attached to the original library argument above asked the following:

> The author supports her point about the need for rehabilitation at the Brookdale Library by citing which of the following?

By previewing this question stem, you know what to look for—evidence, the support provided for the conclusion. If the question asked you to find an assumption, you would read looking for a crucial missing piece of the argument. Previewing the stem allows you to set the tone of your attack on each stimulus, saving time.

2. Untangle the Stimulus.

With the question stem in mind, read the stimulus, paraphrasing as you go. Read actively and critically, pinpointing evidence and conclusion, and forming a sense of how strong or weak the argument is.

3. Think Critically About the Answer.

If you've read the stimulus critically enough, you may know the answer without even looking at the choices. It's much easier to find the correct choice if you have a sense of what you're looking for.

But don't ponder the question for minutes until you're able to write out your own answer—it's still a multiple-choice test, so the right answer is there on the page. Just get in the habit of framing an answer in as much detail as possible first. For instance, say a question for the library argument went like this:

> The author's argument depends on which of the following assumptions about the new building codes?

Having thought about the stimulus argument, an answer to this question may have sprung to mind immediately—that the new codes apply to existing buildings as well as to new buildings under construction. After all, the library will have to be rehabilitated to meet the new codes, according to the author. So an assumption is that the codes apply to existing buildings, and that's the kind of statement you would look for among the choices.

By the way, don't be discouraged if not all questions are good candidates for predicting answers. Some questions just won't have an answer that jumps out at you. But if used correctly, predicting (or **prephrasing**—a word Kaplan uses to mean "get a general sense of what the answer will contain or look like") will really boost your confidence and increase your speed on the section.

KAPLAN EXCLUSIVE

Your prephrase of an answer need not be elaborate or specific. Your goal is to get an idea of what you're looking for in the correct answer.

4. Evaluate the Answer Choices.

Skim the choices looking for something that sounds like what you have in mind. If you couldn't prephrase very specifically, read and evaluate each choice, throwing out the ones that are outside scope. After settling on an answer choice, you may wish to double-check the question stem to make sure that you're answering the question that was asked.

Now try this approach on a genuine Logical Reasoning item:

> A study of twenty overweight men revealed that each man experienced significant weight loss after adding SlimDown, an artificial food supplement, to his daily diet. For three months, each man consumed one SlimDown portion every morning after exercising, and then followed his normal diet for the rest of the day. Clearly, anyone who consumes one portion of SlimDown every day for at least three months will lose weight and will look and feel his or her best.
>
> Which one of the following is an assumption on which the argument depends?
>
> (A) The men in the study will gain back the weight they lost if they discontinue the SlimDown program.
>
> (B) No other dietary supplement will have the same effect on overweight men.
>
> (C) The daily exercise regimen was not responsible for the effects noted in the study.
>
> (D) Women will not experience similar weight reductions if they adhere to the SlimDown program for three months.
>
> (E) Overweight men will achieve only partial weight loss if they do not remain on the SlimDown program for a full three months.

1. Read the Question Stem First.

Quite clearly, this is an Assumption question. Before reading the first word of the stimulus, you know that the conclusion will lack an important piece of supporting evidence. Now turn to the stimulus, already on the lookout for this missing link.

2. Untangle the Stimulus.

The first sentence introduces a study of twenty men using a food supplement, resulting in weight loss for all twenty. The second sentence describes how they used it: once a day for three months, after morning exercise. So far so good; it feels as if it's building up to something. The keyword *clearly* usually indicates that some sort of conclusion follows, and in fact it does, in the third sentence: anyone who has one portion of the product daily for three months will lose weight, too.

Read critically! If you read quickly, the conclusion might seem to say that anyone who follows the same routine as the twenty men will have the same results; but it actually says that anyone who consumes the product in the same way will have the same results. You should have begun to sense the lack of crucial information at this point. The evidence in the second sentence describes a routine that includes daily exercise, whereas the conclusion focuses only on the supplement. The conclusion, therefore, doesn't stem logically from the evidence. This blends seamlessly into Step 3.

3. Think Critically About the Answer.

As expected, the argument is beginning to look as if it has a serious shortcoming. In simplified terms, the argument is: "A bunch of guys did A and B for three months and had X result. If anyone does A for three months, that person will experience X result, too." The author must be assuming that A (the product), not B (exercise), was the determining element. So, you might prephrase: "Something about exercise needs to be cleared up." That's it. All you need is an inkling of what the question is looking for, and in this case it seems that if you don't shore up the exercise issue, the argument is invalid. Turn to Step 4, which is . . .

4. Evaluate the Answer Choices.

Since you were able to prephrase something, it's best to skim the choices looking for it. And there's your idea, stated in a very LSAT-like manner, in (C). At this point, if time is an issue, simply choose (C) and move on. If you have time, quickly check the remaining choices, to find that none of them fits the bill.

In questions based on the recognition of evidence and conclusions in arguments, once you grasp the structure of the argument and have located the author's central assumption, you should be able to answer any question they throw at you. This one takes the form of an Assumption question, but it could just as easily have been a Weaken question:

> Which one of the following, if true, casts the most doubt on the argument above?

Answer: Daily exercise contributed significantly to the weight loss experienced by the men in the study. And here's a Flaw question that could have been based on the same stimulus:

> The author's reasoning is flawed because it . . .

Answer: . . . overlooks the possibility that the results noted in the study were caused by daily exercise rather than by the consumption of SlimDown.

So there you have it—a quick demonstration of how to use the strategies and techniques outlined in this chapter to work through the complete Logical Reasoning process. Apply these techniques on the following practice sets and in the Logical Reasoning sections of your Practice Tests in this book. Pay careful attention to all of the written explanations, even for the questions you got right.

SUMMARY

The basic principles of Logical Reasoning are:

- Understand the structure of arguments.
- Paraphrase the author's point.
- Judge the argument's persuasiveness.
- Answer the question being asked.
- Remember the scope of the argument.
- Eliminate wrong choices first if you have to guess.

The 9 crucial Logical Reasoning question types are:

- Assumption questions: identify unstated, necessary support for the conclusion.
- Strengthen or Weaken questions: support or challenge evidence or assumptions in the stimulus.
- Inference questions: know what must be true if statements in the stimulus are true.
- Flaw questions: focus on general classic fallacies or specific pieces of the argument.
- Method of Argument questions: identify the structure of arguments.
- Parallel Reasoning questions: mimic the structure, not the context, of the stimulus.
- Paradox questions: reconcile apparent inconsistencies.
- Principle questions: identify or apply underlying principles.
- Point at Issue questions: identify how two or more arguments differ.

Kaplan's 4-Step Method for Logical Reasoning

1. Read the question stem first.
2. Untangle the stimulus.
3. Think critically about the answer.
4. Evaluate the answer choices.

LOGICAL REASONING PRACTICE

Set One

Directions: This test consists of questions that ask you to analyze the logic of statements or short paragraphs. You are to choose as the answer to each question the one you consider correct on the basis of your common sense evaluation of the statement and its assumptions. Although a question may seem to have more than one acceptable answer, there is only one answer, and it is the one that does not entail making any illogical, extraneous, or conflicting assumptions about the question. These questions do not presuppose any knowledge of formal logic on your part.

1. In his long and epochal career, Beethoven was both synthesizer and innovator, the supreme classicist who startled the musical world of his time by his bold surges forward toward the chromaticism to come. But because his later music made so much use of unprecedented dissonance, a few cynical critics have suggested that the composer's progressively worsening deafness must have weakened his ability to imagine and produce consistently harmonious music. In other words, he was writing what he misheard, according to these critics. I maintain that, on the contrary, if the deaf Beethoven had been trying to create in a medium he had known intimately but could no longer manipulate successfully, he would have been all the more likely to ________.

   Which one of the following best completes the passage above?

   (A) depend heavily upon the rules of conventional harmony to produce predictable sounds
   (B) compose dissonances from his inability to hear what he had written
   (C) rely upon his own judgment in deciding what type of music to compose
   (D) avoid cynical criticism by composing only consistently harmonious music
   (E) suspect that his ear had become so untrustworthy that he should end his career before full maturation

2. Many factors affect the home-building industry, but the number of single family homes under construction generally rises as interest rates decline. Contractors are able to plan their hiring schedules and order essential building materials in response to reliable predictors of the movement of prevailing interest rates.

   It can be inferred from the passage above that

   (A) the price of building materials rises when interest rates decline
   (B) no factor affecting home building is as reliable a predictor as interest rates
   (C) assessments of growth in the housing industry are sometimes based upon expected fluctuations of interest rates
   (D) a contractor does not order building materials until a hiring schedule is set up
   (E) most housing being built today is single-family housing

3. Experts on the American political process have long agreed that voters like a certain amount of combativeness, even aggressiveness, in a presidential candidate. A poll just after the 1988 election, however, showed that many people had been annoyed or disgusted with the campaign and had not even bothered to vote. In addition, many voters felt that most candidates were "non-presidential." Campaigns that feature combativeness have therefore become counterproductive by causing voters to lose respect for the combative candidate.

   Which one of the following, if true, most seriously weakens the argument?

   (A) Many presidential campaigns have been memorable because they were full of surprises.

   (B) The poll cited does not specifically show that combative campaigning was responsible for voter disaffection.

   (C) Even before 1988, many voters were skeptical about politicians, particularly candidates for President.

   (D) What seems to be aggressiveness is really assertiveness, a necessary quality for keeping one's name in the public eye.

   (E) Political campaigning is a means of giving the voter essential information on which he must base his decision.

4. The federal government currently interferes blatantly in the relationship between parent and child. The Internal Revenue Service provides a child-care or dependent's deduction on the annual income tax return. In effect, the government, by rewarding some providers of support, determines which taxpayers are to be considered worthy enough to care for dependents.

   Which one of the following, if true, weakens the argument above?

   (A) A taxpayer need only attach the appropriate schedule to the tax form to apply for the deduction.

   (B) The deduction is likely to offer a proportionately greater benefit to the lower income taxpayer.

   (C) A child must be living at home with the provider of support in order to qualify as a dependent.

   (D) The deduction actually affects a fairly small percentage of taxpayers.

   (E) The deduction is available to anyone who supplies the principal support of a dependent.

5. Detective-adventure series and other action programming on prime-time television have been criticized for inciting some viewers, male adolescents in particular, to commit acts of violence. The most carefully engineered studies have not, however, supported this assumption. Rather, it seems likely that someone who is frustrated and resentful, and therefore prone to violence, is drawn to the kind of programming that shows characters who release their frustrations in acts of violence.

   Which one of the following would provide the most logical concluding sentence for the paragraph above?

   (A) In fact, action programming probably helps a frustrated viewer release his hostility without resorting to violence.

   (B) Moreover, there are studies that indicate that male adolescents are more likely than other viewers to believe that the world shown in action programming is realistic.

   (C) In other words, an unusual interest in action programming may be an indication of a violence-prone personality rather than an incitement to violence.

   (D) Be that as it may, action programming continues to grow in popularity with the American TV audience.

   (E) Therefore, the reasonable observer of the American scene will conclude that action programming should be banned from primetime viewing hours.

Questions 6–7

Although the legislative process in our democratic government is based on the proposition that Congress must represent the interests of the majority of its constituents, this principle that the majority rules is frequently contradicted by the efforts of lobbyists. Minority interests with the wherewithal to finance hard-sell lobbying campaigns can distort an elected official's sense of public opinion, thereby exercising a destructive influence over political decisions.

6. The argument above depends upon the truth of which one of the following assumptions?

   (A) The democratic process is a reflection of our capitalist economic system.

   (B) The democratic process requires that minority interests be protected by constitutional amendment.

   (C) Minority interests cannot be protected without spending large sums of money on lobbying activities.

   (D) The democratic process cannot function properly unless the activities of big business are restrained.

   (E) The democratic process depends on the ability of all members of society to have equal influence on the legislative process.

7. Which one of the following, if true, would most weaken the argument above?

   (A) The majority opinion on many political issues is ill informed and unconsidered.

   (B) Elected officials are rarely influenced by pressures of lobbying campaigns.

   (C) Interest groups can accumulate large sums of money through fund-raising activities.

   (D) All groups and interests are entitled to hire professional lobbyists to represent their cause.

   (E) There is no clear-cut majority position on many political issues facing Congress.

8. If we reduce the rate of income taxation, people will spend a larger portion of their gross incomes on consumer goods. This will stimulate economic growth and result in higher salaries and thus in higher government revenues, despite a lower rate of taxation.

   Which one of the following arguments most closely resembles the reasoning in the statements above?

   (A) If we reduce the amount of overtime our employees work, production costs will decline and our total income will thus increase.

   (B) If we make it harder to participate in the school lunch program, people will have to pay for more of their food and the farm income will therefore increase.

   (C) If a movie is classified as obscene, more people will want to see it and the morals of the general community will be corrupted more than they would be otherwise.

   (D) If we give our employees more paid holidays, their efficiency while actually on the job will improve and our total productivity will thus increase.

   (E) If we give our children more spending money, they will learn to manage their finances better and will thereby realize the virtue of thrift.

9. If a judge is appointed for life, she will make courtroom decisions that reflect the accumulated wisdom inherent in this country's judicial history, relying upon the law and reason rather than upon trends in political thinking. If, on the other hand, the judge is appointed or elected for short terms in office, her decisions will be heavily influenced by the prevailing political climate. In sum, the outcome of many court cases will be determined by the method by which the presiding judge has been installed in her post.

   Each of the following, if true, provides support for the argument above EXCEPT

   (A) Surveys indicate that judges enjoy their work and want to remain in office as long as possible.

   (B) Judges appointed for life are just as informed about political matters as are judges who must run for re-election.

   (C) The rulings of judges who must run for re-election are generally approved of by the voters who live in their elective districts.

   (D) Most judges appointed for life hand down identical rulings on similar cases throughout their long careers.

   (E) Only judges who are selected for short terms of office employ pollsters to read the mood of the electorate.

10. Advertisement: Savvy shoppers know that the Fall Sale at Thompson's gives you great savings on clothes for the whole family. When you make at least one purchase in each of the Men's, Women's, and Children's departments during the sale, you'll receive a voucher for 50% off any purchase in the Housewares department. If you're working to clothe the family on a budget, don't miss the Fall Sale at Thompson's!

    Which one of the following provides the most serious criticism of the above advertisement?

    (A) Many shoppers may not make a purchase in each department during September.
    (B) The savings advertised are for housewares, not for clothing.
    (C) The length of the sale is not specified in the advertisement.
    (D) A purchase in the Housewares department is much more expensive than a purchase in the Women's department.
    (E) The sale does not take into account other discounts that customers may redeem.

11. It is possible for a panhandler to collect a considerable amount of money from passersby if she can convince them that she is destitute and that begging is the only way for her to help herself. If, on the other hand, passersby get the impression that they are being conned or that the panhandler is just being lazy, they will not give her anything at all.

    Which one of the following statements can be most reliably concluded from the passage above?

    (A) Most panhandlers are unwilling to work.
    (B) If someone begs when she does not need to, people will not give her any money.
    (C) Most passersby would give a panhandler money if they thought that she was not conning them.
    (D) Passersby often base their decision of whether or not to give money to a panhandler on their impressions of her and her honesty.
    (E) People who give money to panhandlers are not influenced by how much change they have in their pockets when they decide the amount of money they will give.

12. Dr. Kells is a better physician than Dr. Li. This is obvious because in a recent survey their mutual patients rated Dr. Kells as the better physician.

    The argument above assumes that

    (A) patient rating is a valid indicator of the quality of a physician
    (B) patients will rate a doctor as "better" if they feel more comfortable with that doctor
    (C) the better doctor will be the one with greater experience
    (D) the better doctor is the one from whose care patients benefit more
    (E) there are no doctors better than Dr. Kells

13. Although temporary and contract employees can play an important role in completing projects and adjusting to seasonal work flow, they are not an adequate substitute for a full-time, permanent staff. In order to thrive, the company needs workers who are not just skilled and efficient, but who have a personal connection to their work and a dedication to the company. A staff made up of contract or temporary employees is incomplete at best.

    The author of this passage assumes that

    (A) temporary employees are detrimental to a company's success
    (B) companies should encourage temporary employees to feel dedicated to their employers
    (C) seasonal work flow is not an important factor in assessing an employee's suitability for work
    (D) temporary employees lack connection and commitment to the companies that hire them
    (E) permanent employees are more skilled and efficient than are temporary employees

Set Two

Directions: This test consists of questions that ask you to analyze the logic of statements or short paragraphs. You are to choose as the answer to each question the one you consider correct on the basis of your common sense evaluation of the statement and its assumptions. Although a question may seem to have more than one acceptable answer, there is only one answer, and it is the one that does not entail making any illogical, extraneous, or conflicting assumptions about the question. These questions do not presuppose any knowledge of formal logic on your part.

1. We gave working parents the opportunity to use a trial membership to our new Flash Fitness Centers. More than 85 percent found this convenient new workout to be very effective. If you're a parent who is crunched for time, Flash Fitness is the quick solution!

   Which one of the following statements is the most serious criticism of the advertisement above?

   (A) Working parents are not necessarily representative of the general population.

   (B) Other fitness centers are just as convenient and effective as Flash Fitness.

   (C) The fact that working parents found Flash Fitness effective does not mean that it was quick.

   (D) "Effective" is a subjective term and makes no representation as to a measurable degree of success.

   (E) Most people do not consider convenience as an important factor when choosing a fitness center.

2. Ranjit was extremely upset when he received a failing grade in his engineering class, because he had attended every class, participated in class discussions, and turned in every project except for the 3-D modeling project. He concluded that the grade was unfair, since other students who had not turned in the 3-D modeling project had passed the class.

   Based on the information contained in the passage, it is reasonable to infer that:

   (A) Ranjit has never failed a class before.

   (B) Ranjit received a failing grade primarily because he didn't turn in the 3-D modeling assignment.

   (C) Ranjit received above-average scores on all of his assignments except the 3-D modeling project.

   (D) Ranjit believes that he received a failing grade primarily because he did not turn in the 3-D modeling project.

   (E) Ranjit's performance was above average in comparison to students in other engineering courses.

3. Several of the older pieces in the City Opera Company's costume shop, made from rare vintage fabrics, have become threadbare and worn from improper storage and exposure to light. Luckily, the original seamstress saved the extra fabric from the creation of these costumes. Utilizing the seamstress's original patterns and these pieces of fabric, the costume designer will be able to restore the costumes to their original fabric quality.

   Which of the following statements, if true, would most strengthen the author's argument?

   (A) The costume designer will be able to duplicate the original seamstress's careful technique.

   (B) The heavy traffic and difficulty in maintaining a steady climate make the costume shop a less than ideal location for storage of the costumes.

   (C) The seamstress anticipated that the costumes would eventually need repairs.

   (D) The fabric that was put aside when the costumes were made has not itself been damaged by improper storage.

   (E) Garment storage techniques were not advanced enough at the time the costumes were made to prevent them from becoming damaged.

4. Due to a dramatic drop in population, Academy B, known as one of the city's best schools, closed. Many of its teachers got jobs in suburban school districts well known for their excellent schools. They returned to Academy B when it reopened two years later and have all remained there; the school is again considered one of the finest in the city.

   Which one of the following can be most reasonably inferred from the statements above?

   (A) The quality of education at Academy B vastly improved only because its teachers worked in other excellent schools.

   (B) Academy B reopened because its board recognized the high quality of the teachers' work.

   (C) When Academy B reopened, some suburban school teachers left their jobs

   (D) The teachers in the district's other schools did not have an opportunity to teach at Academy B when it reopened.

   (E) Although the teachers in the district's other schools were inferior to those at Academy B, the closing of the school had no real effect on the district's quality of education.

5. Proponents of writing programs have reacted with uncritical enthusiasm to recent studies showing an increase in writing programs in high schools. The majority of these classes, however, utilize creative writing techniques rather than the traditional practice in reading texts and writing and revising expository text. Unfortunately, by concentrating on a less practical type of expression, these programs will actually have the undesirable effect of decreasing the numbers of high school graduates who are skilled at expository writing.

   The author's conclusion relies on which of the following beliefs?

   (A) Introducing an expository writing requirement for graduation would lead to the abandonment of most creative writing classes.

   (B) When students have a choice, more of them will enroll in a creative writing course than in an expository writing course.

   (C) Creative writing courses fail to provide the skills necessary to be an effective expository writer.

   (D) Continued emphasis on creative writing courses will eventually reduce the pool of qualified instructors of expository writing.

   (E) Most high school graduates today have at least average skills in expository writing.

6. Figures from other cities conclusively disprove the commonly held belief that magnet school programs in Minneapolis caused the extremely long waiting lists for certain schools. Some cities with magnet school programs have no waiting lists for schools at all, while in other cities with no magnet programs, parents send their children to schools in other areas because the classes in their neighborhood elementary schools are so crowded.

   The author of the argument is assuming which of the following?

   (A) Since magnet school programs offer different programs than other schools, parents' decisions to add their children to the waiting lists must be motivated by an interest in that particular school.

   (B) Since magnet school programs have not caused long school waiting lists in every case, they have not caused the increase in Minneapolis.

   (C) Since magnet school programs in other cities did not cause school waiting lists to grow, their impact has been beneficial.

   (D) Minneapolis's magnet school program fostered long waiting lists because it did not sufficiently anticipate the number of interested families.

   (E) Despite magnet school programs, waiting lists for schools in Minneapolis are minimal.

7. Researchers in the harbor town of Osceola have determined that the channeling of recycled wastewater into the harbor is endangering the health of the town's residents. A sharp increase in cases of the intestinal illness giardia has been directly attributed to bacteria that began to appear in drinking water supplies immediately following the implementation of the wastewater recycling program. The researchers have proposed adding the synthetic enzyme tripticase to the water during recycling. The addition of this enzyme would solve the health problem by eliminating the bacteria that causes giardia.

   Which one of the following statements, if true, most weakens the researchers' argument?

   (A) The tripticase enzyme also acts to break down bacteria causing intestinal conditions other than giardia.

   (B) Globally, giardia is one of the least common and the least severe of all known illnesses related to the consumption of contaminated drinking water,

   (C) No other illnesses aside from giardia have increased significantly in Osceola since the wastewater recycling program began.

   (D) Giardia may be caused by the ingestion of contaminated food as well as contaminated drinking water.

   (E) The tripticase enzyme also breaks down chlorine that is essential to maintaining a safe drinking water supply.

8. Fairfield College's Dean of English noticed that average scores on the year-end freshman English assessment have been significantly lower since 1998 than they were prior to that year. She also realized that in 1998, the freshman English classes had been moved from a 2 P.M. time slot to an 8 A.M. time slot. The dean, pointing out that students perform better when they are wide awake, concluded that test scores would increase if the English class were moved back to the afternoon time slot.

   The Dean's argument assumes that which of the following is true?

   (A) Classroom space could be made available for the English class meeting at 2 P.M.

   (B) Numerous factors could account for the drop in test scores.

   (C) Other colleges with higher English test scores have classes that meet later in the day.

   (D) Students are more likely to be wide awake during the afternoon than they are early in the morning.

   (E) The quality of the English professors' instruction has little or no effect on the students' test scores.

9. It is more expensive to live far from an interstate than near one, not because of the cost of commuting, but because of the decrease in property values associated with proximity to an interstate. Interstates are located in urban areas, and although homes in urban areas generally command higher prices than those in less populated areas, the presence of an interstate nearby can cause a large decrease in property values. The property values of homes far from an interstate are not subject to this decrease. As a result, rural and suburban homes that are far from an interstate are generally more expensive than urban homes that are near one.

   The above argument is based on which one of the following assumptions?

   (A) Interstates are built only in neighborhoods that are made up primarily of single-family homes.

   (B) The property value loss associated with having an interstate nearby is greater than the gain associated with being located in an urban area.

   (C) Urban homes typically have less square footage than homes in suburban and rural areas.

   (D) Homeowners who live near an interstate are more likely to raise their property values by remodeling.

   (E) Most homes have approximately the same property value when factors of location are not taken into consideration.

10. When Han came home from work, she discovered that although the doors and windows were all closed, her security alarm had gone off, something that can happen only if the alarm is set off by strong winds or the vibrations of a large vehicle. Earlier that morning, the alarm had been set off by a large truck passing by, but Han turned off the alarm again before she departed. The forecast called for a 40 percent chance of windy weather. Since the truck had already left the neighborhood when Han left for work, the second alarm must have been activated by a strong wind.

    The speaker's conclusion about how the second alarm was activated assumes which one of the following?

    (A) It is easy to tell the difference between an alarm activated by windy weather and one activated by the vibrations of a large vehicle.

    (B) The vibrations of a vehicle are more likely to set off an alarm than is windy weather.

    (C) No large vehicles have passed by Han's house since the truck left earlier in the morning.

    (D) The alarm was set off because it is too sensitive to movement.

    (E) Every time a large vehicle passes by, the alarm will be set off.

11. From the eighth through the nineteenth century, the Japanese imperial power underwent a period of steady decline. This is often wrongly attributed to a fundamental bias in Japanese society ensuring that clan loyalty was always more important than loyalty to any emperor. A close look at the evidence, however, reveals that even as late as the Kamakura period in the thirteenth and fourteenth centuries, military dictators with the title "shogun" ruled in the name of the emperor and exercised a strong, centralized power.

    Which one of the following, if true, would most seriously weaken the argument?

    (A) Many Japanese followed the shogun because they feared his power and not because they were loyal.

    (B) The Kamakura shogunate collapsed in 1333, and Japan experienced 200 years of civil war.

    (C) The shoguns came from independent clans and ruled without concern for the emperor.

    (D) During the earlier Heian period, from the years 794 to 1185, the power of the shoguns was far less than that of the emperor.

    (E) Many historians believe that geography and the system of taxation were more crucial than clan loyalty in undermining imperial power.

<u>Questions 12–13</u>

The moral condemnation, voiced by some segments of the public, of the students arrested recently while demonstrating at City Hall is an error. We should keep in mind that, more than 200 years ago, our forefathers dumped tea in Boston Harbor in defiance of the British.

12. Which one of the following would be the most effective response for the author's opponents in disputing his argument?

    (A) It is unpatriotic to demonstrate in front of a City Hall.

    (B) Students are too inexperienced to understand the consequences of demonstrations.

    (C) In today's world, one's beliefs and conscience are rarely the motivation behind one's actions.

    (D) The American patriots who threw tea into Boston Harbor had some public support for their cause.

    (E) Simply because some past demonstrations by citizens are considered justified does not mean all such acts are justified.

13. Which one of the following best describes the author's method of argument?

    (A) He attacks the public for its manifest hypocrisy.

    (B) He argues from a general principle of rebellion to a specific instance of that rebellion.

    (C) He argues from a specific instance of rebellion to a general principle concerning the justification of all rebellion.

    (D) He draws an analogy between the students' actions and the actions of patriots now deemed justified.

    (E) He argues from the lack of sufficient evidence concerning the students' actions to a conclusion supporting the students' actions.

Set Three

Directions: This test consists of questions that ask you to analyze the logic of statements or short paragraphs. You are to choose as the answer to each question the one you consider correct on the basis of your common sense evaluation of the statement and its assumptions. Although a question may seem to have more than one acceptable answer, there is only one answer, and it is the one that does not entail making any illogical, extraneous, or conflicting assumptions about the question. These questions do not presuppose any knowledge of formal logic on your part.

1. The problem with arms reduction is that it is an illusory concept benefiting none. Even though designated stockpiles are being reduced, the weapons race continues, as the destructive power of new technologies and remaining arsenals is enhanced in order to maintain the pre-existing firepower. Thus, although it fosters an illusion of progress, arms reduction does nothing to curtail the proliferation of weaponry, and all must continue to live under the constant threat of annihilation.

   Which one of the following, if true, would most strengthen the author's argument?

   (A) Arms reduction allows steady maintenance of the existing balance of power.

   (B) No arms limitation proposals have aimed at completely eliminating a nation's armament stockpile.

   (C) The five largest military powers have increased funding for new weapons in each of the last ten years.

   (D) The distinction between offensive and defensive weapon systems is often merely a matter of interpretation.

   (E) Arms limitation treaties have only accounted for the elimination of fifteen percent of the total firepower possessed by the five largest military powers.

2. These so-called pacifists are either the victims or the propagators of a false logic. They claim that weapons reductions would result in a so-called climate of peace, thereby diminishing the likelihood of conflicts leading to war. But what are the facts? In the past ten years, during which time we have seen increased spending for such defense requirements as state-of-the-art weapons systems and augmented combat personnel, there have been fewer military actions involving our forces than in any previous decade in the twentieth century. Our own installations have not been attacked and our allies have rarely found it necessary to ask for our armed support. In other words, defense readiness is, in the real world, the most efficient peace-making tool.

   Which of the following is an assumption underlying the conclusion of the passage above?

   (A) Military actions involving our forces can be instigated by any of a number of different factors.

   (B) Our buildup of weapons systems and combat personnel has prevented our adversaries from increasing their own spending on defense.

   (C) The increased defense spending of the past ten years has lessened the need for significant military expenditure in future decades.

   (D) At the present time, state-of-the-art weapons systems and the augmentation of combat personnel are equally important to a nation's resources.

   (E) The number of military actions involving our forces would have been greater in the past decade if we had not increased our defense spending.

3. A free press always informs the public of all aspects of a country's current military operations except for cases in which the safety of troops or the success of a mission would be jeopardized by the public's knowing.

   Which one of the following adheres most closely to the principle set forth above?

   (A) A free press would publish editorials supporting a current military campaign, but could repress dissenting opinions regarding the campaign.

   (B) An unfree press would release information on the country's prisoners of war taken during a current military campaign, unless such information would hamper efforts to secure the prisoners' release.

   (C) A free press would accurately report the number of casualties suffered on both sides of a battle, but could withhold information regarding the possible targets for a future military strike.

   (D) An unfree press would print inflammatory accounts of an international event in order to garner public support for an unpopular war.

   (E) A free press would reveal any new information regarding the country's past involvement in secret military operations as soon as that information became available.

4. The Meisman Art Center recently discovered an early work by the renowned painter Marin Dillard, who became famous for work produced during a 10-year period late in her lifetime. This new painting dates to approximately 35 years earlier than her previously known earliest work. What is surprising about the discovery is that, even though a significant amount of time passed between the creation of this and Dillard's later paintings, the style of the new piece is indistinguishable from Dillard's other work. This new discovery helps to elucidate an exciting new facet of Dillard's life and work.

   It can be inferred that the author of the above passage believes that:

   (A) Dillard became famous on the merits of all her work, not just the later pieces.

   (B) Despite the assertions of the art historians who discovered it, the painting in question was not created by Marin Dillard.

   (C) It is likely that the recently discovered painting was actually created much later than experts have claimed.

   (D) Art historians have not been sufficiently thorough in their attempts to make note of stylistic differences between the new piece and Dillard's later work.

   (E) Thirty-five years is an unusually long time for an artist to work without showing any change in artistic style.

5. Salesperson: These computers are marked down dramatically, because two-thirds of the hard drives stop working within a year of their purchase.

   Customer: That isn't a problem. I'll buy three, so I will be certain to have one that continues working after a year.

   The customer's reasoning is faulty in that he mistakenly assumes that

   (A) just because a computer doesn't work in one instance doesn't mean it won't work in another instance
   (B) although the computers don't always continue to work, they are likely to do so for this customer
   (C) one out of any three computers will continue working after a year
   (D) the effectiveness of the computers is not dependent upon who uses them
   (E) the price of three marked-down computers is less than the price of one new computer

6. The human resources department at Luna Systems recently changed its open-door policy, which had allowed employees to view or add information to their human resources portfolios upon request. The portfolios are now accessible only to staff in the human resources department. Many employees are upset with the change—which was initiated by the chair of Human Resources, Andrea McCarthy—and believe that she does not have the company's best interests in mind. However, McCarthy has been a loyal employee of Luna for 12 years, as is clearly evidenced by the records contained in her human resources portfolio.

   The author's conclusion about McCarthy assumes which one of the following?

   (A) Only long-term employees of the human resources department are permitted to add information to employee portfolios.
   (B) Employees' requests to view portfolios are usually motivated by a desire to get a fuller picture of their job performances.
   (C) Salary increases are usually based in part on favorable feedback received from customers and supervisors.
   (D) The open-door policy was instituted to give supervisors a more accurate picture of an employee's performance.
   (E) The information in McCarthy's human resources portfolio is an accurate record of her employment at Luna Systems.

7. Toy Manufacturer: This rubber ball is costly to make. We should switch to a less costly brand of rubber for this product.

   Marketing Analyst: But the ball sells so well because of its superior bouncing properties. No other material performs as well. We should stick with what we know we can sell.

   The speakers above disagree over which one of the following issues?

   (A) Whether the rubber used for this ball is more expensive than other available materials.
   (B) Whether this product regularly meets its sales quotas.
   (C) Whether the company should make the rubber ball from a different brand of rubber.
   (D) Whether customer priorities should factor into product development decisions.
   (E) Whether other rubber materials perform as well as the material currently used.

8. Although Bidwell raises several good points in his criticism of the exclusive nature of the academic arena, his piece as a whole is poorly written, resulting in a confusing and distracting experience for his readers. For example, Chapter 6 accuses academics of dwelling in an "ivory tower" when it discusses their tendency to work in isolation without looking for concrete connections to the world. Perhaps this description was more accurate when Bidwell was a student, but I am certain that college campuses today have neither towers nor white buildings.

   The author of this passage has failed to recognize an instance of which of the following in Bidwell's writing?

   (A) generalization
   (B) deduction
   (C) reasoning through counterexample
   (D) figurative language
   (E) irony

9. Several of the concepts for the company's new advertising campaign can immediately be recognized as effective based on prior knowledge of the market alone. Past experience has shown us, however, that some concepts can be shown to be effective only when the campaign is launched and studies of its effects are undertaken.

   Which of the following can be logically inferred from the passage above?

   (A) It may be impossible to determine the effectiveness of some aspects of the new campaign until after the campaign has launched.
   (B) Many concepts for the company's new advertising campaign are too closely related to prior campaigns to be effective.
   (C) It is likely that there are effective concepts that have not yet been proposed for the company's new campaign.
   (D) The company is less likely to find success with an untested concept than with one that has been launched and studied.
   (E) Many of the concepts that are identified as effective based on prior knowledge of the market have been abandoned before being launched and studied.

10. Holt: The most effective and accurate way of determining the level of need for a food shelf in our neighborhood is by distributing an anonymous questionnaire at the next meeting of the Concerned Neighbors Committee. Nearly all of the meeting attendees are neighborhood residents, and because the responses are anonymous, people will be assured of confidentiality. We can then create an accurate picture of the need for emergency food services in our area.

    Which one of the following provides the most serious criticism of the argument above?

    (A) The plan overlooks the fact that a significant number of people who would use a food shelf may not be members of the Concerned Neighbors Committee.

    (B) The anonymous nature of the questionnaire prevents neighborhood organizations from identifying families who might benefit from a food shelf.

    (C) The plan does not provide a reliable means of determining the level of need for food shelves in adjacent neighborhoods.

    (D) The plan does not distinguish between households that would use a food shelf and those that simply have a tight food budget.

    (E) The plan overlooks the fact that some people surveyed may lie because they are embarrassed by their need for emergency food services.

11. Some commentators have theorized that candidate Steven Perez and incumbent Senator Marlin Ray have a great deal of common ground in their platforms. However, the two candidates could not be more different, as evidenced by the following quotes from the men themselves. Steven Perez eloquently expressed his concern about crime when he said, "Our priority must be increasing police presence to provide safe streets for our children as they walk to school, come home, and fall asleep at night." Compare this to the words of Senator Ray, who said to reporters, "You can hire as many police officers as you like, but one factor in keeping the streets safe is teaching children how to express themselves without violence."

    Which of the following statements offers the most effective criticism of the argument above?

    (A) It assumes that all candidates share the same beliefs about important issues.

    (B) It draws a conclusion about the differences between the two platforms based on information about the candidates' positions on a single issue.

    (C) It confuses the danger of criminals on the street with the danger of violence among children and teenagers.

    (D) It fails to present the argument of the opposing viewpoint.

    (E) It concludes that a public statement is an accurate indication of a politician's beliefs, but provides evidence to the contrary.

12. Alisa is the stockroom coordinator at World Imports, where she is responsible for unpacking new merchandise as it arrives in the store. She estimates that 3 percent of new items in the furniture department are broken or irreparably damaged in transit, while 9 percent of each equally-sized shipment to the kitchen department arrives too damaged to sell. Since these items must be disposed of, increasing total costs, this statistic shows that it costs World Imports three times as much to stock kitchen items as furniture items are.

    Which of the following statements points out a major flaw in the reasoning above?

    (A) The cost of stocking an item is influenced by many factors besides the percentage of each shipment that is damaged in transit.

    (B) The individual shipments on which these breakage rates are based are too small to support statistical generalizations about all shipments.

    (C) Imports Etc., another housewares store, uses a different shipping company and experiences only a 1.5 percent breakage rate for furniture and a 6% breakage rate for kitchen items.

    (D) A certain amount of breakage during shipping is unavoidable, and all import businesses experience similar losses.

    (E) The company's kitchen items have become famous because they are produced in a remote Central American village, making shipping unavoidable.

13. Principal Tsang demands that the English department justify its departure from the prescribed curriculum. By moving away from the texts selected by the school board, she claims, we have left the senior class ill-prepared for the mandatory literature exit exam. What she fails to realize, however, is that the new material we introduced this school year was brought in with the aim of giving students an opportunity to hone their writing skills and experience a broader range of cultures through literature. We expressed these goals in a letter sent to students' parents earlier this fall. As a department, we are baffled by Principal Tsang's opposition to students in this school learning new and important skills.

    Which one of the following points out the principle flaw in the reasoning of the argument?

    (A) There is no guarantee that the new materials will improve students' writing skills.

    (B) The skills gained because of the new curriculum will not necessarily outweigh the skills lost by not studying the previous curriculum.

    (C) Principal Tsang is concerned with the effects of the new curriculum, and not with the intent of the new curriculum.

    (D) The authors' claim concerning the intent of the curriculum change is impossible to verify.

    (E) Students who passed last year's exam had read books from a wide range of cultures.

ANSWERS AND EXPLANATIONS

Set One
1. A
2. C
3. B
4. E
5. C
6. E
7. B
8. D
9. B
10. B
11. D
12. A
13. D

Set Two
1. C
2. D
3. D
4. C
5. C
6. B
7. E
8. D
9. B
10. C
11. C
12. E
13 D

Set Three
1. C
2. E
3. C
4. E
5. C
6. E
7. C
8. D
9. A
10. A
11. B
12. A
13. C

Set One

1. A

You have to fill in the blank. You'll want to get an idea of the direction in which the passage is going so that you can extrapolate to the most likely ending.

The passage begins by labeling Beethoven as both an innovator—meaning he brought music forward, moving towards what the passage says was "the chromaticism to come" (whatever that is)—and a synthesizer, presumably not the Mogue variety but someone who "put it all together," that is, who also worked with classical forms. *But*—a keyword of contrast here—some critics said that Beethoven's innovations (his work with dissonance) were *not* some kind of wonderful experimentation, but merely a manifestation of his increasing deafness—hence, they represent an unharmonious flaw in his later music.

The author doesn't hold with this interpretation. She does, after all, label them "cynical critics." And she says, "I maintain that, on the contrary . . . ," another signal that the author is about to take issue. If Beethoven's deafness was (as is alleged) impairing his ability to handle his musical medium, then he would have been all the more likely to do . . . what? Well, she wants to finish with a statement of a contrary effect. Her argument is: If the cause the cynics describe were, in fact, the case (if deafness made Beethoven less competent), then there would be an opposite effect, an effect something like (A). A less competent Beethoven would have played it safe by producing conventional music.

(B) directly echoes the opinion of the cynical critics—it doesn't stand in contrast to it—so it's not an opinion that would be cited to bolster the author's own feelings about Beethoven. Jumping to (E)—by seeming to agree that Beethoven was losing his abilities towards the end of his career—you can see that (E), too, is more in line with the view of the cynical critics.

(C)'s sentiment is somewhat in line with that of the author; it makes a bit of sense in that it suggests that Beethoven composed what he wanted to compose. But it doesn't act as a clear contrast to the notion that Beethoven composed dissonant music because his hearing was impaired and didn't know what sounds he was making, so it doesn't act in a satisfactory way to fill in the blank.

Finally, (D) brings up the issue of "harmonious music," which you want. But by assigning a motive to Beethoven—that he was trying to defuse critical response—(D) goes far afield. No such reference to motive has a place in the argument as written.

2. C

The stimulus isn't much of an argument, is it? It's a series of flat statements on the topic of interest rates, which are cited as having an inverse relationship with the building of single-family dwellings: as rates go down, construction goes up. In line with that (says the second sentence), contractors order building materials based on predictions of which way interest rates will go. This should make sense. All of this is in line with (C). And remember, when you're asked what can be inferred from the passage, you really want something that must be true—something in line with the scope and point of view. (C) is just a broader rephrasing of the relationship cited in the stimulus and is thus the best answer. (Note that the choice is rendered even more reasonable by its use of the qualifier *sometimes*. Because it's not an extreme statement with no exceptions possible, it's easy to sign on to (C) as a reflection of the author's equally moderate views.)

(A) brings up the cost of building materials, but since the passage says nothing at all about the costs of home building—there isn't a single reference to costs—it goes beyond the scope. You can't infer that those who sell building materials raise their prices in response to the greater demand they expect from the lower interest rates. (B) distorts the paragraph. Interest rates are cited as a good predictor, NOT the best. As for (D), just because the author mentions hiring schedules before mentioning orders for new materials does not mean that one of those things must come first on the builder's agenda. (E) is an unwarranted inference since the author's only concern is one type of dwelling, the single-family home. You cannot fairly extrapolate from this paragraph to any statement about the home-building industry in general.

3. B

The argument of the passage is not closely reasoned, as you may have noticed in the use of "however" in the second sentence. The adverb implies that what follows is a refutation of the first sentence. In fact, there is no such clear, logical relationship: there need not be a conflict between the notion that American voters prefer a combative Presidential candidate and the poll showing voter disaffection in 1988. Because the writer assumes the connection, he concludes that the disaffection, added to the feeling of many voters that the candidates were not "presidential," proves that aggressive candidates are not gaining voter respect. As we have seen, the logical error occurs in the writer's assumption that "people had been annoyed" by the "combativeness, even aggressiveness" of candidates, and not by something else. His argument is seriously weakened, therefore, if, as stated in (B), the poll did not reveal that voters were annoyed by combativeness in the campaign. Furthermore, there is no indication that any of the candidates actually were combative or aggressive.

(A) is completely off the point. The issue is not whether the 1988 campaign was "memorable," but whether it revealed a change in voter attitudes toward combativeness.

(C) refers to a general attitude on the part of many voters, but the passage is confined to an argument about specific attitudes that the author feels were created by specific events of the 1988 election. A prior climate of public skepticism would not damage the argument unless we knew that combativeness did not play a role in those earlier elections.

(D) An attempt is made to soften the charge of aggressiveness by redefining it as a somewhat more admirable and arguably essential quality for a politician. Even if this were true, however, the passage is concerned with public perceptions rather than with a discussion of the merits of what looks like combativeness.

(E) is an interpretation of events which, however legitimate in itself, has no effect on the basic argument of the passage. This choice addresses a general concept, not the specific 1988 campaign and the specific topic of the effectiveness of combative campaigning styles.

4. E

Always watch for tone words; the charge in this stimulus that the government interferes "blatantly," wrongly using its bureaucratic power, alerts you immediately to the author's opinion.

It seems that the IRS gives a child care deduction to certain people who provide support to a dependent. The complaint is that the government exercises unfair control in its choice of which people receive this deduction. The author believes that the government can have no justifiable basis on which to make this decision and is in effect deciding which people are worthy of caring for dependents and which are not.

The choice that most weakens this argument is (E). If the tax deduction is, as (E) says, available to anyone who is the principal supporter of a dependent, then that answers the implicit charge that the government has arbitrarily set itself up to decide people's personal worth. If the IRS, in other words, is using an appropriate criterion that is applied equitably to all, then the charge that the deduction is being selectively used to decide people's worth is groundless.

(A) might have fooled you because it seems to be saying that anyone who wants the deduction can have it. But it really says that anyone who attaches the appropriate schedule may apply for the deduction; they won't necessarily get it. The fact that the IRS will consider anyone doesn't mean that it isn't (as the author alleges) making the final decision on inappropriate criteria, choosing people arbitrarily on the basis of what it deems to be their personal worth. (B) mentions the deduction but is otherwise beyond the argument's scope, going off on the interesting but irrelevant topic of the relative size of the deduction for lower-income taxpayers. As for (C), even if it were true, the government might still be reaching its decision as to who gets the deduction based on improper criteria. All (C) gives us is one of those criteria—the requirement that a dependent be a co-resident. But perhaps the other criteria are just as objectionable as the author seems to feel they are. Finally, (D)'s implication that only a few people will get the deduction is another error in scope, because (D) has nothing to do with the main issue, which is the government's methods or motives. The "weakener" you need has to demonstrate that the government—contrary to what the author believes—is awarding the deduction based on proper criteria.

5. C

The author counters the view that violent TV shows incite people to commit violent acts. Apparently, a correlation has been noticed—and a correlation, of course, is an acknowledgment that two phenomena accompany each other, whether or not they're causally related—between watching TV violence and committing violent acts. Apparently, it's true that people who watch violent shows are more likely to commit violent crimes than those who don't watch those shows. And this finding might well suggest that the TV shows are causing the viewers to commit the crimes. But the author believes that the correlation is better explained in another way—that violence-prone people tend to watch violent shows because they feel an affinity to the violence-prone characters of the shows. So to the author, the critics cited in the first sentence are guilty of confusing cause and effect. The TV shows don't make the viewer violence prone; rather, it's frustration and resentment that make people violence prone and make these people watch violent TV programs.

The passage ends abruptly without a proper conclusion—for obvious reasons, since you're asked to come up with that yourself. The best answer is (C), which takes the author's argument to its logical conclusion: A person's addiction to action TV shows may reveal something about that person's tendency towards violence, but it doesn't indicate an inducement to commit violence.

(A) goes too far. It states that the effect of action shows is salutary. But that doesn't at all follow from the argument, which merely contends that the crime-and-TV-show correlation can be explained in an alternative way. (B) raises the issue of who finds the action programs realistic. This issue comes from left field. You're looking for a summation of the given argument. (B) introduces a new point. (D) is irrelevant—you would never expect a paragraph about whether action TV leads to violence to end with a quick reference to action shows' general popularity. And it's more likely that the author would disagree with (E) than end her discussion with it. In a way, her views are a defense of action programming against the charge of aiding and abetting violent crime. Therefore, (E)'s call for a ban on action shows is uncalled for.

6. E

In the stimulus for questions 6 and 7, the conclusion is expressed in the main clause of the first sentence: Lobbyists have a negative effect on the principle of "the majority rules" as practiced in Congress. The reason for that conclusion—the evidence—comes in the second sentence: Wealthy minority interests can afford to finance lobbyists, who pressure elected officials. These lobbyists make the officials believe that the opinions of the lobby are held by the people at large. So, the argument goes, some people (namely, the rich interest groups) have a greater influence on decision making than do others. And this, it's alleged, thwarts majority rule.

Thinking about a key assumption connecting this evidence to that conclusion—and that's what question 6 asks for—note that the author jumps from the idea that lobbyists distort Congress's sense of public opinion, to the conclusion that lobbyists undermine the majority-rule concept. To make this leap, the author must be assuming that all members of society have to have equal influence on legislation in order for majority-rule to work. All the evidence says is that lobbyists distort Congress's sense of public opinion—it doesn't claim that the opinion of the majority is completely silenced. The majority-rule principle (according to this passage) implies that Congress should represent the interests of the majority of its constituents. So, by asserting that the lobbyists muck things up, the author must be taking for granted that all members of society have to be heard from, have to have equal influence. That's what (E) says.

(A)'s reference to capitalism takes it way, way beyond the scope of the argument. The only connection between money and the argument's content is tangential—the idea that money helps the lobbyists distort Congress's sense of public opinion. (A) blows that out of proportion. (B), meanwhile, is too specific. To say that minority interests have to be protected by constitutional amendment is to propose a specific solution that the author need not be assuming or signing on to. (C) is off the point because the argument is about protecting majority interests—the concept of majority rule is what's allegedly in danger here. (This could be brought up as an objection to (B), as well.) Finally, (D) plays off your possible assumption that the minority interests in the passage are big-business fat cats, but as far as the passage goes, it may be the case that other minority interests, ones not connected with big business at all, engage in lobbying, too.

7. B

Now there's another major assumption at work here—it's not among the answer choices for question 6, but it's the key to question 7. The author is assuming that Congress, bullied and influenced by the lobbyists, goes about the act of legislating under that influence. He's assuming (in short) that lobbyists' efforts are, by and large, successful. But if, as (B) says, it's a rare day when an elected official is at all moved by a lobbying campaign, then the lobbyists are not successful. That in turn defuses the author's concerns about the danger to majority rule. Thus, (B) is an excellent weakener and the correct answer.

(A) is no good because the argument isn't about the quality of the majority opinion; the author is only concerned with whether the majority's opinion is being sufficiently represented. (C) supports the argument: If interest groups can (as it says) raise a lot of cash, they can then use the cash for lobbying purposes—the exact sort of situation that has the author all bent out of shape. As for (D), even if groups are entitled to employ lobbyists, it doesn't weaken the author's claim that the effect of lobbyists is dangerous. There are many things all of us are entitled or permitted to do that may not be good for us or for society. Finally, even if, as (E) says, the majority position were not one definite position but a mush of many, the author wants Congress to have a clear view that that is the case. Despite (E), the lobbyists may still muddy Congress's view, as the author alleges.

8. D

To look for an argument that "resembles" the stimulus is to find parallel reasoning—a structure that is as close as possible to the original. The stimulus says that if you lower taxes, people will buy more things, stimulating economic growth, which in turn will raise salaries, which in turn will bring in more money for the government. You're not concerned here with whether this is a sound program, but with how it's put together. The bottom line is, what you have here is something of a paradox: begin by lowering taxes, which (you'd assume) would lower government revenues, and in the end, government revenues will increase. Engaging in a particular action will (in the end) give you a result that's the opposite of what you expected.

And that's what you get in correct (D). Though it would be reasonable to expect that more employee days off would reduce productivity (since they'd be spending less time on the job), in fact productivity will be greater, the exact opposite effect. The chain of events described in the stimulus may be a little longer—it has more steps—than (D), but its overall shape is very similar.

(A) presents no paradox. You would expect that reducing overtime would bring down costs and increase total income. (B) departs from the stimulus's pattern. It has the government changing the rules about the school lunch program, and farmers—a third party—reaping a benefit. (C)'s plan carries a bit of irony in its assertion that rating a movie "X" ends up corrupting the morals of the community. But as in (B)—and unlike correct (D)—the agent who performs the first action here (the censor) is not the one who reaps the ultimate benefit. (E) may be even less of a paradox than (A). It is not at all surprising that a kid given more practice managing money ends up learning the value of thrift.

9. B

Four of the five answer choices in question 9 support the logic, so you'll be looking for a statement that either weakens it or has no effect on it. The conclusion is that the way a judge came into his or her job, thus how much job security he or she has, often determines how a case will come out—that judges decide differently depending on whether they were elected or appointed for life or only for a short term. In the end, then, the author evidently believes that the wiser judge is the life-term judge.

Since the author provides nothing concrete to back up this claim, the answer choices have many opportunities to support the reasoning. (A) supports the idea that the short-term judges are likely to be moved by the prevailing political climate. If, as (A) says, they really want to keep their jobs, they will be more likely to decide the way the voters want them to decide in order to improve their election chances. Likewise, (C) supports that connection between the approval of the voters (which is necessary for re-election, of course) and the voters' view of the judge's decisions, by showing that short-term judges "happen" to rule in a way the voters approve of. And if you jump ahead to (E), you get perhaps the strongest support for the allegation that short-term judges worry about the mood of the voters—according to (E), they're the only judges who use pollsters, whose sole purpose is to track public opinion.

(D) lends support to the other part of the argument—the view of lifelong judges. (D) implies that those judges, as alleged by the author, do turn a blind eye to the vicissitudes of politics.

You're left with (B), which may in fact weaken the argument. If (B) is right in its claim that long-term judges keep their ear to the political ground as much as short-term judges do, then that damages the distinction between judges raised in the argument. You might have seen this directly—you might have picked (B) right from the start. But it was useful to go through this process and demonstrate how you could have answered it by process of elimination.

10. B

This question asks us to criticize the logic in an advertisement. We are told that the Fall Sale offers savings on clothing. The supporting evidence is that if you purchase clothing in three different departments, you receive a discount off of a purchase in the Housewares department. (B) points out that, although the sale is advertised as offering "great savings on clothes for the whole family," the only discount available is on housewares.

(A) isn't a criticism of the argument because it focuses on people who are outside the scope of the offer, those who won't make the purchases required to get the coupon. As for (C), the length of the sale doesn't affect whether shoppers are saving money on clothes. The comparison in (D) is irrelevant—it may speak to whether or not the shopper saves money overall, but does not address the actual claim made, that the consumer will save money *on clothing*. It's certainly possible that the coupon will help some shoppers save some money—but not, contrary to the ad's claims, on clothes. Similarly, other discounts, (E), don't have any impact on the validity of the claim that this sale will save shoppers money on clothing.

11. D

You're asked for a conclusion. The stimulus argument describes two factors that influence whether or not, and how much, passersby will give to panhandlers. First, if passersby find a panhandler to be destitute and forced to beg, they may give quite a bit of money. Second, and on the other hand, if passersby think they are being conned or that the panhandler is lazy, they won't give anything. Thus, the most reliable conclusion is (D). People decide whether to give to a panhandler based on how they perceive her—as sincere or lazy and dishonest.

As soon as you realize that the passage is only about how people's perceptions influence their reactions, you can eliminate a couple of wrong answers. The passage never tells you whether most panhandlers are lazy or not, (A). The same problem exists in (B). You don't know that some beggars can't fool passersby. (C) is a misreading of the first condition. Appearing truly needy is necessary for getting money from passersby; it need not be sufficient. Furthermore, (C) speaks of most passersby, which needn't be true at all. Perhaps most people never give money to panhandlers. And (E) concludes that a completely new factor, the amount of change one has, doesn't influence the decision making of passersby. There are no grounds for concluding this. The stimulus presents some factors in the decision making, but it never says that these are the only factors.

12. A

This short argument concludes that Dr. Kells is a better physician than Dr. Li. The evidence, which is very brief, is that their patients rate Kells as a better doctor. As always in an assumption question, we're looking for the missing piece that ties the evidence (that patients rate Kells the better doctor) to the conclusion (that Kells IS the better doctor). If the ratings of patients provide a solid basis for determining who is the better doctor, then the argument is solid. That's a perfect match for (A). (B) does nothing to tie ratings to actual quality. Instead, it introduces a new factor, the patients' comfort level with a doctor, which is outside scope. Likewise, (C) and (D) introduce new factors ("greater experience" and "from whose care patients benefit more") without filling the gap between ratings and actual quality. (E) needn't be true for the argument to be valid; the conclusion claims only that Kells is better than Li, not better than *everyone.*

13. D

The author concludes that a staff made up of contract or temporary employees is "incomplete at best." Why? The evidence says it's because a company needs workers who have a personal connection to their work and a dedication to the company. We're looking for the author's assumption—the missing piece that ties the idea that we need dedicated, connected workers to the idea that temporary workers aren't enough. The author must believe that temporary workers *aren't* dedicated and connected. Otherwise, temporary employees would indeed be an acceptable substitute for permanent staff. (D) sums this assumption up nicely. (A) distorts the point; the author states only that temporary staff by themselves are inadequate, not that they cause the company any harm. (B) might be tempting because it suggests a possible remedy for the problem the author raises, but that's not what we've been asked for. We're looking for the missing piece that leads to the conclusion that temporary workers are *not enough*. The idea that they could be encouraged to develop that dedication actually weakens the conclusion. (C) directly contradicts the author's statement that temporary and contract workers can play an important role with regard to seasonal work flow. (E) is another distortion: The passage mentions that skilled and efficient employees are important to a company, but doesn't attribute those qualities to either group.

Set Two

1. C

The conclusion is that for parents who are crunched for time, Flash Fitness is the "quick solution." The evidence, however, doesn't have anything to do with being quick—it tells us that working parents "found this convenient new workout to be very EFFECTIVE." Predict: The fact that the workout was effective doesn't demonstrate that it was quick. There's no evidence for "quick" at all, as set forth in correct choice (C).

Note that none of the wrong choices address quickness, which is the new element introduced in the conclusion. (A) may be true, but it is not a serious criticism of the ad since time-crunched parents are the target audience (and so we really don't care whether the rest of the world would like the program). The information in (B) is irrelevant. The ad makes no claim that Flash Fitness is more effective or convenient than other fitness centers, only that it is an effective and convenient center. (D) may be true, but it's not important, because the conclusion of the argument is that the program is a "quick" solution—we're not trying to prove effectiveness. (E) is also irrelevant. While it may be true that some people are not concerned with convenience when choosing a fitness center, this ad attempts to appeal to those who do have that concern.

2. D

Ranjit thinks it was unfair that he failed the class, because other students who neglected to turn in the same project that he failed to turn in passed the class. Therefore, he must believe that the failure to turn in that project was the *reason* he failed the class, or at least a substantial factor. Note the subtle difference between correct choice (D), which says just that, and wrong choice (B), which suggests that we know the *actual* reason for the failure rather than simply understanding Ranjit's position. All of the information given relates to Ranjit's assessment, *not* to the actual reasons for the grade, and so (B) is beyond the scope of the information provided. We have no information about Ranjit's other classes, and therefore cannot draw any conclusions about his grades in them (as (A) asks us to do). The information in the passage tells us that Ranjit *turned in* all of his other assignments, but nothing about his scores, and (E) takes us even further outside scope by comparing Ranjit's performance to students in other classes—students who were never mentioned in the stimulus.

Whether or not Ranjit has ever failed a class before is irrelevant, since his grade is based on his record in this specific class, so (A) is incorrect. As for (C), Ranjit may have received above-average scores on his other assignments, but then again, he may not. We know only that he turned the assignments in; we have nothing on which to base any inferences about how he did on them. Finally, (E) is incorrect because Ranjit doesn't make any mention of students in other courses; this is outside scope.

3. D

The author concludes that the costume designer will be able to restore the original fabric quality of the garments that have been damaged through improper storage. The evidence? We have access to the original patterns and the original fabric. It's fabric quality that's at issue, so the success or failure of the author's plan hinges on the fabric. If, as the author assumes, it's in its original condition, then it will work and the costumes can be restored to their original fabric quality. Otherwise, the pattern, however detailed, would yield another garment made of damaged fabric. Therefore, (D) would strengthen the argument by providing support for an assumption that is central to the designer's plan.

(A) Is outside scope—our focus is on the quality of the fabric, not the technique. (B) addresses the *causes* of the damage, which are irrelevant to the question of whether or not the fabric quality can be restored. (C) introduces an element—what the original seamstress may or may not have anticipated—that has no bearing on the likelihood that the original fabric quality can be restored. (E) may look tempting at a glance, but it talks about the damage to the *costumes*, not to the remaining fabric—and it's the quality of the remaining fabric that will control the success or failure of the restoration.

4. C

Since this is an Inference question, we're not looking for evidence and conclusion. There's no argument here, just straight information. Summarize what you know as you read: Academy B was known as one of the best schools, but it closed. Many teachers went to good suburban schools, and then when Academy B reopened, they came back, and it's again enjoying an excellent reputation. What else do we *know for sure* based on what we've just read?

You often won't be able to predict the answer to an inference question. Evaluate each in view of what you already know. (C) says that some suburban teachers left their jobs when Academy B reopened. We know that because we know that some Academy B teachers were working as suburban teachers while the Academy was closed, and that they've now returned to Academy B and stayed there.

(A) is incorrect because we don't have enough information to draw any conclusions about the impact of the teachers' experience in the suburban schools. We also have no information about the reasons the school reopened, as (B) asserts, nor about either the quality of other teachers in the district or overall district quality as set forth in (E). (D) might appear tempting because we're told that the teachers from the suburban schools all returned to Academy B and stayed there, but that doesn't mean that there aren't other openings available—only "many" of the teachers went to the suburban schools, and we don't know whether the school reopened with exactly the same number of teachers it had originally, anyway.

5. C

The author's conclusion is that the recent increase in popularity of high school-level writing classes will decrease the number of graduates who are capable of producing effective expository writing. The evidence is that most of these newly popular classes use creative writing techniques. The assumption that links this evidence with the conclusion is that creative writing techniques will not help students become effective expository writers. Correct choice (C) says exactly that: creative writing courses won't give students the skills to be good expository writers. If they WILL, of course, then the argument fails. Incorrect choice (A) brings up the idea of a writing requirement, which is outside scope. The key to this argument is the question as to whether the new classes—which primarily use creative writing techniques—will increase or decrease effective expository writing among high school graduates. (B) makes an irrelevant comparison, which may be tempting at a glance because it contains all the right keywords. As in any assumption question, keep your eye on the gap you're trying to fill between the evidence and conclusion and you won't be misled by choices like this. (D) introduces an entirely new element—that of qualified instructors. (E) is irrelevant to the author's conclusion, which relates to the projected increase/decrease in expository skills, *not* their current level.

6. B

There is no connection between magnet school programs in Minneapolis and long waiting lists for school there, this passage concludes, because no such connection can consistently be found in other cities. Correct choice (B) connects the evidence (magnet schools didn't cause waiting lists in other cities) with the conclusion (therefore, they didn't cause waiting lists in Minneapolis, either). (A) is outside scope; the argument is concerned with the link (or lack thereof) between the magnet program and the waiting lists, not the motivations of the parents *within* that program. (C) introduces another out-of-scope element: the benefits of the magnet programs. Our only concern is with the causal relationship between the magnet programs and the waiting lists. (D) directly contradicts the author, who said the magnet programs were *not* the cause of the waiting lists. (E) is also contradictory; the author states clearly that there are "extremely long" waiting lists for some schools.

7. E

The problem: Channeling recycled wastewater into the harbor seems to have brought dangerous bacteria into this town's drinking water. The solution: Researchers recommend adding the enzyme tripticase to the water to eliminate those pestilent bacteria, which in turn will "solve the health problem." Since you're looking to weaken this argument, ask yourself if there could be a problem with this solution. It removes the bacteria, which will only solve the health problem if tripticase itself doesn't introduce any other problems. If, however, tripticase merely replaces one problem with another, as (E) has it, then the author's conclusion about its effectiveness as a solution is weakened.

(A) Okay, so tripticase is supereffective since it solves the giardia problem as well as others. This certainly doesn't weaken the author's argument that tripticase is an effective solution (even though other illnesses are technically outside the scope).

(B) The frequency and severity of giardia worldwide isn't the issue here—the author addresses the effectiveness of a solution for the health problems of a certain town that originated in response to the channeling of recycled wastewater.

(C) Other illnesses are irrelevant to this consideration, as was mentioned above in (A).

(D) The author discusses water-induced cases of giardia, so cases that arise from other causes aren't within the argument's scope.

When you're asked to weaken or strengthen an argument, remember to evaluate the impact that each answer choice has on that argument without questioning the information you're given. Assume that the stimulus is true, and reconsider it in light of each answer choice. Does the new information make the conclusion more or less plausible? Don't question the information; just focus on its impact on the argument.

8. D

The Dean concludes that moving the English class back to the afternoon would increase student scores, and offers two pieces of evidence for that: the correlation between the change in time slot and the drop in scores, and the fact that students perform better when wide awake. She's making two key assumptions here, either of which could be the correct answer: the first is that there's a causal relationship between the time change and the drop in scores; the second is that the causal relationship is triggered by students not being wide awake at 8:00 A.M. (D) is a perfect match for the second. Remember that some assumption questions will contain more than one possible assumption, and so you should be adaptable in those infrequent instances where your assumption doesn't match.

(A) is not relevant because the dean isn't concerned with whether it is practical to change the class meeting time, only whether test scores would go up if the time were changed. (B) would actually weaken the author's argument, since it suggests that class time may not be the only factor that causes the low test scores. (C) might provide some support for the author's conclusion, but it's not a necessary component of the argument, and the question stem asked for an assumption the argument was based on—that means a necessary but unstated piece of evidence. (E) is outside scope, since the argument relates strictly to the causal relationship between the time change and the drop in scores.

9. B

The argument concludes that it is more expensive to live far from an interstate than near one. The only evidence for this claim is the fact that property values drop in areas that are closer to interstates. However, we're told that most interstates are in urban areas, where property values are higher to start with. In order for the author's conclusion to be true, we must assume that the decline due to proximity to an interstate is greater than the increase due to urban location. (B) states this assumption clearly. Remember that you're looking for something that ties the evidence (being near an interstate lowers property values) to the conclusion (that homes in urban areas near interstates are less expensive than those in suburban/rural areas far from interstates). The core issue is *property values*, and (A) and (C) have nothing to do with property values. Don't fall into the trap of analyzing what impact things like square footage and single-family areas *might* have on property values. (D), far from being a missing component of the argument, would undermine the idea that those homes near the interstate were less expensive. (E) looks tempting because it equalizes costs before taking the location into account—but does nothing to resolve the two competing impacts on the cost (urban location versus proximity to interstate).

10. C

The author concludes that windy weather must have set off the alarm. Her evidence is that only windy weather or a large truck could have done it, and the large truck that had set the alarm off earlier was already gone. The gap between the evidence and conclusion is fairly clear, here—we're presented with evidence that *one specific* truck couldn't have set off the alarm, but perhaps there are other trucks. Our author seems to assume that there were *not* other trucks that could have set off the alarm: a perfect match for (C).

(A) introduces an irrelevant distinction—we're interested only in whether the facts that 1) only wind or a truck could have caused this and 2) the truck Han saw this morning is gone, taken together, mean that wind must have set off the alarm. (B) also raises an irrelevant distinction—and one that would argue *against* the author's conclusion rather than adding supporting evidence. (D) may or may not be true, but it has no impact on the argument, which seeks only to determine that it was wind (versus a truck) that set off the alarm. (E) certainly needn't be true for the author to reach her conclusion—she's attributing the alarm to *wind*, not to a truck. Don't be fooled by familiar language in an answer choice—keep your eye on the gap you identified before you started looking at the choices!

11. C

The author's argument is that the decline the Japanese imperial power underwent was not due to a fundamental bias favoring clan loyalty over loyalty to the emperor. The evidence supporting this claim is that, for hundreds of years during this period of decline, centralized power was held by shoguns, who ruled in the name of the emperor. The assumption here is that the rule of the shoguns was in fact imperial rule rather than clan-based rule. In the passage, you're given little information about this. Choice (C) claims that, in fact, the shoguns were representative of the different clans and ruled with little regard for the emperor. This denies the assumption, and makes the example of the shoguns a piece of evidence for the author's opponents.

(A) does not weaken the argument because you're essentially concerned with *who* held power, rather than *why* they held power. It does deny that there was loyalty involved, but that doesn't greatly weaken the claim made.

(B) gives a piece of history that implies nothing about the type of rule the shoguns exercised, nor about the object of people's loyalty and obedience.

(D) reduces the power of the shoguns during the early part of the period being discussed, and gives it to the *emperor.* Since the author mentions the shoguns as an example of the reach of imperial power, this would tend to *strengthen* his case by showing that loyalty and obedience were given to the emperor, and that the explanation proposed by the author's opponents is off-base.

(E), too, provides another reason for the decline of the imperial power and so would strengthen the author's case, not weaken it.

12. E

The author's conclusion is that the public is in error in its condemnation of the students who were arrested. The evidence is an analogy drawn between the students' actions (which in all likelihood broke the law) and the actions of the patriots in Boston, who dumped tea into the harbor. The implied conclusion here is that since history has justified the violent actions of the patriots, it will probably do the same for the students' actions. The best response to this line of reasoning is to point out that merely because one such incident of rebellion (the Boston Tea Party) has proved justified, is no reason to assume that any such incident is, or will later appear, justified. That's correct choice (E).

(A) fails because it just begs the question. The author is arguing that it may in fact be patriotic, or at least justified, to demonstrate in front of City Hall. So (A) just ignores his argument.

(B) points out that students are too inexperienced to understand the consequences of their demonstration. But is this a reason to condemn their demonstration? Their demonstration could be the morally correct act, yet not be fully understood in all its consequences. So (B) is dealing with a different issue.

(C) is a general, cynical statement, but has no obvious bearing on the argument. Perhaps the students' act was one of those few which are based on beliefs and conscience.

(D) says only that the patriots had some support. Yet we don't know for sure that the students haven't had some support. Secondly, (D) speaks of support for the patriots' cause, whereas it's their actions that the author is using in his analogy.

13. D

As we saw in question 3, the author uses a case of justified rebellion as an analogy to argue that the students' actions may very well have been justified. That's choice (D).

(A) goes too far. He accuses the public of not keeping the patriots in mind, not of purposely ignoring the Boston Tea Party.

(B) and (C) There really is no general principle of rebellion here, as the author compares only two particular instances of rebellion, so (B) and (C) are incorrect.

(E) is incorrect because the author never says that we don't have sufficient evidence to condemn the students. His point is that we're overlooking an important and relevant precedent.

Set Three

1. C

The author concludes that the benefits of arms reduction are merely illusory. The evidence presented is that even though some weapons are reduced, other weapons not covered by the treaty are increased to account for those that are reduced. In other words, if the superpowers agree to cut their tank forces in half, they will also double their navies, or some other arsenal not covered by the reduction treaty. This argument is most strengthened by choice (C). Choice (C) tells us that the five largest military powers have increased funding for new weapons in each of the last ten years. This supports the author's assertion that whatever firepower is reduced by the arms limitation treaties is reacquired through new weapons.

(A) says that the balance of power remains in spite of arms control. However, the balance of power is a proportion, and even though it is unchanged, the amount of firepower might well be reduced.

(B) doesn't strengthen the argument because although no proposals have called for the elimination of weapons, they might still account for a reduction in the number of weapons.

(D) comes from left field, introducing irrelevant outside knowledge. The author lumps all arms together, so this distinction is irrelevant to the argument as given.

(E) actually contradicts the author's claim by stating that fifteen percent of the firepower possessed by the largest military powers really has been cut. Even if this is not a great reduction, it contradicts the author's argument, which is that no reduction has been achieved through arms limitation.

2. E

The author in question 10 refutes some "so-called pacifists" (that's his phrase) who, you learn by inference, have been calling for weapons reductions to create a climate of peace. The author believes that a "climate of peace" has been created by increased military spending, and supports this claim by pointing to the number of attacks on this country and its allies. Fewer attacks, it is said, have occurred, and the author sees a causal connection.

Now the assumption underlying this causal connection is your goal in question 10, and you find it in (E). It has to be true that had defense spending not gone up, the number of attacks on this country and its allies would have increased. Otherwise there would be no causal connection between the two phenomena, as the author claims.

(A) is irrelevant. The author doesn't refer to what causes the attacks but simply asserts that military readiness can prevent them. With regard to (B), the author doesn't tell you how and why more defense spending has prevented military actions, just that it has done so. And the author makes no claim about the future of peace or of military spending, (C). The thrust of the argument is toward the past and what past spending has done. Whether all this readiness can permit future cuts is a matter upon which the author doesn't speculate. Finally, (D)'s equation of weapons and personnel is silly, specious, and irrelevant. Both are mentioned as key elements of the current peace climate, and both have benefited from having more money available. But if the author has an opinion as to which (weapons or personnel) are more valuable, he's keeping it to himself.

3. C

You're asked for a situation that conforms to a principle, so your best bet is to understand the principle thoroughly, and then test the choices against this understanding. The author offers an absolute truth with two restrictions. First the rule: A free press always reports all information about a country's military operations. There are two cases, and only two cases, in which this might not be true. First, if such information would jeopardize the safety of the troops. Second, if such information would jeopardize the success of a mission. With such clear rules, we'll be looking for the answer choice that follows them faithfully.

(A) To make this answer choice work, you'd have to assume that such dissenting opinions would jeopardize the troops and/or the success of the mission. This choice supports no such assumption, so based on the information that it alone provides, it is not consistent with the stimulus' principle.

(B) and (D) discuss unfree presses, and therefore fall outside the scope of the argument. The rules pertain only to a free press, and we can't infer how an unfree press would behave in regard to these issues.

(C) This answer choice succeeds where (A) fails because, while it doesn't directly state that the publication of future military targets would jeopardize the success of a mission, the link between the two is far clearer and more logical. According to the principle, a free press *could* withhold information that endangers the troops or mission, and it's reasonable to say that the info discussed in (C) could fall into that category.

(E) The principle deals with *current* military operations and therefore doesn't shed any light on what's appropriate behavior in regard to previous engagements. Clandestine past military operations are outside the scope.

No correct answer choice will require you to make a significant, unfounded assumption in order to make it work. The right answer choice will be correct on its own merit, without requiring you to introduce extra information.

4. E

Correct (E) is supported by the author's statement that it is "surprising" that Dillard's early and late work are so similar in style, despite the 35-year gap between the two stages. If the author is surprised by this fact, then we can infer that she believes that such a time period would normally be expected to cause a change in the artist's style.

(A) contradicts the passage, which clearly states that Dillard became famous for works produced late in her lifetime. (B), (C), and (D) all indicate some form of skepticism about the discovery or the available information on Dillard's work. However, the author's statement that the newly discovered painting uncovers a new facet of Dillard's life and work clearly indicates that she accepts the historians' identification, examination, and dating of the piece at face value.

5. C

The key to solving a question about a "misunderstanding" is to examine the second person's statement, and see what understanding of the original statement is implied therein. Here, the customer says that he will have at least one functioning computer as long as he purchases three. This is true only if one out of any three given computers would continue working, (C). In reality, of course, the salesperson meant that any given computer has a 1/3 chance of continuing to function.

(A) is incorrect, since the customer's plan would then not be "certain to have" a computer that still worked after a year. (A) would imply that the customer would keep trying computers until he found one that worked, not buy three computers in order to have one that worked. (B) and (D) are incorrect because the identity of the person using the computer (whether it is this customer or another) is outside scope of the stimulus. (E) may be an assumption the customer is making, since he otherwise might be more likely to simply buy a new computer, but we have no evidence that this is what he thought the salesperson said—the only thing we know for sure that he thinks is that if he buys three computers, he'll have one that works.

6. E

There's a lot of information here about the policy change and reaction to it, but the question stem directs us to the end of the stimulus: the author's conclusion "about McCarthy" is simply that she's been a loyal employee for 12 years. How do we know? The author offers her personnel file as evidence. Whether or not we can draw *any* conclusion about McCarthy based on the personnel file depends on the accuracy of the file. If it's accurate, it's a basis to draw conclusions about McCarthy's work history with Luna, but if it's not, then it's useless as evidence. The author, then, must assume that the information in the file is accurate. That's (E). It could be true that only long-term human resources staff can add items to portfolios, (A), but don't lose sight of what you're looking for—we need the missing piece that allows us to draw conclusions about McCarthy's work history at Luna from her personnel file. (B) certainly seems to make sense, but it doesn't plug that gap between McCarthy's personnel file and drawing conclusions about her work history at Luna. (C) provides a good explanation of why employees would want to add information to their portfolios, but fails to address the validity of McCarthy's personnel file as evidence of her loyalty. As for (D), the reason for the policy is irrelevant to this question, since our focus is on the use of McCarthy's personnel file as evidence. Note that all of the wrong answer choices here address the policy change, rather than focusing in on the piece of the stimulus referred to in the question stem. Since the bulk of the text relates to that change, it will be tempting for students who haven't used the question stem to direct their reading to focus there as well.

7. C

This is a Point at Issue question that basically asks, "What are they fighting about?" Look to see where they disagree. The marketing analyst only disputes the manufacturer's conclusion; each person presents completely different evidence. They can only disagree about something that they both discuss, and the only thing that meets that criterion in this dialogue is the conclusion. Therefore, they disagree about whether the company should switch to a less expensive brand of rubber, or (C).

(A) The manufacturer certainly assumes that other brands cost less, but the analyst in no way disputes this or even directly mentions it. Both seem to agree that other brands would cost less.

(B) is not addressed by either person. The analyst mentions sales but not sales *quotas*, and the manufacturer doesn't even get close to discussing sales.

(D), like (B), brings up an issue that neither person directly addresses. Even if you thought the analyst's comments might have some relevance to customer preferences, the analyst never addresses them directly, and the manufacturer never gets near this subject.

(E) is addressed by the analyst, but not by the manufacturer, whose argument deals only with cost.

Notice that all of the wrong answer choices mention issues that would be more relevant to the analyst's comments than the manufacturer's. Don't neglect the first argument; the right answer will have to be something discussed and discussed with different opinions by both people.

8. D

The author believes that Bidwell has incorrectly used the expression "ivory tower," because in her experience, buildings that have towers or are ivory-colored are not to be found on college campuses. However, the passage tells us that Bidwell uses the term when he "discusses [academics'] tendency to work in isolation without looking for concrete connections to the world." Even if you aren't familiar with the terminology, you should recognize that Bidwell isn't claiming that academics reside in tall white buildings. The expression "ivory tower" is an example of figurative language. Bidwell is implying that academics are distant from, and untouched by, the real world. (D) is the correct answer.

If you were unfamiliar with the term "ivory tower," you could have used the context of the passage and the process of elimination to find the answer. To make a generalization, (A), is to draw a general conclusion from a specific set of events or circumstances. The author of this passage generalizes when she states that no college campuses have white buildings or towers, but this is not a generalization that she has failed to see in Bidwell's writing. (B), a deduction, is a conclusion formed on the basis of given information; there's nothing like that in the passage. There is no support for (C); a counterexample is a fact that disproves a generalization, but no generalization is found here. Lastly, irony, (E), is a situation in which the actual result or sequence of events is the opposite of what would be expected. An example of irony would be if the author of this passage discovered that her office were being relocated to the tower area of a white building on campus.

9. A

The stimulus tells us that there are at least two sources of effective concepts for a company's advertising campaign: those that are recognizable as such based on previous knowledge of the market, and those that are shown to be effective only when used to launch a campaign. We don't know which kind the current campaign consists of, or whether it might be a mix. Therefore, we can infer that we may not be able to judge the effectiveness of all aspects of the campaign pre-launch—because we won't if it contains any elements that fall into the latter category.

(B) distorts the role of "prior knowledge" and "past performance" in the stimulus. (C) is probably true—but we have no information in the passage from which to draw that conclusion. Avoid answer choices that seem reasonable but can't be tied directly to the stimulus. Similarly, (D) brings in an element that is not found in the passage. The passage draws a distinction between the two types of concepts, but does not state which of them has more merit. As far as we know, both types are effective and fulfill the company's needs. (E) is outside scope: our concern is the point at which effectiveness can be assessed.

10. A

Mr. Holt concludes that an anonymous survey at the next Concerned Neighbors Committee meeting is the best way to gather accurate information about the need for a food shelf. His evidence is that the people at the meeting are largely from the neighborhood, and the anonymity will encourage them to answer honestly. (A) provides the best criticism of Mr. Holt's logic by pointing out that the sample of neighborhood residents attending the meeting may not be large enough or may not be representative. If the survey might fail to reach a significant number of potential food shelf clients, then Holt's plan will not be effective.

(B) is outside scope. The purpose of the survey is to determine whether there is a need, not to target specific beneficiaries. (C) is also outside scope—we're only looking to determine the need in *this* neighborhood. (D) introduces an irrelevant element. We're only concerned with those who might use a food shelf. If some people lie on the survey,

(E), then its results might be slightly skewed, but the author has taken measures to minimize that by making the survey anonymous, so he hasn't overlooked the issue.

11. B

The author believes that these two opposing quotations reflect the dramatically different platforms of two candidates for a Senate seat. However, a candidate's platform may be made up of many issues, and so one narrow conflict is not sufficient to demonstrate, as the author claims, that there is not "a lot of common ground." Perhaps these two candidates have identical positions on fiscal issues, education, etc. (A) directly contradicts the author's illustration, which shows two candidates who do not share the same beliefs on a particular issue. (C) attempts to mislead by making reference to a familiar detail, but it doesn't reach the core of the argument—that these two candidates don't have a lot of middle ground because they disagree about this one point. (D) is true, but it's not a flaw. A valid argument need not include evidence for the opposing viewpoint. (E) might look tempting, since the author does assume that the candidates' quotations here express the totality of their views on an issue, but he does not provide any evidence to show that this is not the case. Beware of answer choices that start strong and take a wrong turn.

12. A

The author concludes that World Imports spends three times as much on kitchen items as it does on furniture. The evidence is that 3 percent of the furniture arrives at the store too damaged to sell, while 9 percent of the kitchen items arrive in the same condition. While the math might look good, this is a classic case of statistics being used to support a conclusion they don't actually support at all. The author attempts to convince us that since three times as much kitchen merchandise is damaged, it must be three times as expensive to stock kitchen merchandise as furniture. The problem, of course, is that the cost of stocking items is reliant on more than simply the breakage rate. Some items are more expensive than others, some are heavier (and therefore more expensive to ship)...the list could go on. All you really need to know is that other factors impact the cost, leading to correct choice (A).

(B) is tempting, in that inadequate and unrepresentative samples are often at the core of a flaw question, but in this case we have no information about the shipments on which we can make that determination. (C) is simply a distraction; the varying breakage rates at World Imports' competitors have nothing to do with the argument at hand, which deals exclusively with World Imports' products. The mention of competitors takes us outside the scope of the argument. (D) suggests that a minimum amount of breakage is inevitable, but that doesn't impact the assessment of relative costs, which is really what we're interested in. (E) says merely that long distance shipping is unavoidable...this also has no impact on the relationship between breakage and cost.

13. C

The primary flaw in the authors' reasoning is that they respond by defending their *intentions,* while the Principal's concern is clearly for the actual impact. (C) is therefore correct; the issue here is not the motivation behind the change, but the effects that came out of it. (A) and (B) deal with the effectiveness of the new curriculum. But the authors never implied that the curriculum was guaranteed to improve writing skills, (A), or that it would be more beneficial than the old curriculum, (B). They merely stated that the change was well-intentioned. (D) is irrelevant since the Principal is unconcerned with motivations. (E) is outside scope—students who passed last year's exam weren't using the curriculum in question.

Chapter 4: **Logic Games**

- **The 6 basic principles of Logic Games**
- **Sequencing, grouping, and matching skills**
- **Kaplan's 5-Step Method for Logic Games**

Nothing inspires more fear in the hearts of LSAT test takers than Analytical Reasoning, or Logic Games, because the skills tested on the section are unfamiliar. It may help you to reexamine the reason this section is included on the test—the major analytical skills that the Logic Games section is designed to measure:

- Organization: the ability to assimilate efficiently, both in your head and on the page, the formidable amount of data associated with each game
- Mental agility: the ability to maintain enough flexibility to shuffle the data around in different ways for each question
- Memory: the ability to retain the work done in the setup stage while focusing on the new information in each question stem
- Concentration: the ability to keep focused on the task at hand and not let your mind wander

Games are most troublesome to those students who don't have a clearly defined method of attack. And that's where Kaplan's basic principles, game-specific strategies and techniques, and 5-Step Method for Logic Games will help, streamlining your work so you can rack up points quickly and confidently.

 GO ONLINE

Your downloadable study sheet summarizes these principles, strategies, and methods.

THE 6 BASIC PRINCIPLES OF LOGIC GAMES

For many students, Logic Games is the most time-sensitive section of the test. The test makers know that if you could spend hours methodically trying out every choice, you'd probably get everything right. But what does that prove? Who's going to get the sought-after legal position or win the important client—the person who can write the legal brief and prepare the court case in four days, or the person who can do the same job in four hours? It's all about efficiency. And that brings you to the first, and somewhat paradoxical, Logic Games principle.

GO ONLINE

As you read through these principles, consider how each might have improved your Diagnostic Quiz performance.

Slow Down To Go Faster

To gain time in Logic Games, spend time thinking through and analyzing the setup and the rules. This is the most important principle for Logic Games success and the one that's most often neglected, probably because it doesn't seem right intuitively. People with timing problems tend to rush to the questions. But spending a little extra time thinking through the stimulus, the "action" of the game, and the rules, helps you to recognize key issues and make important deductions that will save you time.

Games are structured so that, in order to answer the questions quickly and correctly, you need to search out relevant pieces of information that combine to form valid new **deductions** (inferences). You can either do this once, up front, or you can choose to piece together the same basic deductions—repeating the same work—for each question. For instance, what if two of the rules for a Logic Game are:

- If Bob is chosen for the team, then Eric is also chosen.
- If Eric is chosen for the team, then Pat will not be chosen.

You can, as you read through the rules of the game, treat those rules as two independent pieces of information. But there's a deduction to be made from them: If Bob is chosen, Eric is, too. If Eric is chosen, Pat is not. Therefore, if Bob is chosen, Pat is not chosen. And that deduction will undoubtedly be required in more than one question.

The choice is yours; but the rush-to-the-questions method is inefficient, time-consuming, and stress-inducing. Take the game scenario and the rules as far as you can before moving on to the questions.

Common Elements and Deductions

As the Bob-and-Eric example demonstrates, rules that contain common elements often lead to deductions. Consider the following three rules:

- If Sybil goes to the party, then Edna will go to the party.
- If Jacqui goes to the party, then Sherry will not go to the party.
- If Edna goes to the party, then Dale will go to the party.

Rules 1 and 2 have no entities in common—it doesn't appear you can deduce anything by combining them. Note, however, that even when rules have no common elements, their placement or the way they interact with the numbers may lead to something useful. The same goes for Rules 2 and 3. But since Rules 1 and 3 have Edna in common, a deduction is possible (although not guaranteed). In this case, you can deduce another rule: if Sybil goes to the party, then Dale will go also.

Focus on the Important Rules

Not all rules are equal—some are inherently more important than others. Try to focus first on the concrete ones and the ones that involve the greatest number of the entities or otherwise have the greatest impact on the action.

These are also the rules to turn to first whenever you're stuck on a question and don't know how to set off the chain of deduction.

No "Best" Choice

The answers in Logic Games—like answers to math questions—are objectively correct or incorrect. Therefore, when you find an answer that's definitely right, have the confidence to circle it and move on, without checking the other choices. This is one way to improve your timing on the section.

KAPLAN EXCLUSIVE

Don't overcorrect yourself; just because an answer comes easily (when you know how to approach it) doesn't mean it's wrong.

Use Scratchwork and Shorthand

Developing good scratchwork will help your performance on Logic Games. Although some rare games aren't amenable to scratchwork, for most games you'll find it helpful to create a master sketch that encapsulates the game's information in an easy-to-follow form. This gives your eye a place to gravitate towards when you need information, and helps to solidify in your mind the action of the game, the rules, and whatever deductions you made.

Keep scratchwork simple—you get no points for beautiful diagrams, and the less time you spend drawing the more time you'll have for thinking and answering questions. Pay careful attention to the scratchwork suggestions in the explanations to the games in the Practice Tests.

The goal of the scratchwork is to condense a lot of information into manageable, user-friendly visual cues. Jot down a quick, short form of each rule. Shorthand is useful only if it reminds you at a glance of the rule's meaning. You should never have to look back at the game itself once you get to the questions. It's much easier to remember and apply rules written like so:

B → E

No G in 2

than those written like so:

If Bob is chosen for the team, then Eric is also chosen.

Box 2 does not contain any gumdrops.

But such notation is only helpful if you know what the arrow means and use it consistently. If you develop personal shorthand that's instantly understandable to you, you'll have a decided advantage on test day.

Know What a Rule Means, Not Just What It Says

The LSAT measures critical thinking, and virtually every sentence in Logic Games has to be filtered through some sort of analytical process to be of any use. So it's not enough just to copy a rule off the page (or shorthand it); it's imperative that you think through its full meaning, including any implications it might have. And don't limit this to the indented rules; statements in introductions are very often rules that warrant the same meticulous consideration.

Say a game's introduction sets up a scenario in which you have three boxes, each containing at least two of the following three types of candy—chocolates, gumdrops, and mints—and then you get the following rule:

> Box 2 does not contain any gumdrops.

What does that rule say? *There aren't any gumdrops in Box 2.* But what does that rule *mean* in the context of the game? That Box 2 *does* contain chocolates and mints. Each box contains at least two of three things. If you eliminate one of the three things from any particular box, the other two things *must* be in that box.

Moreover, part of understanding what a rule means is being clear about what the rule *doesn't* mean. Take the rule you saw earlier:

> **Rule:** If Bob is chosen for the team, then Eric is also chosen.
>
> **Means:** Whenever Bob is chosen, Eric is, too.
>
> **Doesn't mean:** Whenever Eric is chosen, Bob is, too.

Remember the discussion of formal logic in the Logical Reasoning chapter, with its *if/then* statements and **sufficient** and **necessary** conditions? If I yell loudly at my cat, he will run away. That means that whenever I yell at him loudly, he runs away. But, just as important, it *doesn't* mean that whenever he runs away, I've yelled at him.

KAPLAN EXCLUSIVE

Don't over-compartmentalize your skills: those used mainly in one LSAT section may be very helpful in another.

Try to Set off Chains of Deduction

When a question stem offers a hypothetical—an *if-clause* offering information pertaining only to that question—use it to set off a new chain of deductions. Consider the following question. (Since this question is excerpted without the accompanying introduction and rules, ignore its specific logic; it's just presented to make a point.)

> If the speedboat is yellow, which one of the following must be true?
>
> (A) The car is green.
> (B) The airplane is red.
> (C) The train is black.
> (D) The car is yellow.
> (E) The train is red.

The stem contains a new "if." The wrong approach is to acknowledge that the speedboat is yellow and then proceed to test out all of the choices. The muddled mental thought process accompanying this approach might sound something like this:

> "All right, the speedboat's yellow, does the car have to be green? Well, let's see, if the speedboat's yellow, and the car is green, then the train would have to be yellow, but I can't tell what color the airplane is, and I guess this is okay, I don't know, I better try the next choice. Let's see what happens if the speedboat's yellow and the airplane is red. . . . "

Stay focused! The question doesn't ask: "What happens if, in addition to this, the car is green?" or "What happens if this is true and the airplane is red?" So why is this confused test taker intent on answering all of these irrelevant questions? Never begin a question by trying out answer choices. Only if you're entirely stuck should you resort to trial and error.

The Correct Approach

Incorporate the new piece of information into your view of the game, creating a new sketch if it helps. Apply the rules and any previous deductions to the new information in order to set off a new chain of deductions. Play out the deductions just as you would have if this had been one of the original rules, but stop after each new deduction and skim your answer choices. You don't want to waste time on unnecessary work after you've found all you need to answer the question.

Know the Logic Games Question Types

You must have a solid command of the limited number of Logic Games question stems. When you take a few seconds to recognize the question type, characterize the answer choices, and apply the appropriate process, your work becomes more efficient—and more accurate.

 GO ONLINE

Start to learn your strengths and weaknesses based on your Diagnostic Quiz results with these question types.

Acceptability Questions

If the question asks which choice would be "acceptable," one answer choice will satisfy all the rules; each wrong choice will violate at least one rule.

New "If" Questions

When the question adds a new "if" condition, treat the "if" as a new rule and draw a new sketch if necessary.

Complete and Accurate List Questions

Answer the other questions first; their sketches will help you answer these. Use the choices to decide what possibilities you have to test.

Could [not] vs. Must [not] Questions

Focus on the nature of the right and wrong answer choices:

If the question reads...	The right answer will be...
Which one of the following statements could be true?	a statement that could be true, and the four wrong choices will be statements that definitely cannot be true (that is, must be false)
Which one of the following statements cannot be true?	a statement that cannot be true, and the four wrong choices will be statements that either must be true or merely could be true

Which one of the following statements must be true?	a statement that must be true, and the four wrong choices will be statements that either cannot be true or merely could be true
All of the following statements could . . . be true EXCEPT	a statement that cannot be true, and the four wrong choices will be statements that either could be true or even must be true
All of the following statements must be true EXCEPT . . .	a statement that either cannot be true, or merely could be true, and the four wrong choices will be statements that must be true
Which one of the following statements could be false?	a statement that cannot be true or could be true or false, and the four wrong choices will be statements that must be true
Which one of the following statements must be false?	a statement that cannot be true, and the four wrong choices will be statements that either must be true or merely could be true

You'll have a chance to see these major Logic Games principles in action when you review the explanations to the games in the Practice Tests in this book.

 KAPLAN STRATEGY

Kaplan's basic principles for success in Logic Games are:

- **Slow down to go faster.**
- **Always use the rules and deductions to work out as much positive, concrete information as you can before moving to the questions.**
- **Know what a rule means, not just what it says.**
- **Use scratchwork and shorthand.**
- **Try to set off chains of deductions.**
- **Know the Logic Games question types.**

THE 3 CRUCIAL LOGIC GAMES SKILLS

Although Logic Games can contain a wide variety of situations and scenarios, certain skills are required again and again. Variations on the following are the most common:

Sequencing

Logic Games requiring **sequencing** skills—those that involve putting entities in order—have long been a test-makers' favorite. In a typical sequencing game, you may be asked to arrange the cast of characters numerically from left to right, from top to bottom, in days of the week, in a circle, and so on. The sequence may be a matter of degree—say, ranking the eight smartest test takers from one to eight. Or it may be based on time, such as one that involves the order of shows broadcast on a radio station. Occasionally there are two or even three orderings to keep track of in a single game.

Strict and Loose Sequences

There are two types of sequence games. In a **strict** sequence game, the placement of entities is very strictly defined. You may be told, for example, that "A is third," or that "X and Y are adjacent," and so on. These are definite, concrete pieces of information, and the game centers around placing as many people into definite spots as possible. In contrast to this, in a **loose** (or "free-floating") sequence game, your job is to rank the entities only in relation to one another. You're usually never asked to fully determine the ordering of the cast of characters. Instead, the relationships between the entities constitute the crux of the game.

Typical Sequence Game Issues

GO ONLINE

As you practice, don't forget to track your progress in your online syllabus.

The following is a list of the key issues in sequencing games, each followed by a corresponding rule—in some cases, with several alternative ways of expressing the same rule. At the end, these rules will be used to build a miniature Logic Game, so that you can see how rules work together to define and limit a game's action.

These rules all refer to a scenario in which eight events are to be sequenced from first to eighth.

Issue	Rule
Which entities are concretely placed in the ordering?	X is third.
Which entities are forbidden from a specific position in the ordering?	Y is not fourth.
Which entities are next to, adjacent to, or immediately preceding or following one another?	X and Y are consecutive. X is next to Y. No event comes between X and Y. X and Y are consecutive in the ordering.
Which entities cannot be next to, adjacent to, or immediately following one another?	X does not immediately precede or follow Z. X is not immediately before or after Z. At least one event comes between X and Z. X and Z are not consecutive in the sequence.
How far apart in the ordering are two particular entities?	Exactly two events come between X and Q.
What is the relative position of two entities in the ordering?	Q comes before T in the sequence. T comes after Q in the sequence.

How a Sequence Game Works

Now see how rules like those above might combine to create a simple Logic Game.

> Eight events—Q, R, S, T, W, X, Y, and Z—are being ordered from first to eighth.
>
> X is third.
>
> Y is not fourth.
>
> X and Y are consecutive.
>
> Exactly two events come between X and Q.
>
> Q occurs before T in the sequence.

KAPLAN EXCLUSIVE

When planning scratchwork for sequencing, consider whether the game is best drawn horizontally or vertically.

How would you approach this simplified game? Remember the first and third basic principles: slow down to go faster and use scratchwork and shorthand. With eight events to sequence from first to eighth, you might draw eight dashes in the margin of your test booklet, maybe in two groups of four (so you can easily determine which dash is which). Then take the rules in order of concreteness, starting with the most concrete—Rule 1, X is third. Fill in your sketch:

__ __ X __   __ __ __ __

The next most concrete rule, Rule 4, tells you that exactly two events come between X and Q. Well, since Q can't obey this rule coming before X, it must come after X—in the sixth space. (Be careful, though. If Rule 4 said "At least two events" rather than "Exactly two events" you couldn't draw this clear conclusion.)

__ __ X __   __ Q __ __

Rule 5 says Q comes before T. Since Q is sixth, T must be either seventh or eighth. To indicate this, you might write T with two arrows pointing to the seventh and eighth dashes. Rule 3 says X and Y are consecutive. X is third, so Y will be either second or fourth. Rule 2 clears up that matter: Y can't be fourth, so it's second:

__ Y X __   __ Q __ __
↖T↗

This is how the rules work together to build a sequence game. The questions might then present hypothetical information that would set off the "chain of deduction" (fifth basic principle). You'll see how this works in the sequencing games on the Practice Tests; pay careful attention to the written explanations.

Grouping

In a pure grouping game, unlike sequencing, there's no call for putting the entities in order. Instead, you'll select a smaller group from the initial group or distribute the entities into more than one subgroup. You're not concerned with what order the entities are in, but rather who's in, who's out, and who can and cannot be with whom in various subgroups. In grouping games, knowing an entity is rejected is as helpful as knowing one is selected.

Selection and Distribution

In **selection** games, you'll be given the cast of characters and told to select a smaller group based on the rules. For example, a game may include eight music CDs, from which you must choose four. Sometimes the test makers specify an exact number for the smaller group, sometimes they don't. In a common variation, the initial group of entities is itself broken into subgroups at the start of the game: an example would be a farmer choosing three animals from a group of three cows and five horses.

In **distribution** games, you're concerned with who goes where rather than with who's chosen and who isn't. Sometimes, every entity will end up in a group—like placing eight marbles into two jars, four to a jar. A common hybrid game combines selection and distribution. For instance, a game might mandate the placement of three marbles in each jar, leaving two marbles out in the cold.

It's important for you to be aware of the numbers that govern each particular grouping game, because although all grouping games rely on the same general skills, you have to adapt these skills to the specific situation. Like sequencing games, grouping games have a language all their own, and it's up to you to speak that language fluently.

Typical Issues—Grouping Games of Selection

The following is a list of the key issues in grouping games of selection, each followed by a corresponding rule—in some cases, with several alternative ways of expressing the same rule. At the end, again, these rules will be used to build a miniature Logic Game.

These rules all refer to a scenario in which you are to select a subgroup of four from a group of eight entities—Q, R, S, T, W, X, Y, and Z.

Issue	Rule
Which entities are definitely chosen?	Q is selected.
Which entities rely on a different entity's selection in order to be chosen?	If X is selected, then Y is selected. X will be selected only if Y is selected. X will not be selected unless Y is selected.
Which entities must be chosen together, or not at all?	If Y is selected, then Z is selected, and if Z is selected, then Y is selected. Y will not be selected unless Z is selected, and vice versa.
Which entities cannot both be chosen?	If R is selected, then Z is not selected. If Z is selected, then R is not selected. R and Z won't both be selected.

How Grouping Games of Selection Work

You can combine these rules to create a rudimentary grouping game of selection:

> A professor must choose a group of four books for her next seminar. She must choose from a pool of eight books—Q, R, S, T, W, X, Y, and Z.
>
> Q is selected.
>
> If X is selected then Y is selected.
>
> If Y is selected, Z is selected, and if Z is selected, then Y is selected.
>
> If R is selected, Z is not selected.

KAPLAN EXCLUSIVE

The rule, "If X is selected, then Y is selected" works only in one direction; if X is chosen, Y must be, but if Y is chosen, X may or may not be.

One good way to deal with this kind of game is to write out the eight letters—four on top, four on the bottom—and then circle the ones that are selected while crossing out the ones that are definitely not selected. Thus, Rule 1 would allow you to circle the Q:

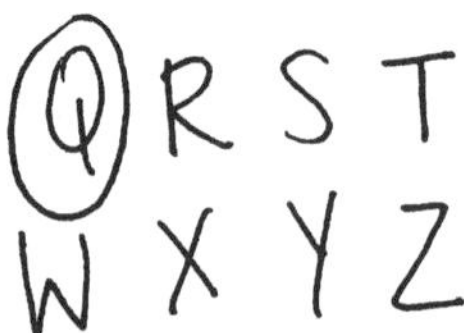

The other rules can't be built into the sketch just yet, since they describe eventualities (what happens if something else happens). Here's where you'd want to use shorthand:

- Rule 2 translates as, "If X, then Y" or "X → Y."
- Rule 3 might be rendered as, "YZ together" (as a reminder to choose them together, if at all).
- Rule 4 could be shorthanded as, "Never RZ" (since R and Z are mutually exclusive).

The rules would then be poised to take effect whenever a question adds new hypothetical information, setting off a chain of deduction. For instance, say a question reads:

If R is selected, which of the following must be true?

This new information puts the rules into motion. R's inclusion sets off Rule 4—"Never RZ"—so you have to circle R and cross out Z:

This would in turn set off Rule 3—"YZ together." Since Z is out, Y is out:

Now Rule 2 comes into play. "X → Y" means that if Y is not chosen, X can't be either (the contrapositive of the rule that X's inclusion would require Y's). So you can take the chain of deduction one step further:

A correct answer to this question, then, might be "X is not selected." And that, in a nutshell, is how a (simplified) grouping game of selection works.

KAPLAN EXCLUSIVE

In selection games, create a roster of entities. Circle those accepted and X-out those rejected.

Typical Issues—Grouping Games of Distribution

Here are the issues involved in grouping games of distribution—along with the rules that govern them.

These rules refer to a scenario in which the members of another group of eight entities—Q, R, S, T, W, X, Y, Z—have to be distributed into three different classes:

Issue	Rule
Which entities are concretely placed in a particular subgroup?	X is placed in Class 3.
Which entities are barred from a particular subgroup?	Y is not placed in Class 2.
Which entities must be placed in the same subgroup?	X is placed in the same class as Z. Z is placed in the same class as X. X and Z are placed in the same class.
Which entities cannot be placed in the same subgroup?	X is not placed in the same class as Y. Y is not placed in the same class as X. X and Y are not placed in the same class.
Which entity's placement depends on the placement of another entity?	If Y is placed in Class 1, then Q is placed in Class 2.

How Grouping Games of Distribution Work

These rules can combine to form a miniature grouping game of distribution.

> Eight students—Q, R, S, T, W, X, Y, and Z—must be subdivided into three different classes—Classes 1, 2, and 3.
>
> X is placed in Class 3.
> Y is not placed in Class 2.
> X is placed in the same class as Z.
> X is not placed in the same class as Y.
> If Y is placed in Class 1, then Q is placed in Class 2.

KAPLAN EXCLUSIVE

For distribution games, draw the subgroups and enter the slots to be filled in for each.

Good scratchwork for games of this type would be to draw three columns in your booklet, one for each of the three classes. Then put the eight entities in the appropriate columns as that information becomes known. Here again, start with the most concrete rule first, which is Rule 1, which definitively places X in Class 3. Rule 2 just as definitively precludes Y from Class 2, so build that into the scratchwork, too:

1	2	3
		X
	No Y	

Rule 3 requires Z to join X in Class 3:

1	2	3
		XZ
	No Y	

Rule 4 prohibits Y from being in the same class as X, so Y can't be in Class 3. But you already know that Y can't be in Class 2. You can deduce, therefore, that Y must go in Class 1. That in turn puts Rule 5 into play: if Y is in Class 1 (as it is here), Q is in Class 2:

1	2	3
Y	Q	XZ
	No Y	

And that, in simplified form, is the dynamic of most grouping games of distribution. For more complex distribution games, check out the Practice Tests.

Matching

As the name implies, **matching** games ask you to match up various characteristics about a group of entities—often many characteristics at once. A game may involve three animals, each assigned a name, a color, and a particular size. It's no wonder test takers get bogged down in these types—there's a lot to keep track of.

Some people dislike matching games because they feel bombarded with information and don't know where to start. Organization is especially crucial. A table or grid can be helpful. Distinguish each characteristic by using CAPS for one category, lowercase for another.

KAPLAN EXCLUSIVE

In matching games, make a list or grid; represent one set of entities in CAPS and one in lowercase. Keep track of the number of slots available.

Remember that thinking must always precede writing. A visual representation of a mental thought process can be invaluable; scribbling thoughtlessly for the sake of getting something down on the page is useless, even detrimental.

Center the sketch around the most important characteristic—the one with the most information attached to it. Going back to the animals example, don't assume that you should organize your sketch around the animals—there may be a better attribute, one that you know more about, that should take center stage. Visualize the action and create a mental picture or a sketch that puts the elements into a logical order. If you think through the scenarios and don't get scared off by their seeming complexity, you can find matching games accessible and even fun.

Typical Matching Game Issues

The following is a list of the key issues in matching games, each followed by a corresponding rule or set of rules.

All of these rules refer to a situation in which you have three animals—a dog, a cat, and a goat. Each animal has a name (Bimpy, Hank, and Jiming), a color (brown, black, or white), and a size (large or small).

Issue	Rule
Which entities are matched up?	The dog is brown. The black animal is small.
Which entities are not matched up?	Bimpy is not white. The goat is not large.
Which entity's matchups depend on the matchups of other entities?	If the cat is large, then Hank is brown. If the white animal is small, then Jiming is not the dog.

Notice that these last rules take the form of *if/then* statements, which means that the contrapositive can be employed.

KAPLAN EXCLUSIVE

Use the contrapositive on all *if/then* rules in Logic Games. It will always yield an important deduction.

Remember, the **contrapositive** is formed by reversing and negating the terms of an *if/then* statement. For the first, you get:

If Hank is NOT brown, then the cat is NOT large.

Taking the contrapositive of the second rule results in this statement:

If Jiming IS the dog, then the white animal is NOT small.

Both of these new pieces of information are just as powerful as any of the indented rules given in the game's introduction.

How Matching Games Work

You know the drill by now. Now take some of the rules above and form them into a minilogic game:

> A rancher owns three animals—a dog, a cat, and a goat. The animals are named Bimpy, Hank, and Jiming, though not necessarily in that order. One of the animals is brown, one is black, and one is white. Two of the animals are large and one is small.
>
> The dog is brown.
> The black animal is small.
> Bimpy is not white.
> The goat is not large.
> If the cat is large, then Hank is brown.

A good way to approach this game would be to set up a grid or chart to keep track of all of the attributes to be matched up:

(animal)	Dog	Cat	Goat
(name) BHJ			
(size) LLS			
(color) br bl wh			

Notice that Rules 1 and 4—the most concrete rules—can be built into the sketch immediately:

(animal)	Dog	Cat	Goat
(name) BHJ			
(size) LLS			not L
(color) ~~br~~ bl wh			

But think about what Rule 4 means, not just what it says. There are only two sizes here—small and large. If the goat is not large, it must be small, and since there are two large animals and only one small animal, you can deduce the size of the other two as well:

(animal)	Dog	Cat	Goat
(name) BHJ			
(size) LLS	L	L	S ~~not~~ L
(color) ~~br~~ bl wh			

KAPLAN EXCLUSIVE

If you can't make a single deduction by combining rules, you probably missed or misinterpreted something—check again.

Once you know that the cat is large, Rule 5 kicks in, telling you that Hank is brown. And since you've already deduced that the brown animal is the large dog, you know that Hank is the large brown dog.

That's how a simple matching game works. The third game of the Logic Games section on the Practice Tests in this book is a typical matching game for you to work on. Pay careful attention to the way in which it's set up, as outlined in the written explanations.

Hybrid Games

KAPLAN EXCLUSIVE

In hybrid games, expect to draw a separate sketch for each action, but consider whether you can combine the sketches.

Many games are "hybrid games," requiring you to combine sequencing, grouping, and/or matching skills (one will be used in discussing Kaplan's 5-step method). It really doesn't matter if you categorize a game as a sequencing game with a grouping element or as a grouping game with a sequencing element, as long as you're comfortable with both sets of skills.

Now that you have some Logic Games background, it's time to see how you can marshall that knowledge into a systematic approach to games.

KAPLAN'S 5-STEP METHOD FOR LOGIC GAMES

1. Overview

Carefully read the game's introduction and rules to establish the **situation**, the **entities** involved, the **action**, and the number **limits** governing the game ("SEAL").

2. Sketch

Make a mental picture of the situation, and let it guide you as you create a sketch or other scratchwork, to help you keep track of the rules and handle new information.

3. Rules

As you think through the meaning and implications of each rule, you have three choices. You can:

- Build it directly into your sketch.
- Jot down the rule in shorthand.

4. Deduction

Look for common elements among the rules; that's what will lead you to make deductions. Treat these deductions as additional rules, good for the whole game.

5. Questions

Read the question stems carefully! Take special notice of words such as *must, could, cannot, not, impossible,* and *except*. Use new "ifs" to set off a new chain of deduction.

Here's how the approach can work with an actual Logic Game:

Questions 1–2

Five workers—Mona, Patrick, Renatta, Saffie, and Will—are scheduled to clean apartments on five days of a single week, Monday–Friday. There are three cleaning shifts available each day—a morning shift, an afternoon shift, and an evening shift. No more than one worker cleans in any given shift. Each worker cleans exactly two shifts during the week, but no one works more than one cleaning shift in a single day.

Exactly two workers clean on each day of the week.
Mona and Will clean on the same days of the week.
Patrick doesn't clean on any afternoon or evening shifts during the week.
Will doesn't clean on any morning or afternoon shifts during the week.
Mona cleans on two consecutive days of the week.
Saffie's second cleaning shift of the week occurs on an earlier day of the week than Mona's first cleaning shift.

1. Which one of the following must be true?
   (A) Saffie cleans on Tuesday afternoon.
   (B) Patrick cleans on Monday morning.
   (C) Will cleans on Thursday evening.
   (D) Renatta cleans on Friday afternoon.
   (E) Mona cleans on Tuesday morning.

2. If Will does not clean on Friday, which one of the following could be false?
   (A) Renatta cleans on Friday.
   (B) Saffie cleans on Tuesday.
   (C) Mona cleans on Wednesday.
   (D) Saffie cleans on Monday.
   (E) Patrick cleans on Tuesday.

Though only two questions accompanying this game, a typical logic game will have 5–7 questions.

1. Overview

You need to schedule 5 workers, abbreviated M, P, R, S, and W, in a particular order during a 5-day calendar week, Monday through Friday. The ordering element tells you that you're dealing with a sequencing task, though a couple of the rules deal with grouping issues—namely, which people can or cannot clean on the same day of the week as each other. That makes this a slightly more complex sequence—but remember, it doesn't matter what you call it, as long as you can do it.

Be very careful about the numbers governing this game; they go a long way toward defining how the game works. There are to be exactly 2 workers per day (never cleaning on the same shift). Each worker must clean exactly 2 shifts, and since workers are forbidden to take 2 shifts in the same day, this means that each worker will clean on exactly 2 days. So, in effect, 10 out of 15 available shifts will be taken, and 5 will be left untouched.

2. Sketch

Go with whatever you feel is the most efficient way to keep track of the situation. Most people would settle on a sketch of the 5 days, each broken up into 3 shifts:

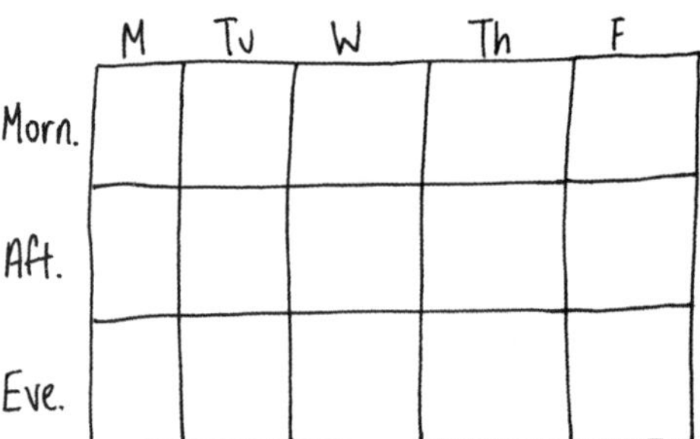

Into this sketch—one letter per box—each entity will have to go twice (each worker does 2 shifts, remember). So your pool of entities to place would be: MMPPRRSSWW. You might want to include 5 X's (or Ø's) for the 5 shifts that won't be taken by anyone.

3. Rules

You've already seen number-related rules hidden in the game's introduction. Now consider this statement from the intro:

> No more than one worker cleans in any given shift.

Make sure you interpret rules like this correctly. You may have to paraphrase its exact meaning. In this case: 2 workers per shift is no good, 3 is out of the question, etc. But it doesn't mean that any given shift must have a worker. If the test makers meant to imply that, they would have written, "Exactly one worker cleans on every given shift." Notice the difference in wording. It's subtle, but it has a huge impact on the game. Now consider the other rules.

You've already handled Rule 1. You may wish to jot down "2 a day," or something like that, to remind you of this important information.

Rule 2: Mona and Will clean on the same days, and that holds for both of the days they clean. Shorthand this any way that seems fitting (one suggestion is to draw MW with a circle around it).

Rules 3 and 4: You can handle these two together because they're so similar. You can shorthand these rules as they are, but you'd be doing yourself a great disservice. Instead, first work out their implications: If Patrick doesn't clean afternoons or evenings, he must clean mornings. If Will doesn't clean mornings or afternoons, he must clean evenings. Always take the rules as far as you can, and then jot down their implications for reference. These can be added directly to your sketch rather than just to your list of rules.

Rule 5: This is pretty self-explanatory; Mona's shifts must be on consecutive days, such as Thursday and Friday. MM might be a good way to shorthand this.

Rule 6: Another sequencing rule—you must place both S's for Saffie on earlier days of the week than the 2 M's, for Mona. That means that Saffie and Mona can't clean on the same day (although you already knew that from Rule 2), and that Mona's shifts can't come before Saffie's. Try shorthanding this as (S . . . S . . . MM).

4. Deduction

This is the crucial stage for most games. Notice that Mona appears in 3 of the 6 indented rules; that's a good indication that combining these rules should lead somewhere useful. Combining Rule 2 and Rule 5 gives you 2 Mona/Will days in a row: Will must be scheduled for evening shifts (remember, you turned Rule 4 into this positive statement). That means that Mona would take the morning or afternoon shift on these consecutive days.

Rule 6 concerns Mona as well: 2 Saffies before the 2 Monas. How is this possible? You need 2 S's on different days to come before the 2 consecutive M's. If Saffie's cleaning shifts are as early in the week as possible, she'll clean on Monday and Tuesday. That means that the earliest day that Mona can clean (and Will as well, thanks to Rule 2) is Wednesday. There's your first key deduction:

> Mona and Will cannot clean on Monday and Tuesday; they must clean Wednesday, Thursday, or Friday.

Do you stop there? Of course not. If you relate this deduction back to Rule 5, it's clear that Mona and Will must clean on Wednesday and Thursday, or on Thursday and Friday. This brings you to another big deduction:

> Either way, Mona and Will must clean on Thursday. Thanks to Rule 4, you can slot in Will for Thursday evening. Mona will then take Thursday morning or afternoon. The other Mona/Will day must be either Wednesday or Friday, to remain consecutive.

KAPLAN EXCLUSIVE

The Logic Games expert knows how to press on when more deductions are possible.

The following sketch shows what your completed sketch may look like, with as many of the rules built into it as possible:

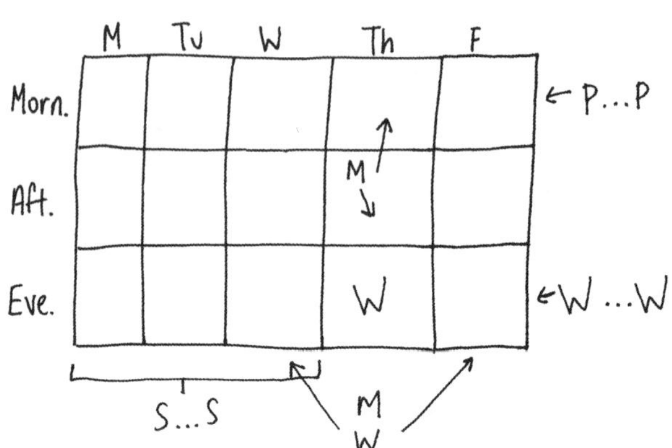

KAPLAN EXCLUSIVE

Trial and error with the answer choices should be your last resort, not your first. It's quicker to follow a chain of deduction.

Now that you've combined the rules and made some big deductions, move on to the questions.

5. Questions

This is where you'll see how all the work you did up front pays off. Question 1 offers no new "if" information; it simply asks what must be true. And since you've already deduced a few things that must be true, you can scan the choices for one that matches any of your newly discovered pieces of information. It doesn't take long to spot choice (C)—your big deduction staring you right in the face. Don't waste time checking the other choices; have the confidence that you've done the right work the right way, circle (C) and move on. (Just for the record, for those of you who are curious, (A), (B), and (D) could be true, but need not be, while (E), as you discovered earlier, is impossible.)

Question 2 contains a hypothetical: no Will on Friday. One glance at your sketch tells you that the second Mona/Will cluster must therefore be placed on Wednesday, next to the Thursday Mona/Will group. Saffie must then clean on Monday and Tuesday, in order to satisfy Rule 6 (although you don't yet know the exact shifts she takes during those days).

That brings you to the two questions that test takers ask all too infrequently: "Who's left?" and more importantly, "Where can they go?" You have 2 P's and 2 R's left to place, with 1 spot on Monday, 1 spot on Tuesday, and 2 spots on Friday open to place them. How can this be done? Friday can't get both P's or both R's (from the last sentence in the introduction), so it will have to get 1 of each, with P in the morning and R in either the afternoon or evening. The other P and the other R will join S on Monday or Tuesday, in either order. Of course, whichever day P is on, he must be in the morning, whereas the exact shifts for R and S are ambiguous.

Look at how far the chain of deductions takes you, beginning with the simple statement in the question stem found on the next page:

2. If Will doesn't clean on Friday, then . . .

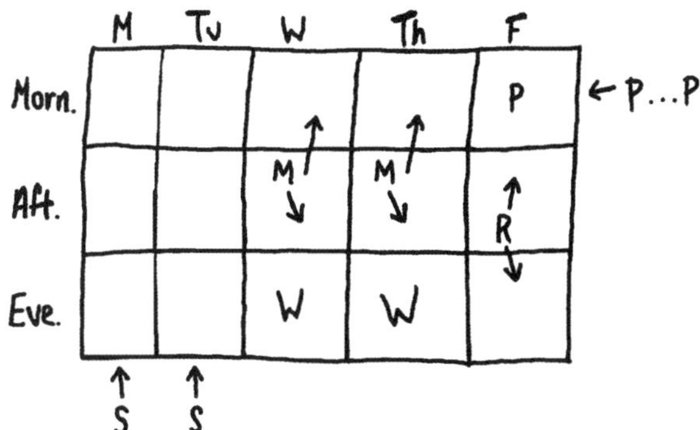

With all of this information at your disposal, you can answer any question correctly. This one asks for a statement that could be false—which means that the four wrong choices will all be things that must be true. And in fact, choices (A) through (D) match the situation in this question perfectly, while (E) merely could be true: Patrick's first cleaning shift of the week could be on Tuesday, but it just as easily could be on Monday as well. (His second shift must be on Friday.) (E) is the only choice that could be false.

READ MORE

Kaplan's *LSAT 180* offers even more Logic Games practice.

Be sure to apply the 5-Step Method and the strategies and techniques discussed when you work through the following practice sets and all your Practice Tests.

SUMMARY

The basic principles of Logic Games are:

- Slow down to go faster.
- Always use the rules and deductions to work out as much positive, concrete information as you can before moving to the questions.
- Know what a rule means, not just what it says.
- Use scratchwork and shorthand.
- Try to set off chains of deductions.
- Know the Logic Games question types.

Types of Games

Sequencing Games: have been the most popular game type, involving putting entities in order (strict or loose), often in time, space, or degree.

Grouping Games: the number of elements is often crucial; it's action involves deciding what entities are included a group (selection), or which group an entity belongs in (distribution).

Matching Games: often complicated games requiring tables or grids, they may involve *if/then* rules that can be handled by using the contrapositive.

Hybrid Games: often the most difficult games that contain elements of two (or more) of the other game types.

Kaplan's 5-Step Method for Logic Games

1. Overview (SEAL)
2. Sketch
3. Rules
4. Deduction
5. Questions

LOGIC GAMES PRACTICE

Set One

Directions: Each group of questions is based on a passage or a set of conditions. You may wish to draw a diagram to answer some of the questions. Choose the best answer for each question.

Questions 1–5

Six people—Matt, Ned, Qi, Stanley, Tonga, and Vladimir—are sitting around a rectangular table with six seats, one at the head of the table, one at the foot, and two on each long side of the table. The chairs are numbered 1 through 6 in a clockwise fashion, beginning with the chair at the head of the table, such that Chairs 1 and 4, 2 and 6, and 3 and 5 are directly across the table from each other.

Consecutively numbered chairs are considered adjacent. Chairs 1 and 6 are also considered adjacent.

Ned is sitting in chair 1 or chair 4.

Stanley and Tonga are sitting in adjacent chairs on one long side of the table.

Qi and Stanley are not sitting in adjacent chairs.

1. Which one of the following could be the seating arrangement of the six people in Chairs 1 through 6, respectively?

   (A) Ned, Vladimir, Tonga, Stanley, Matt, Qi
   (B) Vladimir, Stanley, Tonga, Ned, Matt, Qi
   (C) Qi, Matt, Ned, Stanley, Tonga, Vladimir
   (D) Ned, Tonga, Qi, Vladimir, Stanley, Matt
   (E) Qi, Vladimir, Matt, Ned, Tonga, Stanley

2. If Vladimir is sitting in Chair 4, then which one of the following pairs must be sitting in adjacent seats?

   (A) Matt and Ned
   (B) Matt and Qi
   (C) Ned and Qi
   (D) Ned and Stanley
   (E) Stanley and Vladimir

3. If Qi is sitting in Chair 1, then which one of the following must be sitting adjacent to her?

   (A) Ned
   (B) Matt
   (C) Stanley
   (D) Tonga
   (E) Vladimir

4. If Stanley and Vladimir are sitting in adjacent chairs, then Matt could be sitting in any of the following EXCEPT:

   (A) Chair 1
   (B) Chair 2
   (C) Chair 3
   (D) Chair 5
   (E) Chair 6

5. If Stanley is sitting in Chair 3 and Matt is sitting in Chair 6, then which one of the following pairs CANNOT sit directly across the table from each other?

   (A) Ned and Qi
   (B) Ned and Vladimir
   (C) Qi and Stanley
   (D) Qi and Vladimir
   (E) Stanley and Vladimir

Questions 6–11

A salesperson will display nine cheeses in three groups of three cheeses each. The groups are labeled A, B, and C. Four of the cheeses—F, G, H, and J—are domestic cheeses, and five—P, Q, R, S, and T—are imported cheeses. Each cheese will be displayed in exactly one of the three groups. The display must meet the following conditions:

At least one cheese in each group must be a domestic cheese.
F must be displayed with two imported cheeses.
Q must be displayed in Group C.
S must be displayed in Group A.
Neither F nor J nor R can be displayed in the same group as Q.

6. If both P and T are displayed in Group B, then which one of the following must be true?

(A) F is displayed in Group A.
(B) G is displayed in Group A.
(C) H is displayed in Group A.
(D) J is displayed in Group A.
(E) R is displayed in Group A.

7. Which one of the following statements must be true?

(A) If F and R are displayed together, they are displayed in the same group as S.
(B) If G and H are displayed together, they are displayed in the same group as Q.
(C) If G and T are displayed together, they are displayed in the same group as F.
(D) If H and J are displayed together, they are displayed in the same group as P.
(E) If R and S are displayed together, they are displayed in the same group as J.

8. All of the following are groups of three cheeses that can be displayed together in Group B EXCEPT:

(A) F, P, and R
(B) G, H, and T
(C) G, J, and R
(D) J, P, and T
(E) J, R, and T

9. If G is displayed in Group A, then which one of the following could be true?

(A) H is displayed in Group A.
(B) J is displayed in Group B.
(C) P is displayed in Group A.
(D) R is displayed in Group A.
(E) T is displayed in Group C.

10. If both H and P are displayed in Group B, then which one of the following must be the cheeses displayed in Group A?

(A) F, J, S
(B) F, R, S
(C) F, S, T
(D) J, S, R
(E) J, S, T

11. If J is displayed in Group B, then which one of the following CANNOT be true?

(A) F and R are displayed in the same group.
(B) G and R are displayed in the same group.
(C) H and S are displayed in the same group.
(D) R and S are displayed in the same group.
(E) S and T are displayed in the same group.

Set Two

Questions 1–5

A doctor is scheduled to see seven patients—Quincy, Roland, Selena, Thurman, Vivian, Wilma, and Xavier—between the hours of 9 AM and 5 PM. All appointments last exactly one hour and start at the top of the hour. There are no appointments scheduled during lunch. The schedule for the appointments must conform to the following conditions:

Xavier is scheduled as either the first or last appointment.
Selena's appointment is scheduled earlier than Thurman's appointment.
Thurman's appointment is exactly one hour before Vivian's appointment.
If Roland's appointment is scheduled for 12 PM, then Thurman's appointment is scheduled for 3 PM.
Lunch is scheduled for 1 PM and is one hour long and there are no other breaks scheduled for the day.

1. Which one of the following could be a list of the patients in the order of their scheduled appointments, from 9 AM to 4 PM?

   (A) Xavier, Quincy, Roland, Thurman, Vivian, Selena, Wilma
   (B) Quincy, Selena, Wilma, Roland, Xavier, Thurman, Vivian
   (C) Roland, Quincy, Selena, Wilma, Thurman, Vivian, Xavier
   (D) Xavier, Thurman, Vivian, Wilma, Selena, Roland, Quincy
   (E) Selena, Thurman, Vivian, Roland, Wilma, Quincy, Xavier

2. Which one of the following must be FALSE?

   (A) Roland's appointment is scheduled for 4 PM.
   (B) Quincy's appointment is scheduled for 2 PM.
   (C) Wilma's appointment is scheduled for 10 AM.
   (D) Vivian's appointment is scheduled for 10 AM.
   (E) Selena's appointment is scheduled for 9 AM.

3. If Roland is scheduled for 12 PM, then which of the following must be true?

   (A) Xavier is scheduled for 9 AM.
   (B) Selena is scheduled for 2 PM.
   (C) Wilma is scheduled for 11 AM.
   (D) Quincy is scheduled for 11 AM.
   (E) Vivian is scheduled for 3 PM.

4. Which of the following patients CANNOT be scheduled for 2 PM?

   (A) Quincy
   (B) Roland
   (C) Selena
   (D) Thurman
   (E) Vivian

5. If Roland's appointment is exactly one hour before Thurman's appointment, which choice contains two alternative appointments either of which could be true?

   (A) Quincy's appointment is at 2 PM; Wilma's appointment is at 2 PM.
   (B) Wilma's appointment is at 10 AM; Vivian's appointment is at 10 AM.
   (C) Selena's appointment is at 3 PM.; Vivian's appointment is at 3 PM.
   (D) Thurman's appointment is at 2 PM; Selena's appointment is at 2 PM.
   (E) Roland's appointment is at 12 PM; Thurman's appointment is at 12 PM.

Questions 6–10

Each of six vacationers—Cedric, Dolores, Fredrick, Gloria, Hedwig, and Jorge—will visit one of three cities—Lisbon, Madrid, or Novosibirsk—for exactly one month, according to the following conditions:

Each of the vacationers visits one of the cities with either one or three of the other vacationers, and no two groups contain exactly the same number of tourists.
Hedwig visits a different city than Jorge.
Dolores visits the same city as Gloria.
Cedric visits either Lisbon or Madrid.
If Jorge visits Novosibirsk, Dolores visits Novosibirsk with him.

6. Which of the following could be true for the one month vacation?

(A) Fredrick and Hedwig visit Madrid. Cedric, Dolores, Gloria, and Jorge visit Novosibirsk.
(B) Dolores, Fredrick, Gloria, and Jorge visit Lisbon. Cedric and Hedwig visit Madrid.
(C) Dolores, Gloria, and Jorge visit Lisbon. Cedric, Fredrick, and Hedwig visit Madrid.
(D) Cedric and Fredrick visit Lisbon. Dolores, Gloria, Hedwig, and Jorge visit Madrid.
(E) Cedric, Fredrick, Gloria, and Hedwig visit Lisbon. Dolores and Jorge visit Novosibirsk.

7. Which of the following must be FALSE?

(A) Fredrick visits the same city as Hedwig.
(B) Cedric visits the same city as Hedwig.
(C) Cedric visits the same city as Fredrick.
(D) Jorge visits Lisbon.
(E) Jorge visits Madrid.

8. If Hedwig visits Novosibirsk, which one of the following must be true for the one month vacation?

(A) Cedric visits Lisbon.
(B) Jorge visits Madrid.
(C) Dolores visits Novosibirsk.
(D) Gloria visits Lisbon.
(E) Fredrick visits Novosibirsk.

9. If Gloria visits Madrid, which one of the following must be FALSE?

(A) Fredrick visits Madrid.
(B) Hedwig visits Madrid.
(C) Hedwig visits Novosibirsk.
(D) Jorge visits Novosibirsk.
(E) Jorge visits Lisbon.

10. Which one of the following could be FALSE?

(A) Dolores visits a city with exactly three of the other five students.
(B) Gloria must visit Madrid if Hedwig visits Novosibirsk.
(C) Fredrick must visit Novosibirsk if Jorge visits Novosibirsk.
(D) Gloria visits a city with exactly three of the other five students.
(E) Cedric must visit Lisbon if Fredrick visits Madrid.

Set Three

Questions 1–5

Seven instructors—J, K, L, M, N, P, and Q—teach adult education courses at a community college. Each instructor teaches during exactly one semester: the fall semester, the spring semester, or the winter semester. The following conditions apply:

K teaches during the winter semester.
L and M teach during the same semester.
Q teaches during either the fall semester or the spring semester.
Exactly twice as many instructors teach during the winter semester as teach during the fall semester.
N and Q teach during different semesters.
J and P teach during different semesters.

1. Which one of the following could be an accurate matching of instructors to semesters?

   (A) M: the fall semester; P: the spring semester; Q: the fall semester
   (B) J: the winter semester; L: the winter semester; P: the winter semester
   (C) L: the fall semester; N: the spring semester; P: the winter semester
   (D) J: the fall semester; M: the winter semester; N: the spring semester
   (E) K: the spring semester; L: the winter semester; P: the winter semester

2. Which one of the following cannot be true?

   (A) L teaches during the fall semester.
   (B) M teaches during the spring semester.
   (C) M teaches during the winter semester.
   (D) N teaches during the spring semester.
   (E) P teaches during the fall semester.

3. If exactly one instructor teaches during the spring semester, which one of the following must be true?

   (A) J teaches during the winter semester.
   (B) L teaches during the fall semester.
   (C) M teaches during the winter semester.
   (D) P teaches during the spring semester.
   (E) Q teaches during the fall semester.

4. Each of the following contains a list of instructors who can all teach during the same semester EXCEPT:

   (A) J, K, M
   (B) J, L, M
   (C) K, L, P
   (D) K, P, Q
   (E) L, M, P

5. Which one of the following could be a complete and accurate list of instructors who do not teach during the winter semester?

   (A) J, L, Q
   (B) J, Q
   (C) L, M, Q
   (D) N, P, Q
   (E) N, Q

Questions 6–10

Eight albums are to be played at a party. Two of the albums are country—G and H, three of the albums are dance—J, K, and L, and three of the albums are folk—M, N, and P. The two country albums are to be played consecutively, the three dance albums are to be played consecutively, and the three folk albums are to be played consecutively. The following conditions apply:

Each album is played exactly once.

The dance albums are played after the country albums or after the folk albums, but not after both.

Album N is played before album P and album G is played before album H.

No two albums are played at the same time.

6. Which of the following statements must be false?

    (A) Album G is played first.
    (B) Album G is played seventh.
    (C) Album H is played second.
    (D) Album H is played seventh.
    (E) Album M is played third.

7. Which of the following could be true?

    (A) Album G is played fourth.
    (B) Album G is played eighth.
    (C) Album K is played first.
    (D) Album N is played second.
    (E) Album N is played third.

8. Which of the following CANNOT be an accurate list of the albums that are played second, third, and fourth?

    (A) N, M, J
    (B) P, M, J
    (C) N, P, K
    (D) H, J, K
    (E) H, K, L

9. If album P is played immediately before album M, then which one of the following statements could be true?

    (A) Album P is played first.
    (B) Album P is played sixth.
    (C) Album M is played third.
    (D) Album M is played seventh.
    (E) Album M is played second.

10. If albums K and N are played consecutively, but not necessarily in that order, which of the following statements must be false?

    (A) Album N is played before album M.
    (B) Album J is played before album L.
    (C) Album L is played before album J.
    (D) Album M is played before album H.
    (E) Album G is played before album K.

ANSWERS AND EXPLANATIONS

Answer Key

Set One	Set Two	Set Three
1. B	1. C	1. D
2. B	2. D	2. A
3. D	3. A	3. C
4. A	4. E	4. D
5. D	5. A	5. D
6. E	6. B	6. D
7. B	7. C	7. D
8. B	8. E	8. A
9. E	9. D	9. C
10. B	10. B	10. D
11. C		

Set One

Quesions 1–5

This game involves placing people around a table, and it's pretty straightforward. The table is clearly described, maybe even too clearly. It's awfully wordy for all it has to say.

There is a rectangle in which Chairs 1 and 4 are at opposite ends, the head and foot, with Chairs 2 and 3 adjacent to each other on one side, and Chairs 5 and 6 adjacent on the other. You go clockwise around the table, the rules tell you, and, although you might have figured it out for yourself, you're even told exactly which chairs are opposite which. So this all turns out to be pretty simple to sketch.

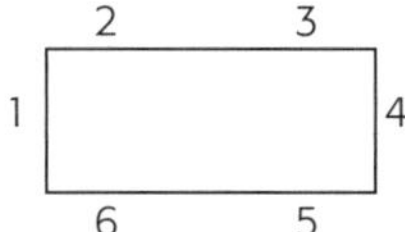

Rule 2 says Ned is in Chair 1 or 4. Of course, that means he is either at the head or foot of the table. You could have written a note to yourself at the top of the page: "N head or foot." And, as a result, each time you drew the table to answer a question, you would have seen that note and remembered right away to put Ned at the bottom or the top of the rectangular table.

Same thing for the other rules. You could have written in big letters "ST" at the top of the page to remind yourself that those two characters, Stanley and Tonga, have to be next to each other along one of the table's two long edges. Alternatively, you might have written "ST = 2 and 3 or 5 and 6." That's just another way of noting the relevant information. And there's no need to do much more with Rule 4 than write something like "Q not = S," a reminder always to separate Qi and Stanley.

1. B

Armed with all that information, you should be able to make short work of question 1, which asks for the one and only one acceptable sequence. Ned has to be in Chair 1 or 4. That means that choice (C) is unacceptable since (C) puts him in Chair 3. Cross out (C); there's no point in ever looking at it again. Next, remember that Stanley and Tonga have to be adjacent, and that eliminates choice (D), which puts two people between S and T in either direction. Moreover, they have to be adjacent along a long side of the table, that is, in Chairs 2 and 3 or 5 and 6. This eliminates choice (A), in which they are next to each other but Stanley is sitting in Chair 4, that is, at the foot of the table.

Nothing seems to have violated Rule 4 yet, but dollars to doughnuts, one choice will. And it turns out to be choice (E). You can't have Q in 1 and S in 6 because that, according to the first rule, counts as adjacency. You're left with choice (B), which must be okay since the other four choices violate rules. (B) is correct, although you needn't bother to check it at this point as long as you're sure the others are wrong. Just choose (B) and move on.

2. B

A quick sketch for question 2 puts V in Chair 4, and should immediately put Ned in Chair 1. Ned has to be in one or the other, and since someone else is in 4, he has to be in Chair 1. On one side of the table, as always, you put Stanley and Tonga. You don't know which side right now. That leaves two people, Qi and Matt, and they, too, will be along one long side of the table. That's all that's left. So, when question 2 asks who has to be next to each other, you should look for Qi and Matt, and you'll find them in correct choice (B). All of the other pairs *could* be adjacent but needn't be. So it's choice (B), and you're done with that one almost as quickly as you started.

3. D

Question 3 can be done very quickly, too. Putting Qi in Chair 1, as you're told to do, means that Ned goes to Chair 4 this time. That leaves Stanley and Tonga, once again, along one of the long sides. But remember Rule 4: you have to separate Qi and Stanley. Therefore, Q, who will have to sit next to either S or T, since she's at the head, will be next to Tonga for sure, choice (D). Ned, choice (A), is opposite Qi. Stanley, choice (C), can't be next to her. And, certainly, either Matt, choice (B), or Vladimir, choice (E), will have to be next to Qi, too, although you cannot choose between them. So it's Tonga, choice (D).

4. A

Question 4 asks, "Where could Matt *not* be?" The rules tell you very little about Matt, so build on the concrete information you're given about the other characters and see where that leaves Matt at the end.

Stanley and Vladimir are next to each other, you're told to assume. Stanley and Tonga are likewise next to each other, right? So, both V and T will flank S at the table. However, you specifically know that Stanley and Tonga take up one long side of the table. This means that Vladimir will have to end up at one end of the table or the other, either the head or the foot. Well, the other end, the head or the foot, is reserved for Ned. So if you look at the answer choices with the head and the foot going to Vladimir and Ned, there's no way that Matt or anyone else, besides those two, could occupy Chair 1 or Chair 4. The former has been chosen as the correct answer, choice (A). As for the others, Matt could take any of those. He and Qi will occupy 2 and 3 or 5 and 6, but more than that you don't know. So it's choice (A).

5. D

Question 5, in its exploration of who can or cannot sit across from whom, explicitly places two people in chairs and allows you to do likewise with a third. Specifically, if Stanley is in Chair 3, Tonga (who again has to be next to Stanley along a long side of the table) has to take the other chair along that side, Chair 2. Stanley in 3, Tonga in 2, and Matt in 6. Now, at this point, a lot depends on the placement of Ned. Both Chair 1, the head, and Chair 4, the foot, are available to him. If Ned is in Chair 1, the head, that is between Tonga on his left and Matt on his right, that leaves two chairs, 4 and 5, available to Qi and Vladimir. But Qi can't take Chair 4 while Stanley is in Chair 3. Rule 4 forbids it. So you would have to have Vladimir in 4 and Qi in 5. Under those circumstances, you would see choice (C), Qi and Stanley opposite each other in Chairs 5 and 3 respectively, and also choice (B), Ned and Vladimir opposite each other at the ends of the table.

But suppose Ned's in Chair 4 at the foot. With Matt in 6, Ned in 4, Stanley in 3, and Tonga in 2, the possibilities are slightly more numerous. Chairs 1 and 5 remain for Qi and Vladimir, with no restrictions as to which one is in which. Under those circumstances, you could certainly have Ned in 4 opposite Qi in 1, leaving Vladimir in 5 opposite Stanley in 3. And thus A and E must be rejected. Either is a possibility. But under no circumstances will you ever see Qi and Vladimir opposite each other (as it turns out, in none of these scenarios did you see that), and that makes choice (D) correct.

Questions 6–11

After previewing the setup and rules, you see that this game asks you to distribute nine cheeses into three groups of three cheeses each—a grouping game of distribution. There are four domestic cheeses—F, G, H, and J—and five imported cheeses—p, q, r, s, and t (it can help to keep the entities separate if you use CAPS for one group and lower case letters for the other). The three groups are A, B, and C. The Key Issues will be:

1) What cheese is in what group?
2) What cheeses can, must, or cannot be selected with what other cheeses?

You've got three groups of three each. Set this up like you might in real life. Just list the three groups with three dashes under each. Be sure you also list the two types of cheeses:

DOMESTIC: F G H J   imported: p q r s t

A: — — —   B: — — —   C: — — —

1) It's best to build a rule directly into the master sketch whenever you can. One of the cheeses in each group must be domestic. Make a note of this in the sketch; placing a "D" under one of the dashes in each group should suffice.

2) You don't know which group F is in, but F must always be accompanied by two imports—no domestics allowed in a group with F.
3) q, an imported cheese, goes in Group C. Build this right into the sketch.
4) s goes in Group A. That's another imported cheese definitely set.
5) Whew. Three rules in one. Be careful when you unpack this rule. Take it one step at a time. First of all, F can't be in the same group as q. Secondly, J can't go in the same group as q, and finally, r can't go with q either. Your mind is probably jumping ahead and combining this rule with Rule 3, and that's a good thing. It means that you're getting used to looking for deductions.

Time to take a closer look at Rule 5 (and Rule 3). Don't just write "No F q." Ask yourself "What does that mean?"—q is in Group C, so F must be in either A or B. J, too, can't go with q. Again, this means that J must go in either Group A or Group B. Finally, r can't go with q, so r must also go in A or B.

Keep going. There's more to be deduced here. F and J and r each must go in either Group A or Group B. Can these entities go in the same group? Rule 2 told you that F must go in a group with two imports. r is an import, so F and r could go in the same group, but J is a domestic. No way could F and J go in the same group. So, F must go in Group A or B, and J must go in the other.

As with all games, take a moment to work through the numbers aspect of the game. Here that means looking at Rule 1. Each group must have at least one domestic cheese. Rule 5 said that F and J (two domestics) can't go with q in Group C, but Group C must have at least one domestic. What domestic cheeses are left? G and H are the only other domestics. One of this pair must ALWAYS go in Group C. You can bet that one or two answer choices will try to put them both elsewhere. Now you're thinking like the test makers.

Finally, it's a good idea to identify the "floaters" in each game. These are those entities that don't appear in any rules or deductions. They will serve to fill in the remaining slots after you've placed all the other entities. Here, the "floaters" are p and t, two imported cheeses.

Here's what you have going into the questions:

DOMESTIC	imported
F G H J	p q r s t

A	B	C
__ s __	__ __ __	G/H q __
D	D	D
F + 2 imp.	F + 2 imp.	No F
J	J	No J
r	r	No r
F ≠ J	F ≠ J	

6. E

You know that each group must have at least one domestic cheese. Because p and t (both imports) are in Group B, the remaining cheese must be domestic. We deduced in Rule 5 that r, an import, must be in Group A or B. The last cheese in B must be domestic, so r must go in Group A, choice (E).

(A) No, F could go in group B with p and t.

(B) No, G could be in Group C.

(C) No, H could be in Group C.

(D) No, J could go in Group B with p and t.

When you're given new information, get it down in the test booklet. Then ask yourself, "What entities does this new information affect?" Go back to your master sketch and the rules.

7. B

A "must be true" question with no new information often signals that the test makers are asking for a key deduction. However, you can tell that that's probably not the case here because of the complex answer choices. Each choice is like a question in itself. You can count on spending a good deal of time here. This question is a candidate for skipping the first time around if you need to preserve time because there's not much to do except try out each choice.

(A) Could F and r be together and not be in the group with s (that's Group A)? Sure they could. Here are the complete groupings that show choice (A) needn't be true: A—J s t, B—F p r, C—G H q.

(B) Could G and H be together and not be in the group with q? No way. We saw up front that J and F can't be with q (Rule 5), and because each group needs at least one domestic, either G or H must be with q. (B) must be true and is the answer. On test day you'd stop right here and go on to the next question. For the record, here are groupings that show the remaining choices needn't be true (you may have come up with other acceptable groupings to dispose of these choices):

(C) and (D) A—J H s , B—F p r, C—G q t

(E) A—F s r, B—J G r, C—H p q

To prove that a choice in a "must be true" question is wrong, find an exception to the choice, an acceptable situation that shows that the choice could be false.

8. B

This takes a slightly different form than most acceptability questions, but it's still an acceptability question. You're asked to find the one unacceptable Group B among the choices. What do we know about Group B? We deduced that either F or J must always go in Group B (see Key Deductions for a reminder of how we deduced that). Every acceptable Group B must therefore contain either F or J. Scan the choices. Choice (B) doesn't include F or J, and it tries to place both G and H in Group B—wrong on both counts. Remember, one of G or H must always go in Group C.

Always keep in mind exactly what the question is asking. If you had mistakenly thought that this question was asking for the one acceptable choice instead of the one unacceptable one, you would have been very confused.

9. E

G is in Group A. In what rules or deductions are you used to dealing with G? Questions 2 and 3 both were answered by realizing that either G or H must go in Group C. Here G is in A, so H must go in Group C. What else do you know about G? G is a domestic cheese, so F, which must be grouped with two imports, can't be in A. The only other choice for F is Group B. F and J can't be in the same group, so J must go in Group A. So far we have G, J and s in Group A, F and r in Group B, and H and q in Group C. Who's left? p and t will fill in the slots: one in Group B and the other in Group C. Don't hesitate to redraw your master sketch whenever needed. Here's what this question's sketch would look like:

A	B	C
G s J	F r p/t	H q p/t

Scan the choices; t could indeed be in Group C. (E) could be true and is the answer.

(A) No, H is in Group C.

(B) No, J is in Group A.

(C) No, p is in Group B or C.

(D) No, r is in Group B.

Work with any new information that you're given. Keep asking yourself, "In what rules and deductions have I seen this entity before?" and "What do I know about this entity?"

10. B

H is a domestic cheese, so F can't join H and p in Group B (Rule 2). Because F can't, J must be the one to fill out Group B. F's only other choice is Group A. r must go in Group A because B is now full. We're looking for Group A, and now we have it: F, r, and s, choice (B).

Only do the work required to answer the question. You could have taken the deductions further and filled out Group C, but there's no need to. The question is asking about Group A, so that's the only group you're interested in.

11. C

What does it mean for J to be in Group B? It means that F must be in Group A—by now, splitting these two entities up between Groups A and B should be instinctual. Other than that, there's not much else to deduce: r, as usual, can go in either A or B, and our perpetual floaters p and t can pretty much go anywhere. What leads to the answer here is the situation of G and H. These two domestic cheeses can both join q in C or they can split up between B and C. The one thing neither of them can do is end up in Group A because that's where F is in this question, and F's companion cheeses are always both imports. (C) is therefore impossible—for H to be displayed with s (in Group A) would mean placing H in the same group as F, which is a no-no.

(A) and (D) No problem here—r can go in Group A with F and s while the remaining entities fill out Groups B and C in any one of a number of different ways.

(B) G and r can join J in Group B as long as H joins q in Group C. Then p and t can fill in the remaining slots in Groups A and C.

(E) The situation just described in (B) above works for this one; just put t in Group A along with F and s and p in Group C along with H and q.

Set Two

Questions 1–5

In this sequencing game, you're asked to put seven patients in order according to their scheduled appointments. The natural way to picture this is to create eight empty spaces with the time of the appointment above each one, starting with 9 AM. Try to find a way to build each rule into the sketch as you read over each one. Create your own visual diagrams, and then compare to the ones shown below. You might like our visual aids better, or you might prefer your own symbols. Either way, the goal is to create a visual language that you can use to help yourself answer all LSAT logic games questions.

Xavier can only have the appointment at 9 AM or 4 PM. Note this limitation on your graph. Selena must come before Thurman, but the rule does not say exactly when. Make a note showing the link between S and T. Thurman and Vivian must be scheduled for back-to-back appointments, with Thurman's being the first. You can combine this with the previous clue to give you a link between S, T, and V. With three letters integrated into this clue, you can expect it will be important.

If Roland is at 12 PM, then Thurman must be scheduled for 3 PM. From a previous clue you know that Vivian must be scheduled at 4 PM. This gives you a connection between R, T, and V, but only if R = 12.

There is one last point to make: Q and W have no limitations placed on them whatsoever. This information may help when determining what "must be true." Since the two elements are identical, what must be true of one will also be true of the other.

Q, R, S, T, V, W, X

S . . . T

\+

TV

=

S . . . TV

if R = 12, T = 3

Q/W

/X (above 9) X/ (above 4)

9 10 11 12 1 2 3 4

X (under 1)

No one can be scheduled for 1 PM, the hour designated for lunch. Place a blocked out X there to designate this.

Before you start with the questions, be sure you have considered all the implications of each rule. Xavier can only be at the two ends of the schedule. Since Selena is before Thurman, and Vivian is directly after Thurman, then Selena must go before both Thurman and Vivian. This means that Selena CANNOT have either the 3 PM or 4 PM appointment.

Now that you've taken the time to consider all the important implications of each rule you should be all set to jump into the questions and rack up some points.

1. C

This is an acceptability question, so grab each rule and see which choices violate that rule. The correct answer is the one that violates no rules. The first rule, Xavier at either 9 AM or 4 PM, eliminates (B). The second rule, Selena is scheduled before Thurman, eliminates (A) and (D). Rule 3, Thurman is immediately before Vivian, doesn't help eliminate any answer choices. However, the fourth rule, placing Roland at 12 PM and Thurman at 3 PM, eliminates answer (E). Only (C) is left.

2. D

This question asks you to identify the one patient who cannot have the designated appointment time given in the answer choices. A good place to begin would be to see which rules, if any, govern the patients in the answer choices. Rule 4 is only relevant if Roland is scheduled for 12 PM, and answer (A) schedules him at 4 PM. There are no limitations governing the placement of Quincy and Wilma, therefore they could be scheduled for 2 PM and 10 AM respectively. Rule 2 states that Selena must be scheduled some time before Thurman, and answer (E) clearly does this by giving Selena the first appointment at 9 AM. Rule 3 states that Vivian must be scheduled immediately after Thurman. Therefore if Vivian is scheduled for 10 AM, Thurman must have the first appointment at 9 AM. However, Rule 2 clearly places Selena before Thurman, and if Thurman is scheduled for 9 AM, there would be place to schedule Selena and Rule 2 would be violated. Therefore (D) must be false.

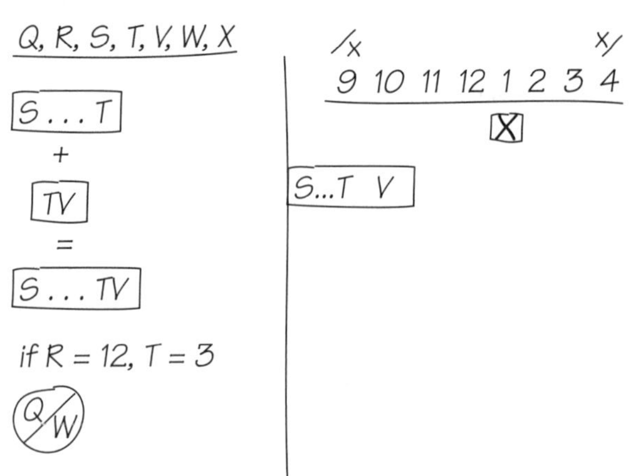

3. A

If Roland is scheduled for 12 PM, then Thurman is at 3 PM and Vivian is at 4 PM. With Vivian in the 4 PM slot, Xavier must be scheduled for 9 AM. Answer (A) is just waiting for you to pick up an easy point.

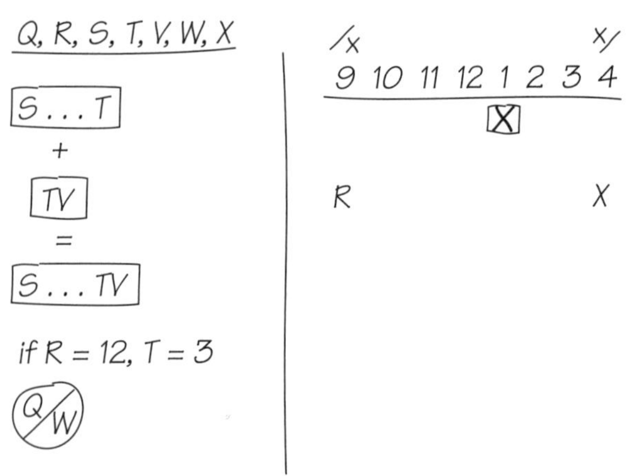

4. E

On your scratch work you should have factored in Rule 5, which gives you the doctor's lunch time. The question asks who can't be scheduled immediately after the doctor's lunch. According to Rule 3, Thurman is scheduled exactly one hour before Vivian, so if Vivian is scheduled for 2 PM, then Thurman must be scheduled for 1 PM, which coincides with the doctor's lunch. Therefore Vivian CANNOT have a 2 PM appointment.

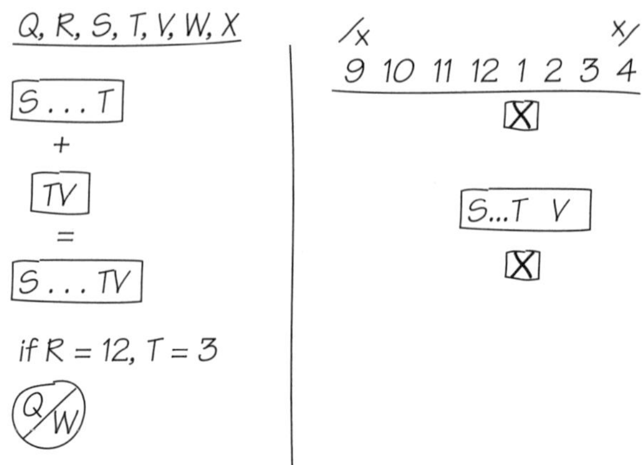

5. A

Some questions, such as this one, will add an extra rule or condition that they want you to incorporate into the existing rules given in the setup to solve for the answer. Follow the same steps you took when you were reading the setup; visualize how the new rule affects the game and think of any deductions or implications the new rule will have. For this question, Roland must now be placed immediately before Thurman, and Thurman is still placed immediately before Vivian. Therefore, Roland, Thurman, and Vivian now form a three-hour chunk of appointments that cannot be separated. Since Selena still has to come before Thurman, the only two places this group of appointments can fit are 10 AM – 12 PM (Roland, Thurman, and Vivian respectively) or 2 PM – 4 PM. If the group is placed in the 10 AM – 12 PM appointments, then Selena must have the 9 AM and Xavier has the 4 PM. This leaves Quincy and Wilma to have the 2 PM and 3 PM appointments and either of them can have the 2 PM.

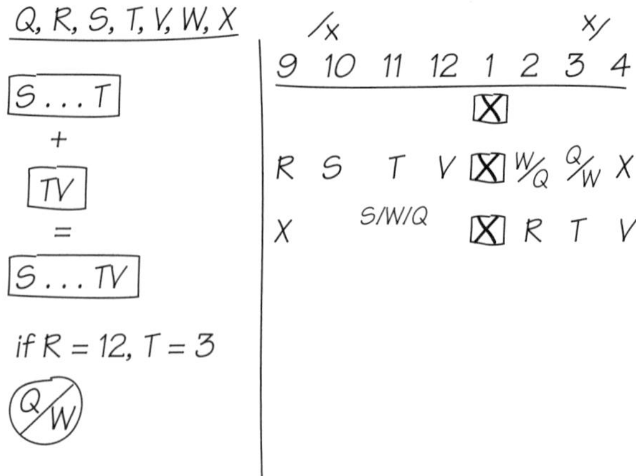

(A) is correct. Vivian would be restricted only to the 12 PM and 4 PM appointments and therefore (B) and (C) are incorrect. Thurman would be restricted to the 11 AM and 3 PM appointments and therefore (D) and (E) are incorrect.

Questions 6–10

This game asks you to distribute six vacationers among three cities: call it a grouping game of distribution. The six vacationers are Cedric, Dolores, Fredrick, Gloria, Hedwig, and Jorge (who can be referred to as C, D, F, G, H, J) and the vacation cities are Lisbon, Madrid, and Novosibirsk (l, m, n). The easiest way to set up the game is to create three columns, one for Lisbon, one for Madrid, and one for Novosibirsk (l, m, and n), and leave room below each to designate which vacationers go to which city.

C, D, F, G, H, J

2·4·0 (one city empty)

No H·J

[DG]

if J_n = [DJ]

. . . .

F*

if J_n = $[DGJ]_n$ and (H crossed out)$_n$

/c l	c/ m	n

Your diagram might look similar to the one pictured above. The first rule states that each vacationer is accompanied by either one or three of the other vacationers. This means that there can only be two groups of vacationers to separate among three cities, so one city will be left empty. The second rule is that Hedwig and Jorge will each be in one of the separate groups. Denote this in some way on your graph. The third rule states that Dolores and Gloria must visit the same city together. The fourth rule states that Cedric must be in Lisbon or Madrid. Place this on your graph in some form. The fifth rule tells you that if Jorge is in Novosibirsk, then Dolores is also in Novosibirsk with him.

Remember to take a closer look at all the rules to see if there are any deductions or implications that can be made with each one. You can deduce from the first rule that you should have one group of two vacationers in any given city and one group of four vacationers in another city. You also know from this rule that one column in your chart, which represents one of the cities, must be left blank. Also, consider the first three rules together. Dolores and Gloria must be in the same city together. If they consist of the group of two vacationers, then the remaining four vacationers must all be together, including Hedwig and Jorge, which violates rule 2. Therefore, Dolores and Gloria must be part of the group of four. Fredrick has no limitations on him.

Finally, if Jorge visits Novosibirsk, then Dolores visits Novosibirsk; therefore Dolores *and* Gloria both visit because they are always together. Since D and G are in the group of four, the fourth person must be Fredrick because Cedric is in either Lisbon or Madrid and Hedwig cannot be in the same city as Jorge. Now, let's see how all this applies to the questions.

6 B

This is the familiar acceptability question. Apply each rule to the answer choices, eliminating all answers that violate a rule. The first rule states that the vacationers are divided into a group of two and a group of four, eliminating (C). The second rule states that Hedwig and Jorge must be in separate cities, so get rid of (D). The third rule states that Dolores and Gloria must be in the same city, eliminating (E). The fourth rule states that Cedric cannot be in Novosibirsk, so choice (A) is out. The remaining answer choice, (B), is the correct response.

7. C

Questions that ask for an answer choice that "must be false" mean that you can eliminate any answer choice that *could* be true. Based on the answer from question 6, eliminate (B) and (D) since they show that Cedric and Hedwig could be together and that Jorge could be in Lisbon. Answer (A) could also be eliminated since it would be possible for Fredrick to visit the same city as Hedwig, with the remaining four vacationers in the second group. The trickiness of this question is in the fact that there are no explicit limitations regarding Cedric and Fredrick. But if you were to place them in the same city, they would either be their own group of two or half of a group of four. If they were their own group of two, then the remaining four vacationers must make up the second group and must contain both Hedwig and Jorge, a clear violation of the second rule. If they were half of a group of four, then the other two vacationers would be either Dolores and Gloria (since they must be together) or Hedwig and Jorge. Both choices leave Hedwig and Jorge together in the same group, a clear violation of the second rule. Therefore (C) must be false—Cedric cannot be in the same city as Fredrick.

8. E

If Hedwig visits Novosibirsk, then Jorge cannot visit Novosibirsk and must be with Cedric in either Lisbon or Madrid. Since there can only be groups of two or four, the remaining three vacationers (Dolores, Fredrick, and Gloria) could all join Hedwig in Novosibirsk or Dolores and Gloria (they must be together) could join Cedric and Jorge in Lisbon or Madrid and Fredrick could join Hedwig in Novosibirsk. Either way, Fredrick is in Novosibirsk, and (E) is correct.

9. D

If Gloria visits Madrid, then Dolores must also be in Madrid. But if Jorge is in Novosibirsk then Dolores and Gloria have to be there with him. So Jorge cannot visit Novosibirsk; (D) is correct.

10. B

Since the question is asking for what "could be false," you can eliminate any answer choice that *must* be true. Remember the deduction you made about Dolores and Gloria? They had to be in the group of four, therefore (A) and (D) must be true and can be eliminated. Remember question 7? You determined that Cedric cannot be in the same city as Fredrick, and since Cedric must be in either Lisbon or Madrid, if Fredrick is in one, then Cedric must be in the other. Eliminate (E) since it must be true. If Jorge visits Novosibirsk, then Dolores and Gloria must also visit Novosibirsk, which means one of the remaining three vacationers (Cedric, Fredrick, or Hedwig) must also visit Novosibirsk to complete the group of four. Cedric must be in Lisbon or Madrid and Hedwig cannot be in the same city as Jorge, therefore Fredrick must be in Novosibirsk and (C) must be true. If Hedwig is in Novosibirsk, Gloria and Dolores could be in any of the three cities. (B) is the only answer choice that could be false.

Set Three

Questions 1–5

Seven instructors—J, K, L, M, N, P, and Q—each teach during exactly one of three semesters. In other words, you have to distribute the seven instructors among the three semesters. So, this is another grouping game of distribution, and the Key Issues will be:

- Which instructors can, must, or cannot teach during which semesters?
- Which instructors can, must, or cannot teach during the same semester as which other instructors?
- How many instructors teach during each semester?

A list of the entities and three columns (one for each of the semesters) will allow you to keep track of the action here.

J K L M N P Q

Fall	Spring	Winter

1) Here's a concrete rule: You can place K in the winter column permanently.

2) Rule 2 is a familiar enough Grouping rule. L and M are always together. "Always LM" captures this.

3) Rule 3 can be built in directly, with arrows pointing to the fall and spring semesters.

4) The winter semester gets twice as many as the fall semester. Okay, what does that mean in the context of this game? With seven instructors, there really aren't that many ways to split them up so that exactly twice as many wind up in the Winter semester. So how many combinations are there? If one instructor taught in the fall, then you'd need two in the winter, and the remaining four would teach during the spring semester. Or, you could have two in the fall, four in the winter, and one in the spring. That's it. It's either 1/4/2 or 2/1/4. You can't have three or more in the fall, since that would force you to have six or more in the winter, and that's no good because there are only seven instructors.

5) and 6) are familiar enough Grouping rules. You cannot have an NQ, and we cannot have a JP.

The Big Deduction here was the 1/4/2 or 2/1/4 breakdown of the instructors. This essentially comes straight out of Rule 4, but if you noticed it at this point, it's okay, too. From here, you could have explored different scenarios, seeing if they set off any chains of inferences, but there wasn't anything else that qualifies as a major deduction. On to the questions!

The Final Visualization

The Questions

1. D

This is a harder Acceptability question than most since we're only given part of the lineup. So you may have been forced to work out scenarios for each choice. Only (B) and (E) contain a straightforward violation of a rule. (According to Rule 6, we can't have J and P together, and according to Rule 1, K teaches during the winter). The rest of the choices require some work:

(A) With Q and M in the fall, you need L there as well (Rule 2). That's three in the fall, which is no good, since it would force you to place six in the winter.

(C) If L is in the fall, then so is M. Since the fall can hold no more, Q must go in the spring (Rule 3).That leaves K, J, P, and N for the winter. But we can't have J and P together, so (C) doesn't work. So (D) is correct by the process of elimination.

(D) For the record: Placing J, M, and N as the stem dictates means you must also place L in the winter. Since the winter now has three instructors, it will need a fourth to satisfy the 2/1/4 distribution. We also need to split up J and P. So you can place Q in the fall and P in the winter, and you have an acceptable arrangement.

Fall	Spring	Winter
J	N	K
Q		M
		L
		P

Acceptability questions are usually quick points, but they can be harder when you only see part of the arrangement. Often, the wrong choices in these questions don't contain obvious violations of the rules. Rather, they violate the rules by virtue of their implications for the other entities.

2. A

This one was quick if you worked out the scenario in (C) from the previous question. In that choice, you saw what happens when you put L in the fall: You need to put M there as well, and you're forced to place J and P together in the winter. So you can never put L (or M, for that matter) in the fall, and choice (A) is correct.

If you didn't see this, you still could have attacked this question strategically by postponing working on it until after you've built some acceptable scenarios from the other questions. (B) must be true in question 18, (E) could be true in question 18, and both (C) and (D) are true in the correct answer to the Acceptability questions.

Postpone working on questions when your work in the other questions will eliminate some choices.

Don't forget about the correct answer to the Acceptability question. It often eliminates a few wrong choices elsewhere.

3. C

If only one instructor teaches in the spring, then we have a 2/1/4 setup. You've seen we can't place L and M in the fall since that would force J and P together in the winter. So L and M teach in the winter, and (C) is correct.

(A), (D), and (E) are all possible only.

(B) is impossible. L teaches in the winter.

Sometimes a game's questions are similar to each other. So once you build some experience, you should be able to make inferences more quickly as the game goes on.

4. D

Here's another question that allows you to benefit from previous work. In the last question, we had K, L, and M together in the winter. They could be joined by either J or P without any violations. Once you know that we can have KLMJ or KLMP together, you can eliminate all four wrong choices because they all contain a subset of one of those groups. You also might have spotted correct choice (D) directly: K must be in the winter, and Q can never be in the winter. So (D) is correct.

Use your previous work whenever possible. It saves time.

5. D

Who doesn't teach in the winter semester? Since the winter semester has either 2 or 4 instructors, either three or five instructors don't teach during the winter semester. So (B) and (E) are wrong. Eliminating the other wrong choices was a little harder:

(A) splits up L and M, in violation of Rule 2.

(C) places J and P in the winter and thus violates Rule 6. So (D) is correct.

(D) For the record, we could place Q and P in the fall, N in the spring, and K, L, M, and J in the winter.

Numbers deductions are key in Grouping games. Always look for minimums and maximums, and then use that information to cut down on your work later on.

Note that the challenge with this game was timing. Lots of people could find the right answers given unlimited time, but the real challenge is to find the right answers as quickly as possible. Take a second look at your work on these questions, and ask yourself how you could have used good test-taking strategies to save time. Then practice these strategies until you apply them automatically.

Questions 6–10

This game involves placing eight albums of three different genres in playing order. Since you are both distributing the albums among the genres and ordering them from first to last, this would be a hybrid game of sequencing and grouping. First, organize the setup. The two country albums are G and H, the three dance albums are J, K, and L, and the three folk albums are M, N, and P. The next part of the setup informs you that all genre albums are to be played consecutively. This means that albums G and H will be played consecutively, albums J, K, and L will be played consecutively, and albums M, N, and P will be played consecutively. Your sketch work should be concerned with organizing the order in which the genres will be played and the order of the albums within each genre. Now take a look at the rules to see what restrictions you will have on the "action" of the game.

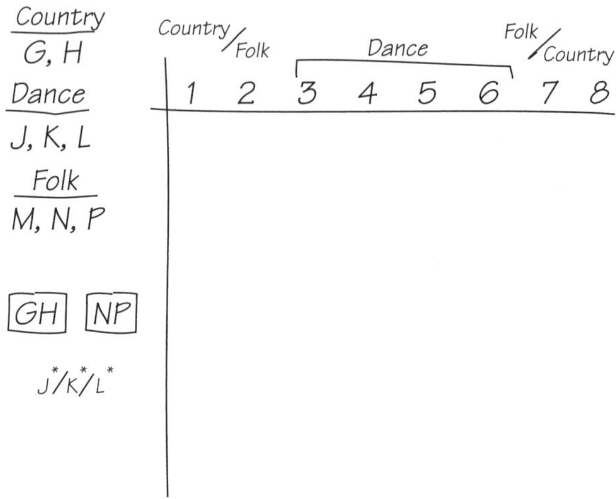

Take a look at the first and last rule. If each album is to be played only once and no two albums can be played at the same time, then you will have exactly eight spaces to place the eight different albums. The next rule—that dance albums are to be played after the country or folk albums but not after both—tells you that the dance albums must be played in the middle. Organize your sketch accordingly.

For the third rule, mark on your sketch under the folk genre that album N is played before album P. This connects N and P in a loose manner. Under the country genre, mark that album G is played before album H. That's another similar connection, this time of GH. Since there are only two albums in the country genre, note that the sequence must always be G then H. Although it's not listed, you can see that at this moment items J, K, and L have no limitations concerning them. This fact may come in handy.

Now take a look at the questions.

6. D

Since the question asks for the one answer that must be false, eliminate any choice that could be true. If the country genre was played first, then album G could be played first, eliminating (A). If the genre sequence was folk-dance-country, and since there are three albums for both folk and dance, then the seventh album would be the first country album and would be album G. Eliminate (B). Following the same setup as (A), if album G is first, then album H must be second. Eliminate (C). However, if album H is played seventh, the country genre must be played last, which means album G would be played eighth and rule 3 would be violated. Therefore (D) must be false. To state it another way, If H is seventh, then to preserve the GH rule G must be sixth, leaving a big hole in the eight spot. That won't do. (E) could be true by following the setup of (B), placing the folk genre first.

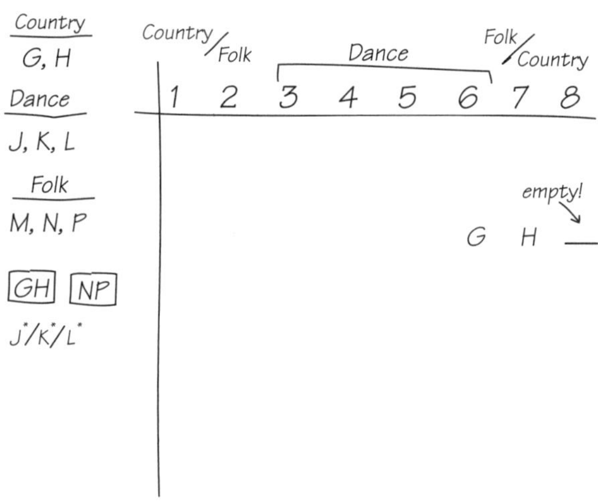

7. D

Since you're looking for the answer choice that *could* be true, all four wrong choices *must* be false. It is usually easier to eliminate what must be false than to play out all of the possibilities. Choice (A) places G, a Country album, second. Country albums can be first and second, but there's another rule involving G—it has to come before H (another Country album). That means that if the Country albums are played first and second, G would have to be first—(A) cannot be true and can be eliminated. The same analysis rules out (B)—if the Country albums are 7th and 8th, then G must be 7th to leave room for H to follow. (C) is impossible because K is a Dance album, and the Dance albums come in the middle, after either Country or Folk. (D) works: MNP could be in slots 1, 2, and 3, respectively. If this isn't immediately apparent, though, just hold on to this choice and move on to (E), which can be authoritatively ruled out because N must precede P. If the Folk albums are in slots 1, 2, and 3, then N can be no later than second without violating the third rule. That leaves only (D).

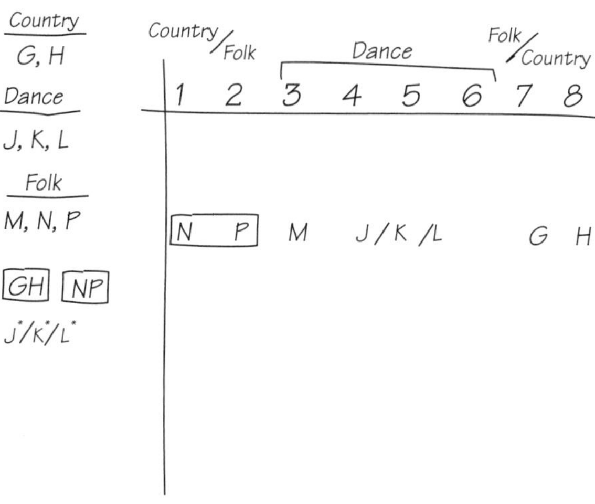

8. A

The question asks which answer choice CANNOT be a list of albums that are played second, third, and fourth. This means you can eliminate all answer choices that could be the albums played second, third, and fourth. If the country genre is played first, then you know that album H must be the second album. Since there are no limitations on the order of the dance albums, both (D) and (E) are possible lists. The remaining three answer choices play the folk genre first, which means that album N must be played before album P. (A) violates this rule. If album N is played second and album M played third, then album P must be played first, which violates rule 3.

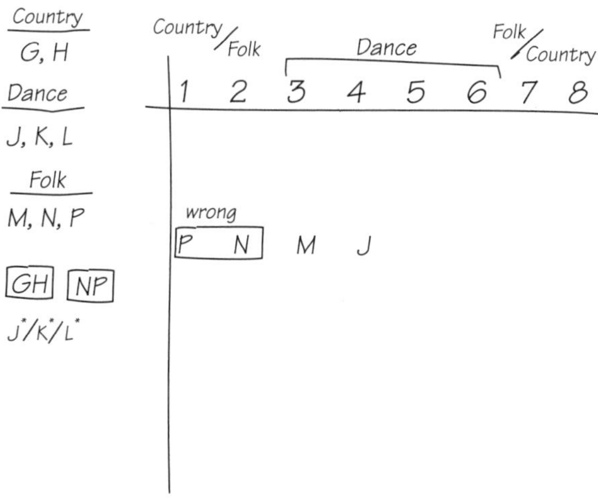

9. C

This question gives you an extra conditional statement to work into the already established rules. If album P is played immediately before album M and album N must be played before album P (rule 2), then the folk genre must be played in the order of N, P, and M. If the folk genre is played first, then album N would be played first, album P would be played second, and album M would be played third. If the folk genre was played last, then album N would be played sixth, album P would be played seventh, and album M would be played eighth. These are the only possible positions for the albums to be played in. (C) is the only choice that could be true.

Country: G, H
Dance: J, K, L
Folk: M, N, P
[GH] [NP]
J*/K*/L*
[NPM]

Country/Folk (1–2), Dance (3–6), Folk/Country (7–8)

1 2 3 4 5 6 7 8
N P M J/ /K L/ G H
or
G H J/K/L/ N P M

10. D

Another condition has been added in this question (albums K and N are to be played consecutively.) It is misleading that the question tells you they do not have to be played in that particular order, because they do. Since album N must be played before album P, as stipulated in rule 3, the folk genre could not be played first, ending with album N and starting the dance genre with album K. Therefore the country genre must be played first. The dance genre, as stipulated in rule 2, must be played second and end with album K, and the folk genre is then played last, starting with album N. (D) must be false since the country genre, which album H belongs to, is played before the folk genre, which album M belongs to.

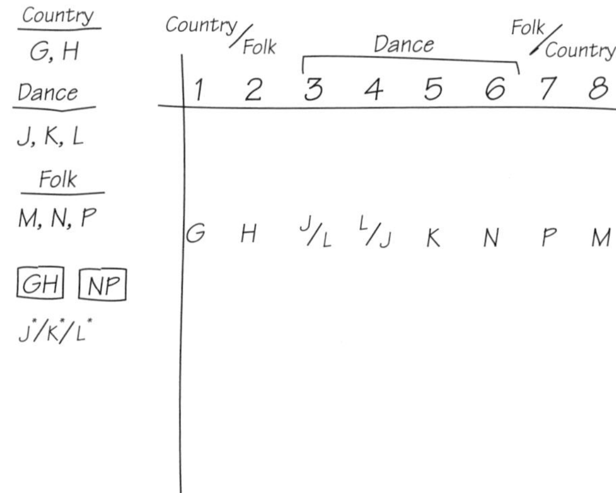

Chapter 5: **Reading Comprehension**

- **The 6 Basic Principles of Reading Comp**
- **The 4 Reading Comp Question Types**
- **Kaplan's 5-Step Method for Reading Comp**

When preparing students for most tests, Kaplan emphasizes that reading for Reading Comp is not like any other reading they'll do. But that isn't as true in the case of the LSAT. Most legal careers will at times involve the selective, methodical approach to reading matter that this test section requires.

The topics for LSAT Reading Comp passages are taken from four areas: social sciences, natural sciences, the humanities, and law. The passages are long, dense, and difficult—like at least some of the material you'll face in law school and your careers. So right now is a good time to start shoring up your reading skills.

> **GO ONLINE**
>
> **How did you do in Reading Comp on your Diagnostic Quiz? Most test takers find the section harder than expected.**

THE 6 BASIC PRINCIPLES OF READING COMP

Improvement in Reading Comp requires patience. You may not see dramatic improvement after taking only one section. But with steady practice, the principles and strategies below will increase your skill and confidence on this section.

Read Critically

The single most important factor in Reading Comp is the basic skill that's relevant on all sections of the test: critical reading. Critical reading involves perspective—the ability to step back from a piece of prose and carefully evaluate it. You get no points for just "getting through" the passage. You must attack—not simply read—passages and questions. If you think in terms of attack, you're less likely to be distracted or to let the densely worded prose confuse you.

The following are some concrete ways to improve the specific critical reading skills necessary for Reading Comp:

- Paraphrase key ideas: Put the author's important concepts into your own words.
- Connect abstract ideas to your own experience: Visualize the subject matter if you can.
- Anticipate where the author is going: Each step of the way, ask: "What could or must follow?"
- Don't let complex words and sentences scare you: You don't have to become expert on the topic.
- Remember that authors are repetitious: Not every sentence adds a new idea.

Use keywords

Like Logical Reasoning arguments, Reading Comp passages are full of structural signals—words or phrases that help the author string ideas together logically. They allow you to infer a great deal about content, even if that content is obscure or difficult. Conclusion signals (*therefore, consequently, thus*) and evidence signals (*because, since*) are extremely helpful, as are contrast signals (*but, however, although, by contrast*), which indicate an opposition or shift in ideas.

A Word About Outside Knowledge

On the LSAT, no outside knowledge is necessary. In Reading Comp, it's not necessary—or even helpful—to know anything about the topics covered in the passages. Everything you'll need to answer every question is included in the passage. This, too, is consistent with legal practice. When you read case law or a statute, it's irrelevant what you believe should be true, or what you read in an article on the way to work. What counts is what the case or statute says. In Reading Comp, correct answers must reflect only what the passage says or implies.

KAPLAN EXCLUSIVE

Mark the passage as you read. Circle names, box dates, underline key sentences—whatever helps you navigate.

However, the passages are always logical, and always reflect ideas that you can understand. Don't read in a vacuum—relate what you read to your world, and recognize the common sense of the text. So use your own knowledge to help you understand the passages, but be careful not to let it interfere with answering questions correctly.

Read for the Topic, Scope, Purpose, and Main Idea

The first third of any passage usually introduces the topic, scope, main idea, and purpose, and the author's attitude. Let's take a closer look at these crucial elements of a Reading Comp passage.

Topic, Scope, and Purpose

Topic and scope are both **objective**, meaning they include no reference to the author's point of view. The difference between them is that the **topic** is broader; the **scope** narrows the topic. Scope is particularly important because of the many answer choices that will be wrong because they depart from it.

The topic/scope distinction ties into the all-important author's **purpose**. The author deliberately narrows the scope by including certain aspects of the broader topic and excluding others. Those choices have to do with why the passage is being written in the first place. We can say that the topic is broadly stated (for instance, a passage's topic might be "solving world hunger"). Scope is narrower (a new technology for solving world hunger) and leads rather quickly to the author's subjective purpose (the author wrote in order to describe a new technology and its promising uses). And this is what turns into the author's main idea.

Main Idea

Almost every passage boils down to one main idea. The primary purpose and main idea are intertwined. Take, for example, the hypothetical passage described above, in which the author had the following purpose.

> The author wrote in order to describe a new technology and its promising uses.

The main idea is simply a more detailed restatement of this without the active verb:

> Biochemical engineering (or whatever new technology is discussed) can help solve world hunger.

Most often, the main idea will be presented early in the passage, but sometimes the author will build up to it more gradually; you may not see the author's purpose or main idea until the very end.

In any case, the main idea appears somewhere in the passage, and when it does, take conscious note of it. For one thing, the purpose of everything else in the passage will be to support this idea. Furthermore, many of the questions are easier to handle when you have the main idea in the forefront of your mind.

Get the Gist of Each Paragraph

The paragraph is the main structural unit of any passage. Find the **gist**, or purpose, of each succeeding paragraph, and attempt to relate it back to the passage as a whole. To do this, ask yourself:

- Why did the author include this paragraph?
- What shift did the author have in mind when moving on to this paragraph?
- What bearing does this paragraph have on the author's main idea?

Use this process to create a roadmap of the passage, tying each paragraph to the structure and main idea. When a question requires you to look back into the passage, this roadmap will help you locate the answer.

Notice Structure and Tone

In a quest to master the content of a passage, test takers are notorious for ignoring the **structure**—how the author says it. One of the keys to success on this section is to understand not only the purpose, but also the structure of each passage, because the questions ask about both.

The following is a list of the classic LSAT passage structures:

- Passages based on differing opinions
- Passages based on a serious problem or situation
- Passages based on a strong opinion
- Passages based on significant new findings (common in science passages)

Many LSAT passages are based on variations of one of these classic structures. Your task is to seek them out actively. Knowing these classic structures can "jump start" your search.

And notice the author's position within these structures—the **tone**. Within the first classic structure, the author may simply relate the two sides of the story, or may at some point jump in and take a side, or even reject the conflicting opinions in favor of a third opinion. Within the third structure, the opinion could be the author's, in which case the author's tone may be opinionated, argumentative, heated, or passionate. On the other hand, the author could simply describe the strongly held opinions of someone else. This author's writing style would be more descriptive, factual, and even-handed.

Notice the difference in tone between the two types of authors. Correct answer choices for a primary purpose question in the former case would use terms like *argue for, propose,* and *demonstrate*, whereas correct choices in the latter case would use terms like *describe* and *discuss*.

Don't Obsess over Details

In school, you probably read to memorize information for an exam. This is not the type of reading that's good for getting points on LSAT Reading Comp. You'll be reading for short-term, not long-term, retention. When you finish the questions on a passage, you're free to promptly forget everything about it.

What's more, it's an open-book test. You can relocate details if you have a good sense of a passage's structure and paragraph topics.

Do the Questions in the Order Best for You

Just as you skip any passage that slows you down too much, get the easy questions before tackling hard ones. After finishing a passage, quickly scan for global questions, especially main idea or primary purpose questions. Doing these first generally helps you solidify your grasp of these concepts, and you should already have answered these questions mentally as you read.

Then do any other global types—questions about the author's overall tone or the organization of the passage. Detail questions, especially those with line references, are good candidates to tackle next. Many test takers benefit from leaving the more difficult Logic or Inference questions for last.

This, of course, is only a rough suggested order. With practice, you may want to revise it to account for your own strengths and the difficulty level of each question. Some Inference questions may be easier than some Detail questions. So, for each question, ask yourself: "Can I answer this question quickly?"

Eliminate Wrong Choices First If You Have to Guess

One or more of the wrong answer choices on any Reading Comp question will fall into patterns you'll learn to recognize. Any wrong choice you can eliminate improves your chance of choosing the correct answer. The common wrong answer types in Reading Comp are:

- **180:** Choices that are exactly the opposite of the correct choice, which are especially common on EXCEPT or strengthen/weaken questions
- **Outside Scope:** Choices that go beyond the scope of the passage or the particular argument being focused on
- **Faulty Use of Detail:** Choices that use language or ideas from the stimulus, but misapply them conspicuously
- **Extreme:** Choices using words like *always, never, none, all,* and *every*, which are most likely wrong unless the language of the argument is extreme
- **1/2 Right, 1/2 Wrong:** Choices that join a correct statement with an incorrect one; don't be hasty and choose your answer without reading the entire choice.

In addition, when you see that any two or more answer choices are very similar, that's a strong signal that they are wrong—only one choice can be correct.

KAPLAN STRATEGY

The basic principles for Reading Comp success are:

- **Read critically.**
- **Read for topic, scope, purpose, and main idea.**
- **Get the gist of each paragraph.**
- **Note structure and tone.**
- **Do the questions in the order that's best for you.**
- **Eliminate wrong choices first if you have to guess.**

THE 4 CRUCIAL READING COMP QUESTION TYPES

While it might be convenient to cover the Reading Comp section in terms of the types of passages that typically appear on it, Kaplan has found that that's not the best way to master the section. In Logic Games, categorizing the games is helpful because grouping, sequencing, and matching games have their own sets of issues.

Such differences don't separate a humanities passage from one on social science, or a natural science passage from one on law; you read them in the same way. But different question types do require different skills sets.

 GO ONLINE

As you read through the question types, pay close attention to those you missed on the Diagnostic Quiz to see why you missed them.

Global Questions

Global questions, which account for 20–25 percent of all Reading Comp questions, ask you to sum up the author's overall intentions, ideas, or passage structure. In general, a Global question choice that zeros in on a detail or the content of one paragraph will be wrong. You'll often find Global questions at the beginning of question sets, and often one of the wrong choices will be a side issue discussed at the tail end of the passage. Scanning the verbs in the answer choices is a good way to take a first cut at the question: The verb in the correct choice must agree with the author's tone.

Main Idea and Primary Purpose

The formats for these questions are pretty self-evident:

- Which one of following best expresses the main idea of the passage?
- The author's primary purpose is to . . .
- Which of the following titles best describes the content of the passage as a whole?

Structure

Another type of Global question asks about the structure of a passage or an argument. The question might read: "Which of the following best describes the organization of the passage?"

Answer choices are usually worded very generally; they focus on the broad layout of the passage as opposed to the specific content. Here are a few possible ways that a passage could be organized:

- A hypothesis is stated and then analyzed.
- A proposal is evaluated, and alternatives are explored.
- A viewpoint is set forth and then subsequently defended.

When choosing among these choices, ask yourself: "Was there a hypothesis here? Was there an evaluation of a proposal or a defense of a viewpoint?" Make yourself identify where the hypothesis or evaluation is—don't think in generalities. These terms may all seem similar, but in fact, they're very different.

Author's Attitude

The tone question asks you to evaluate the author's attitude. Is the author passionate, fiery, neutral, angry, hostile, opinionated, low-key? Here's an example: "The author's tone in the passage can best be characterized as . . . ." Don't confuse the nature of the content with the author's tone—a social science passage based on this century's grisliest murders may be presented in a cool, detached, and strictly informative way.

Logic Questions

Logic questions come in two distinct forms: function questions and reasoning questions.

Function Questions

These questions ask why the author included certain information—what role did it play in the author's overall argument.

KAPLAN EXCLUSIVE

Keep the main idea in mind, even when answering questions that don't ask for it. Even in the Detail questions, correct answers generally echo the main idea in one way or another.

Reasoning Questions

These are similar to Logical Reasoning questions; rely on the skills you learned there to handle them, but remember that the only relevant logic is the logic expressed in the passage.

Answer choices that focus on content rather than structure will be wrong for these Logic questions.

Inference Questions

Inference questions make up 55–60 percent of the Reading Comp section and are similar to Logical Reasoning questions. As you've seen in Logical Reasoning, an **inference** is a statement that must be true based on the passage, but that is contained "between the lines." The answer is strongly implied or hinted at but not stated directly.

So in that respect, Logical Reasoning and Reading Comp inferences are similar. The difference?

- Reading Comp text is tougher to get through than Logical Reasoning prose.

The same rules that apply to inferences in Logical Reasoning also apply to inferences in Reading Comp, and the skills learned there will serve you well here.

Extracting valid inferences from Reading Comp passages often requires recognizing that information can be expressed in different ways. In fact, Inference questions often boil down to an exercise in translation.

Inference questions appear in a variety of different forms:

- It can be inferred from the passage that . . .
- The passage/author suggests/implies that . . .
- The author would probably agree that . . .
- The passage supports which one of the following statements . . .

Usually, some specific information will complete these questions, providing clues as to where in the passage the answer will be. Occasionally, the stem won't contain specific information, in which case you simply have to work your way through the choices until you find the one that's supported by the text. When evaluating the answer choices, keep the relevant ideas firmly in mind. The farther you stray from them to endorse a choice, the more likely it is that this choice will be wrong.

KAPLAN STRATEGY

A good inference:

- **Stays in line with the author's (or proponent's) tone.**
- **Stays within the scope of the passage.**
- **Is neither denied by, nor irrelevant to, the ideas stated in the passage.**

Detail Questions

Detail questions, which makes up roughly 10–20 percent of section, are directly answered in the text. Most students find these the easiest Reading Comp questions, since they're the most concrete. It's fairly simple to identify a Detail question from its stem:

- According to the passage/author . . .
- The author states that . . .
- The author mentions which one of the following as . . .

Sometimes the question provides a line reference, text quoted from the passage, or other clues to where the answer is located. (Just be careful with line references—they'll bring you to the right area, but usually the answer will be found in the lines before or after the referenced line.)

If your roadmap is in the forefront of your mind, it shouldn't take long to locate the relevant detail. And if that fails, as a last resort, you can put that question aside and return to it later, if and when you have the time to search through the passage.

Now that you have the basics of LSAT Reading Comp under your belt, learn the method that combines them all into a single *modus operandi*.

KAPLAN'S 5-STEP METHOD FOR READING COMP

1. Read the Passage Critically.

As outlined in the basic principles, read to determine the main idea and purpose, structure, and tone. Paraphrase ideas, and build your roadmap by noting the gist of each paragraph.

2. Read the Question Stem.

Identify exactly what the question asks. Mark keywords in the question (like *not* and *implies)*, if it helps you to keep focused on what's required. Look for clues—like proper nouns and names, line or paragraph references, or direct quotes—that will lead you to the answer.

3. Research the Relevant Text.

Using your roadmap, at least glance back at any relevant language. Taking the time to locate the information can help you focus your mind and recall the details as precisely as the question demands. Sometimes just establishing that information appears in a particular paragraph will be enough to answer the question.

4. Make a Prediction.

Without wasting much time on it, a prediction of the expected answer (or at least a prephrase, whether in fine detail or the merest hint) will lead you to the correct choice and prevent you from falling for distracters.

5. Go to the Choices.

As with the other question types, the preparation you've done will help you zero in on the right choice. Eliminate wrong choices, if necessary.

Now let's try the 5-step method on an actual LSAT-strength Reading Comp passage.

For the time being, we've just included the question stems of the questions attached to this passage, since you don't want to get into answer choices until later. Remember that on test day, you don't have to do the passages in order, either—pick your best shots.

It has been suggested that post–World War II concepts of environmental liability, as they pertain to hazardous waste, grew out of issues regarding municipal refuse collection and disposal and industrial waste disposal in the period 1880–1940. To a great degree, the remedies available to Americans for dealing with the burgeoning hazardous waste problem were characteristic of the judicial, legislative, and regulatory tools used to confront a whole range of problems in the industrial age.

At the same time, these remedies were operating in an era in which the problem of hazardous waste had yet to be recognized. It is understandable that an assessment of liability was narrowly drawn and most often restricted to a clearly identified violator in a specific act of infringement of the property rights of someone else. Legislation, for the most part, focused narrowly on clear threats to the public health and dealt with problems of industrial pollution meekly if at all.

Nevertheless, it would be grossly inaccurate to assume that the actions of American politicians, technologists, health officials, judges, and legislators in the period 1880–1940 have had little impact on the attempts to define environmental liability and to confront the consequences of hazardous waste. Taken as a whole, the precedents of the late nineteenth through the mid-twentieth century have established a framework in which the problem of hazardous waste is understood and confronted today. Efforts at refuse reform gradually identified the immutable connection between waste and disease, turning eyesores into nuisances and nuisances into health hazards. Confronting the refuse problem and other forms of municipal pollution forced cities to define public responsibility and accountability with respect to the environment. A commitment to municipal services in the development of sewers and collection and disposal systems shifted the burden of responsibility for eliminating wastes from the individual to the community. In some way, the courts' efforts to clarify and broaden the definition of public nuisance were dependent on the cities' efforts to define community responsibility themselves.

The courts retained their role as arbiter of what constituted private and public nuisances. Indeed, fear that the courts would transform individual decisions into national precedents often contributed to the search for other remedies. Nonetheless, the courts remained an active agent in cases on the local, state, and national level, making it quite clear that they were not going to be left out of the process of defining environmental liability in the United States. In the case of hazardous waste, precedents for behavior and remedial action were well developed by 1940. Even though the concept of hazardous waste is essentially a post–World War II notion, the problem was not foreign to earlier generations. The observation that the administrative, technical, and legal problems of water pollution in the 1920s were intertwined is equally applicable to today's hazardous waste problem.

1. According to the author, the efforts by cities to define public responsibility for the environment resulted in which of the following?

2. Which of the following, if substituted for the word *immutable* (line 23), would LEAST alter the author's meaning?

3. With which one of the following statements would the author be most likely to agree?

4. The author's primary purpose is to discuss . . .
5. The tone of the author's discussion of early attempts to deal with waste and pollution problems could best be described as . . .
6. According to the passage, judicial assessments of liability in waste disposal disputes prior to World War II were usually based on . . .
7. The passage suggests that responses to environmental problems between 1880 and 1940 were relatively limited in part because of . . .

KAPLAN EXCLUSIVE

Forget about each passage when you finish it. Approach each new passage as if it were the only one. Stay active and confident.

1. Read the Passage Critically.

The first few sentences introduce the topic: hazardous waste. The scope—the specific angle the author takes on the topic—seems to be the post-World War II concept of environmental liability. It's been suggested that this has some connection to issues from 1880–1940; latter-day remedies are "characteristic of the judicial, legislative, and regulatory tools used to confront a whole range of problems in the industrial age." Since hazardous waste liability concepts had their roots in an era that predated the recognition of hazardous waste, the author believes that liability assessment and the ensuing legislation regarding hazardous waste were both "narrowly drawn."

However, the keyword *nevertheless* at the beginning of the next paragraph indicates that a contrast is coming. This sentence harks back to and solidifies the connection between the actions and policies from 1880–1940 and the concept of environmental liability, which is the author's main idea.

Lines 19–22 ("Taken as a whole . . . confronted today") restate the main idea. There's a description of the gradual recognition of hazardous waste and some repercussions of the efforts to define the problem and assign responsibility. Note that there's some talk about individual versus community responsibility and the role of cities, but don't fuss over the specifics. If there's a question on these issues, you'll know where to look.

The first part of the last paragraph deals with the courts' role. The last three sentences reinforce the main idea.

2. Read the Question Stem.

Don't forget to select the order in which you'll do the questions. Be clear about what each question asks. Look at the question stems for this passage scanning for Global questions—especially *main idea* or *primary purpose*. If you come across the following question, you should attempt it with the passage fresh in your mind:

4. The author's primary purpose is to discuss

3. Research the Relevant Text.

In this case, your roadmap or a quick review of the gist of each paragraph will suffice.

4. Make a Prediction.

If you read critically, you have already formed an idea of the author's purpose.

5. Go to the Choices.

(A) contrasts in the legislative approaches to environmental liability before and after World War II

(B) legislative trends which have been instrumental in the reduction of environmental hazardous wastes

(C) the historical and legislative context in which to view post–World War II hazardous waste problems

(D) early patterns of industrial abuse and pollution of the American environment

(E) the growth of an activist tradition in American jurisprudence

Choice (C) has the right elements: the connection to the author's main idea ("the historical and legislative context . . . to view . . . waste problems") and the correct topic and scope: hazardous waste, post–World War II.

Choice (A) misinterprets the passage structure—there is no such contrast presented. (B) is tempting; legislative trends were discussed, but not in enough depth to be the author's primary purpose. And the discussion hinges on defining liability for hazardous wastes and doesn't specifically discuss any factor "instrumental in the reduction of environmental wastes." (D) and (E) both violate the topic and scope of the passage (notice that neither one even mentions the topic of hazardous wastes).

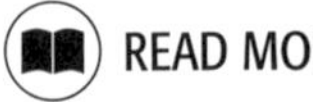

There's plenty of practice with challenging Reading Comp sets in Kaplan's *LSAT 180*.

Question 5, focusing on tone, is another Global question that you may wish to answer early on. Continuing to scan the questions, the one with the line reference, question 2, may have caught your eye. This type simply tests your understanding of a certain word in a particular context, and since it tells you exactly where in the passage the word is, you might try this one next. Questions 1 and 6 are clearly Detail questions, so you should do those next, beginning with the one that seems the most familiar. The Inference questions, 3 and 7, are good to save for last.

Try one Detail question and one Inference question, repeating steps 2–5 of Kaplan's Method.

2. Read the Question Stem.

Here's the complete form (with answer choices) of question 6:

6. According to the passage, judicial assessments of liability in waste disposal disputes prior to World War II were usually based on

    (A) excessively broad definitions of legal responsibility
    (B) the presence of a clear threat to the public health
    (C) precedents derived from well-known cases of large-scale industrial polluters
    (D) restricted interpretations of property rights infringements
    (E) trivial issues such as littering, eyesores, and other public nuisances

Mark keywords (like *according to the passage* and *prior to World War II)*, if it helps you to keep focused on what's required. Look for clues—like proper nouns and names, line or paragraph references, or direct quotes—that will lead you to the answer.

3. Research the Relevant Text.

Pre-World War II judicial assessments of liability should ring a bell—they were discussed in the first paragraph.

4. Make a Prediction.

The answer is " . . . an assessment of liability was narrowly drawn and most often restricted to a clearly identified violator in a specific act of *infringement of the property rights* of someone else. [emphasis added]"

5. Go to the Choices.

The correct choice, (D), is a direct paraphrase.

(E) is a common type of wrong answer; it consists of wording taken straight from the passage, but unfortunately, the wrong part of the passage. Don't choose an answer simply because you recognize some of the words or phrases in it; this is a common trap that snags many careless test takers. (B) is another classic wrong answer—the 180 choice. This choice actually represents the opposite of what's stated or implied in the passage. According to the author, pre-World War II was "an era in which the problem of hazardous waste had yet to be recognized."

2. Read the Question Stem.

3. With which one of the following statements would the author be most likely to agree?

   (A) The growth of community responsibility for waste control exemplifies the tendency of government power to expand at the expense of individual rights.

   (B) Although important legal precedents for waste control were established between 1880 and 1940, today's problems will require radically new approaches.

   (C) While early court decisions established important precedents involving environmental abuses by industry, such equally pressing matters as disposal of municipal garbage were neglected.

   (D) Because environmental legislation between 1880 and 1940 was in advance of its time it failed to affect society's awareness of environmental problems.

   (E) The historical role of U.S. courts in defining problems of hazardous waste and environmental liability provides valuable traditions for courts today.

Note words like *author…most likely agree* to understand that the question asks for an inference.

3. Research the Relevant Text.

You want something the author would agree with; what do you know about the author's opinions? The first sentence of the second paragraph says that it would be *wrong to assume* (an opinion) that the actions of judges and legislators had little impact on defining liability and confronting the issue. This implies that the courts had a positive impact, which is bolstered by lines 21–24 and 39–43.

4. Make a Prediction.

You want a choice that discusses the positive effects of the courts, and one that is in line with the author's tone (in this case factual and evenhanded) as well as the content.

5. Go to the Choices.

Notice how correct choice (E) sounds like an offshoot of the author's main idea. The first sentence of the second paragraph says that it would be wrong to assume that the actions of judges and legislators had little impact on defining liability and confronting the issue. This implies that the courts had a positive impact, which is bolstered by lines 39–43. Combine that with the statement in lines 21–24: "Taken as a whole, the precedents of the late nineteenth through the mid-twentieth century have established a framework in which the problem of hazardous waste is understood and confronted today."

Choice (A) offers a judgment taken from the community/individual responsibility issue, something the author never does; he or she simply says that the burden shifted from one to the other. And there's no reason to believe that the author would agree with (B), either. While he or she would certainly agree with the first part, there's nothing that indicates that the author would advocate radical new approaches for today's problems. Both of these choices fail to match the author's tone and are outside the scope of the passage.

Now apply these techniques in some practice sets.

SUMMARY

The basic principles of Reading Comp are:

- Read critically.
- Read for topic, scope, purpose, and main idea.
- Note structure and tone.
- Get the gist of each paragraph.
- Do the questions in the order that's best for you.
- Eliminate wrong choices if you have to guess.

The Reading Comp question types are:

- Global questions ask the reader to sum up the author's overall ideas, attitudes, or structure.
- Logic questions include function and reasoning questions.
- Inference questions ask what is implied.
- Detail questions ask what is expressly stated.

Kaplan's 5-Step Method for Reading Comp

1. Read the passage critically.
2. Read the question stem.
3. Research the relevant text.
4. Make a prediction.
5. Go to the choices.

READING COMP PRACTICE

Set One

Directions: Each passage in this test is followed by several questions. After reading the passage, choose the best answer to each question. Your replies are to be based on what is stated or implied in the selection.

Passage for Questions 1–7

Various factors influence voter preference in United States presidential elections, but perhaps none is so persuasive as a candidate's performance on nationally televised debates just prior to the election. Newspapers and television news programs generally attempt to provide thorough coverage of the debates, further augmenting the effect of good or bad candidate performances. In this way, the news media fulfill the traditional role of educating the public and enabling voters to make better informed decisions about elected officials. However, the same media that bring live debates into millions of living rooms across the nation also limit the availability of debate coverage by use of "pool" coverage, the sharing of news coverage with other news organizations. When typical pool situations arise, one of the major networks covers the event, and a "feed" is created so other broadcasters may have access to the same coverage. Individual broadcasters are unable to convey a unique account to their viewers. The pool system limits the news-gathering ability of television news organizations and denies viewers an opportunity to gain maximum insight from the debate. The First Amendment freedoms afforded the press exist largely to ensure that the public benefits from the free flow of information. Some commentators suggest that the purpose of a free press is to inform citizens about matters of public concern. Others, however, believe that the value of free press lies in its ability to foster a marketplace of ideas in which the best options prevail. Presidential debates embody all these considerations. Not only do candidates provide information about matters of utmost interest, they also offer diverse views on how to approach the major issues. Given television's ability to further informational and marketplace-of-ideas goals of the First Amendment, debate coverage should be diverse as possible.

What difference does it make whether viewers saw a "tight shot" of one candidate or a "two-shot" of both candidates at a given time? The answer depends on what happens, when it happens, and whether the pool director anticipated it or was fortunate enough to have captured it anyway. It may be argued that none of this matters. The important thing, the argument goes, is that viewers will know generally what happened. According to this line of reasoning, the number of news organizations covering an event—and even which ones—would be irrelevant. But courts have held differently: "It is impossible to treat two news services as interchangeable, and it is only by cross lights from varying directions that full illumination can be secured." Undoubtedly, there are some circumstances in which pool coverage is the only way to cover an event. But these few situations must not foster a casual acceptance of pool implementation in other situations.

1. It can be inferred that the author's primary objection to the pool system of covering presidential debates is that it

   (A) restricts the public's access to a diversity of ideas and information

   (B) limits the number of people who have access to debates on television

   (C) undermines candidates' ability to persuade voters

   (D) dissuades voters from exercising their right to choose between candidates

   (E) contributes to an overreliance by the public on televised accounts of political issues

2. The author would probably assert that the opinion of the court presented in the second paragraph is

   (A) useful but biased
   (B) reflective of an unfortunate trend
   (C) overly permissive
   (D) substantially correct
   (E) commendable but ineffective

3. In the first paragraph, the author cites two opinions concerning the benefits provided to society by a free press primarily in order to

   (A) suggest the range of benefits that potentially would be provided by competitive coverage of presidential debates
   (B) indicate that some of the defenses of pool coverage contradict one another
   (C) criticize the assumptions held by some commentators on journalism
   (D) contend that First Amendment freedoms do not apply to presidential debates
   (E) reconcile different points of view in an effort to reach a more acceptable definition of press freedom

4. It can be inferred from the passage that a proponent of the pool system of debate coverage would be most likely to defend her viewpoint with which of the following remarks?

   (A) Broadcasters rarely betray their political preferences in debate coverage.
   (B) Although imperfect, pool coverage is the only practical means of reporting most political events.
   (C) Presidential debates are too complex to be covered thoroughly by any one broadcaster.
   (D) Broadcasters are prevented by public opinion from presenting biased coverage.
   (E) Small differences in style of coverage do not significantly affect the amount of information conveyed to viewers.

5. The author warns that the use of pool coverage in situations in which it may be needed may lead to other situations in which

   (A) public events covered by the media are subjected to undue analytical scrutiny
   (B) broadcasters accept further limitation of their First Amendment freedoms
   (C) the informational content of news events is diminished
   (D) pool coverage is relied upon when it is in fact undesirable
   (E) broadcasters suffer increasing erosion of their capacity for news gathering

6. The author's argument that the pool system "denies viewers an opportunity to gain maximum insight from the debate" (lines 23–24) would be most WEAKENED if it could be shown that

   (A) candidates' debate performances rarely make a difference of more than a few percent in voting results

   (B) most debate viewers form their opinions primarily on the basis of post-debate commentary presented separately by each network

   (C) candidates' posture and mannerisms during debates are as important in forming voter opinion as their actual words

   (D) few viewers of televised debates bother to read follow-up commentary in newspapers and magazines

   (E) competitive coverage would provide viewers with a wider variety of interpretations on which to base their opinions

7. Which of the following titles best describes the content of the passage?

   (A) Debate Coverage: How It Changes Voters' Opinions

   (B) The "Pool" System: A Limitation on Public Access to Information

   (C) The "Pool" System: Its Benefits Versus Its Impracticalities

   (D) First Amendment Press Rights: How They Conflict with Presidential Politics

   (E) Televised Debates: Their Role in Presidential Politics

Passage for Questions 8–10

It is crucial to question the assumption that for-profit health care institutions have special obligations to help subsidize care for the needy over and above their general obligation as taxpayers. As the for-profits are quick to point out, supermarkets are not expected to provide free food to the hungry poor, and real estate developers are not expected to let the poor live rent free in their housing. Yet food and housing, like health care, are basic necessities for even minimal subsistence. If there are basic human rights to some adequate level of health care, it is reasonable to think there are such rights to food and shelter as well.

Whose obligation is it, then, to secure some basic health care for those unable to secure it for themselves? Assuming that private markets and charity leave some without access to whatever amount of health care that justice requires be available to all, there are several reasons to believe that the obligation ultimately rests with the federal government. First, the obligation to secure a just or fair overall distribution of benefits and burdens across society is usually understood to be a general societal obligation. Second, the federal government is the institution society commonly employs to meet society-wide distributive requirements. With its taxing power, it has the revenue-raising capacities to finance what would be a massively expensive program for an adequate level of health care to be guaranteed to all. This taxing power also allows the burden of financing health care for the poor to be spread fairly across all members of society and not to depend on the vagaries of how wealthy or poor a state or local area happens to be. The federal government also has the power to coordinate programs guaranteeing access to health care for the poor across local and state boundaries. This is necessary both for reducing inefficiencies that allow substantial numbers of the poor to fall between the cracks of the patchwork of local and state programs, and for ensuring that there are not great differences in the minimum of health care guaranteed to all in different locales within our country.

If we are one society, a United States, then the level of health care required by justice for all citizens should not vary greatly in different locales because of political and economic contingencies. It is worth noting that food stamp programs and housing subsidies, also aimed at basic necessities, similarly are largely a federal responsibility. These are reasons for the federal government having the obligation to guarantee access to health care for those unable to secure it for themselves. It might do this by directly providing the care itself or by providing vouchers to be used by the poor in the health care marketplace. How access should be guaranteed and secured—and in particular, to what extent market mechanisms ought to be utilized—is a separate question.

8. The author's primary concern in the passage is to discuss

(A) the level of expenditures required to ensure equitable access to health care for all

(B) measures that might be enacted to carry out a program of subsidized health care

(C) differences among states and localities in the provision of basic social services

(D) whether a national commitment to health care can be reconciled with the federal structure of the United States

(E) which institutions bear the obligation for assuring adequate health services for the poor

9. The author mentions federal "food stamp programs and housing subsidies" (lines 49–50) primarily in order to

   (A) modify a previous point in response to new information
   (B) support his argument by mentioning a comparable situation
   (C) argue that these programs should be modified
   (D) make a concession to a contrasting opinion
   (E) acknowledge that not all programs would benefit from the approach he favors

10. According to the passage, the federal government possesses all the following powers in regard to health care EXCEPT the power to

    (A) raise the revenue to finance health care expenditures
    (B) distribute the costs of health care equitably among different sectors of the country
    (C) ensure that the poor have access to health care regardless of state and local boundaries
    (D) compel private businesses and charities to assume greater responsibility for financing health care for the needy
    (E) set comparable standards for the minimum level of health care in different areas

Set Two

Directions: Each passage in this test is followed by several questions. After reading the passage, choose the best answer to each question. Your replies are to be based on what is stated or implied in the selection.

Passage for Questions 1–7

It is in his attack on the abstract and individualistic doctrine of the "rights of man" that Edmund Burke develops most fully his philosophy of society, and breaks most decisively with the mechanical and atomic political theory which, inherited from John Locke, had dominated the thought of the eighteenth century. Over and against the view of the state as the product of a "contract" among individuals, whose "rights" exist prior to that contract, and constitute the standard by which at every stage the just claim of society on the individual is to be tested, he develops the conception of the individual as himself the product of society, born to an inheritance of rights (which are "all the advantages" for which civil society is made) and of reciprocal duties, and, in the last resort, owing these concrete rights (actual rights which fall short in perfection of those ideal rights "whose abstract perfection is their practical defect") to convention and prescription. Society originates not in a free contract but in necessity, and the shaping factor in its institutions has not been the consideration of any code of abstract pre-existent rights ("the inherent rights of the people") but "convenience."

And, of these conveniences or rights, two are supreme, government and prescription, the existence of "a power out of themselves by which the will of individuals may be controlled," and the recognition of the sacred character of prescription. In whatever way a particular society may have originated—conquest, usurpation, revolution ("there is a sacred veil to be drawn over the beginnings of all government")—in process of time, its institutions and rights come to rest upon prescription. In any ancient community such as that of France or Britain, every constituent factor, including what we choose to call the people, is the product of convention. The privileges of every order, the rights of every individual, rest upon prescription embodied in law or established by usage. This is the "compact or agreement which gives its corporate form and capacity to a state," and, if it is once broken, the people are a number of vague, loose individuals and nothing more. Alas! They little know how many a weary step is to be taken before they can form themselves into a mass, which has a true politic personality.

There is, therefore, no right of revolution, or rebellion at will. The "civil, social man" never may rebel except when he must rebel. Revolution is always the annulment of some rights. It will be judged in the last resort by the degree in which it preserves as well as destroys, and by what it substitutes for what it takes away. At its best, revolution is "the extreme medicine of the constitution," and Burke's quarrel with the Assembly (which ruled during the French Revolution) is that they have made it "its daily bread"; that, when the whole constitution of France was in their hands to preserve and to reform, they elected only to destroy.

1. The primary purpose of the passage is to

(A) expound upon Burke's belief that there exists a sovereign right for citizenry to revolt when one can be assured that they will create a vastly superior, wholly new system of government

(B) explain Burke's unique concept that the state is formed through a pact individuals choose to make, forfeiting some of their inherent rights for longer-term success of the group

(C) determine the extent to which Burke believed in the ability for the individual to govern himself solely as a solitary individual

(D) explain Burke's philosophy of the necessity of societies, the importance of evolved prescriptions, and the impact of these needs on the right of revolution

(E) define Burke's belief that a sovereign ruler must be chosen to lead a society

2. The passage suggests which of the following about the relationship between the individual and revolution?

   (A) The individual has the right to rebel at will, because there is historical precedent for revolution.
   (B) Revolution is inherently destructive to at least some of the rights in any given society.
   (C) It is the individual's choice to pursue revolution, but they should do it only when they intend to totally overhaul the existing system.
   (D) There is no need for revolution, because individuals are free within themselves to alter their realities.
   (E) Revolution is an extension of the individual's agreement with the social contract.

3. The author indicates that, for Burke, the customs that exist regarding how individuals are treated result primarily from

   (A) existing laws and traditions that have evolved in a society, regardless of the origins of those practices or the society itself
   (B) the creation and enforcement of the rules of society by a sovereign ruler
   (C) the individual's decision as to whether to participate in society or to focus on individual freedoms independent of society
   (D) ever shifting trends and societal perspectives
   (E) the manner in which the society was originally formed

4. Each of the following is a component of Locke's philosophy with which the author tells us that Burke disagrees EXCEPT:

   (A) the individual is endowed with the ideal right to choose whether or not to be part of society
   (B) society is subject to reassessment as membership evolves
   (C) society originates from necessity rather than by the will of individuals
   (D) the individual's experience of society is formed by the choices he or she makes
   (E) governments are created by the individual

5. With which of the following statements about Edmund Burke would the author of this passage most likely agree?

   (A) Burke believed that it was critical to avoid change in the predictable rules of society.
   (B) Burke was a free thinker who felt that adaptability and frequent restructuring were key to maintaining effective government.
   (C) Burke was an optimist who sought to demonstrate that society was an individualist's utopia.
   (D) Burke accepted that moderate changes in society were sometimes necessary.
   (E) Burke was an individualist who believed that the needs of members of society were paramount to those of society as a whole.

6. The author indicates that, in Burke's view, revolutionary zeal serves primarily as

    (A) the ultimate solution for the political dissatisfaction of the general populace
    (B) a means of disguising more subtle and manipulative political processes
    (C) an ultimately difficult solution to dissatisfaction with society that may spawn more problems than it solves
    (D) the understandable emotional outpouring of individuals who have discovered that their social contract is being violated
    (E) the conscious decision of citizens to alter their inherent rights

7. Based on the passage, which of the following would be most likely to be the subject of a work by Locke?

    (A) An analysis of the basis of society's right to make claims on individuals
    (B) The right of rulers to dictate social doctrines even in the absence of the consent of the people
    (C) Society's inability to create new social mores
    (D) The importance of tradition and evolved prescription in society's construction
    (E) The importance of a person's social position in determining their worth

Passage for Questions 8–14

A new test can predict the risk of breast cancer recurrence and may identify women who will benefit most from chemotherapy, according to research supported by the National Cancer Institute (NCI). These results suggest that almost half of over 50,000 U.S. women diagnosed with estrogen-dependent, lymph-node negative breast cancer every year are at low risk for recurrence and may not need to go through the discomfort and side effects of chemotherapy.

The test is based on levels of expression (increased or decreased) of a panel of cancer-related genes. This panel is used to predict whether estrogen-dependent breast cancer will come back. Scientists on this study also will present new results indicating that the same test can predict which women benefit most from chemotherapy. Women with low risk of breast cancer recurrence—about half of the women in the recent study—do not appear to derive much benefit from chemotherapy.

The researchers used tissue samples and medical records from women enrolled in clinical trials of the cancer drug tamoxifen, which blocks the effect of estrogen on breast cancer cells. These women had a kind of breast cancer defined as estrogen receptor-positive, lymph node-negative. This kind of breast cancer needs estrogen to grow but has not spread to the lymph nodes. Currently, many American women with this type of breast cancer do receive chemotherapy in addition to hormonal therapy.

Using samples from 447 patients and a collection of 250 genes, 16 cancer-related genes were found that worked best. The scientists created a formula that generates a "recurrence score" based on the expression patterns of these genes in a tumor sample. Ranging from 1 to 100, the recurrence score is a measure of the risk that a given cancer will recur.

The results validate the ability of the recurrence score to predict risk of recurrence. Using biopsy tissue and medical records from another tamoxifen trial, researchers divided 668 women into low, intermediate, and high risk of recurrence groups. Fifty-one percent were in the low risk group (with a score of less than 18); 22 percent were at intermediate risk (recurrence score 18 or higher but less than 31); 27 percent were at high risk (a score of 31 or higher).

These risk group divisions correlated well with the actual rates of recurrence of breast cancer after 10 years. There was a significant difference in recurrence rates between women in the low and high risk groups. In the low risk group, there was a 6.8 percent rate of recurrence at 10 years; in the intermediate and high risk categories these rates were 14.3 and 30.5 percent, respectively. Up to a recurrence score of 50, rates of recurrence increased continuously as the recurrence score increased. These trends held across age groups and tumor size. The same test has also been used to predict how beneficial chemotherapy will be for women with estrogen receptor-positive, lymph node-negative breast cancer that are on tamoxifen.

In the treatment study, women with high recurrence scores, who are representative of about 25 percent of patients with this kind of breast cancer, had a large benefit from chemotherapy in terms of 10 year recurrence-free rates. Women with low recurrence scores, who represent about 50 percent of these patients, derived minimal benefits from chemotherapy. The group under study was not large enough to determine whether chemotherapy is detrimental to the low risk group. "The test has the potential to change medical practice by sparing thousands of women each year from the harmful short- and long-term side effects associated with chemotherapy," said JoAnne Zujewski, M.D., senior investigator in NCI's Cancer Therapy Evaluation Program.

8. With which of the following statements concerning estrogen-dependent, lymph-node negative breast cancer would the author be most likely to agree?

 (A) It is essential that these women all participate in chemotherapy treatment.
 (B) The vast majority of women with estrogen-dependent, lymph-node negative breast cancer are at a high risk for recurrence.
 (C) Chemotherapy is detrimental to women who are in the low risk group for recurrence of estrogen-dependent, lymph-node negative breast cancer.
 (D) A significant percentage of the women diagnosed with this type of cancer do not need to be treated with chemotherapy.
 (E) The drug tamoxifen is the best cure for women with estrogen-dependent, lymph-node negative breast cancer.

9. The author is primarily concerned with discussing

 (A) public interest in breast-cancer drugs and how raised awareness has positively effected patients
 (B) the drawbacks to using drug testing participants as subjects for the recurrence scale
 (C) the benefits of testing levels of expression of certain cancer-related genes to predict the likelihood of recurrence of estrogen-dependent breast cancer
 (D) the effectiveness of the formula that generates a "recurrence score" based on the expression patterns of genes taken from chemotherapy recipients
 (E) comparing and contrasting the benefits and the disadvantages of treating patients with estrogen-dependent breast cancer with chemotherapy

10. According to the study outlined in the passage, which one of the following is an example of a woman who would benefit from chemotherapy?

 (A) One with estrogen receptor-positive, lymph node-negative breast cancer who is at a low risk of recurrence
 (B) One who is not taking tamoxifen to treat her estrogen receptor-positive, lymph node-negative breast cancer
 (C) One who is taking tamoxifen for her estrogen receptor-negative, lymph-node positive breast cancer
 (D) One that had test results showing high levels of increased expression of cancer-related genes.
 (E) One with estrogen receptor-positive, lymph node-negative breast cancer who is at a high risk of recurrence

11. Which one of the following provides the best description of the organization of the passage?

 (A) A medicine is introduced, and its benefits and side effects are described in greater detail.
 (B) A problem is defined, its potential causes are discussed, and a possible solution is presented.
 (C) A process is outlined, its negative consequences are explained, and predictions are made.
 (D) A process is introduced and explained, its efficacy is discussed, and its potential value explained
 (E) A process is critiqued, and its previous history is generalized.

12. Each of the following is mentioned in the passage as a result of the success in assigning recurrence scores to patients being treated for estrogen receptor-positive, lymph node-negative breast cancer EXCEPT:

    (A) Fewer low-risk women will have to undergo chemotherapy as part of their treatment for this form of breast cancer

    (B) More lower-risk women will utilize hormonal therapy to prevent cancer from coming back

    (C) Doctors will be able to more accurately predict the likelihood of recurrence of this type of cancer

    (D) Doctors now know that age groups and tumor size are less important in detecting recurrence than the expression (increased or decreased) of certain cancer-related genes.

    (E) Confirmation of the importance of chemotherapy in treating patients at a high risk of recurrence

13. According to the passage, the likelihood that a woman with estrogen-dependent breast, lymph-node negative cancer will have it recur can best be determined by:

    (A) the age of the woman at the initial onset of cancer

    (B) the level of expression of certain genes

    (C) the size of her initial tumor

    (D) at what point in her treatment tamoxifen therapy is commenced

    (E) whether or not she is undergoing or has undergone chemotherapy

14. It can be inferred from the passage that:

    (A) A patient with a recurrence score of 20 would not be likely to benefit from chemotherapy

    (B) Recurrence levels can be accurately predicted only if the patient is taking tamoxifen

    (C) Chemotherapy can increase the risk of recurrence in patients with low recurrence scores

    (D) Some doctors believe that chemotherapy can negatively impact a patient

    (E) More than half of the women who currently receive chemotherapy as part of their treatment for estrogen-dependent, lympth-node negative breast cancer are unlikely to benefit from it

Set Three

Directions: Each passage in this test is followed by several questions. After reading the passage, choose the best answer to each question. Your replies are to be based on what is stated or implied in the selection.

Passage for Questions 1–6

The Nazi Party leadership's interest in art arose early on, and art confiscations began by 1938. The Nazis wanted to rid Germany of art created during the Weimar Republic, the period of 1924–1930, when Germany was a leading European cultural center, especially in the fields of art, cinema, and literature. Weimar decadence aroused Nazi anger, and Hitler began closing art schools in 1933.

Soon after their rise to power in 1933, the Nazis purged so-called "degenerate art" from German public institutions. Artworks deemed degenerate by the Nazis included modern French and German artists in the areas of cubism, expressionism, and impressionism. Approximately sixteen thousand pieces were removed, and by 1938 the Nazi Party declared that all German art museums were purified. State-sponsored exhibitions of this art followed the Nazi purges, clarifying to Germans which types of modern art were now unacceptable in the new German Reich. Soon after, an auction of 126 degenerate artworks took place in 1939 at the Fischer Gallerie in Lucerne, Switzerland, in order to increase revenues for the party. The auctioned paintings by modern masters, many previously purged from German public institutions, included works by van Gogh and Matisse.

Hitler called for a new art, an art that portrayed the Volk and the Volksgemeinschaft (Volk community) as "a realization not of individual talents or of the inspiration of a lone genius, but of the collective expression of the Volk, channeled through the souls of individual creators." Hitler wanted new cultural and artistic creativity to arise in Germany, with the "folk-related" and "race-conscious" arts of Nazi culture replacing what he called the "Jewish decadence" of the Weimar Republic. According to the Nazis, acceptable and desirable art included Old Flemish and Dutch masters; medieval and Renaissance German artworks; Italian Renaissance and baroque pieces; eighteenth-century French artworks; and nineteenth-century German realist painters depicting the German Volk culture.

Art looting that had begun on an ideological basis became an organized government policy. For Nazi officers seeking social status and promotion within the party, collecting and giving art confirmed one's dedication to promoting Nazi racial ideologies in the Reich. It was a way to emulate Hitler and Göring. Yet some top Nazis deviated from this model. For example, Joseph Goebbles, Reich minister for propaganda, collected artworks by German expressionists, and Foreign Minister Joachim von Ribbentrop acquired impressionist paintings by Manet.

The first official rounds of Nazi confiscations began in Austria after the 1938 Anschluss, the annexation of Austria into the German Reich. Art confiscations in Poland began in 1939. Shortly thereafter, Nazi bureaucratic agencies were established in the newly occupied territories and charged with confiscating art. For example, the collections of Vienna's prominent Jewish families were the first to be taken by the Nazis, and Jews who did not plan to leave "Greater Germany" were required to register their personal property with the local police. Artworks soon paid for exit visas and taxes.

Many who were persecuted by the Nazis or who were political opponents did attempt to flee Germany in the mid 1930s. When the Nazis banned the exportation of paper money, wealthy émigrés began to turn their investments into art. Because the Nazis lacked a useable foreign currency, artworks were often used as an alternative to money. As late as 1939, art could be taken out of Germany only as personal property. Art, thus, became cash for black marketers, Nazis and non-Nazis, and for victims of Nazism who used it as a safe, liquid asset. Almost all European art dealers who bought and sold to Germans and Nazis took advantage of their ignorant or ill-informed clients in the occupied areas, and both occupier and occupied exploited one another.

1. A Jewish art owner who emigrated in 1935 from Hitler's Germany would most likely
   - (A) have had little difficulty taking German currency with them
   - (B) have had to use art as a means of taking their investments with them
   - (C) have been able to leave the country with all of their personal belongings
   - (D) have invested substantial sums of money in paintings by Matisse and van Gogh
   - (E) have received a fair return for their investment when they sold their art to European art dealers
2. The passage is primarily concerned with detailing
   - (A) the ironclad distinctions the Nazi government used to decide which art was "degenerate" and which was acceptable
   - (B) how, during the rule of the Nazi regime, art was used for varying financial purposes
   - (C) the history of the Nazi movement to purge certain types of art and replace them, and the role art came to play in the financial transactions of Germans and the Nazi party
   - (D) the persecution of German, Polish and Austrian individuals who collected what the Nazis deemed "degenerate art"
   - (E) the catastrophic effects of Nazi art "purification" on the German art establishment
3. According to the passage, which one of the following is an example of art that the Nazi government *did* approve of?
   - (A) cubist paintings by modern French and German artists
   - (B) paintings that focus on the self-expression of the individual
   - (C) works by van Gogh and Matisse
   - (D) German folk art that depicted the Volk community in a positive way
   - (E) Polish art
4. It can be inferred from the passage that the Nazi treatment of art in the 1930s was motivated, at least in part, by all of the following EXCEPT:
   - (A) A desire to purge the country of decadent Weimar-era art
   - (B) The confiscation of valuable, saleable works that would earn funds for the government
   - (C) An effort to bring greater focus to acceptable art, like German Renaissance and medieval works
   - (D) A desire to extend the party's actions with regard to art beyond the borders of Germany
   - (E) A desire to promote German impressionist and expressionist painters
5. Which of the following relationships does the author imply?
   - (A) a partial causal link between the belief in individualistic art and "Volk" art
   - (B) a correlation between being Jewish and having your art deemed "degenerate"
   - (C) a connection between the destruction of "degenerate" art and the belief that certain modern art was symbolic of "Weimar decadence"
   - (D) a causal relationship between the black market art trade and the creation of German currency that could be used abroad
   - (E) a direct causal link between collecting art and being termed "degenerate"
6. The author indicates that the Nazi Party intended for art to serve primarily as
   - (A) a means of personal expression for German artists
   - (B) a method for Jewish people to transform German currency into exportable funds
   - (C) a way to establish credibility by showing continuity with the Weimar government
   - (D) a way to promote racial tolerance through folk art and a sense of community
   - (E) a method to propagate the Nazi belief in the racial superiority of the "Volk" people

Passage for Questions 7–12

Women, subjected by ignorance to their sensations, are only taught to look for happiness in love, and adopt metaphysical notions respecting that passion, and frequently in the midst of these sublime refinements they plump into actual vice. These are the women who are amused by the reveries of the stupid novelists, who, knowing little of human nature, work up stale tales, all retailed in a sentimental jargon, which equally tend to corrupt the taste, and draw the heart aside from its daily duties.

Females, in fact, denied all political privileges, and not allowed a civil existence, have their attention naturally drawn from the interest of the whole community to that of the minute parts. The mighty business of female life is to please, and restrained from entering into more important concerns by political and civil oppression, sentiments become events, and reflection deepens what it should, and would have effaced, if the understanding had been allowed to take a wider range.

Unable to grasp any thing great, is it surprising that they find the reading of history a very dry task, and disquisitions addressed to the understanding intolerably tedious, and almost unintelligible? Yet, when I exclaim against novels, I mean when contrasted with those works which exercise the understanding and regulate the imagination. For any kind of reading I think better than leaving a blank still a blank, because the mind must receive a degree of enlargement and obtain a little strength by a slight exertion of its thinking powers.

I have known several notable women, and one in particular, who was a very good woman—as good as such a narrow mind would allow her to be, who took care that her daughters (three in number) should never see a novel. As she was a woman of fortune and fashion, they had various masters to attend them, but as the few books thrown in their way were far above their capacities, or devotion, they neither acquired ideas nor sentiments, and passed their time in dressing, quarrelling with each other, or conversing with their maids by stealth, till they were brought into company as marriageable.

With respect to love, nature, or their nurses, had taken care to teach them the physical meaning of the word; and, as they had few topics of conversation, and fewer refinements of sentiment, they expressed their gross wishes not in very delicate phrases, when they spoke freely, talking of matrimony.

I recollect many other women who, not led by degrees to proper studies, and not permitted to choose for themselves, have indeed been overgrown children; or have obtained, by mixing in the world, a little of what is termed common sense; that is a distinct manner of seeing common occurrences, as they stand detached: but what deserves the name of intellect, the power of gaining general or abstract ideas, or even intermediate ones, was out of the question. Their minds were quiescent, and when they were not roused by sensible objects and employments of that kind, they were low-spirited, would cry, or go to sleep.

The best method, I believe, that can be adopted to correct a fondness for novels is to ridicule them: not indiscriminately, for then it would have little effect; but, if a judicious person, with some turn for humor, would read several to a young girl, and point out both by tones, and apt comparisons with pathetic incidents and heroic characters in history, how foolishly and ridiculously they caricatured human nature, just opinions might be substituted instead of romantic sentiments.

7. The primary purpose of the passage is to

(A) extol the virtues of novels as a means of expanding women's intellectual capacities

(B) refute the belief that women are less educated and intellectually developed than men

(C) explain the relationship between the intellectual limitations placed on women of the time and the role of novels in their lives.

(D catalog the misguided topics most common to novels

(E) explain the feminist bent of most novels and its impact on women's intellectual growth

8. With which of the following statements about the place of women in her society would the author of this passage most likely agree?

   (A) a woman's primary function in society is to generate income
   (B) women, although generally of different character and inclination than men, have the same opportunities that men do
   (C) adult women have rights and responsibilities in society that are equal to those of men
   (D) men are inferior to women, since women are more inclined by nature and their role in society to provide pleasure to others
   (E) The lack of opportunity to involve herself in politics and the life of society is one of the factors that helps to limit a woman's intellectual development.

9. The author cites all of the following as problems EXCEPT:

   (A) the limitations on women's intellectual development make them depressed
   (B) lack of proper sources of education may lead them to believe it is acceptable to swear and speak crudely about sex
   (C) the lack of proper education of women creates a situation where ignorant women are teaching other women to be ignorant
   (D) the lack of access to proper reading material keeps them shamefully unaware of the realities of human sexuality
   (E) women are unable to gain true intellect

10. According to the passage, in the author's time a woman's worth was derived from

   (A) her financial and social standing within the community
   (B) her tendency toward civil-mindedness and political involvement
   (C) her intellectual capabilities and accomplishments
   (D) her ability to please
   (E) her refined manner of speaking

11. Which one of the following statements would most weaken the author's negative portrayal of the impact of novels on women?

   (A) they make women want to focus on love
   (B) they expose women to life outside of their sheltered existences, encouraging them toward vice
   (C)they make reading fun, increasing the chance that women will move on to reading more intellectually challenging works
   (D) they teach women how to please the opposite sex, so that they can be empowered
   (E) they provide enjoyable entertainment for women

12. The text suggests which of the following as a way to get young women to stop reading novels?

   (A) have a person read passages from some novels to young women and make fun of them
   (B) make it clear to young women that all novels deserve their scorn
   (C) mothers should have a serious talk with their children about the inaccuracies and over-simplifications in novels
   (D) an adult should explain to young women that romance is wicked, and so they should not read novels, which glorify love
   (E) force them to read material at a much higher level, so that they can begin to actually develop their intellects

ANSWERS AND EXPLANATIONS

Set One	Set Two	Set Three
1. A	1. D	1. B
2. D	2. B	2. C
3. A	3. A	3. D
4. E	4. C	4. E
5. D	5. D	5. B
6. B	6. C	6. E
7. B	7. A	7. C
8. E	8. D	8. E
9. B	9. C	9. D
10. D	10. E	10. D
	11. D	11. C
	12. B	12. A
	13. B	
	14. D	

1. A

The first passage is pretty straightforward. It revolves around the author's argument that "pool" coverage of presidential debates stifles the news media's ability to gather and present news. Why does the author find such a limitation on the media alarming? She feels that it denies viewers an opportunity to gain maximum insight from presidential debates—that is, it sets limits on the amount and variety of information that the public receives. That's the passage's main point. Be aware that the author is talking about the actual "shooting" of a news event—the visual image broadcast to the viewer. She feels that a diversity of images is needed to fully illuminate an event. Although she concedes at the end of the passage that pool coverage may be the only way to cover *some* events, she cautions against the indiscriminate use of such coverage.

Question 1 asks for the author's primary objection to pool coverage of presidential debates. As noted, the author is primarily concerned with the way pool coverage limits the public's exposure to a variety of viewpoints and information. (A) says exactly that and is the correct answer. The author never charges the pool coverage system with limiting the *number* of people who have access to televised debates. Her point is that it limits the number of *versions* of a debate being offered to people, so (B) is wrong. The author discusses the impact of a candidate's debate performance in the first paragraph. But when examining the effects of pool coverage, the author clearly is thinking of the effect on the public's ability to judge, not on the candidates' ability to persuade, so (C) is out. (D) involves a similar distortion of the passage's contents. The author claims that pool coverage, by limiting the information viewers receive, hinders the public's ability to choose between candidates, not its right to choose. As for (E), the author salutes TV's ability to bring live debates into millions of living rooms across the country. Her argument doesn't include a discussion of the dangers of an "overreliance" by the public on television.

2. D

Take a look at the second paragraph and see what motivates the author's reference to court opinion. The author begins by anticipating a possible counterargument—that it doesn't matter what specific images people see as long as they know generally what happened. This argument would lead a proponent of pool coverage to say that the number of news organizations covering an event is irrelevant. At the end of the paragraph, the author attacks this counterargument by quoting a court decision. That is, she uses the words of the court to defend her views. If you realize this, you don't even have to look at the quote to infer the author's opinion of the court's findings. She must agree with them, right? The only choice that reflects this level of agreement is (D)—"substantially correct." (B) and (C) are way too negative, and (A) and (E) are not positive enough.

3. A

To answer Question 3, take a close look at the second half of the first paragraph. The two benefits of a free press cited there are (1), its ability "to inform citizens about matters of public concern," and (2), its ability "to foster a marketplace of ideas in which the best options prevail." Both benefits are involved when television airs a presidential debate, and the author argues that diversity of coverage would maximize these benefits. (A) paraphrases this argument. The author doesn't mention these benefits as proposed "defenses" of pool coverage, and they certainly don't contradict each other, so (B) is off the mark. (C) is wrong—you more or less know this as soon as you see the verb *criticize*—it just doesn't fit what the author is doing. The same goes for (E); the author does not "reconcile" anything here. In fact, there's no need to—the different views on free press benefits are presented here as being complementary. Finally, (D) is dead wrong—the point of this paragraph is that First Amendment freedoms have a whole lot to do with presidential debates.

4. E

Question 4 asks how a proponent of the pool system would defend her viewpoint. Since the author argues that pool coverage limits the information provided to viewers, you need a choice that would challenge the author's point of view. (A) doesn't address this position. So what if broadcasters only rarely betray their political preferences in debate coverage? Pool coverage still limits viewers to coverage by only one of these broadcasters. (B) could be tempting, too, but it also doesn't attack the author's main argument. The author concedes that pool coverage may be the only way to cover some events. But the drawbacks of such coverage still exist for nonpolitical events—and you might have to forgo "practicality" at some point in deference to larger issues. (C) strengthens the author's argument. If presidential debates are so complex that one broadcaster cannot cover them properly, we should allow coverage by a number of broadcasters. (D) is similar to (A) and is wrong for the same reason. (By the way, when you see that two or more answer on the LSAT are very similar, it's a strong signal that these are wrong. After all, there could be only one "right" answer.) (E) is your last chance—and it's the correct answer. If small differences in style of coverage don't affect the amount of information conveyed to viewers, then the premise to the author's argument is blown out of the water. (E) would be the best remark for a proponent of pool coverage to make in its defense.

5. D

Question 5 is a Detail question. The authorial warning occurs in the last paragraph. There the author expresses the hope that the few situations in which pool coverage is necessary will not "foster ... pool implementation in other situations." Unnecessary pool coverage translates to undesirable pool coverage for the author—so (D) is your answer. (A) comes out of left field—the author never mentions the dangers of analysis-crazed media. (Who knows, she might even welcome such a situation. It would provide the public with a lot of information, wouldn't it?) (B) calls attention to the author's fleeting reference—back in the first paragraph—to the First Amendment freedoms afforded the press. But in her discussion of these freedoms, the author never makes the specific argument that pool coverage violates them. So expanded use of pool coverage couldn't be referred to as a "further limitation."

(C) could have been tempting if you made things difficult for yourself. If you thought, "Well, gee, the author thinks pool coverage limits the informational content of presidential debates, so she probably would claim that expanded use of pool coverage would reduce the informational content of other news events, too." But such logical gymnastics shouldn't be necessary on the LSAT. The same thing goes for (E). The author does think pool coverage limits news gathering, but this point never arises in her final warning.

6. B

Question 6 calls your attention to lines 23–25, but you're actually dealing once again with the author's overall argument. The author feels that the pool system "denies viewers an opportunity to gain maximum insight from the debate" because the sharing of news coverage means that viewers are receiving only one set of images—only one version of the debate—not a wide variety representing various viewpoints. According to the author, this prevents individual broadcasters from conveying a unique account of the debate to their viewers. The question asks you to find an answer that would weaken the author's contention that this limitation adversely affects viewers' ability to make voting decisions.

(A) might be tempting. If debate performances don't sway many voters one way or another, what difference does it make what version of the debate they saw? But (A) doesn't address the author's specific argument concerning the effects of the pool system on voter insight. It doesn't matter if a debate doesn't have a major impact on the outcome of an election. What matters—to the author—is that the public has access to as much information as possible when deciding how to vote. So (A) wouldn't weaken the author's argument. (B) reveals a way to alleviate—if not make irrelevant—the limits that the pool system places on the public's access to a variety of ideas. If networks were to wrap up a debate with their own follow-up commentary, providing the public with a diversity of ideas that they then use as a basis for making voting decisions, then the author's objections to the pool system would be weakened. So (B) looks pretty good, but go on to the other choices. (C), (D), and (E) would all strengthen, not weaken, the author's argument. If (C) is correct, then the author's objections to pool coverage are right on the mark—no amount of post-debate coverage could make up for viewers' having access to only one visual version of a debate. If (D) is correct, the importance of televised coverage—and a variety of it—is emphasized all the more. Finally, (E) just restates the author's argument. "Competitive coverage" means the same thing as elimination of pool coverage.

7. B

Question 7 asks for the title that best describes the content of the passage. Wrong answers in such questions usually involve titles that are either too general or too specific—or those that are totally outside the scope. Take (A), for example. The author doesn't discuss how debate coverage changes voters' opinions, does she? Throw it out! The author also doesn't discuss the benefits or impracticalities of the pool system. Throw (C) out! Does the author discuss how First Amendment press rights conflict with presidential politics? Nope—forget (D). How about (E)? In the first paragraph, the author does touch on the influence exercised by televised presidential debates. But the brunt of the passage involves the pool system and the limitations it imposes on public access to information. That's (B), your answer—the only choice that accurately reflects the author's main concerns.

8. E

The main topic of this passage isn't immediately apparent. The first paragraph leaves you expecting the author to examine the obligations of for-profit health care or the basic human rights to food and shelter. The author's real topic becomes clear only when you reach the second paragraph and its introductory question—"Whose obligation is it to secure basic health care for those unable to secure it for themselves?" According to the author, it's the federal government's obligation; the rest of the passage serves to back up this claim. The second paragraph outlines the powers that enable the federal government to guarantee access to health care for all those who need it. Finally, the third paragraph reiterates the basic right to an adequate level of health care and the government's responsibility to provide it. The author ends by introducing the problem of how the federal government should guarantee access to health care.

Question 8 is a main idea question that takes you back to the beginning of the second paragraph. Remember, that's where the author first introduces his main topic—the question of whose obligation it is to secure basic health care for those unable to secure it for themselves. That's this passage's big idea, and (E), the correct choice, captures it well. Turning now to the wrong answers, (A) is way too specific. The author mentions in the second paragraph that the government's taxing power enables it to raise the money required for health care expenditures, but he doesn't delve into specifics, like the exact level of expenditures that would be required. The same goes for (B) and (C). In the last paragraph, the author only fleetingly discusses the how of his argument, (B). He also mentions that differences among various states and localities in the provision of basic social services could arise, (C), but these differences aren't specifically described, and they don't take up the bulk of the discussion. As for (D), the author's argument presupposes that a national commitment to health care can be reconciled with the federal structure of the United States. Indeed, the author's whole argument is that the federal structure is ideal for assuring access to health care.

9. B

Look at lines 50–51, where the author mentions federal food stamp programs and housing subsidies. Why are these mentioned? The author notes that both are aimed at basic necessities, largely a federal responsibility. He mentions these two already established federal programs in order to support his argument that the federal government should start a *similar* program involving access to health care—another basic necessity. Now, keeping that in mind, you probably could have picked the correct answer, (B), by looking solely at the verbs of the answer choices.

But take a closer look at the wrong answers. As for (A), the author certainly doesn't modify a previous point—in fact, he reiterates his main argument wholesale. And he doesn't argue for the modification of the aforementioned programs, either. He just wishes that a federal health care program would join them, so (C) gets eliminated. The author's reference to food stamp programs and housing subsidies does not involve a "contrasting opinion." As you know, the author sees the existence of these programs as support for his own argument. Since no contrasting opinion is presented, no "concession" can be made to it, and (D) is wrong. The "approach" favored by the author is federal support of programs involving basic human necessities.

Food stamps and housing subsidies are examples of programs that have already benefited from this approach, so (E) doesn't make sense.

10. D

This is a Detail question, and the second paragraph provides you with all the information you need. The author lists the federal government's powers regarding health care. If you managed to remember the nature of these powers, it might have been fairly easy for you to run down through the choices and pick out the one that looked suspicious. Assuming you didn't, compare each with the information in the paragraph. (A) corresponds to the first power cited—the federal government's ability to tax. This power enables it to raise the revenue needed to finance health care expenditures. (B), conveniently enough, corresponds to the second power cited. The government's taxing power ensures that the burden of financing health care would be spread equitably across all members of society. (C) corresponds nicely to the third power—the power to coordinate programs guaranteeing access to health care for the poor across local and state boundaries. The ability to ensure that there are not great differences in the minimum of health care guaranteed to all is the last power cited and one that is paraphrased in (E). This leaves you with (D). Nowhere does the author mention a state power that can compel private businesses and charities to assume greater responsibility for financing health care for the needy. By virtue of being wrong, (D) is the answer.

Set Two

1. D

The author begins the passage by discussing why Edmund Burke's belief in how governments are formed contrasts with his philosophical forefather John Locke's idealistic belief that people choose to join their governments. Unlike Locke, Burke believed that people are the "product of society, born to an inheritance of rights…and of reciprocal duties" and that government and prescription are paramount and limit the "right" of revolution. (D) is the only answer that encompasses the full scope of the passage. (A) distorts the last paragraph, where the author reports that Burke sees the right of revolution as a limited one of last resort. (B) can't be the right answer because Burke felt that people are born into a political system without first consciously making a decision to join it—it is his predecessor Locke who believes that societies are formed voluntarily. (C) contradicts Burke's belief that societies exist of necessity and that individuals exist as "a product of society." Finally, (E) is incorrect because Burke never speaks of a particular *form* of government, only of the importance of government and prescription.

2. B

The author clearly states at the beginning of the second paragraph that "there is, therefore, no right of revolution, or rebellion at will," which eliminates (A). The second paragraph states that "revolution is always the annulment of some rights," leading to correct answer (B). Burke took issue with the way that the French Assembly made totally destroying the existing structure of their government their "daily bread." He believed that the present government should reflect the prescriptions and traditions leading up to it. For this reason, (C) is incorrect. (D) is wrong because the text, while explaining that Burke was not for revolutions, did not say that he was concerned with the individual's freedom. (E) is incorrect because, while Locke's concept of the social contract is discussed (and contrasted with Burke's opinions on how societies are built), revolution is never outlined as an inherent right of the social contract concept.

3. A

Near the end of the first paragraph the author says, "there is a sacred veil to be drawn over the beginnings of all government." He goes on to say "in any ancient community such as that of France or Britain, every constituent factor, including what we choose to call the people, is the product of convention. The privileges of every order, the rights of every individual, rest upon prescription embodied in law or established by usage," leading to correct answer (A). (B) contradicts the idea that the rules are developed over time and passed down through society. (C) lifts language from the passage, but there is no link in the passage between the behavior of individuals and their treatment. (D) is incorrect because the author says the prescriptions that dictate the course of society are evolved and become ingrained, not "ever shifting." (E) is not the correct answer because the author has stated that the origins of a society are cut off from the prescriptions.

4. C

Burke disagreed with Locke's philosophies, which had dominated western political thought of the eighteenth century, for many reasons. Since this is an "EXCEPT" question, it may be most efficient to eliminate the choices that *are* aspects of Locke's philosophy we're told Burke doesn't accept. Correct choice (C) *is* a point of contention between Locke and Burke, but this is Burke's view—Locke believed that individuals "contracted" to form society. If you recognize that immediately, great—if not, eliminate the rest: Burke disagreed with Locke's belief that the individual consciously chose whether or not to be part of the society around them, so eliminate (A). Burke believed that society built upon the prescription and traditions of the past while Locke said that the claims of society were "continually tested" as it evolved, so (B) is not the answer. (D) can be eliminated because Burke felt that the way people are treated depends on the customs their society has built up about an individual's treatment. Like (B), (E) is incorrect because Burke believed that the individual had much less to do with the formation of his or her society, compared to the laws and customs that came before them, whereas Locke believed that the "contract" was subject to continual analysis and modification.

5. D

(D) is the statement that the author would most likely agree with—Burke did recognize that some change was required—and, indeed, that even revolution was occasionally necessary. In the last paragraph, we're told that he believed that the proper role of the assembly was to "preserve *and reform."* The same information contradicts (A). Burke stressed the importance of continuity and tradition in government, so (B) can be eliminated. Both (C) and (E) can be eliminated, as Burke's philosophy focused on society as a whole and eschewed individualism.

6. C

The end of the first paragraph discusses Burke's belief that individuals breaking a society are unprepared for the long, difficult road toward re-establishing society. The last paragraph tells us that revolution necessarily destroys some rights, and should be undertaken only as a last resort because of the difficulty of rebuilding society. (C) sums up these cautionary words. (A) directly contradicts this idea, claiming that revolution is a *good* solution. The whole last paragraph tells us unequivocally that Burke doesn't believe so. (B) is wrong because other political processes are not discussed in relation to revolution. (D), despite inviting familiar language from the passage, can't be right because it was Locke, not Burke, who believed in a social contract that individuals chose to agree to. (E) again lifts language from the passage, but it's language that relates to the formation of society, not to the role of revolution.

7. A

To answer this question correctly, you must clearly recognize that Burke was attacking the ideology of Locke. Only a very small piece of the passage talks about Locke's beliefs, near the beginning of the first paragraph. Being aware of "who said what" in a passage that sets forth more than one point of view is critical. We learn in the first paragraph that Locke was interested in what he termed the social contract, where individuals, who are born with certain rights, decide if they want to join society. Locke also believed that the participation in society and its claim on the rights of the individual was subject to continual reassessment. (A) describes a work that would elaborate on those points. (B) is incorrect because Locke believed the power of society derived from the consent of its members. (C) may look tempting because the passage talks quite a bit about the importance of evolved prescription and pre-existing societal rights—but those are Burke's views, not Locke's. (D) can be eliminated for the same reason. (E) is also not likely, since Locke believed *all* people were born with inherent rights.

8. D

In the first paragraph of the passage, the author states that "the results of the new test "suggest that almost half of over 50,000 U.S. women diagnosed with estrogen-dependent, lymph-node negative breast cancer every year are at low risk for recurrence and may not need to go through the discomfort and side effects of chemotherapy." Paragraph 2 includes a paraphrase of this information, and in the last paragraph, the author reiterates "Women with low recurrence scores, who make up about 50 percent of these patients, derived minimal benefits from chemotherapy." So (D) is the correct answer. Both of these pieces of text contradict wrong answer (A). (B) is incorrect because if almost half of the women diagnosed are at low risk, "the vast majority" can't be at high risk. In fact, information from the study tells us that 27% of the subjects were at high risk. (C) is a distortion—we know chemotherapy isn't especially beneficial to these women, but the author specifically stated that the group hadn't been large enough to determine whether or not it was detrimental. (E) makes a comparison that's never addressed in the passage—the only thing the author tells us categorically is that chemotherapy seems not to be necessary/beneficial for low risk women. He says nothing about what *is* the best course of treatment, though Tamoxifen might be tempting because it's familiar from the passage.

9. C

Since this is a Global question, look at your Topic/Scope/Purpose and your roadmap before the answer choices. We've already determined that the author's purpose here was to inform us about this test and its benefits, which is a perfect match for answer (C). (A) is outside the scope of the passage—there's no mention of public interest nor of a positive impact that's *already* taken place, only the one that is now possible. (B) isn't mentioned at all, although the study group did come from the test-group for another drug. (D) may be tempting, in that the author does tell us that the test seems to be effective, but only one small piece of the passage is devoted to the method, and the correct answer to a global question must encompass the passage as a whole. (E) is incorrect because the specific benefits and disadvantages aren't addressed, only the fact that there are benefits for one group but not the other.

10. E

For this Detail question, begin with your road map and look up the answer. Where did the author talk about who would and would not benefit from chemotherapy? The last paragraph, so look back and see what the passage says. The only information we're given is that women at a high risk of recurrence benefit and those at a low risk do not. So who *would* benefit, as the question asks? Someone at a high risk of recurrence, which is (E). Women with low recurrence scores didn't benefit much from chemotherapy; so, (A) is wrong. (B) introduces an element that's totally outside the scope of the passage—all of the women studied were taking tamoxifen, and (C) also makes the tamoxifen a factor, though we have no means of determining the impact of tamoxifen use on the need for chemotherapy since we have studied only women taking tamoxifen. (D) is wrong because all we're told is that the levels of expression (increased *or* decreased) form the basis for prediction—we don't know the meaning of increased expression in particular.

11. D

This question asks about the general organization of the passage, which you should already have laid out in your road map. Although the details might be a bit complex, the basic structure of the passage isn't too complicated—which is often the case in science-based passages. Correct choice (D) provides a good summary: A process (the new test) is introduced and explained, then its efficacy is discussed (through the data showing the accuracy of its predictions), and finally, the potential benefits (saving women from unnecessary chemotherapy) are set forth. (A) can be eliminated with a glance at the first clause—the passage begins by describing the *test*, not a medicine. Likewise, (B) goes wrong immediately: the passage doesn't begin with a problem, but with an announcement of the new test. (C) starts out right, because a process *is* outlined (the process of testing for levels of expression of a panel of cancer-related genes), but there are no negative consequences described. (E) takes a wrong turn at "critiqued," and another at "generalized." Either of those verbs alone is enough to eliminate this answer choice.

12. B

In a Detail/EXCEPT question, the most efficient approach is generally to locate those items that *are* found in the passage and eliminate them. (A) is stated directly in the first paragraph. Correct choice (B) is a distortion—hormone therapy is mentioned, but the only treatment option that is discussed in terms of its efficacy or necessity is chemotherapy. We're told in paragraphs 5 and 6 that the recurrence scores are reliable, so we can eliminate (C). (D) can be eliminated because paragraph 6 tells us that the correlation between recurrence scores and actual rates of recurrence are consistent regardless of age group and tumor size. The final paragraph indicates that women with high-recurrence risk benefit greatly from chemotherapy, eliminating (E).

13. B

The result of the recurrence score tests is that by looking at "levels of expression (increased or decreased) of a panel of cancer-related genes" scientists can accurately predict the likelihood of recurrence, so (B) is correct. (A) and (C) are directly contradicted when paragraph 6 states that the findings of the study "held across age groups and tumor size," but an efficient approach to this question won't require elimination—it will require only looking up the correct answer and matching it with (B). Tamoxifen, again, is a red herring. It's mentioned in the passage, but not for its own value as a treatment, so (D) can be eliminated. As for (E), there's a correlation between the recurrence score and chemotherapy, but this answer has it backward, suggesting that chemotherapy determines the likelihood of recurrence when the passage tells us that the likelihood of recurrence determines the need for chemotherapy.

14. D

Since this is a wide-open inference question with a stem that provides no direction to the appropriate section of the passage, we'll have to go straight to the answer choices. (A) refers to a patient who falls in the intermediate risk group—a group we know very little about, and nothing in terms of the benefits of chemotherapy. (B) ties the success of the test to tamoxifen. It's true that we've only seen the efficacy of the test in the context of patients taking tamoxifen, but we can't predict that it would be any less accurate in other patients—we simply don't have enough information from the passage to know one way or the other. (C) directly contradicts the last paragraph, which says that we don't have enough information yet to determine whether chemotherapy is detrimental to low risk patients. (D), although similar, refers to the belief of "some doctors," not a provable fact. We know that at least one doctor—the one quoted in paragraph 7—thinks chemotherapy has negative effects because she refers to "harmful short and long-term side effects." Note also the distinction between the language of (D)'s "negatively impact" a patient versus the more specific (and unsupportable) "increase the risk of recurrence" in (C). (E) is close but distorts the numbers—we're told that *almost half* of the women being treated with chemotherapy could do without it, not "more than half."

Set Three

1. B

(B) is the correct answer because paragraph 6 explains that in Hitler's Germany, the currency was non-exportable, and had to be invested into physical art that would later be sold. This directly contradicts (A). As for (C), the only information we're given about personal property in the passage is that Jews who were not leaving "Greater Germany" were required to register it with the police. Likewise, (D) is unlikely since paragraph 2 states that works by these artists were among those confiscated by the Nazis. Paragraph 6 states that most European art dealers took advantage of the political situation in Germany in order to acquire art for less than it was truly worth, so (E) is also unlikely.

2. C

The passage begins by explaining how the Nazi party undertook to purge certain art (particularly that of the Weimar era) that it deemed decadent, describes that process in more detail, and then sets forth the role that art came to play in financial transactions—a perfect match for (C). (A) can be eliminated readily for two reasons: It's too strong in its terminology ("ironclad distinctions") and it addresses only a small portion of the passage and therefore can't be the correct answer to a global question. (B) is tempting because the passage does discuss how art was used by the individual and the German government during this time for various financial purposes, but it also fails to take in the passage as a whole. Paragraphs 5 and 6 refer to the treatment and experiences of Jewish people, and how art played a role in that, but there is no indication that art collecting was a cause of the persecution or that those who collected art were singled out, so (D) is incorrect. It, too, focuses in on one specific aspect of the passage rather than the global aspects. The effects of Hitler's attitudes about art on the German art world are not the main focus of the piece—it is merely one of the facts the passage touches upon, so (E) is incorrect.

3. D

In paragraph 3, the author explains that Hitler wanted German artists to aspire to creating "a new art, an art that portrayed the Volk and the *Volksgemeinschaft* (Volk community) as 'a realization not of individual talents or of the inspiration of a lone genius, but of the collective expression of the Volk, channeled through the souls of individual creators.'" The paragraph goes on to explain that Hitler wanted new German art to be "folk-related" and "race-conscious", taking the place of what he believed to be decadent artists of the previous Weimar regime. So, (D) is correct. In the passage's second paragraph, cubist art is one of the types of art listed as being considered degenerate by the Nazis, so (A) is out. (B) can't be right because paragraph three explained that Hitler wanted artists to focus on creating what he felt was a "collective expression of the Volk," not the artistic expression of the individual. In paragraph 2, the passage lists masterworks by van Gogh and Matisse as some of the "degenerate" artwork that the Nazi government auctioned off to raise money for the regime, so (C) is wrong. The only reference to art in Poland comes in paragraph 5, where the author tells us that art was confiscated in Poland after 1939. The passage doesn't even state explicitly whether this was Polish art, or simply art that was in Poland at that time, and certainly makes no claim of Nazi approval, so (E) is wrong.

4. E

(E) is the exception, because paragraph 2 states this type of art was exactly the type to incur the label "degenerate." There is mention of party officials collecting such art in paragraph four, but it's set forth as a deviation, not a party goal. (A) is incorrect because paragraph 1 states that Hitler detested the art of the Weimar period of government that came before it, which the passage states he termed "Jewish decadence" in paragraph 3. (B) is incorrect, because the Nazi Government profited greatly from the art they chose to censor, as outlined in paragraph 2. Paragraph 3 discusses what art of the past and present Hitler wanted to support, and German Renaissance and medieval works were among them, so (C) is not the exception. (D) is not the exception either, because paragraph 5 discusses the systematized censorship of art in Austria and Poland.

5. B

(B) is correct because Hitler clearly hated Jewish people and wanted to eradicate their "degeneracy" from Germany in what he saw as its many forms. One of the motivations for the artistic changes set in motion by the Nazi party was to rid Germany of the "Jewish decadence" of Weimar era. In paragraph three Hitler's belief that art's new direction needed to be in a more collective, less individual approach is discussed, so (A) is not correct. (C) is incorrect because the passage never discusses destruction of art, just that art deemed "degenerate" was sold to make the Nazi party more money. (D) is wrong because paragraph 6 states that "When the Nazis banned the exportation of paper money, wealthy émigrés began to turn their investments into art. Because the Nazis lacked a useable foreign currency, artworks were often used as an alternative to money." So, the black market trade did not cause the creation of a useable currency abroad. Paragraph 4 explains that "For Nazi officers seeking social status and promotion within the party, collecting and giving art confirmed one's dedication to promoting Nazi racial ideologies in the Reich." So (E) is wrong.

6. E

Paragraph 3 describes Hitler's interest in fostering a new type of art, which is "race conscious" and "folk related," so (E) is the correct answer. (A) is incorrect because that same paragraph discourages individualism in art. (B) is a tantalizing choice, because paragraph 6 does discuss how Jewish people were forced to invest in art in order to take their money with them when they left Germany, but the passage does not say that the Nazis intended this to be a means of assistance for the Jews. This was just a side result of the policies the Nazi Party had concerning their currency. Hitler wished to eradicate what he saw as their "decadent" attitude from the German art world during the Weimar era, so (C) is incorrect. (D) is incorrect because Hitler believed that art should champion the "Volk" people, and that other races were inferior.

7. C

We already determined during our passage overview that the author was primarily concerned with explaining the restrictions on women's intellectual development and the way that novels played into those limitations: that's a close match for (C). (A), is clearly incorrect because it directly contradicts the author's negative attitude toward the value of novels. The answer also can't be (B), since she *does* believe men receive better educations than women do. The author discusses the topics common to novels only briefly—it's neither a "catalog" nor the main focus of the passage. Remember that correct to a global question must take in the passage as a whole. (E) is incorrect because the novel's sentimentality and simplistic ideas about how women should be focused on romance—the antithesis of feminism—are part of the reason Wollstonecraft dislikes them, as she explains in paragraph 1.

8. E

In the second paragraph, the author tells us that women's lack of access to political participation narrows their view and "sentiments turn to events," which is a match for (E). (A) directly contradicts paragraph two's assertion that the primary business of female life is to please, and (B) is contradicted in various places, in particular paragraph 2's mention of the denial of political privileges and paragraph six's note that many women were not led to proper studies nor "permitted to choose for themselves." These same references contradict answer (C). The author makes no reference to the superiority or inferiority of men versus women—only their respective rights and positions in society. Therefore, (D) is a distortion.

9. D

Wollstonecraft is concerned (in paragraph 5) that women learn about sex even without a good education, but in a crude and unrefined way, so (D) is correct. The same paragraph describes how that improper learning leads to crude expression, so (B) can't be the exception. In paragraph 7, Wollstonecraft is concerned that women either stay intellectually childish, or only learn some street-smart common sense, but never "what deserves the name of intellect, the power of gaining general or abstract ideas, or even intermediate ones;" consequently (E) can't be the exception. She also states in paragraph six that these women's minds were inactive from not being used, which caused them to be "low-spirited, and they "would cry, or go to sleep," so (A) is not the exception. In paragraphs 4 and 5 she discusses a mother who tries to raise her daughters to be what she knows to be well-educated, but because she herself was only educated as a woman, she did not know what her daughters' education was missing; (C) is not the exception either.

10. D

In the second paragraph of the passage Wollstonecraft says, "the mighty business of female life is to please," so (D) is correct. In this paragraph Wollstonecraft also notes that women are denied political privileges and opportunities that might act to get them involved in the working toward the greater good, so (B) is incorrect. Women were unable to work or have money of their own, so (A) is wrong. (C) can't be right, because the main point of Wollstonecraft's passage is that women are not provided with the means to develop any true intellect at all. (E) is a distortion—the coarseness of speech of certain women was mentioned in the passage, but not with regard to defining a woman's worth.

11. C

Even though Wollstonecraft is not in favor of women reading novels, she does concede in paragraph 3 that she thinks that any type of reading is "better than leaving a blank still a blank, because the mind must receive a degree of enlargement and obtain a little strength by a slight exertion of its thinking powers." If reading novels were a gateway to reading more intellectually stimulating books, Wollstonecraft's opposition to novels would be negated, so (C) is correct. (E) is wrong, because Wollstonecraft would agree that many women find novels enjoyable, but that that is precisely the problem with them, since novelists "work up stale tales, all retailed in a sentimental jargon, which equally tend to corrupt the taste, and draw the heart aside from its daily duties" (paragraph one). Likewise, (A) and (D) are wrong because one of Wollstonecraft's main objections to novels is that she feels that novelists tend to focus on love and base sexuality. She states in paragraph 2 that "the mighty business of female life is to please," which keeps them from "entering into more important concerns by political and civil oppression," and she is upset that for these women love takes on a supreme importance, and "sentiments become events, and reflection deepens what it should, and would have effaced, if the understanding had been allowed to take a wider range." (B) is also wrong, because Wollstonecraft would agree that novels encourage women toward vice, and that point supports her negative conclusions about novels.

12. A

In paragraph 7 Wollstonecraft states that she feels that the best way to curb young women's fondness for novels is have a "judicious person, with some turn for humor," read several novels to a young woman, and "point out both by tones, and apt comparisons with pathetic incidents and heroic characters in history, how foolishly and ridiculously they caricatured human nature, just opinions might be substituted instead of romantic sentiments." Consequently, (A) is correct. She cautions that an adult not make fun of all novels, since that would "have little effect," so (B) is wrong. (C) is incorrect because Wollstonecraft believed a sense of humor is needed to really prove how silly and inaccurate novels are. Throughout the passage Wollstonecraft bemoans the preoccupation women have with romantic love, but while she appears to feel that this besmirches the grandeur of love, she never states that love itself is evil, so (D) is wrong. As we saw in the example she provides in paragraphs 4 and 5, making young women read books that are much too difficult for them is only going to discourage them from reading quality texts, pushing them toward less illuminating interests, so (E) is also incorrect.

Chapter 6: **Writing Sample**

- **Sample essay topics and responses**
- **The 8 basic Writing Sample principles**
- **Kaplan's 4-Step Method for the Writing Sample**

The Writing Sample comes at the end of your LSAT day. It consists of a scenario followed by two possible courses of action or an argument for you to assess. You'll have 35 minutes to make a written case for your position.

This section tests your ability to evaluate an argument or to write a clear, concise, and persuasive argument. No outside knowledge whatsoever is required.

You will need to have a pencil to write the essay, as well as scrap paper to plan out your response before you actually write it. Your essay must be confined to the space provided, which is roughly the equivalent of two sheets of standard lined paper. You won't be given additional paper, so you'll have to keep your argument concise. Usually, two or three paragraphs will be enough. Note that there's really no time or space to change your mind or radically alter your essay once you've begun writing, so *plan your argument out carefully before beginning to write*. Make sure to write as legibly as you can.

READ MORE

The Writing Sample may be crucial in some admissions decisions. Take it seriously and read on.

The Writing Sample is ungraded, but it is sent to law schools along with your LSAT score. Many law schools use the Writing Sample to help make decisions on borderline cases or to decide between applicants with otherwise comparable credentials. Granted, it may not carry the same weight as the scored sections of the test, but since it can impact on your admission chances, your best bet is to take it seriously.

SAMPLE ESSAY TOPICS

Effective June 2005, the LSAT Writing Sample requires a response to one of two types of prompt. The first, the "Decision" prompt, offers a brief introduction outlining a choice to be made. That's followed by two bullet-pointed criteria that should guide your decision. Finally, the two alternatives that you're to choose from are described in a paragraph each. The second type, the "Argument" prompt, offers a

short paragraph expressing a point of view—an argument with a conclusion and supporting evidence. You are asked to analyze the effectiveness of the argument by examining its line of reasoning and the nature of its evidence.

The Decision Essay

The following is an example of the first type of Writing Sample topic:

> The *Daily Tribune*, a metropolitan newspaper, is considering two candidates for promotion to business editor. Write an argument for one candidate over the other with the following considerations in mind:
>
> - The editor must train new writers and assign stories.
> - The editor must be able to edit and rewrite stories under daily deadline pressure.
>
> Laura received a B.A. in English from a large university. She was managing editor of her college newspaper and served as a summer intern at her hometown daily paper. Laura started working at the *Tribune* right out of college and spent three years at the city desk covering the city economy. Eight years ago, the paper formed its business section, and Laura became part of the new department. After several years covering state business, Laura began writing on the national economy. Three years ago, Laura was named senior business and finance editor on the national business staff; she is also responsible for supervising seven writers.
>
> Palmer attended an elite private college where he earned both a B.S. in business administration and an M.A. in journalism. After receiving his journalism degree, Palmer worked for three years on a monthly business magazine. He won a prestigious national award for a series of articles on the impact of monetary policy on multinational corporations. Palmer came to the *Tribune* three years ago to fill the newly created position of international business writer. He was the only member of the international staff for two years and wrote on almost a daily basis. He now supervises a staff of four writers. Last year, Palmer developed a bimonthly business supplement for the *Tribune* that has proved highly popular and has helped increase the paper's circulation.

READ MORE

LSAC offers a wide sampling of other essay topics with their practice tests. The more of them you examine, the more likely that you'll have relevant ideas prepared for test day.

The Argument Essay

The following is an example of the second type of topic:

> The following appeared in a memo from the secretary of the state's new teacher development committee:
>
> "The problem of poorly performing teachers that has plagued the state public school system is bound to become a good deal less serious in the future. The state has initiated comprehensive guidelines that oblige state teachers to complete a number of required credits in education and educational psychology at the graduate level before being certified."
>
> Discuss how well-reasoned you find this argument.

THE 8 BASIC WRITING SAMPLE PRINCIPLES

Here are the most important rules of thumb to remember when attacking the Writing Sample:

KAPLAN EXCLUSIVE

In an Argument essay, use the terminology you learned in Logical Reasoning, especially for Assumption, Flaw, and Method of Argument questions.

Use Scrap Paper to Plan Your Essay

The proctors give you scrap paper for a reason—so use it. Make yourself a rudimentary outline, listing the points you want to make in each paragraph. Ideally, you should know what you want to say and how you want to say it before putting pencil to paper.

Don't Obsess Over Your Position

Nobody really cares whether you consider the argument strong or which choice you make (for example, whether you choose to support Laura or Palmer in the sample above). What's important is how well you support your position. Generally, the Decision alternatives are written to be pretty evenly matched, so there's no right or wrong answer, just a well-supported or ill-supported position.

Get Right to the Point

The first sentence should immediately offer a statement of your position. Assume that the reader is already familiar with the situation; there's no need to waste time describing the scenario.

Use a Clear, Simple Essay Format

Since the essay topics have only two possible structures, you can decide in advance how you will structure your response. One possibility for the Decision essay is the "winner/loser" format, in which the first paragraph begins with a statement of choice and then discusses the reason why your choice (the winner) is superior. The next paragraph focuses on why the other alternative (the loser) is not as good and should end with a concluding sentence reaffirming your decision. Another possibility is the "according to the criteria" format, in which the first paragraph would discuss both the winner and the loser in light of the first criterion, and the second paragraph would discuss them both in light of the second criterion. For an Argument essay, you can write one paragraph on each specific flaw or strength you identify in the prompt.

Whether you adopt one of these formats or use one of your own, the most important thing is that your essay be coherent in its reasoning. The more organized your essay is, the more persuasive it will be.

Mention But Downplay, the Opposing View

Use sentence structures that allow you to do this, such as, "Even though Palmer won a prestigious national award . . . " and then attempt to demonstrate why this is really no big deal. This is an example of mentioning yet downplaying one of the loser's strengths. Try to do the same thing for at least one of the winner's obvious weaknesses. Doing so demonstrates that you see the full picture. Recognizing and dealing with possible objections makes your argument that much stronger.

Don't Simply Repeat Facts From the Prompt

Try instead to offer an *interpretation of the facts in light of the stated criteria*. If you're arguing for Laura in the Decision topic, you can't state simply that "Laura was named senior business and finance editor on the national business staff" and expect the reader to infer that that's a good thing. For all we know, being in that position may be a detriment when it comes to the criteria—training new writers and working under daily deadline pressure. It's up to you to indicate why certain facts about the winner are positive factors in light of the criteria, and vice versa for facts about the loser. Merely parroting what's written in the topic won't win you any points with the law schools.

Write Well

KAPLAN EXCLUSIVE

Readers will be prejudiced against your Writing Sample if it's hard to decipher. If your writing is bad, print.

It sounds obvious, of course, but you should try to make your prose as clean and flawless as you can. Some people get so entangled in content that they neglect the mechanics of essay writing. But spelling, grammar, and writing mechanics are important. Use structural signals to keep your writing fluid and clear, and use transitions between paragraphs to keep the entire essay unified. Above all, write or print legibly.

Budget Your Time Wisely

We suggest spending roughly five to seven minutes reading the topic and planning out your essay. Use the scrap paper provided to jot down a quick outline of the points you intend to make. Then spend about 25 minutes writing the essay. This should be plenty of time; remember, you're only looking at three or four paragraphs at the most. This schedule will leave about three to five minutes at the end to proofread your essay for spelling and grammar.

KAPLAN'S 4-STEP METHOD FOR THE WRITING SAMPLE

1. Prompt

Before you start to write, be sure you understand which type of prompt you have and the scenario it presents. Writing off-topic suggests that you are unable to focus your ideas, or that you don't care.

2. Plan

If you have a Decision prompt, decide which alternative you will support based on the number and quality of your supporting examples. It doesn't have to be your real opinion, but you must express a clear opinion and support it with the types of reasoning you learned in Logical Reasoning.

If you have an Argument prompt, consider whether there are logical flaws in the argument using our Logical Reasoning skills. Consider counterexamples or alternative explanations, look for questionable assumptions underlying the reasoning. Remember that you are not asked for your own opinion, only for an assessment of the opinion offered.

Always plan your approach thoroughly before you start to write. Essays that wander aimlessly, or start with one opinion but change to another halfway through, are unpleasant to read and make an overall bad impression.

3. Produce

Use most of your time to write the essay. Think through each sentence before starting to write it. Start a new paragraph for each new idea. Stick to your plan.

4. Proofread

Don't skip this step. Save a couple of minutes to make sure you haven't left out words (or even sentences) that are necessary for the reader to follow your reasoning. Planning to proofread also helps ensure that you will complete the essay.

GO ONLINE

Your downloadable study sheet summarizes these strategies.

Now try Kaplan's 4-Step Method using the Argument sample prompt:

> Directions:
>
> For this essay, you are presented with an argument that offers reasons for drawing a particular conclusion. In your essay, analyze and evaluate the writer's reasoning and use of evidence. For example, you might consider what questionable assumptions underlie the thinking and what alternative explanations or counterexamples might weaken the conclusion. You might discuss what sort of evidence would strengthen or refute the argument, what changes in the argument would make it more logically sound, and what, if anything, would help you better evaluate its conclusion.
>
> The following appeared in a memo from the secretary of the state's new teacher development committee:
>
> "The problem of poorly performing teachers that has plagued the state public school system is bound to become a good deal less serious in the future. The state has initiated comprehensive guidelines that oblige state teachers to complete a number of required credits in education and educational psychology at the graduate level before being certified."
>
> Discuss how well-reasoned you find this argument.

1. Prompt

Note that the directions for the Argument essay provide you with a checklist of factors to consider: "questionable assumptions...and...alternative explanations or counterexamples," "evidence [that] would strengthen or refute the argument... changes [that] would make it more logically sound, [or] would help you better evaluate its conclusion."

Take the argument apart. It's about teacher performance in the state public schools. The conclusion is that there will be fewer poorly performing teachers in the future. The evidence offered is that the state now has comprehensive guidelines requiring credits in education and educational psychology. What does that assume?

The connection between the evidence and the conclusion isn't clear: the writer assumed that credits in education will improve teacher performance, and that the current, poorly performing teachers haven't already met this new standard of training, and that newly certified teachers will replace the poorly perfoming (but already certified) teachers in the system.

2. Plan

Select the points you will make. Analyze the use of evidence and determine whether there's anything relevant that's not discussed. What does "poorly performing" mean? Can you think of anything that would make the argument stronger? In this case, evidence supporting one or more of the assumptions identified would do that.

When you have established the points you'll make, determine the order in which you'll write them. Address all the ways the assumptions seem unsupported. You might also recommend new evidence you'd like to see and explain why. Plan your opening to make your position clear. Lead with your best arguments.

3. Produce

Then use your notes as a working outline. In this case, since you have determined that there are serious flaws, your response might look like this:

> The argument that improved academic training, ensured by requiring credits in education and psychology, will substantially alleviate the current problem of poorly performing teachers may seem logical at first glance. However, the conclusion relies upon undefined terms and assumptions for which there is no clear evidence.
>
> First, the writer assumes that the required courses will produce better teachers. In fact, the courses might be entirely irrelevant to the teachers' failings. Suppose, for example, the main problem lies in cultural and linguistic gaps between teacher and student; graduate-level courses that do not address these specific issues would be of little use. The notion that the coursework will make better teachers would be strengthened by a clear definition of "poor perfomance" in the classroom and by evidence that the training will address the relevant issues.
>
> Furthermore, the writer assumes that poorly performing teachers currently in the schools have not already met this standard of training. The argument would be strengthened considerably if the writer provided evidence of a direct correlation between teachers' educational backgrounds and their level of effectiveness in the classroom.

KAPLAN EXCLUSIVE

In a Decision essay, bring up factors that aren't listed, but that you think are relevant to the decision maker's choice—just be sure to cover the listed criteria as well.

Finally, the writer provides no evidence that poorly performing teachers currently working will either stop teaching in the near future or will undergo additional training. In its current form, the argument implies that only brand-new teachers—those not previously certified—will receive the specified training. If this is the case, the bright future that the writer envisions may be decades away.

In order to support the conclusion that the guidelines will, in effect, solve the state's problem, the writer must first define the scope of the problem more clearly and demonstrate a more complete understanding of the need for and benefits of the new requirements.

4. Proofread

Make sure that your transitions are clear, and that your ideas are fully expressed on the page.

SAMPLE ESSAY

Using the Decision sample prompt (repeated below) write an essay, using the next two lined pages, and observing the thirty five-minute time limit. Then check your essay, making sure it observes the basic principles outlined above.

> The *Daily Tribune*, a metropolitan newspaper, is considering two candidates for promotion to business editor. Write an argument for one candidate over the other with the following considerations in mind:
>
> - The editor must train new writers and assign stories.
> - The editor must be able to edit and rewrite stories under daily deadline pressure.
>
> Laura received a B.A. in English from a large university. She was managing editor of her college newspaper and served as a summer intern at her hometown daily paper. Laura started working at the *Tribune* right out of college and spent three years at the city desk covering the city economy. Eight years ago, the paper formed its business section, and Laura became part of the new department. After several years covering state business, Laura began writing on the national economy. Three years ago, Laura was named senior business and finance editor on the national business staff; she is also responsible for supervising seven writers.
>
> Palmer attended an elite private college where he earned both a B.S. in business administration and an M.A. in journalism. After receiving his journalism degree, Palmer worked for three years on a monthly business magazine. He won a prestigious national award for a series of articles on the impact of monetary policy on multinational corporations. Palmer came to the *Tribune* three years ago to fill the newly created position of international business writer. He was the only member of the international staff for two years and wrote on almost a daily basis. He now supervises a staff of four writers. Last year, Palmer developed a bimonthly business supplement for the *Tribune* that has proved highly popular and has helped increase the paper's circulation.

Sample Response

Compare your answer to the following sample response:

> Both candidates are obviously qualified, but Laura is the better choice. For one thing, Laura has been working at the *Tribune* for eleven years, and has therefore had plenty of opportunity to learn the workings of the paper. For another, her experience has been in national rather than international business, and national business will certainly be the focus of the *Tribune*'s financial coverage. In her current capacity, she is responsible for writing and editing articles while simultaneously overseeing the work of a staff of seven. Clearly, then, Laura can work under deadline pressure and manage a staff, a capability she demonstrated at an early age as the managing director of her college newspaper. Although Laura's academic credentials may not measure up to Palmer's, her background in English, her history of steady promotions, and her work as senior national business writer—combined with a solid business knowledge and obvious drive for accomplishment—will certainly spur the department to journalistic excellence.
>
> Palmer's résumé is admirable but is nonetheless inferior to Laura's. True, Palmer has evidently done a fine job managing the international section, but his staff numbers only four, and the scope of the venture is smaller than Laura's. True, Palmer's articles on the impact of monetary policy did win an award in the past, but since he has been working for the *Tribune,* no such honors have been forthcoming. Not only does Palmer lack the English literature background that Laura has, but he also lacks her long experience at the *Tribune.* Furthermore, Palmer's editing experience seems slight, considering the length of his current tenure and the size of his staff, and while he demonstrates competence in the area of international business, he has little experience in the national business area.
>
> In light of these circumstances, the newspaper would meet its stated objectives best by promoting Laura to the position of business editor.

This generally well-reasoned and well-written essay would be an asset to any applicant's law school admissions file. The writer states his or her choice in the first sentence and then substantiates this choice in a paragraph on the winner and a paragraph on the loser. Notice the way this writer acknowledges, yet rebuts, the winner's flaws and the loser's strengths. Whether or not one agrees with the choice of Laura over Palmer, the essay definitely makes an organized, well-reasoned case for the choice–and that, after all, is what the law schools will be looking for.

KAPLAN EXCLUSIVE

It's a big mistake to leave the Writing Sample unfinished. Be strict with yourself, so that you'll have at least a few minutes left at the end to read over what you've written.

Do the two practice essays provided in the following pages. You'll find additional prompts and sample responses in your online syllabus. For even more practice, write Argument essays that critique your own Decision essays. This analysis will improve your skills for both essay types.

SUMMARY

The basic Writing Sample principles are:

- Use scrap paper to plan your essay.
- Don't obsess over your position.
- Get right to the point.
- Use a clear, simple essay format.
- Mention but downplay the opposing view.
- Don't simply repeat facts from the prompt.
- Write carefully.
- Budget your time wisely.

Kaplan's 4-Step Method for the Writing Sample

1. Prompt
2. Plan
3. Produce
4. Proofread

WRITING SAMPLE PRACTICE

Essay One

Directions: The scenario presented below describes two choices. In your essay, argue *for* one choice and *against* the other, based on the two specified criteria and the facts provided. There is no right or wrong answer.

Newlyweds Lauren and Michael Tompkins are moving to Centerville, a large city with an active downtown and a network of suburbs. Michael will be starting a new job at a prestigious investment-banking firm and Lauren will be attending graduate school. Keeping the following considerations in mind, write an argument supporting one of the two housing options described.

- The Tompkins have $20,000 in savings.
- The Tompkins are planning on starting a family in a few years.

The couple is considering buying a two-bedroom condo in a renovated building downtown. It is within walking distance of Michael's office and near other amenities like restaurants, clubs, museums, and movie theatres, but a trip to the supermarket will entail a long bus ride. Lauren will also have to ride the bus or take the train to the university, which is located in the suburb of Hillsdale. Should the couple buy a car, they will have to pay monthly for parking in the building. Their monthly mortgage and maintenance fees would be $1000, and the parking fee is an extra $200 per month.

The Tompkins are also considering renting a three-bedroom house with a driveway in historic Millston, a suburb adjacent to Hillsdale and about 30 minutes outside of the city. The house, though old, is in good condition and the landlord lives next door. There is a commuter rail station a few blocks from the house that runs both downtown and to the university in Hillsdale, though given the house's suburban location, a car be very useful. With the money they would have used for a down payment on the condo, the Tompkins could afford a new car. Millston also has excellent public schools. If the Tompkins sign a two-year lease, the rent including utilities will be $850 per month.

Sample Response

The Tompkins should buy the condo in downtown Centerville rather than rent the house in Millston. Given their $20,000 in savings, real estate will prove to be a better investment than a new car for this young couple. Even though the condo seems to cost more in the short run, in the long run it will more than pay for itself. Michael will likely be required to work long hours, whereas Lauren's schedule will be more flexible, making proximity to his job a priority. The Tompkins should take advantage of this time before they have children to live in the city and enjoy an urban lifestyle. Michael's job gives him excellent earning potential, so if Lauren finds the commute to her classes via public transportation to be too inconvenient, the couple will soon be able to afford a used car and the additional charge to park it in their building.

The suburban house would be a better choice if the Tompkins already had children. Its advantages (larger size, good schools) would be most appealing to a larger family. Since the Tompkins plan to wait a few years before having a child, these advantages are negated by the long commute for Michael and the lack of investment in the rental property. Even though a new car would be nice, it too makes more sense once the couple has kids. Although they would be paying less each month for the house, paying for a rental when they can afford to buy does not make good financial sense.

It would not be prudent for the Tompkins make living arrangements best suited to a family with children when their plans to have a baby are still several years off. In these few years, they may decide to move somewhere else entirely, in which case they will be able to make a profit on selling their condo rather than take a loss on the rental of the house.

Comments: This essay makes a good case for the writer's choice of the condo over the house. The writer states his or her opinion in the first sentence and then clearly emphasizes the strengths of the condo option in the first paragraph. The second paragraph acknowledges the attractions of the house, but convincingly argues that the condo is still a better choice for the Tompkins family. This is the kind of essay law schools will be looking for.

Essay Two

Directions: For this essay, you are presented with an argument that offers reasons for drawing a particular conclusion. In your essay, analyze and evaluate the writer's reasoning and use of evidence. For example, you might consider what questionable assumptions underlie the thinking and what alternative explanations or counterexamples might weaken the conclusion. You might discuss what sort of evidence would strengthen or refute the argument, what changes in the argument would make it more logically sound, and what, if anything, would help you better evaluate its conclusion.

The following appeared in a sportswriter's column in a local newspaper.

"In order to boost our baseball team's record and revenues, the owner of the Harrisford Hawks should spend more money on hiring the hottest free agents. Baseball clubs that offer annual salaries of over 10 million dollars to star players attract the best talent, producing teams that win championships. When the Salsbury Sharks signed Robby LaRose for 11 million dollars last year, they won the division championship. If we adopted a similar policy, the resulting rise in fan enthusiasm and ticket sales would more than make up for the expense. Increased media coverage of known "star" players would also spur fans' interest. Besides, our rivals are doing this already, and if we don't follow their lead we will never be in serious World Series contention."

Discuss how well-reasoned you find this argument.

SAMPLE RESPONSE

This writer asserts that by spending more money to hire renowned players, the owner of the Harrisford Hawks would increase the team's overall standing and profits. While his argument follows a logical structure, it is based on many assumptions and unsupported generalizations.

The author assumes, without offering support, that ball clubs that offer higher salaries produce winning teams. However, hiring one or two "star" players doesn't guarantee a cohesive team. Sometimes these individuals are most interested in personal glory, and they may not mesh well with the existing team.

Even if the team's record did improve after this type of acquisition, the team wouldn't necessarily win championships. Information about the current record of the Hawks would be relevant here, as a single excellent player can't make a mediocre team into champions. While the author offers an example of a rival team that won the division championship after paying a lot for a free agent, he implies but does not prove the cause-and-effect relationship. Perhaps the other team had a history of success.

The author also fails to support the assumption that revenue from increased ticket sales would cover the expense of hiring a star player. While fans are more likely to come see a winning team or a celebrated player, the owner still is taking a big risk by spending over 10 million dollars up front. It would strengthen the argument if he could show that the revenue of the Salsbury Sharks increased after the acquisition of Robby LaRose.

While hiring prominent players for high salaries may boost a team's performance and profits, this author makes too many assumptions and offers too little evidence to be convincing. The strategy is risky because one star does not guarantee a winning team, let alone one that is profitable. The author does not provide examples of equivalent teams that improved their records and revenue in this way.

Comments: The writer sums up the argument offered briefly, then gets right to the point about assumptions and generalizations. Each paragraph clearly develops one aspect of the argument's weakness, and the conclusion draws together all the points made. It's clear that this writer had a well-developed plan before she started to write. The language avoids any distracting errors, and draws intelligently on the vocabulary and skills learned in Logical Reasoning.

Chapter 7: **The Final Week**

Is it starting to feel like your whole life is a buildup to the LSAT? You've known about it for years, worried about it for months, and now spent weeks in solid preparation for it. As the test gets closer, you may find your anxiety is on the rise.

You shouldn't worry. After the preparation you've received from the Kaplan's LSAT Comprehensive Program, you're in good shape for the test. To calm any pretest jitters you may have, though, let's go over a few strategies for the days before the test.

THE WEEK BEFORE THE TEST

The week or so leading up to the test should be all about keeping up your skills but avoiding burnout and anxiety. You should do the following:

- Recheck your admission ticket for accuracy; if corrections are necessary, they must be made in writing.
- Practice getting up as early as you'll have to on test day and review test material, preferably your most recent Practice Tests.
- Visit the testing center if you haven't already. This is a good way to ensure that you don't get lost on the day of the test and know where to park. See the actual room where your test will be administered and take notice of little things—like the kind of desk you'll be working on, whether the room is likely to be hot or cold. Remember, you must be on time—the proctors won't wait for you and you won't be allowed in after testing has begun.

Practice Timing

Most test centers have a clock on the wall that the proctor will use to time the test, but don't take anything for granted—your test center may not (stranger things have been known to happen). You should definitely bring along your own timing device, such as a watch or a stopwatch, so long as it doesn't make any noise (devices that beep on the hour or sound an alarm at specified times are prohibited from the testing site). The LSAC specifically prohibits timing devices that have functions other than strictly telling time, so you should be careful in your selection.

 GO ONLINE

Print a copy of your downloadable Study Sheet to take with you on test day.

It's also best to practice using a timing routine that you'll follow during the real test. Some students find it helpful to set their watches at 25 past the hour for the scored sections, often 11:25. This way, they know that the section will end exactly when their watch says 12:00. Others reset their watches exactly on the hour at the beginning of each section, and know that every section will end thirty-five minutes later. Still others synchronize their watches with the room clock and follow the proctor's timing guidelines. It doesn't matter which procedure you adopt, or even if you come up with one of your own, just as long as you use it consistently, so that keeping track of time on test day is second nature.

THE DAY BEFORE THE TEST: AN LSAT SURVIVAL KIT

Avoid doing intensive studying the day before the test. There's little you can do to help yourself at this late date, and you may exhaust yourself and burn out.

Put together an "LSAT survival kit" containing the following items:

- Your admission ticket
- Appropriate photo ID
- A non-beeping timepiece
- Copy of a logic game you've already done (look it over to warm you up and boost confidence)
- A few No. 2 pencils (slightly dull points fill the ovals best)
- Pencil sharpener
- Eraser
- Aspirin, antacid, and tissues
- CD player or iPod
- Some water and high-energy, natural sugar snacks (apples, bananas, nuts, trail mix) for the break

Take the night off entirely. Go to see a movie or watch some TV. Try not to think about the test. Get to bed early.

THE DAY OF THE TEST

Get up early, leaving yourself plenty of time.

Read something to warm up your brain—you don't want the LSAT to be the first written material your brain tries to assimilate that day.

Dress in layers for maximum comfort; you'll be able to adjust to the testing room's temperature.

In traveling to the test center, leave yourself enough time for traffic and mass transit delays.

Be ready for a long day. Total testing time, remember, is three hours and 30 minutes. When you add the administrative paperwork before and after, and the 10- to 15-minute break in the middle, you're looking at an experience of four and a half to six hours.

Test Center Procedures

Don't get flustered when they fingerprint you and check your ID as you enter the testing room—this is standard operating procedure. The test administrators do this because occasionally they have reason to believe that some test takers are not exactly who they say they are. If you're on the up and up, you'll have nothing to worry about.

After the test booklets are handed out, and you've filled out all of the required information, the test will begin. Your proctor should write the starting and ending time of each section on a blackboard in front of the room, and will usually announce the time remaining at specified intervals, such as when there's ten minutes remaining, five minutes remaining, and one minute remaining.

Taking the Test

Here are some last-minute reminders to help guide your work on the test:

- Confidence is key. Accentuate the positives, and don't dwell on the negatives!
- Remember you can get a lot of questions wrong and still score high—so don't panic when faced with difficult material.
- Don't get bogged down in the middle of any section. At the end of every section are questions that may be really easy—get to them!
- Transfer your answers methodically; don't leave any answers blank. To ensure accuracy, say the question number and choice to yourself (silently, of course) as you grid.
- Give all five choices a fair shot in Logical Reasoning and Reading Comp, time permitting. For Logic Games, go with the objectively correct answer as soon as you find it.
- Don't be alarmed by extra-tough questions at the beginning, especially in Logical Reasoning. It happens. Skip past tough ones and come back to them later, making sure to circle them in the test booklet.
- Preview the Logic Games before you launch into them. The third or fourth game could be the easiest one. Skip over any Reading Comp passage that slows you down too much, and come back to it later.
- Don't try to figure out which section is unscored. It can't help you, and you may be wrong.

KAPLAN EXCLUSIVE

Don't forget your stress-management techniques during the test. Breathe deeply, stretch, and relax as needed. Imagine yourself succeeding.

Test Rhythm

Between sections 1 and 2, 2 and 3, and 4 and 5, the proctor will say only: "Time's up on this section. Go on to the next section."

Notice that there's no break here—you must go immediately from one section to the next. Also, if you finish a section early, you're not allowed to move on to another section. They're pretty strict about this one, so watch your step. If you have extra time, spend it looking back over your work on that section alone.

After section 3, you'll be instructed to close your test booklets and take a 10- to 15-minute break. Pay no attention to people's nervous chatter during the break. Some will say it's the hardest test since the dawn of time; others will say it's so easy they can't believe it. Either kind of comment can rattle you. Instead, put on your headphones and tune into your iPod's LSAT playlist or a favorite CD.

After the break, you'll return to the testing room for the remaining sections. Then, after section 5, your test materials will be collected, and the Writing Sample materials will be handed out.

KAPLAN EXCLUSIVE

During the break, avoid nervous chatter about how hard the test is or which section was experimental. Have a snack and listen to your CD player or iPod.

After the Writing Sample is collected, the test ends and you're free to get on with your life. For most of you, this means getting back to the rest of the application and admission process we will talk about in the section titled, "Getting into Law School." In the short term, however, this signals the beginning of a well-deserved night out to unwind.

AFTER THE TEST

Cancellation and Multiple Scores Policy

Unlike many things in life, the LSAT allows you a second chance. If you end the test feeling that you've really not done as well as you could have, you have the option of canceling your score. Canceling a test means that it won't be scored. It will just appear on your score report as a cancelled test. No one will know how well or poorly you really did—not even you.

How to Cancel

There are two ways you can cancel your score:

1. You can cancel your score immediately after the test, by blackening both bubbles on the Score Cancellation Section and signing your name to cerify the statement.
2. You can mail or fax the signed cancellation form to Law Services within nine calendar days of the test.

Kaplan strongly advises against cancelling your score immediately. There's no reason to rush this important decision. Moreover, answer-sheet cancellations are processed with the tests, so confirmation won't be received for 4–5 weeks; if the cancellation was not properly completed, you won't have any chance to correct the error.

When Should You Cancel

When deciding whether to cancel your score, a good rule of thumb is to make an honest assessment of whether you'll do better on the next test. Wishful thinking doesn't count; you need to have a valid reason to believe that the next time would be different. Remember, no test experience is going to be perfect. If you were distracted by the proctor's hacking cough this time around, next time you may be even more distracted by construction noise, or a cold, or the hideous lime-green sweater of the person sitting in front of you.

Two legitimate reasons to cancel your test are illness and personal circumstances that cause you to perform poorly on that particular day. Also, if you feel that you didn't prepare sufficiently, then it may be advisable to cancel your score and approach your test preparation a little more seriously the next time.

But keep in mind that test takers historically underestimate their performance, especially immediately following the test. They tend to forget about all of the things that went right and focus on everything that went wrong. So unless your performance is terribly marred by unforeseen circumstances, don't cancel your test immediately—at least sleep on the decision for one or two nights, and if you still feel you want to do it again, then send in the form. Just remember, cancellations are permanent. Once the form is sent, you can't change your mind.

What the Schools Will See

If you do cancel your test and then take it again for a score, your score report will indicate that you've canceled a previous score. Since it won't be scored, you don't have to worry about this score showing up on any subsequent score report. If you take more than one test without canceling, then all the scores will show up on each score report, so the law schools will see them all. Most law schools average LSAT scores, although there are a few exceptions. Check with individual schools for their policy on multiple scores.

POST-LSAT FESTIVITIES

After all the hard work you've done preparing for and taking the LSAT, you want to make sure you take time to celebrate afterwards. Plan to get together with friends the evening after the test. Relax, have fun, let loose. After all, you've got a lot to celebrate. You prepared for the test ahead of time. You did your best. You're going to get a good score.

So start thinking about all of the great parties you'll be attending at the law school of your choice.

GO ONLINE

Take the online survey to let us know how you did (and how well we prepared you)!

| PART THREE |

Real LSAT Practice Tests and Explanations

How to Calculate Your Score

Step 1

For each practice test add together your total number correct for all four sections. This is your raw score.

Section I (# correct) ______

Section II (# correct) ______

Section III (# correct) ______

Section IV (# correct) ______

Total Correct (raw score) ______

Step 2

Find your raw score on the table below and read across to find your scaled score and your percentile.

Raw Score	Scaled Score	Percentile Rank	Raw Score	Scaled Score	Percentile Rank	Raw Score	Scaled Score	Percentile Rank
0	120	0	34	138	9	68	157	70
1	120	0	35	138	9	69	158	70
2	120	0	36	139	10	70	158	74
3	120	0	37	140	13	71	159	77
4	120	0	38	140	13	72	160	77
5	120	0	39	140	13	73	160	80
6	120	0	40	141	15	74	161	80
7	120	0	41	142	17	75	162	83
8	121	0	42	142	17	76	162	83
9	122	0	43	143	20	77	163	86
10	122	0	44	144	23	78	164	88
11	123	0	45	144	23	79	164	88
12	124	0	46	144	23	80	165	88
13	124	0	47	145	26	81	166	90
14	125	0	48	146	29	82	166	92
15	126	1	49	146	29	83	167	92
16	126	1	50	147	33	84	168	93
17	127	1	51	147	33	85	168	95
18	128	1	52	148	37	86	169	95
19	129	1	53	148	37	87	170	96
20	130	2	54	149	41	88	171	96
21	130	2	55	150	45	89	172	97
22	130	2	56	150	45	90	173	97
23	131	2	57	150	45	91	174	98
24	132	3	58	151	50	92	174	98
25	133	3	59	151	50	93	175	98
26	133	3	60	152	54	94	176	99
27	133	3	61	153	58	95	177	99
28	134	4	62	154	58	96	178	99
29	135	5	63	154	58	97	179	99
30	136	6	64	155	62	98	180	99
31	136	6	65	155	66	99	180	99
32	137	8	66	156	66	100	180	99
33	137	8	67	157	70	101	180	99

Practice Test 1

Practice Test 1

Section I: **Logical Reasoning**

Time—35 minutes
25 questions

Directions: The questions in this section are based on the reasoning contained in brief statements or passages. For some questions, more than one of the choices could conceivably answer the question. However, you are to choose the best answer; that is, the response that most accurately and completely answers the question. You should not make assumptions that are by commonsense standards implausible, superfluous, or incompatible with the passage. After you have chosen the best answer, blacken the corresponding space on your answer sheet.

1. Before the printing press, books could be purchased only in expensive manuscript copies. The printing press produced books that were significantly less expensive than the manuscript editions. The public's demand for printed books in the first years after the invention of the printing press was many times greater than demand had been for manuscript copies. This increase demonstrates that there was a dramatic jump in the number of people who learned how to read in the years after publishers first started producing books on the printing press.

   Which one of the following statements, if true, casts doubt on the argument?

   (A) During the first years after the invention of the printing press, letter writing by people who wrote without the assistance of scribes or clerks exhibited a dramatic increase.

   (B) Books produced on the printing press are often found with written comments in the margins in the handwriting of the people who owned the books.

   (C) In the first years after the printing press was invented, printed books were purchased primarily by people who had always bought and read expensive manuscripts but could afford a greater number of printed books for the same money.

   (D) Books that were printed on the printing press in the first years after its invention often circulated among friends in informal reading clubs or libraries.

   (E) The first printed books published after the invention of the printing press would have been useless to illiterate people, since the books had virtually no illustrations.

2. Bevex, an artificial sweetener used only in soft drinks, is carcinogenic for mice, but only when it is consumed in very large quantities. To ingest an amount of Bevex equivalent to the amount fed to the mice in the relevant studies, a person would have to drink 25 cans of Bevex-sweetened soft drinks per day. For that reason, Bevex is in fact safe for people.

   In order for the conclusion that Bevex is safe for people to be properly drawn, which one of the following must be true?

   (A) Cancer from carcinogenic substances develops more slowly in mice than it does in people.

   (B) If all food additives that are currently used in foods were tested, some would be found to be carcinogenic for mice.

   (C) People drink fewer than 25 cans of Bevex-sweetened soda per day.

   (D) People can obtain important health benefits by controlling their weight through the use of artificially sweetened soft drinks.

   (E) Some of the studies done on Bevex were not relevant to the question of whether or not Bevex is carcinogenic for people.

3. Harry: Airlines have made it possible for anyone to travel around the world in much less time than was formerly possible.

   Judith: That is not true. Many flights are too expensive for all but the rich.

   Judith's response shows that she interprets Harry's statement to imply that

   (A) the majority of people are rich

   (B) everyone has an equal right to experience world travel

   (C) world travel is only possible via routes serviced by airlines

   (D) most forms of world travel are not affordable for most people

   (E) anyone can afford to travel long distances by air

GO ON TO THE NEXT PAGE.

4. Nutritionists have recommended that people eat more fiber. Advertisements for a new fiber-supplement pill state only that it contains "44 percent fiber."

The advertising claim is misleading in its selection of information on which to focus if which one of the following is true?

(A) There are other products on the market that are advertised as providing fiber as a dietary supplement.

(B) Nutritionists base their recommendation on medical findings that dietary fiber protects against some kinds of cancer.

(C) It is possible to become addicted to some kinds of advertised pills, such as sleeping pills and painkillers.

(D) The label of the advertised product recommends taking three pills every day.

(E) The recommended daily intake of fiber is 20 to 30 grams, and the pill contains one-third gram.

5. Many environmentalists have urged environmental awareness on consumers, saying that if we accept moral responsibility for our effects on the environment, then products that directly or indirectly harm the environment ought to be avoided. Unfortunately it is usually impossible for consumers to assess the environmental impact of a product, and thus impossible for them to consciously restrict their purchases to environmentally benign products. Because of this impossibility there can be no moral duty to choose products in the way these environmentalists urge, since ______.

Which one of the following principles provides the most appropriate completion for the argument?

(A) a moral duty to perform an action is never based solely on the effects the action will have on other people

(B) a person cannot possibly have a moral duty to do what he or she is unable to do

(C) moral considerations should not be the sole determinants of what products are made available to consumers

(D) the morally right action is always the one whose effects produce the least total harm

(E) where a moral duty exists, it supersedes any legal duty and any other kind of duty

6. Advertisement: Anyone who exercises knows from firsthand experience that exercise leads to better performance of such physical organs as the heart and the lungs, as well as to improvement in muscle tone. And since your brain is a physical organ, your actions can improve its performance, too. Act now. Subscribe to *Stimulus*: read the magazine that exercises your brain.

The advertisement employs which one of the following argumentative strategies?

(A) It cites experimental evidence that subscribing to the product being advertised has desirable consequences.

(B) It ridicules people who do not subscribe to *Stimulus* by suggesting that they do not believe that exercise will improve brain capacity.

(C) It explains the process by which the product being advertised brings about the result claimed for its use.

(D) It supports its recommendation by a careful analysis of the concept of exercise.

(E) It implies that brains and muscle are similar in one respect because they are similar in another respect.

GO ON TO THE NEXT PAGE.

Questions 7–8

Coherent solutions for the problem of reducing health-care costs cannot be found within the current piecemeal system of paying these costs. The reason is that this system gives health-care providers and insurers every incentive to shift, wherever possible, the costs of treating illness onto each other or any other party, including the patient. That clearly is the lesson of the various reforms of the 1980s: push in on one part of this pliable spending balloon and an equally expensive bulge pops up elsewhere. For example, when the government health-care insurance program for the poor cut costs by disallowing payments for some visits to physicians, patients with advanced illness later presented themselves at hospital emergency rooms in increased numbers.

7. The argument proceeds by
   (A) showing that shifting costs onto the patient contradicts the premise of health-care reimbursement
   (B) attributing without justification fraudulent intent to people
   (C) employing an analogy to characterize interrelationships
   (D) denying the possibility of a solution by disparaging each possible alternative system
   (E) demonstrating that cooperation is feasible by citing an instance

8. The argument provides the most support for which one of the following?
   (A) Under the conditions in which the current system operates, the overall volume of health-care costs could be shrunk, if at all, only by a comprehensive approach.
   (B) Relative to the resources available for health-care funding, the income of the higher-paid health-care professionals is too high.
   (C) Health-care costs are expanding to meet additional funds that have been made available for them.
   (D) Advances in medical technology have raised the expected standards of medical care but have proved expensive.
   (E) Since unfilled hospital beds contribute to overhead charges on each patient's bill, it would be unwise to hold unused hospital capacity in reserve for large-scale emergencies.

9. The commercial news media emphasize exceptional events such as airplane crashes at the expense of those such as automobile accidents, which occur far more frequently and represent a far greater risk to the public. Yet the public tends to interpret the degree of emphasis the news media give to these occurrences as indicating the degree of risk they represent.

   If the statements above are true, which one of the following conclusions is most strongly supported by them?
   (A) Print media, such as newspapers and magazines, are a better source of information than are broadcast media.
   (B) The emphasis given in the commercial news media to major catastrophes is dictated by the public's taste for the extraordinary.
   (C) Events over which people feel they have no control are generally perceived as more dangerous than those which people feel they can avert or avoid.
   (D) Where commercial news media constitute the dominant source of information, public perception of risk does not reflect actual risk.
   (E) A massive outbreak of cholera will be covered more extensively by the news media than will the occurrence of a rarer but less serious disease.

10. A large group of hyperactive children whose regular diets included food containing large amounts of additives was observed by researchers trained to assess the presence or absence of behavior problems. The children were then placed on a low-additive diet for several weeks, after which they were observed again. Originally nearly 60 percent of the children exhibited behavior problems; after the change in diet, only 30 percent did so. On the basis of these data, it can be concluded that food additives can contribute to behavior problems in hyperactive children.

    The evidence cited fails to establish the conclusion because
    (A) there is no evidence that the reduction in behavior problems was proportionate to the reduction in food-additive intake
    (B) there is no way to know what changes would have occurred without the change of diet, since only children who changed to a low-additive diet were studied
    (C) exactly how many children exhibited behavior problems after the change in diet cannot be determined, since the size of the group studied is not precisely given
    (D) there is no evidence that the behavior of some of the children was unaffected by additives
    (E) the evidence is consistent with the claim that some children exhibit more frequent behavior problems after being on the low-additive diet than they had exhibited when first observed

GO ON TO THE NEXT PAGE.

11. In 1990 major engine repairs were performed on 10 percent of the cars that had been built by the National Motor Company in the 1970s and that were still registered. However, the corresponding figure for the cars that the National Motor Company had manufactured in the 1960s was only five percent.

Which one of the following, if true, most helps to explain the discrepancy?

(A) Government motor vehicle regulations generally require all cars, whether old or new, to be inspected for emission levels prior to registration.

(B) Owners of new cars tend to drive their cars more carefully than do owners of old cars.

(C) The older a car is, the more likely it is to be discarded for scrap rather than repaired when major engine work is needed to keep the car in operation.

(D) The cars that the National Motor Company built in the 1970s incorporated simplified engine designs that made the engines less complicated than those of earlier models.

(E) Many of the repairs that were performed on the cars that the National Motor Company built in the 1960s could have been avoided if periodic routine maintenance had been performed.

12. No mathematician today would flatly refuse to accept the results of an enormous computation as an adequate demonstration of the truth of a theorem. In 1976, however, this was not the case. Some mathematicians at that time refused to accept the results of a complex computer demonstration of a very simple mapping theorem. Although some mathematicians still hold a strong belief that a simple theorem ought to have a short, simple proof, in fact, some simple theorems have required enormous proofs.

If all of the statements in the passage are true, which one of the following must also be true?

(A) Today, some mathematicians who believe that a simple theorem ought to have a simple proof would consider accepting the results of an enormous computation as a demonstration of the truth of a theorem.

(B) Some individuals who believe that a simple theorem ought to have a simple proof are not mathematicians.

(C) Today, some individuals who refuse to accept the results of an enormous computation as a demonstration of the truth of a theorem believe that a simple theorem ought to have a simple proof.

(D) Some individuals who do not believe that a simple theorem ought to have a simple proof would not be willing to accept the results of an enormous computation as proof of a complex theorem.

(E) Some nonmathematicians do not believe that a simple theorem ought to have a simple proof.

13. If you climb mountains, you will not live to a ripe old age. But you will be bored unless you climb mountains. Therefore, if you live to a ripe old age, you will have been bored.

Which one of the following most closely parallels the reasoning in the argument above?

(A) If you do not try to swim, you will not learn how to swim. But you will not be safe in boats if you do not learn how to swim. Therefore, you must try to swim.

(B) If you do not play golf, you will not enjoy the weekend. But you will be tired next week unless you relax during the weekend. Therefore, to enjoy the weekend, you will have to relax by playing golf.

(C) If you work for your candidate, you will not improve your guitar playing. But you will neglect your civic duty unless you work for your candidate. Therefore, if you improve your guitar playing, you will have neglected your civic duty.

(D) If you do not train, you will not be a good athlete. But you will become exhausted easily unless you train. Therefore, if you train, you will not have become exhausted easily.

(E) If you spend all of your money, you will not become wealthy. But you will become hungry unless you spend all of your money. Therefore, if you become wealthy, you will not become hungry.

14. Marine biologists had hypothesized that lobsters kept together in lobster traps eat one another in response to hunger. Periodic checking of lobster traps, however, has revealed instances of lobsters sharing traps together for weeks. Eight lobsters even shared one trap together for two months without eating one another. The marine biologists' hypothesis, therefore, is clearly wrong.

The argument against the marine biologists' hypothesis is based on which one of the following assumptions?

(A) Lobsters not caught in lobster traps have been observed eating one another.

(B) Two months is the longest known period during which eight or more lobsters have been trapped together.

(C) It is unusual to find as many as eight lobsters caught together in one single trap.

(D) Members of other marine species sometimes eat their own kind when no other food sources are available.

(E) Any food that the eight lobsters in the trap might have obtained was not enough to ward off hunger.

GO ON TO THE NEXT PAGE.

15. Eight years ago hunting was banned in Greenfield County on the grounds that hunting endangers public safety. Now the deer population in the county is six times what it was before the ban. Deer are invading residential areas, damaging property, and causing motor vehicle accidents that result in serious injury to motorists. Since there were never any hunting-related injuries in the county, clearly the ban was not only unnecessary but has created a danger to public safety that would not otherwise exist.

Which one of the following, if true, provides the strongest additional support for the conclusion above?

(A) In surrounding counties, where hunting is permitted, the size of the deer population has not increased in the last eight years.

(B) Motor vehicle accidents involving deer often result in damage to the vehicle, injury to the motorist, or both.

(C) When deer populations increase beyond optimal size, disease and malnutrition become more widespread among the deer herds.

(D) In residential areas in the county, many residents provide food and salt for deer.

(E) Deer can cause extensive damage to ornamental shrubs and trees by chewing on twigs and saplings.

16. Comets do not give off their own light but reflect light from other sources, such as the Sun. Scientists estimate the mass of comets by their brightness: the greater a comet's mass, the more light that comet will reflect. A satellite probe, however, has revealed that the material of which Halley's comet is composed reflects 60 times less light per unit of mass than had been previously thought.

The statements above, if true, give the most support to which one of the following?

(A) Some comets are composed of material that reflects 60 times more light per unit of mass than the material of which Halley's comet is composed.

(B) Previous estimates of the mass of Halley's comet which were based on its brightness were too low.

(C) The total amount of light reflected from Halley's comet is less than scientists had previously thought.

(D) The reflective properties of the material of which comets are composed vary considerably from comet to comet.

(E) Scientists need more information before they can make a good estimate of the mass of Halley's comet.

17. Office manager: I will not order recycled paper for this office. Our letters to clients must make a good impression, so we cannot print them on inferior paper.

Stationery supplier: Recycled paper is not necessarily inferior. In fact, from the beginning, the finest paper has been made of recycled material. It was only in the 1850s that paper began to be made from wood fiber, and then only because there were no longer enough rags to meet the demand for paper.

In which one of the following ways does the stationer's response fail to address the office manager's objection to recycled paper?

(A) It does not recognize that the office manager's prejudice against recycled paper stems from ignorance.

(B) It uses irrelevant facts to justify a claim about the quality of the disputed product.

(C) It assumes that the office manager is concerned about environmental issues.

(D) It presupposes that the office manager understands the basic technology of paper manufacturing.

(E) It ignores the office manager's legitimate concern about quality.

GO ON TO THE NEXT PAGE.

Questions 18–19

When Alicia Green borrowed a neighbor's car without permission, the police merely gave her a warning. However, when Peter Foster did the same thing, he was charged with automobile theft. Peter came to the attention of the police because the car he was driving was hit by a speeding taxi. Alicia was stopped because the car she was driving had defective taillights. It is true that the car Peter took got damaged and the car Alicia took did not, but since it was the taxi that caused the damage this difference was not due to any difference in the blameworthiness of their behavior. Therefore Alicia should also have been charged with automobile theft.

18. The statement that the car Peter took got damaged and the car Alicia took did not plays which one of the following roles in the argument?
    (A) It presents a reason that directly supports the conclusion.
    (B) It justifies the difference in the actual outcome in the two cases.
    (C) It demonstrates awareness of a fact on which a possible objection might be based.
    (D) It illustrates a general principle on which the argument relies.
    (E) It summarizes a position against which the argument is directed.

19. If all of the claims offered in support of the conclusion are accurate, each of the following could be true EXCEPT:
    (A) The interests of justice would have been better served if the police had released Peter Foster with a warning.
    (B) Alicia Green had never before driven a car belonging to someone else without first securing the owner's permission.
    (C) Peter Foster was hit by the taxi while he was running a red light, whereas Alicia Green drove with extra care to avoid drawing the attention of the police to the car she had taken.
    (D) Alicia Green barely missed hitting a pedestrian when she sped through a red light ten minutes before she was stopped by the police for driving a car that had defective taillights.
    (E) Peter Foster had been cited for speeding twice in the preceding month, whereas Alicia Green had never been cited for a traffic violation.

20. According to sources who can be expected to know, Dr. Maria Esposito is going to run in the mayoral election. But if Dr. Esposito runs, Jerome Krasman will certainly not run against her. Therefore Dr. Esposito will be the only candidate in the election.

    The flawed reasoning in the argument above most closely parallels that in which one of the following?
    (A) According to its management, Brown's Stores will move next year. Without Brown's being present, no new large store can be attracted to the downtown area. Therefore the downtown area will no longer be viable as a shopping district.
    (B) The press release says that the rock group Rollercoaster is playing a concert on Saturday. It won't be playing on Friday if it plays on Saturday. So Saturday will be the only day this week on which Rollercoaster will perform.
    (C) Joshua says the interviewing panel was impressed by Marilyn. But if they were impressed by Marilyn, they probably thought less of Sven. Joshua is probably right, and so Sven will probably not get the job.
    (D) An informant says that Rustimann was involved in the bank robbery. If Rustimann was involved, Jones was certainly not involved. Since these two are the only people who could have been involved, Rustimann is the only person the police need to arrest.
    (E) The review said that this book is the best one for beginners at programming. If this book is the best, that other one can't be as good. So this one is the book we should buy.

GO ON TO THE NEXT PAGE.

21. The initial causes of serious accidents at nuclear power plants have not so far been flaws in the advanced-technology portion of the plants. Rather, the initial causes have been attributed to human error, as when a worker at the Browns Mills reactor in the United States dropped a candle and started a fire, or to flaws in the plumbing, exemplified in a recent incident in Japan. Such everyday events cannot be thought unlikely to occur over the long run.

Which one of the following is most strongly supported by the statements above?

(A) Now that nuclear power generation has become a part of everyday life, an ever-increasing yearly incidence of serious accidents at the plants can be expected.
(B) If nuclear power plants continue in operation, a serious accident at such a plant is not improbable.
(C) The likelihood of human error at the operating consoles of nuclear power generators cannot be lessened by thoughtful design of dials, switches, and displays.
(D) The design of nuclear power plants attempts to compensate for possible failures of the materials used in their construction.
(E) No serious accident will be caused in the future by some flaw in the advanced-technology portion of a nuclear power plant.

22. There is a widespread belief that people can predict impending earthquakes from unusual animal behavior. Skeptics claim that this belief is based on selective coincidence: people whose dogs behaved oddly just before an earthquake will be especially likely to remember that fact. At any given time, the skeptics say, some of the world's dogs will be behaving oddly.

Clarification of which one of the following issues would be most important to an evaluation of the skeptics' position?

(A) Which is larger, the number of skeptics or the number of people who believe that animal behavior can foreshadow earthquakes?
(B) Are there means other than the observation of animal behavior that nonscientists can use to predict earthquakes?
(C) Are there animals about whose behavior people know too little to be able to distinguish unusual from everyday behavior?
(D) Are the sorts of behavior supposedly predictive of earthquakes as pronounced in dogs as they are in other animals?
(E) Is the animal behavior supposedly predictive of earthquakes specific to impending earthquakes or can it be any kind of unusual behavior?

23. Defendants who can afford expensive private defense lawyers have a lower conviction rate than those who rely on court-appointed public defenders. This explains why criminals who commit lucrative crimes like embezzlement or insider trading are more successful at avoiding conviction than are street criminals.

The explanation offered above would be more persuasive if which one of the following were true?

(A) Many street crimes, such as drug dealing, are extremely lucrative and those committing them can afford expensive private lawyers.
(B) Most prosecutors are not competent to handle cases involving highly technical financial evidence and have more success in prosecuting cases of robbery or simple assault.
(C) The number of criminals convicted of street crimes is far greater than the number of criminals convicted of embezzlement or insider trading.
(D) The percentage of defendants who actually committed the crimes of which they are accused is no greater for publicly defended than for privately defended defendants.
(E) Juries, out of sympathy for the victims of crimes, are much more likely to convict defendants accused of violent crimes than they are to convict defendants accused of "victimless" crimes or crimes against property.

GO ON TO THE NEXT PAGE.

24. Many major scientific discoveries of the past were the product of serendipity, the chance discovery of valuable findings that investigators had not purposely sought. Now, however, scientific research tends to be so costly that investigators are heavily dependent on large grants to fund their research. Because such grants require investigators to provide the grant sponsors with clear projections of the outcome of the proposed research, investigators ignore anything that does not directly bear on the funded research. Therefore, under the prevailing circumstances, serendipity can no longer play a role in scientific discovery.

Which one of the following is an assumption on which the argument depends?

(A) Only findings that an investigator purposely seeks can directly bear on that investigator's research.

(B) In the past few scientific investigators attempted to make clear predictions of the outcome of their research.

(C) Dependence on large grants is preventing investigators from conducting the type of scientific research that those investigators would personally prefer.

(D) All scientific investigators who provide grant sponsors with clear projections of the outcome of their research receive at least some of the grants for which they apply.

(E) In general the most valuable scientific discoveries are the product of serendipity.

25. Police statistics have shown that automobile antitheft devices reduce the risk of car theft, but a statistical study of automobile theft by the automobile insurance industry claims that cars equipped with antitheft devices are, paradoxically, more likely to be stolen than cars that are not so equipped.

Which one of the following, if true, does the most to resolve the apparent paradox?

(A) Owners of stolen cars almost invariably report the theft immediately to the police but tend to delay notifying their insurance company, in the hope that the vehicle will be recovered.

(B) Most cars that are stolen are not equipped with antitheft devices, and most cars that are equipped with antitheft devices are not stolen.

(C) The most common automobile antitheft devices are audible alarms, which typically produce ten false alarms for every actual attempted theft.

(D) Automobile owners who have particularly theft-prone cars and live in areas of greatest incidence of car theft are those who are most likely to have antitheft devices installed.

(E) Most automobile thefts are the work of professional thieves against whose efforts antitheft devices offer scant protection.

STOP

IF YOU FINISH BEFORE TIME IS CALLED, YOU MAY CHECK YOUR WORK ON THIS SECTION ONLY. DO NOT WORK ON ANY OTHER SECTION IN THE TEST.

Practice Test 1

Section II: Analytical Reasoning

Time—35 minutes
24 questions

Directions: Each group of questions in this section is based on a set of conditions. In answering some of the questions, it may be useful to draw a rough diagram. Choose the response that most accurately and completely answers each question and blacken the corresponding space on your answer sheet.

Questions 1–7

Seven consecutive time slots for a broadcast, numbered in chronological order 1 through 7, will be filled by six song tapes—G, H, L, O, P, S—and exactly one news tape. Each tape is to be assigned to a different time slot, and no tape is longer than any other tape. The broadcast is subject to the following restrictions:

L must be played immediately before O.
The news tape must be played at some time after L.
There must be exactly two time slots between G and P, regardless of whether G comes before P or whether G comes after P.

1. If G is played second, which one of the following tapes must be played third?
   (A) the news
   (B) H
   (C) L
   (D) O
   (E) S

2. The news tape can be played in any one of the following time slots EXCEPT the
   (A) second
   (B) third
   (C) fourth
   (D) fifth
   (E) sixth

3. If H and S are to be scheduled as far from each other as possible, then the first, the second, and the third time slots could be filled, respectively, by
   (A) G, H, and L
   (B) S, G, and the news
   (C) H, G, and L
   (D) H, L, and O
   (E) L, O, and S

4. If P is played fifth, L must be played
   (A) first
   (B) second
   (C) third
   (D) fourth
   (E) sixth

5. What is the maximum number of tapes that can separate S from the news?
   (A) 1
   (B) 2
   (C) 3
   (D) 4
   (E) 5

6. Which one of the following is the latest time slot in which L can be played?
   (A) the third
   (B) the fourth
   (C) the fifth
   (D) the sixth
   (E) the seventh

7. The time slot in which O must be played is completely determined if G is assigned to which one of the following time slots?
   (A) the first
   (B) the third
   (C) the fourth
   (D) the fifth
   (E) the sixth

GO ON TO THE NEXT PAGE.

Questions 8–12

Doctor Yamata works only on Mondays, Tuesdays, Wednesdays, Fridays, and Saturdays. She performs four different activities—lecturing, operating, treating patients, and conducting research. Each working day she performs exactly one activity in the morning and exactly one activity in the afternoon. During each week her work schedule must satisfy the following restrictions:

She performs operations on exactly three mornings.

If she operates on Monday, she does not operate on Tuesday.

She lectures in the afternoon on exactly two consecutive calendar days.

She treats patients on exactly one morning and exactly three afternoons.

She conducts research on exactly one morning.

On Saturday she neither lectures nor performs operations.

8. Which one of the following must be a day on which Doctor Yamata lectures?
   (A) Monday
   (B) Tuesday
   (C) Wednesday
   (D) Friday
   (E) Saturday

9. On Wednesday Doctor Yamata could be scheduled to
   (A) conduct research in the morning and operate in the afternoon
   (B) lecture in the morning and treat patients in the afternoon
   (C) operate in the morning and lecture in the afternoon
   (D) operate in the morning and conduct research in the afternoon
   (E) treat patients in the morning and treat patients in the afternoon

10. Which one of the following statements must be true?
    (A) There is one day on which the doctor treats patients both in the morning and in the afternoon.
    (B) The doctor conducts research on one of the days on which she lectures.
    (C) The doctor conducts research on one of the days on which she treats patients.
    (D) The doctor lectures on one of the days on which she treats patients.
    (E) The doctor lectures on one of the days on which she operates.

11. If Doctor Yamata operates on Tuesday, then her schedule for treating patients could be
    (A) Monday morning, Monday afternoon, Friday morning, Friday afternoon
    (B) Monday morning, Friday afternoon, Saturday morning, Saturday afternoon
    (C) Monday afternoon, Wednesday morning, Wednesday afternoon, Saturday afternoon
    (D) Wednesday morning, Wednesday afternoon, Friday afternoon, Saturday afternoon
    (E) Wednesday afternoon, Friday afternoon, Saturday morning, Saturday afternoon

12. Which one of the following is a pair of days on both of which Doctor Yamata must treat patients?
    (A) Monday and Tuesday
    (B) Monday and Saturday
    (C) Tuesday and Friday
    (D) Tuesday and Saturday
    (E) Friday and Saturday

GO ON TO THE NEXT PAGE.

Questions 13–18

Each of seven judges voted for or else against granting Datalog Corporation's petition. Each judge is categorized as conservative, moderate, or liberal, and no judge is assigned more than one of those labels. Two judges are conservatives, two are moderates, and three are liberals. The following is known about how the judges voted:

If the two conservatives and at least one liberal voted the same way as each other, then both moderates voted that way.

If the three liberals voted the same way as each other, then no conservative voted that way.

At least two of the judges voted for Datalog, and at least two voted against Datalog.

At least one conservative voted against Datalog.

13. If the two moderates did not vote the same way as each other, then which one of the following could be true?
    (A) No conservative and exactly two liberals voted for Datalog.
    (B) Exactly one conservative and exactly one liberal voted for Datalog.
    (C) Exactly one conservative and all three liberals voted for Datalog.
    (D) Exactly two conservatives and exactly one liberal voted for Datalog.
    (E) Exactly two conservatives and exactly two liberals voted for Datalog.

14. Which one of the following must be true?
    (A) At least one conservative voted for Datalog.
    (B) At least one liberal voted against Datalog.
    (C) At least one liberal voted for Datalog.
    (D) At least one moderate voted against Datalog.
    (E) At least one moderate voted for Datalog.

15. If the three liberals all voted the same way as each other, which one of the following must be true?
    (A) Both moderates voted for Datalog.
    (B) Both moderates voted against Datalog.
    (C) One conservative voted for Datalog and one conservative voted against Datalog.
    (D) One moderate voted for Datalog and one moderate voted against Datalog.
    (E) All three liberals voted for Datalog.

16. If exactly two judges voted against Datalog, then which one of the following must be true?
    (A) Both moderates voted for Datalog.
    (B) Exactly one conservative voted for Datalog.
    (C) No conservative voted for Datalog.
    (D) Exactly two liberals voted for Datalog.
    (E) Exactly three liberals voted for Datalog.

17. Each of the following could be a complete and accurate list of those judges who voted for Datalog EXCEPT
    (A) two liberals
    (B) one conservative, one liberal
    (C) two moderates, three liberals
    (D) one conservative, two moderates, two liberals
    (E) one conservative, two moderates, three liberals

18. If the two conservatives voted the same way as each other, but the liberals did not all vote the same way as each other, then each of the following must be true EXCEPT:
    (A) Both conservatives voted against Datalog.
    (B) Both moderates voted for Datalog.
    (C) At least one liberal voted against Datalog.
    (D) Exactly two liberals voted for Datalog.
    (E) Exactly five of the judges voted against Datalog.

GO ON TO THE NEXT PAGE.

Questions 19–24

An official is assigning five runners—Larry, Ned, Olivia, Patricia, and Sonja—to parallel lanes numbered consecutively 1 through 5. The official will also assign each runner to represent a different charity—F, G, H, J, and K—not necessarily in order of the runner's names as given. The following ordering restrictions apply:

The runner representing K is assigned to lane 4.
Patricia is assigned to the only lane between the lanes of the runners representing F and G.
There are exactly two lanes between Olivia's lane and the lane of the runner representing G.
Sonja is assigned to a higher-numbered lane than the lane to which Ned is assigned.

19. Which one of the following is a possible assignment of runners to lanes by the charity they represent?

	1	2	3	4	5
(A)	F	G	H	K	J
(B)	G	H	J	K	F
(C)	G	K	F	J	H
(D)	H	J	G	K	F
(E)	J	H	F	K	G

20. The lane to which Patricia is assigned must be a lane that is
(A) next to the lane to which Larry is assigned
(B) next to the lane to which Ned is assigned
(C) separated by exactly one lane from the lane to which Ned is assigned
(D) separated by exactly one lane from the lane to which Olivia is assigned
(E) separated by exactly one lane from the lane to which Sonja is assigned

21. If Olivia is assigned to lane 2, which one of the following assignments must be made?

	Charity	Lane
(A)	F	1
(B)	G	5
(C)	H	1
(D)	H	3
(E)	J	5

22. Which one of the following is a complete and accurate list of runners each of whom could be the runner representing F?
(A) Larry, Ned
(B) Patricia, Sonja
(C) Larry, Ned, Olivia
(D) Larry, Ned, Sonja
(E) Ned, Patricia, Sonja

23. If Ned is the runner representing J, then it must be true that
(A) the runner representing G is assigned to lane 1
(B) the runner representing H is assigned to lane 2
(C) Larry is the runner representing K
(D) Olivia is the runner representing F
(E) Patricia is the runner representing H

24. If Larry represents J, which one of the following could be the assignment of runners to lanes?

	1	2	3	4	5
(A)	Larry	Olivia	Ned	Patricia	Sonja
(B)	Larry	Ned	Olivia	Sonja	Patricia
(C)	Larry	Sonja	Patricia	Ned	Olivia
(D)	Ned	Olivia	Larry	Patricia	Sonja
(E)	Ned	Sonja	Olivia	Patricia	Larry

STOP

IF YOU FINISH BEFORE TIME IS CALLED, YOU MAY CHECK YOUR WORK ON THIS SECTION ONLY. DO NOT WORK ON ANY OTHER SECTION IN THE TEST.

Practice Test 1

Section III: **Reading Comprehension**

Time—35 minutes
27 Questions

Directions: Each passage in this section is followed by a group of questions to be answered on the basis of what is <u>stated</u> or <u>implied</u> in the passage. For some of the questions, more than one of the choices could conceivably answer the question. However, you are to choose the <u>best</u> answer; that is, the response that most accurately and completely answers the question, and blacken the corresponding space on your answer sheet.

The labor force is often organized as if workers had no family responsibilities. Preschool-age children need full-time care; children in primary school need care after school and during school vacations. Although day-care services can resolve some scheduling conflicts between home and office, workers cannot always find or afford suitable care. Even when they obtain such care, parents must still cope with emergencies, such as illnesses, that keep children at home. Moreover, children need more than tending; they also need meaningful time with their parents. Conventional full-time workdays, especially when combined with unavoidable household duties, are too inflexible for parents with primary child-care responsibility.

Although a small but increasing number of working men are single parents, those barriers against successful participation in the labor market that are related to primary child-care responsibilities mainly disadvantage women. Even in families where both parents work, cultural pressures are traditionally much greater on mothers than on fathers to bear the primary child-rearing responsibilities.

In reconciling child-rearing responsibilities with participation in the labor market, many working mothers are forced to make compromises. For example, approximately one-third of all working mothers are employed only part-time, even though part-time jobs are dramatically underpaid and often less desirable in comparison to full-time employment. Even though part-time work is usually available only in occupations offering minimal employee responsibility and little opportunity for advancement or self-enrichment, such employment does allow many women the time and flexibility to fulfill their family duties, but only at the expense of the advantages associated with full-time employment.

Moreover, even mothers with full-time employment must compromise opportunities in order to adjust to barriers against parents in the labor market. Many choose jobs entailing little challenge or responsibility or those offering flexible scheduling, often available only in poorly paid positions, while other working mothers, although willing and able to assume as much responsibility as people without children, find that their need to spend regular and predictable time with their children inevitably causes them to lose career opportunities to those without such demands. Thus, women in education are more likely to become teachers than school administrators, whose more conventional full-time work schedules do not correspond to the schedules of school-age children, while female lawyers are more likely to practice law in trusts and estates, where they can control their work schedules, than in litigation, where they cannot. Nonprofessional women are concentrated in secretarial work and department store sales, where their absences can be covered easily by substitutes and where they can enter and leave the work force with little loss, since the jobs offer so little personal gain. Indeed, as long as the labor market remains hostile to parents, and family roles continue to be allocated on the basis of gender, women will be seriously disadvantaged in that labor market.

1. Which one of the following best summarizes the main idea of the passage?
   (A) Current trends in the labor force indicate that working parents, especially women, may not always need to choose between occupational and child-care responsibilities.
   (B) In order for mothers to have an equal opportunity for advancement in the labor force, traditional family roles have to be reexamined and revised.
   (C) Although single parents who work have to balance parental and career demands, single mothers suffer resulting employment disadvantages that single fathers can almost always avoid.
   (D) Although child-care responsibilities disadvantage many women in the labor force, professional women (such as teachers and lawyers) are better able to overcome this problem than are nonprofessional women.
   (E) Traditional work schedules are too inflexible to accommodate the child-care responsibilities of many parents, a fact that severely disadvantages women in the labor force.

GO ON TO THE NEXT PAGE.

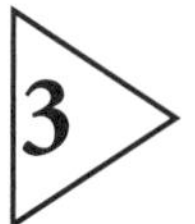

2. Which one of the following statements about part-time work can be inferred from the information presented in the passage?
   (A) One-third of all part-time workers are working mothers.
   (B) Part-time work generally offers fewer opportunities for advancement to working mothers than to women generally.
   (C) Part-time work, in addition to having relatively poor wages, often requires that employees work during holidays, when their children are out of school.
   (D) Part-time employment, despite its disadvantages, provides working mothers with an opportunity to address some of the demands of caring for children.
   (E) Many mothers with primary child-care responsibility choose part-time jobs in order to better exploit full-time career opportunities after their children are grown.

3. It can be inferred from the passage that the author would be most likely to agree with which one of the following statements about working fathers in two-parent families?
   (A) They are equally burdened by the employment disadvantages placed upon all parents—male and female—in the labor market.
   (B) They are so absorbed in their jobs that they often do not see the injustice going on around them.
   (C) They are shielded by the traditional allocation of family roles from many of the pressures associated with child-rearing responsibilities.
   (D) They help compound the inequities in the labor market by keeping women from competing with men for career opportunities.
   (E) They are responsible for many of the problems of working mothers because of their insistence on traditional roles in the family.

4. Of the following, which one would the author most likely say is the most troublesome barrier facing working parents with primary child-care responsibility?
   (A) the lack of full-time jobs open to women
   (B) the inflexibility of work schedules
   (C) the low wages of part-time employment
   (D) the limited advancement opportunities for nonprofessional employees
   (E) the practice of allocating responsibilities in the workplace on the basis of gender

5. The passage suggests that day care is at best a limited solution to the pressures associated with child rearing for all of the following reasons EXCEPT:
   (A) Even the best day care available cannot guarantee that children will have meaningful time with their parents.
   (B) Some parents cannot afford day-care services.
   (C) Working parents sometimes have difficulty finding suitable day care for their children.
   (D) Parents who send their children to day care still need to provide care for their children during vacations.
   (E) Even children who are in day care may have to stay home when they are sick.

6. According to the passage, many working parents may be forced to make any of the following types of career decisions EXCEPT
   (A) declining professional positions for nonprofessional ones, which typically have less conventional work schedules
   (B) accepting part-time employment rather than full-time employment
   (C) taking jobs with limited responsibility, and thus more limited career opportunities, in order to have a more flexible schedule
   (D) pursuing career specializations that allow them to control their work schedules instead of pursuing a more desirable specialization in the same field
   (E) limiting the career potential of one parent, often the mother, who assumes greater child-care responsibility

7. Which one of the following statements would most appropriately continue the discussion at the end of the passage?
   (A) At the same time, most men will remain better able to enjoy the career and salary opportunities offered by the labor market.
   (B) Of course, men who are married to working mothers know of these employment barriers but seem unwilling to do anything about them.
   (C) On the other hand, salary levels may become more equitable between men and women even if the other career opportunities remain more accessible to men than to women.
   (D) On the contrary, men with primary child-rearing responsibilities will continue to enjoy more advantages in the workplace than their female counterparts.
   (E) Thus, institutions in society that favor men over women will continue to widen the gap between the career opportunities available for men and for women.

GO ON TO THE NEXT PAGE.

Critics have long been puzzled by the inner contradictions of major characters in John Webster's tragedies. In his *The Duchess of Malfi*, for instance, the Duchess is "good" in demonstrating the obvious tenderness and sincerity of her love for Antonio, but "bad" in ignoring the wishes and welfare of her family and in making religion a "cloak" hiding worldly self-indulgence. Bosola is "bad" in serving Ferdinand, "good" in turning the Duchess' thoughts toward heaven and in planning to avenge her murder. The ancient Greek philosopher Aristotle implied that such contradictions are virtually essential to the tragic personality, and yet critics keep coming back to this element of inconsistency as though it were an eccentric feature of Webster's own tragic vision.

The problem is that, as an Elizabethan playwright, Webster has become a prisoner of our critical presuppositions. We have, in recent years, been dazzled by the way the earlier Renaissance and medieval theater, particularly the morality play, illuminates Elizabethan drama. We now understand how the habit of mind that saw the world as a battleground between good and evil produced the morality play. Morality plays allegorized that conflict by presenting characters whose actions were defined as the embodiment of good or evil. This model of reality lived on, overlaid by different conventions, in the more sophisticated Elizabethan works of the following age. Yet Webster seems not to have been as heavily influenced by the morality play's model of reality as were his Elizabethan contemporaries; he was apparently more sensitive to the more morally complicated Italian drama than to these English sources. Consequently, his characters cannot be evaluated according to reductive formulas of good and evil, which is precisely what modern critics have tried to do. They choose what seem to be the most promising of the contradictory values that are dramatized in the play, and treat those values as if they were the only basis for analyzing the moral development of the play's major characters, attributing the inconsistencies in a character's behavior to artistic incompetence on Webster's part. The lack of consistency in Webster's characters can be better understood if we recognize that the ambiguity at the heart of his tragic vision lies not in the external world but in the duality of human nature. Webster establishes tension in his plays by setting up conflicting systems of value that appear immoral only when one value system is viewed exclusively from the perspective of the other. He presents us not only with characters that we condemn intellectually or ethically and at the same time impulsively approve of, but also with judgments we must accept as logically sound and yet find emotionally repulsive. The dilemma is not only dramatic: it is tragic, because the conflict is irreconcilable, and because it is ours as much as that of the characters.

8. The primary purpose of the passage is to
   (A) clarify an ambiguous assertion
   (B) provide evidence in support of a commonly held view
   (C) analyze an unresolved question and propose an answer
   (D) offer an alternative to a flawed interpretation
   (E) describe and categorize opposing viewpoints

9. The author suggests which one of the following about the dramatic works that most influenced Webster's tragedies?
   (A) They were not concerned with dramatizing the conflict between good and evil that was presented in morality plays.
   (B) They were not as sophisticated as the Italian sources from which other Elizabethan tragedies were derived.
   (C) They have never been adequately understood by critics.
   (D) They have only recently been used to illuminate the conventions of Elizabethan drama.
   (E) They have been considered by many critics to be the reason for Webster's apparent artistic incompetence.

10. The author's allusion to Aristotle's view of tragedy in lines 11–13 serves which one of the following functions in the passage?
   (A) It introduces a commonly held view of Webster's tragedies that the author plans to defend.
   (B) It supports the author's suggestion that Webster's conception of tragedy is not idiosyncratic.
   (C) It provides an example of an approach to Webster's tragedies that the author criticizes.
   (D) It establishes the similarity between classical and modern approaches to tragedy.
   (E) It supports the author's assertion that Elizabethan tragedy cannot be fully understood without the help of recent scholarship.

11. It can be inferred from the passage that modern critics' interpretations of Webster's tragedies would be more valid if
   (A) the ambiguity inherent in Webster's tragic vision resulted from the duality of human nature
   (B) Webster's conception of the tragic personality were similar to that of Aristotle
   (C) Webster had been heavily influenced by the morality play
   (D) Elizabethan dramatists had been more sensitive to Italian sources of influence
   (E) the inner conflicts exhibited by Webster's characters were similar to those of modern audiences

GO ON TO THE NEXT PAGE.

12. With which one of the following statements regarding Elizabethan drama would the author be most likely to agree?
    (A) The skill of Elizabethan dramatists has in recent years been overestimated.
    (B) The conventions that shaped Elizabethan drama are best exemplified by Webster's drama.
    (C) Elizabethan drama, for the most part, can be viewed as being heavily influenced by the morality play.
    (D) Only by carefully examining the work of his Elizabethan contemporaries can Webster's achievement as a dramatist be accurately measured.
    (E) Elizabethan drama can best be described as influenced by a composite of Italian and classical sources.

13. It can be inferred from the passage that most modern critics assume which one of the following in their interpretation of Webster's tragedies?
    (A) Webster's plays tended to allegorize the conflict between good and evil more than did those of his contemporaries.
    (B) Webster's plays were derived more from Italian than from English sources.
    (C) The artistic flaws in Webster's tragedies were largely the result of his ignorance of the classical definition of tragedy.
    (D) Webster's tragedies provide no relevant basis for analyzing the moral development of their characters.
    (E) In writing his tragedies, Webster was influenced by the same sources as his contemporaries.

14. The author implies that Webster's conception of tragedy was
    (A) artistically flawed
    (B) highly conventional
    (C) largely derived from the morality play
    (D) somewhat different from the conventional Elizabethan conception of tragedy
    (E) uninfluenced by the classical conception of tragedy

GO ON TO THE NEXT PAGE.

Cultivation of a single crop on a given tract of land leads eventually to decreased yields. One reason for this is that harmful bacterial phyto-pathogens, organisms parasitic on plant hosts, increase in the soil surrounding plant roots. The problem can be cured by crop rotation, denying the pathogens a suitable host for a period of time. However, even if crops are not rotated, the severity of diseases brought on by such phytopathogens often decreases after a number or years as the microbial population of the soil changes and the soil becomes "suppressive" to those diseases. While there may be many reasons for this phenomenon, it is clear that levels of certain bacteria, such as *Pseudomonas fluorescens*, a bacterium antagonistic to a number of harmful phytopathogens, are greater in suppressive than in nonsuppressive soil. This suggests that the presence of such bacteria suppresses phytopathogens. There is now considerable experimental support for this view. Wheat yield increases of 27 percent have been obtained in field trials by treatment of wheat seeds with fluorescent pseudomonads. Similar treatment of sugar beets, cotton, and potatoes has had similar results.

These improvements in crop yields through the application of *Pseudomonas fluorescens* suggest that agriculture could benefit from the use of bacteria genetically altered for specific purposes. For example, a form of phytopathogen altered to remove its harmful properties could be released into the environment in quantities favorable to its competing with and eventually excluding the harmful normal strain. Some experiments suggest that deliberately releasing altered nonpathogenic *Pseudomonas syringae* could crowd out the nonaltered variety that causes frost damage. Opponents of such research have objected that the deliberate and large-scale release of genetically altered bacteria might have deleterious results. Proponents, on the other hand, argue that this particular strain is altered only by the removal of the gene responsible for the strain's propensity to cause frost damage, thereby rendering it safer than the phytopathogen from which it was derived.

Some proponents have gone further and suggest that genetic alteration techniques could create organisms with totally new combinations of desirable traits not found in nature. For example, genes responsible for production of insecticidal compounds have been transposed from other bacteria into pseudomonads that colonize corn roots. Experiments of this kind are difficult and require great care: such bacteria are developed in highly artificial environments and may not compete well with natural soil bacteria. Nevertheless, proponents contend that the prospects for improved agriculture through such methods seem excellent. These prospects lead many to hope that current efforts to assess the risks of deliberate release of altered microorganisms will successfully answer the concerns of opponents and create a climate in which such research can go forward without undue impediment.

15. Which one of the following best summarizes the main idea of the passage?

(A) Recent field experiments with genetically altered *Pseudomonas* bacteria have shown that releasing genetically altered bacteria into the environment would not involve any significant danger.

(B) Encouraged by current research, advocates of agricultural use of genetically altered bacteria are optimistic that such use will eventually result in improved agriculture, though opponents remain wary.

(C) Current research indicates that adding genetically altered *Pseudomonas syringae* bacteria to the soil surrounding crop plant roots will have many beneficial effects, such as the prevention of frost damage in certain crops.

(D) Genetic alteration of a number of harmful phytopathogens has been advocated by many researchers who contend that these techniques will eventually replace such outdated methods as crop rotation.

(E) Genetic alteration of bacteria has been successful in highly artificial laboratory conditions, but opponents of such research have argued that these techniques are unlikely to produce organisms that are able to survive in natural environments.

16. The author discusses naturally occurring *Pseudomonas fluorescens* bacteria in the first paragraph primarily in order to do which one of the following?

(A) prove that increases in the level of such bacteria in the soil are the sole cause of soil suppressivity

(B) explain why yields increased after wheat fields were sprayed with altered *Pseudomonas fluorescens* bacteria

(C) detail the chemical processes that such bacteria use to suppress organisms parasitic to crop plants, such as wheat, sugar beets, and potatoes

(D) provide background information to support the argument that research into the agricultural use of genetically altered bacteria would be fruitful

(E) argue that crop rotation is unnecessary, since diseases brought on by phytopathogens diminish in severity and eventually disappear on their own

GO ON TO THE NEXT PAGE.

17. It can be inferred from the author's discussion of *Pseudomonas fluorescens* bacteria that which one of the following would be true of crops impervious to parasitical organisms?
    (A) *Pseudomonas fluorescens* bacteria would be absent from the soil surrounding their roots.
    (B) They would crowd out and eventually exclude other crop plants if their growth were not carefully regulated.
    (C) Their yield would not be likely to be improved by adding *Pseudomonas fluorescens* bacteria to the soil.
    (D) They would mature more quickly than crop plants that were susceptible to parasitical organisms.
    (E) Levels of phytopathogenic bacteria in the soil surrounding their roots would be higher compared with other crop plants.

18. It can be inferred from the passage that crop rotation can increase yields in part because
    (A) moving crop plants around makes them hardier and more resistant to disease
    (B) the number of *Pseudomonas fluorescens* bacteria in the soil usually increases when crops are rotated
    (C) the roots of many crop plants produce compounds that are antagonistic to phytopathogens harmful to other crop plants
    (D) the presence of phytopathogenic bacteria is responsible for the majority of plant diseases
    (E) phytopathogens typically attack some plant species but find other species to be unsuitable hosts

19. According to the passage, proponents of the use of genetically altered bacteria in agriculture argue that which one of the following is true of the altered bacteria used in the frost-damage experiments?
    (A) The altered bacteria had a genetic constitution differing from that of the normal strain only in that the altered variety had one less gene.
    (B) Although the altered bacteria competed effectively with the nonaltered strain in the laboratory, they were not as viable in natural environments.
    (C) The altered bacteria were much safer and more effective than the naturally occurring *Pseudomonas fluorescens* bacteria used in earlier experiments.
    (D) The altered bacteria were antagonistic to several types of naturally occurring phytopathogens in the soil surrounding the roots of frost-damaged crops.
    (E) The altered bacteria were released into the environment in numbers sufficient to guarantee the validity of experimental results.

20. Which one of the following, if true, would most seriously weaken the proponents' argument regarding the safety of using altered *Pseudomonas syringae* bacteria to control frost damage?
    (A) *Pseudomonas syringae* bacteria are primitive and have a simple genetic constitution.
    (B) The altered bacteria are derived from a strain that is parasitic to plants and can cause damage to crops.
    (C) Current genetic-engineering techniques permit the large-scale commercial production of such bacteria.
    (D) Often genes whose presence is responsible for one harmful characteristic must be present in order to prevent other harmful characteristics.
    (E) The frost-damage experiments with *Pseudomonas syringae* bacteria indicate that the altered variety would only replace the normal strain if released in sufficient numbers.

GO ON TO THE NEXT PAGE.

In 1887 the Dawes Act legislated wide-scale private ownership of reservation lands in the United States for Native Americans. The act allotted plots of 80 acres to each Native American adult. However, the Native Americans were not granted outright title to their lands. The act defined each grant as a "trust patent," meaning that the Bureau of Indian Affairs (BIA), the governmental agency in charge of administering policy regarding Native Americans, would hold the allotted land in trust for 25 years, during which time the Native American owners could use, but not alienate (sell) the land. After the 25-year period, the Native American allottee would receive a "fee patent" awarding full legal ownership of the land.

Two main reasons were advanced for the restriction on the Native Americans' ability to sell their lands. First, it was claimed that free alienability would lead to immediate transfer of large amounts of former reservation land to non-Native Americans, consequently threatening the traditional way of life on those reservations. A second objection to free alienation was that Native Americans were unaccustomed to, and did not desire, a system of private landownership. Their custom, it was said, favored communal use of land.

However, both of these arguments bear only on the transfer of Native American lands to non-Native Americans; neither offers a reason for prohibiting Native Americans from transferring land among themselves. Selling land to each other would not threaten the Native American culture. Additionally, if communal land use remained preferable to Native Americans after allotment, free alienability would have allowed allottees to sell their lands back to the tribe.

When stated rationales for government policies prove empty, using an interest-group model often provides an explanation. While neither Native Americans nor the potential non-Native American purchasers benefited from the restraint on alienation contained in the Dawes Act, one clearly defined group did benefit: the BIA bureaucrats. It has been convincingly demonstrated that bureaucrats seek to maximize the size of their staffs and their budgets in order to compensate for the lack of other sources of fulfillment, such as power and prestige. Additionally, politicians tend to favor the growth of governmental bureaucracy because such growth provides increased opportunity for the exercise of political patronage. The restraint on alienation vastly increased the amount of work, and hence the budgets, necessary to implement the statute. Until allotment was ended in 1934, granting fee patents and leasing Native American lands were among the principal activities of the United States government. One hypothesis, then, for the temporary restriction on alienation in the Dawes Act is that it reflected a compromise between non-Native Americans favoring immediate alienability so they could purchase land and the BIA bureaucrats who administered the privatization system.

21. Which one of the following best summarizes the main idea of the passage?
    (A) United States government policy toward Native Americans has tended to disregard their needs and consider instead the needs of non-Native American purchasers of land.
    (B) In order to preserve the unique way of life on Native American reservations, use of Native American lands must be communal rather than individual.
    (C) The Dawes Act's restriction on the right of Native Americans to sell their land may have been implemented primarily to serve the interests of politicians and bureaucrats.
    (D) The clause restricting free alienability in the Dawes Act greatly expanded United States governmental activity in the area of land administration.
    (E) Since passage of the Dawes Act in 1887, Native Americans have not been able to sell or transfer their former reservation land freely.

22. Which one of the following statements concerning the reason for the end of allotment, if true, would provide the most support for the author's view of politicians?
    (A) Politicians realized that allotment was damaging the Native American way of life.
    (B) Politicians decided that allotment would be more congruent with the Native American custom of communal land use.
    (C) Politicians believed that allotment's continuation would not enhance their opportunities to exercise patronage.
    (D) Politicians felt that the staff and budgets of the BIA had grown too large.
    (E) Politicians were concerned that too much Native American land was falling into the hands of non-Native Americans.

GO ON TO THE NEXT PAGE.

23. Which one of the following best describes the organization of the passage?

(A) The passage of a law is analyzed in detail, the benefits and drawbacks of one of its clauses are studied, and a final assessment of the law is offered.

(B) The history of a law is narrated, the effects of one of its clauses on various populations are studied, and repeal of the law is advocated.

(C) A law is examined, the political and social backgrounds of one of its clauses are characterized, and the permanent effects of the law are studied.

(D) A law is described, the rationale put forward for one of its clauses is outlined and dismissed, and a different rationale for the clause is presented.

(E) The legal status of an ethnic group is examined with respect to issues of landownership and commercial autonomy, and the benefits to rival groups due to that status are explained.

24. The author's attitude toward the reasons advanced for the restriction on alienability in the Dawes Act at the time of its passage can best be described as

(A) completely credulous

(B) partially approving

(C) basically indecisive

(D) mildly questioning

(E) highly skeptical

25. It can be inferred from the passage that which one of the following was true of Native American life immediately before passage of the Dawes Act?

(A) Most Native Americans supported themselves through farming.

(B) Not many Native Americans personally owned the land on which they lived.

(C) The land on which most Native Americans lived had been bought from their tribes.

(D) Few Native Americans had much contact with their non-Native American neighbors.

(E) Few Native Americans were willing to sell their land to non-Native Americans.

26. According to the passage, the type of landownership initially obtainable by Native Americans under the Dawes Act differed from the type of ownership obtainable after a 25-year period in that only the latter allowed

(A) owners of land to farm it

(B) owners of land to sell it

(C) government some control over how owners disposed of land

(D) owners of land to build on it with relatively minor governmental restrictions

(E) government to charge owners a fee for developing their land

27. Which one of the following, if true, would most strengthen the author's argument regarding the true motivation for the passage of the Dawes Act?

(A) The legislators who voted in favor of the Dawes Act owned land adjacent to Native American reservations.

(B) The majority of Native Americans who were granted fee patents did not sell their land back to their tribes.

(C) Native Americans managed to preserve their traditional culture even when they were geographically dispersed.

(D) The legislators who voted in favor of the Dawes Act were heavily influenced by BIA bureaucrats.

(E) Non-Native Americans who purchased the majority of Native American lands consolidated them into larger farm holdings.

STOP

IF YOU FINISH BEFORE TIME IS CALLED, YOU MAY CHECK YOUR WORK ON THIS SECTION ONLY. DO NOT WORK ON ANY OTHER SECTION IN THE TEST.

Practice Test 1

Section IV: Logical Reasoning

Time—35 minutes
25 questions

Directions: The questions in this section are based on the reasoning contained in brief statements or passages. For some questions, more than one of the choices could conceivably answer the question. However, you are to choose the best answer; that is, the response that most accurately and completely answers the question. You should not make assumptions that are by commonsense standards implausible, superfluous, or incompatible with the passage. After you have chosen the best answer, blacken the corresponding space on your answer sheet.

1. In 1974 the speed limit on highways in the United States was reduced to 55 miles per hour in order to save fuel. In the first 12 months after the change, the rate of highway fatalities dropped 15 percent, the sharpest one-year drop in history. Over the next 10 years, the fatality rate declined by another 25 percent. It follows that the 1974 reduction in the speed limit saved many lives.

   Which one of the following, if true, most strengthens the argument?

   (A) The 1974 fuel shortage cut driving sharply for more than a year.
   (B) There was no decline in the rate of highway fatalities during the twelfth year following the reduction in the speed limit.
   (C) Since 1974 automobile manufacturers have been required by law to install lifesaving equipment, such as seat belts, in all new cars.
   (D) The fatality rate in highway accidents involving motorists driving faster than 55 miles per hour is much higher than in highway accidents that do not involve motorists driving at such speeds.
   (E) Motorists are more likely to avoid accidents by matching their speed to that of the surrounding highway traffic than by driving at faster or slower speeds.

2. Some legislators refuse to commit public funds for new scientific research if they cannot be assured that the research will contribute to the public welfare. Such a position ignores the lessons of experience. Many important contributions to the public welfare that resulted from scientific research were never predicted as potential outcomes of that research. Suppose that a scientist in the early twentieth century had applied for public funds to study molds: who would have predicted that such research would lead to the discovery of antibiotics—one of the greatest contributions ever made to the public welfare?

   Which one of the following most accurately expresses the main point of the argument?

   (A) The committal of public funds for new scientific research will ensure that the public welfare will be enhanced.
   (B) If it were possible to predict the general outcome of a new scientific research effort, then legislators would not refuse to commit public funds for that effort.
   (C) Scientific discoveries that have contributed to the public welfare would have occurred sooner if public funds had been committed to the research that generated those discoveries.
   (D) In order to ensure that scientific research is directed toward contributing to the public welfare, legislators must commit public funds to new scientific research.
   (E) Lack of guarantees that new scientific research will contribute to the public welfare is not sufficient reason for legislators to refuse to commit public funds to new scientific research.

GO ON TO THE NEXT PAGE.

3. When workers do not find their assignments challenging, they become bored and so achieve less than their abilities would allow. On the other hand, when workers find their assignments too difficult, they give up and so again achieve less than what they are capable of achieving. It is, therefore, clear that no worker's full potential will ever be realized.

   Which one of the following is an error of reasoning contained in the argument?

   (A) mistakenly equating what is actual and what is merely possible
   (B) assuming without warrant that a situation allows only two possibilities
   (C) relying on subjective rather than objective evidence
   (D) confusing the coincidence of two events with a causal relation between the two
   (E) depending on the ambiguous use of a key term

4. Our tomato soup provides good nutrition: for instance, a warm bowl of it contains more units of vitamin C than does a serving of apricots or fresh carrots!

   The advertisement is misleading if which one of the following is true?

   (A) Few people depend exclusively on apricots and carrots to supply vitamin C to their diets.
   (B) A liquid can lose vitamins if it stands in contact with the air for a protracted period of time.
   (C) Tomato soup contains important nutrients other than vitamin C.
   (D) The amount of vitamin C provided by a serving of the advertised soup is less than the amount furnished by a serving of fresh strawberries.
   (E) Apricots and fresh carrots are widely known to be nutritious, but their contribution consists primarily in providing a large amount of vitamin A, not a large amount of vitamin C.

<u>Questions 5–6</u>

The government provides insurance for individuals' bank deposits, but requires the banks to pay the premiums for this insurance. Since it is depositors who primarily benefit from the security this insurance provides, the government should take steps to ensure that depositors who want this security bear the cost of it and thus should make depositors pay the premiums for insuring their own accounts.

5. Which one of the following principles, if established, would do most to justify drawing the conclusion of the argument on the basis of the reasons offered in its support?

   (A) The people who stand to benefit from an economic service should always be made to bear the costs of that service.
   (B) Any rational system of insurance must base the size of premiums on the degree of risk involved.
   (C) Government-backed security for investors, such as bank depositors, should be provided only when it does not reduce incentives for investors to make responsible investments.
   (D) The choice of not accepting an offered service should always be available, even if there is no charge for the service.
   (E) The government should avoid any actions that might alter the behavior of corporations and individuals in the market.

6. Which one of the following is assumed by the argument?

   (A) Banks are not insured by the government against default on the loans the banks make.
   (B) Private insurance companies do not have the resources to provide banks or individuals with deposit insurance.
   (C) Banks do not always cover the cost of the deposit-insurance premiums by paying depositors lower interest rates on insured deposits than the banks would on uninsured deposits.
   (D) The government limits the insurance protection it provides by insuring accounts up to a certain legally defined amount only.
   (E) The government does not allow banks to offer some kinds of accounts in which deposits are not insured.

GO ON TO THE NEXT PAGE.

7. When individual students are all treated equally in that they have identical exposure to curriculum material, the rate, quality, and quantity of learning will vary from student to student. If all students are to master a given curriculum, some of them need different types of help than others, as any experienced teacher knows.

If the statements above are both true, which one of the following conclusions can be drawn on the basis of them?

(A) Unequal treatment, in a sense, of individual students is required in order to ensure equality with respect to the educational tasks they master.
(B) The rate and quality of learning, with learning understood as the acquiring of the ability to solve problems within a given curriculum area, depend on the quantity of teaching an individual student receives in any given curriculum.
(C) The more experienced the teacher is, the more the students will learn.
(D) All students should have identical exposure to learn the material being taught in any given curriculum.
(E) Teachers should help each of their students to learn as much as possible.

8. George: Some scientists say that global warming will occur because people are releasing large amounts of carbon dioxide into the atmosphere by burning trees and fossil fuels. We can see, though, that the predicted warming is occurring already. In the middle of last winter, we had a month of springlike weather in our area, and this fall, because of unusually mild temperatures, the leaves on our town's trees were three weeks late in turning color.

Which one of the following would it be most relevant to investigate in evaluating the conclusion of George's argument?

(A) whether carbon dioxide is the only cause of global warming
(B) when leaves on the trees in the town usually change color
(C) what proportion of global emissions of carbon dioxide is due to the burning of trees by humans
(D) whether air pollution is causing some trees in the area to lose their leaves
(E) whether unusually warm weather is occurring elsewhere on the globe more frequently than before

9. Student representative: Our university, in expelling a student who verbally harassed his roommate, has erred by penalizing the student for doing what he surely has a right to do: speak his mind!

Dean of students: But what you're saying is that our university should endorse verbal harassment. Yet surely if we did that, we would threaten the free flow of ideas that is the essence of university life.

Which one of the following is a questionable technique that the dean of students uses in attempting to refute the student representative?

(A) challenging the student representative's knowledge of the process by which the student was expelled
(B) invoking a fallacious distinction between speech and other sorts of behavior
(C) misdescribing the student representative's position, thereby making it easier to challenge
(D) questioning the motives of the student representative rather than offering reasons for the conclusion defended
(E) relying on a position of power to silence the opposing viewpoint with a threat

10. Famous personalities found guilty of many types of crimes in well-publicized trials are increasingly sentenced to the performance of community service, though unknown defendants convicted of similar crimes almost always serve prison sentences. However, the principle of equality before the law rules out using fame and publicity as relevant considerations in the sentencing of convicted criminals.

The statements above, if true, most strongly support which one of the following conclusions?

(A) The principle of equality before the law is rigorously applied in only a few types of criminal trials.
(B) The number of convicted celebrities sentenced to community service should equal the number of convicted unknown defendants sentenced to community service.
(C) The principle of equality before the law can properly be overridden by other principles in some cases.
(D) The sentencing of celebrities to community service instead of prison constitutes a violation of the principle of equality before the law in many cases.
(E) The principle of equality before the law does not allow for leniency in sentencing.

GO ON TO THE NEXT PAGE.

11. Scientific research at a certain university was supported in part by an annual grant from a major foundation. When the university's physics department embarked on weapons-related research, the foundation, which has a purely humanitarian mission, threatened to cancel its grant. The university then promised that none of the foundation's money would be used for the weapons research, whereupon the foundation withdrew its threat, concluding that the weapons research would not benefit from the foundation's grant.

Which one of the following describes a flaw in the reasoning underlying the foundation's conclusion?

(A) It overlooks the possibility that the availability of the foundation's money for humanitarian uses will allow the university to redirect other funds from humanitarian uses to weapons research.

(B) It overlooks the possibility that the physics department's weapons research is not the only one of the university's research activities with other than purely humanitarian purposes.

(C) It overlooks the possibility that the university made its promise specifically in order to induce the foundation to withdraw its threat.

(D) It confuses the intention of not using a sum of money for a particular purpose with the intention of not using that sum of money at all.

(E) It assumes that if the means to achieve an objective are humanitarian in character, then the objective is also humanitarian in character.

12. To suit the needs of corporate clients, advertising agencies have successfully modified a strategy originally developed for political campaigns. This strategy aims to provide clients with free publicity and air time by designing an advertising campaign that is controversial, thus drawing prime-time media coverage and evoking public comment by officials.

The statements above, if true, most seriously undermine which one of the following assertions?

(A) The usefulness of an advertising campaign is based solely on the degree to which the campaign's advertisements persuade their audiences.

(B) Only a small percentage of eligible voters admit to being influenced by advertising campaigns in deciding how to vote.

(C) Campaign managers have transformed political campaigns by making increasing use of strategies borrowed from corporate advertising campaigns.

(D) Corporations are typically more concerned with maintaining public recognition of the corporate name than with enhancing goodwill toward the corporation.

(E) Advertising agencies that specialize in campaigns for corporate clients are not usually chosen for political campaigns.

13. The National Association of Fire Fighters says that 45 percent of homes now have smoke detectors, whereas only 30 percent of homes had them 10 years ago. This makes early detection of house fires no more likely, however, because over half of the domestic smoke detectors are either without batteries or else inoperative for some other reason.

In order for the conclusion above to be properly drawn, which one of the following assumptions would have to be made?

(A) Fifteen percent of domestic smoke detectors were installed less than 10 years ago.

(B) The number of fires per year in homes with smoke detectors has increased.

(C) Not all of the smoke detectors in homes are battery operated.

(D) The proportion of domestic smoke detectors that are inoperative has increased in the past ten years.

(E) Unlike automatic water sprinklers, a properly functioning smoke detector cannot by itself increase fire safety in a home.

14. Advertisement: HomeGlo Paints, Inc., has won the prestigious Golden Paintbrush Award given to the one paint manufacturer in the country that has increased the environmental safety of its product most over the past three years for HomeGlo Exterior Enamel. The Golden Paintbrush is awarded only on the basis of thorough tests by independent testing laboratories. So when you choose HomeGlo Exterior Enamel, you will know that you have chosen the most environmentally safe brand of paint manufactured in this country today.

The flawed reasoning in the advertisement most closely parallels that in which one of the following?

(A) The ZXC audio system received the overall top ranking for looks, performance, durability, and value in *Listeners' Report* magazine's ratings of currently produced systems. Therefore, the ZXC must have better sound quality than any other currently produced sound system.

(B) Morning Sunshine breakfast cereal contains, ounce for ounce, more of the nutrients needed for a healthy diet than any other breakfast cereal on the market today. Thus, when you eat Morning Sunshine, you will know you are eating the most nutritious food now on the market.

(C) The number of consumer visits increased more at Countryside Market last year than at any other market in the region. Therefore, Countryside's profits must also have increased more last year than those of any other market in the region.

(D) Jerrold's teachers recognize him as the student who has shown more academic improvement than any other student in the junior class this year. Therefore, if Jerrold and his classmates are ranked according to their current academic performance, Jerrold must hold the highest ranking.

(E) Margaret Durring's short story "The Power Lunch" won three separate awards for best short fiction of the year. Therefore, any of Margaret Durring's earlier stories certainly has enough literary merit to be included in an anthology of the best recent short fiction.

15. The consistency of ice cream is adversely affected by even slight temperature changes in the freezer. To counteract this problem, manufacturers add stabilizers to ice cream. Unfortunately, stabilizers, though inexpensive, adversely affect flavor. Stabilizers are less needed if storage temperatures are very low. However, since energy costs are constantly going up, those costs constitute a strong incentive in favor of relatively high storage temperatures.

Which one of the following can be properly inferred from the passage?

(A) Even slight deviations from the proper consistency for ice cream sharply impair its flavor.

(B) Cost considerations favor sacrificing consistency over sacrificing flavor.

(C) It would not be cost-effective to develop a new device to maintain the constancy of freezer temperatures.

(D) Stabilizers function well only at very low freezer temperatures.

(E) Very low, stable freezer temperatures allow for the best possible consistency and flavor of ice cream.

16. Edwina: True appreciation of Mozart's music demands that you hear it exactly as he intended it to be heard; that is, exactly as he heard it. Since he heard it on eighteenth-century instruments, it follows that so should we.

Alberto: But what makes you think that Mozart ever heard his music played as he had intended it to be played? After all, Mozart was writing at a time when the performer was expected, as a matter of course, not just to interpret but to modify the written score.

Alberto adopts which one of the following strategies in criticizing Edwina's position?

(A) He appeals to an academic authority in order to challenge the factual basis of her conclusion.

(B) He attacks her judgment by suggesting that she does not recognize the importance of the performer's creativity to the audience's appreciation of a musical composition.

(C) He defends a competing view of musical authenticity.

(D) He attacks the logic of her argument by suggesting that the conclusion she draws does not follow from the premises she sets forth.

(E) He offers a reason to believe that one of the premises of her argument is false.

GO ON TO THE NEXT PAGE.

17. Since the introduction of the Impanian National Health scheme, Impanians (or their private insurance companies) have had to pay only for the more unusual and sophisticated medical procedures. When the scheme was introduced, it was hoped that private insurance to pay for these procedures would be available at modest cost, since the insurers would no longer be paying for the bulk of health care costs, as they had done previously. Paradoxically, however, the cost of private health insurance did not decrease but has instead increased dramatically in the years since the scheme's introduction.

Which one of the following, if true, does most to explain the apparently paradoxical outcome?

(A) The National Health scheme has greatly reduced the number of medical claims handled annually by Impania's private insurers, enabling these firms to reduce overhead costs substantially.

(B) Before the National Health scheme was introduced, more than 80 percent of all Impanian medical costs were associated with procedures that are now covered by the scheme.

(C) Impanians who previously were unable to afford regular medical treatment now use the National Health scheme, but the number of Impanians with private health insurance has not increased.

(D) Impanians now buy private medical insurance only at times when they expect that they will need care of kinds not available in the National Health scheme.

(E) The proportion of total expenditures within Impania that is spent on health care has declined since the introduction of the National Health scheme.

18. In clinical trials of new medicines, half of the subjects receive the drug being tested and half receive a physiologically inert substance—a placebo. Trials are designed with the intention that neither subjects nor experimenters will find out which subjects are actually being given the drug being tested. However, this intention is frequently frustrated because________.

Which one of the following, if true, most appropriately completes the explanation?

(A) often the subjects who receive the drug being tested develop symptoms that the experimenters recognize as side effects of the physiologically active drug

(B) subjects who believe they are receiving the drug being tested often display improvements in their conditions regardless of whether what is administered to them is physiologically active or not

(C) in general, when the trial is intended to establish the experimental drug's safety rather than its effectiveness, all of the subjects are healthy volunteers

(D) when a trial runs a long time, few of the experimenters will work on it from inception to conclusion

(E) the people who are subjects for clinical trials must, by law, be volunteers and must be informed of the possibility that they will receive a placebo

19. It takes 365.25 days for the Earth to make one complete revolution around the Sun. Long-standing convention makes a year 365 days long, with an extra day added every fourth year, and the year is divided into 52 seven-day weeks. But since 52 times 7 is only 364, anniversaries do not fall on the same day of the week each year. Many scheduling problems could be avoided if the last day of each year and an additional day every fourth year belonged to no week, so that January 1 would be a Sunday every year.

The proposal above, once put into effect, would be most likely to result in continued scheduling conflicts for which one of the following groups?

(A) people who have birthdays or other anniversaries on December 30 or 31

(B) employed people whose strict religious observances require that they refrain from working every seventh day

(C) school systems that require students to attend classes a specific number of days each year

(D) employed people who have three-day breaks from work when holidays are celebrated on Mondays or Fridays

(E) people who have to plan events several years before those events occur

GO ON TO THE NEXT PAGE.

20. Graphologists claim that it is possible to detect permanent character traits by examining people's handwriting. For example, a strong cross on the "t" is supposed to denote enthusiasm. Obviously, however, with practice and perseverance people can alter their handwriting to include this feature. So it seems that graphologists must hold that permanent character traits can be changed.

    The argument against graphology proceeds by

    (A) citing apparently incontestable evidence that leads to absurd consequences when conjoined with the view in question

    (B) demonstrating that an apparently controversial and interesting claim is really just a platitude

    (C) arguing that a particular technique of analysis can never be effective when the people analyzed know that it is being used

    (D) showing that proponents of the view have no theoretical justification for the view

    (E) attacking a technique by arguing that what the technique is supposed to detect can be detected quite readily without it

<u>Questions 21–22</u>

Historian: There is no direct evidence that timber was traded between the ancient nations of Poran and Nayal, but the fact that a law setting tariffs on timber imports from Poran was enacted during the third Nayalese dynasty does suggest that during that period a timber trade was conducted.

Critic: Your reasoning is flawed. During its third dynasty, Nayal may well have imported timber from Poran, but certainly on today's statute books there remain many laws regulating activities that were once common but in which people no longer engage.

21. The critic's response to the historian's reasoning does which one of the following?

    (A) It implies an analogy between the present and the past.

    (B) It identifies a general principle that the historian's reasoning violates.

    (C) It distinguishes between what has been established as a certainty and what has been established as a possibility.

    (D) It establishes explicit criteria that must be used in evaluating indirect evidence.

    (E) It points out the dissimilar roles that law plays in societies that are distinct from one another.

22. The critic's response to the historian is flawed because it

    (A) produces evidence that is consistent with there not having been any timber trade between Poran and Nayal during the third Nayalese dynasty

    (B) cites current laws without indicating whether the laws cited are relevant to the timber trade

    (C) fails to recognize that the historian's conclusion was based on indirect evidence rather than direct evidence

    (D) takes no account of the difference between a law's enactment at a particular time and a law's existence as part of a legal code at a particular time

    (E) accepts without question the assumption about the purpose of laws that underlies the historian's argument

GO ON TO THE NEXT PAGE.

23. The workers at Bell Manufacturing will shortly go on strike unless the management increases their wages. As Bell's president is well aware, however, in order to increase the workers' wages, Bell would have to sell off some of its subsidiaries. So, some of Bell's subsidiaries will be sold.

The conclusion above is properly drawn if which one of the following is assumed?

(A) Bell Manufacturing will begin to suffer increased losses.

(B) Bell's management will refuse to increase its workers' wages.

(C) The workers at Bell Manufacturing will not be going on strike.

(D) Bell's president has the authority to offer the workers their desired wage increase.

(E) Bell's workers will not accept a package of improved benefits in place of their desired wage increase.

24. One sure way you can tell how quickly a new idea—for example, the idea of "privatization"—is taking hold among the population is to monitor how fast the word or words expressing that particular idea are passing into common usage. Professional opinions of whether or not words can indeed be said to have passed into common usage are available from dictionary editors, who are vitally concerned with this question.

The method described above for determining how quickly a new idea is taking hold relies on which one of the following assumptions?

(A) Dictionary editors are not professionally interested in words that are only rarely used.

(B) Dictionary editors have exact numerical criteria for telling when a word has passed into common usage.

(C) For a new idea to take hold, dictionary editors have to include the relevant word or words in their dictionaries.

(D) As a word passes into common usage, its meaning does not undergo any severe distortions in the process.

(E) Words denoting new ideas tend to be used before the ideas denoted are understood.

25. Because migrant workers are typically not hired by any one employer for longer than a single season, migrant workers can legally be paid less than the minimum hourly wage that the government requires employers to pay all their permanent employees. Yet most migrant workers work long hours each day for eleven or twelve months a year and thus are as much full-time workers as are people hired on a year-round basis. Therefore, the law should require that migrant workers be paid the same minimum hourly wage that other full-time workers must be paid.

The pattern of reasoning displayed above most closely parallels that displayed in which one of the following arguments?

(A) Because day-care facilities are now regulated at the local level, the quality of care available to children in two different cities can differ widely. Since such differences in treatment clearly are unfair, day care should be federally rather than locally regulated.

(B) Because many rural areas have few restrictions on development, housing estates in such areas have been built where no adequate supply of safe drinking water could be ensured. Thus, rural areas should adopt building codes more like those large cities have.

(C) Because some countries regulate gun sales more strictly than do other countries, some people can readily purchase a gun, whereas others cannot. Therefore, all countries should cooperate in developing a uniform international policy regarding gun sales.

(D) Because it is a democratic principle that laws should have the consent of those affected by them, liquor laws should be formulated not by politicians but by club and restaurant owners, since such laws directly affect the profitability of their businesses.

(E) Because food additives are not considered drugs, they have not had to meet the safety standards the government applies to drugs. But food additives can be as dangerous as drugs. Therefore, food additives should also be subject to safety regulations as stringent as those covering drugs.

STOP

IF YOU FINISH BEFORE TIME IS CALLED, YOU MAY CHECK YOUR WORK ON THIS SECTION ONLY. DO NOT WORK ON ANY OTHER SECTION IN THE TEST.

Practice Test 1

Writing Sample

SIGNATURE _______________ / / DATE

LSAT WRITING SAMPLE TOPIC

The city of Stockton must choose an event to inaugurate its new auditorium, an open-air stage with seats for about 15,000 people and a surrounding lawn with room for 30,000 more. Write an argument in favor of hiring either of the following performers with these considerations in mind.

- The city hopes the inaugural performance will raise as much money as possible to pay off the auditorium's construction loans.
- The city wants to obtain considerable positive publicity for the new auditorium.

Astrani, one of the legends of popular music, is giving a farewell concert tour before retiring. He has proposed holding the final three concerts in Stockton; because of his elaborate sets and costumes, tickets would be sold only for the auditorium's seats and no lawn seating would be available. Astrani never allows souvenirs to be sold at his concerts, but the city will receive 20 percent of the proceeds from ticket sales. If the tour ends in Stockton, a well-known director will film the historic event and plans to release a full-length feature which will share the final shows with fans around the world.

A number of prominent bands have organized "Animal-Aid" to raise money for endangered species. The concert has already generated significant attention in the press and a number of important arenas competed for the privilege of hosting the event. Stockton's new auditorium is the organizer's first choice as the site for the all-day concert and the city would be allowed to design and sell souvenirs commemorating the event. While tickets would be available for both the seats and surrounding lawn, all of the proceeds from ticket sales would go to "Animal-Aid." The auditorium's security expert is concerned that the facility's novice staff may not yet have the experience to handle a large crowd during an all-day event.

GO ON TO THE NEXT PAGE.

STOP

IF YOU FINISH BEFORE TIME IS CALLED, YOU MAY CHECK YOUR WORK ON THIS SECTION ONLY.
DO NOT WORK ON ANY OTHER SECTION IN THE TEST.

Practice Test 1: **Answer Key**

Section I Logical Reasoning	Section II Analytical Reasoning	Section III Reading Comprehension	Section IV Logical Reasoning
1. C	1. C	1. E	1. D
2. C	2. A	2. D	2. E
3. E	3. C	3. C	3. B
4. E	4. C	4. B	4. E
5. B	5. E	5. D	5. A
6. E	6. C	6. A	6. C
7. C	7. D	7. A	7. A
8. A	8. B	8. D	8. E
9. D	9. C	9. A	9. C
10. B	10. E	10. B	10. D
11. C	11. E	11. C	11. A
12. A	12. E	12. C	12. A
13. C	13. B	13. E	13. D
14. E	14. C	14. D	14. D
15. A	15. E	15. B	15. E
16. B	16. A	16. D	16. E
17. B	17. E	17. C	17. D
18. C	18. B	18. E	18. A
19. C	19. E	19. A	19. B
20. B	20. D	20. D	20. A
21. B	21. B	21. C	21. A
22. E	22. D	22. C	22. D
23. D	23. B	23. D	23. C
24. A	24. A	24. E	24. D
25. D		25. B	25. E
		26. B	
		27. D	

Answers and Explanations

SECTION I: LOGICAL REASONING

1. C

The author concludes in the last sentence that more people were able to read directly after the invention of the printing press. The evidence provided is the greater demand for the new printing press books relative to the demand for expensive manuscript copies. In short, the argument is: More books were bought, therefore more people could read. In making this argument, the author assumes that the number of books sold is directly related to the number of people who can read, but maybe existing readers simply bought more books when the press made them cheaper. (C) breaks down the assumption by implying that the same number of people were buying a greater number of books.

(A) shifts the scope from reading to writing. You can infer no relevant connection between letter writing and *learning* to read, and even if you could (A) would strengthen the argument rather than weaken it.

(B) basically says that people who can read can also write. Like (A), it has no bearing on the relative number of *readers* before the press and after.

(D) and (E) give information about the post-printing press world only, so they are irrelevant. You have no way of knowing whether *earlier* manuscript copies circulated in a manner similar to that described in (D), or whether the manuscript copies *before* the press were also useless to illiterate people (E). Further, even if a comparison to the previous era had been made, neither (D) nor (E) would weaken the argument. If anything, more frequent book lending and decreased utility to the illiterate would strengthen the notion that more books sold implies that more people learned how to read.

- The main issue here is one of *comparison*. You're not concerned simply with determining that there were lots of readers after the invention of the printing press, which (D) and (E) seem to suggest. Rather, you need to know whether there were *more* readers after the invention of the press than before, so (D) and (E) are irrelevant.
- Watch those scope shifts! Reading and writing may conjure up similar images in your mind, but are certainly two different things. You should cross off choices like (A) and (B) quickly.
- Read critically! The phrase "this demonstrates that . . ." strongly suggests that what comes next (i.e., what is *being* demonstrated) is the conclusion, while what comes before (what *does* the demonstrating) is the evidence for this conclusion.

2. C

The author here concludes that Bevex is safe for people based on the evidence that a person would need to drink 25 cans of Bevex-sweetened drinks a day for it to be harmful. Although it may seem unlikely, nothing in the stimulus prevents a person from drinking 25 cans of Bevex drinks a day. Thus, the author must be assuming that people don't drink that many cans of Bevex-sweetened drinks, (C).

(A) offers an irrelevant comparison. What does the developmental time for mice cancer relative to that of human cancer have to do with Bevex? There's also a scope shift here: The issue is whether or not Bevex, which causes cancer in mice, *can* cause cancer in people, not *how long* such a cancer would take to develop.

(B) Other food additives are also bad for mice? This has nothing to do with the safety of Bevex for humans, and so is outside the scope—not a necessary element of the argument.

(D) The health benefits of weight control are outside the scope.

(E) refers to non-relevant studies on Bevex which, basically, is a flat-out announcement that this choice is beyond the scope and not necessary to the argument.

- A stem that asks "what must be true in order to draw this conclusion?" is indirectly asking, "What is the central assumption?" Treat it like any other assumption question.
- An assumption is a piece of information that is *necessary* to an argument. An outside-the-scope statement is a statement that is *irrelevant* to an argument. Therefore, if a choice is outside the scope of the argument, it need not be assumed.
- The phrase "For that reason . . ." tells you that what's coming up is the conclusion.

3. E

Here you get a little communication breakdown between Harry and Judith. The stem alerts you right away that you're concerned with Judith's response, so begin there. Paraphrasing, Judith essentially says, "Not true. Lots of people can't afford to fly." So she must have thought she heard, "Most people (or anyone) can afford to fly." Scanning the choices, you find this in (E).

The other choices provide various opportunities to misinterpret Harry's statement, but you only want *Judith's* misinterpretation.

(A) addresses the wealth of people in general, while Judith is only responding to the affordability of flight.

(B) introduces the *right* to experience travel, which is far removed from the financial ability of people to do so, the only issue involved in Judith's response.

(C) Judith's response addresses only the affordability of flight, so you have no reason to think that Harry's statement implies (C).

(D) shifts the scope away from airlines to other forms of travel, which are not addressed by Judith or by Harry.

- Always read the question stem first in Logical Reasoning. Here, you're asked to determine how Judith interprets Harry's statement, which means that the focus is truly on Judith. Often, the simplest approach to a "crossed-wires" question like this is to read the second person's statement first in order to prephrase what that person must have thought she heard.
- Go where the points are! The stem strongly suggests that what Harry actually says is of little importance, and that Judith's statement is paramount here. And this example provides a great reminder for your LSAT prep in general: Your job is not to master every line of printed material on the test, but rather to rack up points. If you can get this point by blowing past Harry, do it.

4. E

The ads for the new pill state only that it contains 44 percent fiber. Based on the nutritionists' recommendation, it is fair to assume that the ads mean to imply that people will get lots of fiber by taking these pills; after all, it is a fiber supplement. But you should always be suspicious when an argument (especially an advertisement!) employs percentages. Could it be that the ads are trying to suggest that by taking these pills, one would receive 44 percent of the fiber she needs? The more likely interpretation (the one the advertisers don't want people to see) is that the pill *itself* may be made up of 44 percent fiber, which doesn't mean that it contains a lot of fiber *relative to the amount of fiber one needs*. If (E) is true, these pills actually contain very little fiber—only 1/60 to 1/90 of the recommended daily intake. If this is the case, that 44 percent number is misleading; such a minuscule amount would hardly count as a supplement at all. If (E) is true, the ads should focus on the actual amount of fiber these pills add to one's diet, not on the irrelevant statistic offered, namely, how much of each pill is made up of fiber. (It is clear why the ads don't focus on the correct info; no one who knew the truth would buy such a useless product.)

(A) brings up other products, while the focus here is on these fiber pills only.

(B) addresses the basis of the nutritionists' recommendation, which isn't part of the advertisement itself.

(C) What does addiction to other types of pills have to do with the validity of these fiber ads?

(D) offers a classic example of a scope shift by referring to the *label* on the actual product while you're interested specifically in the product's *advertisement*.

- You may have found this stem a bit complex. Feel free to skip a question like this temporarily and return to it later if time permits. It's better to move on than to allow any one question to sap your confidence or your time, especially at the beginning of a section.
- If you understand how percentages differ from raw numbers, you won't mistake one for the other. A large percentage of something little is often, in actual terms, little. Here, the 44 percent figure is meant to sound impressive, but in actual terms it may amount to very little fiber. If (E) is true, the impression given by the 44 percent figure is misleading.

5. B

Essentially, the author says that it is impossible for consumers to avoid environmentally harmful products and that, therefore, consumers can't be held morally accountable for not avoiding them. Stated in more general terms, the author grants moral exemption for things beyond one's control. An appropriate concluding principle to the

Section IV

1.	Ⓐ Ⓑ Ⓒ Ⓓ Ⓔ	9.	Ⓐ Ⓑ Ⓒ Ⓓ Ⓔ	17.	Ⓐ Ⓑ Ⓒ Ⓓ Ⓔ	25.	Ⓐ Ⓑ Ⓒ Ⓓ Ⓔ
2.	Ⓐ Ⓑ Ⓒ Ⓓ Ⓔ	10.	Ⓐ Ⓑ Ⓒ Ⓓ Ⓔ	18.	Ⓐ Ⓑ Ⓒ Ⓓ Ⓔ	26.	Ⓐ Ⓑ Ⓒ Ⓓ Ⓔ
3.	Ⓐ Ⓑ Ⓒ Ⓓ Ⓔ	11.	Ⓐ Ⓑ Ⓒ Ⓓ Ⓔ	19.	Ⓐ Ⓑ Ⓒ Ⓓ Ⓔ	27.	Ⓐ Ⓑ Ⓒ Ⓓ Ⓔ
4.	Ⓐ Ⓑ Ⓒ Ⓓ Ⓔ	12.	Ⓐ Ⓑ Ⓒ Ⓓ Ⓔ	20.	Ⓐ Ⓑ Ⓒ Ⓓ Ⓔ	28.	Ⓐ Ⓑ Ⓒ Ⓓ Ⓔ
5.	Ⓐ Ⓑ Ⓒ Ⓓ Ⓔ	13.	Ⓐ Ⓑ Ⓒ Ⓓ Ⓔ	21.	Ⓐ Ⓑ Ⓒ Ⓓ Ⓔ	29.	Ⓐ Ⓑ Ⓒ Ⓓ Ⓔ
6.	Ⓐ Ⓑ Ⓒ Ⓓ Ⓔ	14.	Ⓐ Ⓑ Ⓒ Ⓓ Ⓔ	22.	Ⓐ Ⓑ Ⓒ Ⓓ Ⓔ	30.	Ⓐ Ⓑ Ⓒ Ⓓ Ⓔ
7.	Ⓐ Ⓑ Ⓒ Ⓓ Ⓔ	15.	Ⓐ Ⓑ Ⓒ Ⓓ Ⓔ	23.	Ⓐ Ⓑ Ⓒ Ⓓ Ⓔ		
8.	Ⓐ Ⓑ Ⓒ Ⓓ Ⓔ	16.	Ⓐ Ⓑ Ⓒ Ⓓ Ⓔ	24.	Ⓐ Ⓑ Ⓒ Ⓓ Ⓔ		

☐ # right in Section IV

☐ # wrong in Section IV

GO ONLINE

Be sure to add your scores to your syllabus.

LSAT PRACTICE TEST 1 ANSWER SHEET

Remove (or photocopy) the answer sheet and use it to complete the practice test.

How to Take the Practice Tests

Before taking each test, find a quiet place where you can work uninterrupted for about two and a half hours. Make sure you have a comfortable desk and several No. 2 pencils.

Each Practice Test includes four scored multiple-choice sections. Keep in mind that on the actual LSAT, there will be an additional multiple-choice section—the experimental section—that will not contribute to your score, plus an unscored Writing Sample.

Once you start a Practice Test, don't stop (except for a 5- to 10-minute break after the second section) until you've gone through all four sections. Remember, you can review any questions within a section, but you may not go back or forward a section.

Good luck!

Start with number 1 for each section. If a section has fewer questions than answer spaces, leave the extra spaces blank.

Section I

1.	A B C D E	9.	A B C D E	17.	A B C D E	25.	A B C D E	
2.	A B C D E	10.	A B C D E	18.	A B C D E	26.	A B C D E	
3.	A B C D E	11.	A B C D E	19.	A B C D E	27.	A B C D E	# right in Section I
4.	A B C D E	12.	A B C D E	20.	A B C D E	28.	A B C D E	
5.	A B C D E	13.	A B C D E	21.	A B C D E	29.	A B C D E	
6.	A B C D E	14.	A B C D E	22.	A B C D E	30.	A B C D E	
7.	A B C D E	15.	A B C D E	23.	A B C D E			# wrong in Section I
8.	A B C D E	16.	A B C D E	24.	A B C D E			

Section II

1.	A B C D E	9.	A B C D E	17.	A B C D E	25.	A B C D E	
2.	A B C D E	10.	A B C D E	18.	A B C D E	26.	A B C D E	
3.	A B C D E	11.	A B C D E	19.	A B C D E	27.	A B C D E	# right in Section II
4.	A B C D E	12.	A B C D E	20.	A B C D E	28.	A B C D E	
5.	A B C D E	13.	A B C D E	21.	A B C D E	29.	A B C D E	
6.	A B C D E	14.	A B C D E	22.	A B C D E	30.	A B C D E	
7.	A B C D E	15.	A B C D E	23.	A B C D E			# wrong in Section II
8.	A B C D E	16.	A B C D E	24.	A B C D E			

Section III

1.	A B C D E	9.	A B C D E	17.	A B C D E	25.	A B C D E	
2.	A B C D E	10.	A B C D E	18.	A B C D E	26.	A B C D E	
3.	A B C D E	11.	A B C D E	19.	A B C D E	27.	A B C D E	# right in Section III
4.	A B C D E	12.	A B C D E	20.	A B C D E	28.	A B C D E	
5.	A B C D E	13.	A B C D E	21.	A B C D E	29.	A B C D E	
6.	A B C D E	14.	A B C D E	22.	A B C D E	30.	A B C D E	
7.	A B C D E	15.	A B C D E	23.	A B C D E			# wrong in Section III
8.	A B C D E	16.	A B C D E	24.	A B C D E			

paragraph must be, at the very least, highly consistent with this general theme, and the completion must also be completely consistent with the statement "because of this impossibility there can be no moral duty." Perhaps you were able to prephrase the kind of principle the test-makers are after: "One can't be held morally accountable for actions that are impossible to avoid." This is what you get in (B).

If you had trouble prephrasing an answer here, you could still get the point by eliminating the wrong choices. Each wrong choice fails either because it shifts the scope, or doesn't provide the proper follow-up to the first part of the final sentence; that is, it ignores the notion of the impossible situation consumers face in following the environmentalists' recommendation.

(A) It is the unavoidable nature of an action that is in question here, not its effects.

(C) The stimulus focuses on the morality of consumption, not production, so (C) goes astray and cannot logically complete the argument.

(D) brings up the new concept of "least total harm," and ignores the issue of the conundrum faced by consumers trying to act in the way the environmentalists urge. This impossibility to act in this way is the central theme of the passage, and the principle in (D) has nothing to do with it at all.

(E) brings up other kinds of duty, but the author speaks only of moral duty, so this choice goes beyond the scope of the argument.

- Anticipating where the author is going is always a helpful strategy for dealing with Logical Reasoning stimuli and Reading Comp passages. However, a fill-in-the-blank question rewards you *directly* for your ability to predict where the author is going.

6. E

Here you get another advertisement, and it's easy to pick out the main point— "Subscribe to this magazine." The rest of the ad tells you *why* you should subscribe: The brain is a physical organ and since physical organs benefit from exercise, it follows that the brain will benefit from exercise. This magazine will exercise the brain, therefore this magazine will benefit the brain. What's the method? The ad compares the brain and muscles in the sense that they are both physical organs, and then reasons that since exercise helps one (muscles) it will also help the other (the brain). With all the comparisons being made here, the word "similar" in choice (E) should jump out. The ad implies that brains and muscles must be similar in one respect (they will both benefit from exercise) because they are similar in another (they are both physical organs).

(A) What experimental evidence?

(B) The ad may begin rather brusquely by stating that "anyone who exercises knows..." but it certainly does not ridicule anyone, so choice (B) will not do.

(C) The ad never explains how the magazine "exercises your brain"—it simply employs an analogy to attempt to demonstrate *that* it does. The "process" itself is never explained.

(D) Most ads, this one included, don't offer a careful analysis of anything. They offer soundbites, and sometimes, as in this case, a comparison. When you look closely, you see that there is no "careful analysis."

- The LSAT uses words very precisely. A "careful analysis" (D) is just that: something a scientist, scholar, or researcher might provide, not what you get in this light sales pitch. "Experimental evidence" in (A) is simply off the mark too. Put each choice through its paces, and if what it offers is not in the stimulus, cross it off.

7. C

Here's a second Method of Argument question in a row, so once again, you should pay attention to the logical structure as you read. First comes the claim that a reduction in health care costs won't happen within the current "piecemeal payment" system. Why? Because in this system there's an incentive to shift the financial burden to someone else. This is illustrated by the notion of a "pliable spending balloon"—push in on one part and an equally expensive bulge pops up in another. It's likely you've seen this argumentative technique before: When an author says that a health-care system, for example, *is like a balloon*, she is making an analogy. A suitable prephrase for this author's method would be "a claim is made, explained, and illustrated by analogy." Choice (C) gets the point.

(A) Shifting of cost to the patient is mentioned as a minor detail, but the "premise" of health-care reimbursement is not mentioned at all.

(B) is excessively negative in tone; the author speaks of flaws in the system, not of fraud by the people involved.

(D) No alternatives are mentioned, much less disparaged.

(E) goes against the passage: The instance cited in the last sentence is an example of a previous *failure* of an analogous system, not a demonstration of the feasibility of cooperation.

- The wrong choices in a Method of Argument question all fail to address the central structure of the argument. Try each choice out rigorously. Ask yourself: "Is this in here? Is this the way the argument proceeds?" You may have skimmed past the balloon analogy in your initial reading of the stimulus, but a thorough test of (C) would force you to ask "Is there an analogy here?" Actively searching the stimulus for an analogy, the balloon should then jump off the page, so to speak.

8. A

Now you're asked for an inference, and there's really no way to proceed here except by testing out the choices. Luckily, the first one fits the bill, and you can derive this inference from an interpretation of the first sentence. As you'll recall, the claim was that within the current "piecemeal" system, the problem of reducing health-care costs cannot be solved. What this means is that *if* a solution is to be found, it must come from something other than a "piecemeal" system, and (A)'s "comprehensive approach" is just the ticket. Translate "non-piecemeal" as "comprehensive," and you have choice (A).

Each of the other choices goes beyond the scope, and here you also find a few unjustified value assessments.

(B) You can't infer anything about the income of health-care professionals relative to available funding. The system's out of whack, for sure, but how the income of health-care professionals fits into the equation is never addressed.

(C) attempts to explain the rise in health care costs in a manner inconsistent with the author's explanation. Additional funds are not the problem; shift of burden is.

(D) The passage concerns the cost, not the quality of medical care. Furthermore, the issue of medical "technology" is so far from the scope that you can cut this choice for this word alone.

(E) goes way beyond the scope, dealing with the wisdom (a value assessment) of hospital capacity utilization and the issue of "large-scale emergencies."

- Some Inference questions are vulnerable to prephrasing; namely, questions with stimuli involving formal logic. If you see two or more statements that can be combined, go ahead and combine them and then scan the choices for the result. This is just like the process of making deductions in Logic Games. But in a stimulus like this one, the statements don't link up as easily, and the test-makers are most likely looking for an interpretation or paraphrase of one particular part of the passage. In this case, it's best to move right on to evaluating the choices.

9. D

Here's another Inference question, and a perfect place to enact the advice in the bullet point immediately above. It's possible to prephrase an answer, but it's still closer to the open-ended type of passage than the formal logic type, so simply evaluating the choices will be the best way to go unless a prephrase comes to mind. The statements in the stimulus center on the emphasis of the news media on spectacular events and the public's interpretation of this emphasis. The public links the amount of media attention to the actual risk of the events described, even though this may lead to a discrepancy between the perceived risk and the actual risk of certain events. The media gives more attention to more dramatic but statistically less risky accidents, and so if the public depends on the news media, the public will have a skewed idea of these risks. Taken together, this is precisely what the conclusion in choice (D) states.

(A) offers an irrelevant comparison. "Commercial media" includes both print and broadcast media, and the author draws no distinction between them.

(B) The author addresses the *results* of the media's behavior, not the *cause* of it. Whether the media pander to the "public's taste" is not a concern of the author.

(C) The passage gives you no basis on which to assess or infer anything about this issue of "control." You can assume that of the examples listed, planes and cars, many people would feel that they have more control driving than flying. But, first of all, this is an opinion that is not supported one way or the other by the passage. Secondly, these are just two examples that illustrate the author's overall point. For all you know, other "spectacular" events that are perceived as dangerous may be events over which people feel they have more control.

(E) attempts to make a specific prediction based on the statements given. However, it's hard to tell from the information given which would be the more "exceptional event," and so you cannot infer which event would receive more extensive coverage.

- Inferring a conclusion is different from forming a general inference. The latter could come as a result, interpretation, or combination of any part of the stimulus. It's not unusual for a general inference to be derived from a single sentence of a long stimulus. An example of this is question 8 above, in which (A) is simply an interpretation of the first sentence. An inferred conclusion, however, must take account of the overall movement of the passage; it must reflect where the author is going with the argument.

10. B

A large group was studied and a percentage of members exhibited behavioral problems. A dietary change was made and a decrease in this percentage was observed. Therefore, the author concludes, the change in diet caused the behavioral change. Such an argument necessarily assumes that no other factors may have influenced this behavioral change. The fact that no control group was used in the study to see if any other factors might be contributing to the behavioral change is a flaw in the study and in its interpretation by the author. The observed changes might have occurred in a control group as well, perhaps due to the extra attention the children received while involved in the study, or to other factors that may have been present. Choice (B) describes this flaw.

(A) is a true statement—no evidence is given relating the quantity of additives to the quantity of behavioral problems, but then again, no claims are made regarding this relationship, either. So the argument doesn't logically require such support.

(C) is also a true statement, but it's not a flaw since the percentage, not the actual *number* of problem children, is the issue here.

(D) is irrelevant, since the children who were *unaffected* by the dietary change are outside the scope of the argument.

(E) offers an alternative interpretation of the study, but goes beyond the scope by mentioning the *frequency* of behavioral problems. The author is concerned only with the percentage of children exhibiting behavioral problems, not with the specific *frequency* of those problems.

- In a Flaw question, steer clear of choices that fault the author for failing to provide information that the author has no obligation to provide. Evidence of a "proportionate reduction" (A), the exact number of problem children (C), and evidence regarding children unaffected by additives (D) are all irrelevant to the argument at hand. It is true that the author doesn't supply these pieces of evidence, but don't let that fool you: they are beyond the scope of her specific argument, so she doesn't have to address them.

11. C

When asked to explain a discrepancy in the stimulus, the first step is to locate the discrepancy. The unusual thing in the situation described is that a smaller percentage of the *older* cars had engine work done. One might think that a greater percentage of older cars would need repairs, but notice that the stimulus refers to which automobiles *had* repairs, not which *needed* them. If the cars from the 1960s are probably in more need of repair, why have a greater percentage of 1970s cars received repairs? Maybe you tried to prephrase an answer. You're dealing with percentages again, not raw numbers, so fewer older cars on the road wouldn't make for a good answer. Maybe you considered the economics associated with repairs: If a car is worth $500, and engine repairs cost $1,000, it probably doesn't make much financial sense to get the car repaired. This is the idea that gets the point: If older cars are not worth the expense, and are scrapped instead of repaired, then the statistics described in the stimulus are understandable. (C) nicely clears up the discrepancy.

(A) Inspection for emission levels probably would turn up more problems in older cars, which suggests that the older cars would have a greater percentage of repairs, so (A) only deepens the mystery.

(B) New cars are out of the scope based on the dates provided in the passage. Even if you considered the 1970s cars "new" (at least, newer than cars from the 1960s), this choice would, like (A), make the facts even less understandable.

(D) Whether or not simplified car engines result in fewer repairs is pretty shaky, but even if they did, (D) would also suggest that the sixties models would need more repairs.

(E) chastises those negligent sixties car owners for not maintaining their cars, but it doesn't mention 1970s cars, and thus does nothing to explain the discrepancy.

- When attempting to resolve a discrepancy, be wary of choices that further confound the odd result or finding found in the stimulus.
- When the discrepancy revolves around two groups or things (which is usually the case), quickly eliminate any choice, like (E) here, that offers information that relates to only one of them. A true resolution to such a discrepancy must be based on a fact that in some way relates to both groups.

12. A

Here you have an example of the type of formal logic inference question alluded to in the bullet point of question 8. How do you know formal logic is involved? There are three sentences. The first begins with "*no* mathematicians," the second with "*some* mathematicians," and the third with "*some* mathematicians." And in fact, despite the seemingly technical nature of the stimulus, the correct inference can be derived directly from a combination of the first and third sentences: No current mathematician would flatly refuse to accept a lengthy proof. But some mathematicians (that means current ones) still believe that simple theorems should have simple proofs. Since both of these statements are about the same group, current mathematicians, you can combine them: Some mathematicians (current ones) who believe proofs should be simple would not flatly refuse to accept a lengthy one—again, because of the first sentence: no current mathematician would reject a lengthy proof.

(B) and (E) The statements in the stimulus don't say anything about *non*-mathematicians, so these two choices are outside the scope.

(C) and (D) both discuss "individuals" and not specifically "mathematicians." While it may be true that the term "individuals" includes mathematicians, it also includes everyone else, and that's too general for this argument.

- It's crucial to translate statements correctly: "...some mathematicians *still* hold a strong belief..." means that these are *current* mathematicians, the same ones that appear in sentence 1, but not the same as the 1976 mathematicians in the second sentence. This is how you know to combine the first and third sentences; they both speak of a common group.
- The beauty of formal arguments is that they usually operate within strictly defined parameters. Therefore, when a choice offers a term that isn't perfectly within this boundary, such as "non-mathematician" or "individual," you can be reasonably sure that that choice is beyond the scope.

13. C

In question 13 you get more practice with formal logic in the form of a Parallel Reasoning question. Since it's just a straight parallel question (and not parallel flaw), characterize the conclusion. The conclusion is conditional—if one thing occurs, then another will occur. Now check the conclusions for each of the answer choices. In this question (like many parallel questions), you won't have to go any further than that to find the correct answer.

(A) concludes definitely—"you must try to." Eliminate it.

(B) has a conditional conclusion, but the format doesn't match—it isn't "if one thing occurs, another will," but "if you *want* one thing to occur, then you must do another." A little tougher to recognize, but definitely not a match. Eliminate it.

(C) A perfect match. If one thing, then another—the conclusion is a match, so hold on to this for now. You could check the evidence and confirm, but it won't be necessary for this question, since a quick check of all five choices will show that this is the only matching conclusion.

(D) Close, but this says "If one thing then *not* another. That's not a match and can be eliminated.

(E) Same pattern as (D). Eliminate it.

- The amount of formal logic on the LSAT varies from test to test, and from section to section. Formal logic is all over Logic Games, and it shows up in Logical Reasoning mainly in Inference and Parallel Reasoning questions like this one.

14. E

Here's a pleasant topic: lobster cannibalism. The argument is short, to the point, and missing a major chunk (so to speak), which is good because you're asked to find the author's assumption. Marine biologists theorize that trapped lobsters eat one another in response to hunger. The author refutes this claim by pointing out cases in which several lobsters trapped together for weeks or months did *not* eat one another. Notice, however, that there's nothing in the author's evidence that gives you an idea of how hungry the lobsters were, or how much food they had at the time they were trapped. For all you know, these lobsters could make do for much more than two months before getting hungry enough to eat one another. The author assumes that the lobsters she cites in her evidence were hungry lobsters. If they weren't hungry, then she has no business trampling on the marine biologists' theory.

(A) Lobsters that *aren't* in traps? They are outside the trap *and* outside the scope.

(B) and (C) are irrelevant. Neither affects the validity of the biologists' hypothesis (or, more to the point, the author's claim that the hypothesis is wrong).

(D) Other species of marine life are outside the scope; nothing about them can help fill the void in this argument about lobsters.

- Strong unqualified conclusions such as "the hypothesis is clearly wrong" are much more difficult to defend than qualified conclusions such as "the theory is *probably* wrong" or "the evidence *seems to show* the hypothesis is *unlikely*." Often, the assumption in arguments containing strong unqualified conclusions involves an alternative explanation or possibility—that is, a factor that the author has overlooked.
- Some question stems are a little wordy and introduce characters with whom you're not yet familiar. Don't let this throw you. Use that information to direct your reading of the stimulus and focus in on the pieces that will help you to answer the question.

15. A

The author is not happy about the ban on hunting: the deer population has multiplied by six, and the large deer population has caused property damage and accidents. Therefore, the author feels that the ban on hunting was unnecessary and has created safety hazards "that would not otherwise exist." But do you know for sure that the increase in the deer population was caused by the ban on hunting? The author assumes that the population explosion was *caused* by the ban on hunting because the increase came *after* the ban on hunting. Implicit in this assumption is the belief that the deer population would not have grown if the ban *weren't* enacted. Granted, there does seem to be a rational connection between fewer deer being shot and more deer being alive, but the author hasn't ruled out other factors. Choice (A) compensates for this weakness by showing how the deer population has *not* grown in nearby locales where hunting is allowed, suggesting that the deer population would not have grown in Greenfield if hunting had not been banned; (A) bolsters the author's assumption, and in so doing strengthens the argument.

(B) lends support only to evidence already given—that deer are often the unwitting cause of injury and accidents. It's not necessarily true that this is a direct result of the ban on hunting, however, since deer could probably wander on to the street whether or not hunting kept their population in check.

(C) is concerned with the welfare of the deer. While this might strengthen one type of argument against the ban on hunting, it doesn't strengthen the author's point that the increase in the number of deer is bad for *people*.

(D) doesn't do much either way. It may bring up a possible alternative explanation for the growth in the deer population, but it doesn't even do that well since you don't know whether the residents provided sustenance for the deer before the ban or only since it was enacted.

(E) provides more evidence for the statement that deer cause damage, but the author's conclusion isn't merely that damage occurs—it's that the damage is a result of the ban on hunting.

- One of the surest ways to strengthen an argument is to shore up a central assumption.
- Make sure you strengthen the right argument, that is, the one that's on the page. As shown above, many of the wrong choices lend support to arguments other than the one the author is making. This is why it's important to keep the author's conclusion firmly in mind while you evaluate the choices.
- Strengthening an argument is not the same as proving it. Correct choice (A) doesn't objectively *prove* that the ban was unnecessary and has created new risks to the public, as the author maintains, but it does increase the likelihood that the author is on target.
- Learn to recognize the kind of "after, therefore caused by" style of reasoning demonstrated in this argument. An author can't say that X causes Y based on evidence that Y came after X. Such an argument assumes that no other factor is responsible for Y.

16. B

The stem tells you to look for a valid inference. Scientists estimate the mass of comets by their brightness. It was recently discovered that the material in Halley's comet is less reflective than was once thought—that is, it reflects less light per unit of mass. Well, then, it follows that the comet must be bigger, or, rather, more massive than previously thought. With this thought in mind, (B) shines—the previous estimates based on its brightness were too low. The key here (and this may have been tricky to some) is to understand that the total amount of light given off is constant. So if it is discovered that much less light is reflected *per unit* of mass, yet the overall light reflected is the same, then it must be true that the comet is larger than previously thought. While scientists thought Halley's comet was a smaller comet shining very brightly, it is in fact a larger comet that gives out much less light per unit of mass.

(A) could be true based on the statements in the stimulus, but then again it could also be false. Maybe all comets are made of the same material; who knows? While this statement is not inconsistent with the stimulus, neither is it supported by the stimulus.

(C) claims that the total amount of light is less than previously thought, but this seems rather unlikely. Total amount of light is what the scientists have been using to make their estimates, and, as mentioned above, in this case you need to take this to be constant. The *interpretation* of the total amount of reflected light is what has come into question, not the amount itself.

(D) As in (A), you can't infer anything about the properties of other comets. This statement may or may not be true; you have no way of knowing from this passage.

(E) Brightness is still an effective way to estimate the mass of comets, which means that the newly received information can lead to a good estimate of the mass of Halley's comet. You therefore can't infer that more info is necessary.

- If you notice a pattern in the kinds of questions that give you trouble, make a habit of skipping those questions during your first run through the section. Some students shy away from numerical Logical Reasoning questions, and that's okay. If you had trouble interpreting what "60 times less light per unit of mass" meant, then this question may have been a good one to put off until later.

17. B

Next is an argument over paper. Previewing the stem, as always, you see that you're asked to critique the stationer's response to the office manager's comment. The office manager strongly implies that recycled paper is inferior. An appropriate response would address this concern, perhaps by stating that "recycled paper is not inferior," and then backing up that claim with good, solid evidence. The stationer does indeed address the issue, saying that recycled paper is not necessarily inferior, but then goes off on a tangent discussing the history of recycling in the production of paper. Now really, who cares about paper from the beginning of time? The stationer's evidence is irrelevant to the issue at hand: whether the recycled paper of today, the kind the office manager would use, is inferior. This is the stationer's major flaw—he fails to provide relevant evidence to support his claim in the defense of recycled paper, (B).

(A) If anything, the little history lesson indicates the stationery supplier *assumes* the office manager's ignorance on the topic.

(C) and (D) The environmental aspect of paper recycling and the basic technology of paper manufacturing aren't addressed in either side of the dialogue, so these choices can be eliminated.

(E) The stationer *does* explicitly address the manager's concern about quality by saying that recycled paper is not necessarily inferior, and then attempts to present evidence to back this up. The failure is in the *nature* of the evidence (it's irrelevant to current quality), not that he doesn't address the issue.

- It often helps to imagine how you would react to the various scenarios presented in Logical Reasoning. Since you know from the stem that you're to critique the second person's response, you can put yourself in the place of the first person, who would likely respond to the stationer: "Thanks for the history lesson, Jack, but I don't see what that has to do with the paper for our letters." When you put yourself in the place of the office manager, it's easier to see how the stationer's response is irrelevant.

18. C

The stem alerts you to the important statement: Peter's car got damaged, but Alicia's did not. You're asked to determine the purpose of this statement, so you'll need to examine the context in which it appears. Alicia and Peter committed the same offense—they borrowed cars without permission. Both were caught, but only Peter was punished. The author feels that Peter was punished only because the car he was driving was damaged while in his possession, although not by him. And here's the purpose of the statement mentioned in the stem: The author implies that equal crimes deserve equal punishment and, acknowledging the difference in the two situations, argues that this difference really shouldn't affect the magnitude of the offense since Peter didn't cause the damage. The author *acknowledges but downplays* the difference in situations. Someone might object to his argument by pointing out that Peter's car was damaged while Alicia's was not. Realizing this, the author mentions the damage done to the car to illustrate his awareness of the situation and to head off possible objections to the argument based on this fact—a preemptive strike, if you will.

Wrong choices (A), (B), and (D) all contradict the general gist of the argument:

(A) The different outcomes highlighted in the stem wouldn't support the conclusion that equal crimes deserve equal punishment, since the crimes would not then be equal after all. The author argues that this difference in results isn't relevant; she certainly doesn't use the difference to support her argument.

(B) It is clear from the conclusion and the overall tone of the passage that the author doesn't feel that the difference in outcomes is justified.

(D) The statement in question is not used to directly support the argument—it's meant to address a thorny issue in advance in order to get it out of the way. Furthermore, the statement concerns a specific difference in the results of this particular situation; it therefore is not even a "general principle."

(E) The statement in question is a minor detail the author counter-argued, not a summary of anything, and certainly not a central focus of the argument.

- Use sentence structure to help you understand Logical Reasoning stimuli. The structure "It is true that . . ., *but* . . ." strongly suggests that the author is admitting a fact, but attempting to downplay or dismiss it. This kind of prephrased notion accords nicely with correct choice (C).
- Use the skills you develop on other LSAT sections wherever they may apply. This variation of a Logical Reasoning Method of Argument question is very similar to the popular Reading Comp "purpose of detail" question.

19. C

No use rehashing the argument; it's all analyzed in question 18. You're looking for a statement that cannot be true, so simply try out the choices.

(A) Would justice have been better served if Peter had received only a warning? It's possible; it's certainly not inconsistent with the idea of equal punishment, since Peter and Alicia committed the same crime and Alicia got off with just a warning. Since (A) could be true, it can't be the answer, and you should move on.

(B) Is it possible that this is Alicia's first offense of this nature? Sure. If Peter is a first offender too, then you still have the possibility of equal crimes.

(C) essentially says that Peter was engaged in unsafe and illegal behavior when he hit the cab, while Alicia was well behaved. Can this be true? No: This choice contradicts the author's notion that the difference in the two cases was not due to any difference in the culpability of the two offenders. For that matter, it also directly contradicts the statement that the cab driver was at fault for Peter's accident. (C) can't be true, and is the answer. For the record:

(D) tells you that Alicia wasn't all that well behaved even before she was caught for the busted taillights. This is possible; this transgression is said to have occurred at an earlier time and thus is not connected to her apprehension. Since this information doesn't provide a major difference in the relevant circumstances of the respective cases, (D) could be true and is not the answer.

(E) offers up another historical difference between the offenders, not a difference between the offenses, so like all of the other wrong choices it's not inconsistent with the author's argument.

- A statement that "could be true" is any statement that does not flatly contradict the stimulus. Such a statement need not be inferable, probable, or even likely; as long as it doesn't go directly against anything in the stimulus, it theoretically could be true. In a "could be true EXCEPT" question, the correct choice will be the one that truly conflicts with the information in the stimulus; that is, the choice that cannot be true.

20. B

This is a parallel Flaw question, so our approach is a little different—you want to characterize the flaw in the stimulus and then check the answer choices for the corresponding flaw. The evidence in the argument states that if one particular candidate runs, another will not. The conclusion, though, says that *no one* else will run. So the argument makes a general conclusion (no one will run against Esposito) from specific evidence (Krasman will not run against Esposito). It overlooks the possibility that someone else might run against Esposito. You need to find the answer choice that is flawed in the same way.

(A) The problem here is a scope shift—the evidence is about not being able to attract large stores, but the conclusion is about not being "viable as a shopping district." It's similar in spirit to the stimulus, and a tempting wrong answer choice for the test taker who doesn't know to characterize the flaw specifically, but it's not a match for the flaw you identified.

(B) A perfect match. The evidence says the group won't play on a specific day, and the conclusion says it won't play on *any* day but Saturday. Just like the stimulus, this argument bases a broad conclusion on very narrow evidence—and overlooks the possibility that the band will play on any of the days not mentioned.

(C) The conclusion here is a very specific prediction, which is all you need to recognize in order to know that this argument doesn't match the "specific evidence/general conclusion" pattern of the stimulus.

(D) There's no flaw here. That's all you need to know, since you're looking to match the flaw that appeared in the stimulus. Eliminate.

(E) Another scope shift, from "the best one for a specific group" to "the one you should buy." That's a flaw, but not the same one you saw in the stimulus. Eliminate.

- Notice how the second sentence of correct choice (B) is written in reverse order compared with its counterpart in the original. The original was of the form "If X, then not Y." In (B), the second sentence reads "Not Y, if X." Logically, this is the same thing: "If it is raining, the car will not be dry" is equivalent to "The car will not be dry if it is raining." The correct choice is allowed to reverse a term, as long as it remains logically parallel to the original.

21. B

You're told in this Inference question that all nuclear accidents thus far have been caused by human error. Now jump to the last sentence, which requires a bit of a translation because of the double negative employed. "*cannot* be thought *unlikely*" means "it is thought likely." So the author essentially says in the last sentence that such everyday events of human error are likely to continue into the future. If human error won't end, and human error is the cause of nuclear accidents, you can infer that nuclear accidents are likely to occur again. Aside from the double negatives, it's a fairly straightforward inference. (B)'s "not improbable" means "probable, likely," so (B) is a close paraphrase of the inference.

(A) is a bit excessive; an "ever-increasing incidence of accidents" is a major exaggeration of "not unlikely." You can't infer that there will be more incidents every succeeding year from evidence that merely suggests that these incidents will probably happen.

(C) also goes overboard by suggesting that nothing can be done about the likelihood of human error.

(D) refers to nuclear power plant design, while the argument focuses on human error. The construction material for plants is outside the scope, and there's no way you can infer anything about them.

(E) attempts to make an absolute prediction about the technology side of the issue, but this prediction is not inferable: Just because an accident caused by a flaw in technology has never happened doesn't mean it never will.

- This question provides a good example of the way the test makers test your ability to translate tricky phrases. The passage and the correct choice both contain double negatives, and it's up to you to translate them into a more manageable form. "NOT UNlikely" means "likely." "NOT IMprobable" means "probable." Correctly translating complex phrases into simpler ones is not unimportant for LSAT success.

22. E

This question stem is somewhat unusual and complex: It asks you which question would elicit answers that would be relevant to evaluating a part of the stimulus, namely, the skeptics' position. That's a good place to start: The skeptics' position is that unusual animal behavior doesn't really predict earthquakes. It is a coincidence, they say, since unusual behavior is not really unusual; at any given time, some dogs will be behaving oddly. It may be hard to prephrase an answer here—your best bet is to evaluate each choice in light of each one's possible relevance to this issue. Choice (E) raises the most relevant question: How unusual is the unusual behavior anyway? If the so-called "unusual behavior" can be anything from barking to running in circles, then the skeptics may have a point, and the behavior may only be remembered because it came just before an earthquake. If, however, a dog stands up on its hind legs and does a jig immediately preceding an earthquake *and at no other time,* the skeptics' argument is weakened. The answer to the question posed in (E) would allow you to better evaluate the skeptics' position, which is why (E) gets the point.

The wrong choices, predictably, go outside of the scope, since anything that's relevant to the argument is necessarily *within* the scope.

(A) offers an irrelevant comparison. Who cares which group is more numerous? The issue is which group is *correct*.

(B) asks if there are other ways to predict earthquakes, but the issue in the stimulus is whether or not this one particular method, observing animal behavior, is reliable.

(C) asks about other animals, but the skeptics have focused their skepticism on dogs. Besides, even the non-skeptics in our stimulus wouldn't be likely to base their belief on behavior that is indistinguishable from normal behaviors.

(D) also focuses on other animals and thus strays from the apparent focus of the skeptics. Also, how *pronounced* the behavior is *isn't* the point—the point is how *unusual* the behavior is.

- "Relevant data" questions are fairly rare on the LSAT, but when they do appear they can be challenging since there will often be a variety of things that might be helpful in evaluating the argument. This makes it difficult to prephrase an answer to the question. Two thoughts that should help you test the choices in such a question: First, consider the various possible answers to each question (most can be answered with a yes or a no) and then see whether the different answers would lead to a different evaluation of the issue in question. Secondly, pay close attention to the scope of the argument; the wrong choices will be irrelevant and can therefore be eliminated.

23. D

The argument boils down to this: White-collar criminals are less likely to be convicted because they can afford expensive defense lawyers. A common assumption central to many such arguments of causality is that there are no other reasons for the stated result, in this case the lower conviction rate. If there is a greater percentage of the falsely accused in white collar crimes, these alleged criminals would be less likely to be convicted for reasons other than their expensive defense lawyers—it's simply a case that a greater percentage of them are innocent. This alternative explanation of the facts damages the argument that the smaller percentage of convictions for white-collar crimes *is due to the efforts of expensive lawyers*. Choice (D) supports the stimulus by ruling out this possible alternative explanation: By saying that the percentage of truly guilty defendants represented by public lawyers is no greater than the percentage guilty represented by private lawyers, (D) lends support to the idea that it *is* the attorney who makes the difference in the outcome of the case.

(A) is inconsistent with the notion that there is a higher conviction rate among street criminals. If street criminals can afford expensive lawyers, then, according to the argument, you would expect little difference in the conviction rate of white collar and street criminals.

(B) The relative skill level of *most* prosecutors has no effect on this argument. The prosecutors that *actually* handle white-collar cases could still be those few prosecutors that have the required skills.

(C) You are interested in the conviction *rate*, a percentage, not in the absolute number of convictions.

(E) weakens the argument by suggesting that there is a reason *other than* the effects of high-priced lawyers that impacts on the cited difference in conviction rates: Juries are simply more comfortable convicting street criminals as opposed to white collar criminals.

- In many arguments that assert causality (expensive lawyers *cause* fewer convictions), the author ignores possible alternative explanations. In other words, the author assumes that nothing else but the factor she cites could have led to the result. A choice that offers such an alternative weakens the argument by breaking down that central assumption. Conversely, a choice that eliminates from consideration a likely alternative—as (D) does here—strengthens the argument by shoring up the central assumption that nothing *else* led to the stated result.

24. A

Due to funding restrictions, scientists are bound to ignore findings that are not directly related to the goals of the funded research. Therefore, according to the author, serendipity (a kind of luck that yields unexpected happy results) can no longer play a role in discovery. In other words, since all findings must be directly related to goals, serendipity can't play a role in research. The author assumes that anything that researchers are not purposely looking for can't be directly related. It certainly seems possible, after all, that research might bring unexpected findings that *are* related, that *can* be used because, although unexpected, they do bear on the stated goals of the research. This assumption is described in (A).

(B) contradicts the stimulus' assertion that serendipity, and not clear predictions, played a major role in past scientific discovery.

(C) The author does not venture into the territory of the personal preference of the scientists. Nothing, therefore, need be assumed about this in order for the conclusion regarding the death of scientific serendipity to stand.

(D) gets things backwards: Those who receive grants must provide clear projections, which does not necessarily mean that those who provide clear projections must get grants. Even if the opposite of (D) is true, if some scientists who provide clear projections don't get grants, the argument remains unaffected because it's structured around those scientists who *do* receive their grants.

(E) brings up the concept of "value," which is outside the scope of this argument. The value of a finding isn't necessarily related to the way in which it was found. Nothing regarding "value" need be assumed.

- In order for a statement to meet the definition of an assumption, it must be both missing, meaning *unstated*, and required, meaning *necessary* for the argument to work.
- All assumptions stay within the scope of the argument. Notice how "findings purposely sought" in correct choice (A) is right in line with the major theme of the passage, whereas scientists' *preferences* (C) and the *value* of findings (E) are outside the scope.

25. D

The first step in resolving an apparent paradox is to locate it. Police statistics show that anti-theft devices reduce the risk of car theft. However, insurance companies claim that cars with such devices are *more likely* to be stolen. And therein lies the apparent paradox: cars with anti-theft devices appear to be both more likely *and* less likely to be stolen. Resolution of this inconsistency lies in the fact that the groups in the two statistical claims are not identical. The police statistics refer to a reduction in risk: One car with the device is less likely to be stolen than is *the same car* without the device. The insurance industry stats, however, compare different groups of cars—those with the devices to those without. So it is possible for the anti-theft devices to both reduce the overall risk of car theft for a single car and increase the likelihood of theft for that car *in comparison to cars without the device*. If (D) is true, the scenario makes sense: It allows for the police statistics to be true—the same car is less likely to be stolen with an anti-theft device than without it—while still allowing for the insurance industry claims to be true, since these are the cars that are both most likely to be stolen and, perhaps because they are so attractive to thieves, most likely to have an anti-theft device.

(A) Time is not in question in the argument. Whenever the theft *is* reported, it will find its way into the statistics, and the apparent paradox will still exist.

(B) approaches the issue from the wrong perspective. In both the police and the insurance industry claims, the issue is the change in the risk percentage from one level to another depending on the installation of the device. (B) offers general information that does not impact on the issue of the *increase* or *reduction* of risk associated with the device. (B) can be a true statement and still offer no help in resolving the paradox.

(C) doesn't help to explain either claim, much less how they could be true together. If certain anti-theft devices tend to produce many false alarms for every actual attempted theft (C), then the devices seem *less* valuable as crime prevention devices, since people presumably won't pay attention to alarms that almost always "cry wolf." But this still wouldn't explain why cars equipped with these devices are *more* likely to be stolen, and it seems inconsistent with the notion that these devices are effective in preventing car thefts.

(E) undermines in the same way as (C) the claim that the devices are effective in preventing thefts, but still wouldn't explain why cars equipped with the devices are more likely to be stolen than their unequipped counterparts. So (E) does nothing to solve the mystery.

- Often, LSAT "apparent paradoxes" are based on subtle scope shifts. Once you pick out the shift in scope, you're better able to debunk the paradox—that is, show that the situation is not paradoxical at all. In this case, the key was noticing the difference between the statistical claims: The police stats speak of one car's comparative risk with and without the device. The insurance industry's claims, on the other hand, speak of the likelihood that a car that will be stolen comes from the group of cars with the device or the group of cars without it.

SECTION II: ANALYTICAL REASONING

GAME 1—Broadcast News

The Action

"Seven consecutive time slots" immediately suggests a sequencing game, and that's exactly what you get in Game 1. A slight oddity is introduced, but it turns out to be inconsequential: Six of the seven entities are song tapes with letter names, while the last entity is referred to as a "news tape." Usually such a differentiation between entities means something, but here it doesn't—if you call the news tape N, you simply have seven lettered entities to fit into seven time slots, which is as familiar a game action as any you'll see on the Logic Games section. You're told that no tapes share a time slot, and no tape is longer than any other, which are just loophole closers. So far then, any tape can be slotted anywhere.

The Initial Setup

A roster of the entities and seven dashes on your page should do it for an initial setup—there's no need to get any fancier than that. You can include the news tape, N, alphabetically between L and O, or keep N separate for now, just in case this tape takes on some special significance in the game. (As you'll see, it doesn't—N will be regarded as just another entity.)

G H L O P S and N

__ __ __ __ __ __ __

The Rules

1) Rule 1 is a traditional sequencing rule that pairs up a couple of entities in a specific order. The upshot is that you'll always have LO somewhere in the list, and you can simply denote this as ALWAYS LO.
2) Rule 2 links up nicely with Rule 1, and you probably didn't have to wait until you got to Step 4 of the Kaplan Method to combine these rules to create an even bigger cluster: LO....N. Song tape O comes immediately after L, and then N must come some time after that. The dots remind you that it's okay for other tapes to come between O and N; the rule is satisfied as long as N is anywhere to the right of LO.
3) Don't let the wordiness of Rule 3 intimidate you: All it says is that two tapes must come between G and P, but G and P can appear in either order. This allows for two possibilities: G _ _ P or P _ _ G.

Deductions

In a game so basic, there's often not much in the way of deductions. However, there are usually some implications of the rules that are worth noting. Take, for example, our main LO...N bloc. What does this tell you about L? **L can't be played in slots six or seven, right?** If it were, there wouldn't be enough room for N at the end, and possibly O as well. Similarly, **N can't be played in slots one or two,** because that would shove L, O, or both off the map at the beginning of the sequence. These may not seem like major deductions, but these limitations directly help you bag a few questions, notably questions 2 and 6.

The Final Visualization

Here's what you have to work with heading into the questions:

G H L O P S and N

__ __ __ __ __ __ __

Always LO...N

G __ __ P or P __ __ G

The Big Picture

- Shorthanding a rule on the page will help you to solidify the rule in your mind and to convince yourself that you've interpreted the rule correctly. The wordiness of Rule 3 can be reduced to the convenient shorthand indicated above, and if you had any doubt as to the correct interpretation of that rule, working out the two concrete possibilities on your page should have helped to ease such doubt.
- The purpose of shorthand is to relieve you of the burden of returning to the written rules on the page. Re-reading the text of Rules 1 and 2 takes longer than eyeballing the LO...N bloc created by those rules.

- Not all entities fulfill the same roles within a game. Some entities, like L, O, and N here, are major players: They form blocs that practically scream for attention in many questions. Blocs are important in that they often offer a starting point in the questions—something to immediately focus on when you don't know where to begin.
- On the other side of the spectrum from the major players are the "floaters." These entities are by no means unimportant. While you may begin your work in many of the questions with your blocs and high-profile entities, you'll often be called upon to fill in the ordering with the more unrestricted entities. That's why it's a good idea to at least take notice of the entities bound by few, or even no, restrictions. Here, H and S are not mentioned at all in the rules, and both are completely free to roam throughout the schedule to fill in the gaps left by the others.
- A familiar game type with seven questions is a great place to begin work on the Logic Games section. Here, the test makers were kind and put this game right up front. But sometimes they hide these easier games later on in the section. Preview the section quickly before jumping into the first game. Hopefully, you'll find the one that's easiest for you, and there's nothing better for your confidence (and your score) than to get off to a fast start on the easiest game on the section.

The Questions

1. C

Whenever you see a new "if" in the question stem, get the information into a new sketch and see where it leads. Placing G into the second slot kicks Rule 3 into effect, forcing P into slot five; that's the only way that exactly two time slots will fit between G and P as mandated by Rule 3. That leaves the LO...N bloc as your next major concern. The LO pair physically fits into slots three and four or slots six and seven, but the latter case leaves no room for N. So L must be played third, and O fourth. The stem asks which tape must be third, and there you have it: L, choice (C).

- Usually a sequencing game will begin with an acceptability question, giving you the opportunity to try out the rules and pick up an easy point. But even though this game lacks a standard acceptability question, a question like this one is a nice substitute—you get to try your hand at the rules and "get acquainted" with the game. Use the first few questions to reinforce your understanding of the game.
- Don't let slightly odd conventions throw you off. It's obvious from this first question that "the news" tape will be referred to as such throughout the game, but to you it's plain old "N."

2. A

You've already given N all the consideration that question 2 requires. Recall N's limitations, discussed in the Deductions section above: N cannot be played first, because then there would be no room for the LO pair before it, and N can't be played second, because even if you squeeze O into slot one, L would be left out in the cold. You're looking for the time slot that N can't take, so it's either one or two. The test makers chose "second" for (A).

- You need not draw something new for every question. Non-"if" questions, especially, are sometimes answerable based on your knowledge of the game and the sketching you did up front.
- Don't waste time on additional choices after you've found a choice that works. N *cannot* be second, so that's all you need to know to select (A). You don't have to *also* prove that slots three, four, five, and six are okay for N; they *must* be, since there can be only one correct answer. It doesn't hurt to notice that you're implicitly told that N can take any slot from three to six; for all you know, this information may come in handy later. If you noticed this, great. But if you spent time *checking* (B) through (E) "just for good measure," you need to work on how you prioritize your time.

3. C

Here, the two free agents, H and S, are to be slotted as far from each other as possible. "How far is that?" is the question that should come to mind. You may as well try placing them on opposite sides of the ordering, that is, in slots one and seven. And it doesn't matter which is on which side, since neither H nor S has any relationship to any other entity, thus making them functionally identical. Trying it out, you find that it is possible to place H and S on opposite ends of the ordering, as long as L and O take slots three and four, respectively. If this pair is in any other consecutive slots between two and six, there's no way to satisfy Rule 3. A little trial and error shows that L and O must be in slots three and four, surrounded by G and P, in either order, in two and five. N is left for slot six.

Now, you're asked about the first three slots, and while there's some variability in slots one and two (slot one can be H or S, and slot two can be G or P), slot three is definitely reserved for L, so our best bet is to check the choices for that. This narrows the possibilities down to (A) and (C), and (A) is out for two reasons: First, G H L is an impossible way to start the sequence under any circumstances: Rule 1 would force O into slot four, while Rule 3 would have it going to P. That's enough to eliminate (A). The other problem with (A) is that it doesn't fulfill the requirement in the stem: H, in slot two, is not the furthest it could be from S. That leaves (C): H G L is a possible beginning for the ordering under these circumstances, as long as you flesh it out with O P N S, in that order.

- Don't be afraid of a little trial and error—taking a few extra seconds to test out various arrangements before hitting the choices often pays off in a big way. Shrewd test takers look for ways to eliminate choices in bunches. Here, playing with the possibilities until noting that L is a definite for slot three is the way to kill (B), (D), and (E) in one fell swoop. Remember, though, that you have to make good judgments about the use of your time—a question that requires playing out different scenarios may be best left until the end of the game, not just to save time but because you may do some directed work on other questions that will help you find the answer.

4. C

What happens when P is fifth? G is second, and you're right back at question 1 again. Lucky for us, since you've already worked through this scenario: As you saw there, when G is second and P is fifth, L must be third, (C).

- "Too easy," you're thinking? Every Logic Games section has its share of low, medium, and high difficulty points, and the way to master the timing of the section and finish in 35 minutes is to snap up the easy points quickly, leaving extra time for the more difficult games and questions.

- Don't be surprised to see the same question asked in different forms. As you get on in a game, strive to use previous work whenever possible to help answer questions, or at least eliminate a few choices. And in fact, you get another opportunity to apply this strategy in question 5.

5. E

What's the greatest number of tapes you can get between S and N? As mentioned just above, you can use our previous orderings to help you out here. You've seen the same partial ordering in questions 1 and 4:

_ G L O P _ _

Can you get all the tapes between S and N? Sure; if the familiar GLOP sequence occupies slots two through five, you can place S into slot one and N into slot seven (which leaves H for slot six), and you're done. It is possible to fit all five of the other tapes between S and N, (E).

- When asked for a maximum in any situation, start with the greatest number possible. It makes no sense to test whether three time slots can come between S and N; even if the answer is yes, you'd still have to test four, and then five. Start at the highest number and work your way down. The same principle applies to handling the stem in question 3 here, in which you're asked to put as much distance as possible between H and S. Conversely, when asked for a *minimum*, start testing the smallest possible number and work your way up.
- The ordering above is not the only one that proves that S and N can be separated by all of the other tapes; S H P L O G N is another example. You could have gotten the point by constructing any one of a number of acceptable orderings that place S first and N last. But you're interested in *saving time*, and it's fastest to use previous work that's already down on the page.

6. C

Another quick point for work already done: You thought through L's limitations up front, so this one shouldn't take much more than a few seconds. Since both O and N must come after L, L cannot be played sixth or seventh, which means the latest slot possible for L is fifth, (C). And placing L fifth causes no other violations, as the ordering "G H S P L O N" readily proves.

- Don't be surprised to find a "gimme" late in the game. The questions are not presented in order of difficulty, and sometimes the test makers reward those who reach the end of games with a quick and easy point.

7. D

You're looking for a time slot for G that will decisively fix the time slot for O, and once again previous work in questions 1 and 4 can help you out. In both of those questions, G was second, which forced L to be third and O to be fourth. "Second," which would therefore be a viable answer, is conspicuously absent; notice how the choices jump right from "first" to "third." This is not a problem, though, once you remember that G and P are interchangeable in this game. You can switch

_ G L O P _ _

from questions 1 and 4 to

_ P L O G _ _

without altering the logic in any way. P in two and G in five would thus force the same situation you've seen a number of times—L in 3 and O in 4. So placing G in slot five fixes O in slot four, and (D) is correct for the final question of this first game.

For the record:

(A) If G is first, then P is fourth, and O can be slotted third or sixth.

(B) If G is third, then P is sixth, and O can be slotted second or fifth.

(C) If G is fourth, then P could be first, in which case O can be slotted third or sixth.

(E) If G is sixth, then P is third, and O can be slotted second or fifth.

- Again, it's fastest to rely on previous work, but it's not the only way to get the answer. You may have resorted to trying out the choices, in which case the method would be to put G first, then third, then fourth, and so on, each time testing for whether O can be fit into more than one possible slot. When you try G fifth, you'll find O is limited to slot four, confirming (D) as the correct answer. This is a valid method, and *will* get the point. But since you've seen a situation very much like this before, the better and *faster* way is to consult earlier work.

GAME 2—Doctor's Activities

The Action

Next you come face to face with the hectic world of one Doctor Yamata, who performs various activities during the course of a week. Scheduling events or activities during days of a week, mornings and afternoons, isn't too unusual—this common everyday scenario is the foundation of a number of games you'll encounter in a Kaplan course. One odd feature of this one, though, is the actual days of the week; notice that Thursday is missing (probably golf day). Hopefully you didn't breeze by this little wrinkle. The action mainly involves distributing four activities over the course of a week, which places the game in the grouping camp. Most schedule games have a heavy sequencing element, but here there's really only one true sequencing rule, Rule 3. And the questions don't really hinge on normal sequencing aspects, such as "before" and "after." So call this a grouping game of distribution with a slight sequencing element attached. You're asked to distribute activities over the course of a slightly irregular workweek.

The Initial Setup

A chart indicating the mornings and afternoons of Yamata's workdays (don't forget, no Thursday!) is in order here, with the activities listed underneath. There are numerous ways to shorthand the activities: For convenience, use L for lecturing, O for operating, T for treating patients, and C for conducting research.

	M	T	W	Th	F	S
AM				X		
PM				X		

L O T C

Note that the intro paragraph specifies that exactly one activity will be performed during each morning and afternoon shift, which eliminates the possibility of placing multiple letters in a single box. Our job, then, is to fill each box (time slot) with exactly one letter (activity) as directed by the rules and questions.

The Rules

1) Rule 1 narrows things down nicely—three of the five boxes in our top morning row will be filled with O's. You're not sure which yet, but it's a start. Sketch in "OOO" to the right of the morning row.
2) Rule 2 is an if-then rule, common to grouping games of distribution. If O Mon, no O Tues. Naturally, you want to think through the contrapositive, and get that down on the page as well: If O Tues, no O Mon. It's possible at this point to combine this with Rule 1, since both deal with operating. But hold off for now and wait until Step 4 of the Kaplan Method; you'll piece it all together below in the Deductions section.
3) Here's the sequencing rule alluded to: you need to place L's in the afternoon row on "exactly two *consecutive* calendar days." This raises the question "what *are* "consecutive calendar days" in this setup?" Here's where the missing Thursday comes into play. In Yamata's schedule, consecutive calendar days are Monday and Tuesday, Tuesday and Wednesday, and Friday and Saturday—*not Wednesday and Friday*. Wednesday and Friday are not "consecutive calendar days." For now, indicate the consecutive L's on the page, and move on.
4) Rule 4 tells you that you'll need to fit exactly one T in the morning row and exactly three T's in the afternoon row—another significant fact that you'll come back to in a jiffy.
5) Conducting research, C, gets into the act, or at least into the top morning row, exactly once. Indicate that near your other morning notes.
6) No L's or O's on Saturday, which turns out to be a key piece of information that allows you to blow this game wide open.

Deductions

Before reading these deductions, go back over the game and the rules and try to piece the puzzle together yourself. If you had no trouble the first time, and feel you got most or all of the deductions, that's great; you probably breezed through the questions, and you need not repeat this exercise. If you had trouble with this game, Step 4 of the Kaplan Method is the skill you need to work on, and this is a great game on which to practice making deductions.

Here's the objective: **It may take a few minutes, but it's possible to deduce a full five of the ten calendar slots, and to narrow the other five down to a few possible activities.** When you've gone as far as you can go, check your work against the following Deductions.

Begin with the afternoon lectures. You need to place two L's on consecutive calendar days, and you know two major things: There can be no lecture on Saturday (Rule 6), so Friday-Saturday is impossible for the two consecutive L's; and, as discussed above, *Wednesday and Friday are not consecutive calendar days*. That means that the two afternoon lectures must be on Monday-Tuesday or on Tuesday-Wednesday. Either way, then, **Tuesday afternoon is devoted to lecturing, and the other afternoon lecture must be on Monday or Wednesday.** You also know that you must place exactly three T's in the afternoon slots (Rule 4), which along with the two L's completes the afternoon roster. Well, what slots are available? You just deduced that one L is on Tuesday afternoon. If the other afternoon L is scheduled for Monday, then treating patients would fall on Wednesday, Friday, and Saturday afternoons. If, however, the other afternoon L is on Wednesday, then treating patients would take place on Monday, Friday, and Saturday afternoons. Either way, **the good doctor must treat patients on Friday and Saturday afternoons. The other afternoon T will fall on Monday or Wednesday, whichever is not taken up by the remaining afternoon lecture**.

What about the morning time slots? The entities are set; you're to distribute 3 O's, 1 T, and 1 C into the five morning slots (Rules 1, 4, and 5). There's lots of information regarding the operating days, and operating takes up three of the five morning slots, so begin there. No O on Saturday—Rule 6 forbids it. That makes it easier: **Saturday morning will be devoted to treating patients or conducting research**, and you can focus on distributing 3 O's into the first four days—Monday, Tuesday, Wednesday, and Friday. And Rule 2 narrows down the possibilities even further: If she operates on Monday, then she doesn't operate on Tuesday, which means she must operate on Wednesday and Friday. Similarly, if she operates on Tuesday, then she doesn't operate on Monday (the contrapositive of Rule 2), and must again operate on Wednesday and Friday to satisfy Rule 1. Either way, **Yamata must operate on Wednesday and Friday mornings, and the third operating morning will be on Monday or Tuesday. Whichever activity is not on Saturday morning, T or C, will fall on Monday or Tuesday morning, the slot not taken by the final O.**

The Final Visualization

Whew! It may seem like a lot of time to spend up front, but as you'll see, compiling this great information into one sketch makes for quick, stress-free questions later on. Here's the load of deductions you have to work with heading into the questions:

O

	M	T	W	Th	F	S	
AM	O	X	O	X	O	T/C	OOO C T
PM	L/T	L	L/T	X	T	T	LL TTT

If O Mon then no O Tues
If O Tues then no O Mon

The Big Picture

- Some games have no significant Deductions. Others are *entirely based* on Deductions. The rest fall somewhere in the middle, containing one or two major deductions that make the questions more manageable. Granted, you can get points in this game without working through the steps described above, but this will probably take you much longer; you may be forced to re-invent the wheel for every question, and that involves time and stress. The most efficient and timely way to handle a game is to piece as much together as possible before hitting the questions. The point of your Logic Games practice is to hone and reinforce this skill. If you got most or all of the deductions on your own the first time around, great! Keep doing what you're doing. If not, use games like this as an opportunity to get to that level. That's what practice is for.
- Critical reading is essential for success on every section of the LSAT. Just because there's much less text in the Logic Games section than in the others doesn't mean you can read less carefully. In fact, just the opposite is the case: The relative brevity of the games makes every rule, every line, even every *word* that much more important—just think of the difference between "exactly" and "at least." And speaking of reading critically...
- When a rule like Rule 3 here uses a phrase like "consecutive calendar days," stop to make sure you know what that means *in the context of the game*. Here, Wednesday and Friday are not "consecutive calendar days." Those who overlooked this fact were in for a rough time of it.

The Questions

8. B

Tuesday afternoon is a definite lecture. Armed with our Deductions, question 8 is a definite five-second point.

(A), (C), (D) and (E) As you've seen, the second afternoon lecture must be on either Monday or Wednesday, so (A) and (C) are possible only, while (D) and (E) are flat out impossible.

9. C

As you deduced, operating is a must for Wednesday morning, which narrows the choices down to (C) and (D). The Wednesday afternoon activity must be either lecturing or treating patients, which confirms (C) and eliminates (D) as the possible schedule for Wednesday.

Questions 10 and 11 follow question 12.

12. E

Right off the sketch: Treating patients is the activity for Friday and Saturday afternoon, (E).

- Like many battles, this game is won or lost in the planning stage, that is, in the setup. Proper work up front saves time, cuts down on stress, and boosts confidence during Step 5 of the Kaplan Method, answering the questions. If you've put in the work, this is the reward.
- While questions 10 and 11 require a little more thought, the answers to questions 8, 9, and 12 can be simply read off the final sketch, which is why you should do them together. If you've started honing your time management skills, you may have even done the questions in this order. When so much has been deduced, try scanning the questions for things that have already been determined (non-ifs are a good bet).
- In Logic Games, confidence is key—don't second-guess yourself. If you've made deductions up front, *use them*. Trust your Final Visualization: It's based on your understanding of the game, and if you took

your time and were careful, there's no reason to doubt your work now. The questions *should* largely be falling into your lap—that's your reward for all your great thinking up front.

10. E

Another non-if, but this one's a little more involved. Still, all you need to do is check the choices against the sketch.

(A) Must Yamata treat patients on both shifts of a single day? She treats patients in the afternoon on Saturday, but could conduct research Saturday morning. Friday has T in the afternoon and O in the morning. And the final afternoon T could be on Wednesday, a day on which she operates in the morning. So (A) need not be true.

(B) Must she conduct research and lecture on the same day? No—the two afternoon L's could be scheduled for Tuesday and Wednesday, both days on which Yamata can perform operations in the morning.

(C) Must she conduct research and treat patients on the same day? No—Yamata could treat patients on Wednesday, Friday, and Saturday afternoons, while conducting research only on Monday morning.

(D) Must she lecture and treat patients on the same day? No—the one morning T can be placed on Saturday, far away from the two afternoon L's.

(E) must be correct. And in fact, there's no way to avoid having at least one day containing a lecture and operation. One lecture is always Tuesday, and the other is Monday or Wednesday. If it's on Monday, then you have L's Monday and Tuesday, and exactly one operation must fall on either Monday or Tuesday morning. If, however, the second afternoon lecture is on Wednesday, then that's all you need to know: Yamata must operate on Wednesday morning, so no matter how you space out the afternoon lectures, there will always be at least one day containing both a lecture and operation.

- The more writing you do up front—that is, the more deductions you make—the less writing you'll need to do during the questions stage. In most cases, you won't need to lift your pencil for a non-if question; just follow the directions in the stem and look for the answer in your master sketch, or check each choice against the sketch, as the case may be.
- Here's another way to save time: When trying out choices, if you've eliminated four, choose the other by process of elimination without checking it. This goes back to the point made above regarding confidence: If you have it, you trust your work, and are comfortable penciling in (E) without bothering to check it, because you know that (A) through (D) are wrong, and there has to be *some* answer. Less confident gamesters, on the other hand, think "Oh no, I may have done something wrong. Better work out (E) . . ." Try to get out of this habit; work through a remaining choice only if you're *really* unsure of your work on the others.
- In a "must be true" question, the correct answer often involves one or more of the most restricted entities. If you need to try out the choices, you can possibly save some time by trying these choices first.

11. E

Here's our first "if" question—suppose that Yamata operates on Tuesday. No problem; that means that the days for operations are set at Tuesday, Wednesday, and Friday, and you're interested in when she can possibly treat patients. According to Rule 4, she must treat patients on exactly three afternoons; that alone eliminates (A) and (B), which include only two afternoons. Furthermore, you know from our work up front that she must treat patients Friday and Saturday afternoons; in fact, that's the answer to question 12, and allows you to delete (C), which leaves out Friday afternoon. (D) falls by the wayside, because operating is scheduled for Wednesday morning. (E) is all that remains, and represents a perfectly valid schedule for treating patients.

- Notice how the if-clause in the stem was unnecessary, as you were able to eliminate all of the wrong choices straight from the rules and deductions. Occasionally the test makers will throw in a superfluous "if"—but it doesn't happen often. In any case, don't worry if you think you can answer the question without enacting the if-clause; this situation is not without precedent.

GAME 3—Conservatives, Moderates, and Liberals

The Action

You're presented with seven judges, each of whom voted either for or against a petition. One way to look at this is that each entity is either in or out, which strongly suggests grouping—specifically a grouping game of selection. The entities are two conservatives, two moderates, and three liberals.

The Initial Setup

First, get the basics down on the page. Since it's a Selection game, start with a list of the entities; as you work through the rules, circle the fors and cross out the againsts.

C C M M L L L

The Rules

4) A quick scan of the rules tells you that Rule 4 is the most concrete, and you can put this information right into the sketch: At least one conservative votes against Datalog, which means that you can cross out one C.

3) While you're at it, you may as well take care of Rule 3, and save the two conditional rules for last. Rule 3 tells you that at least 2 judges vote for Datalog, and at least 2 against. Take a moment to give some thought to what this rule means. There are seven judges, and they all vote. That means that a requirement for at least two fors and at least two againsts strictly limits our possible breakdowns—you could have a 2-5 split or a 3-4 split. Those are the only possibilities that comply with this rule.

1) Now the if-thens: If both conservatives and at least one liberal voted the same way, then both moderates voted that way as well. Thanks to Rule 4, you can take this one step further (although if this didn't jump out at you, you'd save this for the Deduction step). You know from that rule that at least one conservative said nay. Thus, if both conservatives and at least one liberal voted the same way, then that way must be against. The rule then tells you that under these circumstances, the two moderates will vote against as well:

~~C~~ ~~C~~ ~~M~~ ~~M~~ ~~L~~ L L

Now you may have taken this rule even further, or you may have waited until Step 4 of the Kaplan Method. If you handled the rules in order from 1 to 4, that's probably what you did, but since you've already incorporated Rules 3 and 4, continue. Since you still need two votes in favor of the petition (Rule 3), in this situation the two remaining liberals must have voted for it. So Rule 1, if enacted, really boils down to this:

If both Cs vote against and 1 L votes against, then:

~~C~~ ~~C~~ ~~M~~ ~~M~~ ~~L~~ (L) (L)

Remember, though, that this rule is conditional—what you just played out happens only **if** 2 conservatives and 1 liberal vote the same. This doesn't, therefore, go in your master sketch—if you thought this through in advance, a little sketch off to the side to reflect the implications of this rule is in order.

2) If the three liberals voted the same, then neither conservative voted that way, which is to say that both conservatives voted the other way. You can shorthand this any way that makes sense to you. Here's one possibility:

If Ls the same, then Cs opposite

Now take a further look at the implications of this rule in "Deductions."

Deductions

You've already worked through a few implications of the rules by combining the more concrete Rules 3 and 4 with the first two if-then rules. But a little extra thought will reveal one more major thing—did you see it? It's derived by combining Rules 2 and 4.

If the three liberals voted the same, then both conservatives voted the opposite, and you know from Rule 4 that at least one conservative voted against. So the situation works if all three liberals voted *for* the petition, in which case both conservatives must have voted against. But the other option is impossible: If all the liberals voted *against* the petition, then Rule 2 would require that both conservatives vote *for* it. But that would violate Rule 4, so it's impossible for all three liberals to vote against the petition. Which means, driving this thought to completion, that **at least one liberal must have voted for the petition**. This insight bags questions 14 and 15 directly, and is just useful knowledge throughout. Circle an L (and you can make your shorthand for Rule 2 more specific thanks to this deduction). Now you're ready to attack the questions.

The Final Visualization

Here's what a good final sketch might look like:

~~C~~ C M M L Ⓛ L

at least 2 FOR
at least 2 AGAINST
if both Cs AGAINST and 1 L AGAINST, then both Ms AGAINST and 2 Ls FOR
if all Ls FOR, then both Cs AGAINST

The Big Picture

- Use your experience on previous games to help you grasp the action of each game you face. While the games each have different characters and settings, their logical structures repeat over and over again. Here, voting for or against a petition is the same as any other yes/no decision for an entity—deciding whether an entity goes on a boat trip or not, sits on a committee or not, is selected as a book for a course or not, and so on. In each case, each entity is either in or out. Seen in this light, this game is nothing more than a standard grouping game of selection, and should be treated as such.
- You need not tackle the rules in the order given on the page. A concrete rule like Rule 4 here is a good rule to begin with because it allows you to add information directly into the sketch, which often makes it easier to assimilate the other rules. Getting something definite on the page gives you some substance around which the more abstract rules can be worked out.
- Always drive information toward the concrete. "If the two conservatives voted the same way . . ." in Rule 1 means something very definite in light of Rule 4. It means "if both conservatives voted *against* . . ." Always translate statements in light of the other information at your disposal. Here's a tangible example of how handling the concrete Rule 4 first pays off when dealing with the more abstract Rule 1.

The Questions

13. B

If the moderates split their votes, then one voted for and the other voted against. Quickly jot this down in a new sketch:

~~C~~ C ~~M~~ Ⓜ Ⓛ L L

The contrapositive of Rule 1, which you should have noted earlier in the setup stage, is that if the moderates split their votes, then it cannot be true that both conservatives and at least one liberal voted the same way. But following this train of thought gets a little messy, because there are a few different ways to ensure this doesn't happen. The better method here, since you're dealing with a "could be true" question, is to test the choices against the sketch just created and eliminate those that contradict the information.

(A) The voting arrangement that would result from (A) would violate Rule 1: you would have both conservatives and one liberal voting against the petition, which, according to Rule 1, would force both moderates to vote against as well. But the stem has it otherwise.

(B) works. It looks like this:

~~C~~ Ⓒ ~~M~~ Ⓜ Ⓛ ~~L~~ ~~L~~

However, don't play it out until you consider whether the remaining choices can be quickly eliminated—what *can't* happen is far more concrete than what *might* happen.

(C) violates Rule 2—if all three liberals voted for the petition, then both conservatives would have to vote against, but (C) has one of the conservatives voting in favor of the petition.

(D) and (E) both violate Rule 4, which requires at least one "nay" among the conservatives.

- Don't hesitate to re-draw a master sketch when new information is given; it takes very little time to jot down a few Cs, Ms, and Ls on the page. Plus, you'll then have representative scenarios to look back on later.

14. C

Here's the reward for the deduction described above—you deduced that at least one liberal must have voted for the petition. That's because if all the liberals voted no, Rule 2 would have both conservatives voting yes. But Rule 4 disallows that, which means that it cannot be true that all the liberals voted against, which in turn means that at least one liberal must have voted in favor of the petition, (C).

(A) and (B) No, all the liberals could vote in favor of the petition, in which case both conservatives would vote against.

(D) and (E) The moderates can swing all possible ways; as you saw in question 13, they can split their votes. On the other hand, both can vote for, or both can vote against, so (D) and (E) both *could* be true, but need not be.

- If you didn't make the "liberal" deduction early on, you're forced to work it out here. That's not the end of the world—the game is not all lost. The important thing is to realize that the answer here is something that must be true without any conditional circumstances—that is, without being derived from a hypothetical—which means that it must be true for the *entire game*, not just for this question. If it's not already in your master sketch, build it in as if it were a given rule.
- If you must resort to testing the choices in a "must be true" question, try to *prove the exception*. For example, in (A), to test whether at least one conservative must have voted for the petition, see if it's possible that *no* conservatives voted for it. Since this *is* possible, you've proven an exception to (A), which shows that (A) need not be true and should be crossed off. However, this is a time consuming process compared to the direct approach, and when it's necessary you should consider leaving that question until the end of the game.

15. E

Now, whether you made the deduction regarding the liberals early on, or just now in the previous question, you can and should use this information to bag question 15. If all three liberals voted the same way . . . yup, that's right, they must all vote *for*, because it's impossible for all of them to vote against, for reasons elaborated just above and in the "Deductions" section. And there's the point in (E).

With the liberals all voting for the petition, Rule 2 mandates that both conservatives vote against. So here's what you know of the voting so far:

Ȼ Ȼ M M Ⓛ Ⓛ Ⓛ

(A), (B) and (D) As Rule 1 is not in effect here, the moderates are totally free to vote any old way: both for, both against, or one each way. So these three choices all *could* be true, but need not be.

(C) is impossible—as shown above, both conservatives have to vote "nay" in this situation.

- Use your work on the first few questions to pick up insights you may have missed during the setup stage. If you made the deductions you discussed earlier, then questions 14 and 15 should have been a breeze. This is why you should strive to make deductions up front. But if you didn't see these things, then at least you could have picked up these points now, and in the process seen that at least one liberal must always vote yes, and that Rule 2 is only applicable in one direction—if the three liberals vote together, it must be for, not against.

16. A

Your job in this one is to figure out how you can fit exactly two no votes (which means five votes for) into the sketch. You already know one definite no, a conservative thanks to Rule 4. And you've seen, most recently in question 15, the case in which both conservatives vote against the petition. Filling out the rest in line with the stem's mandate results in this arrangement:

Ȼ Ȼ Ⓜ Ⓜ Ⓛ Ⓛ Ⓛ

No problems there; but is this the only way to get a 2-5 breakdown of "nays" to "yeas"? Giving the second *against* to one of the moderates doesn't work—then all three liberals vote *for*, which according to Rule 2 means that both conservatives would have to vote *against*. But if the second (and therefore last) against goes to a moderate, the other conservative would have to vote in favor, which cannot be. So it's impossible for a moderate here to cast the second against vote, which means both moderates must vote for the petition, (A).

You may have waited until you worked out the other possible scenario before moving to the choices, in which case you would have worked out this arrangement:

This is the only other way to satisfy the stem, which again confirms that (A) must be true. As for the wrong choices, they all *could* be true, but need not be: (C) and (E) are true in the first possible scenario but not in the second. (B) and (D) are true in the second but not in the first.

- Some "if" questions specify an exact occurrence, and others, like this one, are more vague. You're told that exactly two judges voted against, but you're not told *which*—that would give it all away. So you must make it concrete. Ask yourself "How can this happen?"—and the first thing to do is to see if it's happened before in earlier questions. That gets you halfway there, but you still have to inquire if there are *other* possible ways to place exactly two votes against, and in this case, there is one more possible scenario. Armed with the only two possible voting schemes, you can answer any question thrown your way.
- In a "must be true" question, scan the choices whenever you discover something new. Here, you could have picked up the point as soon as you noticed that the second against couldn't go to a moderate.

17. E

We're looking for the choice that contains the list of judges that cannot be a complete and accurate list of judges in favor of the petition. Before jumping into complicated scenarios, see if you can derive the answer by checking the choices against the concrete rules, Rules 3 and 4. Rule 4 is easy—there must always be at least one conservative voting against the petition, so if any choice contains two conservatives, that must be the answer (remember, the entities in the choices represent judges voting *for* the petition). No luck. But Rule 3 does the trick. Are there any choices that would result in a lack of two judges on either side? Yes: (E) uses every judge but one conservative, which would result in six "yeas" and only one "nay." Just add 'em up—six judges voting in favor of the proposal is a direct violation of Rule 3.

- Translate complex-sounding stems into a workable framework—something that will inform your attack on the question. When asking if certain judges can constitute a "complete and accurate list of those judges who voted for Datalog," the test makers are really asking whether you can circle those judges and cross out the rest. Translated this way, the test for each choice is fairly straightforward.
- Always keep the numbers aspect of the game in the forefront of your mind—sometimes, as here, working out the numbers will lead to a shortcut. All you had to do was add up the number of judges in (E) to see that it's impossible for all the members in that group of judges to vote yes to the petition.
- All rules are *not* created equal: Concrete rules like Rules 3 and 4 are usually easier to work with than conditional rules like Rules 1 and 2, so gravitate toward the concrete whenever you have a choice of rules with which to begin your attack on a question.

18. B

Take it one step at a time: The conservatives voted the same way, which means (thanks to Rule 4) that they both voted no. Next you're told that the liberals didn't all vote the same way. You deduced (and saw later in question 14) that at least one liberal must vote for the petition, so now you know that at least one must vote against. So far then, this is how the votes went:

~~C~~ ~~C~~ M M L Ⓛ ~~L~~

This situation triggers Rule 1—both conservatives and at least one liberal voted the same way, against—which means that both moderates must vote against as well. But wait—you may as well complete the voting: With only one *for* vote out of six so far, Rule 3 requires that the remaining liberal vote for the petition, resulting in:

~~C~~ ~~C~~ ~~M~~ ~~M~~ Ⓛ ~~L~~ Ⓛ

Every choice conforms to this arrangement except (B), which is impossible (and therefore correct): Under these circumstances, both moderates must have voted against, not for the petition.

- Take complicated stems apart. When a stem contains more than one new "if" incorporate one at a time into a new sketch, and then see how the resulting situation is affected by the rules.
- Read the stems carefully, and don't overlook the word EXCEPT. It's capitalized to make it stand out on the page, but in the heat of the moment some test takers do all the right work but then miss this word, and answer the wrong question. It's a shame to miss a point for this reason, and since the Logic Games section contains such a variety of stems (*must be true, could be true, must be false, could be false, is impossible, cannot be true,* and so on), it's not a bad idea to double-check each stem just before moving to the choices, just to make sure you're answering the question that was asked.

GAME 4—Runners and Charities

The Action

Next up you have runners in five consecutively numbered lanes, which immediately suggests sequencing, and indeed, you will be concerned with the order of the runners in the five lanes. But you have another concern as well—the runners are also matched up with charities, so in fact the game is a sequencing/matching hybrid.

The Initial Setup

Since there are two levels to this sequence, put the lane numbers on the page with the runners and charities listed off to the side, like so:

	1	2	3	4	5
LNOPS					
fghjk					

With this setup, you have space in your sketch to insert the line of runners, as well as space for the charities the runners represent. As this also makes the match-ups of runners to charities readily apparent, both game actions can be accommodated within this one simple sketch.

The Rules

1) Nice and concrete: you can insert k right into lane 4 in the lower line of our sketch. And, since each runner represents a different charity, cross k off your list.
2) is slightly complex in that it posits a relationship between runner P and charities f and g. The use of the word "only" in this rule tells you that no other runner besides P comes between charities f and g, so whether it's fPg or gPf, this trio will form a solid bloc somewhere in the sketch. Jot this down off to the side for now, and come back to analyze its implications during Step 4 of the Kaplan Method. Keep your notations in a structure consistent with your sketch.

```
  P           P
f __ g   or  g __ f
```

3) Rule 3 also deals with both a runner and charity, in this case runner O and charity g:

O__ ______ O
g or g

4) Here's a straightforward sequencing rule involving only runners:

N . . . S

is a perfect reminder of this, and you're ready to combine the rules and see what you can deduce.

Deductions

Now, remember what you said back in Game 2 (and applied in Game 3): One of the best ways to find deductions is to focus on duplications—entities that appear in more than one rule, and here, that entity is charity g. So investigate the possible lanes for charity g. Rule 1 places charity k in lane 4, which severely restricts g's position: In order to satisfy Rule 2 (that is, to get P between g's lane and f's lane), g's lane can only be lanes 1, 3, or 5—that k in 4 prevents any other possibility. But lane 3 is impossible for g because of Rule 3: If g is in 3, there's no way to get exactly two lanes between g and runner O. Therefore, you have limited options. **Charity g must be in either lane 1 or lane 5**, so it's worth investigating what happens in both cases. And, in either case, f must be in Lane 3.

OPTION 1:

If g is in lane 1, then runner P is in lane 2, followed by charity f in lane 3 (Rule 2). Rule 3 kicks in, forcing runner O to lane 4, along with charity k, which is always in that lane. That leaves charities h and j to float between lanes 2 and 5, and runners N, S, and free agent L to fill in remaining lanes 1, 3, and 5, so long as N precedes S (Rule 4). This first option, therefore, boils down to this:

	1	2	3	4	5
NSL		P		O	
	g	h/j	f	k	h/j

You may note that in this option lane 5 must go to runner S or L, as N can't be in 5. You can write this in if you like, or simply deal with the remaining runners accordingly in each question.

OPTION 2:

If g is in lane 5, then runner P is in lane 4 (along with k), and charity f takes lane 3, again thanks to Rule 2. Rule 3 forces O into lane 2. Again, charities h and j will float, this time between lanes 1 and 2. And again, runners N, S, and L will take lanes 1, 3 and 5, with N before S in 1 or 3 and S or L in 5. Here's this second option:

	1	2	3	4	5
N...S L		O		P	
	h/j	h/j	f	k	g

Notice that **charity f is in lane 3** in both options, which means that this is another solid deduction that must hold for the entire game.

The Final Visualization

This now consists of the two options on the page. Every acceptable ordering and match-up will have to correspond to one of these two options, which will lighten our workload considerably when it comes to answering the questions.

The Big Picture

- When a major entity in the game is limited to one of two positions, it's usually worth working out what happens in each case. The resulting scenarios are "limited options," and when you can reduce the possibilities down to a pair of options, your work in the questions will be greatly reduced.
- Once again, it may seem like a lot of work up front, but working out limited option scenarios actually goes faster than you might imagine if you work methodically and keep your cool. The opportunity for some quick and easy points should be incentive enough to take the little bit of extra time.
- Don't be intimidated by a game that has more than one game action; if you can handle a basic sequencing game, and are comfortable with matching games, then a hybrid of the two need not be unusually difficult. If you use your experience from past games to help you handle each game action, you shouldn't have unusual difficulty with a game that combines those actions.

- In games that contain more than one group of entities, it's imperative that you keep them straight. Here, some rules are about the runners, some about the charities, and some about both. As you'll see below, the same goes for the questions. Pay careful attention to the information thrown your way, and continually ask yourself which group is the relevant one for the task at hand. Use different notation for each group, like the capital and lower-case letters you've used above.

- The beauty of limited options is that the full range of possibilities for each entity is pretty much established on the page. So when a question asks about a specific entity, you need only to find that entity in each option and note how it behaves.

The Questions

19. E

This Acceptability question is your first opportunity to use the options you created—note that you're concerned only with charities here. You deduced that in both options, charity f must be in lane 3, which allows you to quickly eliminate (A), (B), and (D). Of the remaining choices, (C) violates Rule 1—k must be in lane 4—which is why the ordering in (C) doesn't jibe with either of the options listed on the page. (E) remains and gets the point.

- Acceptability questions aren't just quick points—they're useful tools, providing you with a first-hand opportunity to see how the rules and entities interrelate, and to test out any deductions or limited option scenarios you may have come upon in the setup stage.
- Even if you hadn't worked out the two options above, an acceptability question is always eminently doable using the Kaplan method—just take each rule in turn and check each choice against it until only one choice remains.

20. D

In Option 1, P is in lane 2 and O is in lane 4. In Option 2, they're reversed: O is in 2 and P is in 4. Either way, (D) has it right: P and O must be separated by exactly one lane.

(A) In Option 1, P is in lane 2 and L can take lane 5.

(B) and (C) In Option 2, P is in lane 4 and N can be in lane 1. So contrary to both (B) and (C), it's possible to have exactly two lanes between the lanes of P and N.

(E) is impossible: In Option 1, S is either right next to P or separated by two lanes from P; in Option 2, S, in lanes 3 or 5, is always right next to P.

21. B

Here's your first "if" question, and it steers you clearly toward Option 2, the only option in which O is in lane 2. All you need to do is check the choices against Option 2, looking for the assignment that must be made. Charity g in lane 5 is the one the test makers chose, (B).

(A) and (D) are impossible—charity f must always be in lane 3.

(C) is only possible; in Option 2, h *could* be in lane 1, but could also be in lane 2, with j in 1.

(E) No—in Option 2, charity j must be in either lane 1 or 2.

- In a game in which you're able to create limited options, use the if-clauses in the question stems to direct you to the option that's in effect. Very often, the new "if" will lead to one and only one of the options, which narrows down the possible arrangements even further and makes your work that much easier.

22. D

Rule 2 directly rules out Patricia as f's representative, as Patricia must run in the lane *between* the lanes of charities f and g. That eliminates (B) and (E). Both Larry and Ned appear in all of the remaining choices, so those runners must be part of the correct list, and you need not bother with them. The question then boils down to Olivia and Sonja. If neither can represent f, then (A) is it. If only O can, then you choose (C), and if Sonja can, (D) is the winner. A glance at either option on the page confirms that Sonja can represent f, a charity that you know is always in lane 3.

- Look for shortcuts when putting together a "complete and accurate list." If you've eliminated some choices, and the remaining ones all have certain entities in common, then those entities must be part of the list, and need not be checked. Zero in on the *differences* between the remaining choices, and look for the simplest test that will allow you to single out the winner.

23. B

For the sake of comparison, approach this question without the benefit of the limited options worked out above. Ned is to represent charity j, and you need to determine what must be true. For all you know, there are lots of ways this can happen, and as there's not much information on Ned (only Rule 4, which doesn't narrow things down much) and *no* information on charity j (a "free agent"), you have no choice but to pop N and j into lanes and see how they fare.

What about lane 1? If N represents j in lane 1, nothing is triggered directly, so you'd better consider the large bloc of entities, the fPg bloc. With charity k always in lane 4, and j now in lane 1, the only way to space charities f and g with exactly one lane between them for P would be to place them in lanes 3 and 5, with P in lane 4. But f and g could theoretically go in either order, so which is in 3 and which is in 5? You just have to try it out, in which case you find that g in 3 is impossible, because there would be no way to satisfy Rule 3. (More perceptive test takers might realize at this point that g can *never* be in 3, but others who proceed piecemeal like this may not realize this and think that this observation only applies to this question, thereby diminishing the value of this important insight.) So in this case, with N representing j in lane 1, charity f must be in 3 and charity g in 5, which forces runner O and the one remaining charity, h, into lane 2.

Whew! Are you done? No; all you've done is prove that N *can* represent j in lane 1, which would help you in a "could be true question," but is only part of the battle in a "must be true" question. For all you know, N and j can occupy other lanes, so you now have to test out other scenarios. What about N and j in lane 2? The only way to place the fPg bloc would be to place them again in lanes 3, 4, and 5, respectively, but this leads to a violation: Rule 3 would then force O into lane 2, but you've just placed N there.

Moving along, could N and j take lane 3? No, because there's no way to then place the fPg bloc at all. Lane 4 is off limits, because charity k already occupies that space, and lane 5 is no good, because N can never be in lane 5, lest it violate Rule 4.

So after this somewhat lengthy analysis, you've proven that there's only one lane in which N can represent charity j, and it leads to this scenario:

	1	2	3	4	5
N...S L	N	O	S/L	P	S/L
	j	H	f	k	g

Now you're in a position to recognize for sure what must be true—charity h's runner is assigned to lane 2, (B). All of the other choices here must be false:

(A) No, charity g's runner is assigned to lane 5.

(C) No, Patricia represents charity k here.

(D) and (E) No, Olivia represents charity h here.

- It's hard to backtrack to this piecemeal approach once you've worked out the two possible scenarios, the limited options. But the exercise makes a point: If you take the rules at face value, and don't look for implications, deductions, or limited options up front, many Logic Games questions will require the kind of extensive work described here. You can eventually arrive at the right answers, but the section would probably take longer than 35 minutes. This "brute force" approach to Logic Games is like coming at a wooden door with a hammer rather than a key. You may get in eventually, but at what cost? In Logic Games, the cost of a plodding approach is *time*. It does no good to get every question you attempt right, if you only get to half the questions. Incidentally . . .
- With the benefit of using our limited options, question 23 would go something like this: In Option 1, j is either in lane 2, represented by P, or lane 5, a lane off limits to N (Rule 4). This means that Option 2 must be in effect here, the option in which j is either in lanes 1 or 2. If j is to be matched up with N, it must be in lane 1, because O takes lane 2 in this option. That leaves charity h for lane 2, (B). Limited options allow you to see quickly what must happen when N and j pair up.

24. A

Finally, you're looking for an acceptable ordering of runners if Larry is matched with charity j. Your options help you immediately: No matter what, O and P must take lanes 2 and 4, in either order. But three of the five choices—(B), (C), and (E)—don't conform to this, and can be axed on this basis alone. That leaves (A) and (D), both acceptable orderings in general, but obviously one will not accord with the mandate in the stem. Both have O in lane 2 and P in lane 4, which places this scenario squarely in Option 2. In that Option, charity j is either in lane 1 or lane 2, and if L is to be matched with j, it must be in lane 1, leaving N and S to lanes 3 and 5, respectively (Rule 4). L O N P S works, and therefore could be the assignment of runners to lanes under these conditions.

- It's important to know how to look for and work out limited options within games, but it's also vital to know how to *use* them to answer questions. Just because you generate the options doesn't necessarily guarantee success on the game. Go back, if necessary, and review how the options on the page were best used to generate quick points, and resolve to investigate limited option scenarios whenever the opportunity arises.

SECTION III: READING COMPREHENSION

Passage 1—Working Women

Topic and Scope

Working parents in the labor force; specifically, the problems that working mothers face in a world that seems hostile to their goals and responsibilities

Purpose and Main Idea

The author's purpose is to describe the conditions in the workplace that disadvantage working parents, especially women. The main idea surfaces in its full form at the end: If the job market continues to be inflexible, and thus hostile toward parents, and if women still have to bear most of the burden of child care, then women will continue to be disadvantaged in the labor market.

Paragraph Structure

Paragraph one describes how the labor force is structured in such a way that workers' family responsibilities are ignored. Examples are given that demonstrate how regular full-time workdays, combined with everyday chores, don't allow the flexibility needed by parents who are responsible for child care. The topic is evident, but the specific focus on women's difficulties is yet to come.

Paragraph two introduces the notion that among working parents, women suffer the disadvantages of the workplace more than men. There's also a second point made here that further complicates the plight of the working mother—women are under greater cultural pressure to take responsibility for child care than men.

Paragraphs three and four spell out in greater detail the specific problems of working mothers. Paragraph three focuses on the disadvantages of part-time work, while paragraph four outlines the problems of mothers who work full-time. The final sentence of the passage is a reflection of the first sentence, but with a particular emphasis on the problems of women. If workplace conditions and cultural standards don't change, women will continue to be seriously disadvantaged in the labor market.

The Big Picture

- Always keep your eye out for the author's main idea, no matter where in the passage it may appear. Don't always expect the main idea to jump out of the first paragraph; in some passages, the main idea doesn't fully emerge until the end. This is the case here: The first three paragraphs establish the topic and scope, and offer many examples that support the author's own skepticism that emerges fully in the last sentence.
- Very often, the scope of the passage will be clearly defined by the end of the first paragraph, but that's not always the case. Remain open to slight shifts, particularly, a narrowing of the scope as the passage develops. In paragraph one, the scope seems to include "working parents," but paragraph two suggests that the author is concerned mainly with the case of women. The examples presented in the last two paragraphs bear this out.

The Questions

1. E

This Global question asks about the passage's big idea, which is developed throughout but emphasized in the last sentence. You should be able to prephrase this answer: you're looking for a statement to the effect that women have great difficulty pursuing a career while raising children. (E) tells you that traditional workplace organization is too rigid, which makes it difficult for working parents to both work and care for their children. Furthermore, this especially disadvantages working mothers, which is precisely the author's message.

(A) Nothing in the passage suggests that the author believes that life will get easier for working parents, or that there is a trend toward flexibility in the working world, so this isn't the main idea.

(B) captures some of the flavor of the author's feelings, but the author's criticism is directed more toward the inflexibility of the working world than toward traditional family roles. Sure, the author feels that cultural pressures on women to care for children exacerbate the problem, but this isn't the main message. In any case, you cannot infer that changes in traditional family roles are *necessary* for equal opportunity.

(C) is beyond the scope of the passage, since you have hardly any information about single parents and their work life and none about a comparison between single mothers and single fathers.

(D) centers on a comparison that the author never makes. The author makes a point of saying in the last paragraph that *both* professional and nonprofessional working mothers are disadvantaged by inflexible work schedules, but never indicates which group is better at dealing with the situation. (Even if this comparison were indicated, it still wouldn't be the main idea of the passage.)

- In Global questions, beware of choices like (B) that capture only part of the author's true intent. (B) correctly notes the author's skepticism, but directs it toward the wrong target.

2. D

Part-time work is the subject of paragraph three. The last sentence of this paragraph tells you that although part-time work isn't personally enriching, it does allow women "flexibility to fulfill their family duties" (line 37). In the context of this passage, women's family duties include primary child-rearing responsibilities. Choice (D) connects the phrase "family duties" to its meaning in the context of the passage, and that's why (D) is inferable.

(A) erroneously reverses the statistic in the second sentence of the third paragraph, so look back there. One-third of working mothers work part-time; but you certainly can't conclude from this that one-third of part-time workers are working mothers. Familiar language in answer choices can mislead you if you attempt to rely on memory rather than the text.

(B) According to the passage, part-time work is intrinsically flawed because it offers little opportunity for challenge or advancement. But there's no basis for comparing working mothers to *women in general* in this respect. You can't infer that part-time work is more limiting for working mothers than it is for women in general.

(C) is not inferable because the passage doesn't indicate anything about part-time employees working during holidays. The closest the passage comes to "holidays" is the talk about "vacations" in paragraph one, but this has no relation to the discussion of part-time work in paragraph three.

(E) attempts to combine two unrelated elements. The passage discusses part-time work and full-time work, but does not discuss the possibility of part-time work *leading to* full-time careers. Again, this is a connection you cannot make.

- For many Reading Comp Inference questions, you'll need to translate a word or phrase into its meaning within the larger context of the passage.
- Beware of choices that attempt to combine two or more elements of the passage in a way that the author never intends. Many wrong choices, like (C) and (E) here, use the passage's language but distort its ideas.

3. C

You're looking for another inference: something left unsaid that's nonetheless strongly supported. Working fathers in two-parent families are discussed in paragraph two: When both parents work, cultural pressures put the primary responsibility for child rearing on women. If women in two-parent families have primary child-rearing responsibilities, you can infer that working fathers, thanks to these cultural traditions, have secondary, or lesser, child-rearing responsibilities.

(A) contradicts the theme of the passage. The author makes it clear that women bear the greater brunt of the labor market disadvantages in the two-parent working couple.

(B) is outside the scope; you know nothing about the possible workaholic tendencies of husbands that might lead them to ignore injustice.

(D) and (E) both heap blame on men themselves for women's problems in the labor force, but the issue of who is to blame is never really addressed in the passage. You're told that the labor market works against the priorities of parents, but you can't infer from this that working fathers in two-parent families compound the problem (D), or are the ones responsible for the "traditional roles" (E)—the author simply cites cultural pressures as the cause for this. Blame, if anywhere, must go to the system and society itself; ascribing it to this specific group, "working fathers in two-parent families," is unwarranted.

- Read critically! There's a big difference between saying "this system is terrible" and saying "here's who to blame." The author does a lot of the former, and little if any of the latter. Recognizing this allows you to axe (D) and (E) quickly.

4. B

We've seen that the author believes that inflexible work schedules and gender-based allocation of family roles are the reasons why working mothers occupy a disadvantaged place in the work force. But this question asks for the most troublesome barrier for working parents, not just mothers, so the answer must have something to do with the rigidity of work schedules. This is supported in lines 12–15 ("conventional workdays . . . are too inflexible for parents"); paragraph three (working mothers are forced to take part-time work for the flexibility, but at the expense of the benefits of full-time work); and paragraph four (professionals and nonprofessionals alike have to sacrifice in all kinds of ways in order to secure the flexibility needed to raise children).

(A) is barking up the wrong tree: The author says nothing about a lack of full-time jobs available to women; rather, full-time work is not practically feasible for many working mothers, which is not the same as saying that it's not *available*.

(C) and (D) focus on details about part-time work and nonprofessional employees, but neither is important enough to be cited as the "most troublesome barrier" facing working parents. Both of these details are part of the larger problem, which is that the inflexible structure of the workplace forces some parents to even consider such positions in the first place.

(E) The allocation of workplace responsibilities based on gender is outside the scope. The author doesn't deal with gender-based issues in the workplace, but rather with the factors that determine whether certain kinds of people (working parents) can even take certain jobs in the first place.

- Prephrase answers to the fullest extent possible. This may seem like a detail-oriented question, but in truth it's really asking you what the author thinks is the biggest problem with the system, and that question is answered throughout the passage: Inflexible schedules create all kinds of problems for working parents.

- Expect at least two (and sometimes even three) questions in a Reading Comp set to be very similar. The reason for this is that the test makers like to test the main idea in different ways. Despite their differences, questions 1 and 4 in this set test the same basic thing, and notice the similarity in the wording of their respective correct choices: 1(E): "Traditional work schedules are too inflexible . . .," 4(B): "the inflexibility of work schedules." Don't be scared off if the answers you chose for two different questions seem too much alike.

5. D

The focus is on day care here, and your knowledge of the passage structure should help you to quickly focus in on lines 5–12 of paragraph one where the inadequacies of day care are addressed. You're asked for the exception; which reason wasn't addressed?

Check off the answer choices that you find in the text. All of the points raised in the choices are mentioned in this paragraph except for the point brought up in (D). Although school vacations are mentioned in the second sentence, this topic is used to illustrate the notion that school-age children need care when school is not in session. It has no connection to the issue of day care; the author never says or implies that day care for preschool children is interrupted during vacations.

(A) Day care's inability to guarantee parent-child quality time comes up in lines 10–12.

(B) and (C) Affording and finding suitable day care, (B) and (C) respectively, are issues discussed in the third sentence.

(E) The problem of sick children comes up in the fourth sentence.

- If you make a good mental roadmap of the passage as you read through, you won't have to waste time finding the relevant area of the passage for each particular question. Here, the mention of the limitations of day care should have directed you right to paragraph one.

6. A

In this EXCEPT question you're asked to locate a type of career decision working parents might face that's *not* discussed by the author. Refer back to the passage to eliminate those the author does mention. The specific issue and conflicts are addressed in the last two paragraphs, so start there. In the end, you should have found that the decision in (A) is the odd one out: Although the author mentions both professional and nonprofessional jobs and the circumstances that both entail, the author never states or implies that working parents are forced to decline professional jobs for nonprofessional ones.

(B) Taking part-time over full-time work appears in paragraph three, where the author writes about compromises that working mothers make.

(C) and (D) Taking jobs with less responsibility and pursuing less desirable specializations both appear in paragraph four. If you caught the basic gist of that paragraph, you probably were able to axe these choices without having to refer back to the passage.

(E) is another choice that may not have required a glance back to the passage; it's a main focus of the whole passage, and is suggested throughout, but most particularly at the beginning of the third paragraph.

- In Reading Comp, be on the lookout for choices that mention things stated in the passage, but relate them to one another in ways the author didn't. The author does deal with professional and nonprofessional positions, but not in the way presented in (A). Because this is an EXCEPT question, (A) is our answer. In creating a choice like this, the test makers are trying to separate careful from careless readers.

7. A

The final question of this passage asks for the choice containing the sentence that would best follow the concluding sentence. The best place to start is by taking another look at that concluding sentence: women will continue to be disadvantaged in the labor market as long as the market is hostile toward parents and as long as family roles are based on gender. Well, if women continue to be disadvantaged, it makes sense to say that men will continue to be advantaged; that is, they will do better in the labor market. (A) logically follows from the argument. This is not to say that this is the direction the author has to go if she decides to continue the passage, but it does make for an appropriate and logical continuation.

(B) is unwarranted. You have no reason to believe that men are unwilling to do anything about employment barriers. In addition, it changes the subject from the matter at hand—the current and future state of parents in the job market.

(C) is also an unlikely continuation because it discusses "salaries," an issue barely touched on in the passage.

(D) refers to men with primary child-raising responsibilities, but the passage presents no information about their role in the workplace.

(E) tries to relate gender-related societal traditions to gender differences in career opportunities, but there's no indication that this is where the author is going with all this. (E) makes it sound as if the first thing causes the other, whereas the author discusses societal institutions only as a part of a larger problem.

- Note how closely related (A) is to the author's message throughout the passage; it is a logical corollary to the theme "working women are *especially* disadvantaged in the labor force." The point is, even when you're asked to go beyond the passage, the correct answer will be based strongly on what the author has actually said.

Passage 2—John Webster

Topic and Scope

Elizabethan playwright John Webster and how critics misinterpret his work

Purpose and Main Idea

The author's purpose is to describe how the criticism of the contradictions in the characters of Webster's tragedies is misdirected. The main idea is that critics have been confused by the contradictory nature of Webster's characters because of certain mistaken assumptions they have made about the playwright himself.

Paragraph Structure

Paragraph one sets up the main idea but doesn't quite get there. First you're told that the critics are confused by the contradictory nature of Webster's characters. Then the author provides examples of the contradictory nature of Webster's characters. Aristotle is cited as believing that contradiction is necessary for tragedy, and the paragraph ends with another hint that the critics are off base.

The author delivers her main point in the first sentence of paragraph two. Critics have been confused by the contradictory nature of Webster's characters because of certain mistaken assumptions they have made about the playwright himself. According to the author, critics have assumed that Webster was a typical Elizabethan playwright, and as such intended to create characters who were meant to be either good or evil, but not both. Thus, when Webster's characters exhibit both good and evil tendencies, critics have ascribed this to incompetence on the part of the playwright, rather than to deliberate design on his part. The author takes exception to this view, saying that Webster intentionally created characters that were grey rather than black and white, characters that were both good and evil. According to the author, Webster was not a typical Elizabethan playwright. This is what has led to confusion and, ultimately, to mistaken judgments about his competence.

The Big Picture

- A passage like this one is a good place to begin your work on the Reading Comp section because the purpose and structure are fairly easy to grasp. After some brief background facts are presented in the first paragraph, the author's message appears at the beginning of the second paragraph, while the rest of the passage just fleshes out that message.
- Always take note of the author's allegiances. Here, they are hinted at in the beginning paragraph, and then fully expounded in the rest of the passage: The author is pro Webster and against the critics' judgments.
- Don't be intimidated by the length of the second paragraph. A paragraph like this is not broken up because it essentially harps on the same point throughout—it provides support for the author's position that the critics have misinterpreted Webster's work. With only two paragraphs, the passage's structure is not difficult to discern.

The Questions

8. D

The most straightforward kind of Global question simply asks about the author's purpose in writing the passage: The author wrote this passage in order to take issue with critics over their interpretation of Webster's characters. In the second paragraph, the author explains how critics have misunderstood Webster's characters and provides a more plausible interpretation of those characters' inconsistencies. Put another way, then, the author's purpose in writing this passage is to offer a more convincing alternative explanation, (D).

(A) There is no ambiguity requiring clarification here. The critics' position is clear; the author simply disagrees with it and offers her own take on the matter.

(B) The author doesn't support the mainstream view of Webster's work, but rather tears it down and supplies what she considers to be a more plausible explanation.

(C) has some truth to it—the author *does* propose an answer to the problem of the contradictory nature of Webster's characters, but there's no unresolved question at issue in the passage. As mentioned in the explanation to (A) above, the critics have a definite point of view about Webster's work and the author has simply taken issue with this view.

(E) is perhaps trickier than the rest. The author's purpose isn't to describe two opposing viewpoints; she offers an opposing viewpoint to counter that of the critics. Furthermore, the author doesn't categorize viewpoints—she simply rejects one in favor of another.

- You've already done the work for Global questions as you read, so prephrase and stay focused. If you do, you'll be less likely to be swayed by the wrong choices, which often *sound impressive*, even when they're not on target.
- If you're forced to eliminate, be strategic. Understanding the structure of the passage allows you to eliminate many wrong choices in a "purpose" question. Here, there's no ambiguous assertion (A) or unresolved question (C) built into the structure of this passage. Understanding the general thrust of the argument—here's what the critics say, here's how the author counters—should be enough to allow you to axe these choices.

9. A

Here's an Inference question about the works that most influenced Webster's own tragedies. The best way to approach this question is to quickly re-read the section that deals with influences on Webster's plays, namely lines 30–38. Here you're told that Webster was influenced by earlier Italian dramas, whose characters, unlike those in the morality play, are not black and white, but rather morally complex, both good and evil. That's essentially what (A) says in a slightly different way.

(B) is wrong on two counts: For one thing, Webster *was* influenced by Italian sources. For another, the other Elizabethan tragedies referred to in (B) were based on earlier morality plays that were English, not Italian.

(C) you can't conclude that critics don't adequately *understand* Italian drama just because they have failed to evaluate Webster's tragedies in light of this genre. All you know from the passage is that critics apparently feel that this genre is not relevant to understanding Webster's work, a different point entirely.

(D) Italian dramas, according to the passage, have *not* been used as a basis for interpreting Elizabethan drama. Rather, Elizabethan works have been interpreted as an outgrowth of earlier morality plays, a non-Italian genre. (The lone exception to this rule that you're aware of is the author's use of Italian drama to understand the work of John Webster, a single, non-traditional Elizabethan playwright.)

(E) contradicts the passage. Critics have considered Webster's work to be incompetent because they have always evaluated it in light of earlier morality plays, rather than Italian drama. Indeed, the author attacks critics precisely for failing to examine Webster's work in light of Italian drama.

- Make sure you're familiar with the various kinds of wrong answer types. In Inference questions, a common wrong choice is the one that brings up an irrelevant issue, such "critics' *understanding* of Italian dramas" in (C). Nothing can be inferred about this. However, the other wrong choices, (B), (D), and (E), fall into another category; they all contradict information in the passage. If a choice is the least bit inconsistent with the passage, it can't be the valid inference you seek.

10. B

Why did the author mention Aristotle's view of tragedy? In lines 11–13 you see that Aristotle implied that character inconsistencies are a *natural* part of tragedies, *and yet* Webster's critics still view these inconsistencies as eccentric. The keywords "and yet" are extremely helpful. Aristotle is cited as an authority supporting the notion that character inconsistency is essential to tragedy, *and yet* the critics ignore this evidence and still believe that Webster's vision is eccentric. So the author cites Aristotle to bolster her own argument that Webster's conception was not eccentric. Translate "not eccentric" as "not idiosyncratic" and you have (B).

(A) and (C) both contradict the thrust of the passage. Aristotle's view is introduced in order to bolster the author's *dissenting* view of Webster's work, not the mainstream view of critics, with which the author does not agree. So (A) is out. (C) is out for much the same reason; the author approves of Aristotle's view of tragedy, which is precisely why she cites it. She criticizes the critics' view, not the doctrines of Aristotle.

(D) For one thing, the author is not out to establish the similarity between classical and modern approaches to tragedy—that's beyond the more narrow purpose of this passage. Furthermore, since Aristotle and most modern critics seem to *disagree* on the nature of tragedy, how could introducing Aristotle's view establish a similarity between classical and modern approaches?

(E) starts off pretty well: "supports the author's assertion . . ." but is all downhill from there. This passage is about one Elizabethan playwright, John Webster; it's not about Elizabethan tragedy in general. Like (D), this choice is much too broad in scope. Not only that, but the author doesn't seem to be particularly fond of recent scholarship, so (E) also goes against the thrust of the passage.

- When a question asks for the function of a detail, consider purpose and how the detail fits into that purpose. Is the detail an opposing point of view that the author will try to discredit? Is it there to provide a contrast to the author's opinion? Is it there to support the author's opinion? In this case, if you were able to recognize the Aristotle reference as support for the author's view, you'd be able to narrow the choices down to (B) and (E).

11. C

What piece of information would make the critics' interpretations of Webster's tragedies more valid? Well, a good place to start would be with a reminder of what, according to the author, makes those interpretations *invalid*. It's the same idea you've been harping on thus far: The author believes that the critics mistakenly assume that Webster based his tragedies on earlier morality plays. So, if Webster *had* actually based his tragedies on earlier morality plays, with their black and white characters, yet his own tragedies still featured morally ambiguous characters, you could safely conclude that he was, as the critics contend, incompetent.

(A) Webster's tragic vision would seem more competent, not less, if it were based on the duality of human nature.

(B) Aristotle was mentioned to uphold the validity of employing contradiction in tragedy, so again, the fact that Webster's vision conforms to Aristotle's would only *support* the author's argument, rather than increase the validity of the critics' interpretation.

(D) According to the author, the critics' position is based on the assumption that Elizabethan dramatists, including Webster, were primarily influenced by the English morality play, not by the Italian dramatists. It's hard to see how disputing this assumption would bolster the critics' position.

(E) The modern audience is outside the scope; it could have no bearing on how and why Webster created his characters, and thus no bearing on the critics' interpretation of them.

- Interpret the wording in the stem in order to determine your task for each question. Most stems are self-explanatory, but others, like this one, are more complex and tricky. Essentially, this is a Strengthen question disguised as an Inference question.
- Be on the lookout for that common wrong-answer type, the *180* choice—a choice that provides the opposite of what you're looking for. Here, (A) and (B) support the notion that Webster *was* on target with his tragic vision, that his characters' duality was *not* due to his own artistic incompetence. This is the opposite of something that would strengthen the critics' interpretation.

12. C

You're looking for a statement about Elizabethan drama with which the author would agree. By now, you know that the author thinks that Webster was an exception to the rule that Elizabethan drama in general was heavily influenced by the morality play, which points you directly to choice (C).

(A) comes from out of the blue; nowhere in the passage does the author state or imply that the skill of Elizabethan dramatists has been overestimated recently. The author only argues that Webster's work should not be evaluated according to the same criterion used to judge the work of other Elizabethan dramatists.

(B), (D), and (E) all go against the author's point of view. Contrary to (B), the author doesn't think that Webster's works are typical of Elizabethan drama, just the opposite. (D) is out for the same reason: Since Webster's works were different, it's wrong to evaluate them in light of mainstream Elizabethan drama. As for (E), the author flatly says that mainstream Elizabethan drama was influenced by the morality play, not by Italian and classical sources.

- Don't be surprised when some questions merely ask you for what you've known all along. Don't look for a trick or think to yourself "it can't be this simple." Expect that some questions will revolve around the clear themes from the passage—these are the points that you need to rack up confidently and quickly in order to buy time for the more difficult ones.

13. E

Question 13 is very similar to question 11, and both are tied closely to the passage's main idea: how critics have wrongly assessed Webster's works. In question 11, you reiterated the main point that critics have assumed (wrongly) that Webster was influenced by earlier morality plays. They have done so because *most* Elizabethan dramatists were influenced by morality plays. Choice (E) says this, only substituting "same sources as his contemporaries" for "morality plays."

(A) Critics have found Webster's characters, in contrast to those of other Elizabethan dramatists, morally ambiguous, not black and white.

(B) 180. As you've seen over and over, the author's point is that critics have assumed (albeit incorrectly) that Webster's works derived from morality plays, which were English, not Italian.

(C) Critics have attributed Webster's alleged artistic flaws to his supposed inability to copy the style of the earlier morality play, rather than to ignorance of the classical definition of tragedy.

(D) Lines 38–43 tell you that critics have found that Webster's tragedies provide at least some basis for character analysis.

- Often two or more questions in a Reading Comp set will test the same concept. Use your work on earlier questions to help you answer later questions whenever possible. (And in this case, there's a good reason for the similarity: Both questions are tied to the author's main idea.)

14. D

The last question in this set asks about the author's view of Webster's conception of tragedies. All along you've seen that the author feels that Webster was not an incompetent Elizabethan playwright, but rather simply had a *different conception* of tragedy than most Elizabethan playwrights—a conception based on Italian drama rather than the English morality play. Lines 30–35, in fact, make this very point; (D) is the answer.

All four wrong choices contradict the author's point of view:

(A) Critics, not the author, consider Webster's conception of tragedy to be flawed.

(B) The author thinks Webster's conception of tragedy was unusual for, not typical of, an Elizabethan playwright.

(C) The author argues that Webster's tragedies derived from Italian drama, not the morality play.

(E) The author thinks that the morally complex nature of the characters in Webster's tragedies is fully consistent with Aristotle's classical conception of tragedy.

- The word "implies" in a question stem suggests an Inference question, but some inferences are so close to the actual text that they seem almost like explicit details. All along you've discussed how the author believes Webster's vision of tragedy was different and unique among his Elizabethan contemporaries. (D) simply reiterates this point.
- For the third question in a row, most of the wrong choices are inconsistent with the information in the passage. When there are two or more points of view in a passage (here you have the author vs. the critics), make sure you keep them straight in your mind. Know at all times who is arguing *what*. Then you'll be less likely to attribute a point of view to the wrong group and to fall for a 180 choice.

Passage 3—Phytopathogens

Topic and Scope

Agriculture; specifically, the effects of using genetically altered bacteria for specific agricultural purposes

Purpose and Main Idea

The author's purpose is to describe a debate over the agricultural benefits of using genetically altered bacteria on crops. The main idea, not fully evident until the second and third paragraphs, is that some are encouraged by the research in this field, while others still remain skeptical.

Paragraph Structure

Paragraph one essentially establishes the lingo for the passage. It begins with some brief background information (the impact of phytopathogens, crop rotation, and "suppressive soil" on agricultural yields), and then moves on to the topic at hand: Phytopathogens, or "bad" bacteria—"bad" because they're harmful to crops—may be suppressed by putting "good" bacteria such as *Pseudomonas fluorescens* into the soil. The rest of the first paragraph simply provides some evidence in support of this point by citing increased crop yields.

In paragraph two you learn that increased crop yields suggest that putting genetically altered "good" bacteria into the soil might be beneficial to agriculture in general. A few examples are given, and you find out that there are both proponents and opponents of such a course of action.

Paragraph three simply takes the debate a step further by giving you additional information about the work being done by the proponents—those who want to use genetically altered bacteria on the soil.

The Big Picture

- Although some test takers get flustered by natural science passages, they're really not much different from social science or humanities passages. Sure, they often contain some technical words or phrases, but these will be defined and explained in the passage. And they often compensate for the technical language with a very clear passage structure. As with all passages, nail down the author's purpose, structure, and main idea, and you'll be in a position to answer most if not all of the questions.
- Never try to memorize details—many of them will not be tested. Instead, keep in mind the big idea, in this case that there is a debate over whether releasing genetically altered bacteria into the soil is a good idea. *That such a debate is taking place* is the message the author wants to convey.
- Strive to understand the author's place in the argument. This author's tone, despite the seemingly rosy ending, can only be described as neutral and objective. He cites examples as well as the proponents' case and the opponents' reservations about bacterial use in agriculture. And in the end, it is "many" (not necessarily including the author) who are encouraged by the prospects for the procedure. Detached, objective, informative; not at all unusual for a natural science passage.

The Questions

15. B

As is often the case, the first question in the set is a standard Global question asking the main idea. As discussed, the author is interested in conveying the notion that some people out there favor the use of genetically altered bacteria as a means for improving agricultural yields, while others oppose this course of action. (B) captures the spirit of this precisely.

(A), (C), and (E) are all too narrow in scope to qualify as the main idea. The passage's main message is that there's a *debate* going on in the scientific community about whether genetically altered bacteria will improve agriculture. The author discusses recent research and experiments because they support this message, which means that they're nothing more than supporting details. Moreover, (A) and (C) can also be thrown out on the grounds that they're unequivocally positive in tone—they completely ignore the concerns of the opponents of genetically altered bacteria.

(D) Crop rotation is never characterized as "outdated," nor is there any suggestion of getting rid of it. It is merely mentioned in the beginning as background information. This passage isn't about the possible effects of genetic research on crop rotation; it's about a debate over the efficacy of using genetic engineering to boost agriculture, a different issue.

- Don't lose sight of the forest for the trees! In a passage like this some test takers will focus exclusively on the scientific jargon and lose sight of the fact that the author's real purpose is to alert the reader to the existence of a *debate* over the cited procedure. If you came out of the passage with that notion intact, you should have had no problems with this question.
- Once again, watch out for choices like (D) that combine elements from the passage in ways the passage did not. Choices that use the passage's language but distort its ideas are common in both Global and Inference questions.

16. D

Next up is another "function of a detail" question. This is just like question 10 in the previous passage, which asked you why Aristotle was mentioned by the author. The same procedure applies: Locate the detail and try to understand the role it plays in context. The stem directs you to the first paragraph, where *Pseudomonas fluorescens* appears. Here you find out that this bacterium seems to suppress harmful phytopathogens, thereby contributing to improved crop yields. In the first sentence of the second paragraph, the author cites this fact—"These improvements in crop yields. . ."—in support of the belief that putting genetically altered bacteria into the soil might be a good thing for agriculture. In other words, the author uses this example to show how the position advocated by the proponents regarding genetically altered bacteria might have evolved. Choice (D) makes this point, employing slightly different language.

(A) contradicts information in the passage. In lines 13-14, the author specifically says that there may be a number of reasons, not just one, for soil suppressivity.

(B) Even if the "treatment of wheat seeds" is the same thing as "spraying wheat fields," there's still no explanation as to *why* the yields increased, only that they did increase.

(C) The passage never details any "chemical processes." Even if it had, that's not *why* the author discussed *Pseudomonas fluorescens*.

(E) The author never says or implies that crop rotation is unnecessary (see first bullet point below). Moreover, the author never says or implies that phytopathogens "eventually disappear on their own"; this is an exaggeration.

- Choice (E) here is the second choice so far that is wrong because it distorts the example of crop rotation mentioned in the first paragraph (choice (D) in question 15 is the other). The "distortion" is a common wrong answer type, and if you're hazy on what is meant by this, simply compare these two choices to what is actually said about crop rotation in the passage. Hopefully you'll see how these choices distort the example, and you'll be able to recognize similar kinds of distortions in other wrong choices.
- If you find yourself stumbling over the lingo in the passage, feel free to abbreviate, just as you do in Logic Games. There's no reason to mentally stumble over the term "harmful phytopathogens" again and again; you can just as easily think of them as the "bad p-things."

17. C

According to line 4, "phytopathogens" are parasitic. So crops "impervious" to parasites cannot be harmed by phytopathogens. Such crops will therefore not be helped by the addition of *Pseudomonas fluorescens* to the soil around them; after all, the reason for adding this bacterium to the soil in the first place is to protect crops from harmful phytopathogens. This benefit would be absent for crops that are impervious to parasites, which points to (C).

(A) Nothing in the passage says or suggests that the presence or absence of *Pseudomonas fluorescens* in the soil around crops is in any way connected to the susceptibility of crops to phytopathogens. In other words, *Pseudomonas fluorescens* may be present whether or not there are parasites for it to act against.

(B) and (D) The passage doesn't provide you with any facts about these crops mentioned in the stem—those that are resistant to phytopathogens—so you can't infer anything about their growth patterns or their effects on other crops.

(E) is out for much the same reason as (A): All you know about "impervious" crops is that they're immune to phytopathogenic bacteria. You can't infer from this how much of such bacteria surrounds these plants in comparison to other crops. There may be a lot, there may be a little; all you know for sure is that no matter how much surrounds the roots of these plants, it has no detrimental effect.

- Since you know nothing of these new plants mentioned in the stem, any valid inference must relate back to something you know about from the passage. This is why any choice that discusses only elements related to the new topic (impervious plants) must be wrong. How could you know anything about their growth patterns, (B) and (D)? This strongly suggests that the answer will in some way have to relate back to *Pseudomonas fluorescens,* which narrows the choices down to (A) or (C).

18. E

As you know by now, crop rotation is discussed at the beginning of the passage, so look there. The author says that crop rotation cuts down on the problem posed by phytopathogens by denying them a "suitable host." This is how crop rotation can cure the problem of decreased yield. Working straight from the language, plants that "deny phytopathogens a suitable host" must be *unsuitable* hosts. This suggests that not every phytopathogen can attach to every host, which in turn means that specific phytopathogens must attack specific kinds of plants. All of this points directly to (E).

(A) According to the passage, crop rotation seems to help crops not by making *them* stronger, but rather by making their environment less harmful.

(B) If anything, lines 8–18 seem to suggest that the number of *Pseudomonas fluorescens* bacteria in the soil increases when crops are *not* rotated. What happens to their number when crops *are* rotated is anyone's guess.

(C) Compounds produced by the roots of crop plants are outside the scope of the passage. Nothing allows you to infer what kind of compounds such roots might produce, let alone what connection this might have to the benefits of crop rotation.

(D) Although you know that phytopathogenic bacteria cause crop disease, there's no information in the passage that would indicate that they're responsible for *most* crop diseases. More importantly, as in (C), even if you could agree to this, what connection does this have to the way in which crop rotation increases yield?

- Make sure you answer the actual question that is asked. The question here isn't "what can be generally inferred from the passage?" The question is "what can be inferred regarding the way in which crop rotation increases yield?" That's a big difference. Critical reading is rewarded not just in the passage but also in the stems and answer choices. Just like a Detail stem, this kind of specific inference stem will direct you to the right place to research the answer in the passage.

19. A

In this one, you're interested in what proponents of genetic engineering think about the altered bacteria used in the frost-damage experiments, and that's outlined in lines 41–45. Line 41, specifically ("Proponents, on the other hand, argue that . . ."), announces that this is where the answer is likely to be found. The proponents assert that genetically altered bacteria used in these experiments differ from the naturally occurring bacteria *only* in that one gene—the one that causes frost damage—has been removed from the altered bacteria, which brings you to (A).

(B) distorts a detail brought up in lines 54–56, which, in any case, has nothing to do with the frost-damage experiments.

(C) Those who favor the use of altered bacteria never make any comparison between the safety and effectiveness of the altered bacteria used in the frost-damage experiments and naturally occurring *Pseudomonas fluorescens.* They merely claim that the altered bacteria in these experiments are safer than the phytopathogenic bacterium from which it was derived, *Pseudomonas syringae*.

(D) Proponents claim that the altered bacteria will attack one type of phytopathogen, the one that causes frost damage to crops; nowhere do they say or imply that the altered bacteria fought against "several types of naturally occurring phytopathogens."

(E) This claim is never made by the supporters of genetic engineering; in fact, they never discuss anything regarding the number of bacteria released. If anything, it is the *opponents* who speak of "large-scale release" of genetically altered bacteria, and not in the specific context of the frost-damage experiments at that.

- Formal logic terms have the same meaning on all three sections of the LSAT. While you encounter formal logic most often in Logic Games, and then in Logical Reasoning, formal logic terms do pop up in Reading Comp passages as well. Here, the proponents assert that the bacteria in question is altered "only" by the removal of the responsible gene; a correct translation of this is that this bacteria differs from the original only in that it has one fewer gene, (A).

- Detail questions that ask what is stated or argued will be answerable straight from the passage, so your main job is to locate the relevant text. Correct choice (A) here is simply a slight rewording of lines 41–45.

20. D

Again you're concerned with the frost-damage issue, but this time you're asked what, if true, would weaken the proponents' argument. You just reviewed their argument for the sake of the previous question, so it should be fresh in our minds: These proponents claim that the new bacteria, which is the old minus the one harmful gene, limits frost damage without causing any harmful effects. Well, if it were true that the deletion of one gene could indeed cause harmful effects, this argument would be weakened. (D) leads you in that direction: If the gene removed from the original pathogenic bacteria may very well be responsible for protecting the crop in other ways, then removing this gene may thus endanger the crop and therefore warrant the opponents' fear of "deleterious results."

(A) Primitive and simple? So what? This has no bearing on the argument that the altered bacteria are safer because it doesn't contain the gene that causes frost damage.

(B) is entirely consistent with the proponents' argument, so it obviously doesn't weaken their argument. They never claimed that the altered bacteria derived from anything *but* a harmful phytopathogen. Indeed, their claim is that they're turning a harmful bacterium into a beneficial one by altering its genetic structure.

(C) Commercial production of genetically altered bacteria is irrelevant to the issue of the safety of such bacteria, which is after all the cornerstone of the proponents' argument.

(E) The info in (E)—how the altered variety works most efficiently—doesn't address the safety issue. Instead, it speaks to the effectiveness of the altered bacteria, a different issue entirely.

- When you see a Weaken question in Reading Comp, use the same strategies you use in Logical Reasoning. Remember, an argument can only be weakened on its own terms, which in this case is safety and harm to crops. Choice (D) addresses this issue. Wrong choices (A), (C), and (E) do not, and must be eliminated. Choice (B) is within the scope, as it deals with the "harmful to crops" issue, but as you saw, (B) is perfectly consistent with the proponents' argument and is therefore not a weakener.
- Use your work on one question to help you answer related questions. Question 19 forced you to review the argument of the proponents of the use of genetically altered bacteria in frost-damage experiments. Question 20 asks you to weaken this same argument, so you need waste no time in familiarizing yourself with the issue at hand, and you can jump right into attacking this argument.

Passage 4—The Dawes Act

Topic and Scope

Legislation regulating the private ownership of reservation lands for Native Americans—specifically, the stated and actual intentions of the legislators behind the Dawes Act

Purpose and Main Idea

The author's purpose is to describe the Dawes Act and the reasons advanced for a particular restriction in the act, and then to discredit these reasons and argue that another factor may have influenced this legislation. The main idea doesn't become evident until the final paragraph, but it's not a difficult one to grasp: The author thinks that the clause in the Dawes Act restricting land sales for 25 years had nothing to do with protecting the interests of Native Americans, but rather was intended to serve the interests of government bureaucrats and, by extension, politicians.

Paragraph Structure

Paragraph one introduces the Dawes Act, a piece of legislation that dealt with land ownership by Native Americans. This paragraph simply provides you with some facts about the act: Under its terms, each Native American adult was granted limited ownership of 80 acres of land, which they could use but not sell for 25 years.

In paragraph two you find out two reasons *why* Native Americans were restricted from selling their land: This would prevent the sale of Native American land to non-Native Americans and thus preserve the Native American way of life; secondly, Native Americans were not really ready for, or interested in, full private ownership because of their tradition of communal land use.

Paragraph three questions the validity of this rationale on the grounds that it doesn't explain why Native Americans were prohibited from selling land to each other, or to the tribe.

This leads directly into paragraph four, in which the author's purpose in writing the passage becomes clear. As stated above, the author feels that the real motivation for the "restriction on alienation" clause was self-interest on the part of government bureaucrats and politicians, not the wellbeing of Native Americans, as originally stated. That's the author's message, and it's spelled out in a bit more detail in the remainder of this paragraph.

The Big Picture

- As you read, continually ask "why is the author telling me this?" Why are you told the specifics of the Dawes Act in paragraph one? You don't know by the end of that paragraph—which is a good clue that the purpose and main idea are yet to come. Paragraph two offers two reasons for the "restriction of sale" clause in the act. Why are you told this? Still not sure; this *could* be a purely descriptive passage, but there are still two paragraphs to go. In paragraph three, things really heat up; the author objects to the reasons cited in the previous paragraph, and this objection sets up the crucial paragraph four, in which an entirely new interpretation of the true intentions of the "restriction on alienation" clause is put forth. A careful reader, asking the right questions along the way, can discern not only the main idea wherever it appears, but also the *structure* of the passage: paragraphs one and two supply background; paragraph three questions a previous account of the facts; and paragraph four provides the author's hypothesis and main idea.
- Use the definitions provided in the passage, and substitute simpler words for complex ones whenever possible. In the first paragraph, "alienate" is defined in parentheses as "sell." Forms of the more complicated term appear throughout the rest of the passage—"alienability" and "alienation," for example. In paraphrasing the passage as you read, simply substitute the easier word "sell" whenever these words appear. The more you translate and simplify the author's ideas, the better you'll understand the passage.

The Questions

21. C

You start off with another standard Global question asking about the main idea of the passage. Well, as just mentioned, the author's main message appears at the end of the passage; she disagrees with the stated reasons for the restriction on Native American land sales contained in the Dawes Act, and instead posits her own theory that this restriction was meant to serve the interests of bureaucrats and politicians, not Native Americans. The first three paragraphs of the passage lay the foundation for this message, and the last paragraph delivers it. Whenever you're dealing with a Global question, you should already have determined the answer during your reading of the passage, so don't get distracted—use the work you've already done to pick up quick points.

(A) is way too broad in scope: This passage is specifically about the Dawes Act, not about general U.S. government policy toward Native Americans. Secondly, as far as the Dawes Act was concerned, it was intended to serve the interests of bureaucrats and politicians, not non-Native Americans, who were specifically precluded by the act from purchasing Native American land.

(B) can also be eliminated for a couple of reasons. For one thing, it's much too narrow in scope: Communal land use is discussed only briefly in the second and third paragraphs. More importantly, the author never makes the claim that communal land use is necessary if Native Americans are to preserve their way of life; all you know is that they favored this form.

(D) is a true statement—the Dawes Act *did* expand U.S. government activity in the area of land administration. But is that why the author wrote the passage, to point this out? Or does this fact lead somewhere bigger? Indeed it does; it acts as support for the notion that bureaucrats and politicians, not Native Americans, benefited from the clause in the Dawes Act restricting land sales. Anything that supports a larger point can't be the main idea (see bullet point below).

(E) twists a detail in the passage. According to the Dawes Act, Native Americans could not sell their land for 25 years. After that period of time was up, they were free to sell, and presumably some did so. In any case, the author's interest in the Dawes Act lies elsewhere.

- A choice may contain true information based on the passage and yet still not be the main idea. Take (D), for instance: Even if you had trouble recognizing the author's main idea, the fact that the true statement in (D) is used in the passage to lead somewhere else, to something bigger, is enough to tell you that (D) itself isn't the main idea. Anything that supports a *larger* point can't be the main idea of the passage.

22. C

This question asks which reason for the end of land allotment best supports the author's conception of politicians. The best place to start is with a consideration of the author's opinion of politicians, which should be at the forefront of your mind because it ties directly in with the main idea. In lines 48–51, the author makes politicians out to be totally self-interested individuals who support policies that tend to increase their own political influence. If the reason for the end of land allotment was that it failed to serve political interests, as (C) has it, then you would be more likely to believe that the author's characterization of politicians is correct.

(A) is out because the author doesn't believe that politicians are motivated by concern for the welfare of others; they're out for their own, not the Native Americans', interests.

(B) would provide evidence of a certain kind of mean-spiritedness or anti-Native American stance on the part of the politicians, but the author doesn't suggest this at all; she simply says that politicians are motivated by self-interest in this matter, not that they have any particular problem with the Native Americans' conception of land use.

(D) The author says that politicians *favor* the growth of government bureaucracy because this enhances prospects "for the exercise of political patronage." Politicians therefore wouldn't push for an end to allotment on the grounds that the BIA, a part of the government's bureaucracy, had become too big; according to the author, this is what politicians want.

(E) Again, the author is convinced that politicians would never push for an end to a policy solely on the basis of that policy's effect on others. If (E) is the true reason for the end of allotment, then the author hasn't portrayed the politicians very well.

- Treat a Strengthen question in Reading Comp the same as you would in Logical Reasoning: Focus in on the relevant argument, and see what effect, if any, each choice has on it. The only difference here is that the stem directs you right to the relevant material (in this case, the author's view of politicians), whereas in Logical Reasoning you often have to first pinpoint the author's conclusion yourself.

23. D

This Global question deals specifically with the organization of the passage, which provides for a quick and easy point for those test takers who pay careful attention to the passage structure as they read. You discussed above how the first paragraph describes the Dawes Act, the second paragraph discusses the official explanation behind one of its clauses (restriction on selling land), the third paragraph takes issue with the official explanation, and the last paragraph sets out an entirely different rationale for the clause (political self-interest). (D) contains all of these elements, and is correct.

(A) immediately goes off track; the legislative *process* leading to the enactment of the Dawes Act is never mentioned, much less analyzed in detail. Moreover, no final assessment of the law itself is given—all you get is an analysis of the rationale behind one of its clauses.

(B) You're never told about the history of the Dawes Act, and the author never advocates its repeal. After all, line 54 tells you that "the allotment was ended in 1934."

(C) is a bit more plausible than (A) or (B), especially up until the end of the choice, but it goes wrong when it speaks of studying the lasting effects of the Dawes Act. That's simply not what the author does. Again, the author is interested in explaining the "real" (as opposed to the official) rationale behind one of its clauses, the land sales clause.

(E) This passage is about the political overtones of *one particular clause of one particular law*; it's not about the overall legal status of Native Americans in matters of land ownership and commercial autonomy, although it does touch on these issues.

- An "organization of the passage" question in RC is similar to a Method of Argument question in LR. In both cases, test every element of the choice to see whether that element is indeed part of the passage or argumentative structure. If even one thing in the choice doesn't match, then throw that choice out.
- Notice how many of the wrong choices can be eliminated for the same reason: They deal with the Dawes Act in general while the author is primarily concerned with only one of its clauses.

24. E

Next up is a question that asks about the author's attitude toward the official explanation behind the land sales clause of the Dawes Act. This answer can definitely be predicted, and you quite possibly were able to answer this one without a look back to the passage; the whole main idea of the passage revolves around this very attitude. The only reason the author offers her own interpretation of the motivations behind the land sales clause is because she is very dissatisfied with the "official" explanation. That immediately rules out any choice with a positive sentiment, such as (A)'s "credulous" and (B)'s "approving." It also rules out neutrality, (C)'s "indecisive."

No, the author's attitude is *negative*, and so the question boils down to *how* negative: Is she "mildly questioning," (D), or "highly skeptical," (E)? You may have needed to return to the text to select between these two remaining choices, but you shouldn't have had any trouble finding clues in the third paragraph and the beginning of the fourth. In particular, notice how the author calls the official explanation "empty." This is enough to confirm the author's attitude as highly skeptical; "mildly questioning" is too weak. If the author only "mildly" questioned the official rationale for the clause, the opposition in the third paragraph wouldn't be so strongly stated, and the author may not have seen the need to provide her own hypothesis. And she wouldn't have used the word "empty" to describe the official explanation.

- When asked to describe the author's attitude toward something, first break it down to positive, negative, or indifferent. This should help you eliminate between 2 and 4 wrong choices. Then, if necessary, look for clues in the passage to narrow your choice down to the winner.
- Critical readers understand how even small words can provide a world of meaning. Think about it: If you were arguing a point with a friend, and your friend said your argument was "empty," you would not get the impression that he was "mildly questioning" your notion, so "highly skeptical" is a better description of his opinion. And the same is true here. That one little word in line 38 confirms (E) as the correct choice.

25. B

In this question, you're asked to infer something about Native American life before the Dawes Act, so it makes sense to review what the Dawes Act was all about. It was intended to give ownership of land to Native Americans (albeit with the proviso that they couldn't sell it for 25 years). This strongly suggests that before the Dawes Act, Native Americans didn't own land, doesn't it? Why else would the government adopt a law to give ownership to them? It doesn't make sense to give land to someone who already owns that land. (B) is inferable, and it's nicely qualified too; notice how it says "not many" rather than "no." You may not be able to infer that "no" Native Americans owned their own land; there may have been a few exceptions. But from the way the law is described, you *can* infer that few Native Americans owned their own land immediately before the passage of the Dawes Act.

(A) The way in which Native Americans supported themselves is not tied to the issue of land ownership. You don't have enough information to infer that most Native Americans supported themselves through farming.

(C) goes against the grain of the passage. If Native Americans had bought land from their tribes before the Dawes Act, why would there be any need for this act? Native Americans, after all, would already have owned their own land.

(D) doesn't make much sense at all: There's no necessary connection between the degree of contact between Native and non-Native Americans and the issue of land ownership.

(E) If anything, the opposite is suggested: The government might have had the impression that many Native Americans *would* sell their land to non-Native Americans; this was one of the reasons advanced for the restriction. But you say *might* because the author argues that this was not the *true* reason for the land sales restriction. In any case, you can't draw the inference in (E) based on the information contained in the passage.

- Don't read extra facts or interpretations into the passage: Under the sway of (A), you may have reasoned that the government enacted the Dawes Act because most Native Americans were farmers without title to the land which they worked. But while there may be some logic in this line of thought, nothing in the passage supports this notion. Don't take a logical leap simply because it leads to a credible-sounding idea; stay within the framework of the passage.

26. B

Here's a Detail question regarding, not surprisingly, the author's main area of concern, the land sales clause of the Dawes Act. And hopefully you didn't let the long stem confuse you; it simply asks how land ownership for the first 25 years differed from land ownership thereafter. And you know this; it's all part of the background information of the first paragraph. Lines 5–15 tell you that during the first 25 years of ownership, a Native American landowner could not sell his land; he had only limited title. After 25 years of ownership, however, the Native American landowner was granted full title to the land, giving the landowner the right to sell the land.

(A) and (D) As far as you know, the government never placed any sort of conditions on how Native Americans could use their land.

(C) has the facts backward. The government had control over land sales during the *first* 25 years, but no control after that.

(E) There's no mention of the government asking Native Americans to pay a fee to develop their land.

- Don't be intimidated by the length or wordiness of a question stem. This stem is basically a long-winded way of asking about what you already know and have known since paragraph one: According to the clause, after 25 years, the Native Americans could freely sell their land. Before that, they couldn't.

27. D

Lastly, you're asked to determine which of five possible facts would strengthen the author's argument regarding the motivation for the Dawes Act. This takes you right back to the author's main idea, which is that the restriction on selling was included to benefit bureaucrats, which, in turn, benefited politicians. All of this is made clear in the middle of the last paragraph. Choice (D) underscores the influence of BIA bureaucrats on the legislators who enacted the act, and therefore supports the author's argument and gets the point.

(A) would, if anything, tend to weaken, rather than strengthen, the author's argument. The author views politicians as self-interested individuals, but non-Native Americans who owned land next to Native American land were inferably hurt by the Dawes Act to the extent that they were unable to purchase land from Native American landowners for 25 years. Thus, if politicians who owned land next to Native American land had voted for such a piece of legislation, this could not be considered self-interested behavior.

(B), (C), and (E) The "facts" brought up in these remaining choices are all outside the scope of the author's main argument. Remember, the argument is based on the behavior and motivations of *bureaucrats* and *politicians*, not on the behavior of Native Americans or non-Native American land purchasers. How these groups behave may be of some interest to us, but does not affect the gist of the author's argument because that argument centers on other groups.

- When asked to strengthen or weaken an argument, immediately eliminate choices that fall outside the scope. Since this author's main idea focuses on the true motivations of politicians and bureaucrats, you can immediately narrow the choices in this question down to (A) and (D).
- Main idea, purpose, and structure, taken together, form the cornerstone of every LSAT RC passage. If you can nail these down, you'll be ready for the questions. You've seen this before, of course, in this program, or in a class or workshop, perhaps. Look back over the correct answers to questions 21–27 and notice how almost every question in this set revolved in some way around these elements. Resolve now to continually improve your ability to pick out the main idea, purpose, and structure of every RC passage you read, and when test day arrives, you'll be able to make your way through this section with confidence.

SECTION IV: LOGICAL REASONING

1. D

You're asked to strengthen the argument, which centers around two specific events: reduction in the speed limit and the marked decrease in the rate of highway fatalities over the next ten years. At this point you can probably guess what the author's conclusion will be: that the first event (the change in speed limit) caused the second event (the steady decrease in the rate of highway fatalities). Sure enough, the author concludes in the last sentence that the reduced speed limit saved lives. A reduction in the speed limit followed by a decline in the fatality rate *suggests* that there may be cause and effect at work, but it doesn't *prove* it. What this argument needs is more evidence that, in fact, there *is* a causal relationship between speed limits and highway fatalities. Choice (D) provides this: If drivers driving over 55 mph are more likely to suffer or cause fatalities, then you have greater reason to believe that the author's argument—lowering the speed limit to 55 mph reduced the fatality rate—is on target.

(A) The stimulus discusses fatality *rates*, that is, fatalities per some given number of drivers. Having fewer people driving due to the fuel shortage has no bearing on the argument, because the author is concerned with the fatality *rate*, and not the sheer number of drivers.

(B) The twelfth year? First of all, year twelve is outside the scope; the argument is nicely contained in years one through eleven after the reduction in the speed limit. Secondly, the fact that the rate didn't continue downward indicates nothing; perhaps the life-saving potential of the 55 mph speed limit was fully realized after eleven years.

(C) actually weakens the argument by providing an alternative explanation for the reduction in the fatality rate. Contrary to the author's assertion, it could have been the seat belts, rather than the speed limit, that saved lives during the period mentioned.

(E) If (E) is true, then it's possible that driving *faster* may save more lives in those cases where many people are speeding. Therefore, (E) may weaken the argument by suggesting that a reduction in speed didn't save lives after all.

- Anticipate as you read; this keeps you one step ahead of the game. Many Logical Reasoning arguments are structurally similar, so you're likely to come upon the same kinds of arguments again and again. Here, once you're told about a reduction in the speed limit and then a decline in the fatality rate, it's almost a lock that the author is going to conclude that the first caused the second. And speaking of causality . . .
- No doubt you've seen the "X happened, then Y happened, therefore X caused Y" form of argument before (or if you're at the beginning of your preparation, you certainly will see it in the future). Even in cases like this one, where a causal relationship seems plausible, the author still must provide substantive proof of causality, and here, (D) adds the kind of solid evidence the argument is lacking.

2. E

The author's point of view jumps forcefully off the page from the second sentence: "Such a position ignores the lessons of experience." So you know right away that the author is arguing against the "position" in the first sentence: the refusal of some legislators to commit public money to research lacking a clearly defined public benefit. Predictably, the author's rationale for arguing against this position comes next: Many unexpected, yet socially beneficial discoveries have emerged from just such research. Antibiotics are offered as an example of a hugely beneficial discovery that was accidentally born out of the seemingly unrelated study of molds. Where is the author going with all this? You may have been able to prephrase, at least in spirit, if not word for word, the point the author is leading toward: The legislators are wrong—specifically, they are wrong to refuse to fund research solely because that research isn't *guaranteed* to benefit the public welfare. (E) is a close paraphrase of this idea.

(A) is overly optimistic: The author's notion that you can't know for sure whether a given research program will benefit society is a far cry from arguing that *any* public funding for scientific research will *necessarily* enhance the public good.

(B) is too broad, for it necessarily leads to an absurd result: Suppose the predicted "general outcome" of a new research effort was utter failure, something with no public use, or something that would even harm the public? Would legislators *really* be willing to fund such research? According to (B), simply knowing the outcome would result in funding, but this is far from the point the author is trying to make.

(C) While the author may possibly agree with (C), still, this isn't the main point she's trying to make. The author's evidence is not presented in order to lament what could have been the case for past discoveries, but rather to show what the unexpected results of past research can tell you about the shortsightedness of the legislators' current position.

(D) The author believes that legislators should fund research, but not, as (D) has it, because this would ensure that the research is *directed* toward the public good. Rather, she promotes funding because you can't be sure what research, regardless of its direction, will ultimately increase the public good.

- Use your critical reading skills in the Logical Reasoning section, where applicable. The second sentence highlighted above is a clear indicator of authorial purpose, much like the kind of statements you're trained to look for in RC passages. Such a sentence is of the utmost importance: This one tells you that this author thinks the legislators' view is wrong, and the rest of the stimulus exists as evidence for this notion. That alone is almost enough to get the point, or at least narrow the choices down considerably.
- Don't confuse a statement with which the author might agree, like (C) here, with the author's main point. It's very possible for a statement to be consistent with the author's argument without it being the main point she's trying to make.

3. B

The stem tells you you're looking for a Flaw. First you get evidence: Workers who aren't challenged become bored and achieve less than they're capable of. As if that weren't bad enough, employers face another risk: Workers who find their jobs *too* challenging get discouraged, and they, too, achieve less than they are capable of. The last sentence is the conclusion, indicated clearly by the keyword "therefore." Workers, the author concludes, cannot possibly realize their full potential. This is only true if there is no middle ground—a healthy amount of challenge: not too much, not too little. The conclusion is therefore based on the assumption that the two extremes mentioned in the evidence are the only possibilities. But nothing in the evidence precludes the existence of just the right amount of challenge, which would allow for full realization of a worker's potential. (B) describes this flaw. As *Goldilocks* teaches us, this porridge is too hot, this porridge is too cold, but this porridge is *just right*.

(A) The whole argument aims to show that what is actual—workers' actual achievements—never matches what is possible—their potential achievements—so the author *isn't* falsely equating the actual and the possible.

(C) The author reasons from general principles of cause and effect: "If a worker isn't challenged (or is *too* challenged), then . . ." But no clue is given as to whether these are, or are intended to be "objective" or "subjective." The principles themselves aren't the problem; the logic bogs down in the author's failure to consider that these principles don't describe all possible levels of challenge in the workplace.

(D) accuses the author of confusing correlation (coincidence of two events) with causation. But the author *does* provide evidence for causality in the form of a middle term for both cases. Unchallenging work leads to *boredom* and too-difficult work leads to *discouragement*, so the problem with this argument is not the confusion of coincidence and causality.

(E) Only a few key terms are included in the argument: assignments, challenging, achieve, and potential. None of these, however, is hard to understand or decipher. There is no such ambiguity here; each of these terms is clear.

- Read critically, especially when the stem tells you there is a problem with the argumentation. In such cases, always keep an eye out for alternative possibilities or explanations that the author ignores. When an author assumes without evidence that no such alternative exists, then the omission of this alternative possibility is usually the source of the Flaw.
- Look at the Kaplan process at work. Here's the optimal chain of events in getting this point: Previewing the stem tells you to break the argument into evidence and conclusion and look for the gap; prephrasing leads you to question "What if the challenge is just right?"; and scanning the choices with this thought in mind leads to correct choice (B). Your preparation task is to continually hone this process so it will be as close to automatic as possible by test day.

4. E

Another misleading ad; you'll recall you saw one back in section 1, question 4, and now you get one in this section, question 4. You're asked to find the statement that, if true, would make the ad misleading. The claim is that the soup provides good nutrition. The evidence for this claim is signaled by the keyword phrase "for instance," which turns out to be one example of the soup's nutritional value—a warm bowl of this tomato soup provides more units of vitamin C than does a serving of carrots or apricots. Presumably, this comparison is intended to astound us, as the exclamation mark makes clear.

But there are a lot of holes to be punched in this argument, and hopefully you were able to prephrase at least one or two. First off, vitamin C is only one nutrient. If the soup has nothing else to offer, then the ad is a bit misleading because consumers might reasonably expect a food to provide more than one type of nutrient. Secondly, you don't know that the comparison is fair: Just how much vitamin C do apricots or carrots have? To get even pickier, just how big is the soup bowl, and how many carrots or apricots make "a serving"? The test makers chose to exploit the second ambiguity in (E): if carrots and apricots aren't particularly good sources of vitamin C, then the fact that the soup provides *more* vitamin C isn't as impressive as it's meant to sound. And since that's the only support offered for the claim, the ad would be misleading if (E) were true.

(A) Carrots and apricots don't have to provide all the vitamin C a person needs in order for them to be rich in vitamin C. Even if most people get their vitamin C elsewhere, carrots and apricots might still be excellent sources of vitamin C, in which case the validity of the ad is not undermined.

(B) The ad hypes a cup of *warm* soup, not room temperature soup that's been lying around for a long time, so this fact doesn't affect the advertisement's claim.

(C) Bully for the soup; let the company use this information in its next ad. Tomato soup's strengths in other respects wouldn't make this ad misleading.

(D) Strawberries and their vitamin C content are irrelevant. The ad stands or falls on the relevance of the comparison of the soup's vitamin C content with that of apricots and carrots. As long as the soup is nutritious, it doesn't matter how the soup compares to other foods.

- Always focus on the scope of the argument presented. Here, the argument is not simply that the soup is nutritious, but rather that it's nutritious *for a specific reason*—more vitamin C than apricots and carrots. If the ad is misleading, there must be some breakdown between this evidence and the claim, which means that the right answer will almost surely contain info about apricots and carrots. This alone narrows the choices down to (A) and (E). You won't always be able to prephrase a Strengthen or Weaken question directly, because there's almost always more than one possible way to affect the argument—but keeping your eye on the hole is the trick. You're looking for an answer a choice that says "just because the soup has more Vitamin C than carrots and apricots doesn't necessarily mean it's nutritious."

5. A

You're looking for the principle that best supports the argument's conclusion. The argument begins with a statement of contrast, signaled by the keyword "but": Deposit insurance is *provided* to individuals, but *paid for* by banks. Since (here's evidence) depositors are the primary beneficiaries of deposit insurance, those depositors who want the insurance (here's the conclusion) should pay for it—not a very complicated argument. Depositors should pay for deposit insurance because it's designed to benefit them, not the banks. The author is appealing to the more general principle that those who benefit from something should be those who pay for that something. Replace "something" with the more specific "economic service," and you have correct choice (A).

(B) The argument centers on who benefits and who pays. Risk and the *level* of payments have nothing to do with the argument, so the principle in (B) is of no help.

(C) The economic rationale for when to provide deposit insurance doesn't help this argument at all. The issue is who should *pay* for deposit insurance, not *whether* it should be offered.

(D) The argument is about what should happen in the case of "depositors who want this security." The right to refuse a service that one *doesn't* pay for is an entirely separate issue that's outside the scope.

(E) is such a broad principle that you can't be sure how it relates to the author's argument. It's quite possible that relieving banks of the burden of paying deposit insurance premiums, and forcing depositors to do so, *would* alter the behavior of corporations and individuals in the marketplace. In that case, the principle in (E) would stand in opposition to the argument, which posits that the government *should* step in to change the current practice.

- Often, the principle that supports an argument is nothing more than a slightly more general restatement of the argument itself. Here, if you substitute "deposit insurance" for "economic service" in (A), it's easy to see how the principle in (A) and the author's main point are nearly identical.

6. C

The assumption here is tough to prephrase. The argument, you'll recall, is that since depositors benefit from deposit insurance, they should pay the premiums. At present, the banks pay. But what if, in fact, the banks simply pass this cost on to the depositors? This is not an unusual business practice; a store with property taxes to pay on a new parking lot, for example, may increase its prices to cover the cost, and the same may be true here. The author must believe that the banks do not defer the cost in this way, because if they did, then the argument that the government should make depositors pay these premiums directly would make no sense because they'd *already* be paying them. If, contrary to (C), banks *always* pass the cost of the premiums along to the depositors, then the depositors are really paying the premiums and there is no injustice in the situation, and therefore no need for the government to step in.

(A) Insuring loans made by banks? This is outside the scope of the argument, which concerns *deposit* insurance, so (A) isn't a necessary part of this argument.

(B) The argument centers on government-provided deposit insurance; private insurance of deposits is a different issue. Whether other types of deposit insurance can exist is irrelevant and therefore need not be assumed.

(D) *How much* protection the government provides is one step removed from the focus of the argument, which is about who should *bear the cost*. The author's argument that the burden of cost should be shifted is in no way dependent on the existence of any such insurance protection limit.

(E) seems to contradict the argument: The statement "depositors who *want* this security" strongly implies that depositors have the choice of insured or uninsured accounts. This suggests, contrary to (E), that the government *does* allow banks to offer some uninsured accounts.

- The wrong choices in Assumption questions are often outside the scope like (A) and (B), or run contrary to the argument, as in the case of (E) here. Notice how "in the scope" correct choice (C) is—the argument is specifically about who pays the cost of deposit insurance, and this is exactly the issue addressed in (C).

7. A

Here's a stimulus about education, and you're asked to infer a conclusion. Take inventory of the information in the stimulus: First you learn that exposure to identical curriculum results in unequal learning by students—specifically, some students will learn more, better, and faster than others. If more equal results are to be achieved (if you want all the students to master the material), some will require different types of teaching from others. In the first sentence, the author defines equal treatment as identical exposure to curriculum; you can infer from this that she considers *different* exposure to curriculum to be "unequal" treatment. In this context, the last sentence means that equal results—i.e., the equal mastery of the curriculum—requires *unequal* treatment, (A). The author is leading toward the main point that unequal treatment is necessary for equal educational results.

(B) The word "quantity" comes up only in the context of learning—in (B), the notion of the quantity of *teaching* appears. The author argues that different students may need different *types* of help; but that's not enough to infer how the "quantity of teaching" may affect the rate and quality of learning.

(C) All you can infer from the reference to experienced teachers is that the author believes that these teachers agree with her premise stated in the second sentence. This doesn't, however, allow you to infer any kind of connection between experienced teachers and successful students; more information is necessary for this.

(D) A 180 answer choice—identical exposure leads to variances in learning. (D) is the exact opposite of the author's call for "different types of help" that's necessary for all students to master the material.

(E) seems like a nice sentiment, and the author may well agree with it. It isn't, however, inferable from these statements. The "different types of help" necessary for mastery is a vague and undefined notion; it doesn't mandate that teachers teach as much as they can to every student. After all, this intensive attention may not be the kind of help some students need.

- Beware of red herrings. The closing remark "as any experienced teacher knows. . ." may be a secondary piece of support—an appeal to authority. But in relation to the main argument, it's just a flourish, and is not really required in a logical sense. Such references are often used to generate wrong choices like (C).

8. E

Talk about a scope shift! George supports a conclusion about global warming with evidence from his town. George says that global warming *is* occurring because his town has recently exhibited an unusual warming trend, but you know that that could be a coincidence. What you really need to know in evaluating George's argument is whether the trends cited in his town are truly global trends—is the rest of the world getting warmer too? If so, his conclusion may hold up. If not, you have no reason to believe that George's experience is an indicator of a global trend.

(A) Whether there are other causes of global warming is irrelevant. George merely argues that global warming *is occurring* on the basis of recent weather in *his* area.

(B) you know as much about the leaves as you need to know: they're three weeks late in changing color. Whether they're three weeks late from September 1 or some other date doesn't matter. What *is* relevant is whether the rest of the world's leaves also turned later than usual.

(C) How the carbon dioxide gets into the atmosphere is irrelevant; the fact is that it's there, scientists predict global warming because of it, and George agrees. Why George agrees forms the basis of his argument—it is around this issue that our inquiry into his argument must occur.

(D) distorts the leaves example: Leaves are important only insofar as they've turned color late. Trees *losing* leaves, and possible causes for this, have no relation to George's theory, and thus are also irrelevant.

- When an author employs such a large shift in scope, any one of a number of questions could be asked regarding the argument, but recognizing the assumption will open the door to all of them. Here, George assumed that the experience in his town was representative of a global trend. Recognizing that disparity between the scope of the evidence (here, local weather) and the scope of the conclusion (global warming) will lead to the answer in all evidence/conclusion based question types.
- Information that is not relevant to an argument is often irrelevant because it is outside the scope. Your reaction to the wrong choices in a question like this should be "who cares?" When that reaction strikes you, it's usually a sign to cross that choice off quickly.

9. C

The student rep argues that the university has wrongly punished a student who was expelled for verbally harassing his roommate. The dean's response begins "But what you're saying is that our university should endorse verbal harassment"—to which the student rep would probably respond "No, I'm not saying that at all; all I'm saying is that the punishment is wrong." The dean mischaracterizes the representative's position as an argument that the university should *endorse* verbal harassment, probably because that position is much easier to attack, (C). Upon careful inspection, you see that the student rep may defend the right to free speech, but never says the university should endorse harassment. The student rep has a perfect right to believe in a middle ground: a position from which the university neither endorses verbal harassment nor tramples on free speech.

(A) The conflict centers on the reasons for the expulsion; no one mentions the *process* by which the student was expelled (was it done by mail, in person, etc.).

(B) The rep argues about verbal harassment and free speech, and the dean argues about the same. The dean distorts the rep's argument, but does not point out a distinction between speech and other sorts of behavior.

(D) is wrong on both counts. The dean doesn't question the student representative's motives; if she did, she would say something about the rep's intentions, something she never does. Moreover, she *does* offer reasons for the expulsion, just not good reasons in the context of this debate.

(E) There's no threat made by the dean. The dean's argument rests on the claim that endorsing verbal harassment would be a threat to the *university*. So although she mentions a threat, she doesn't make one.

- In dialogue questions, you're often asked to critique the second speaker's response. Sometimes the second speaker misinterprets the first speaker's remarks; other times he or she attempts to cleverly argue around them. In either case, it's often helpful to put yourself in the place of the first speaker, and imagine how you might respond to the second person's comeback. Here, when the dean says "you say that . . .", the first speaker would likely retort "I said no such thing." This notion, or prephrase, leads nicely to (C)'s "misdescribes the representative's position."

- Offering bad reasons is not the same as offering no reasons at all. Some choices in flaw questions accuse the author of presenting no evidence to back up a conclusion. If you're going to select a choice like this, make sure that in fact there *is no* evidence presented (which is fairly rare on the LSAT), as opposed to the case in which evidence, albeit faulty, *is* offered.

10. D

When you need to infer a conclusion from the stimulus, it's best to think about where the argument is leading. It pays to be famous: According to the first sentence, celebrities convicted of crimes are increasingly being sentenced to community service, whereas unknown convicts almost always get locked up for the same crimes. Doesn't sound very fair, does it?

Next, you find out that the principle of equality before the law does not permit celebrity status to affect the sentencing of criminals. This principle seems to directly conflict with the example in the first sentence. If, in fact, celebrities are getting off easier because of their celebrity status, then some judges out there aren't paying much attention to the principle of equality before the law. That's the one solid conclusion that's inferable from the passage. Some of the punishments described in the first sentence *conflict* with the principle described in the second, and it seems as though the author stopped just short of presenting the conclusion contained in (D).

(A) points out that the principle of equality is getting sidestepped, but it does so too strongly. The stimulus implies only that the principle is getting sidestepped in *some cases* dealing with celebrities, and you can't therefore infer that the principle is overlooked in *most types* of criminal trials.

(B) The passage compares the punishments of unknown and famous defendants who have committed similar crimes. (B) ignores the "similar crimes" feature of the argument and broadly suggests that equal numbers of both groups be sentenced to community service. This is not where the author is going, as the types of crimes committed by these groups and the relative number of criminals in each group may be very different. Furthermore, (B) is a strongly prescriptive statement; it out-and-out says what *should* be done. While this passage *could* have a recommendation appended to it, the author has given no indication that he's headed in that direction.

(C) It's not at all clear that sentencing celebrities to community service is in line with "another principle," as (C) has it, nor is it clear that this overriding of the principle of equality before the law is "proper," as is also implied by (C).

(E) Leniency is a new and ambiguous term, which is a good reason to kill this choice right away. For all you know, the principle of equality before the law is compatible with leniency; nothing forbids this, so (E) isn't the conclusion you seek.

- When asked to infer a conclusion, think to yourself: "Where is the author going with all this?" The answer must be more than just a statement with which the author would likely agree; it must encompass the overarching idea the author set out to express when he or she sat down to write.
- A prephrase of an answer need not be eloquent or pretty to be effective. "Hey, these ideas conflict . . ." is a valid way of thinking about the notions presented in the first and second sentences. From there, it's a short jump to (D), which states that the example in sentence one violates the principle in sentence two.

11. A

The stem tells you that there's a flaw in the foundation's conclusion, so you need to find the disconnect between the evidence and the conclusion. The humanitarian-minded foundation gives a certain university an annual grant for scientific research, but hesitated when it discovered that the physics department began to work on weapons-related research. The foundation, feeling, no doubt, that weapons research would be incompatible with its humanitarian mission, threatened to cancel the grant. In response, the university assured the foundation that none of the foundation's money would fund the weapons research, whereupon the foundation went ahead and bestowed the grant because it concluded that the money wouldn't benefit the weapons research.

The foundation's reasoning boils down to this: Since our money won't be *spent on* weapons research, our providing money won't *benefit* the weapons research. That's a little optimistic, isn't it? The university could, after all, take the foundation's money, use it to fund only humanitarian research, and then divert *other* funding from the humanitarian projects to the weapons research. Maybe you were able to prephrase (A): Just because the weapons research won't receive the foundation's money doesn't assure that the foundation's money won't *indirectly* aid the weapons research.

(B) Overlooking the possibility in (B) isn't a logical problem. The question is whether the grant will benefit the weapons research in the physics department. If other departments are up to no good, then those bad departments might benefit from money diverted from the physics department, but the weapons research in the physics department would still be unaffected, and that's the point at issue.

(C) It's fairly obvious that the university did make its promise in order to retain the grant, and it's unlikely anyone at the foundation missed this point. Understanding the motivation of the university isn't relevant to the issue of whether the weapons research will benefit from the grant.

(D) Neither the foundation nor the university expects that the grant money won't be used, so (D) is not a proper criticism of the foundation's logic.

(E) Discussion of means and ends is simply confusing; no such distinction is raised in the stimulus between an objective and the means to that objective. The only "objective" that can be discerned here is the university's desire to conduct research to build weapons, and the foundation folks certainly don't believe anything about that objective is humanitarian in character.

- Some choices will evoke an immediate response of "huh?" True, if you misunderstand the argument or overlook something important in the stimulus, a choice that appears utterly baffling can turn out to be the correct answer. But if you've understood the argument fairly well, and come upon a choice that just seems out of left field, even difficult to understand, chances are it's wrong.
- Always keep your eyes peeled for alternative possibilities. In this one, a valid possibility (that the funding may indirectly benefit weapons research) is overlooked by one party, and that forms the basis of its faulty reasoning.

12. A

This question presents an interesting twist: It's a "weaken the argument" question, but the argument to be weakened is in the answer choices, and the weakener is the stimulus. This means a greater time investment and an adaptation of your process, which may mean this is a good question to skip and come back to at the end.

In the stimulus you find that an advertising strategy developed for and used by political campaigns has now successfully been applied to corporate accounts. The strategy is to design controversial ads that will become news, generate media attention, and evoke public responses from officials. Thus, the companies get a lot more exposure than they pay for. You don't have to look very far for the choice that's incompatible with this notion; (A) directly violates the "get something for nothing" principle behind the strategy. This strategy flies in the face of the assertion in (A), which says that the usefulness of an ad campaign is based *solely* on the degree to which the ads themselves persuade people. (A) does not consider extra media coverage or public comment by officials to be relevant to an ad's effectiveness. If the statements in the stimulus are true, then (A) is seriously weakened by the fact that some ads are successful thanks to a factor besides persuading the public—namely because they make the news and generate free publicity for the client.

(B) makes too much of the mention of political campaigns: Even though the strategy was originally developed for political campaigns, this is just a little side note—the stimulus focuses on corporate ads, not political ads, so (B) is unaffected by the stimulus.

(C) The assertion that political campaigns have borrowed strategies from corporate advertising is unaffected by the fact that corporate advertising has returned the compliment.

(D) This assertion is actually *strengthened* by the stimulus argument. If, as the stimulus says, ads are now designed to be controversial for maximum exposure value, then it makes sense that name recognition is a bigger priority than the generation of goodwill.

(E) No contradiction here: It's possible for one realm of advertising to borrow strategies from another without the same agencies handling both kinds of campaigns. The stimulus talks about a borrowing of ad strategy, not ad agencies, so the stimulus in no way weakens the assertion in (E).

- Considering the hundreds, and possibly thousands of Logical Reasoning questions you will do for practice before your test, it is highly unlikely that you will come across a question type that's entirely different from anything you've seen. You may, however, find a question that differs slightly from its usual appearance. Don't panic! Simply relate the question to the kinds you're familiar with, and proceed from there.

13. D

Here's the basic argument in which you need to locate an assumption: The likelihood of the early detection of fires hasn't risen even though the percentage of homes with smoke detectors has. This is because over half of these smoke detectors don't work. But what if, ten years ago, the same problem existed? If, ten years ago, over half of the smoke detectors didn't work, then early detection of fires should be more, not less common now. If the same percentages of detectors were inoperative then as now, then the sheer increase in the percentage of homes with detectors would make early detection more likely now than ten years ago. Therefore, in order for the conclusion to stand, this must not be the case—the percentage of inoperative detectors must be *higher* now; otherwise, the author's argument gets smoked out. Adding (D) to the scenario, the conclusion can be properly drawn. If you deny (D), the argument falls apart.

(A) is unnecessary. In fact, it's quite possible that no new smoke detectors have been installed in the last ten years. How can this be? If there are far fewer houses than there were ten years ago, and the ones that no longer exist are ones that didn't have smoke detectors (maybe they burned down...), then the percentage of homes with smoke detectors would have risen, exactly as the stimulus says, yet *no* smoke detectors need have been installed in the last ten years. This is an extreme case, but the fact that it's logically possible proves that (A) is not a necessary part of this argument.

(B) and (E) The number of fires (B) and the putting out of fires (E) are both issues one step removed from the crux of the argument, which is the likelihood of *early detection* of fires. Smoke detectors don't prevent or put out fires, after all, they just report them—which means that these two choices are outside the scope of the argument, and as such are not necessary assumptions.

(C) Why couldn't *all* smoke detectors be battery operated? Nothing in the argument requires that some smoke detectors aren't battery-operated, as (C) claims. Everything the author says could be true even if every smoke detector ran on batteries—the "other" malfunctions that aren't battery-related could simply be caused by a different part of battery-operated detectors.

- Always be aware of the raw numbers that lurk behind every percentage. The percentage of homes that have smoke detectors is affected by both the number of homes with detectors *and* the total number of homes. If the percentage of houses with smoke detectors has risen, you can't necessarily conclude that *more* detectors were installed, because the other side of the equation might have changed: As you saw in (A), there could instead be *fewer* total houses.
- Always pay attention to the scope of the argument. Here, (B) and (E) are smoke from other fires.

14. D

The first Parallel Reasoning question on the section is based on an ad for HomeGlo Paints, and the stem alerts you to the fact that the reasoning is flawed. Your task, then, is to characterize the flaw, and here it's a scope shift. The award is given to the product that has most *increased* its environmental safety over the last three years, yet the argument concludes that HomeGlo is the *most* environmentally safe brand of paint in the country today. "Most improved" is not necessarily synonymous with "most environmentally safe." You need to find the choice that commits the same error. Check the choices, bearing in mind that you can use the Kaplan technique of comparing conclusions to quickly eliminate a few.

(A) Also contains a scope shift, but it's a different one—you're looking for an answer choice that confuses improvement with overall quality.

(B) The "*most* nutritious food" seems to match the conclusion of the original. However, like (A), there's no element of improvement here. The cereal is allegedly the healthiest cereal on the market. From this, the conclusion generalizes the cereal's top health ranking to *all* foods, which is a fallacy, but not the one found in the stimulus.

(C) again, this argument is flawed by a scope shift (from visits to profits), but there's no question of improvement vs. overall quality.

(E) Likewise, the scope shift here is between one particular story and the same author's earlier stories—a flaw, but not the one you're looking for.

(D) Contains the same flaw as the stimulus—most improved performance isn't the same thing as "best" performance.

15. E

There are so many different elements to this Inference question that a prephrase is not likely to jump to mind here—the best you can do is follow the logic, making sure you understand exactly what information you are (and are not) given, and eliminate the choices that attempt to combine the statements in ways not supported by the stimulus.

Slight changes in freezer temperature are bad for the consistency of ice cream. The ill effects of these changes can be minimized through the use of stabilizers, but that has its own drawback: stabilizers detract from the ice cream's flavor. So at this point it looks like a trade-off: In order to prevent a possible consistency problem resulting from temperature change, a small loss in flavor may have to be tolerated. Stabilizers, however, are less necessary (a good thing) if really low storage temperatures are maintained. But even that's a problem. Very low storage temperatures are expensive. So again you've got a trade-off. Consistency is at risk—it can be preserved by using stabilizers or very low storage temperatures, but neither of these is a perfect solution, because stabilizers detract from flavor and low storage temperatures are expensive. As mentioned above, there's a lot swirling around in this one, so the best thing to do is keep the tradeoffs in mind and move on to carefully evaluate each choice.

(A) posits an unsupported connection between consistency and flavor. No such connection is stated or implied in the passage. Deviations in storage temperature affect ice cream's consistency, and stabilizers affect its flavor, but (A) mistakenly has deviations in consistency affecting flavor.

(B) 180. As stated in the last sentence, cost considerations favor high storage temperatures due to the increasing cost of energy, and high temperatures require the use of stabilizers, which maintain consistency but adversely affect flavor. So cost considerations favor sacrificing flavor for consistency, not the other way around.

(C) is way off the mark: Nothing in the passage allows you to infer that new technologies would be too costly to develop.

(D) goes against the grain of the passage. You're told that at low temperatures stabilizers are less necessary, which strongly implies that stabilizers are used mainly to maintain the consistency of ice cream stored at relatively high temperatures. Consequently, to say that these stabilizers function well *only* at low temperatures seems to contradict the evidence.

(E) must be inferable, by process of elimination. To preserve consistency it is necessary to have either very low storage temperatures or stabilizers. If you want the best taste, however, you have to avoid the stabilizers. So, to produce the best consistency *and* the best taste in ice cream, you need low, stable freezer temperatures.

- A common wrong answer type in Inference questions is the unwarranted comparison or connection, illustrated nicely in (A) here. It appears often when the stimulus contains two or more groups or elements, such as this argument's "consistency" and "flavor." If there's no stated or implied connection between the two, cross off any choices that attempt to assert that there is.

16. E

As is often the case in a dialogue question, you're asked about how the second person responds to the first, so first get a grip on Edwina's argument so you can see how Alberto's response proceeds. Edwina's conclusion, signaled by the keywords "it follows that," is that you should hear Mozart's music on eighteenth-century instruments. Her evidence for this is that "true appreciation" requires hearing it the way Mozart intended, but this is precisely the point at which Alberto strikes: He questions whether the manner in which Mozart *intended* his music to be heard is in fact the manner in which he actually heard it. What makes you think this is so?— he asks Edwina. It's possible that there's a difference in how Mozart heard his music performed and how he intended it to be played; as evidence, Alberto presents the fact that eighteenth-century performers were expected to *modify* the scores they were given. Essentially then, Alberto presents a reason to believe that Edwina's argument relies upon a false premise, (E).

(A) Alberto appeals to an historical fact, yes, but not to an academic authority (see the second bullet point below).

(B) Alberto attempts to show that the creative license of the eighteenth-century performer extended even to changing the written score. This is not intended to make Edwina more appreciative of performers, though. Rather, it's intended to smash the important connection she draws between what an eighteenth-century performer delivered and what Mozart intended to hear.

(C) "Musical authenticity" is certainly an ambiguous term in this context, but Alberto doesn't attack any view about what is authentic music. Rather, he confines his attack to Edwina's assertion that Mozart heard his music as he intended it to be played. There is no other "competing view" of musical authenticity presented here.

(D) confuses Alberto's point of contention. He doesn't attack the logic that binds Edwina's conclusion to her premises. Instead, he attacks one of the premises itself, the one that says that Mozart heard his music as he intended it to sound.

- It's important in every Logical Reasoning question to understand the author's or speaker's conclusion, and what evidence is used to back it up. But in some questions, like question 16, correctly making this distinction leads directly to the answer. Alberto, in his first sentence, directly attacks part of Edwina's argument. If you recognized that the part under attack is her evidence, you should have gravitated toward (E). Remember, on the LSAT, the word "premise" is simply another word for "evidence."
- An "appeal to authority" is a very specific thing; citing facts by themselves does not constitute an appeal to authority. "The venerable Professor So-and-So" or "The Prestigious Committee on Such-and-Such" are examples of an academic authority. If you chose (A), look back until you convince yourself that no such authority figure appears in this debate.
- Take a look back at (E), and make sure you understand the difference between an attack on an author's *overall* logic—that is, the relationship between evidence and conclusion—and an attack on the evidence itself.

17. D

The stem alerts you to the existence of a paradox in the stimulus—an apparent conflict that you'll be called upon to resolve. So what's strange or unusual about the information in the passage? The mystery appears to be that the cost of private health insurance rose dramatically at a time when it was expected to fall. Due to the new health scheme, the only medical costs that Impanians must pay are those for unusual and sophisticated treatments; it was hoped these procedures could be covered by inexpensive, private insurance. Since the private insurance companies would only rarely have to pay off on such claims (because the policies would cover only *unusual* treatments), it was expected that such insurance would be affordable. Not so—the cost of these policies soared. It's our job to find the choice that could explain this unexpected result.

In a Paradox question, you may not prephrase exactly, but you need to focus in on the *kind* of evidence you're looking for. The expectation that private policies would be modestly priced was based on the notion that the companies wouldn't have to pay off on them often—unusual treatments are supposedly rare. The fact that the cost of these policies *has* increased dramatically strongly suggests that the companies *are* incurring more medical costs than expected, and anything that leads you in that direction will help solve the mystery. (D) gets you there: If the shrewd Impanians buy these policies only when they know they'll need the kind of care these policies cover, then it's easier to understand why, despite the original expectations, the cost of these policies has increased.

(A) deepens the mystery: If insurers' overhead costs have been substantially reduced, you'd have even more reason to expect them to offer cheaper policies.

(B) is also of no help. If 80 percent of all costs are now footed by the National Health scheme, private insurers should have much less to pay, and the expectation of modest costs still seems reasonable.

(C) suggests that while the poorer Impanians use the National Health Scheme, most, if not all of them, haven't bought private health insurance. Yet, since these people *never* had private health insurance, their failure to purchase it now doesn't explain why policy costs have risen.

(E) The slice of the expenditure pie occupied by health care in the overall Impanian economy isn't relevant here—the apparent discrepancy concerns an unexpected change *within* the health care system, not health care's relative place in the economy as a whole. (If you could conclude from (E) that insurers' costs have risen, then it might explain the paradox. But you can't, so it doesn't.)

- The first step in a Paradox question is to understand the nature of the surprising event, finding, situation, or discrepancy. Only then will you be able to confidently settle on the choice that does away with the apparent conflict.
- It's not unusual in Paradox questions to find choices that deepen the mystery rather than solve it. Make

sure you don't accidentally choose one of these choices simply because it has *some* effect on the situation—the effect you're looking for here is resolution.

18. A

Next you need to fill in the blank, which in this case represents an explanation, signaled by the word "because." The situation is fairly straightforward: Half the test subjects in clinical trials for new medicines receive the actual drug, while the others get a placebo, a substance that has no physiological effect. Neither experimenters nor patients are supposed to know who gets what, but alas, this intention is often frustrated because . . . and that's all you get; you have to fill in the remaining piece of the argument.

It's not difficult to prephrase a general explanation: There must be something about the drug or placebo that makes it possible to tell who got which. The placebo, by definition, should have no noticeable effects. Therefore, if one of the two substances produces marked effects on the subjects who receive it, that substance should be the drug. This is the general idea behind correct choice (A), which says that the drug may have side effects that the experimenters recognize. For example, if half the subjects lose their hair within days of taking the medication, this would be a pretty strong indication that those subjects were in fact getting a drug and not a placebo. (A) provides a plausible explanation for why it's not always possible to keep the recipients of the drug and the placebo a secret.

(B) would, if true, most likely *confuse* the experimenters. If subjects getting the placebo often display physical changes, they should be harder to differentiate from those getting the real drug (assuming that those getting the drug will also display some improvement or at least some change).

(C) and (E) merely tell you what kind of subjects are chosen for certain drug trials, which does nothing to explain how experimenters would come to realize which of these subjects are receiving the drug. Neither choice contains any information about what happens during the experiment; the particulars of the selection procedure are therefore irrelevant to the explanation you seek.

(D) would, if anything, make it tougher for the experimenters to determine who's getting the real drug. If experimenters can't observe the experiment for its entire run, then it's less likely they'll notice something that tips them off.

- Fill-in-the-blank questions are fairly rare on the LSAT, but they do appear from time to time. They're not, however, an entirely different breed of question; often, they work just like Inference questions, or in a case like this, like a Paradox question: Why, if the trials are designed with a particular intention in mind, is this intention often frustrated? If a fill-in-the-blank question appears on your test, try to nail down its "action," and use your knowledge from other question types, where applicable, to solve it.

19. B

Ever wonder what day of the week your birthday (or an anniversary or holiday) will fall on during any given year? You'll never need to wonder again, according to this author, if her plan is enacted. Simply place the last day of each year, and that pesky extra day added every four years, into "limbo," and January 1 will fall on a Sunday every year. This is because 52 weeks times seven days a week equals 364, not 365, the number of days in the current calendar. Get rid of that last day (well, you can't get rid of it altogether, but you *can* call it something different, like "Extra Day," or "blue" for that matter), and the year would divide up perfectly into weeks, and the beginning of every year would fall on the same day of the week. In fact, *every* date on the calendar would always fall on the same day of the week. Then, according to the author, scheduling conflicts will be resolved, because everyone will always know on which day of the week the important events of their lives fall.

If you got the gist of the stem, however, you'd know in advance that this proposal will not clear up conflicts in every possible situation, and you're looking for that situation that would continue to result in the kind of scheduling conflicts the new plan is intended to eliminate. It's not easy to prephrase an answer here, so the best approach is probably to evaluate the situations in each choice, asking yourself "will the new method work here?"

(B) contains the situation that throws the system off kilter, because it contains a stipulation based not on dates, or days of the week—which will all be constant under the new plan—but rather on *an interval* containing a *raw number* of days. This will be fine until the end of the year (or until the designated special time in a leap year) when the extra day is added in. The extra day counts as a day to the religious observers of (B), even though it's not referred to as one of the normal days of the week. If religious workers have to refrain from work every seventh day, their day of rest will vary from year to year (see the bullet point below).

(A) points out dates that might fall outside of a week. This might seem distressing to you, assuming you had an anniversary on one of these dates, but it wouldn't force a conflict. Why not? The "extra" days are not part of any week, and so they won't *change* days of the week from year to year. The anniversaries would be scheduled for these "non-week" dates just as though they fell regularly in a week.

(C) just requires that a certain number of days be devoted to school. This isn't a problem, because there would still be plenty of days for school. Remember, all that would change under the author's proposal is the day of the week upon which a calendar day would fall, not the number of days in a year.

(D) is no problem, either. Since every calendar day would fall on the same day of the week, the new system would merely standardize three-day weekends. So if July 4th (or whatever) formed a three-day weekend one year, then it would form a three-day weekend next year, and so on, forever. Eerie, perhaps, but not a conflict.

(E) These people would benefit from the new calendar. As long as the events they're planning don't occur at the very end of the year, they'll know exactly what day of the week the event will fall on simply by consulting the current year's calendar.

- In questions involving numerical elements, it sometimes helps to formulate a quick example in order to test a choice. If you work out the situation in (B), you see that it *will* cause scheduling conflicts from year to year: Suppose on a non-leap year (to make it easier) such an employee designates the first Sunday of the year as the day of rest. For the next 52 weeks, every Sunday will be the day of rest. But then the next Sunday will be postponed until the beginning of the next year and there will be an extra day between week 52 and the first week of the next year, which means that the day off at the end of the year will fall on the makeup day, and seven days from then will be the following Saturday. For these people, the system doesn't work—their day of rest will vary from year to year.

20. A

The stem here announces a Method of Argument question, and also tells you that the argument is directed against graphology. The graphologists' claim comes in the first sentence: Handwriting can reveal permanent character traits. But the author is skeptical: People who want to be deemed "enthusiastic" can simply work on crossing their "t's" in a stronger fashion. And then comes the final sentence, which may have sounded bizarre if you didn't recognize its tone. How can graphologists believe that "permanent" character traits can be changed? They can't: "Permanent" means unchangeable, and the author knows this. The author, in this final sentence, is being sarcastic, in order to make the point that the graphologists' view, when confronted by his evidence, leads to an absurd result. The author prefaces his evidence with the word "obviously," which is meant to show, as correct choice (A) has it, that this evidence is "incontestable"—and it does indeed sound reasonable that people could alter their handwriting to include the features that denote good character traits, as the author proposes. This evidence, when combined with the graphologists' view, leads to an absurd result, the impossible changing-permanent character trait. (A) cites the correct method here.

(B) A platitude is a commonplace or banal remark. The author doesn't dismiss the claim that handwriting reveals permanent character traits as being a platitude. He implies that the claim is *absurd*, not commonplace.

(C) The author presents evidence to suggest the incoherence of graphology theory in general, not to say that it can never work when people are aware that this kind of analysis is being used. The author intends to show, by implication, that the entire theory is flawed. He *doesn't* set out specifically to show that the method will be ineffectual in one particular circumstance, that is, when people are aware of its use.

(D) is subtle, but wrong. The author doesn't dismiss graphology's claims as "unjustified"—that would entail saying that the claim is simply not backed up by sufficient evidence. This is not the author's approach; rather, he works to show that the claim is absurd because it implies a contradiction, namely, changeable permanent characteristics.

(E) The author never says that permanent character traits can be detected without graphology—he doesn't criticize graphology for being *unnecessary*.

- Every element in the correct answer to a Method of Argument question must match the structural elements of the argument. Nothing in the correct choice can be superfluous. So, in (A), the apparently incontestable evidence is the idea that people can change their handwriting, the absurd consequence is the idea that permanent character traits can be altered, and the view in question is the idea that graphology can identify permanent character traits. If any piece doesn't match, the answer can't be correct.

- Some choices in Method of Argument questions are wrong because what the choice posits is "just not there." There's no better way to eliminate such choices than to simply recognize that what they say is going on in the argument is "just not there." Choices (B) and (D) are particularly good examples of this: General principle? Explicit criteria? They're "just not there."

21. A

Two points hinge on a dispute between an historian and a critic, and the first point is awarded for correctly characterizing the critic's method of argument. First the historian's argument: During the third Nayalese dynasty, a law taxing timber imports from Poran was enacted. So, although you have no actual evidence of the timber trade, you do have evidence that a law concerning timber trade was put into effect, which *suggests* the existence of a timber trade. The critic finds this reasoning flawed. She grants that the historian's conclusion may well be true—Nayal may indeed have imported timber from Poran—but this conclusion isn't supported by the evidence: It ignores the fact that many laws now exist governing activities that people no longer engage in. Her point, then, is that the historian's argument is flawed because it overlooks the possibility that any given law (specifically, the ancient Nayalese law) may be out of date and thus not truly reflect the activity of a particular era. In suggesting that evidence regarding today's statute books is relevant to the argument concerning ancient Poran and Nayal, the author is, as (A) has it, implying an analogy between present and past. Specifically, she implies that modern day laws and ancient laws are alike in that both can outlive their usefulness.

(B) The critic doesn't identify any principles at all, preferring to point to the specific example of a few outdated laws.

(C) is actually a better description of the *historian's* argument. He's the one who explains that the timber trade is established as a possibility, but not a certainty. The critic's response merely *recognizes* that this trade is a possibility and then goes on to attack the significance that the historian attaches to the Nayalese law.

(D) The critic attacks the historian's "indirect" evidence by implying that similar evidence in the modern period wouldn't necessarily support the same kind of conclusion. But she never offers a list of things that such indirect evidence could be checked against in order to prove its validity. In short, the critic never mentions any specific criteria.

(E) The critic uses an example of modern law to make a point about the old Nayalese law; thus, she isn't pointing out dissimilarities in laws—in fact, just the opposite.

22. D

Now to pick up the second point related to this debate; you're asked for the flaw in the critic's response. The historian's argument rests on the evidence that the Nayalese law was *enacted* in the third dynasty. So he's banking on the notion that a law regulating a non-existent trade wouldn't be enacted, which seems to make sense. The critic shifts the scope away from "enacted" to "exists"—she argues that just because a law is on the books doesn't mean that it's up-to-date. But this is an unfair response, because "enacted," a word that the critic evidently missed, rules out this possible objection. It's highly unlikely that a law would be out of date at the time it was enacted. In order to truly weaken the historian's argument, the critic would need to offer examples of laws that were irrelevant when they were first put into effect. Her mistake is therefore to overlook the fact that the historian's evidence concerns the *enactment* of a law, not its mere *existence*, (D).

(A) The critic's evidence *doesn't* contradict the possibility of no timber trade between the ancient nations, and thus she *does* provide evidence consistent with this possibility. Remember than in logical terms, "consistent" means nothing more than "not contradictory." However, this is not a flaw in her reasoning. It's perfectly acceptable for this to be the case; you would almost expect her evidence to lean in that direction. Moreover, the critic's response attacks the historian's reasoning, not his conclusion that timber was probably traded.

(B) The current laws cited are intended to illustrate outdated laws, not outdated *timber* laws. They need not have anything to do with the timber trade because the author is citing these laws only to show that laws in general (and that would include ancient Nayalese tariffs) can be outdated.

(C) The distinction between direct and indirect evidence is not lost on the critic. She attacks the historian's reference to the Nayalese tariff, which is pretty clearly stated as indirect evidence. The critic's flaw is that she misses or misinterprets a concept *contained* in this indirect evidence ("enactment"), not that she fails to recognize the evidence as indirect.

(E) The critic doesn't accept the historian's assumption, but rather misunderstands it. The critic thinks the historian is assuming that the existence of a law at a particular time indicates that the activity it regulates also exists at that time. As you've seen, however, the historian is assuming only that the *enactment* of a law at some time indicates the existence of the activity it regulates at that time.

- In two-question stimuli, you can attack the questions in any order you like. If you immediately noticed the scope shift and hence the flaw in the critic's response, you may have jumped right to Flaw question 22 while the flaw was fresh in your mind. Section management techniques are crucial because they offer you yet another way to take control of the test.
- This dialogue offers a nice example of how most scope shifts are born: A word or phrase is either ignored, or subtly changed into something else. The historian said "enacted," but a careful reading of the critic's response reveals that the critic heard "existed." Why is the LSAT this picky? Because the practice of law itself is about the interpretation of laws and statutes, whose meanings hinge on the precise definitions of the words used.

23. C

The argument is missing a large chunk, as you may have noticed from the abrupt conclusion at the end (and also from the stem which tells you that there's a necessary assumption to be filled in here). The author concludes that some subsidiaries will be sold. Why? Because that's the only way to raise wages and avoid a strike. The author must be assuming that there will be no strike, (C). Then and only then does it make sense to say for sure that subsidiaries will be sold, specifically to raise the money to increase the workers' wages.

(A) forecasts increased losses. This is a completely new concept, and you can't conclude anything from it, including the conclusion here that subsidiaries will be sold.

(B) Selling the subsidiaries has been presented as a requirement for raising workers' wages. If, as (B) says, workers' wages *aren't* going to go up, then the author's conclusion becomes truly mystifying, rather than necessary.

(D) Suppose that the president doesn't have the power to authorize the pay increase. Does that contradict the conclusion? No. You don't care who can or will authorize the pay increase, only whether or not the workers are going to get it.

(E) just reinforces one of the premises, namely, the one saying that the workers insist on increased wages. Because this adds nothing new to the argument, it can't justify the conclusion.

- Formal logic is often hidden within seemingly casual arguments. The stimulus argument has a casual tone, but it's actually a formal argument comprised of two conditional statements. First, you get the word "unless" in the first sentence, a word which is used in a very precise way on the LSAT. The correct interpretation of this statement is: *if* the workers *don't* get more money, *then* they'll strike. Sentence two can be translated into a common if-then statement: *if* workers' wages are to increase, *then* some subsidiaries have to go. If you recognized and understood the precise meanings of these formal logic statements, you may have had an easier time with the question.

24. D

This stem offers two important pieces of information. First, you're looking for an assumption, and second, you're told what the argument entails: a "method... for determining how quickly a new idea is taking hold." As you read through the stimulus, you need to focus on this method and determine what assumption it relies on.

The method is presented right off the bat. One way to find out how quickly a new idea is taking hold among people is to see how fast the words that describe the new idea pass into everyday language. The second sentence elaborates on this notion: you can tell when a word has passed into everyday usage by consulting experts, namely dictionary editors.

So the notion underlying the method is this: If the vocabulary associated with a new idea has found acceptance, then so has the idea itself. That's true *if* the words, as they pass into common usage, continue to refer to the idea. If the words have passed into usage with altered meanings, then the connection between the words and the idea is severed and you cannot infer the popularity of the latter from the popularity of the former. In order for the method described to work, it must be assumed that no such distortion occurs along the way, as (D) points out.

(A) Just because the author describes dictionary editors as being vitally concerned with words that enter common usage, he needn't assume that they *aren't* professionally interested in lots of other things, such as (A)'s rarely used words.

(B) demands too much of the editors. They need only have an informed opinion about when new words have been accepted into everyday speech. They don't have to have "exact numerical criteria."

(C) The causality expressed in (C) runs counter to the proposed method. Dictionary editors follow new words to see if they become popular enough to be included in a dictionary. The method proposed by the author involves consulting dictionary editors to see if a new idea *has* taken hold, not using editors to *help* ideas take hold by including certain words in their dictionary.

(E) Far from helping the argument, (E) would sink it. If the words tend to be used before the ideas they represent are understood, then a word's passing into everyday speech wouldn't allow you to infer that the idea it represents has been embraced.

25. E

Last up is a Parallel Reasoning question, so you'll begin by characterizing the conclusion. It's a recommendation—specifically, that one thing should be brought more in line with another.

(A) The conclusion is a recommendation, but not that one thing should be made more comparable to another. Eliminate it.

(B) does tell you that one thing should be made more like another. Keep it for now. However, on your second pass through, you'll compare the evidence. The stimulus evidence says that one thing is like another (migrant workers put in similar work schedules to those of full-time workers). There's no such comparison in (B), so it will be eliminated as well.

(C) Another recommendation, but this one relates to the development of a uniform policy, not bringing one specific thing in line with another. Eliminate.

(D) Recommendation relates to who should make a decision, not the substance of the treatment of two particular groups. Eliminate.

(E) Conclusion first—standards applied to one category should be the same as standards applied to another. That's a match. Now look at the evidence. It points to a common element between the two groups, just like the stimulus. It's a match!

- This question contains a lot of text, and it may have been wise to skip it in order to return to any others you left behind during the section. There is no one right order in which to attack the questions, but if you continuously decide the order that's best for you, including which ones to skip and hold off until later, and when it's appropriate to return to them, then you're taking matters into your own hands, and you're on the right track.

Practice Test 2

LSAT PRACTICE TEST 2 ANSWER SHEET

Remove (or photocopy) the answer sheet and use it to complete the practice test.

How to Take the Practice Tests

Before taking each test, find a quiet place where you can work uninterrupted for about two and a half hours. Make sure you have a comfortable desk and several No. 2 pencils.

Each Practice Test includes four scored multiple-choice sections. Keep in mind that on the actual LSAT, there will be an additional multiple-choice section—the experimental section—that will not contribute to your score, plus an unscored Writing Sample.

Once you start a Practice Test, don't stop (except for a 5- to 10-minute break after the second section) until you've gone through all four sections. Remember, you can review any questions within a section, but you may not go back or forward a section.

Good luck!

Start with number 1 for each section. If a section has fewer questions than answer spaces, leave the extra spaces blank.

Section I

1. A B C D E	9. A B C D E	17. A B C D E	25. A B C D E	☐
2. A B C D E	10. A B C D E	18. A B C D E	26. A B C D E	
3. A B C D E	11. A B C D E	19. A B C D E	27. A B C D E	# right in Section I
4. A B C D E	12. A B C D E	20. A B C D E	28. A B C D E	
5. A B C D E	13. A B C D E	21. A B C D E	29. A B C D E	☐
6. A B C D E	14. A B C D E	22. A B C D E	30. A B C D E	
7. A B C D E	15. A B C D E	23. A B C D E		# wrong in Section I
8. A B C D E	16. A B C D E	24. A B C D E		

Section II

1. A B C D E	9. A B C D E	17. A B C D E	25. A B C D E	☐
2. A B C D E	10. A B C D E	18. A B C D E	26. A B C D E	
3. A B C D E	11. A B C D E	19. A B C D E	27. A B C D E	# right in Section II
4. A B C D E	12. A B C D E	20. A B C D E	28. A B C D E	
5. A B C D E	13. A B C D E	21. A B C D E	29. A B C D E	☐
6. A B C D E	14. A B C D E	22. A B C D E	30. A B C D E	
7. A B C D E	15. A B C D E	23. A B C D E		# wrong in Section II
8. A B C D E	16. A B C D E	24. A B C D E		

Section III

1. A B C D E	9. A B C D E	17. A B C D E	25. A B C D E	☐
2. A B C D E	10. A B C D E	18. A B C D E	26. A B C D E	
3. A B C D E	11. A B C D E	19. A B C D E	27. A B C D E	# right in Section III
4. A B C D E	12. A B C D E	20. A B C D E	28. A B C D E	
5. A B C D E	13. A B C D E	21. A B C D E	29. A B C D E	☐
6. A B C D E	14. A B C D E	22. A B C D E	30. A B C D E	
7. A B C D E	15. A B C D E	23. A B C D E		# wrong in Section III
8. A B C D E	16. A B C D E	24. A B C D E		

Section IV

1. Ⓐ Ⓑ Ⓒ Ⓓ Ⓔ	9. Ⓐ Ⓑ Ⓒ Ⓓ Ⓔ	17. Ⓐ Ⓑ Ⓒ Ⓓ Ⓔ	25. Ⓐ Ⓑ Ⓒ Ⓓ Ⓔ
2. Ⓐ Ⓑ Ⓒ Ⓓ Ⓔ	10. Ⓐ Ⓑ Ⓒ Ⓓ Ⓔ	18. Ⓐ Ⓑ Ⓒ Ⓓ Ⓔ	26. Ⓐ Ⓑ Ⓒ Ⓓ Ⓔ
3. Ⓐ Ⓑ Ⓒ Ⓓ Ⓔ	11. Ⓐ Ⓑ Ⓒ Ⓓ Ⓔ	19. Ⓐ Ⓑ Ⓒ Ⓓ Ⓔ	27. Ⓐ Ⓑ Ⓒ Ⓓ Ⓔ
4. Ⓐ Ⓑ Ⓒ Ⓓ Ⓔ	12. Ⓐ Ⓑ Ⓒ Ⓓ Ⓔ	20. Ⓐ Ⓑ Ⓒ Ⓓ Ⓔ	28. Ⓐ Ⓑ Ⓒ Ⓓ Ⓔ
5. Ⓐ Ⓑ Ⓒ Ⓓ Ⓔ	13. Ⓐ Ⓑ Ⓒ Ⓓ Ⓔ	21. Ⓐ Ⓑ Ⓒ Ⓓ Ⓔ	29. Ⓐ Ⓑ Ⓒ Ⓓ Ⓔ
6. Ⓐ Ⓑ Ⓒ Ⓓ Ⓔ	14. Ⓐ Ⓑ Ⓒ Ⓓ Ⓔ	22. Ⓐ Ⓑ Ⓒ Ⓓ Ⓔ	30. Ⓐ Ⓑ Ⓒ Ⓓ Ⓔ
7. Ⓐ Ⓑ Ⓒ Ⓓ Ⓔ	15. Ⓐ Ⓑ Ⓒ Ⓓ Ⓔ	23. Ⓐ Ⓑ Ⓒ Ⓓ Ⓔ	
8. Ⓐ Ⓑ Ⓒ Ⓓ Ⓔ	16. Ⓐ Ⓑ Ⓒ Ⓓ Ⓔ	24. Ⓐ Ⓑ Ⓒ Ⓓ Ⓔ	

\# right in Section IV

\# wrong in Section IV

GO ONLINE

Be sure to add your scores to your syllabus.

Practice Test 2

Section I: **Logical Reasoning**

Time—35 minutes
25 questions

Directions: The questions in this section are based on the reasoning contained in brief statements or passages. For some questions, more than one of the choices could conceivably answer the question. However, you are to choose the best answer; that is, the response that most accurately and completely answers the question. You should not make assumptions that are by commonsense standards implausible, superfluous, or incompatible with the passage. After you have chosen the best answer, blacken the corresponding space on your answer sheet.

1. Of all the surgeons practicing at the city hospital, the chief surgeon has the worst record in terms of the percentage of his patients who die either during or immediately following an operation performed by him. Paradoxically, the hospital's administrators claim that he is the best surgeon currently working at the hospital.

   Which one of the following, if true, goes farthest toward showing that the administrators' claim and the statistic cited might both be correct?

   (A) Since the hospital administrators appoint the chief surgeon, the administrators are strongly motivated to depict the chief surgeon they have chosen as a wise choice.
   (B) In appointing the current chief surgeon, the hospital administrators followed the practice, well established at the city hospital, of promoting one of the surgeons already on staff.
   (C) Some of the younger surgeons on the city hospital's staff received part of their training from the current chief surgeon.
   (D) At the city hospital those operations that inherently entail the greatest risk to the life of the patient are generally performed by the chief surgeon.
   (E) The current chief surgeon has a better record of patients' surviving surgery than did his immediate predecessor.

2. Between 1971 and 1975, the government office that monitors drug companies issued an average of 60 citations a year for serious violations of drug-promotion laws. Between 1976 and 1980, the annual average for issuance of such citations was only 5. This decrease indicates that the government office was, on average, considerably more lax in enforcing drug-promotion laws between 1976 and 1980 than it was between 1971 and 1975.

   The argument assumes which one of the following?

   (A) The decrease in the number of citations was not caused by a decrease in drug companies' violations of drug-promotion laws.
   (B) A change in enforcement of drug-promotion laws did not apply to minor violations.
   (C) The enforcement of drug-promotion laws changed in response to political pressure.
   (D) The government office should not issue more than an average of 5 citations a year to drug companies for serious violations of drug-promotion laws.
   (E) Before 1971 the government office issued more than 60 citations a year to drug companies for serious violations of drug-promotion laws.

GO ON TO THE NEXT PAGE.

3. Sheila: Health experts generally agree that smoking a tobacco product for many years is very likely to be harmful to the smoker's health.

   Tim: On the contrary, smoking has no effect on health at all: although my grandfather smoked three cigars a day from the age of fourteen, he died at age ninety-six.

   A major weakness of Tim's counterargument is that his counterargument

   (A) attempts to refute a probabilistic conclusion by claiming the existence of a single counterexample
   (B) challenges expert opinion on the basis of specific information unavailable to experts in the field
   (C) describes an individual case that is explicitly discounted as an exception to the experts' conclusion
   (D) presupposes that longevity and health status are unrelated to each other in the general population
   (E) tacitly assumes that those health experts who are in agreement on this issue arrived at that agreement independently of one another

4. The case of the French Revolution is typically regarded as the best evidence for the claim that societies can reap more benefit than harm from a revolution. But even the French Revolution serves this role poorly, since France at the time of the Revolution had a unique advantage. Despite the Revolution, the same civil servants and functionaries remained in office, carrying on the day-to-day work of government, and thus many of the disruptions that revolutions normally bring were avoided.

   Which one of the following most accurately characterizes the argumentative strategy used in the passage?

   (A) demonstrating that the claim argued against is internally inconsistent
   (B) supporting a particular position on the basis of general principles
   (C) opposing a claim by undermining evidence offered in support of that claim
   (D) justifying a view through the use of a series of persuasive examples
   (E) comparing two positions in order to illustrate their relative strengths and weaknesses

5. A person can develop or outgrow asthma at any age. In children under ten, asthma is twice as likely to develop in boys. Boys are less likely than girls to outgrow asthma, yet by adolescence the percentage of boys with asthma is about the same as the percentage of girls with asthma because a large number of girls develop asthma in early adolescence.

   Assuming the truth of the passage, one can conclude from it that the number of adolescent boys with asthma is approximately equal to the number of adolescent girls with asthma, if one also knows that

   (A) a tendency toward asthma is often inherited
   (B) children who develop asthma before two years of age are unlikely to outgrow it
   (C) there are approximately equal numbers of adolescent boys and adolescent girls in the population
   (D) the development of asthma in childhood is not closely related to climate or environment
   (E) the percentage of adults with asthma is lower than the percentage of adolescents with asthma

6. Harry Trevalga: You and your publication have unfairly discriminated against my poems. I have submitted thirty poems in the last two years and you have not published any of them! It is all because I won the Fenner Poetry Award two years ago and your poetry editor thought she deserved it.

   Publisher: Ridiculous! Our editorial policy and practice is perfectly fair, since our poetry editor judges all submissions for publication without ever seeing the names of the poets, and hence cannot possibly have known who wrote your poems.

   The publisher makes which one of the following assumptions in replying to Trevalga's charges of unfair discrimination?

   (A) The poetry editor does not bear a grudge against Harry Trevalga for his winning the Fenner Poetry Award.
   (B) It is not unusual for poets to contribute many poems to the publisher's publication without ever having any accepted for publication.
   (C) The poetry editor cannot recognize the poems submitted by Harry Trevalga as his unless Trevalga's name is attached to them.
   (D) The poetry editor's decisions on which poems to publish are not based strictly on judgments of intrinsic merit.
   (E) Harry Trevalga submitted his poems to the publisher's publication under his pen name.

GO ON TO THE NEXT PAGE.

7. In a study of the effect of radiation from nuclear weapons plants on people living in areas near them, researchers compared death rates in the areas near the plants with death rates in areas that had no such plants. Finding no difference in these rates, the researchers concluded that radiation from the nuclear weapons plants poses no health hazards to people living near them.

   Which one of the following, if true, most seriously weakens the researchers' argument?

   (A) Nuclear power plants were not included in the study.
   (B) The areas studied had similar death rates before and after the nuclear weapons plants were built.
   (C) Exposure to nuclear radiation can cause many serious diseases that do not necessarily result in death.
   (D) Only a small number of areas have nuclear weapons plants.
   (E) The researchers did not study the possible health hazards of radiation on people who were employed at the nuclear weapons plants if those employees did not live in the study areas.

8. It was once believed that cells grown in laboratory tissue cultures were essentially immortal. That is, as long as all of their needs were met, they would continue dividing forever. However, it has been shown that normal cells have a finite reproductive limit. A human liver cell, for example, divides 60 times and then stops. If such a cell divides 30 times and then is put into a deep freeze for months or even years, it "remembers" where it stopped dividing. After thawing, it divides another 30 times—but no more.

   If the information above is accurate, a liver cell in which more than 60 divisions took place in a tissue culture CANNOT be which one of the following?

   (A) an abnormal human liver cell
   (B) a normal human liver cell that had been frozen after its first division and afterward thawed
   (C) a normal cell that came from the liver of an individual of a nonhuman species and had never been frozen
   (D) a normal liver cell that came from an individual of a nonhuman species and had been frozen after its first division and afterward thawed
   (E) an abnormal cell from the liver of an individual of a nonhuman species

9. Complaints that milk bottlers take enormous markups on the bottled milk sold to consumers are most likely to arise when least warranted by the actual spread between the price that bottlers pay for raw milk and the price at which they sell bottled milk. The complaints occur when the bottled-milk price rises, yet these price increases most often merely reflect the rising price of the raw milk that bottlers buy from dairy farmers. When the raw-milk price is rising, the bottlers' markups are actually smallest proportionate to the retail price. When the raw-milk price is falling, however, the markups are greatest.

   If all of the statements above are true, which one of the following must also be true on the basis of them?

   (A) Consumers pay more for bottled milk when raw-milk prices are falling than when these prices are rising.
   (B) Increases in dairy farmers' cost of producing milk are generally not passed on to consumers.
   (C) Milk bottlers take substantially greater markups on bottled milk when its price is low for an extended period than when it is high for an extended period.
   (D) Milk bottlers generally do not respond to a decrease in raw-milk prices by straightaway proportionately lowering the price of the bottled milk they sell.
   (E) Consumers tend to complain more about the price they pay for bottled milk when dairy farmers are earning their smallest profits.

GO ON TO THE NEXT PAGE.

Questions 10–11

If the public library shared by the adjacent towns of Redville and Glenwood were relocated from the library's current, overcrowded building in central Redville to a larger, available building in central Glenwood, the library would then be within walking distance of a larger number of library users. That is because there are many more people living in central Glenwood than in central Redville, and people generally will walk to the library only if it is located close to their homes.

10. Which one of the following, if true, most strengthens the argument?
    (A) The public library was located between Glenwood and Redville before being moved to its current location in central Redville.
    (B) The area covered by central Glenwood is approximately the same size as that covered by central Redville.
    (C) The building that is available in Glenwood is smaller than an alternative building that is available in Redville.
    (D) Many of the people who use the public library do not live in either Glenwood or Redville.
    (E) The distance that people currently walk to get to the library is farther than what is generally considered walking distance.

11. Which one of the following, if true, most seriously weakens the argument?
    (A) Many more people who currently walk to the library live in central Redville than in central Glenwood.
    (B) The number of people living in central Glenwood who would use the library if it were located there is smaller than the number of people living in central Redville who currently use the library.
    (C) The number of people using the public library would continue to increase steadily if the library were moved to Glenwood.
    (D) Most of the people who currently either drive to the library or take public transportation to reach it would continue to do so if the library were moved to central Glenwood.
    (E) Most of the people who currently walk to the library would remain library users if the library were relocated to central Glenwood.

12. Light utility trucks have become popular among consumers who buy them primarily for the trucks' rugged appearance. Yet although these trucks are tough-looking, they are exempt from the government's car-safety standards that dictate minimum roof strength and minimum resistance to impact. Therefore, if involved in a serious high-impact accident, a driver of one of these trucks is more likely to be injured than is a driver of a car that is subject to these government standards.

    The argument depends on the assumption that
    (A) the government has established safety standards for the construction of light utility trucks
    (B) people who buy automobiles solely for their appearance are more likely than other people to drive recklessly
    (C) light utility trucks are more likely than other kinds of vehicles to be involved in accidents that result in injuries
    (D) the trucks' rugged appearance is deceptive in that their engines are not especially powerful
    (E) light utility trucks are less likely to meet the car-safety standards than are cars that are subject to the standards

13. Five years ago, during the first North American outbreak of the cattle disease CXC, the death rate from the disease was 5 percent of all reported cases, whereas today the corresponding figure is over 18 percent. It is clear, therefore, that during these past 5 years, CXC has increased in virulence.

    Which one of the following, if true, most substantially weakens the argument?
    (A) Many recent cattle deaths that have actually been caused by CXC have been mistakenly attributed to another disease that mimics the symptoms of CXC.
    (B) During the first North American outbreak of the disease, many of the deaths reported to have been caused by CXC were actually due to other causes.
    (C) An inoculation program against CXC was recently begun after controlled studies showed inoculation to be 70 percent effective in preventing serious cases of the illness.
    (D) Since the first outbreak, farmers have learned to treat mild cases of CXC and no longer report them to veterinarians or authorities.
    (E) Cattle that have contracted and survived CXC rarely contract the disease a second time.

GO ON TO THE NEXT PAGE.

Questions 14–15

Economist: Some policymakers believe that our country's continued economic growth requires a higher level of personal savings than we currently have. A recent legislative proposal would allow individuals to set up savings accounts in which interest earned would be exempt from taxes until money is withdrawn from the account. Backers of this proposal claim that its implementation would increase the amount of money available for banks to loan at a relatively small cost to the government in lost tax revenues. Yet, when similar tax-incentive programs were tried in the past, virtually all of the money invested through them was diverted from other personal savings, and the overall level of personal savings was unchanged.

14. The passage as a whole provides the most support for which one of the following conclusions?
    (A) Backers of the tax-incentive proposal undoubtedly have some motive other than their expressed aim of increasing the amount of money available for banks to loan.
    (B) The proposed tax incentive is unlikely to attract enough additional money into personal savings accounts to make up for the attendant loss in tax revenues.
    (C) A tax-incentive program that resulted in substantial loss of tax revenues would be likely to generate a large increase in personal savings.
    (D) The economy will be in danger unless some alternative to increased personal savings can be found to stimulate growth.
    (E) The government has no effective means of influencing the amount of money that people are willing to put into savings accounts.

15. The author criticizes the proposed tax-incentive program by
    (A) challenging a premise on which the proposal is based
    (B) pointing out a disagreement among policymakers
    (C) demonstrating that the proposal's implementation is not feasible
    (D) questioning the judgment of the proposal's backers by citing past cases in which they had advocated programs that have proved ineffective
    (E) disputing the assumption that a program to encourage personal savings is needed

16. Although all birds have feathers and all birds have wings, some birds do not fly. For example, penguins and ostriches use their wings to move in a different way from other birds. Penguins use their wings only to swim under water at high speeds. Ostriches use their wings only to run with the wind by lifting them as if they were sails.

    Which one of the following is most parallel in its reasoning to the argument above?
    (A) Ancient philosophers tried to explain not how the world functions but why it functions. In contrast, most contemporary biologists seek comprehensive theories of how organisms function, but many refuse to speculate about purpose.
    (B) Some chairs are used only as decorations, and other chairs are used only to tame lions. Therefore, not all chairs are used for sitting in despite the fact that all chairs have a seat and some support such as legs.
    (C) Some musicians in a symphony orchestra play the violin, and others play the viola, but these are both in the same category of musical instruments, namely string instruments.
    (D) All cars have similar drive mechanisms, but some cars derive their power from solar energy, whereas others burn gasoline. Thus, solar-powered cars are less efficient than gasoline-powered ones.
    (E) Sailing ships move in a different way from steamships. Both sailing ships and steamships navigate over water, but only sailing ships use sails to move over the surface.

GO ON TO THE NEXT PAGE.

Questions 17–18

Jones: Prehistoric wooden tools found in South America have been dated to 13,000 years ago. Although scientists attribute these tools to peoples whose ancestors first crossed into the Americas from Siberia to Alaska, this cannot be correct. In order to have reached a site so far south, these peoples must have been migrating southward well before 13,000 years ago. However, no such tools dating to before 13,000 years ago have been found anywhere between Alaska and South America.

Smith: Your evidence is inconclusive. Those tools were found in peat bogs, which are rare in the Americas. Wooden tools in soils other than peat bogs usually decompose within only a few years.

17. The point at issue between Jones and Smith is

(A) whether all prehistoric tools that are 13,000 years or older were made of wood

(B) whether the scientists' attribution of tools could be correct in light of Jones's evidence

(C) whether the dating of the wooden tools by the scientists could be correct

(D) how long ago the peoples who crossed into the Americas from Siberia to Alaska first did so

(E) whether Smith's evidence entails that the wooden tools have been dated correctly

18. Smith responds to Jones by

(A) citing several studies that invalidate Jones's conclusion

(B) accusing Jones of distorting the scientists' position

(C) disputing the accuracy of the supporting evidence cited by Jones

(D) showing that Jones's evidence actually supports the denial of Jones's conclusion

(E) challenging an implicit assumption in Jones's argument

19. Editorial: It is clear that if this country's universities were living up to both their moral and their intellectual responsibilities, the best-selling publications in most university bookstores would not be frivolous ones like *TV Today* and *Gossip Review*. However, in most university bookstores the only publication that sells better than *Gossip Review* is *TV Today*.

If the statements in the editorial are true, which one of the following must also be true on the basis of them?

(A) People who purchase publications that are devoted primarily to gossip or to television programming are intellectually irresponsible.

(B) It is irresponsible for university bookstores to carry publications such as *Gossip Review* and *TV Today*.

(C) Most people who purchase publications at university bookstores purchase either *TV Today* or *Gossip Review*.

(D) Many people who attend this country's universities fail to live up to both their moral and their intellectual responsibilities.

(E) At least some of this country's universities are not meeting their moral responsibilities or their intellectual responsibilities or both.

Questions 20–21

Saunders: Everyone at last week's neighborhood association meeting agreed that the row of abandoned and vandalized houses on Carlton Street posed a threat to the safety of our neighborhood. Moreover, no one now disputes that getting the houses torn down eliminated that threat. Some people tried to argue that it was unnecessary to demolish what they claimed were basically sound buildings, since the city had established a fund to help people in need of housing buy and rehabilitate such buildings. The overwhelming success of the demolition strategy, however, proves that the majority, who favored demolition, were right and that those who claimed that the problem could and should be solved by rehabilitating the houses were wrong.

20. Which one of the following principles, if established, would determine that demolishing the houses was the right decision or instead would determine that the proposal advocated by the opponents of demolition should have been adopted?
   (A) When what to do about an abandoned neighborhood building is in dispute, the course of action that would result in the most housing for people who need it should be the one adopted unless the building is believed to pose a threat to neighborhood safety.
   (B) When there are two proposals for solving a neighborhood problem, and only one of them would preclude the possibility of trying the other approach if the first proves unsatisfactory, then the approach that does not foreclose the other possibility should be the one adopted.
   (C) If one of two proposals for renovating vacant neighborhood buildings requires government funding whereas the second does not, the second proposal should be the one adopted unless the necessary government funds have already been secured.
   (D) No plan for eliminating a neighborhood problem that requires demolishing basically sound houses should be carried out until all other possible alternatives have been thoroughly investigated.
   (E) No proposal for dealing with a threat to a neighborhood's safety should be adopted merely because a majority of the residents of that neighborhood prefer that proposal to a particular counterproposal.

21. Saunders' reasoning is flawed because it
   (A) relies on fear rather than on argument to persuade the neighborhood association to reject the policy advocated by Saunders' opponents
   (B) fails to establish that there is anyone who could qualify for city funds who would be interested in buying and rehabilitating the houses
   (C) mistakenly equates an absence of vocal public dissent with the presence of universal public support
   (D) offers no evidence that the policy advocated by Saunders' opponents would not have succeeded if it had been given the chance
   (E) does not specify the precise nature of the threat to neighborhood safety supposedly posed by the vandalized houses

---

22. For the writers who first gave feudalism its name, the existence of feudalism presupposed the existence of a noble class. Yet there cannot be a noble class, properly speaking, unless both the titles that indicate superior, noble status and the inheritance of such titles are sanctioned by law. Although feudalism existed in Europe as early as the eighth century, it was not until the twelfth century, when many feudal institutions were in decline, that the hereditary transfer of legally recognized titles of nobility first appeared.

   The statements above, if true, most strongly support which one of the following claims?
   (A) To say that feudalism by definition requires the existence of a nobility is to employ a definition that distorts history.
   (B) Prior to the twelfth century, the institution of European feudalism functioned without the presence of a dominant class.
   (C) The fact that a societal group has a distinct legal status is not in itself sufficient to allow that group to be properly considered a social class.
   (D) The decline of feudalism in Europe was the only cause of the rise of a European nobility.
   (E) The prior existence of feudal institutions is a prerequisite for the emergence of a nobility, as defined in the strictest sense of the term.

GO ON TO THE NEXT PAGE.

23. Mayor Smith, one of our few government officials with a record of outspoken, informed, and consistent opposition to nuclear power plant construction projects, has now declared herself in favor of building the nuclear power plant at Littletown. If someone with her past antinuclear record now favors building this power plant, then there is good reason to believe that it will be safe and therefore should be built.

The argument is vulnerable to criticism on which one of the following grounds?

(A) It overlooks the possibility that not all those who fail to speak out on issues of nuclear power are necessarily opposed to it.

(B) It assumes without warrant that the qualities enabling a person to be elected to public office confer on that person a grasp of the scientific principles on which technical decisions are based.

(C) It fails to establish that a consistent and outspoken opposition is necessarily an informed opposition.

(D) It leads to the further but unacceptable conclusion that any project favored by Mayor Smith should be sanctioned simply on the basis of her having spoken out in favor of it.

(E) It gives no indication of either the basis of Mayor Smith's former opposition to nuclear power plant construction or the reasons for her support for the Littletown project.

24. Advertisement: In today's world, you make a statement about the person you are by the car you own. The message of the SKX Mach-5 is unambiguous: Its owner is Dynamic, Aggressive, and Successful. Shouldn't you own an SKX Mach-5?

If the claims made in the advertisement are true, which one of the following must also be true on the basis of them?

(A) Anyone who is dynamic and aggressive is also successful.

(B) Anyone who is not both dynamic and successful would misrepresent himself or herself by being the owner of an SKX Mach-5.

(C) People who buy the SKX Mach-5 are usually more aggressive than people who buy other cars.

(D) No car other than the SKX Mach-5 announces that its owner is successful.

(E) Almost no one would fail to recognize the kind of person who would choose to own an SKX Mach-5.

25. The great medieval universities had no administrators, yet they endured for centuries. Our university has a huge administrative staff, and we are in serious financial difficulties. Therefore, we should abolish the positions and salaries of the administrators to ensure the longevity of the university.

Which one of the following arguments contains flawed reasoning that most closely parallels the flawed reasoning in the argument above?

(A) No airplane had jet engines before 1940, yet airplanes had been flying since 1903. Therefore, jet engines are not necessary for the operation of airplanes.

(B) The novelist's stories began to be accepted for publication soon after she started using a computer to write them. You have been having trouble getting your stories accepted for publication, and you do not use a computer. To make sure your stories are accepted for publication, then, you should write them with the aid of a computer.

(C) After doctors began using antibiotics, the number of infections among patients dropped drastically. Now, however, resistant strains of bacteria cannot be controlled by standard antibiotics. Therefore, new methods of control are needed.

(D) A bicycle should not be ridden without a helmet. Since a good helmet can save the rider's life, a helmet should be considered the most important piece of bicycling equipment.

(E) The great cities of the ancient world were mostly built along waterways. Archaeologists searching for the remains of such cities should therefore try to determine where major rivers used to run.

S T O P

IF YOU FINISH BEFORE TIME IS CALLED, YOU MAY CHECK YOUR WORK ON THIS SECTION ONLY. DO NOT WORK ON ANY OTHER SECTION IN THE TEST.

Practice Test 2

Section II: **Analytical Reasoning**

Time—35 minutes
24 questions

Directions: Each group of questions in this section is based on a set of conditions. In answering some of the questions, it may be useful to draw a rough diagram. Choose the response that most accurately and completely answers each question and blacken the corresponding space on your answer sheet.

Questions 1–5

A gymnastics instructor is planning a weekly schedule, Monday through Friday, of individual coaching sessions for each of six students—H, I, K, O, U, and Z. The instructor will coach exactly one student each day, except for one day when the instructor will coach two students in separate but consecutive sessions. The following restrictions apply:

H's session must take place at some time before Z's session.
I's session is on Thursday.
K's session is always scheduled for the day immediately before or the day immediately after the day for which O's session is scheduled.
Neither Monday nor Wednesday can be a day for which two students are scheduled.

1. Which one of the following is a pair of students whose sessions can both be scheduled for Tuesday, not necessarily in the order given?
   (A) H and U
   (B) H and Z
   (C) K and O
   (D) O and U
   (E) U and Z

2. If K's session is scheduled for Tuesday, then which one of the following is the earliest day for which Z's session can be scheduled?
   (A) Monday
   (B) Tuesday
   (C) Wednesday
   (D) Thursday
   (E) Friday

3. Which one of the following must be true?
   (A) If U's session is scheduled for Monday, H's session is scheduled for Tuesday.
   (B) If U's session is scheduled for Tuesday, O's session is scheduled for Wednesday.
   (C) If U's session is scheduled for Wednesday, Z's session is scheduled for Tuesday.
   (D) If U's session is scheduled for Thursday, Z's session is scheduled for Friday.
   (E) If U's session is scheduled for Friday, Z's session is scheduled for Thursday.

4. Scheduling Z's session for which one of the following days determines the day for which U's session must be scheduled?
   (A) Monday
   (B) Tuesday
   (C) Wednesday
   (D) Thursday
   (E) Friday

5. If H's session is scheduled as the next session after U's session, which one of the following could be true about H's session and U's session?
   (A) U's session is scheduled for Monday, and H's session is scheduled for Tuesday.
   (B) U's session is scheduled for Thursday, and H's session is scheduled for Friday.
   (C) They are both scheduled for Tuesday.
   (D) They are both scheduled for Thursday.
   (E) They are both scheduled for Friday.

GO ON TO THE NEXT PAGE.

Questions 6–12

A square parking lot has exactly eight lights—numbered 1 through 8—situated along its perimeter as diagramed below.

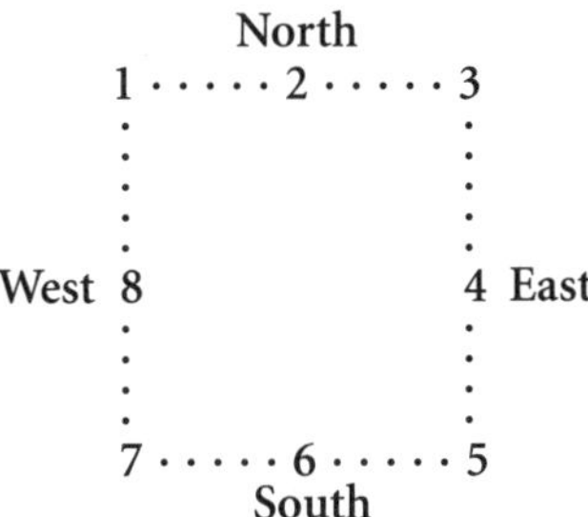

The lot must always be illuminated in such a way that the following specifications are met:

At least one of any three consecutively numbered lights is off.
Light 8 is on.
Neither light 2 nor light 7 is on when light 1 is on.
At least one of the three lights on each side is on.
If any side has exactly one of its three lights on, then that light is its center light.
Two of the lights on the north side are on.

6. Which one of the following could be a complete and accurate list of lights that are on together?
   (A) 1, 3, 5, 7
   (B) 2, 4, 6, 8
   (C) 2, 3, 5, 6, 8
   (D) 3, 4, 6, 7, 8
   (E) 1, 2, 4, 5, 6, 8

7. Which one of the following lights must be on?
   (A) light 2
   (B) light 3
   (C) light 4
   (D) light 5
   (E) light 6

8. If light 1 is off, which one of the following is a light that must also be off?
   (A) light 3
   (B) light 4
   (C) light 5
   (D) light 6
   (E) light 7

9. Which one of the following statements must be true?
   (A) If light 2 is on, then light 6 is off.
   (B) If light 3 is on, then light 2 is on.
   (C) If light 4 is on, then light 3 is off.
   (D) If light 5 is off, then light 4 is on.
   (E) If light 6 is off, then light 1 is on.

10. If light 5 is on, which one of the following could be true?
   (A) Light 1 is off and light 6 is off.
   (B) Light 1 is on and light 7 is on.
   (C) Light 2 is off and light 4 is on.
   (D) Light 2 is off and light 6 is off.
   (E) Light 6 is on and light 7 is on.

11. If light 4 is on, each of the following statements must be true EXCEPT:
   (A) Light 1 is on.
   (B) Light 2 is on.
   (C) Light 5 is off.
   (D) Light 6 is on.
   (E) Light 7 is off.

12. Suppose that it is no longer part of the specifications that two lights on the north side be on. If all of the other original specifications remain the same, and if exactly one light on the north side is on, which one of the following statements could be false?
   (A) Light 1 is off.
   (B) Light 2 is on.
   (C) Light 3 is off.
   (D) Light 4 is on.
   (E) Light 5 is on.

GO ON TO THE NEXT PAGE.

Questions 13–17

Seven children are to be seated in seven chairs arranged in a row that runs from west to east. All seven children will face north. Four of the children are boys: Frank, Harry, Ivan, and Joel. Three are girls: Ruby, Sylvia, and Thelma. The children are assigned to chairs according to the following conditions:

Exactly one child sits in each chair.
No boy sits next to another boy.
Ivan sits next to and east of the fourth child in the row.
Sylvia sits east of Ivan.
Frank sits next to Ruby.

13. What is the maximum possible number of different pairs of chairs in which Frank and Ruby could sit?
    (A) one
    (B) two
    (C) three
    (D) four
    (E) five

14. Which one of the following statements must be false?
    (A) Both Harry and Joel sit east of Frank.
    (B) Both Harry and Ruby sit east of Frank.
    (C) Both Harry and Joel sit west of Frank.
    (D) Both Harry and Ruby sit west of Frank.
    (E) Both Joel and Ruby sit east of Frank.

15. If Thelma sits next to Ivan, and if Frank sits next to Thelma, which one of the following statements could be false?
    (A) Both Frank and Ivan sit east of Ruby.
    (B) Both Frank and Ruby sit west of Thelma.
    (C) Both Frank and Sylvia sit east of Ruby.
    (D) Both Frank and Thelma sit west of Sylvia.
    (E) Both Frank and Ruby sit west of Joel.

16. If Frank does not sit next to any child who sits next to Ivan, which one of the following statements could be true?
    (A) Harry sits west of Frank.
    (B) Joel sits west of Ivan.
    (C) Ruby sits west of Frank.
    (D) Thelma sits west of Frank.
    (E) Thelma sits west of Ruby.

17. If Frank sits east of Ruby, which one of the following pairs of children CANNOT sit next to each other?
    (A) Frank and Thelma
    (B) Harry and Ruby
    (C) Harry and Sylvia
    (D) Ivan and Ruby
    (E) Joel and Ruby

GO ON TO THE NEXT PAGE.

Questions 18–24

The organisms W, X, Y, and Z respond to the antibiotics ferromycin, ganocyclene, and heptocillin in a manner consistent with the following:

Each of the organisms responds to at least one of the antibiotics.

No organism responds to all three antibiotics.

At least two but not all four or the organisms respond to ferromycin.

If W responds to any antibiotic, then X responds to that antibiotic.

If an organism responds to ferromycin, then it responds to ganocyclene.

Y responds to ferromycin.

18. Each of the following can be true EXCEPT:
    (A) W responds to heptocillin.
    (B) X responds to ganocyclene.
    (C) X responds to heptocillin.
    (D) Y responds to heptocillin.
    (E) Z responds to ganocyclene.

19. Which one of the following could be true?
    (A) W, X, and Z all respond to ferromycin.
    (B) W, X, and Z all respond to ganocyclene.
    (C) W and exactly one other organism respond to ganocyclene.
    (D) W responds to more of the antibiotics than X does.
    (E) More of the organisms respond to ferromycin than to ganocyclene.

20. Which one of the following could be true?
    (A) Exactly one of the organisms responds to ferromycin.
    (B) All four of the organisms respond to heptocillin.
    (C) At least one of the organisms responds both to ferromycin and to heptocillin.
    (D) At least one of the organisms responds neither to ganocyclene nor to heptocillin.
    (E) At least one of the organisms responds to ganocyclene but does not respond to ferromycin.

21. If X does not respond to ferromycin, then which one of the following must be true?
    (A) W responds to ganocyclene.
    (B) X responds to ganocyclene.
    (C) X responds to heptocillin.
    (D) Z responds to ferromycin.
    (E) Z responds to heptocillin.

22. If any of the organisms responds to two of the antibiotics, then which one of the following is true about such an organism?
    (A) It must respond to ferromycin.
    (B) It must respond to ganocyclene.
    (C) It must respond to heptocillin.
    (D) It cannot respond to ferromycin.
    (E) It cannot respond to ganocyclene.

23. If none of the organisms responds to heptocillin, then which one of the following must be true?
    (A) W responds to ferromycin.
    (B) X responds to ferromycin.
    (C) Z responds to ferromycin.
    (D) Exactly three of the organisms respond to ganocyclene.
    (E) Exactly four of the organisms respond to ganocyclene.

24. If three of the organisms respond to exactly the same set of antibiotics as each other, and if Z does not respond to ferromycin, then each of the following must be true EXCEPT:
    (A) W responds to ferromycin.
    (B) X responds to ganocyclene.
    (C) Z responds to ganocyclene.
    (D) W responds to exactly the same set of antibiotics as Y.
    (E) X responds to exactly the same set of antibiotics as Y.

STOP

IF YOU FINISH BEFORE TIME IS CALLED, YOU MAY CHECK YOUR WORK ON THIS SECTION ONLY. DO NOT WORK ON ANY OTHER SECTION IN THE TEST.

Practice Test 2

Section III: Reading Comprehension

Time—35 minutes
27 Questions

Directions: Each passage in this section is followed by a group of questions to be answered on the basis of what is stated or implied in the passage. For some of the questions, more than one of the choices could conceivably answer the question. However, you are to choose the best answer; that is, the response that most accurately and completely answers the question, and blacken the corresponding space on your answer sheet.

After thirty years of investigation into cell genetics, researchers made startling discoveries in the 1960s and early 1970s which culminated in the development of processes, collectively known as recombinant deoxyribonucleic acid (rDNA) technology, for the active manipulation of a cell's genetic code. The technology has created excitement and controversy because it involves altering DNA—which contains the building blocks of the genetic code.

Using rDNA technology, scientists can transfer a portion of the DNA from one organism to a single living cell of another. The scientist chemically "snips" the DNA chain of the host cell at a predetermined point and attaches another piece of DNA from a donor cell at that place, creating a completely new organism.

Proponents of rDNA research and development claim that it will allow scientists to find cures for disease and to better understand how genetic information controls an organism's development. They also see many other potentially practical benefits, especially in the pharmaceutical industry. Some corporations employing the new technology even claim that by the end of the century all major diseases will be treated with drugs derived from microorganisms created through rDNA technology. Pharmaceutical products already developed, but not yet marketed, indicate that these predictions may be realized.

Proponents also cite nonmedical applications for this technology. Energy production and waste disposal may benefit: genetically altered organisms could convert sewage and other organic material into methane fuel. Agriculture might also take advantage of rDNA technology to produce new varieties of crops that resist foul weather, pests, and the effects of poor soil.

A major concern of the critics of rDNA research is that genetically altered microorganisms might escape from the laboratory. Because these microorganisms are laboratory creations that, in all probability, do not occur in nature. their interaction with the natural world cannot be predicted with certainty. It is possible that they could cause previously unknown perhaps incurable diseases. The effect of genetically altered microorganisms on the world's microbiological predator-prey relationships is another potentially serious problem pointed out by the opponents of rDNA research. Introducing a new species may disrupt or even destroy the existing ecosystem. The collapse of interdependent relationships among species, extrapolated to its extreme, could eventually result in the destruction of humanity.

Opponents of rDNA technology also cite ethical problems with it. For example, it gives scientists the power to instantly cross evolutionary and species boundaries that nature took millennia to establish. The implications of such power would become particularly profound if genetic engineers were to tinker with human genes, a practice that would bring us one step closer to Aldous Huxley's grim vision in *Brave New World* of a totalitarian society that engineers human beings to fulfill specific roles.

1. In the passage, the author is primarily concerned with doing which one of the following?
   (A) explaining the process and applications of rDNA technology
   (B) advocating continued rDNA research and development
   (C) providing evidence indicating the need for regulation of rDNA research and development
   (D) summarizing the controversy surrounding rDNA research and development
   (E) arguing that the environmental risks of rDNA technology may outweigh its medical benefits

2. According to the passage, which one of the following is an accurate statement about research into the genetic code of cells?
   (A) It led to the development of processes for the manipulation of DNA.
   (B) It was initiated by the discovery of rDNA technology.
   (C) It led to the use of new treatments for major diseases.
   (D) It was universally heralded as a great benefit to humanity.
   (E) It was motivated by a desire to create new organisms.

GO ON TO THE NEXT PAGE.

3. The potential benefits of rDNA technology referred to in the passage include all of the following EXCEPT
   (A) new methods of waste treatment
   (B) new biological knowledge
   (C) enhanced food production
   (D) development of less expensive drugs
   (E) increased energy production

4. Which one of the following, if true, would most weaken an argument of opponents of rDNA technology?
   (A) New safety procedures developed by rDNA researchers make it impossible for genetically altered microorganisms to escape from laboratories.
   (B) A genetically altered microorganism accidentally released from a laboratory is successfully contained.
   (C) A particular rDNA-engineered microorganism introduced into an ecosystem attracts predators that keep its population down.
   (D) Genetically altered organisms designed to process sewage into methane cannot survive outside the waste treatment plant.
   (E) A specific hereditary disease that has plagued humankind for generations is successfully eradicated.

5. The author's reference in the last sentence of the passage to a society that engineers human beings to fulfill specific roles serves to
   (A) emphasize the potential medical dangers of rDNA technology
   (B) advocate research on the use of rDNA technology in human genetics
   (C) warn of the possible disasters that could result from upsetting the balance of nature
   (D) present *Brave New World* as an example of a work of fiction that accurately predicted technological developments
   (E) illustrate the sociopolitical ramifications of applying genetic engineering to humans

6. Which one of the following, if true, would most strengthen an argument of the opponents of rDNA technology?
   (A) Agricultural products developed through rDNA technology are no more attractive to consumers than are traditional crops.
   (B) Genetically altered microorganisms have no natural predators but can prey on a wide variety of other microorganisms.
   (C) Drugs produced using rDNA technology cost more to manufacture than drugs produced with traditional technologies.
   (D) Ecosystems are impermanent systems that are often liable to collapse, and occasionally do so.
   (E) Genetically altered microorganisms generally cannot survive for more than a few hours in the natural environment.

Acknowledgment is made to the following sources from which material has been adapted for use in this test:
From "Stopping a 'Gruesome Parade of Horribles': Criminal Sanctions to Deter Corporate Misuse of Recombinant DNA Technology" by Richard Kevin Zepfel, Southern California Law Review, Volume 59, pages 641–665. © 1986 by the University of Southern California. Used by permission.

GO ON TO THE NEXT PAGE.

Gray marketing, the selling of trademarked products through channels of distribution not authorized by the trademark holder, can involve distribution of goods either within a market region or across market boundaries. Gray marketing within a market region ("channel flow diversion") occurs when manufacturer-authorized distributors sell trademarked goods to unauthorized distributors who then sell the goods to consumers within the same region. For example, quantity discounts from manufacturers may motivate authorized dealers to enter the gray market because they can purchase larger quantities of a product than they themselves intend to stock if they can sell the extra units through gray market channels.

When gray marketing occurs across market boundaries, it is typically in an international setting and may be called "parallel importing." Manufacturers often produce and sell products in more than one country and establish a network of authorized dealers in each country. Parallel importing occurs when trademarked goods intended for one country are diverted from proper channels (channel flow diversion) and then exported to unauthorized distributors in another country.

Trademark owners justifiably argue against gray marketing practices since such practices clearly jeopardize the goodwill established by trademark owners: consumers who purchase trademarked goods in the gray market do not get the same "extended product," which typically includes pre- and postsale service. Equally important, authorized distributors may cease to promote the product if it becomes available for much lower prices through unauthorized channels.

Current debate over regulation of gray marketing focuses on three disparate theories in trademark law that have been variously and confusingly applied to parallel importation cases: universality, exhaustion, and territoriality. The theory of universality holds that a trademark is only an indication of the source or origin of the product. This theory does not recognize the goodwill functions of a trademark. When the courts apply this theory, gray marketing practices are allowed to continue because the origin of the product remains the same regardless of the specific route of the product through the channel of distribution. The exhaustion theory holds that a trademark owner relinquishes all rights once a product has been sold. When this theory is applied, gray marketing practices are allowed to continue because the trademark owners' rights cease as soon as their products are sold to a distributor. The theory of territoriality holds that a trademark is effective in the country in which it is registered. Under the theory of territoriality, trademark owners can stop gray marketing practices in the registering countries on products bearing their trademarks. Since only the territoriality theory affords trademark owners any real legal protection against gray marketing practices, I believe it is inevitable as well as desirable that it will come to be consistently applied in gray marketing cases.

7. Which one of the following best expresses the main point of the passage?
   (A) Gray marketing is unfair to trademark owners and should be legally controlled.
   (B) Gray marketing is practiced in many different forms and places, and legislators should recognize the futility of trying to regulate it.
   (C) The mechanisms used to control gray marketing across markets are different from those most effective in controlling gray marketing within markets.
   (D) The three trademark law theories that have been applied in gray marketing cases lead to different case outcomes.
   (E) Current theories used to interpret trademark laws have resulted in increased gray marketing activity.

8. The function of the passage as a whole is to
   (A) criticize the motives and methods of those who practice gray marketing
   (B) evaluate the effects of both channel flow diversion and parallel importation
   (C) discuss the methods that have been used to regulate gray marketing and evaluate such methods' degrees of success
   (D) describe a controversial marketing practice and evaluate several legal views regarding it
   (E) discuss situations in which certain marketing practices are common and analyze the economic factors responsible for their development

9. Which one of the following does the author offer as an argument against gray marketing?
   (A) Manufacturers find it difficult to monitor the effectiveness of promotional efforts made on behalf of products that are gray marketed.
   (B) Gray marketing can discourage product promotion by authorized distributors.
   (C) Gray marketing forces manufacturers to accept the low profit margins that result from quantity discounting.
   (D) Gray marketing discourages competition among unauthorized dealers.
   (E) Quality standards in the manufacture of products likely to be gray marketed may decline.

GO ON TO THE NEXT PAGE.

10. The information in the passage suggests that proponents of the theory of territoriality would probably differ from proponents of the theory of exhaustion on which one of the following issues?
    (A) the right of trademark owners to enforce, in countries in which the trademarks are registered, distribution agreements intended to restrict distribution to authorized channels
    (B) the right of trademark owners to sell trademarked goods only to those distributors who agree to abide by distribution agreements
    (C) the legality of channel flow diversion that occurs in a country other than the one in which a trademark is registered
    (D) the significance consumers attach to a trademark
    (E) the usefulness of trademarks as marketing tools

11. The author discusses the impact of gray marketing on goodwill in order to
    (A) fault trademark owners for their unwillingness to offer a solution to a major consumer complaint against gray marketing
    (B) indicate a way in which manufacturers sustain damage against which they ought to be protected
    (C) highlight one way in which gray marketing across markets is more problematic than gray marketing within a market
    (D) demonstrate that gray marketing does not always benefit the interests of unauthorized distributors
    (E) argue that consumers are unwilling to accept a reduction in price in exchange for elimination of service

12. The author's attitude toward the possibility that the courts will come to exercise consistent control over gray marketing practices can best be characterized as one of
    (A) resigned tolerance
    (B) utter dismay
    (C) reasoned optimism
    (D) unbridled fervor
    (E) cynical indifference

13. It can be inferred from the passage that some channel flow diversion might be eliminated if
    (A) profit margins on authorized distribution of goods were less than those on goods marketed through parallel importing
    (B) manufacturers relieved authorized channels of all responsibility for product promotion
    (C) manufacturers charged all authorized distributors the same unit price for products regardless of quantity purchased
    (D) the postsale service policies of authorized channels were controlled by manufacturers
    (E) manufacturers refused to provide the "extended product" to consumers who purchase goods in the gray market

GO ON TO THE NEXT PAGE.

Any study of autobiographical narratives that appeared under the ostensible authorship of African American writers between 1760 and 1865 inevitably raises concerns about authenticity and interpretation. Should an autobiography whose written composition was literally out of the hands of its narrator be considered as the literary equivalent of those autobiographies that were authored independently by their subjects?

In many cases, the so-called edited narrative of an ex-slave ought to be treated as a ghostwritten account insofar as literary analysis is concerned, especially when it was composed by its editor from "a statement of facts" provided by an African American subject. Blassingame has taken pains to show that the editors of several of the more famous antebellum slave narratives were "noted for their integrity" and thus were unlikely to distort the facts given them by slave narrators. From a literary standpoint, however, it is not the moral integrity of these editors that is at issue but the linguistic, structural, and tonal integrity of the narratives they produced. Even if an editor faithfully reproduced the facts of a narrator's life, it was still the editor who decided what to make of these facts, how they should be emphasized, in what order they ought to be presented, and what was extraneous or germane. Readers of African American autobiography then and now have too readily accepted the presumption of these eighteenth- and nineteenth-century editors that experiential facts recounted orally could be recorded and sorted by an amanuensis-editor, taken out of their original contexts, and then published with editorial prefaces, footnotes, and appended commentary, all without compromising the validity of the narrative as a product of an African American consciousness.

Transcribed narratives in which an editor explicitly delimits his or her role undoubtedly may be regarded as more authentic and reflective of the narrator's thought in action than those edited works that flesh out a statement of facts in ways unaccounted for. Still, it would be naive to accord dictated oral narratives the same status as autobiographies composed and written by the subjects of the stories themselves. This point is illustrated by an analysis of Works Progress Administration interviews with ex-slaves in the 1930s that suggests that narrators often told interviewers what they seemed to want to hear. If it seemed impolitic for former slaves to tell all they knew and thought about the past to interviewers in the 1930s, the same could be said of escaped slaves on the run in the antebellum era. Dictated narratives, therefore, are literary texts whose authenticity is difficult to determine. Analysts should reserve close analytic readings for independently authored texts. Discussion of collaborative texts should take into account the conditions that governed their production.

14. Which one of the following best summarizes the main point of the passage?
    - (A) The personal integrity of an autobiography's editor has little relevance to its value as a literary work.
    - (B) Autobiographies dictated to editors are less valuable as literature than are autobiographies authored by their subjects.
    - (C) The facts that are recorded in an autobiography are less important than the personal impressions of its author.
    - (D) The circumstances under which an autobiography was written should affect the way it is interpreted as literature.
    - (E) The autobiographies of African Americans written between 1760 and 1865 deserve more careful study than they have so far received.

15. The information in the passage suggests that the role of the "editor" (lines 23–24) is most like that of
    - (A) an artist who wishes to invent a unique method of conveying the emotional impact of a scene in a painting
    - (B) a worker who must interpret the instructions of an employer
    - (C) a critic who must provide evidence to support opinions about a play being reviewed
    - (D) an architect who must make the best use of a natural setting in designing a public building
    - (E) a historian who must decide how to direct the reenactment of a historical event

16. Which one of the following best describes the author's opinion about applying literary analysis to edited autobiographies?
    - (A) The author is adamantly opposed to the application of literary analysis to edited autobiographies.
    - (B) The author is skeptical of the value of close analytical reading in the case of edited autobiographies.
    - (C) The author believes that literary analysis of the prefaces, footnotes, and commentaries that accompany edited autobiographies would be more useful than an analysis of the text of the autobiographies.
    - (D) The author believes that an exclusively literary analysis of edited autobiographies is more valuable than a reading that emphasizes their historical import.
    - (E) The author believes that the literary analysis of edited autobiographies would enhance their linguistic, structural, and tonal integrity.

GO ON TO THE NEXT PAGE.

17. The passage supports which one of the following statements about the readers of autobiographies of African Americans that were published between 1760 and 1865?
    (A) They were more concerned with the personal details in the autobiographies than with their historical significance.
    (B) They were unable to distinguish between ghostwritten and edited autobiographies.
    (C) They were less naive about the facts of slave life than are readers today.
    (D) They presumed that the editing of the autobiographies did not affect their authenticity.
    (E) They had little interest in the moral integrity of the editors of the autobiographies.

18. Which one of the following words, as it is used in the passage, best serves to underscore the author's concerns about the authenticity of the autobiographies discussed?
    (A) "ostensible" (line 2)
    (B) "integrity" (line 18)
    (C) "extraneous" (line 27)
    (D) "delimits" (line 39)
    (E) "impolitic" (line 51)

19. According to the passage, close analytic reading of an autobiography is appropriate only when the
    (A) autobiography has been dictated to an experienced amanuensis-editor
    (B) autobiography attempts to reflect the narrator's thought in action
    (C) autobiography was authored independently by its subject
    (D) moral integrity of the autobiography's editor is well established
    (E) editor of the autobiography collaborated closely with its subject in its editing

20. It can be inferred that the discussion in the passage of Blassingame's work primarily serves which one of the following purposes?
    (A) It adds an authority's endorsement to the author's view that edited narratives ought to be treated as ghostwritten accounts.
    (B) It provides an example of a mistaken emphasis in the study of autobiography.
    (C) It presents an account of a new method of literary analysis to be applied to autobiography.
    (D) It illustrates the inadequacy of traditional approaches to the analysis of autobiography.
    (E) It emphasizes the importance of the relationship between editor and narrator.

GO ON TO THE NEXT PAGE.

A conventional view of nineteenth-century Britain holds that iron manufacturers and textile manufacturers from the north of England became the wealthiest and most powerful people in society after about 1832. According to Marxist historians, these industrialists were the target of the working class in its struggle for power. A new study by Rubinstein, however, suggests that the real wealth lay with the bankers and merchants of London. Rubinstein does not deny that a northern industrial elite existed but argues that it was consistently outnumbered and outdone by a London-based commercial elite. His claims are provocative and deserve consideration.

Rubinstein's claim about the location of wealth comes from his investigation of probate records. These indicate the value of personal property, excluding real property (buildings and land), left by individuals at death. It does seem as if large fortunes were more frequently made in commerce than in industry and, within industry, more frequently from alcohol or tobacco than from textiles or metal. However, such records do not unequivocally make Rubinstein's case. Uncertainties abound about how the probate rules for valuing assets were actually applied. Mills and factories, being real property, were clearly excluded; machinery may also have been, for the same reason. What the valuation conventions were for stock-in-trade (goods for sale) is also uncertain. It is possible that their probate values were much lower than their actual market values; cash or near-cash, such as bank balances or stocks, were, on the other hand, invariably considered at full face value. A further complication is that probate valuations probably took no notice of a business's goodwill (favor with the public) which, since it represents expectations about future profit-making, would today very often be a large fraction of market value. Whether factors like these introduced systematic biases into the probate valuations of individuals with different types of businesses would be worth investigating.

The orthodox view that the wealthiest individuals were the most powerful is also questioned by Rubinstein's study. The problem for this orthodox view is that Rubinstein finds many millionaires who are totally unknown to nineteenth-century historians; the reason for their obscurity could be that they were not powerful. Indeed, Rubinstein dismisses any notion that great wealth had anything to do with entry into the governing elite, as represented by bishops, higher civil servants, and chairmen of manufacturing companies. The only requirements were university attendance and a father with a middle-class income.

Rubinstein, in another study, has begun to buttress his findings about the location of wealth by analyzing income tax returns, which reveal a geographical distribution of middle-class incomes similar to that of wealthy incomes revealed by probate records. But until further confirmatory investigation is done, his claims can only be considered partially convincing.

21. The main idea of the passage is that
   (A) the Marxist interpretation of the relationship between class and power in nineteenth-century Britain is no longer viable
   (B) a simple equation between wealth and power is unlikely to be supported by new data from nineteenth-century British archives
   (C) a recent historical investigation has challenged but not disproved the orthodox view of the distribution of wealth and the relationship of wealth to power in nineteenth-century Britain
   (D) probate records provide the historian with a revealing but incomplete glimpse of the extent and location of wealth in nineteenth-century Britain
   (E) an attempt has been made to confirm the findings of a new historical study of nineteenth-century Britain, but complete confirmation is likely to remain elusive

22. The author of the passage implies that probate records as a source of information about wealth in nineteenth-century Britain are
   (A) self-contradictory and misleading
   (B) ambiguous and outdated
   (C) controversial but readily available
   (D) revealing but difficult to interpret
   (E) widely used by historians but fully understandable only by specialists

23. The author suggests that the total probate valuations of the personal property of individuals holding goods for sale in nineteenth-century Britain may have been
   (A) affected by the valuation conventions for such goods
   (B) less accurate than the valuations for such goods provided by income tax returns
   (C) less, on average, if such goods were tobacco-related than if they were alcohol-related
   (D) greater, on average, than the total probate valuations of those individuals who held bank balances
   (E) dependent on whether such goods were held by industrialists or by merchants or bankers

GO ON TO THE NEXT PAGE.

24. According to the passage, Rubinstein has provided evidence that challenges which one of the following claims about nineteenth-century Britain?
    (A) The distribution of great wealth between commerce and industry was not equal.
    (B) Large incomes were typically made in alcohol and tobacco rather than in textiles and metal.
    (C) A London-based commercial elite can be identified.
    (D) An official governing elite can be identified.
    (E) There was a necessary relationship between great wealth and power.

25. The author mentions that goodwill was probably excluded from the probate valuation of a business in nineteenth-century Britain most likely in order to
    (A) give an example of a business asset about which little was known in the nineteenth century
    (B) suggest that the probate valuations of certain businesses may have been significant underestimations of their true market value
    (C) make the point that this exclusion probably had an equal impact on the probate valuations of all nineteenth-century British businesses
    (D) indicate that expectations about future profit-making is the single most important factor in determining the market value of certain businesses
    (E) argue that the twentieth-century method of determining probate valuations of a business may be consistently superior to the nineteenth-century method

26. Which one of the following studies would provide support for Rubinstein's claims?
    (A) a study that indicated that many members of the commercial elite in nineteenth-century London had insignificant holdings of real property
    (B) a study that indicated that, in the nineteenth century, industrialists from the north of England were in fact a target for working-class people
    (C) a study that indicated that, in nineteenth-century Britain, probate values of goods for sale were not as high as probate values of cash assets
    (D) a study that indicated that the wealth of nineteenth-century British industrialists did not appear to be significantly greater when the full value of their real property holdings was actually considered
    (E) a study that indicated that at least some members of the official governing elite in nineteenth-century Britain owned more real property than had previously been thought to be the case

27. Which one of the following, if true, would cast the most doubt on Rubinstein's argument concerning wealth and the official governing elite in nineteenth-century Britain?
    (A) Entry into this elite was more dependent on university attendance than on religious background.
    (B) Attendance at a prestigious university was probably more crucial than a certain minimum family income in gaining entry into this elite.
    (C) Bishops as a group were somewhat wealthier, at the point of entry into this elite, than were higher civil servants or chairmen of manufacturing companies.
    (D) The families of many members of this elite owned few, if any, shares in iron industries and textile industries in the north of England.
    (E) The composition or this elite included vice-chancellors, many of whom held office because of their wealth.

STOP

IF YOU FINISH BEFORE TIME IS CALLED, YOU MAY CHECK YOUR WORK ON THIS SECTION ONLY. DO NOT WORK ON ANY OTHER SECTION IN THE TEST.

Practice Test 2

Section IV: **Logical Reasoning**

Time—35 minutes
25 questions

Directions: The questions in this section are based on the reasoning contained in brief statements or passages. For some questions, more than one of the choices could conceivably answer the question. However, you are to choose the best answer; that is, the response that most accurately and completely answers the question. You should not make assumptions that are by commonsense standards implausible, superfluous, or incompatible with the passage. After you have chosen the best answer, blacken the corresponding space on your answer sheet.

1. The cafeteria at Acme Company can offer only four main dishes at lunchtime, and the same four choices have been offered for years. Recently mushroom casserole was offered in place of one of the other main dishes for two days, during which more people chose mushroom casserole than any other main dish. Clearly, if the cafeteria wants to please its customers, mushroom casserole should replace one of the regular dishes as a permanent part of the menu.

   The argument is most vulnerable to criticism on the grounds that it fails to consider

   (A) the proportion of Acme Company employees who regularly eat lunch in the company cafeteria
   (B) whether any of the ingredients used in the cafeteria's recipe for mushroom casserole are included in any of the regular main dishes
   (C) a desire for variety as a reason for people's choice of mushroom casserole during the days it was offered
   (D) what foods other than main dishes are regularly offered at lunchtime by the cafeteria
   (E) whether other meals besides lunch are served in the Acme Company cafeteria

2. When old-growth forests are cleared of tall trees, more sunlight reaches the forest floor. This results in a sharp increase in the population of leafy shrubs on which the mule deer depend for food. Yet mule deer herds that inhabit cleared forests are less well-nourished than are herds living in old-growth forests.

   Which one of the following, if true, most helps to resolve the apparent paradox?

   (A) Mule deer have enzyme-rich saliva and specialized digestive organs that enable the deer to digest tough plants inedible to other deer species.
   (B) Mule deer herds that inhabit cleared forests tend to have more females with young offspring and fewer adult males than do other mule deer populations.
   (C) Mule deer populations are spread throughout western North America and inhabit hot, sunny climates as well as cool, wet climates.
   (D) As plants receive more sunlight, they produce higher amounts of tannins, compounds that inhibit digestion of the plants' proteins.
   (E) Insect parasites, such as certain species of ticks, that feed primarily on mule deer often dwell in trees, from which they drop onto passing deer.

3. Genevieve: Increasing costs have led commercial airlines to cut back on airplane maintenance. Also, reductions in public spending have led to air traffic control centers being underfunded and understaffed. For these and other reasons it is becoming quite unsafe to fly, and so one should avoid doing it.

   Harold: Your reasoning may be sound, but I can hardly accept your conclusion when you yourself have recently been flying on commercial airlines even more than before.

   Which one of the following relies on a questionable technique most similar to that used in Harold's reply to Genevieve?

   (A) David says that the new film is not very good, but he has not seen it himself, so I don't accept his opinion.
   (B) A long time ago Maria showed me a great way to cook lamb, but for medical reasons she no longer eats red meat, so I'll cook something else for dinner tonight.
   (C) Susan has been trying to persuade me to go rock climbing with her, claiming that it's quite safe, but last week she fell and broke her collarbone, so I don't believe her.
   (D) Pat has shown me research that proves that eating raw green vegetables is very beneficial and that one should eat them daily, but I don't believe it, since she hardly ever eats raw green vegetables.
   (E) Gabriel has all the qualifications we have specified for the job and has much relevant work experience, but I don't believe we should hire him, because when he worked in a similar position before his performance was mediocre.

GO ON TO THE NEXT PAGE.

4. All people residing in the country of Gradara approve of legislation requiring that certain hazardous wastes be disposed of by being burned in modern high-temperature incinerators. However, waste disposal companies planning to build such incinerators encounter fierce resistance to their applications for building permits from the residents of every Gradaran community that those companies propose as an incinerator site.

Which one of the following, if true, most helps to explain the residents' simultaneously holding both of the positions ascribed to them?

(A) High-temperature incineration minimizes the overall risk to the human population of the country from the wastes being disposed of, but it concentrates the remaining risk in a small number of incineration sites.

(B) High-temperature incineration is more expensive than any of the available alternatives would be, and the higher costs would be recovered through higher product prices.

(C) High-temperature incineration will be carried out by private companies rather than by a government agency so that the government will not be required to police itself.

(D) The toxic fumes generated within a high-temperature incinerator can be further treated so that all toxic residues from a properly operating incinerator are solids.

(E) The substantial cost of high-temperature incineration can be partially offset by revenue from sales of electric energy generated as a by-product of incineration.

5. Elena: While I was at the dog show, every dog that growled at me was a white poodle, and every white poodle I saw growled at me.

Which one of the following can be properly inferred from Elena's statement?

(A) The only white dogs that Elena saw at the dog show were poodles.

(B) There were no gray poodles at the dog show.

(C) At the dog show, no gray dogs growled at Elena.

(D) All the white dogs that Elena saw growled at her.

(E) Elena did not see any gray poodles at the dog show.

Questions 6–7

Derek: We must exploit available resources in developing effective anticancer drugs such as the one made from mature Pacific yew trees. Although the yew population might be threatened, the trees should be harvested now, since an effective synthetic version of the yew's anticancer chemical could take years to develop.

Lola: Not only are mature yews very rare, but most are located in areas where logging is prohibited to protect the habitat of the endangered spotted owl. Despite our eagerness to take advantage or a new medical breakthrough, we should wait for a synthetic drug rather than threaten the survival of both the yew and the owl, which could have far-reaching consequences for an entire ecosystem.

6. Which one of the following is the main point at issue between Lola and Derek?

(A) whether the harvesting of available Pacific yews would have far-reaching environmental repercussions

(B) whether the drugs that are effective against potentially deadly diseases should be based on synthetic rather than naturally occurring chemicals

(C) whether it is justifiable to wait until a synthetic drug can be developed when the capacity for producing the yew-derived drug already exists

(D) the extent of the environmental disaster that would result if both the Pacific yew and the spotted owl were to become extinct

(E) whether environmental considerations should ever have any weight when human lives are at stake

7. Lola's position most closely conforms to which one of the following principles?

(A) Unless people's well-being is threatened, there should be no higher priority than preserving endangered plant and animal populations.

(B) Medical researchers should work with environmentalists to come to an agreement about the rate of the Pacific yew and the spotted owl.

(C) Environmental concerns should play a role in decisions concerning medical research only if human lives are not at stake.

(D) Only medical breakthroughs that could save human lives would justify threatening the environment.

(E) Avoiding actions that threaten an entire ecosystem takes precedence over immediately providing advantage to a restricted group of people.

GO ON TO THE NEXT PAGE.

8. The director of a secondary school where many students were having severe academic problems impaneled a committee to study the matter. The committee reported that these students were having academic problems because they spent large amounts of time on school sports and too little time studying. The director then prohibited all students who were having academic problems from taking part in sports in which they were active. He stated that this would ensure that such students would do well academically.

   The reasoning on which the director bases his statement is not sound because he fails to establish that

   (A) some students who spend time on sports do not have academic problems
   (B) all students who do well academically do so because of time saved by not participating in sports
   (C) at least some of the time the students will save by not participating in sports will be spent on solving their academic problems
   (D) no students who do well academically spend time on sports
   (E) the quality of the school's sports program would not suffer as a result of the ban

9. It can safely be concluded that there are at least as many trees in Seclee as there are in Martown.

   From which one of the following does the conclusion logically follow?

   (A) More trees were planted in Seclee in the past two years than in Martown.
   (B) Seclee is the region within which Martown is located.
   (C) Martown is suffering from an epidemic of tree-virus infection.
   (D) The average annual rainfall for Seclee is greater than the average annual rainfall for Martown.
   (E) The average number of trees cut down annually in Martown is higher than in Seclee.

Questions 10–11

A distemper virus has caused two-thirds of the seal population in the North Sea to die since May 1988. The explanation for the deaths cannot rest here, however. There must be a reason the normally latent virus could prevail so suddenly: clearly the severe pollution of the North Sea waters must have weakened the immune system of the seals so that they could no longer withstand the virus.

10. The argument concerning the immune system of the seals presupposes which one of the following?

    (A) There has been a gradual decline in the seal population of the North Sea during the past two centuries.
    (B) No further sources of pollution have been added since May 1988 to the already existing sources of pollution in the North Sea.
    (C) There was no sudden mutation in the distemper virus which would have allowed the virus successfully to attack healthy North Sea seals by May 1988.
    (D) Pollution in the North Sea is no greater than pollution in the Mediterranean Sea, off the coast of North America, or in the Sea of Japan.
    (E) Some species that provide food for the seals have nearly become extinct as a result of the pollution.

11. Which one of the following, if true, most strongly supports the explanation given in the argument?

    (A) At various times during the last ten years, several species of shellfish and seabirds in the North Sea have experienced unprecedentedly steep drops in population.
    (B) By reducing pollution at its source, Northern Europe and Scandinavia have been taking the lead in preventing pollution from reaching the waters of the North Sea.
    (C) For many years, fish for human consumption have been taken from the waters of the North Sea.
    (D) There are two species of seal found throughout the North Sea area, the common seal and the gray seal.
    (E) The distemper caused by the virus was a disease that was new to the population of North Sea seals in May 1988, and so the seals' immune systems were unprepared to counter it.

GO ON TO THE NEXT PAGE.

12. It is clear that none of the volleyball players at yesterday's office beach party came to work today since everyone who played volleyball at that party got badly sunburned and no one at work today is even slightly sunburned.

    Which one of the following exhibits a pattern of reasoning that most closely parallels that in the argument above?

    (A) Since everyone employed by TRF who was given the opportunity to purchase dental insurance did so and everyone who purchased dental insurance saw a dentist, it is clear that no one who failed to see a dentist is employed by TRF.

    (B) Since no one who was promoted during the past year failed to attend the awards banquet, evidently none of the office managers attended the banquet this year since they were all denied promotion.

    (C) Since the Donnely report was not finished on time, no one in John's group could have been assigned to contribute to that report since everyone in John's group has a reputation for getting assignments in on time.

    (D) Everyone with an office on the second floor works directly for the president and, as a result, no one with a second floor office will take a July vacation because no one who works for the president will be able to take time off during July.

    (E) Since all of the people who are now on the MXM Corporation payroll have been employed in the same job for the past five years, it is clear that no one who frequently changes jobs is likely to be hired by MXM.

<u>Questions 13–14</u>

The dean of computing must be respected by the academic staff and be competent to oversee the use of computers on campus. The only deans whom academics respect are those who hold doctoral degrees, and only someone who really knows about computers can competently oversee the use of computers on campus. Furthermore, the board of trustees has decided that the dean of computing must be selected from among this university's staff. Therefore, the dean of computing must be a professor from this university's computer science department.

13. Which one of the following is an assumption on which the argument depends?

    (A) Academics respect only people who hold doctoral degrees.

    (B) All of this university's professors have obtained doctoral degrees.

    (C) At this university, every professor who holds a doctoral degree in computer science really knows about computers.

    (D) All academics who hold doctoral degrees are respected by their academic colleagues.

    (E) Among this university's staff members with doctoral degrees, only those in the computer science department really know about computers.

14. Which one of the following statements, if true, would weaken the argument?

    (A) There are members of this university's staff who hold doctoral degrees and who are not professors but who really know about computers.

    (B) There are members of this university's philosophy department who do not hold doctoral degrees but who really know about computers.

    (C) Computer science professors who hold doctoral degrees but who are not members of this university's staff have applied for the position of dean of computing.

    (D) Several members of the board of trustees of this university do not hold doctoral degrees.

    (E) Some members of the computer science department at this university are not respected by academics in other departments.

GO ON TO THE NEXT PAGE.

Questions 15–16

Consumer advocate: Under the current absence of government standards for food product labeling, manufacturers are misleading or deceiving consumers by their product labeling. For example, a certain brand of juice is labeled "fresh orange juice," yet the product is made from water, concentrate, and flavor enhancers. Since "fresh" as applied to food products is commonly understood to mean pure and unprocessed, labeling that orange juice "fresh" is unquestionably deceptive.

Manufacturer: Using words somewhat differently than they are commonly used is not deceptive. After all, "fresh" can also mean never frozen. We cannot be faulted for failing to comply with standards that have not been officially formulated. When the government sets clear standards pertaining to product labeling, we will certainly comply with them.

15. On the basis of their statements above, the consumer advocate and the manufacturer are committed to disagreeing about the truth of which one of the following statements?
    (A) In the absence of government standards, common understanding is the arbiter of deceptive labeling practices.
    (B) Truthful labeling practices that reflect common standards of usage can be established by the government.
    (C) The term "fresh" when it is applied to food products is commonly understood to mean pure and unprocessed.
    (D) Terms that apply to natural foods can be truthfully applied to packaged foods.
    (E) Clear government standards for labeling food products will ensure truthful labeling practices.

16. Which one of the following principles, if established, would contribute most to a defense of the manufacturer's position against that of the consumer advocate?
    (A) In the absence of government definitions for terms used in product labeling, common standards of understanding alone should apply.
    (B) Government standards for truthful labeling should always be designed to reflect common standards of understanding.
    (C) People should be free, to the extent that it is legal to do so, to exploit to their advantages the inherent ambiguity and vagueness in language.
    (D) When government standards and common standards for truthful labeling are incompatible with each other, the government standards should always take precedence.
    (E) In their interpretation of language, consumers should never presume that vagueness indicates an attempt to deceive on the part of manufacturers unless those manufacturers would reap large benefits from successful deception.

17. Certain items—those with that hard-to-define quality called exclusivity—have the odd property, when they become available for sale, of selling rapidly even though they are extremely expensive. In fact, trying to sell such an item fast by asking too low a price is a serious error, since it calls into question the very thing—exclusivity—that is supposed to be the item's chief appeal. Therefore, given that a price that will prove to be right is virtually impossible for the seller to gauge in advance, the seller should make sure that any error in the initial asking price is in the direction of setting the price too high.

    The argument recommends a certain pricing strategy on the grounds that
    (A) this strategy lacks a counterproductive feature of the rejected alternative
    (B) this strategy has all of the advantages of the rejected alternative, but fewer of its disadvantages
    (C) experience has proven this strategy to be superior, even though the reasons for this superiority elude analysis
    (D) this strategy does not rely on prospective buyers' estimates of value
    (E) the error associated with this strategy, unlike the error associated with the rejected alternative, is likely to go unnoticed

GO ON TO THE NEXT PAGE.

18. In order to control the deer population, a biologist has proposed injecting female deer during breeding season with 10 milligrams of a hormone that would suppress fertility. Critics have charged that the proposal poses health risks to people who might eat the meat of treated deer and thereby ingest unsafe quantities of the hormone. The biologist has responded to these critics by pointing out that humans can ingest up to 10 milligrams of the hormone a day without any adverse effects, and since no one would eat even one entire deer a day, the treatment would be sale.

    The biologist's response to critics of the proposal is based on which one of the following assumptions?

    (A) People would be notified of the time when deer in their area were to be treated with the hormone.
    (B) The hormone that would be injected into the deer is chemically similar to hormones used in human contraceptives.
    (C) Hunting season for deer could be scheduled so that it would not coincide with breeding season.
    (D) The hormone in question does not occur naturally in the female deer that would be injected.
    (E) Most people do not consider deer meat to be part of their daily diet and eat it only on rare occasions.

19. A recent survey conducted in one North American city revealed widespread concern about the problems faced by teenagers today. Seventy percent of the adults surveyed said they would pay higher taxes for drug treatment programs, and 60 percent said they were willing to pay higher taxes to improve the city's schools. Yet in a vote in that same city, a proposition to increase funding for schools by raising taxes failed by a narrow margin to win majority approval.

    Which one of the following factors, if true, would LEAST contribute to an explanation of the discrepancy described above?

    (A) The survey sample was not representative of the voters who voted on the proposition.
    (B) Many of the people who were surveyed did not respond truthfully to all of the questions put to them.
    (C) The proposition was only part of a more expensive community improvement program that voters had to accept or reject in total.
    (D) A proposition for increasing funds for local drug treatment centers also failed to win approval.
    (E) The proposition to raise taxes for schools was couched in terminology that many of the voters found confusing.

<u>Questions 20–21</u>

So-called environmentalists have argued that the proposed Golden Lake Development would interfere with bird-migration patterns. However, the fact that these same people have raised environmental objections to virtually every development proposal brought before the council in recent years indicates that their expressed concern for bird-migration patterns is nothing but a mask for their antidevelopment, antiprogress agenda. Their claim, therefore, should be dismissed without further consideration.

20. Which one of the following questionable argumentative techniques is employed in the passage?

    (A) taking the failure of a given argument to establish its conclusion as the basis for claiming that the view expressed by that conclusion is false
    (B) rejecting the conclusion of an argument on the basis of a claim about the motives of those advancing the argument
    (C) using a few exceptional cases as the basis for a claim about what is true in general
    (D) misrepresenting evidence that supports the position the argument is intended to refute
    (E) assuming that what is true of a group as a whole is necessarily true of each member of that group

21. For the claim that the concern expressed by the so-called environmentalists is not their real concern to be properly drawn on the basis of the evidence cited, which one of the following must be assumed?

    (A) Not every development proposal opposed in recent years by these so-called environmentalists was opposed because they believed it to pose a threat to the environment.
    (B) People whose real agenda is to block development wherever it is proposed always try to disguise their true motives.
    (C) Anyone who opposes unrestricted development is an opponent of progress.
    (D) The council has no reason to object to the proposed Golden Lake Development other than concern about the development's effect on bird-migration patterns.
    (E) When people say that they oppose a development project solely on environmental grounds, their real concern almost always lies elsewhere.

GO ON TO THE NEXT PAGE.

22. Psychologists today recognize childhood as a separate stage of life which can only be understood in its own terms, and they wonder why the Western world took so long to see the folly of regarding children simply as small, inadequately socialized adults. Most psychologists, however, persist in regarding people 70 to 90 years old as though they were 35 year olds who just happen to have white hair and extra leisure time. But old age is as fundamentally different from young adulthood and middle age as childhood is—a fact attested to by the organization of modern social and economic life. Surely it is time, therefore, to acknowledge that serious research into the unique psychology of advanced age has become indispensable.

Which one of the following principles, if established, would provide the strongest backing for the argument?

(A) Whenever current psychological practice conflicts with traditional attitudes toward people, those traditional attitudes should be changed to bring them in line with current psychological practice.

(B) Whenever two groups of people are so related to each other that any member of the second group must previously have been a member of the first, people in the first group should not be regarded simply as deviant members of the second group.

(C) Whenever most practitioners of a given discipline approach a particular problem in the same way, that uniformity is good evidence that all similar problems should also be approached in that way.

(D) Whenever a society's economic life is so organized that two distinct times of life are treated as being fundamentally different from one another, each time of life can be understood only in terms of its own distinct psychology.

(E) Whenever psychologists agree that a single psychology is inadequate for two distinct age groups, they should be prepared to show that there are greater differences between the two age groups than there are between individuals in the same age group.

23. Sabina: The words used in expressing facts affect neither the facts nor the conclusions those facts will support. Moreover, if the words are clearly defined and consistently used, the actual words chosen make no difference to an argument's soundness. Thus, how an argument is expressed can have no bearing on whether it is a good argument.

Emile: Badly chosen words can make even the soundest argument a poor one. After all, many words have social and political connotations that influence people's response to claims expressed in those words, regardless of how carefully and explicitly those words are defined. Since whether people will acknowledge a fact is affected by how the fact is expressed, the conclusions they actually draw are also affected.

The point at issue between Emile and Sabina is whether

(A) defining words in one way rather than another can alter either the facts or the conclusions the facts will justify

(B) a word can be defined without taking into account its social and political connotations

(C) a sound argument in support of a given conclusion is a better argument than any unsound argument for that same conclusion

(D) it would be a good policy to avoid using words that are likely to lead people either to misunderstand the claims being made or to reason badly about those claims

(E) a factor that affects neither the truth of an argument's premises nor the logical relation between its premises and its conclusion can cause an argument to be a bad one

GO ON TO THE NEXT PAGE.

24. Most disposable plastic containers are now labeled with a code number (from 1 to 9) indicating the type or quality of the plastic. Plastics with the lowest code numbers are the easiest for recycling plants to recycle and are thus the most likely to be recycled after use rather than dumped in landfills. Plastics labeled with the highest numbers are only rarely recycled. Consumers can make a significant long-term reduction in the amount of waste that goes unrecycled, therefore, by refusing to purchase those products packaged in plastic containers labeled with the highest code numbers.

Which one of the following, if true, most seriously undermines the conclusion above?

(A) The cost of collecting, sorting, and recycling discarded plastics is currently higher than the cost of manufacturing new plastics from virgin materials.

(B) Many consumers are unaware of the codes that are stamped on the plastic containers.

(C) A plastic container almost always has a higher code number after it is recycled than it had before recycling because the recycling process causes a degradation of the quality of the plastic.

(D) Products packaged in plastics with the lowest code numbers are often more expensive than those packaged in the higher-numbered plastics.

(E) Communities that collect all discarded plastic containers for potential recycling later dump in landfills plastics with higher-numbered codes only when it is clear that no recycler will take them.

25. Despite a steady decrease in the average number of hours worked per person per week, the share of the population that reads a daily newspaper has declined greatly in the past 20 years. But the percentage of the population that watches television daily has shown a similarly dramatic increase over the same period. Clearly, increased television viewing has caused a simultaneous decline in newspaper reading.

Which one of the following, if true, would be most damaging to the explanation given above for the decline in newspaper reading?

(A) There has been a dramatic increase over the past 20 years in the percentage of people who tell polltakers that television is their primary source of information about current events.

(B) Of those members of the population who do not watch television, the percentage who read a newspaper every day has also shown a dramatic decrease.

(C) The time people spend with the books and newspapers they read has increased, on average, from 1 to 3 hours per week in the past 20 years.

(D) People who spend large amounts of time each day watching television are less able to process and remember printed information than are those who do not watch television.

(E) A typical television set is on 6 hours a day, down from an average of 6 1/2 hours a day 5 years ago.

STOP

IF YOU FINISH BEFORE TIME IS CALLED, YOU MAY CHECK YOUR WORK ON THIS SECTION ONLY. DO NOT WORK ON ANY OTHER SECTION IN THE TEST.

Practice Test 2

Writing Sample

SIGNATURE _______________ / / ____
DATE

LSAT WRITING SAMPLE TOPIC

The English department at Corbett University must choose a text for the college's first-year composition course. Write an argument in favor of selecting either of the following texts with these considerations in mind:

- The department has a strong commitment to teaching basic writing skills, such as grammar and essay organization.
- The department wants to increase the students' enthusiasm for and interest in writing.

During the three years that the department has used The Standard Textbook of English, instructors in other departments have reported significant improvement in students' writing skills. Nicknamed "The Best and the Dullest," the text contains classic essays from both ancient and modern authors and is organized to illustrate the various forms of the essay—such as narration, exposition and persuasion. The essays average more than 10 pages, and almost all are written in a formal style. While students find some of the subjects foreign, they feel the materials covered are often useful in their other coursework.

A new text, *The Modern Writer*, contains both an introduction describing the basics of grammar and a number of journalistic essays by contemporary authors. The pieces are typically short (only 2 to 3 pages) and explore topics of interest to most college students, such as popular music and career planning. The style of the essays tends to be informal, even colloquial. Each chapter contains several essays on a given topic and exercises designed to aid students in developing essays of their own. Although the introduction provides an adequate overview of basic grammar, the text does not discuss the essay form.

GO ON TO THE NEXT PAGE.

STOP

IF YOU FINISH BEFORE TIME IS CALLED, YOU MAY CHECK YOUR WORK ON THIS SECTION ONLY. DO NOT WORK ON ANY OTHER SECTION IN THE TEST.

Practice Test 2: **Answer Key**

Section I Logical Reasoning		Section II Analytical Reasoning		Section III Reading Comprehension		Section IV Logical Reasoning	
1.	D	1.	D	1.	D	1.	C
2.	A	2.	B	2.	A	2.	D
3.	A	3.	D	3.	D	3.	D
4.	C	4.	D	4.	A	4.	A
5.	C	5.	A	5.	E	5.	C
6.	C	6.	C	6.	B	6.	C
7.	C	7.	B	7.	A	7.	E
8.	B	8.	B	8.	D	8.	C
9.	D	9.	D	9.	B	9.	B
10.	B	10.	A	10.	A	10.	C
11.	B	11.	B	11.	B	11.	A
12.	E	12.	E	12.	C	12.	D
13.	D	13.	C	13.	C	13.	E
14.	B	14.	C	14.	D	14.	A
15.	A	15.	E	15.	E	15.	A
16.	B	16.	B	16.	B	16.	C
17.	B	17.	D	17.	D	17.	A
18.	E	18.	D	18.	A	18.	D
19.	E	19.	B	19.	C	19.	D
20.	B	20.	E	20.	B	20.	B
21.	D	21.	D	21.	C	21.	A
22.	A	22.	B	22.	D	22.	D
23.	E	23.	E	23.	A	23.	E
24.	B	24.	C	24.	E	24.	C
25.	B			25.	B	25.	B
				26.	D		
				27.	E		

Answers and Explanations

SECTION I: LOGICAL REASONING

1. D

Sounds like a paradox to be reconciled—the language is a bit unusual, but the task is the same as in any other Paradox question. The first thing you need to do is identify what seems to be wrong, and the language of the stimulus makes that easy—the word "Paradoxically" in the final sentence points to the apparent contradiction. The best surgeon has the worst fatality record. Why might that be?

Perhaps you were able to prephrase a specific answer here; if not, you at least should have gone into the choices with a clear idea of the seeming inconsistency, along with a general notion of what would clear it up: something that makes it understandable that the surgeon considered the best can also be the one who loses the most patients. (D) serves this purpose: The fact that the chief surgeon gets the hardest cases, the ones that entail "the greatest risk to life," explains why he may lose the most patients without suffering damage to his reputation.

(A) would explain why the administrators would praise the chief surgeon to the heavens even if he were a bumbling fool, but that's not what you're looking for. You need to show how the administrators' claim could be *correct*—that the chief surgeon is the best they've got, despite the fact that he loses the most patients.

(B) provides info on how the chief became the chief, but doesn't touch on the mystery at hand.

(C) Training in what—how to kill people? There's nothing about the chief's training activities that lends a clue as to why so many of his patients don't pull through despite his great skill.

(E) The hospital is looking up! Still, this doesn't solve the paradox, which has nothing to do with any comparison between this chief and the last one. The fact that you don't know the perceived skill level of the previous chief surgeon doesn't help matters either.

- Try to stay one step ahead of the game. The question stem doesn't confirm that you're dealing with a Paradox question, but strongly suggests it. Reconciling things or disposing of an "apparent discrepancy" is the action of the typical Paradox question. Approach the stimulus as you would any other paradoxical situation; see what's the big surprise, and consider ways in which it may not be so odd after all.
- It helps to restate the paradox to yourself as a means of testing the choices. Ask yourself "if he's the best, why does he lose the most patients?" Follow that up with "because he trained some younger surgeons on the staff," (C), or "hey, you should have seen the *last* guy," (E). Huh? Viewed in this context, these choices are clearly irrelevant. They don't answer the question at hand.

2. A

What's assumed? Find the evidence and the conclusion, and think about what's necessary to connect them. You can dispose of all the numbers and figures as you reduce the argument down to its basics: Because the average number of citations is down in a later period as compared to an earlier period, the agency that issues the citations must be easing up. Does something seem odd about that? Aren't there other possibilities? Maybe the companies are simply cleaning up their act and not engaging as much in the activities that would warrant citations? The author, though, assumes that there are no other possible explanations. Otherwise, how would she jump to the conclusion that the government office is more lax in enforcing the laws based simply on the decrease of citations? This argument works only if the decrease in citations was not caused by something else. That's what you get in (A).

(B) The issue of minor violations is outside the scope of this argument, which deals with a change in the number of citations for *serious* violations.

(C) Why the government office is supposedly more lax regarding this matter is never explored; you're told only that it is. Like (B), the issue dealt with here (reasons for the change in policy) is outside the scope—you're only concerned with *whether* enforcement policies have become more lax.

(D) This choice is prescriptive, which rules it out as a possible assumption. The author merely states a fact (the decrease) and infers a conclusion based on that fact. Nothing about what the office should or should not do plays into the argument. The argument is not lacking a mandate regarding the maximum number of citations the office should issue.

(E) is outside the scope. What happened *before* 1971 takes you beyond the relevant time frame here.

- The key to successful paraphrasing is getting rid of as much wording as you can. Boil the argument down to its essence. The fact that the author is talking about citations for violations of drug promotion laws issued by a government agency is largely ornamental; the same logic could have appeared in a stimulus about a decrease in failing grades issued by a teacher. Zero in on the logic of the various stimuli, and you'll begin to recognize logical patterns that will be of great help on test day.
- If you can determine that a choice is outside the scope of the argument, you can be sure that that choice need not be assumed in order for the argument to work.

3. A

Tim's argument is a counterargument—a response to Sheila's statement—and you're asked to spot where Tim goes wrong. Sheila cites an argument that's familiar to you all from the sides of cigarette boxes: smoking over time may be dangerous to one's health. Tim begs to differ, and you wait with bated breath to see how Tim can make such a sweeping statement as "smoking has no effect on health at all."

Enter Grandpa who, according to Tim, smoked like a fiend since an early age but died at the ripe old age of ninety-six. There's plenty to prephrase here: Maybe Tim's grandfather was severely ill his whole life as a result of smoking; the evidence Sheila cites doesn't say smoking will kill people at an early age, only that it will make them unhealthy. More blatantly, however, you may have noticed how Tim overlooks the qualified nature of Sheila's statement—long-term smoking is "very likely" to cause health problems, which doesn't mean that every single person who smokes for years will become ill. Surely, the single case of Tim's grandfather cannot counter the reasonably qualified position of the experts; even a few thousand such exceptions among the millions who smoke are not inconsistent with their view. Using bigger words, (A) describes the failure of Tim's counterargument. "Very likely" from the stimulus matches up with "probabilistic," while grandpa is the "single counterexample."

(B) It doesn't matter that the experts don't know about the specific good fortune of Tim's grandfather; they're probably aware themselves of smokers who don't follow the pattern they outline. But even if they're not, the real problem is that Tim's evidence is simply not sufficient to counter the experts' general proposition, not that the experts are unaware of the example he uses.

(C) is just not there: In neither argument do you hear of any exceptions to the experts' position that would possibly discount Tim's evidence in advance.

(D) If anything, Tim assumes that there *is* a connection between longevity and health. By citing the case of his grandfather, he's implying that grandpa's ripe old age indicates that he was a healthy long-term smoker. This implication is a large part of his attempt to rebut the experts' claim.

(E) Tim never addresses the method by which the experts achieved consensus on this issue. His argument deals only with their specific claim, and in no way assumes anything about how they came to settle on that claim. For all it matters to Tim's argument, the experts may have formulated their opinion as a group.

- Prephrase answers whenever you can—and in argument-based questions that should be most of the time. Evaluating each answer choice should be a last resort.

4. C

Next you're asked to recognize how the author makes her point—a Method of Argument question. An example (the French Revolution) is cited as evidence for a claim (the positives of revolutions outweigh the negatives). *"but . . ."* —and you know enough of this contrast keyword to anticipate where things are going from here—the example isn't a good one: other circumstances made it easy for France to avoid the disruptions typical of revolutions. What these other circumstances are you really needn't worry about at this point, because you know from reading the stem that answering the question may not require this specific information. In fact, all you need to grasp is the general structure just mentioned above to at least eliminate a handful of choices and zero in on the winner. Take the choices in order and match each one to the structure you've discerned thus far:

(A) The claim that societies get more good than bad out of revolutions is merely supported by one example that the author believes doesn't make the case. The author says that the evidence doesn't adequately support the conclusion; she doesn't argue or demonstrate that the argument is internally inconsistent.

(B) The first half is believable, if you take "a particular position" to mean the notion that the claim cited in the first sentence may not be true. But are "general principles" used to support this position? No. Very specific evidence regarding societal realities of the French Revolution are presented to refute what is "typically regarded as the best evidence" for the claim.

(C) Is the author opposed to the claim? She certainly seems to be, although she may not state her opposition outright. But she does go to great lengths to knock out the evidence by arguing that using the case of the French Revolution to support the claim is misguided. France's "unique advantage," bureaucratic stability, is her evidence that Revolutionary France is not a good example with which to support the claim. If you knock out the best evidence for a claim, you undermine the claim as well. All of which matches the strategy in (C).

(D) There is no "series" of persuasive examples used to make the author's case. Dismissing the main example in support of the claim argued against is more like it.

(E) What two positions? There's only one claim here, there's no comparison per se, and there's nothing pertaining to strengths and weaknesses (the "strengths" part may be a distortion of the notion of France's "unique advantage"). (E) is far from the method employed here.

- In Method of Argument questions, you must switch gears and concern yourself less with the specifics and more with the mechanics of the argument. Try to paraphrase the argument in general terms as you go along; that will make it easier to deal with the kind of abstract answer choices that often accompany MOA questions.
- "Internally inconsistent" doesn't simply mean "bad"—it means that the argument contains contradictory premises. The author doesn't make that case here, even though she does strongly suggest that the claim doesn't hold water.

5. C

Although the format of the question is a little odd, you're just looking for a missing piece of evidence. The stem tells you that the conclusion you're looking to support is that the number of adolescent boys with asthma is approximately equal to the number of adolescent girls with asthma. What evidence do you already have to support that idea? Asthma is twice as likely to strike boys than girls in kids under ten, and boys are less likely to outgrow it. Yet the percentages of boys and girls with asthma equal up around adolescence, because that's when a lot of girls develop the disease.

Now, you're looking for a piece of information that would allow you to conclude that the *number* of cases of asthma of adolescent boys and girls is roughly the same. Notice how you're jumping from evidence regarding percentages to a conclusion regarding raw numbers. To argue that the fact that the same percentage of two groups share a characteristic means that the same *number* in each group share that characteristic, it must be assumed that the number of people in each group is roughly identical.

Try some numbers: Say that 50% of the adolescent boys and 50% of the adolescent girls have asthma. But if there are 50 million girls in this group and only 20 million boys, then it can't be claimed that the actual number of cases in each group is equal too. If (C) is true—if the number of adolescent boys is roughly the same as the number of adolescent girls in the population—then and *only* then would it be valid to conclude that the number of adolescent boys and girls with asthma is roughly equal, based on the fact that their *percentages* are equal.

(A) and (D) How people *get* asthma is irrelevant to the numbers/percentages issue. You're concerned here with the issue of how many people in a certain age group have asthma, not with how people get or don't get the disease, so these choices don't help you form the conclusion called for in the stem.

(B) You're concerned with the tally of *adolescents* with asthma. The info in (B) is far removed from this.

(E) offers an irrelevant comparison between asthmatic adults and adolescents. But again, the argument specifically centers on a comparison between two groups of adolescents, and adults have nothing to do with this.

- Use the stem to direct your attack on the question—which includes the decision to put it off until later if you so choose. It's obvious from the stem that this is another question involving numbers, and if you've determined that these aren't your strong suit, don't hesitate to put it off based on the stem alone.
- The jump from percentages to numbers always entails the danger of distortion; take special care to think about the raw numbers that determined the percentages in the first place. Percentage info may be totally misleading, depending on the numbers that make them up—and the test makers often take

advantage of that fact. Take, for example, the cited fact that boys under ten are twice as likely as girls under ten to get asthma. But what if there are ten times more girls than boys in this age group? Even though boys are more *likely* victims, the raw numbers would strongly suggest that there are actually more girls in this age group with asthma than boys.

6. C

A rare full-named character makes an appearance in this one: Poet Harry Trevalga claims that none of the poems he submitted was published due to a vengeful editor's jealousy over Harry's winning a prize she thought she deserved. "No way!" says the publisher: All the submissions are anonymous to the editor, so she couldn't have even known which poems were his. You're looking for an assumption underlying the publisher's response, and again, you may have been able to prephrase something here. What if there's some other way the editor could have known which poems were his? Certainly some poets have distinctive styles, right? This would surely sink his rebuttal, so he must be assuming that there is no other way she could possibly recognize his work. (C) states this assumption.

(A) Grudge or no grudge, the basis of the publisher's response is that the editor couldn't have unfairly dismissed Trevalga's work even if she tried. She can despise him for winning the award for all the publisher cares; his defense lies in another arena.

(B) Whether or not Trevalga's case is *typical* is beside the point, since the point at issue is the possibility of discrimination against his work.

(D) weakens the publisher's argument by suggesting that other factors (e.g., the "I hate you because you won the award that should have been mine!" factor) besides merit may come into play. It would be better for the publisher's argument to reassure Harry that merit, and only merit, is the deciding factor in choosing poems to publish.

(E) Since the poems are judged without names, nothing need be assumed about what name Trevalga may have used. The publisher's whole point is that names are irrelevant, implying that Harry got dinged simply because his poems don't make the grade.

7. C

The stem tells you you're looking for a weakener, so you can attack the stimulus looking for gaps between the evidence and the conclusion. First the study itself (evidence): Researchers compared the death rates of people who live near nuclear weapons plants with the death rates of people who live in areas without these plants. The researchers concluded that, because there was no difference in *death rates*, radiation from nuclear weapons plants poses no *health hazards* to people who live near them. (C) explains that exposure to radiation can cause health problems that won't necessarily kill you, which weakens the argument by demonstrating that equal death rates don't mean equal health.

(A) talks about nuclear power plants, which are beyond the scope. This study is only concerned with nuclear *weapons* plants.

(B) raises the issue of death rates, information that might even *strengthen* this specious argument by giving more information to imply that nukes don't cause deaths.

(D) The number of areas with nuclear weapons plants is pretty much outside the scope, and only serves to strengthen the idea that you shouldn't worry about these plants. (D) is no weakener.

(E) goes beyond the scope as well. The researchers' conclusion is only pertinent to people living near nuclear weapons plants, and so (E)'s reference to an additional study can't weaken the self-contained conclusion of this argument.

- Always pay attention to the scope of the conclusion, and note when the author makes extreme claims like "nuclear weapons plants pose no health hazards at all." Such conclusions are hard to support and easy to weaken. In this stimulus—and in many stimuli—the scope of the evidence is much narrower than what's claimed in the conclusion.

8. B

The question stem tells you you're looking for an inference about a particular kind of liver cell. People used to think that cells would divide forever, on into infinity, but it's been discovered that normal cells have a limit on the number of times they can divide. The author then brings up the example of a normal human liver cell, which divides 60 times, before stopping forever. Even if this kind of cell is frozen, you're told, it will pick up where it left off if thawed, and, no matter what, it will only divide 60 times. You're asked about a hypothetical liver cell that divides *more* than 60 times. What do you know? Normal human liver cells only divide 60 times, so this cell can't be both normal and human. And thus (B) leaps up and begs to be chosen as the choice that this cell can't be.

(A), (C), (D), and (E) are all outside the scope. You only know about normal human cells. But (A) refers to an abnormal cell, and (C), (D) and (E) refer to nonhuman cells. Since such cells don't fall under the limitations posed by the stimulus, any of them could have divided over 60 times.

- The whole question is largely a matter of scope. The scope of the author's inquiry is normal human liver cells, only; notice how all of the other choices are outside this scope.

9. D

The stem says you need to make an inference, but tells you nothing more. Keep that in mind as you go through the stimulus. Hmm, milk trends. The LSAT occasionally has these "as one goes up, the other goes down" questions, and if you have trouble following upward and downward trends you should skip such questions at first, and come back if you have time. That said, the only logical attack is to plunge in with care—breaking it down into manageable chunks.

First of all, people complain that milk bottlers take huge markups on the bottled milk they sell to consumers. According to the author, these complaints are most likely to arise when they are least warranted (or deserved) considering the spread between the price bottlers pay for raw milk and the price they charge the consumer for the bottled milk. Well, when do these complaints occur? When the bottled milk price rises. That makes sense, right? The consumer sees the expensive milk on the shelf, and complains.

But according to the author, these increases just reflect the rise in the price of raw milk. At this point, the time of the most complaints, the spread between the raw milk price and the bottled milk price is actually the smallest. So the bottlers are making less money on the deal, even though the consumers are complaining the most. Yet when the raw-milk price is falling, the bottlers make the most money, since the spread is greater. What can you infer from all of this? If the bottlers make more money, and have a greater spread, or markup, when the raw-milk price is down, then you must infer that milk bottlers don't immediately lower the price of bottled milk in a corresponding amount when the raw milk price goes down. This is what (D) says.

(A) It needn't be true that consumers are actually paying more for milk when raw-milk prices fall. All you know is that bottlers don't lower the price to reflect the drop in raw-milk price—the price could stay the same, or even be lowered slightly but not proportionately to the drop in raw-milk prices.

(B) brings in dairy farmers, who are way beyond the scope, so you needn't assume anything about how their costs might affect the price of tea in China, or milk in Kansas, or whatever.

(C) Since you're only given information about circumstances when prices rise and fall, you can't make any inferences about extended periods of time.

(E) again goes outside the scope with dairy farmers, about whom nothing can be inferred.

- An inference must be true based on the stimulus. Don't pick a choice like (A) that is merely plausible or even probable. If it *could* be false, it's wrong.

10. B

The author claims that *if* the library shared by Redville and Glenwood were relocated from central Redville to central Glenwood, *then* a larger number of library users would be within walking distance of the library. Well, first of all, realize that, although the two buildings are described by terms such as "overcrowded" and "larger," the conclusion is not based on these characteristics—it's only based on the number of people who will be within walking distance of the building.

Moving on, the evidence provided is that there are many more people living in central Glenwood than in central Redville, and most people will walk to the library only if it's near their house. To strengthen the argument, you need to fill in a missing piece. There are more people living in central Glenwood than in central Redville, but you don't know anything about the area of either city. If Glenwood has more people but they're spread out over a larger area, then maybe moving the library won't place it within walking distance for more people. So it would be to the argument's advantage to show that the two areas are around the same size. (B) says just this, supporting the argument by making its evidence even more relevant.

(A) Where the library *was* doesn't help convince you that the library should either move or stay where it is. The library's previous location is outside the scope.

(C) You're only concerned with how accessible the library will be for walkers, so the size of the building is outside the scope. This could be a tempting choice for the test taker who didn't clearly break down evidence and conclusion, since size and overcrowding is mentioned in the stimulus.

(D) Since you're concerned with people who can walk to the library, (D)'s mention of people who don't live in either town can neither strengthen nor weaken this argument.

(E) If people currently walk farther than standard walking distance, then perhaps the new library will cater to these people more readily. But you can't assume that, because you don't know where they're walking *from*; (E) is too vague to have any effect on the argument.

- To strengthen an argument, look to bolster an assumption in that argument. If you can fill in a missing piece, you've made the argument stronger.

11. B

Now you must weaken the same argument, which, you'll recall, says that if the library were moved to Glenwood, it would be within walking distance of a larger number of library users. But what the evidence actually told you was that it would be in walking distance of more *people*. That doesn't mean that all, or even most, of these people are library users. If (B) were true—if there are fewer potential library users in central Glenwood than there are now in central Redville, then the claim that moving the library would put it within walking distance of more library users would be substantially weakened. Its main assumption would be torn down. So (B) is correct.

(A) It makes sense that, since the library's now in Redville, more Redvillians than Glenwoodians are walking there. The choice doesn't say anything about the *potential* number of walking users if the library were moved, so it's no weakener.

(C) has it backward. The prediction that library use would grow after the Glenwood move tends to strengthen, not weaken the argument.

(D) mentions non-walking library users, which is outside the scope of the argument. Knowing that some people drive or ride to the library has no impact on the different potential for *walking* library users after a change in library location.

(E) doesn't affect the numbers you're concerned with—those library users who will be able to walk to the library before and after the proposed move.

- Some LSAT arguments contain more than one weakness. Here, for example, the strengthener and weakener picked up on different assumptions. So it's not always possible to precisely prephrase a strengthener or weakener. But you can still spot either one by analyzing the connection between evidence and conclusion.

12. E

As should be clear from the question stem, you're looking for an assumption. The author tells you that light utility trucks are now popular, and that consumers like their rugged looks. The trucks, however, are exempt from safety standards for roof strength and resistance to impact. That's the evidence, and the conclusion is that, in a serious, high-impact crash, a driver of a light utility truck is more likely to be hurt than is a driver of a car that must meet the government safety standards.

So what's the author assuming? Well, for the likelihood of injury to be higher, the actual roof strength and resistance to impact for the trucks would have to be lower than that of cars that fall under government regulation. In order to draw her conclusion, then, the author would have to assume that the trucks wouldn't meet the standards required of those cars. This is what (E) tells you.

(A) is clever but outside the scope. You needn't assume that there *are* any safety standards for light utility trucks—all you know is that the trucks are exempt from certain standards that apply to cars. Whether these trucks have any safety standards besides the ones mentioned doesn't play into the argument.

(B) goes way too far. The author doesn't talk at all about the likelihood of accidents, which is implied here by the idea of reckless driving. She only discusses the likelihood of injuries *if* an accident happens to occur.

(C) makes the same insinuations as (B), but again you have no reason to believe that the trucks have more accidents than do cars or other kinds of vehicles. Even if that's false, the argument could *still* be viable—it's all about what will happen *if* accidents occur.

(D) mentions the power of the trucks' engines, which is beyond the scope here. There's absolutely no reference to engine power, stated or implied. Remember, an assumption is something that the author must be taking for granted as true. No way is the author counting on the trucks' being "deceptively rugged."

13. D

A Weaken question, so you have to identify evidence and conclusion. The keywords, "It is clear, therefore" point you right to the conclusion—CXC has increased in virulence over the past five years. What's the evidence? Five years ago, during the first outbreak of a cattle disease called CXC in North America, the death rate was 5 percent of all reported cases. Today though, the death rate of all reported cases is over 18 percent. The author attributes this increase in death rate to increased virulence, but is it the only possible explanation?

No...the author assumes that increased virulence is the cause, and overlooks the possibility that there's some other reason the numbers are increasing. (D) explains that farmers can now treat mild cases of CXC but don't bother reporting them. If this were true, then there would be fewer mild cases in the pool, and so it would be more likely that a reported case would be a fatal one. That's another explanation for the increased reported death rate, and thus weakens the author's conclusion that CXC became more virulent in the last five years.

(A) If it were true that many recent CXC deaths were attributed to another disease, then there would be *even more* recent fatalities from CXC than the author assumes. This would be a strengthener, not a weakener!

(B) also tends to strengthen the argument, by claiming that many deaths reported to be CXC five years ago were actually caused by something else. Again, that would imply that the fatality group five years ago was even smaller.

(C) The question is whether you can conclude based on these statistics that CXC has become more virulent over the past five years. The inoculation program has nothing to do with the strength of the disease, and so can't weaken (or in any way impact) the argument.

(E) is outside the scope, since information about survivors won't affect the disease pool. There's no way to tell how and if these survivors would have any impact on the data here.

- Many LSAT questions concern percents, but don't get caught up in the numbers. Many are more manageable when you consider alternative possibilities.

14. B

Questions 14 and 15, an Inference and a Method of Argument respectively, have the same stimulus. And for all its length and variety of jargon, this one is really not so tough if you break it down. Some people, namely policymakers, think that the country needs a higher level of personal savings if continued economic growth is to be assured. And a certain plan would let people have savings accounts in which the interest would be tax-exempt until money is withdrawn from the account.

The people who support that proposal claim that it would increase personal savings, giving banks more money to loan, and not costing the government much in lost taxes. The down side, the author explains, is that when this kind of plan was tried in the past, almost all the money that went into these tax-deferred accounts came out of other kinds of accounts. Do you see that? People just *moved* their money—they didn't put *more* money in.

For question 14, you have to draw a conclusion from all this. The author presents a plan to make personal savings more desirable and thus stimulate growth, but then explains that, when similar programs were tried in the past, they were unsuccessful. What's the next step? That this program probably won't be successful either! Since no distinction is made between this program and those that took place in the past, why should this one succeed? Choice (B) outlines this conclusion quite nicely. The proposed plan, just like the others, probably won't attract enough savings to make up for the loss in taxes.

(A) brings up the backers' motives—you don't have any information about their motives in the stimulus, and so can't draw any conclusions about them.

(C) distorts the terms in the passage, trying to link lost taxes to increased savings in a way that the author never does. The plan calls for increasing savings while not losing much in taxes. The author believes this won't work, period—there's no way to conclude that a *different* program, one that resulted in lots of lost taxes, would result in higher savings.

(D) you have no reason to believe that the economy is on the verge of disaster. The only thing you know is that some policymakers think that, for continued growth, more savings are needed. If anything, the allusion to "continued" economic growth indicates that the economy is *not* currently in trouble.

(E) is out in left field as well, since you can't conclude that there's *no* effective way that the government can influence savings. You just know that *this* plan probably won't work. Other plans that might be more effective go unmentioned.

- Choices that question arguers' motives are almost never correct on the LSAT.
- Beware of answer choices that are too extreme. The author here merely suggests that this plan won't work because similar programs didn't achieve the desired result. (B)'s "is *unlikely* to attract..." fits this tone perfectly. (A)'s "undoubtedly," (D)'s "*will* be in danger," and (E)'s "*no* effective means..." are all too extreme.

15. A

You're not done—you still have a Method question to dispose of. How does the author criticize the program? Well, she shows that the overall level of personal savings probably won't change, considering past programs' rate of success. If the level won't change, then the loss in taxes won't be compensated for. Since the planners are counting on a rise in savings, you can say that the author shoots down the main support for the plan. Phrased a little differently, (A) says just this: She challenges the premise—the idea of a rise in savings—on which the plan is based.

(B) There's no disagreement expressed here, since you only know about the plan of certain policymakers. The author doesn't point out any opposing views among this group, so (B) is out.

(C) is tempting because it reflects the tone of the author's pessimism, but it's not the *implementation* that she sees as impossible, but the possible inefficacy of a plan based on a shaky premise.

(D) also tries to lead you into temptation by mentioning "past cases." But it's not that the backers approved the plans that didn't work—there's no evidence that these particular folks were involved with those plans at all. Although the author uses the unsuccessful programs to point out the potential failure of the program in question, no one is questioning the judgment of the proposal's backers.

(E) is way off: The author only has a problem with this particular program, since she believes that it won't be successful. The author never disputes the *necessity* of a program to boost personal savings.

- Stick to the basic facts in a Method of Argument question. Here, some people believe something is necessary. The author never disputes this—goodbye (E). They propose a plan, but similar plans didn't work in the past. Did *these* particular people advocate these past plans? No way to tell: goodbye (D). Nowhere is any disagreement among the policymakers brought up, so (B) is out as well. So three of the five choices simply conflict with the basic structure of the passage. The good critical reader should be able to narrow this one down to (A) and (C) fairly readily.

16. B

Find the conclusion, then search for the argument with a parallel conclusion. It's also possible to begin with the evidence, but in this and many similar questions, the conclusion is the simplest piece, so it's the easiest to match up.

Looking at the stimulus, you see that the conclusion is "some birds do not fly." Pretty clear. All the rest of the information is just backing this up by explaining that, though all birds have feathers and wings, some birds use them for different purposes. Find the parallel.

(A) compares ancient philosophers with modern biologists, discussing their goals for study. There's no comparison in the stimulus conclusion, so you can eliminate this one.

(B) The word "therefore" is a great structural signal telling you that a conclusion is coming. There you find "not all chairs are used for sitting in." This could be rephrased as "Some chairs are not used for sitting in" and that's parallel to "some birds do not fly." Keep it and check the remaining conclusions—if you're left with more than one answer choice, you can check the evidence and find that this argument has the same kinds of evidence, giving examples of chairs that aren't used for sitting. Furthermore, "seat" and "support" match up perfectly with "feathers" and "wings" as two characteristics of the respective categories (chairs and birds). (B) is parallel and correct.

(C) Two things are in the same category—no "some are not." Eliminate.

(D) A comparison between two things—eliminate.

(E) A distinction between two things—not a match. That eliminates all but (B), and you'll never even have to look at the evidence.

- Parallel Reasoning questions can be time consuming, but a methodical, piece-by-piece approach will increase your speed and your accuracy.

17. B

The next two questions share a dialogue stimulus. The first is a Point at Issue question, and in order to answer it, you have to find the answer choice that is addressed by both speakers and about which their positions conflict.

(A) There's no discussion whatsoever of rock, iron, bronze, etcetera—neither speaker takes a position, so this one's out.

(C) There's no debate at all about the dating of the tools—it's the attribution of the tools to a certain group of people that's in question. Eliminate.

(D) Jones talks about when these peoples must have migrated, but Smith doesn't mention it at all—eliminate.

(E) brings up Smith's evidence. Well, all Smith says is that the tools in question were found in peat bogs where wood doesn't decompose as fast as in regular soils. Neither one raises the question about whether the tools are dated correctly in the first place.

- In Point at Issue questions, the correct answer will be 1) an issue that both speakers address; and 2) an issue on which they have *different* opinions. Take this methodical approach to the answer choices.

18. E

You need to find Smith's method of argument—the way in which she responds to Jones. She says that Jones' evidence is unconvincing, and points out that Jones has based his argument on the lack of wooden tools dating before 13,000 years ago. Jones has assumed that, because these tools weren't found, they never existed. Smith blows this apart by pointing out the soil problem, thus attacking Jones' major assumption. This is best expressed in (E).

(A) Smith doesn't cite any studies at all in her retort.

(B) Smith doesn't think that Jones is misrepresenting the scientists' position; she's just unconvinced by Jones' argument.

(C) is a little tricky, because Smith does dispute the accuracy of Jones' argument, but it's not the supporting evidence that's in question—it's the validity of Jones' assumption that the tools in question didn't exist.

(D) says that Smith accuses Jones of a self-contradiction, but if that were the case you'd hear Smith say, "Your evidence proves just the opposite point."

- Many Method of Argument choices provoke the "huh?" response. If you see a choice that seems out of left field, just cross it off with confidence. Don't waste time re-reading the stimulus and never bend over backward for an answer choice. Look for the one that is unquestionably correct.

19. E

Next up is a classic Inference question—"if this is true, then what else must be true?"—and the stimulus is set up in standard if/then format: *If* universities were living up to their moral and intellectual responsibilities, *then* the bestsellers in college bookstores wouldn't be fluff like *TV Today* and *Gossip Review*. The contrapositive is: If the best-selling publications in most university bookstores ARE *TV Today* and *Gossip Review*, then some of this country's universities **must not be** fulfilling their moral or intellectual responsibilities.

With that in mind, you can move to the second sentence of the editorial, and look!—that's just the first part of the contrapositive you just created. Well, if all this must be true, then you need the choice that completes that contrapositive, (E)—some of the universities aren't meeting their moral responsibilities or their intellectual responsibilities.

(A) talks about individuals who read these publications, while the stimulus focuses on universities, so (A) needn't be true.

(B) goes too far, because the author is concerned that these publications are *bestsellers*, not that they are stocked in the first place.

(C) would like to fool you into thinking that, because in most university bookstores *Gossip Review* and *TV Today* sell better than any other publication, most purchasers in all university bookstores must buy one of those two. Not necessarily! It's possible that most people who buy books at university bookstores purchase *neither* of the two, while the number of people who *do* buy these is large enough to make these the bestsellers.

(D) is hopelessly vague—you don't even know for sure that the people who are buying this trash from university bookstores are people who attend these schools. Also, (D) is much like (A) in that it focuses on individuals rather than on universities, and nothing about individuals need be true in this context.

- When confronted with an if/then statement, stop to think through the contrapositive, and you'll be well on your way to answering the question.

20. B

It's another two-question stimulus for questions 20 and 21, the fourth one in this section, and for this one you have two very different question stems. The former is a tangled and wordy one, asking you to find the principle involved, while the latter is a straightforward Flaw stem.

Speaker Saunders starts by telling you about last week's neighborhood meeting, at which everyone agreed about a certain problem—a row of abandoned houses was a threat to the safety of the community. Saunders goes on to say that no one disputes that the problem has now gone away: since the houses have been torn down, there's no more problem. The stimulus gets a little thornier here, as Saunders goes on to explain that *some* people thought that the buildings, which were in pretty good shape, shouldn't be demolished, since the city had a fund that would help people who need housing to buy and fix up buildings like the ones in question. Saunders then concludes that, since the demolition was so successful in eradicating the problem, those who favored it must be right, and those who opposed it must be wrong.

Question 20 is a somewhat unusual Principle question—you're asked for a principle that would resolve the issue either way, not simply support one conclusion or outcome. That means detailed prephrasing isn't realistic—you'll probably have to check each answer choice. Carefully compare the actual facts as laid out by Saunders to the wording in each choice:

(A) explains that, in this kind of dispute, the plan that results in the most housing for people should be adopted. Okay, that means the opponents' proposal, right? But wait, there's more. (A) goes on to say that this is true *unless* the building is a threat to safety. Well, these buildings were a threat!—and you have no way of knowing whether they would continue to be a threat after the renovation; (A) thus gives you no clear option as to what should be done in this circumstance, so it can't be the principle you seek.

(B) says that when there are two proposals to solve a community problem, and when only one of them would preclude trying the other, then the one that doesn't close off the other possibility should be adopted. This seems like the perfect choice. You know that demolishing the buildings precluded trying the other plan—rehabilitating the buildings. So, according to this principle, the neighborhood should have adopted the opponents' plan and tried to rehabilitate the buildings—if that had failed, *then* the wrecking ball could be called in. (B) provides a coherent plan that allows you to resolve the conflict, and so it's correct.

(C) leaves you hanging, as (A) did. Yes, the opponents' plan calls for government funding, so by that token the demolition plan should be chosen. Yet you know that the government funds for these projects *have* been secured. So, again, the evil "unless" eliminates this choice.

(D) tells you that the neighborhood can't choose demolition until all other possibilities have been investigated. Well, you don't know if *all* other plans were looked into, so (D) won't let you choose demolition, yet it also doesn't give you any clue about whether the opponents' plan should have been adopted or not. Too vague.

(E) says that no proposal should be chosen merely because of a majority opinion favoring that proposal. Well, the majority favored demolition, and so this principle tells you that the buildings shouldn't be demolished on this ground alone. You don't know anything about how a decision *can* be made from this principle—just how it *can't* be.

- Section management strategies are crucial on the LSAT. Look at the length of this one: Between the stimulus, the long and complicated stem, and the lengthy choices, it takes up an entire side of the page! Skip it temporarily if it intimidates you—some test takers preferred to tackle the shorter and simpler question 21 first. Look to take control of the test in every possible way you can.

21. D

So what's the flaw? Saunders claims that, since the demolition strategy worked, those who favored it must be right and those who opposed it must be wrong. But he doesn't consider the idea that the opposing plan might *also* have worked—maybe it would even have worked *better* given a chance. He doesn't even try to show that the demolition plan was the only alternative; he neglects the possibility that the opposing plan, if adopted, might have also solved the safety problem. Saunders supplies no evidence against the opposing plan, as (D) correctly points out, so it's premature for him to declare the rehab proponents wrong.

(A) You don't know what kind of scare tactics Saunders and his buddies may have used in the actual meeting, but these aren't a factor in this argument, which comes after the fact.

(B) has more to do with the opposing side. In order for the rehab folks to fully make their case, *they* would eventually have to establish that there were eligible people interested in participating in the program. Saunders, however, certainly doesn't need to furnish this kind of information.

(C) You know that there *was* some vocal public dissent, and Saunders doesn't try to pretend that there wasn't. He makes no claim of "universal public support."

(E) Everyone agreed that the houses were a safety threat, and the specific nature of the danger isn't part of the dispute between the demolition supporters and the opposing faction. Saunders need not elaborate on this.

- Don't fault the author for not supplying info that's not directly relevant to the issue at hand. The flaw must relate to something that's central to the argument.
- When an author or speaker claims "these people are wrong," he or she must supply evidence for this assertion. Here, Saunders pronounces the rehab supporters wrong simply based on the success of the demolition plan. He needs more ammo than that, as (D) rightfully points out.

22. A

The stem asks for the claim most strongly supported by the stimulus. The author begins by explaining that, for the creators of the name "feudalism," the existence of a noble class was essential for the very existence of feudalism. The author goes on to explain that there can't be a noble class unless the titles that indicate superior status as a noble and the inheritance of those titles are both sanctioned by law. Next you're told that feudalism existed in Europe as early as the eighth century, even though it wasn't until the twelfth century that the inheritance of noble titles was recognized by the law.

This is pretty bizarre: Feudalism apparently existed in the eighth century even though legal recognition of title inheritance—one of the conditions of a noble class, and by extension feudalism—didn't happen until the twelfth century. Something doesn't match up, but it's not easy to prephrase a proper inference here. You have to go to the choices.

(A) is a valid inference; it plays off of the discrepancy in the dates cited in the stimulus. If feudalism requires the existence of a noble class, then history is distorted, since feudalism did exist before the twelfth century, but not in the terms of the definition given. The definition must therefore be inappropriate, which is essentially what (A) says.

(B) There *was* a dominant class before the twelfth century under some definitions, even though the class in question doesn't live up to the nobility definition.

(C) confuses the idea of legal status—it's not that these "nobles" were legally but not socially noble; it's that they couldn't live up to the definition posed by those who invented the name "feudalism."

(D) There's no causation implied in the relationship between the decline of feudalism and the rise of nobility. The author mentions the correlation only to point out the gap in the definition of feudalism from an historical perspective.

(E) has it all backward: The definition in the stimulus says that nobility must exist before feudalism can exist, while (E) says the opposite.

- Pay attention when the author defines terms. When that happens, the definition will usually be the key to the question.

23. E

You're asked to find the flaw, so begin with evidence and conclusion. Mayor Smith, in the past, has opposed nuclear power plant projects, and the record shows that her decisions have been informed and consistent. The mayor has now shown support for building a nuclear power plant in Littletown. According to the author, if someone like Mayor Smith with a past anti-nuke record now thinks that a nuclear power plant is okay, you should believe that the plant will be safe and should be built. But where's the evidence? There are no studies to show that it'll be safe, or even profitable, or efficient, or anything. All you know is that, if Mayor Smith thinks it's okay, then it's okay with the author. (E) picks up on the lack of relevant evidence, so it's correct.

(A) You know that Mayor Smith, the subject of the argument, spoke out against nukes in the past, and so you needn't consider a lack of information about people who don't speak out to be a flaw in this argument—they're outside the scope of the stimulus.

(B) implies that the author is assuming that Mayor Smith must know everything about the technical details of the power plant for her to make decisions about it. You have no reason to believe that the author thinks this—she could have well-informed advisors, or this could simply be an uninformed decision. It's all based on the mayor's reputation, so (B) is not a good critique.

(C) The author claims that Smith's opposition in the past was outspoken, consistent, and informed, and that's all she needs to say on the matter. She need not establish that consistent and outspoken opposition *always* leads to informed opposition.

(D) goes too far, since the author doesn't bring up any other issues—her argument is confined to the power plant. Although this choice does touch on the idea of an appeal to authority, it pushes the idea too far.

- Your practice with LR questions should make you pretty sensitive to the kinds of evidence that authors put forth, as well as when evidence is faulty and when no evidence is given at all. The fact that someone favors a position does not, by itself, constitute evidence. Why does the good mayor here favor the plants now when she was vehemently opposed to them in the past? A good question—and one the author conveniently sidesteps.

24. B

Next up is an advertisement-type stimulus that appears occasionally on the LSAT—this one for a car, the impressive-sounding SKX Mach-5. According to the ad, you are defined by your car in today's society. The message sent by this car—call it the Mach for short—is that its owner is Dynamic, Aggressive, and Successful. That's the main premise here, and the ad concludes with a typical Madison Avenue tagline: "Shouldn't you own one?"

This is essentially a formal logic statement hidden in casual language: If one owns a Mach, then one declares oneself dynamic, aggressive, and successful. What must be true based on this information? Choice (B), which tells you that a person who is *not* dynamic and successful would be misrepresenting himself or herself by owning a Mach. To own a Mach-5 when you're a sluggish, passive flop would *certainly* be misrepresentation, according to the logic of the ad.

(A) *could* be true, but it needn't be so. If one owns a Mach, then one must be pronouncing oneself dynamic, aggressive, and successful. Whether one actually *is* these things or is misrepresenting oneself, as (B) suggests, is another story. But of course there are all the non-Mach owners, who could easily pronounce themselves, and actually be, any combination of those adjectives, or none of the above. So (A) is far from inferable.

(C) Mach owners must be stating that they're "Aggressive," with a Capital A, but are not necessarily more aggressive than owners of other cars.

(D) is like (C)—you don't know about any other cars; as far as you know, other cars announce the success of their owners too.

(E) is concerned with most people recognizing that Mach owners are dynamic, aggressive, and successful, but you can't infer this from the ad. Just because Mach owners announce their traits through their car doesn't mean they actually possess those traits or, if they do, that they're apparent to almost everyone.

- If the statements in the stimulus can be translated into if/then format, inference questions become more manageable. Then the contrapositive can yield the answer, or at least get you one step closer.

25. B

For this Parallel Reasoning question, apply the Kaplan "compare the conclusions" strategy. First of all, you're told that the great universities in medieval times endured for centuries, and they had no administrators. The university in question has tons of administrators, and the university's in bad financial shape. So, concludes the author, you should get rid of the administrators to ensure that the university will endure.

Hmm. Sounds like correlation mistaken for causation. Who's to say that a lack of administrators was the *reason* that the great medieval universities endured? The best way to start to seek a parallel to this flawed argument is to look for a parallel to the conclusion, in the form of "You should (strong recommendation)."

If you eliminate choices with this in mind, only (B), (D), and (E) are possible. Choice (A) concludes with "Jet engines aren't necessary," and (C) concludes with "new methods of control are needed." Both of these are ruled out by their conclusions, which are more statements of fact than strong recommendations. And actually, (D) isn't so great either—while it does include the word "should," determining how something should be considered is more of a value judgment than the kind of direct recommendation found in the original. So you're down to (B) and (E) without even considering the evidence.

(B) commits the same correlation-causation flaw as the original argument. The author of (B) makes it seem as if the computer is the magic element in the novelist's success, just as the lack of administration "caused" the medieval universities to endure. In both cases, it's argued that mimicking the successful element will lead to success in a different case, but both ignore the fact that these elements may not in fact *cause* these successes. (B) it is.

(E) doesn't contain the correlation-causation idea, since there's no plan to change a bad situation by copying a different situation. The recommendation in (E) is actually a reasonable one, given the evidence in the first sentence.

- The correlation/causation flaw shows up in many question types. Be dubious of all claims of causation, or situations in which a belief in causation is clearly implied. When the author concludes or implies that A caused B, consider the possibility that B caused A, that some other factor caused both, or that they're simply correlated with no causal relationship at all.

SECTION II: ANALYTICAL REASONING

Game 1—Gymnastic Schedule

The Action

"Weekly schedule" is a sure sign of sequencing, and indeed, you are mainly concerned with ordering students throughout a five-day period from Monday through Friday. One small wrinkle, though: There are six students for the five days, so exactly one day will get two students, whose sessions will be "separate but consecutive." This two-student day lends a very small grouping element to the game, but so small in fact that we'll just consider this to be a standard sequence with a minor twist. If you took a peek at the rules, you'd notice that all but the last deal with typical sequencing concerns.

The Initial Setup

No great difficulty picturing this setup; simply get the days of the week and students down on the page and you're ready to see what the rules have in store for the aspiring gymnasts: ("No days free" is a good reminder of the stipulation in the intro paragraph that aside from the double-student day, the coach meets with exactly one student each day.)

H I K O U Z

_ _ _ _ _
M T W Th F

NO DAYS FREE

The Rules

2) No reason not to jump right to the most concrete rule of the bunch: Student I is on Thursday, so build that right into the sketch.

1) Standard sequencing fare: H . . . Z should help you to remember this. You should make a mental note, however, that due to the slight wrinkle (the two-student day), this rule does not necessarily imply that H's session will be on an earlier day of the week than Z's. It must come "some time before," which leaves open the possibility that H can be the first student of the two-student day with Z's lesson later that day.

3) Here's the more standard adjacency type of sequencing rule that you're used to: K and O must fall on consecutive days of the week, in either order. KO or OK will remind you of this.

4) Monday and Wednesday will have one student, so the two-student day will be Tuesday, Thursday, or Friday.

Deductions

Not much to combine here, is there? Notice that no entity appears in more than one rule, a fact that makes it less likely that a big deduction will exist. Trying out a few scenarios leads to the conclusion that the possibilities are not very limited thus far, which means that the best bet is to move right on to the questions.

The Final Visualization

This contains all that we'll take with you into the questions:

H I K O U Z

_ _ _ *I* _
M T W Th F
(1) (1)
H...Z
KO or OK
NO DAYS FREE

- Before you jump into the rules in the order given on the page, scan them for something concrete to build into your sketch. Sometimes, having something definite down on the page will make the more abstract rules easier to handle.
- The action of the game informs how the rules play out, which is why the first step in tackling a Logic Game is to determine the game action and note the limitations it implies. Rule 1 must be properly understood in the context of *this* game, which includes one two-person day; it would mean something else in a standard sequencing scenario in which this wrinkle didn't exist.
- Critical reading is crucial in Logic Games. They may not sound much different, but the phrases "some time before" in Rule 1 and "the day immediately before or after" in Rule 3 mean very different things. As noted above, the former allows for sessions on the same day, while the latter does not.
- Always turn negatives into positives. You're less interested in where things are *not* than where they *must* or *could* be.

- It's worthwhile noticing which entities are unrestricted. Here, U has no limitations, and is therefore the "floater." Often, such an entity will be used to shore up an ordering while the other entities are behaving as prescribed.

The Questions

1. D

The game gets off to a nasty start with this "could be true" question—with no big deductions at your disposal, there's not much to do but try out the choices. You could postpone this one for later, hoping to see a pair among the choices show up together on Tuesday in another question, but that's not all that likely, so you may as well simply get to it. First, you can check to see if any choices directly violate a rule, and in fact (C) does—Rule 3: K and O, scheduled for immediately consecutive days, can never be on the same day. It would nice if a choice contained I who must be on Thursday, but no such luck, so from here you'll just have to test the remaining choices:

(A) Can H and U pair up on Tuesday? Nope—that leaves no room for the KO bloc. With H and U taking up the double day, there's no way to get K and O on consecutive days without doubling up somewhere else. And that means that *any* pair that doesn't include either K or O for Tuesday will result in the same violation. This insight effectively eliminates (B) and (E), and you've already axed (C) for the reason stated above, so (D) must be correct. If you test it out, you'll see that

```
KOH  IZ

M  T  W  Th  F
   U
```

is a valid ordering, confirming (D) as the pair that could be scheduled for Tuesday.

- You need to bring an arsenal of strategies to bear on the Logic Games section. You'll sometimes have to resort to your second or third preferred option in tackling a question (testing out choices is pretty low on the list because it can be time intensive), but even then a little thinking on your feet can go a long way. Here, you considered postponing the question, and decided against it. Then you tried to kill a few choices directly, but only eliminated one. Then you resigned yourself to simply testing out the remainders, but noticed something in the process of testing out (A) that allowed you to eliminate all the others as well. You may not have followed this exact path, but the point should be clear: Good LG test takers have, and employ, many weapons.

2. B

K is on Tuesday, so get that into a new sketch. Not much to work with, but the question's specificity tells you where to go next—find the earliest spot for Z. The earliest day is Monday, and while Rule 1 would allow H and Z on Monday (as long as H went first), Rule 4 forbids it—the double-student day can't be Monday. What about Tuesday for Z? No problem there:

```
M  T  W  Th  F
H  K  O  I   U
   Z
```

This ordering takes care of the stem and satisfies all the rules, proving that Tuesday, (B), is the earliest day for Z under these circumstances.

- When asked for the earliest day for some event, start with the earliest day possible and work your way up. When asked for the latest, or biggest, or the maximum, etc. in any situation, start up top and work your way down. This approach saves time.

3. D

Ouch. A non-if "must be true" question is perfectly welcome when there's a big deduction up front, but what must be true here given no new information? Nothing, really, except maybe something negative like "Z cannot be scheduled for Monday"—but the choices here are all themselves hypotheticals.

This is a great question to leave for last, though the task is made a little easier by using work from the previous two questions. The schedule you formed in question 2 allows you to axe (E)—there you see that U can be on Friday while Z need not be on Thursday. And the schedule you created in question 1 shows that U and O could both be on Tuesday, effectively killing (B). The rest, however, you'll have to work out:

(A) If U is on Monday, does H have to be on Tuesday? The test is to see whether you can place H on some other day. And you can: If K and O are on Tuesday and Wednesday (in either order), then H can be on Thursday with Z on Friday. So (A) need not be true.

(C) With U on Wednesday, K and O can take Monday and Tuesday, leaving H and Z for Thursday and Friday, respectively. So U on Wednesday does not force Z into Tuesday, and you can cross off (C).

(D) is all that's left, so it must be correct. For the record: With U on Thursday, the KO pair must be scheduled during two consecutive days between Monday and Wednesday. To get H before Z, H must take the leftover day before Thursday while Z is slotted for Friday.

- Always refer back to your previous work when asked about what could be true. In this case, you may have even held off on question 3 until you got a few more orderings under your belt from questions 4 and 5. An excellent idea, which unfortunately wouldn't have helped in this case, as the orderings created in those questions don't allow you to eliminate any further choices here. But the thought is correct, and the goal of this kind of practice is to form good habits by test day.

4. D

This requires some trial and error, but a little cleverness makes the job easier. You're asked to find the day for Z that would fix U's position in the schedule. The shortcut here is to recognize that the end of the week will probably pose more restrictions given the fact that I is already placed on Thursday. Testing out Z on those days at the end, you'll find that Thursday, (D), is indeed the spot for Z that would fix U's time slot as well: If Z is on Thursday with I, then the double-student day is used up. The adjacent KO bloc will have to fall on consecutive days between Monday and Wednesday (in either order), and H's session must also be before Thursday to satisfy Rule 1.

Either way, U is the only student left for Friday. All of the other choices leave U an option of at least two days in the ordering. (Note: If you started testing from the beginning, you would have noticed, as you pointed out above in question 2, that Z can never be scheduled for Monday. If Z's on Monday, then H would have to come before Z on Monday (Rule 1), setting up a situation that would violate Rule 4.)

- Remember your arsenal of strategies? Here's another example of good question strategy that the better LG test takers try to employ. If you have no other choice but to try out choices, see whether some choices are more likely candidates than others, and jump right to those first. It won't always work, but here that strategy is rewarded. You're looking for a situation that will fully restrict U's placement, so you may as well gravitate toward the part of the schedule that's most restricted *to begin with*; and that's the area around I.

5. A

You get some info to work with here, but once again you're faced with the prospect of testing out various scenarios. The schedule from question 1 applies, as H's session could be immediately after U's in that one, but unfortunately none of the choices conform to that schedule. And there's not even a likely candidate here as in the previous question, so you really have no choice but to try 'em out. Luckily, (A) comes through as the winner, as illustrated by the following schedule:

M	T	W	Th	F
U	H	Z	I	O
				K

There are other ways to space out Z, K, and O from the middle to end of the week, but all you need is one instance that works with respect to H and U to choose (A) for this "could be true" question. As for the rest:

(B) With U doubling up with I on Thursday, it's not possible to put H on Friday and still have H's session before Z's (Rule 1). Sure, you could put Z later on Friday, but then you'd have two two-student days, in violation of the numbers rule in the intro.

(C) Scheduling both H and U on Tuesday causes the same problem you saw back in question 1—there would be no way to place the consecutive KO pair without doubling up somewhere else.

(D) With I already on Thursday (Rule 2), placing this pair there would result in three Thursday students. No good.

(E) If H and U were on Friday, then Rule 1 would force Z onto Friday's roster as well, overburdening the poor coach with three Friday lessons. Again, no good.

- In a "could be true" question, as soon as you've found a scenario that works, circle it and move on. But if you're not sure whether an option will work, don't waste time testing it out until you've checked to see which choices can be readily eliminated.

Game 2—Parking Lot Lights

The Action

Lighting the parking lot—that's your job here. A picture is provided, illustrating the location of eight lights around a square lot. And what exactly are you called on to do? It's nothing fancy; you're simply to decide whether each light is on or off. Some understood this game action to be similar to that of a grouping game of selection—each light being either in or out, on or off. If that conception helped you, great. You can just as easily group this one in the "oddball" category—a spatial arrangement game with a selection element.

The Initial Setup

There's nothing initially to draw; your best bet is to work off the picture on the page. There's plenty of room on the bottom of the page to recreate the square when necessary. But it's worth deciding at this point how you're going to indicate whether a light's on or off. A simple but effective solution is to circle a number whose light is on and put an X through a number whose light is off.

The Rules

2) No reason not to jump to the simplest and most concrete rule of the bunch: Light 8 is on. Circle it.

1) This one needs some interpretation. "At least one of any three consecutively numbered lights is off." First of all, what are consecutively numbered lights? Well, there's no special definition provided, so lights 1, 2, and 3, for example, or 6, 7, 8. All this rule tells you is that if any consecutive trio of lights like these are all on, that's a violation. In other words, if lights 2 and 3 are on, then 1 and 4 must be off.

But wait a minute: What about the trio 7, 8, 1, or 8, 1, 2? The lights in each of these trios are physically adjacent to one another in the picture, but certainly wouldn't be considered "consecutively numbered." It's a good question, but this possible slight ambiguity is taken care of by Rule 3. In the meantime, your task is to represent the rule on the page. Perhaps you came up with "NO 3 CONSEC ON" or something to that effect that will enable to you to quickly access this restriction.

3) The safest way to handle Rule 3 is to first translate it into if/then form: "IF 1 ON, THEN 2 OFF AND 7 OFF." Did you work through the contrapositive? "IF 2 OR 7 OR BOTH ON, THEN 1 OFF." Get both down on your page.

As just mentioned, this rule turns the possible ambiguity alluded to above into a moot point: Since 1 and 2 can never be on at the same time, and 1 and 7 can never be on at the same time, you don't have to worry about the trios 8, 1, 2 and 7, 8, 1. The test makers probably didn't mean for these to qualify as "consecutively numbered" trios, but Rule 3 makes the issue irrelevant.

4) "AT LEAST ONE ON EACH SIDE" captures the gist, although as shorthand it's not much shorter than the original. You may have simply chosen to remember this rule, or circle it on the page. If you were unsure of the meaning, again, try out an example. Lights 5, 6, and 7, for example—the three south-side lights—cannot all be off. If two of them are off, then the other one must be on. The west side, of course, automatically satisfies this rule thanks to Rule 2's illumination of light 8.

5) This requires care as well: If a side has exactly one light on, then it has to be the middle light. Perhaps another quick example is in order to clarify this: Light 5 cannot be the only illuminated light on the south side; *that* would violate this rule. Again, the shorthand is a little problematic; there's just no really concise way to say this. Come up with some written way to express this, or commit it to memory, or circle it on the page. Here, just say "IF EX 1 ONE ON, THEN MIDDLE." As long as you know what the rule *means*, you'll be okay.

6) Finally, a rule that's a little more specific than some of the previous ones—two northern lights are on, which means two out of the trio 1, 2, 3. And that, thankfully, leads you right to a big deduction. Did you see it?

Deductions

Hopefully upon registering the final rule you asked yourself "which two can they be?" 1 and 2? Nope—Rule 3 forbids it. Which means you're talking either 1 and 3, or 2 and 3. One of those pairs of northern lights must be on to satisfy Rule 6. In either case, **light 3 must be on** and one of the questions, question 7, is answered already. Circle light 3 in your master sketch, and you're ready to roll.

The Final Visualization

You can redraw the sketch as needed, when new information arrives. But expect to be able to get some quick points simply by referring to the master sketch created around the picture on the page:

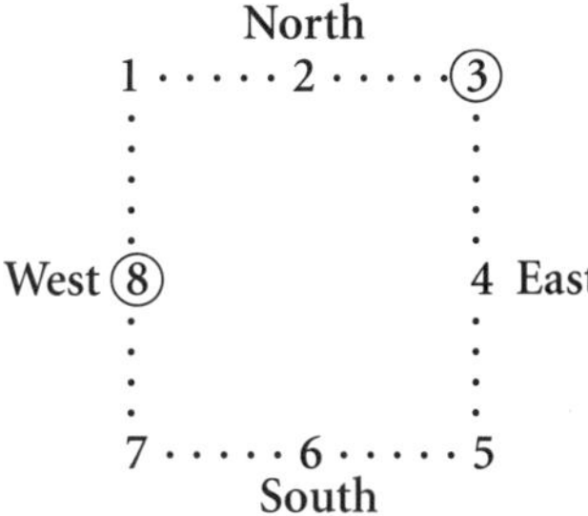

No 3 Consecutive On	
If 1 On	*2 off and 7 off*
If 2 or 7 both On	*1 off*
At least one on each side	
If Ex 1 On	*Middle*

The Big Picture

- How do you know when to postpone a game for later in the section? Many factors play into this decision.
  - Certainly when the action is unfamiliar and seems unmanageable, that's a good reason to hold off. This game may be a little unusual, but the action is fairly straightforward—turning lights on or off.
  - Another factor in postponing is the nature of the rules: Are they complex or straightforward? Wordy or concise? Difficult or easy to shorthand? The rules in this game seem to fall more into the difficult category, although some test takers who handled them okay found the questions fairly manageable.
- In this section, most found Game 3 simpler than this one, but Game 4 more difficult. If you skipped this game to get to the basic sequencing Game 3 (or better yet, if you jumped right to Game 3 to lead off the section), then you're doing the right thing in taking control of the test.
- Sometimes, the easiest way to grasp an abstract rule is to think through examples that would violate it. This is a good way to come to terms with what a difficult rule really means.
- Some games contain rules that just aren't all that amenable to shorthand. Try your best to capture the gist of each such rule in some form, or, if need be, simply circle the rule on the page.

The Questions

6. C

Shouldn't have had much trouble here if you used the Kaplan Method for this Acceptability question. Rule 2 is the easiest to check—light 8 must be included in any "complete and accurate" list of illuminated lights, but (A) begs to differ, and must be axed. (A) also violates Rule 3 by having lights 1 and 7 on together, and (E) violates the same rule by lighting up both 1 and 2. No good. Rule 1 gets rid of (D); 6, 7, and 8 are consecutive and therefore can't all be on at the same time. (D) also violates Rule 6, a rule that is also not met by (B), which fails to light two lights on the north side. (You may have chucked (B) and (E) right away by noticing that they don't reflect the big deduction above—that 3 is always on.) The losers are chock full of violations here. (C) remains and gets the point.

- Move swiftly in Acceptability questions to apply the Kaplan technique of comparing what you know to the choices, and throwing out the violators. Also feel free to use any deductions you made up front to speed your work.

7. B

Here's the reward for those of you who worked out the implications of Rule 6 as you did above: Light 3 must be on because of a combination of Rules 3 and 6 (see "Deductions").

- If you miss a deduction up front, but are forced to make it in the course of answering a non-if "must be true" question, recognize that what you've discovered is not particular to that question but holds for the entire game. Build that information right into the sketch and use it the rest of the way.

8. B

If you're on top of the rules, a glance at the master sketch should be enough to answer this one. Light 1 is up north, and you know something special about the northern lights—two of them must be on. If 1 is off, then 2 and 3 are on, which has a direct implication for light 4: Rule 1 insists that under these conditions, light 4 must be off. Luckily, that's exactly what you're looking for. If 1 is off, then 4 must be off—(B).

- Don't jump into drawing a new sketch until you're sure that you need one. Many questions, like this one, are manageable by just consulting your master sketch.

9. D

No new info to add here, so you have a choice. You can either hold off on question 9 until you have more possible scenarios worked out in the final three questions (although question 12 doesn't help in this case because it involves a rule change), or you can just plow through the choices. If you were feeling good with the game to this point, and were having no problem using the sketch to eyeball the situations posed by the choices, then tackling this one now wouldn't be a terrible mistake. For the sake of continuity, you'll work through each choice here, but for the record, (A) can be eliminated from the correct answer to question 6 (which you should have noticed in either case); (B) can be axed thanks to the arrangement to be worked out in question 11, and (E) thanks to the correct choice of question 10. Choice (C) falls to the big deduction (a.k.a. the answer to question 7), as light 3 can never be off. So the method of using other work allows you to narrow the choices all the way down to (D). Here's how it would have gone if you handled the question in the order presented:

(A) Correct choice (C) in Acceptability question 6 offers you a valid collection of lights that are on: 2, 3, 5, 6, and 8. Clearly, since this is acceptable, (A) is not—if light 2 is on, light 6 can be on, too.

(B) If 3 is on (and you know by now it's *always* on), must 2 be on? No; you can satisfy Rule 6 by turning on light 1 instead, which is fine as long as 7 is off.

(C) Light 3 is never off. A quick elimination thanks to your big deduction.

(D) Yup: If 5 is off, then you're left with only light 3 blazing on the east side. That's a no-no according to Rule 5—better send some juice over to light 4, pronto. So (D) must be true. If 5 is off, then 4 must be on. For the record:

(E) is out-and-out false: If southern middle light 6 is off, then 5 and 7 must be on (Rules 4 and 5). And if 7 is on, then 1 is off, contrary to (E).

- Use your previous work to eliminate choices whenever possible. And in some cases, you may even wish to skip a question temporarily so that the ones that come after will in effect *become* "previous work" upon your return to the skipped question.

10. A

You certainly may have benefited from jotting down a new sketch to incorporate question 10's hypothetical—circle light 5 along with 8 and 3 and you're ready to go. The first thing to notice is that light 4 must be off; otherwise Rule 1 is violated with 3, 4, and 5 on simultaneously. You're looking for a choice that could be true under these circumstances, so it's on to the choices.

(A) And you don't have to look far: It's quite possible for lights 1 and 6 to be off here, provided that 2 and 7 are on. So (A) it is. (Note that this eliminates (E) in question 9.) On test day, you would circle (A) and move on, but for the record, here's how the others pan out:

(B) directly contradicts Rule 3—1 and 7 can never be on together.

(C) denies what you've just deduced—that 4 must be off any time 5 is on.

(D) is perhaps the trickiest one to eliminate, because it forces many rules into play. But ultimately it fails, too, and here's why: If both 2 and 6 are off, then 1 must be on (Rule 6), and 7 must be on (Rule 5). But firing up both 1 and 7 violates Rule 3, so (D) isn't possible.

(E) would create a consecutive 5, 6, 7 trio, not to mention a 6, 7, 8 trio, both of which are expressly forbidden by Rule 1.

- In Logic Games, when you find a choice early in the list of choices that works, take it and move on. This is one effective way to store up time that you may need at the end of the section.

11. B

You may or may not have created a new sketch for question 10, but it certainly helps here to plot out the chain of deductions. A circle around light 4 demands an X through lights 2 and 5 (lest you end up with three consecutive lights illuminated). Light 1 must therefore be the other light on up north (Rule 6). And with 1 on, 7 is off, thanks to Rule 3. That leaves 6 as the only light left to illuminate the south side, and Rule 4 tells you that the south side can't go dark. So there you have it, the entire lighting design, so to speak: 1, 3, 4, 6, and 8 on; 2, 5, and 7 off. Every choice matches up except (B).

- In a "must be true" question, it pays to scan the list of choices as soon as you make each deduction—no sense doing more work than you need to. But in a "must be true EXCEPT" question, you've got a lot of deductions to make simply because you have four choices containing true statements to rule out. Better in this case to just roll with the deductions and expect to fill in most, if not all of the info possible. Then you can simply compare the choices to your sketch, looking for the odd man out.

12. E

Uh-oh, they're shaking things up. No sooner is the "two northern lights" rule lifted than you're told that exactly one light's on up there. No problem, you know which one it is—must be the middle one, light 2, because of Rule 5. For the first time, you get to go back on the big deduction and cross out light 3 along with light 1. You need at least one light on for the east side, and with 3 off, it's down to 4 and 5. You've seen this before: If only the end light, light 5, were on, then Rule 5 would be violated. So at least middle light 4 must be on, and light 5 could, but need not, be on as well. The choice that could be false, therefore, is (E); maybe yes, maybe no. All of the others are definite.

- In a "could be false" question, the wrong choices all must be true. (Note that this stem is essentially asking the same thing as the previous question.) Make sure you're adept at characterizing the right and wrong choices for every type of question they can throw at you; know in advance to testing the choices how the right and wrong ones will behave.
- Use your judgment as to whether or not to deal with a rule change question or put it off for later. In the worst-case scenario, such a question will require a lot of new work and just may not be worth the time and effort. But if you're in a groove on the game, you may wish to play right through. If not, it's certainly okay to have taken a stab at the first six questions, and the seventh rule-changer may be expendable. (Do try, of course, to return at the end to any questions you skip if there's time.) Whichever approach you take, be sure to remember that since they've removed a rule, the work you do for this question *can't* be used to answer any other.

Game 3—Seven Children In Chairs

The Action

Back to the basics here: "Seven chairs arranged in a row" immediately denotes sequencing as the game action. The entities, children, are split into boys and girls, but that's not so tough to incorporate. And that west to east business, with all children facing north?—simply a different way of describing the kids' relationships to one another. The reference to "facing north" suggests that there may be a left-right element to the game, which turns out not to be the case. So it simply boils down to seven chairs, seven kids, putting them in order—you've seen this (or will before we're through with you) dozens of times.

The Initial Setup

Since the east-west thing seems to play a big part in the questions, there's no harm in jotting down a W and E to remind yourself at a glance which children are east of and west of each other. Get the boys and girls down on the page, throw in seven chairs, and you're ready to see how the seating arrangement will be determined.

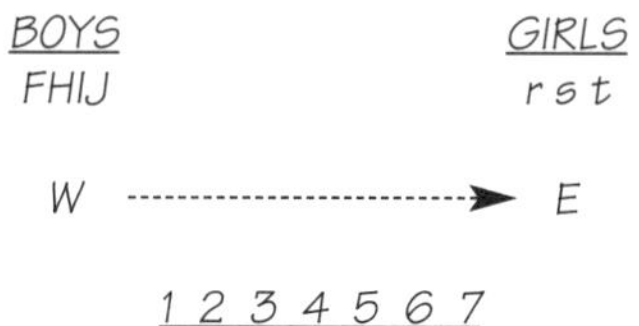

The Rules

1) Talk about strict. No fun for these kids; one kid per chair. Just a loophole-closer that you most likely assumed anyway.

2) It's hard to wait for Step 4 of the Kaplan Method to consider the implications of Rule 2: There are four boys, and none of them sits next to any other one. Well, that's not so easy to do in a sequence of only seven kids, is it? Your reaction to each rule is supposed to be "what does this mean" in the context of this game—and you needn't postpone a deduction until Step 4 if it jumps right out at you. Hopefully you saw that the only way to space out four non-adjacent entities in a sequence of seven is to place them in spots 1, 3, 5, and 7—there's simply no other way. At this point, just put a b for boy over those slots in your sketch, and a g for girl over the others. (Boy, girl, boy, girl . . . how quaint.)

3) Here's the most concrete rule of the bunch, one that you may have jumped to right away: It requires a touch of interpretation, but essentially means that Ivan is 5th. Chairs 5, 6, and 7 are the chairs east of chair 4, and the only one of those next to 4 is 5.

4) "East of" in this game means to the right, so this boils down to the usual sequencing notation I . . . S. Perhaps you thought this through in accordance with the deduction stated above. Hold off until Step 4 and deal with it in Deductions below.

5) Fr or rF must appear somewhere in the ordering.

Deductions

You jumped all over Rule 2 above; it seemed natural to work through the implications of the rule at that point. If you didn't think it through then, you probably did so now. As you recall, you deduced that boys must sit in chairs 1, 3, 5, and 7, which leaves the girls in chairs 2, 4, and 6. Now you can combine that with Rules 3 and 4. Since Ivan is in chair 5, and Sylvia must be east of that, Sylvia must be in chair 6 or chair 7. But 7 is a boy's chair, so Sylvia must sit in chair 6. Is that it?

Don't stop there; what else can you deduce? With Sylvia in 6, the other girls, Ruby and Thelma, must split chairs 2 and 4. And Frank, who must sit next to Ruby, must therefore sit in either chair 1 or chair 3. This latter piece of information comes in especially handy throughout the questions. (You could take it one step further by noticing that either Harry or Joel must occupy chair 7, but the game isn't won or lost on this tidbit.)

The Final Visualization

This reflects the rules and all the deductions discussed above:

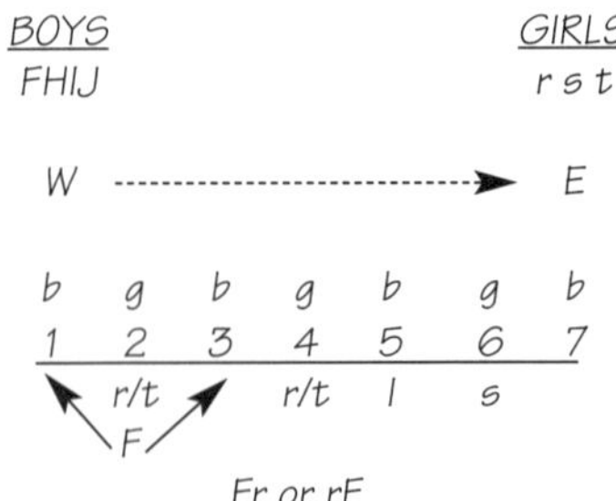

The Big Picture

- When the proctor says "turn the page and begin work on Section X" and you find yourself faced with Logic Games, quickly look through the section and determine the most efficient order in which to attack the games. In this section, many found this game to be a good place to start. It may not seem like a big deal, because you plan to get to every game anyway. But the psychological advantage of diffusing anxiety at the beginning of the section by totally crunching the first game you do is immense—and if you do end up running out of time, you don't want to miss easy points that you would have picked up quickly if only you'd gotten to those questions. A garden-variety Sequencing game like this may be just the ticket.
- Don't let a little wrinkle in a game fluster you; "west of" and "east of" are nothing more than "to the left of" and "to the right of."
- Deduce as much as you can up front. It's optimal to determine exactly where an entity must go: s in 6 is an example of that. The next best thing is to limit an entity's position to one of two spots, and here, r, t, and F all fall into that category. As mentioned above, knowing that F must be in 1 or 3 turns out to be especially helpful.
- Notice the entities that aren't restricted by any rules. Here, H and J are interchangeable "floaters" who will be used to fill in the gaps in the ordering. If you deduced that one of them must be in chair 7, even better.
- When the entities of a game fall into different categories (such as boys and girls here), you may wish to differentiate the groups on your page. Using uppercase and lowercase letters is a tried and true method. If that helps you, use it (though here, there didn't seem to be much chance of confusing the boys and girls).

The Questions

13. C

The major challenge of question 13 is figuring out exactly what they're looking for, so a careful reading is in order. First of all, what *is* a "pair of chairs in which Frank and Ruby can sit"? Check it out: you see from the sketch that Frank can be in chair 1 with Ruby in chair 2, so chairs 1 and 2 together count as one acceptable pair for this couple linked by Rule 5. Keeping Ruby in 2, Frank can move to 3 without a hitch, so there's a second pair, chairs 2 and 3. But Ruby can also be in chair 4 when Frank's in 3, so 3 and 4 together counts as the third pair. Any others? Nope, so three it is, (C).

- Read the stems carefully, and take as much time as you need to fully decipher the task at hand. There's no way here to come up with an accurate number if you're hazy on what's being asked.

14. C

Next you're to find a statement that must be false, which means that each wrong choice will either be true or possibly true. Notice how all the choices involve Frank, which is nice because you know plenty about Frank's prospects. In fact, simply recognizing that Frank can be in the first chair gets rid of (A), (B), and (E), since if Frank were to take chair 1, *everyone* would be east of him. Upon analysis, you see that (C) is the impossibility you seek: you deduced up front that Frank must sit in 1 or 3. But even if you slide Frank down as far east as possible—that is, chair 3—there's no way to fit both free agents Harry and Joel west of him, because either Ruby or Thelma must take chair 2. (D) is possible: One of the boy floaters, in this case Harry, can hang out with Ruby on the west side of Frank—H in 1, R in 2, and F in 3 would do the trick. But you can't get both Harry and Joel west of Frank: one of those guys has to be in the easternmost chair 7.

- Use your deductions; this work is done to save you time in the questions.
- Don't immediately rush to use your pencil. Become adept at eyeballing your shorthand and master sketch to eliminate choices and pick up points in non-if questions like this one.

15. E

Good solid info is offered in this one, so get it all down in a new sketch.

Ivan's in chair 5, so if Thelma's next to him, she must be in chair 4, because you've already slotted Sylvia for chair 6. The stem also tells you that Frank is next to Thelma, so put F in chair 3, which leaves Ruby for chair 2. Free agents Harry and Joel will float between chairs 1 and 7. You're looking for something that could be false, and you can shorten your work by scanning the choices for Harry and Joel; after all, they're the only ones not fully restricted here. Only Joel appears, and way down in (E). Lo and behold, Joel's elusive nature does in fact make (E) the correct choice. (E) would be true if Joel's in chair 7, but would be false if Joel's in chair 1.

- If most entities are set in a particular question, and you're asked for something that could be *false*, you may be able to save a bit of time by scanning the choices for the one or two entities that still have some leeway; chances are the right answer will have something to do with them. The fact that Joel could be in chair 1 or chair 7 in this case means (E) could be false.

16. B

You already have Frank's location narrowed down to either 1 or 3, and the information in the stem allows you to deduce it must be 1. How? Because chair 3 is next to chair 4, which *does* seat a child sitting next to Ivan (who you know is in 5). The stem says Frank can't sit in such a seat, so Frank goes to 1, which forces Ruby into 2 (Rule 5) and Thelma into chair 4. Once again, you're left with the two free agents, H and J, this time floating between chairs 3 and 7. Checking the choices, you see that only (B) could be true—if Joel's in 3 and Harry's in 7, then Joel indeed would be sitting west of Ivan. All of the others are impossible. (You may have eliminated (A), (C), and (D) quickly on account of the fact that with Frank in chair 1, ain't nobody west of him.)

- Sometimes the test makers will use slightly obscure language to toughen up an otherwise simple game. Once you make the new information concrete, all that's left is to plug away. And if you've done good work up front, *that* should be the easy part.

17. D

If you're not yet convinced of the importance of the Frank deduction, here's another question that falls pretty easily thanks to the fact that Frank must be in 1 or 3. If Frank took chair 1, he wouldn't be east of Ruby as the stem demands; so Frank must sit in chair 3 with Ruby in chair 2. That again lands Thelma in chair 4, which again leaves 1 and 7 for Harry and Joel to fight over. Again, everyone's placed but those two. From this ordering, you can see quite readily that the only pair that cannot be next to each other is the duo of Ivan and Ruby—Frank and Thelma come between them. Choice (A) contains folks that *are* next to each other, while the others contain pairs that could be, depending on where Harry and Joel sit.

- Nothing says the last question of a game must be a killer, or even difficult. Question 17 posed the same basic challenge as the previous two: to digest the information in the stem and to use it to trigger deductions based on what you already know.

Game 4—Organisms And Antibiotics

The Action

The key verb phrase in the opening paragraph here is "respond to"; each organism responds to the three antibiotics in some manner, so you're dealing with a matching game. Does W get F, or G, or H—or some combination thereof? No doubt that's what the rules are going to help you to decide, and the same goes of course for the other three organisms. No tricks here.

The Initial Setup

The simplest way to match up the entities in two groups is to list the definite entities horizontally in columns across your page (here, the four organisms) and place the choices for those entities off to the side, to be filled in as needed. A simple list or grid like so will suffice, and certainly won't take long to draw or recopy when necessary:

	W	X	Y	Z
FGH				

The Rules

6) Keeping with the Kaplan strategy of beginning with the most concrete information, a quick scan of the rules reveals that Y responds to F, so draw it in. Having incorporated this, you may have been drawn to the other rules about F:

5) Anywhere you place an F, you'll also have to place a G, so you may as well place a G under organism Y since you just placed an F there from Rule 6. Off to the side, you'll want to indicate "If F, then G." The contrapositive should be readily apparent: "If no G, then no F."

3) Rule 3 is about F too, but this one you'll have to shorthand off to the side. Did you simply make the rule shorter, by writing something to the effect of "2 but not 4 Fs"? If you did, you need to remind yourself to ferret out the *implications* of the rules: that is, to turn negatives into positives and state the meaning of the rules as clearly as possible. "2 or 3 Fs" is much better. That's what the rule really *means* in the context of this game.

There's no indication that any of the remaining rules should be given priority at this point, so jump back to the beginning. As it turns out, Rules 1 and 2 can be combined on the fly:

1) and 2) Each organism responds to at least one antibiotic, but no organism responds to all three. You can and should perform the same simple arithmetic as above to deduce that each organism will respond to either 1 or 2 antibiotics. "Each gets 1 or 2" is one of many ways to remind you of this.

4) Lastly, Rule 4: Whatever antibiotics W gets, X gets too. Take a few seconds to work out the implications of this. Whatever goes in the W column must also appear in the X column. But does it work the other way around? No. If W responds to two antibiotics, then X must have the same two. But if W gets only one—for example, G—then X must get G but can also get one more antibiotic, F or H.

Deductions

You've already begun your deductive work by piecing together the number information above. You saw that **each organism will respond to either 1 or 2 antibiotics**, and also that **exactly 2 or 3 organisms will respond to F**. You also went right ahead and put FG into the Y column, and now, factoring in Rule 2, you can safely conclude that **organism Y, responding to F and G, is done and fully accounted for**.

What else? You can combine Rules 2 and 5 to deduce that **no organism responds to both F and H**. F requires G, and adding H as well would violate Rule 2. And here's one more thing you may have noticed (but if you didn't, is not a huge drawback): What happens if W responds to F? Then so does X (Rule 4). And you know that Y responds to F (Rule 6), so Z cannot because then all four would be responding to F, in violation of Rule 3. Stated simply: **If W responds to F, then Z doesn't respond to F**. If you saw this, great, if not, no biggie; you probably had the opportunity to work through this at some point during the questions. You won't even bother including it in the master sketch. And speaking of which:

The Final Visualization

Here is all the information you have at your disposal to dispose of the seven questions hanging in the balance:

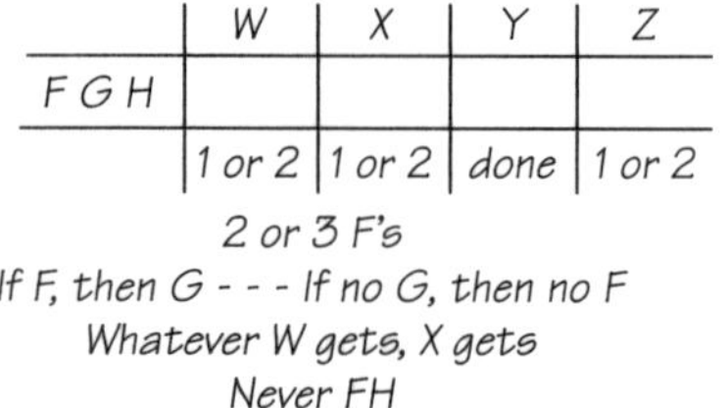

W X Y Z
FGH
1 or 2 | 1 or 2 | done | 1 or 2
2 or 3 F's
If F, then G - - - If no G, then no F
Whatever W gets, X gets
Never FH

The Big Picture

- Don't let impressive-sounding terminology throw you off your rhythm in Logic Games. "Organisms" and "antibiotics" sound more complicated than, say, "boys" and "girls," but they stand for the same thing—two groups of entities that need to be matched up. Same goes for the lengthy names of the antibiotics themselves; treat these simply as any other entities F, G, and H.
- Don't make things hard on yourself! Some test takers make the game more complex than it really is. This is a straightforward matching scenario, no twists. So a simple list on the page of the entities to be linked up is the simplest and most effective way to go.
- Number information is crucial in grouping and matching games. Always take any info regarding

numbers as far as you can, and always try to turn negative statements into positive ones. "Not all four respond to F" in this case *means* one, two, or three *do* respond to F. Combining that with "at least two," you can narrow it down to two or three.

The Questions

18. D

May as well begin by checking your deductions, looking for the odd man out here. And your previous work with Y takes you where you need to go. You saw that since Y gets F (Rule 6), and therefore gets G (Rule 5), it cannot get H also because that would violate Rule 2. (D) is the impossibility here; all the rest work just fine.

- In a "can be true EXCEPT" question, all four wrong answers present situations that are possible, so you can notice these things and build that information into your conception of the game, or at least remain aware that you can refer back to these choices to see a number of match-ups that are possible.

19. B

You've most likely deduced enough up front to knock these choices out quickly, so take 'em one at a time. You're looking for something that's possible:

(A) Since Y already has F, linking W, X, and Z with F would result in four F's—a direct violation of Rule 3.

(B) No problem here: Nothing prohibits four Gs across the board. You need to get one more F in there to take care of Rule 3, but other than that, smooth sailing.

(C) If W responds to G, then so does X (Rule 4), and you already know that Y responds to G. So (C) is impossible: If W responds to G, then at least two more that you know of must respond to G as well.

(D) directly contradicts Rule 4: Whatever W gets, X gets, so there's no way W can respond to *more* antibiotics than X.

(E) Same thought as (D), only stemming from Rule 5: Whatever gets F, gets G; so there can't be more organisms with F than G.

- In Logic Games, when you're fully satisfied that a choice does the trick, circle it and move on, even if it appears early on in the list of choices. If you still feel the desire to check the other choices, you need to work up the extra confidence necessary to allow you to save time wherever you can.

20. E

Same drill as 19. You're looking for what could be true, so test the choices until something possible appears. Unfortunately, you have to wait until the bottom of the list in (E): Rule 5 states that wherever there's F, there's G. This doesn't work the other way around. While Y has both F and G, it's perfectly possible for at least one of the other organisms to have G without F. In fact, consulting the partial arrangement worked out for correct choice (B) in question 19 confirms this: it's possible that G is linked to all four while only two organisms respond to F. (E) could be true. As for the others:

(A) directly contradicts Rule 3—you need 2 or 3 F's here.

(B) As you saw earlier, Y cannot respond to H because it already responds to F and G and no organism is allowed to respond to all three.

(C) Here's another deduction you worked out above: Since whatever responds to F must also respond to G (Rule 5), no organism that responds to F may respond to H because that would lead to a prohibited threesome.

(D) is the trickiest of the bunch because it's stated in the negative. Is it possible for any organisms to be without G and H? Well, Rule 1 reminds you that each organism must match up with at least one antibiotic, and if G and H are out, then F is the only one left. But a solo F is against the rules—Rule 5 in particular, which states that wherever F appears, G appears.

- The corollary to the bullet point in question 19 is that if you've confidently eliminated four choices, the other one must be correct and *need not be checked*. The underlying element common to both pieces of advice is *confidence* in your work. When you've determined that (A) through (D) are impossible, you simply *know* that the answer must be (E). It may take only a few seconds to verify it, but those few seconds, and all those "few seconds" accumulated on similar examples throughout the section, add up to time you may sorely need by the end of the section.

21. D

The first new "if" of the game: No F for X. The contrapositive of Rule 4 tells you that whatever X doesn't get, W doesn't get, so no F for X also means no F for W. You still need another F to satisfy Rule 3, so Z must respond to F, as well as to G thanks to Rule 5. Do you have your answer yet? Yup—(D) must be true, and gets the point. (A), (B), and (C) can, but need not, be true, while (E) is flat-out impossible: If

Z responds to H, then Z's got the trifecta, all three antibiotics—and you know of course that that's not allowed.

- In a "must be true" question, scan the choices as soon as you make a deduction or two. Here, there's no need to worry about the status of W and X after you've determined that they can't get F. Once you've figured out where F must be, you have enough info to nail the question. In a more difficult question, the test makers might force you to work out the remaining possibilities, and might state the choices more abstractly in accordance with this. But you never know how far they want you to go, so if you can take a quick shot, do it. If need be, you can always go further.

22. B

There are many ways to go about this one. One quick way is to plot out the possibilities and check them against the choices. The only pairs of antibiotics an organism can respond to are FG and GH. The only other pair that can be formed from the three antibiotics is FH, and you've seen a number of times why this pair doesn't work (where F goes, G goes, therefore no H—all that Rule 2 and Rule 5 business). So call FG option 1, and GH option 2. Checking the choices:

(A) Not in option 2 it doesn't.

(B) Yup. Either way, G is called into service. That's the answer, and naturally you'd move on immediately. But for the record:

(C) No H in option 1.

(D) Sure it can—right there in option 1.

(E) Such an organism *must* respond to G.

- There are often a number of routes into a question. Here, you may have noticed that you already have an example that matches the situation described in the stem—Y responds to two antibiotics, F and G. This alone gets rid of (C), (D), and (E), as it proves that an acceptable twosome *need not* include H and *could* include F and G. From here it's a hop, skip, and jump to concluding that G is the one that's required no matter what. Follow up on whatever seems the most practical approach. If you get the point quickly and confidently, you really can't argue with any approach you take.

23. E

H is off the market for the sake of this question, which means that this scenario is going to be dominated by Fs and Gs. But wait a minute: Wherever F is, G is. And wherever F *isn't*, G is going to have to be there, too, since H is temporarily out of the picture. Bottom line: G is ubiquitous; omnipresent so to speak. Or, another way to put it is (E). (D) is obviously wrong if (E) is right; there must be four Gs, not three. (A) and (B) bite the dust if you give an FG pair to Z and solo Gs to W and X. However, you can also place FG pairs under W and X, with a solo G in Z's slot, contrary to the assertion in (C).

- Even in more complicated questions, it may be possible to deduce the answer directly. If not, use your pencil and plot out arrangements in order to eliminate choices. Often, you'll be able to axe more than one choice with any particular arrangement.

24. C

The second if-clause is more concrete than the first, so it's wise to begin there. If Z doesn't get F, then Z gets G or H or both. So far so good. But that plays into the more abstract new information, which tells you that three of the four organisms respond to the same set of antibiotics. Since Y responds F, and Z doesn't, and you still need at least two F's listed, Z must be the odd organism out: W, X, and Y must therefore be the three identical ones. Each of those responds to both F and G, while Z responds to G or H or both, as noted above. That tells you almost everything you could possibly know about the situation, and all the choices match this scenario except for (C): it's possible that Z responds to only H.

- If a question has more than one new "if" added, work with the more concrete information first. That will make it easier to piece together the implications of the more abstract information in the stem.

SECTION III: READING COMPREHENSION

Passage 1—rDNA

Topic and Scope

Recombinant deoxyribonucleic acid—specifically, the controversy surrounding rDNA research's potential effects

Purpose and Main Idea

The author comes across as neither advocate nor critic of this technology, despite acknowledging both its potential benefits and hazards. The author's intent, it seems, is to set out both sides of a controversial issue.

Paragraph Structure

The first paragraph tells you that the development of rDNA technology "has created excitement and controversy" in the scientific world because it permits scientists to engage in genetic engineering.

Paragraph two gives you a bit of information about the technology itself.

The third and fourth paragraphs describe the potential benefits of this technology, while the fifth and sixth describe its potential hazards.

The Big Picture

- The information above is all you really need to take away from this passage. As usual, there are a lot of details. Note where they appear, but don't try to memorize them. Remember, always read for purpose and structure rather than for content. The former two will get you the points.
- When you see an unfamiliar scientific term like "recombinant deoxyribonucleic acid," how should you react? Should you freak out? Should you hyperventilate? Of course not! What you should do is come up with a simple reference for the term. Here, the passage does it for you by shortening recombinant deoxyribonucleic acid to just rDNA. But it won't always be that convenient; sometimes you're going to have to do the work yourself. If that's the case, treat these words as you would, say, strange names in a logic game.
- Science passages aren't more difficult than social science or humanities passages. In fact, if you don't let unfamiliar terms intimidate you, they're often quite straightforward. Don't try to deal with scientific terminology on the scientifically minded author's own terms: reduce scientific terms to your own, simpler ones.

The Questions

1. D

First up is a Global question asking the author's purpose. The author's intent is to discuss the debate over rDNA technology, noting the arguments of both proponents and opponents of the technology, without taking sides on the matter. That points directly to (D).

(A) completely ignores the most important element of the passage, the controversy surrounding rDNA. (A) would be closer to correct if the passage consisted of only paragraphs two through four.

(B), (C) and (E) have the wrong tone. Phrases like "advocating continued...research" in (B), "providing evidence...for regulation of...research" in (C), and "arguing that the...risks...may outweigh its...benefits" in (E) are out of sync with the neutral tone of the passage. They suggest that the author takes some sort of stand on rDNA technology, which is simply not the case here. Additionally, none of these choices mentions the scientific controversy that's at the heart of the passage (the controversy between supporters and critics of rDNA technology).

- For Global questions, incorrect choices will always misrepresent either the tone or content of the passage; often they will misrepresent both.

2. A

Next up is a specific detail question about genetic codes. You should have noted that these codes are discussed in the first paragraph. In the first sentence, you're told outright that research into genetic codes led to the development of rDNA technology, which makes (A) the answer.

(B) has the causal relationship backward: Research into genetic codes paved the way for the discovery of rDNA technology.

(C), (D) and (E) can each be eliminated for a couple of reasons. For one thing, the issues raised in these choices apply to rDNA technology, not to research on genetic codes. Moreover, the third paragraph makes it clear that new medical treatments, (C), may become a reality in the future; they don't exist today. Likewise, the fifth and sixth paragraphs make it clear that praise for this technology, (D), has been far from universal. As for (E), the passage never says or implies that the development of rDNA technology was motivated by a desire to create new lifeforms; indeed, the passage tells you that many scientists oppose the technology because it gives humanity this capability.

- Construct a strong roadmap as you read so you won't waste precious time trying to relocate details later.

3. D

You're asked to identify something that isn't cited in the passage as a potential benefit of rDNA technology. Well, the best way to approach this all/EXCEPT question is to identify the potential benefits of rDNA technology, and eliminate the corresponding choices. That's because you know where to find the potential benefits: they're listed in the third and fourth paragraphs: Potential non-medical benefits in the areas of waste treatment, (A), agriculture, (C), and energy production, (E), are noted in paragraph four, while potential medical benefits, including new knowledge, (B), are brought up in paragraph three. By process of elimination, then, you're left with (D). If you read the last half of the third paragraph carefully, you'll notice that a potential benefit of rDNA technology is the development of new drugs, not less expensive ones. So, (D) is correct.

- When you're asked about passage details, take the few extra seconds to look back at the appropriate text; you'll avoid costly mistakes. Don't base your answers on your memory of the passage; go back and check.

4. A

This one allows you to use your Logical Reasoning skills as you weaken an argument put forward by opponents of rDNA technology: Which of five scenarios would most undercut their position? As in Logical Reasoning, attack this question by asking yourself what these folks say. The fifth paragraph tells you that they are extremely worried about laboratory safety: extremely worried that new organisms created there will escape into, and wreak havoc on, the environment. However, if some sort of unbreachable containment system were to be developed, laboratory safety would no longer be an issue, and critics of rDNA technology would have the wind taken right out of their sails, right? Choice (A) is thus the best weakener here.

(B) tends to bolster the argument that laboratories are unsafe and that the threat of escape is justified. In any case, that one bug might be successfully contained doesn't render less valid the fears that others might escape and cause trouble.

(C) The fact that an rDNA-produced microorganism has its number kept in check by predators doesn't counteract the opponents' claim that it may still cause damage to the ecosystem. The fact that it can survive at all in the world outside the laboratory suggests that the opponents' argument may still be justified.

(D) It sounds like this particular creation is in check, but what does this say about the general possibility that microorganisms will escape, which, is after all, the chief worry of opponents? This danger still looms, regardless of the seeming success of the organisms highlighted in (D).

(E) Opponents are worried about the potential for rDNA technology to *cause* disease. The notion of eradicating disease may bolster the supporters' argument, but that doesn't mean it necessarily weakens the opposing side.

- Strengthen/Weaken questions in Reading Comp function in the same way as Strengthen/Weaken questions in Logical Reasoning.

5. E

You need to determine the role in the passage of a specific reference. To do this, you must understand the context in which it appears. That can be accomplished by reading the lines around the reference itself. In this particular case, then, you need to read and understand the last paragraph. So, what's being said? Simply put, opponents of rDNA technology fear that it could be misused to create some sort of nightmarish totalitarian society. That makes (E) the answer.

(A) is out because the critics' opposition to rDNA technology on medical grounds appears in lines 41–47—way earlier than the last sentence.

(B) Opponents, not supporters, of rDNA technology refer to the possibility of a grim future in which people are genetically engineered to serve a specific function. Also, remember that you're being asked why the *author* does something, and you decided above that this author is simply describing or summarizing an issue, not taking sides or "advocating" anything.

(C) True, critics of rDNA technology fear that its use could lead to a natural disaster, but the reference in the last sentence of the passage has nothing to do with this fear.

(D) Huxley's *Brave New World (*a fascinating book, for those of you who haven't already read it) is introduced as an example of how society *might* develop in the future if rDNA technology is misused. That's entirely different from saying that it "accurately predicted technological developments."

- Keep your eyes open for answer choices that speak of things that may be supported in the text yet are irrelevant to the question at hand. Somewhere, someone is worried about the type of disaster mentioned in (C), but that has nothing to do with the purpose of the author's reference in the final sentence.

6. B

The final question in this set is exactly like question 4, except that you're asked to identify a scenario that would *strengthen*, rather than weaken, an argument made by opponents of rDNA technology. Once again, start by asking yourself about their arguments. By now, you know that they oppose this technology on medical, environmental and ethical grounds. As the fifth and sixth paragraphs tell you, they think that rDNA technology has the potential to cause great harm to both the natural environment and human society. So look for a situation in which rDNA technology causes this sort of harm. Such a scenario is outlined in (B): If invulnerable organisms were to get loose in nature, they could very well cause an ecological catastrophe similar to the one sketched in the fifth paragraph.

(A) and (C) After all, it's the supporters who claim that it will result in agricultural and medical benefits. The opponents don't address these issues, so (A) and (C) are irrelevant to their argument.

(D) and (E) would weaken, rather than strengthen, the critics' case. If as (D) says the environment is unstable to start with and prone to sudden collapse, then would releasing laboratory-created organisms into it be much of an additional risk? Maybe not. And if as (E) says, genetically altered organisms can't survive in nature for more than a few hours, then what damage could they do? Probably not too much, right?

- RC questions can be very closely related to each other. Use your work on the easier one to give you a head start on the harder one.

Passage 2—Gray Marketing

Topic and Scope

Gray marketing, a practice that involves the sale of trademarked products through unauthorized channels

Purpose and Main Idea

At first, the passage is merely descriptive, but the author reveals his true feelings in the third paragraph, setting forth an argument to establish that gray marketing should be curtailed.

Paragraph Structure

The first couple of paragraphs give some general background information on gray marketing, basically defining it and then telling you how it occurs within a specific region and across international boundaries.

Only in the third paragraph do you begin to get a sense of what the author thinks about gray marketing, when he or she argues that it's unfair to trademark owners, essentially by stating that their opposition to it is justified.

In paragraph four, the author reviews three legal theories for regulating gray marketing activities, and concludes that only the last of them—territoriality—is both workable and just. The final sentence clearly reveals the author's position: He thinks it's "inevitable" that the territoriality interpretation will win the day.

The Big Picture

- Generally, passages in which the author's point of view isn't apparent early are harder to handle than passages that have a clear purpose in paragraph one. Consider saving them for later in your section.
- This is a very dense passage, and it makes no sense to try to absorb all of the details as you read through it. But notice how neat its structure is. The first two paragraphs discuss how gray marketing works, the third describes why it's unfair, and the last evaluates proposed legal remedies. That's what you should

be getting out of the text: full comprehension of the structure, not the content. If you identify and keep this structure in mind, you shouldn't have any trouble relocating details when necessary.

The Questions

7. A

The first one in the set is a Global question, so you should already have predicted this answer as you read the passage. Well, in the context of a general discussion of gray marketing—what it is, how it works, whom it injures, and how it is addressed by the legal system—the author denounces the practice as unfair to trademark owners and recommends a legal remedy for it. (A) catches all of this.

None of the incorrect choices really captures either the author's negative attitude toward gray marketing or optimistic outlook about placing legal controls on it. But they can all be eliminated for other reasons as well.

(B) and (D) are both too narrow in scope. The passage goes well beyond a mere description of how gray marketing works, (B), and "the futility of trying to regulate it" flies in the face of the author's prediction at the end. The passage also goes beyond a general description of legal decisions involving the practice, (D). Another problem with (D) is that, according to the author, two of the three theories result in the same legal outcome.

(C) and (E) are outside the scope of the passage. Nothing is ever said to the effect that putting a stop to gray marketing within markets is a different ball game than putting a stop to it across markets, (C). In fact, at the beginning of the last paragraph, the author makes a point of telling you that current legal theories for controlling gray market activities have thus far been applied only to cases across markets. As for (E), the passage never claims that current legal theories have increased the amount of gray marketing activity. True, two of them do nothing to curb it, but that's very different from saying that they encourage it.

- Wrong choices, especially in Global questions, will often be wrong for a couple of reasons. Demand a choice that does the job unequivocally.
- Some wrong choices bring up two things from the passage but compare or combine them in a way that the passage doesn't.

8. D

Next up is another Global question. Again, you're looking for the choice that accurately summarizes both the tone and content of the entire passage. That's (D). The author describes gray marketing in the first two paragraphs, denounces it in the third, and judges several legal theories for regulating it in the last paragraph.

(A) is outside the scope of the passage. The author really has nothing critical to say about gray marketers, but rather criticizes the practice itself.

(B) and (C) are, in contrast, too narrow in scope. While the first three paragraphs discuss channel flow diversion, parallel importation, and their harmful effects, (B) completely ignores the legal dimension of gray marketing. And while (C) addresses the legal dimension of gray marketing, it totally ignores all of the stuff in the first three paragraphs.

(E) is way too broad in scope. This passage is about one specific marketing practice: gray marketing.

- In Global questions, watch out for choices that mention a detail from the passage but blow it up into the main idea.

9. B

Now you need a specific argument against gray marketing. You should have gone directly to the third paragraph, since the author's arguments against the practice appear there—that's the benefit of mapping the passage as you read. In the last sentence of this paragraph, you're told that authorized dealers may not want to promote a product that is being sold for lower prices by gray marketers, (B).

(A), (C) and (E) The author never claims that gray marketing damages manufacturers by making it difficult to track sales efforts, (A), by lowering profit margins, (C), or by lowering product quality, (E).

(D) has it backward: The author's argument is that gray marketing hurts manufacturers, not unauthorized dealers, whom the author would clearly like to get rid of.

- Paying attention to the terms of the argument helps you eliminate "outside the scope" choices with confidence.

10. A

Legal matters, the theories of territoriality and exhaustion, should have pointed you to the last paragraph. Lines 48–59 reveal that these two theories differ on the rights of manufacturers: According to the exhaustion theory, manufacturers have no legal right to regulate the way in which distributors sell products to the public, while the territoriality theory holds that manufacturers do have such a right in countries where they have registered their trademarks. That's what (A) says in a slightly different way.

(B) is a bit trickier. Once again, territoriality and exhaustion differ only on the issue of whether manufacturers have the right to exercise control over the way in which distributors sell products to the public; these theories are not concerned with the issue of manufacturer sales to distributors.

(C) is out because territoriality turns a blind eye to gray marketing practices in countries where manufacturers have not registered their trademarks. So, in these cases, it's not different from exhaustion.

(D) and (E) The theories in question have nothing whatsoever to do with either consumer preferences, (D), or the marketing value of trademarks, (E); territoriality and exhaustion deal exclusively with the rights of manufacturers. So the issues in these two choices are outside the scope.

- Success in Reading Comp depends on knowing where to look up details. That's why your roadmap of the passage is so important.

11. B

The stem's reference to the effect of gray marketing on "goodwill" should send you to the third paragraph. The concept of goodwill is introduced as part of the author's argument against gray marketing, isn't it? Gray marketing, the author contends, is an unjust practice because it threatens the business reputations of manufacturers: reputations that they have built up by treating consumers properly. This points straight to (B).

(A) The author doesn't fault manufacturers (the trademark owners) for anything; and, indeed, is very sympathetic to their position. Perhaps you axed this one because of the phrase "consumer complaints," an issue that shows up nowhere in the passage.

(C) The difference between gray marketing within and across markets, which comes up in the first couple of paragraphs, is completely irrelevant to the issue of goodwill. Besides, the author never says that gray marketing across markets is a tougher problem than gray marketing within markets.

(D) can be tossed out for the simple reason that threats to goodwill injure manufacturers, not gray marketers.

(E) The fact that some consumers purchase gray market products indicates that they are willing to sacrifice service in order to get a reduced price. In any case, this isn't the reason the author talks about goodwill.

- When dealing with a Logic question about the role of a detail, it's important to understand the context in which that detail appears.

12. C

This question asks you to characterize the author's feelings about the possibility of legal action to control gray marketing. In the last sentence of the passage, the author says that legal protection is both "inevitable and desirable," and this conclusion is based on evidence beginning with the keyword "Since." The use of such words suggests that the author's attitude is one of measured confidence or "reasoned optimism," (C).

(A), (B) and (E) "Resigned tolerance," (A), "utter dismay," (B), and "cynical indifference," (E)—all negative or strongly negative in tone—are completely out of sync with the author's positive attitude.

(D) "[U]nbridled fervor," on the other hand, is far too exuberant a phrase to summarize the author's more low-key outlook.

- Many people have problems questions that ask about the author's attitude because they try to answer such questions on a "hunch." Don't rely on your own feelings to infer something about the author's—go to the text for support!

13. C

The topic is "channel flow diversion," which is also the topic of the first paragraph. By telling you that some authorized distributors take advantage of manufacturer quantity discounts to enter the gray market, lines 10–15 suggest how channel flow diversion, the term for gray marketing within a local market, might be lessened—get rid of quantity discounts. That's what (C) says, albeit in somewhat different language.

(A) Gray marketing is not going to be impeded as long as profit margins are lower on goods sold through authorized channels. Besides, the passage never says that parallel importing, the term for gray marketing across national boundaries, has any impact on channel flow diversion.

(B) The way to decrease channel flow diversion is to make it economically unattractive to potential gray marketers: It's difficult to see how relieving authorized distributors of advertising responsibilities, (B), would accomplish this.

(D) Manufacturers already determine post-sale service policies, yet this apparently hasn't cut into the amount of channel flow diversion taking place.

(E) Manufacturers have never provided an "extended product" to consumers who buy in the gray market, yet this hasn't impeded channel flow diversion either.

- Here's a prime example of an Inference question that doesn't require you to do much more than recognize that information in the passage can be expressed in different terms. As always on the LR and RC sections, the ability to paraphrase text is key.

Passage 3—African American Autobiographies

Topic and Scope

African American autobiographies—specifically, the difference in literary quality between autobiographies authored directly by their subjects as opposed to those composed by second-hand editors

Purpose and Main Idea

The author writes to alert you to the literary difference between the two forms of narrative mentioned above. The main idea is that authentic narratives trump the edited versions; only the former warrant close analytic readings, while those compiled by editors should be recognized as such and viewed in light of their origin.

Paragraph Structure

The first paragraph lays out the main question of the passage: Are autobiographies written by editors equivalent to those actually written by their subjects? African American narratives between 1760 and 1865 are the autobiographies in question, and you have to wait for paragraph two for the author's answer to the question posed in the last sentence.

In paragraph two, the author's message becomes quite clear: From the point of view of literary analysis, there's a big difference between these two forms of autobiography; only those actually written by the subjects themselves, it is argued, are authentic representations of the African American experience. This is essentially the passage's big idea.

Paragraph three simply refines and reinforces this message. Narratives in which editors make it a point to stay out the way, so to speak, are better than ones in which the editor's voice is obtrusive, but these are still not as good as the real thing—stories told directly by the subjects themselves. An example of this is given, and the author reinforces the main point by stating that close readings should be reserved for the authentic documents.

The Big Picture

- Like most passages, this one contains a lot of details. Again, don't waste time trying to memorize them; it's much more important to grasp *purpose* and *structure* than to assimilate details.
- Don't be put off by long paragraphs; even these can usually be broken down into fairly simple ideas. Follow the flow and try to summarize, as you did above, the most important thing to take out of such long blocks of text.
- Keywords are especially important, but sometimes they come packaged as phrases instead of single words. Nonetheless, keep your ear attuned to anything that announces authorial purpose, structure, or logic. Note the phrase "This point is illustrated by..." in paragraph three—this tells you you're about to see an example. Use that information to keep ahead of the game.

The Questions

14. D

First up is a Global question looking for the author's main point. As you just got through saying, the big idea is that autobiographies put together by editors are fundamentally different from those untouched by any but the subject's hand. In a literary sense, the latter is an authentic representation of the African American experience; the former is not. All of this leads straight to (D). The phrase "circumstances under which" etc. adequately covers the ground covered by the passage, and nicely mirrors the wording of the last sentence of the passage.

(A) According to lines 19–27, (A) is a true statement: In the author's view, the integrity of editors has no bearing on the literary value of edited autobiographies. But this is nothing more than a detail in the second paragraph; it's way too narrow in scope to be considered the passage's main idea.

(B) is true as well: The author thinks that edited autobiographies are less valuable as literature than are "dictated" ones. But dictated autobiographies are mentioned only in the third paragraph. The passage revolves around the difference between edited and unedited autobiographies. Dictated autobiographies are just one type of edited autobiography.

(C) plays on a detail. The author never claims that personal impressions are more important than facts, but rather contends that personal impressions affect the way in which facts are set down. In any case, this certainly can't be considered the passage's main idea.

(E) The author *does* seem to believe that African American autobiographies need to be studied more carefully—that's apparent throughout the passage, especially at the end of the second and third paragraphs. But this choice doesn't mention the fundamental difference between edited and unedited autobiographies, the theme that's at the heart of this passage.

- Just because something may be true or is strongly supported by the information in the passage doesn't mean that it suffices as the passage's main idea. Be selective! Go with the one that encompasses the most essential elements of the passage.

15. E

You're asked to apply what you know of editors from the passage to an external situation, specifically looking for the one that exhibits the same type of role as editors as that role is portrayed in the passage. So begin by asking yourself what part editors played in molding collaborative autobiographies. According to lines 23–27, editors took the facts provided by the subject of the autobiography and presented those facts in the way they thought was most appropriate. Looking over the answer choices, this role is closest to that of historians whose job it is to reenact historical events. Like editors, these historians would take a bunch of facts and present them in the way they felt was proper. (E) gets the point.

The roles in the other choices don't involve the interpretation of historical facts. This is most obviously true of the artist in (A) and the architect in (D). The worker in (B) interprets instructions, not facts. And the critic in (C) deals with the strengths and weaknesses of a work of art, not with facts.

16. B

What does the author think about applying literary analysis to edited autobiographies? You already know the author's opinion of such works: They're inauthentic because they can distort the subject's life experiences and feelings. This attitude strongly suggests that the author has doubts about "close analytic readings" of these texts, right? What's the point of closely analyzing a work that's inauthentic? Indeed, in the penultimate sentence of the last paragraph, the author explicitly states that "analysts should reserve close analytic readings for independently authored (i.e., unedited) texts." (B) is the one that expresses this attitude.

(A) is too extreme. In the last sentence of the passage, the author says that literary analysis of edited autobiographies must come to grips with "the conditions that governed their production." In other words, the author's not "adamantly opposed" to all literary analysis of edited works; he or she just thinks that one particular type of literary analysis, the close analytic reading of texts, is inappropriate for edited works.

(C) and (E) twist details in paragraph two: Nowhere does the author advocate analyzing prefaces, footnotes, and commentaries (C); if anything, the author feels these have served as red herrings, masking the lack of authenticity of edited texts. As for (E), linguistic, structural, and tonal integrity are contrasted in the passage to the moral integrity of editors. Nowhere does the author state or imply that analysis enhances these.

(D) raises an issue that the author never addresses—the historical reading of such narratives.

- Learn to recognize classic wrong answer types so that you can eliminate such choices quickly. Here you have a good mix: extreme (A); distortion (C) and (E); and outside the scope (D).

17. D

Next you're asked about past readers of African American autobiographies. These readers are mentioned only once, in lines 28–37. There, you're told that they, like the editors, believed that edited autobiographies were no less genuine a representation of the African American consciousness than unedited works. That makes (D) the answer.

(A), (C), and (E) You simply aren't told what aspect of the autobiographies most interested earlier readers (A), whether they were more knowledgeable about the facts of slave life than contemporary readers (C), or whether they were interested in the moral integrity of the editors, (E). (A) and (C) present comparisons that are simply unwarranted; there's no support for them at all. (E), on the other hand, tries to connect the moral integrity issue in some way to these earlier readers, but there's no support for this connection anywhere.

(B) makes no sense at all, since "ghostwritten" autobiographies, according to the first sentence of the second paragraph, are edited autobiographies.

- Another wrong answer type, common in Logical Reasoning questions as well, is the unwarranted or irrelevant comparison. These can be tempting because they often involve recognizable elements or characters from the passage, but simply compare them in a way that's unsupported by the text.

18. A

The stem is a bit on the long side, but essentially you're after the word that reveals the author's skepticism about the authenticity of edited autobiographies. That's really what the question's asking, right? Choice (A)'s "ostensible" fits the bill. As it's used in the passage, ostensible means "supposed" or "presumed." Using the word "ostensible" to describe the authorship of the narratives is the author's way of saying right off the bat that he's doubtful of the authenticity of some of these works. Any study of these autobiographies supposedly ("ostensibly") written by the subjects themselves would, according to the author, raise concerns about authenticity.

If you didn't see this, you might still have gotten the correct answer through process of elimination. None of the other words refers to the author's feelings about edited autobiographies. In fact, each refers to ideas and issues discussed considerably later. "Integrity," (B), and "delimits," (D), relate to the editors of autobiographies, rather than to the author's attitude toward the works themselves. Similarly, "extraneous," (C), relates to the facts that appear in edited autobiographies, while "impolitic," (E), relates to people being interviewed in the 1930s.

- If you have trouble with a wordy or complicated question stem, you may wish to consider postponing the question for later. Remember, you need not work through every question to get a top score. Just remember to fill in a guess for any question you don't get to.

19. C

You can make quick work of question 19, dealing with "close analytic readings" of texts. As you mentioned back in question 16, the author thinks that close analytic readings are useful only in cases where autobiographies have been written by their subjects. Lines 56–57 explicitly make this point. (C), which says exactly the same thing, is one of the easier points on this section.

(A), (D) and (E) all mention an editor, so they can be eliminated right off the bat. It's edited collaborative texts that the author specifically says shouldn't receive close readings.

(B) raises an issue that's outside the scope of the passage (though it sounds good, doesn't it?).

- Not every question in a Reading Comp set tests a different concept. Often, the issues in various questions are related, so, just as in Logic Games, use your work and thinking from previous questions to help you with later ones when possible.

20. B

Why bring up Blassingame?—asks the final question of the set. To determine this, it's important to grasp the context in which he's discussed. The name isn't too hard to find; Blassingame is cited by the author in the beginning of paragraph two as someone who believes that editors were honest, and therefore would not have played fast and loose with the facts. Directly after this point is made, the author goes on to say that personal integrity is *not* the issue (note the "however"); what *is* at issue, according to the author, is the "linguistic, structural, and tonal integrity" of autobiographies produced by editors. In other words, Blassingame is introduced as an example of a scholar with a misplaced emphasis when it comes to the study of African American autobiography. And that's (B).

(A) is out because Blassingame's point of view contradicts, rather than supports, the author's point of view.

(C) Blassingame's method of studying autobiographies is in line with the one that has traditionally been used by scholars. If anyone has a new idea about how to look at autobiographies, it's the author.

(D) is a bit tricky if you don't keep context in mind. Remember, what the author *really* objects to is Blassingame's assessment of the editor's role, not his adherence to the traditional approach to literary analysis of African American autobiography.

(E) distorts information in the passage: The author doesn't think the editor-narrator relationship is important; if anything, he or she thinks that it causes problems. In any case, this isn't the reason why Blassingame appears in the text.

- Logic function questions test whether you're up on what the author's up to, such as why he includes a word, an example, a paragraph, and so on. Keywords help the author to tell the story in a coherent manner, and by extension help you to keep tabs on the author. The contrast keyword "however" is the key to this question.

Passage 4—Rubinstein's Theory

Topic and Scope

Wealth in Britain; specifically, Rubinstein's theory of wealth and power in 19th-century Britain

Purpose and Main Idea

The author's purpose is to evaluate Rubinstein's work; his specific Main Idea is that Rubinstein has made a valuable contribution to the question, but hasn't entirely proven his case.

Paragraph Structure

In the first paragraph, the author tells you that Rubinstein's theory takes issue with the traditional, Marxist interpretation of 19th-century British history; in contrast to Marxist historians, Rubinstein argues that real wealth lay with a commercial elite in London, rather than with northern industrialists.

The second paragraph tells you about the evidence that Rubinstein uses to substantiate his view; specifically, investigations of probate records. Such records do seem to show more commercial fortunes than industrial ones, but the keyword "However" alerts you to a complication: these investigations don't fully make Rubinstein's case because of ambiguities inherent in the probate valuation process.

Paragraph three goes on to say that Rubinstein also disagrees with the Marxist interpretation of history with respect to the connection between wealth and power; according to him, the rich were not necessarily the most powerful people in society.

The final paragraph tells you that Rubinstein has begun to strengthen his views by collecting evidence from tax records. The last sentence, introduced with the contrast keyword "But," reinforces the author's point that you can't fully accept Rubinstein's theory without further proof.

The Big Picture

- Coming into the passage you don't need to know anything about Rubinstein or his theory. All the information you need to answer the questions is in the passage. So don't worry when a passage mentions a theory. You have everything you need.
- When a theory is presented, try to determine the author's position on the matter. The questions will test whether you've picked up on it. This author finds Rubinstein's theory "provocative," but only "partially convincing."

The Questions

21. C

First up is a typical Global question, so you've already done the work necessary to answer this question. Now, as you just finished saying, this passage is about Rubinstein's theory of the distribution of wealth and power in 19th-century Britain, a theory the author finds intriguing, but still insufficiently documented to displace the traditional view of 19th-century Britain. (C) is the closest to this.

(A) contradicts the author's message: Rubinstein's theory, according to the author, is not strong enough to overturn the traditional, Marxist interpretation of history. Besides, this passage is primarily about Rubinstein's theory, not about the Marxist view of history.

(B) is out because the author never tells you what sort of relationship between wealth and power he or she expects to find in new data. Additionally, this choice completely misses the message of the passage, which (again) is that a new theory has emerged to challenge the orthodox view of 19th-century Britain.

(D) is a true statement: The passage says that probate records are indeed a revealing, though imperfect, source of information about the location of wealth in 19th-century Britain. The problem with (D) is that it's simply too narrow in scope to qualify as the big idea of the passage—a discussion of the benefits and drawbacks of examining probate records is limited to the second paragraph.

(E) is also too narrow. Furthermore, the author never says that confirmation of Rubinstein's theory "is likely to remain elusive"; to say that Rubinstein hasn't gotten it 100% right yet is not to predict that he won't someday.

- The correct answer to a Global question must reflect the scope of the entire passage.

22. D

In the first part of the second paragraph, the author notes that probate records provide interesting information about the distribution of wealth in 19th-century Britain. But in the remainder of the paragraph, he or she notes that there are a number of problems concerning the correct interpretation of these records. So choice (D) is the answer—it touches both bases.

(A), (B) and (C) Remember, the author thinks that probate records are eye opening, though hard to interpret. Of (A), (B) and (C), only (B)'s "ambiguous" and (C)'s "controversial" capture a sense of this feeling. But the second parts of these choices don't fit the bill: "outdated" gets the time frame wrong, and "readily available" is outside the scope of the issue. (A), meanwhile, is way too critical.

(E) Rubinstein, as far as you know, is the only historian to have worked with these records. Moreover, the author never says or implies that only specialists are able to decipher them.

- Many Reading Comp choices can be eliminated because of a single word or phrase that conflicts with the author's tone or opinion on a certain matter.

23. A

You're interested in whether the author thinks that probate records accurately reflect the value of 19th-century "goods for sale." This issue comes up in lines 28–34, where the author more or less tells you that probate values for such goods may have been dependent upon valuation conventions. That's (A).

(B) is out for the simple reason that the author never draws a comparison between the accuracy of probate and income tax records.

(C) is out because the author never draws a comparison between tobacco- and alcohol-related goods. As a matter of fact, the only thing the author says about tobacco and alcohol is that people in these industries tended to make more money than people in textiles or metals.

(D) Lines 30–34 tell you that (D) is the opposite of what the author believes: Probate values for bank balances were higher.

(E) The author never implies that valuation conventions for goods for sale were dependent upon a person's occupation. Rather, the author says that general probate valuations, in contrast to goods for sale valuations, may have been affected by occupation: but that's a completely different story.

- Don't bend over backward for an answer choice. Look for the one choice that the test makers have set up to be excellent. Choices that require you to make up a story in order for them to work are always wrong.

24. E

Now you're asked specifically about Rubinstein's challenge to the orthodox view of 19th-century Britain. Rubinstein challenges the orthodox view on two points: (1) he claims that a London-based commercial elite, rather than a northern industrial elite, was the true center of wealth, and (2) he claims that there was no relationship between wealth and power. Either of these views would be satisfactory as the right answer; the test makers picked the second, (E).

(A) and (D) are too vague: Both Rubinstein and the traditionalists believe that the distribution of wealth between commerce and industry was unequal, (A), and that a governing elite can be identified, (D). It's the specifics of this economic inequality and the precise makeup of this elite that they disagree on. The claims in (A) and (D) don't reflect these nuances.

(B) The claim that the tobacco and alcohol industries were more lucrative than the textiles and metals industries, (B), is based on Rubinstein's research—it's not a point of contention between him and the traditionalists.

(C) If you stop reading too soon, desperate for an answer, you're tempted by poor choices like (C): the existence of a London-based commercial elite is actually a claim made by Rubinstein himself.

- Many LSAT Reading Comp passages present multiple views, and it's up to you to keep them straight. Use your Roadmap to keep track of who says what.

25. B

This one asks why the author points out that "goodwill" was excluded from 19th-century probate valuations. Since you're being asked why a detail has been included in the passage, the context in which it appears is all-important. If you look back at lines 28–39, you'll find that the exclusion of goodwill is brought up in the midst of a general discussion about why many 19th-century British businesses were undervalued in probate records. That makes (B) the answer.

(A) and (E) are outside the scope: The author doesn't say that little was known about the concept of goodwill in the 19th century, (A); nor does the author ever make a comparison between 19th- and 20th-century probate valuation methods, (E).

(C) If anything, the author implies that the exclusion of goodwill may have had an unequal impact across different types of business.

(D) is wrong for a couple of reasons. First, the author's interested only in 19th-century British businesses, not businesses in general. Second, the author never says that goodwill is "the most important factor in determining the market value of certain businesses."

- If you keep your focus on the scope of the passage in your initial read, you won't be distracted by choices that violate it.

26. D

Now you need to determine which of five studies would support Rubinstein's claims. As mentioned in question 24, Rubinstein makes two basic claims: (1) true wealth was in the hands of a commercial elite in London, not in the hands of a northern industrial elite, and (2) there was no direct link between wealth and power. So, you're looking for a study that would support one or both of these claims. (D) fits the bill: Rubinstein's claim about the location of wealth, after all, rests on probate records, which don't include the value of real property. If it were to be discovered that real property did not, in fact, add to the riches of industrialists, this finding would tend to confirm Rubinstein's belief that true wealth lay in the hands of a London-based commercial elite.

(A) would tend to undermine Rubinstein's claim that real wealth in 19th-century Britain was in the hands of a London-based commercial elite.

(B) A study that indicated that working-class people targeted northern industrialists would support the traditional, Marxist view of 19th-century Britain. Rubinstein, as you know, opposes this view.

(C), too, would tend to undermine Rubinstein's claims: If the probate values of goods for sale in that era were found to be lower than probate values of cash assets, this would indicate that industrialists had more wealth in comparison to members of the commercial elite than Rubinstein seems to think. That is, this would tend to confirm one of the uncertainties that the author suggests could limit the value of Rubinstein's theory.

(E) would tend to undermine Rubinstein's claim that there was no connection between money and power.

- In Reading Comp and in Logical Reasoning, you have to be clear as to *which* argument you're strengthening or weakening. Expect a few 180 choices to tempt those that get this backward.

27. E

Now you're asked to pick the scenario that would cast the most doubt on Rubinstein's argument about the connection between wealth and power. Well, as paragraph three tells you, Rubinstein argues that there was no such connection in 19th-century Britain: Wealth, in other words, didn't automatically give one power, and lack of wealth didn't automatically exclude one from power. So, if it was to be shown that there *was* indeed some sort of tangible connection between wealth and power—that possession of wealth *did* lead to power—this would certainly weaken Rubinstein's argument. (E) makes this connection, and therefore casts the most doubt on Rubinstein's wealth-power hypothesis.

(A) To enter the ruling elite, according to Rubinstein, one needed only two things: a university degree and a father with a middle-class income. (A), therefore, would tend to strengthen, rather than weaken, Rubinstein's argument.

(B) and (C) present irrelevant comparisons. (B) compares the relative importance of the two factors Rubinstein claims are prerequisites for power; but Rubinstein never compares them with *each other*, so nothing about this damages his claim. Maybe schooling is more crucial than income, maybe the other way around, who knows? As for (C), the wealth of powerful bishops compared with that of powerful civil servants and company bosses is also irrelevant. These powerful bishops may have had a little more dough than the other members of the elite, but that doesn't mean they were truly wealthy by societal standards. In other words, the fact that they were a little better off financially than the others doesn't weaken Rubinstein's opposition to the claim that power resides in the hands of society's wealthiest.

(D) tends to weaken the traditional Marxist claim, not Rubinstein's argument. The Marxists are the ones who saw the textile and iron barons of the north as the power elite, the ones against which the workers waged their battle.

- Strengthen and Weaken the Argument questions are mainstays of the Logical Reasoning section, but don't be surprised if a few pop up on your RC section as well.
- Make sure you focus on the right argument. There are three here: the traditional Marxist view, Rubinstein's view that this traditional view is incorrect, and the author's view that Rubinstein's critique is provocative but incomplete. If you keep them straight from the beginning, then Strengthen/Weaken questions should be a whole lot easier.

SECTION IV: LOGICAL REASONING

1. C

If you read the question stem first, as the Kaplan LR Method requires, you know exactly what you're looking for: something the author fails to consider. That's a specific kind of logical flaw.

Paraphrase the argument: The Acme cafeteria can only offer four main dishes, and they've offered the same ones for years. When mushroom casserole was offered for two days in place of one of the other dishes, the masses went wild—they loved it. The author concludes that the only way to make these people happy is to now offer mushroom casserole in place of one of the other dishes. It's likely you were able to prephrase what's wrong with this picture: The author sees the mushroom casserole itself as being the catalyst for the seeming popularity of the dish, but while it *could* be true that most people are desperately enamored with mushroom casserole, it seems quite likely that people were simply starving for some variety. Choice (C) spells out this alternative explanation for the mushroom craze, and makes you wonder how many times a person can eat mushroom casserole before getting tired of it? Making this dish a permanent part of the menu, based merely on the evidence of two days, may not be such a great idea after all, if you consider that the need for variety may have driven people to it.

(A) The proportion of employees who eat at the cafeteria has nothing to do with the argument; it's not *who's* eating, but rather *what's being eaten* that matters.

(B) The ingredients of the dishes, and especially the possibility of overlap among the dishes, are outside the scope.

(D) and (E) Only "main dishes at lunchtime" are addressed, so other dishes and other meals are also outside the scope of the argument.

- Reading the question stem first tells you specifically what your focus should be when you read through the stimulus; in this case, what factor in the argument is going right over the author's head? (Of course, it must also be a factor that's *relevant* to the argument. The author also "fails to consider" why the sky is blue, but that's not part of the argument's scope.)

2. D

There's a paradox afoot in question 2, so the first step is to isolate the surprise. Reduced to its basics, the argument reads like this: Even though clearing forests of tall trees results in more sunlight and thus more leafy shrubs, upon which mule deer depend for food, mule deer that live in cleared forests aren't as well-nourished as are herds living in un-cleared forests. So more leafy shrubs *should* mean well-nourished mule deer, but in fact lead to the opposite. What's going on?

Clearly, there's something you're not being told about the leafy shrubs or the greater quantity of sunlight that may explain away this surprising fact, but it's not easy to prephrase the exact resolution. Move to the choices, looking for an additional factor that will solve the mystery.

(A) doesn't address the paradox; it talks about differences between mule deer and other deer, an issue that's outside the scope.

(B) introduces a distinction within the mule deer population between those that live in cleared forests and those that don't, but it doesn't address the problem of less well-nourished deer. It would only be useful if you had some reason to think that females with young offspring are generally less well nourished than adult males—but you've no reason to believe this.

(C) Huh? You're not looking for trivia tidbits regarding the mule deer, fascinating as they may be. You're demanding specific information regarding why mule deer with supposedly more food are less well nourished—and this isn't it.

(D) is, finally, a satisfying answer, even though it fails to mention deer at all. It directly addresses the reason why sunny forests produce less well-nourished deer. If increased sunlight actually leads to the creation of food that is not digestible, as (D) says, the deer can eat to their little hearts' content and they won't reap any benefits. (D) is directly relevant to the mystery at hand, and offers the best resolution.

(E) might help explain why deer might become *better* nourished when the forest is cleared of tall trees, because the parasites wouldn't have a jumping-off point. In terms of resolving the paradox at hand, (E) is of no help at all.

- When you see the word "paradox" in a question stem, think "surprise." A situation that should appear a certain way or lead to a certain logical result instead leads somewhere totally different. Your job in resolving the paradox (or "seeming discrepancy") is to find the choice that explains the surprise.

3. D

Your task in this Parallel Reasoning question is to find the argument that mimics Harold's response to Genevieve. Genevieve gives concrete reasons supporting her argument, and while acknowledging that her reasoning is sound, Harold dismisses it because she herself flies often. So locate the choice in which someone discounts a conclusion on the grounds that the person making a recommendation doesn't follow her own advice.

(A) doesn't include a person giving concrete reasons: it's simply a person saying "Thumbs down." Furthermore, the judgment regards something the person *hasn't* done, not something the person does despite his or her own judgment.

(B) isn't saying why a person should or shouldn't do anything. No judgment is offered at all. This person simply isn't cooking lamb tonight because her friend doesn't eat it. This may make sense if she's having Maria over for dinner, but it has no relation to Harold's logic.

(C) would be closer if Susan had given concrete, sound reasons why rock climbing is safe but nevertheless refused to do it herself. But no: Susan says it's safe, *does* go ahead and do it, and then breaks her collarbone. You can't exactly fault this person for doubting her safety claim.

(D) Bingo. Here you have a person who presents valid evidence to support a statement, but whose argument is dismissed since she doesn't practice what she preaches.

(E) isn't even a reply to someone else's argument, so you can cross it off right away.

- The best way to deal with most Parallel Reasoning questions is to characterize the conclusion. Then, if necessary after checking the conclusion against the answer choices, do the same with the evidence. The content won't lead you to the correct answer; accurately identifying its *structure* will.

4. A

Next up you need to find an explanation for why certain residents seem to hold two contradictory opinions at once. On the one hand, all Gradarans want hazardous waste to be burned in high-temperature incinerators—they want laws to that effect to be passed. But companies that are trying to build the incinerators in question can't find any place to build them because people who live in Gradaran communities are protesting the building permit applications. What's the average Gradaran on the street saying?

The old NIMBY argument: "Not in *my* backyard! I want the incinerator to get rid of that waste, but I don't want to have to look at it, or smell it, or be potentially harmed by it." This is basically what (A) says. Incineration of this kind is great for the population at large, but it has risks for the people closest to the incineration sites. (A) explains how Gradarans can simultaneously hold both opinions cited; if (A) is true, these opinions don't really conflict at all.

(B) and (E) raise the issue of cost, but that's not a factor, as far as you know, in the people's decision making. So no appeal to cost will explain why the Gradarans hold seemingly opposing positions, or will help to resolve them.

(C) is off the subject too, since you don't know anything about how the use of private companies to carry out the incineration will influence public opinion. No help.

(D) seems to try to make the incinerators seem safe, if that's what turning toxic waste fumes into solids means. But that has nothing to do with the paradox at hand. The specifics of the process have no bearing on the seemingly conflicting positions.

- When seeking to resolve an apparent conflict, stick closely to the scope of the contradiction. Here there's an ambiguity regarding the residents' support for the overall plan. Issues such as cost or who will carry it out are beyond this scope.

5. C

The stimulus is only one sentence; Elena doesn't have to say too much to reveal her deep-seated paranoia regarding white poodles. While the question stem should be, "Why didn't someone tell Elena not to attend dog shows?" it's not. So you mustn't spend precious time concerning yourself with Elena's fragile emotional state.

In this one sentence, Elena really makes two interdependent statements: Every dog that growled at her was a white poodle (All X were Y), and every white poodle she saw growled at her (All Y were X). So you know that if you don't have one, you can't have the other, right? It could never be true that, at the dog show, a white poodle looked at her and didn't growl. It could also never be true that a dog that growled at her wasn't a white poodle. There's no point in guessing what the correct inference will be, since it could be one of many, so look through the choices until you find the answer.

(A) You can't infer (A), because you don't know whether or not Elena saw any other dogs. She may have seen a hundred other white breeds—she may have seen none.

(B) is not inferable either. Remember, all you know about is Elena's bad karma with white poodles. There very well could have been lots of gray poodles at the show, or any other color, for that matter—you have no way of knowing. If there *were* dogs of other colors there, you know for sure that they didn't growl at Elena. Speaking of which. . .

(C) is the answer for just that reason. Because all dogs that aren't white poodles have been excluded from the growling category, (C) must be true.

(D) If you knew that the only type of white dog that Elena saw was a white poodle, then (D) would be true, but you can't know this for certain.

(E) Once again, you can't know anything about any type of dog that isn't a white poodle except that it didn't growl at her. Maybe she saw some gray poodles, maybe she didn't.

- Understanding and interpreting if/then statements is an absolute necessity in Logic Games, but it's important for Logical Reasoning, too.

6. C

Questions 6 and 7 share the same stimulus, a conversation between Derek and Lola. Essentially, Derek argues that you need to harvest yew trees now to develop an anticancer drug, because an effective man-made drug would take too long to develop. Lola takes the "friend of nature" stance, arguing that it's more important to protect the rare yew trees and the endangered spotted owl, and therefore you should wait for a synthetic drug to be manufactured.

Skimming through Derek's argument, what stands out? How about "you must exploit..." and "the trees should be harvested now." If you can get an effective anticancer drug *now*, Derek says, why wait? Lola's key words, "Despite our eagerness..." and "you should wait rather than threaten..." shows that she believes there is a justifiable alternative to chopping down rare trees and killing off animals. These keywords clue you in on the main point at issue: to wait or not to wait. Only (C) deals with the delay issue, so it's the correct choice here.

(A) Derek doesn't argue that harvesting yews won't have repercussions—in fact, he allows that it may—so (A) is off base.

(B) Neither Derek nor Lola seems particularly concerned with whether drugs *in general* should be synthetic or natural, so (B) isn't a point of contention either. What worries them are the specific considerations that are entailed in this particular decision—namely, waiting a long time versus threatening the ecosystem.

(D) doesn't work because Derek doesn't quantify the environmental impact of harvesting yew trees, nor does he even mention the spotted owl.

(E) is too broad, specifically in its use of the word "ever": Derek and Lola are talking about a specific set of circumstances, not a plan of action in general. To blow this disagreement up into a general conflict between environmental and human needs is too extreme.

- In dialogue questions, try to boil down the speakers' key points and don't get bogged down in detail. If you do reduce the respective arguments to their most basic formulations, the point at issue should emerge fairly clearly—it's the one both parties address, and take different positions on.
- When prose is dense (and even when it isn't), look for the basic grammatical clues to help you get a handle on the argument.

7. E

For the second question of this two-parter, you're asked to identify the principle to which Lola's position most closely conforms. In simpler terms, what general thing must Lola believe in order to argue as she does?

Recap Lola's argument: She believes that it's more important to protect the ecosystem from long-lasting damage than it is to provide a resource that would quickly enable a new medical breakthrough. In other words, weighing the pros and cons, Lola thinks the cancer cure can wait for a synthetic solution since adopting Derek's plan will damage the ecosystem. This notion of prioritizing is captured in every element of (E): The action that threatens an ecosystem and that should be avoided is harvesting the yews; avoiding this action is more important to Lola than immediately helping the restricted group, the cancer sufferers.

(A) If anything, the principle in (A) works against Lola's position. The wellbeing of cancer patients is certainly threatened, so one who subscribes to the principle in this one would ostensibly favor harvesting the yews to provide quicker relief to the sufferers.

(B) Neither medical researchers nor environmentalists are mentioned in Lola's argument, so it's extremely doubtful that this principle can form the bedrock of Lola's argument. Furthermore, the tone isn't right—nothing suggests that Lola would favor the kind of compromise indicated in (B).

(C) and (D) Neither of these principles can underlie Lola's position, as human lives *are* at stake and you *do* presumably have a situation in which human lives can be saved. Believers in these principles would in all likelihood sacrifice the environmental concerns and support Derek's call to harvest the yews. But Lola goes the other way.

- The wrong choices in Principle questions often present notions that support the opposite of the argument in question. Here, a number of wrong choices conform somewhat to *Derek's* position. This is a good reminder of the importance of keeping the various positions straight, which is of course a skill that holds you in good stead on Reading Comp as well.

8. C

From the question stem, you know that there's a flaw in the reasoning—specifically, something that's necessary to the argument isn't established. Your job is to figure out what that might be. A committee's study states that certain students weren't excelling academically because they spent too much time playing sports and too little time studying. Based on this finding, a school director decides to prohibit those students from playing sports. This, he thinks, will guarantee that they'll do well. Does this make any sense?

Evidently not, or else the test makers wouldn't have designated this a Flaw question. Picture the jock in your homeroom who goofed off during school and only cared about sports. If he suddenly wasn't allowed to play any sports, would he necessarily spend his newfound free time pursuing the academic life? What's the guarantee that schoolwork would suddenly become a priority? It's possible, but hardly a sure thing. This is the error in the director's reasoning—that time is all that's needed to turn these jocks into brains. (C) hits on the omission in the director's argument.

(A), (B), and (D) The scope of the argument is very specific—athletes with academic problems. Jocks who *don't* have trouble in school, (A), and academic stars in general, (B) and (D), are outside this scope. In other words, the director need not establish that some sporty students *don't* have academic problems (A), because he's only worried about the ones who do. Likewise, the director also needn't establish anything about students who *don't* have academic problems. The relationship between academic performance and sports participation is only described for bad students. The director need not prove that academic success is totally incompatible with playing sports, as (B) and (D) would have it, in order to propose that the academically challenged athletes re-prioritize their time.

(E) What would happen to the sports program as a result of the ban is outside the scope of the argument, which simply concerns the director's prohibition and his reason for it. Whether or not the teams decline has nothing to do with whether or not the banned students' schoolwork would improve.

- Don't fault an author, speaker, or in this case, character for not doing something he or she is not *logically obligated* to do. Sure, many of these choices describe things the director failed to establish, but that's only half the question. The other half, of course, is: was it necessary to establish these things? (C) is the only choice that contains an omission that the director absolutely needs to establish in defending his ban.

9. B

What fact could be provided that would lead you to conclude that there are at least as many trees in Seclee as there are in Martown? There has to be some sort of relationship between the two regions for this to be true.

(A) isn't much help. You don't know how many trees were in Seclee or Martown before the planting; for all you know, Seclee was totally treeless before the planting and Martown was a veritable rain forest.

(B) does provide that crucial relationship. If Martown is in Seclee, then every tree in Martown must be in Seclee, and so Seclee must have at least as many trees as Martown. So (B)'s the answer.

(C) doesn't tell you anything helpful. Martown could be choked with tree growth and Seclee could be a wasteland for all you know. They may not be healthy trees in Martown, but that doesn't matter.

(D) You'd need all sorts of additional information for (D) to help you reach any conclusion, so you know it's no good. Rainfall, indeed.

(E) Since you don't know how many trees both towns started out with, you can't know which has more now. Again, no help.

- This question wasn't your standard Inference question. Usually you reason from the stimulus to the correct answer, not the other way around. You always need to be ready for the possibility that the test makers will put a different spin on a familiar question type.

10. C

Two more questions for the price of one; questions 10 and 11 deal with the seals of the North Sea. It appears that distemper is a virus that has caused two-thirds of the seals in the North Sea to die off since May 1988. The virus can't be totally to blame, however, since it's been there (albeit latent) for a while. The author concludes that it must be the severe pollution that has caused the seals to become vulnerable to the disease.

So essentially there's a cause and effect argument at work here. The first question asks you what the author is assuming in coming to this conclusion. Whenever you're faced with a causal argument, consider alternative possibilities. In concluding that the pollution is to blame, the author is assuming that no other possible cause is at work; (C) plays off this issue. If there was a sudden mutation in the distemper virus, there would be an alternate explanation for the death of the poor lovable seals, and the author's argument would be greatly weakened. Therefore, in implicating the pollution as the cause of death, the author *must* presuppose that no such mutation occurred.

(A) The author isn't claiming there has been such a decline over the last 200 years, nor is such a claim relevant to his argument.

(B) The argument would actually be stronger *without* (B), so it can't be the assumption. If further sources of pollution *have* been added since May 1988, it would only support the author's contention that pollution was the cause of the decline in seal population.

(D) too can only weaken the argument, as it suggests that pollution levels in the North Sea, at least relative to other bodies of water, is not that high. But since you have no way of knowing what the levels are at in these other seas, (D) offers nothing more than irrelevant comparisons that are far from necessary pieces of this argument.

(E) isn't necessary for the author's argument either. The author isn't arguing that the seals are dying because their food is gone, but because the seals themselves are becoming sick. The seals' food species can be surviving quite nicely in the polluted water of the North Sea, and the author's argument about the seals' immune systems would still hold.

- Keep your mind open to alternative explanations at all times, especially in arguments involving cause and effect relationships. Recognizing possibilities that the author overlooks can assist you in a number of question types, including Assumption, Strengthen/Weaken, and Flaw.

11. A

Next you're asked to find the choice that supports the explanation for the drop in seal population, so find the choice that either discounts plausible alternative explanations or shores up the pollution account offered by the author.

(A) accomplishes the latter: It bolsters the idea that the North Sea pollution has weakened the seals' immune system by making it likely that the same thing has happened to other North Sea species. (A) may not *prove* the author's case, but it doesn't have to: it makes you more likely to believe that pollution *is* the factor at work here, as the author contends. If you didn't think that (A) went far enough, you should at least have been able to eliminate the others for familiar reasons.

(B) and (E) both weaken the author's argument—(B) by suggesting that pollution in the North Sea isn't that severe, and (E) by suggesting an alternate explanation for the seals' sudden acquisition of distemper.

(C) is outside the scope: The fact that fish have been taken out of the water for human consumption doesn't tell you anything about the pollution level of the water or about the effect of pollution on seals.

(D) The author doesn't distinguish between different kinds of seals, so (D) has no effect on the argument either.

- The job of a strengthener is not to *prove* an argument, nor does a weakener have to *disprove* it. They simply make the argument more or less *likely*—and that's the test you should have in mind when evaluating choices in these kinds of questions.
- Choices that fall outside the scope of an argument can have no bearing on the argument's validity.

12. D

Most of the time, your best bet in Parallel Reasoning is to express the conclusion in abstract terms and throw out the choices that depart from that; then do the same for the pieces of evidence, until all you're left with is the credited choice.

Here, the conclusion says that it is clear that no one in a certain group did something. However, the conclusion isn't particularly helpful in making eliminations in this question, so you'll have to move on and characterize the evidence. Everyone in one group shares a characteristic, and no one in a second group has that characteristic.

(A) can be eliminated based on the conclusion—it interjects the negative "no one who *failed* to do something."

(B) Also fails to match up because of the negatives it introduces, but this time they're in the evidence.

(C) This evidence relates to having a "reputation" for doing something, not a direct statement (as you saw in the stem) that members of the group *had* done something. Eliminate.

(D) works on both counts, though it might be tough to recognize at first since the terms are reversed—make sure you take the time to break down each piece in *logical* terms.

(E) You can get rid of (E) just by looking at its conclusion, which refers to what is "likely" to happen. There's nothing that corresponds to this in the original.

- Pay no attention at all to the fact that in the original stimulus the conclusion is the first sentence, whereas in (D) the conclusion is placed in the middle. As a matter of fact, the test writers often deliberately mix up the order of the sentences in the correct answer to a Parallel Reasoning question to throw you off the track. Keep in mind that the decision of where to place the conclusion in the argument—beginning, middle or end—is a stylistic choice rather than a logical one.
- Remember, you can handle the questions in any order you want. A time-consuming question like this one may be well worth postponing.

13. E

The stimulus for questions 13 and 14 concerns a decision regarding the hiring of a dean of computing. There are several qualifications to be demonstrated. The dean must be: 1) respected by the academic staff, and 2) competent to oversee the use of computers on campus. In order for the dean to be respected, he must 3) hold a doctoral degree. In order to competently oversee the use of computers he must 4) really know about computers. Makes sense so far. Furthermore, he must 5) already be on the university staff. The conclusion is that the dean of computing must therefore be a professor from the computer science department.

Question 13 asks you for the assumption upon which this argument depends. Well, the author made a "logical leap" (or "illogical leap," as the case may be) from the idea that the dean must know a lot about computers, to the conclusion that the dean will have to come from the computer science department. It makes sense that a professor from the computer science department would be *eligible* for the job, but it doesn't make sense to automatically rule out other departments' professors without supporting evidence. In doing so, the author assumes that no one outside the computer science department could fulfill all of the qualifications. (E) gets at this point: The author assumes that only those in the computer science department really know about computers.

(A) Replace the word "people" with "deans" and you'd have a restatement of the evidence in the second sentence. As written, what academics think about *people* in general is outside the scope, which means that nothing about this need be assumed.

(B) It's not necessary for all of the professors to have doctoral degrees, only the ones qualified for this position.

(C) Every professor? Again, you're not concerned with all of them, only the one who is to be chosen.

(D) takes the issue too far. When it comes to respect, all you care about is what kind of *dean* the academic staff respects. Whether *all* eggheads with doctorates are respected is another issue, and one that's not particularly relevant to the issue at hand.

- Read carefully! As far as respect is concerned, the author tells you only what kind of *dean* earns respect from academics. Respect for people in general (A) or for "all academics" (D) is a broader topic, and therefore nothing about these things need be assumed here. If you understood the limited scope of the "respect requirement," you should have been able to axe these two choices quickly.

14. A

Question 14 asks you to find the statement that would weaken the argument, and (A) challenges the author's conclusion that the dean must be a professor. The members of the university staff described in this choice fulfill all the requirements outlined by the author, yet they aren't professors. If they exist (and you are to assume they do from the "if true" clause in the stem), then one of them could be chosen, and the author's final pronouncement would be inaccurate; (A) thus weakens the argument.

(B) One of the main stipulations for candidacy is having a doctoral degree. The academics described in this choice do not challenge the author's conclusion in any way.

(C) What does it matter that these other professors applied? The author isn't making any claims about who will *apply* for the position. This choice is simply outside the scope of the argument.

(D) offers another peripheral tidbit of information that doesn't address the argument in the slightest. The board of trustees makes a cameo appearance by mandating the final requirement that the new dean must come from the university staff. What credentials the members of this board of trustees possess have no bearing on the author's conclusion—the doctoral requirement pertains only to candidates for the position.

(E) would weaken the argument if the author had claimed that *any one* of the members of the computer science department is qualified to be the dean of computing. But she didn't, so it doesn't.

15. A

Another double-question stimulus. And a wordy stimulus it is at that. As always, see if you can pare it down to a manageable amount of information.

The consumer advocate believes that manufacturers are misleading customers with their product labeling. The example used is the term "fresh." According to the advocate, the common understanding of the word "fresh" does not apply to the actual product. So, to sum up the advocate's position, not using words according to their commonly understood definition is a misleading act. The manufacturer, however, counterargues that such an act is not deceptive, since words can have other, equally valid meanings. If there are no rules with which to comply, there can't be anything deceptive about such labeling.

Question 15 asks what the two are disagreeing about. Recap the principle behind the dispute. The advocate argues that in the absence of laws governing labeling practices, common understanding should be used as a guideline. Under that interpretation, she considers the orange juice label deceptive. But the manufacturer says that in the absence of standards, other definitions could suffice, since "fresh" can also signify something besides the "common" meaning. Based on this reasoning, the manufacturer feels the label is *not* deceptive. They therefore disagree about (A)—whether, in the absence of standards, common meaning determines deception or not. The advocate thinks it does; the manufacturer thinks it does not.

(B) Neither party says or suggests the government *couldn't* institute truthful labeling requirements.

(C) The Manufacturer doesn't dispute this point, raised by the consumer advocate, but only says the term can also have other meanings.

(D) The consumer advocate's argument doesn't target natural foods—and takes no position on what can be done truthfully—only on what's being done deceptively. Eliminate.

(E) The consumer advocate doesn't ever mention what could or should occur *after* government standards are created; she's only concerned with the here and now, which means the absence of government standards.

- The answer to a Point at Issue question must contain an issue that's addressed by both parties to the dispute. If either party has nothing to say on a particular issue addressed in a choice, cross that choice off.

16. C

Now for part two: "Which principle would strengthen the manufacturer's argument?" The manufacturer says, in short, that it's okay to play with the meaning of words so long as the government doesn't prohibit it. Look for a choice that provides that freedom.

(A) reiterates the advocate's stance; that's definitely not going to help the manufacturer's position in the least.

(B) would also work against the manufacturer: Sticking to common usages would preclude the fancy wordplay the manufacturer employs to condone what the advocate feels are deceptive labeling practices. The manufacturer would want the freedom to use alternative meanings. The creation of standards that reflect common understandings could only hurt his case.

(C) This principle is just what the manufacturer was trying to communicate, however crudely. There could be several meanings for any one word, so why can't I use them as long as there's no legal prohibition? If this principle were established, this point would be strengthened considerably, so (C) is correct. For the record:

(D) is nonsensical, because government standards don't exist in this scenario, so any judgment about them is beside the point.

(E) is beyond the scope, since the motivation behind the manufacturer's labeling practices isn't addressed, nor is the consumers' take on the issue a factor in this argument.

17. A

This is a quirky Method of Argument question, and a glance at the stem tells you that you need to find the grounds that the author uses to recommend a certain strategy. What's it all about?

First of all, items with the quality of exclusivity have an odd property: The items, when they become available, sell very quickly even though they're very expensive. You're then told that trying to sell an exclusive item cheaply is a mistake. Why? Because it makes people doubt its exclusivity. You then have the conclusion of the argument—signaled by "therefore." Given that it's almost impossible for a seller to gauge a correct price for an item in advance, the seller should be sure that any error is on the side of setting the price too high. That way, a seller won't price an exclusive item too low, and thus endanger the perception of its exclusivity, which is, after all, its chief appeal.

This is a Method of Argument question, so put the argument into more abstract terms. How does the author promote the strategy of setting prices too high? By explaining that setting prices too low will endanger the item's appeal, while setting the price too high doesn't entail this risk. So he recommends one strategy by pointing out a counterproductive feature of the alternative plan. That's (A).

(B) The author doesn't present any advantages of the alternate plan, so this can't be right.

(C) The author doesn't talk about past experience at all, and although the quality of exclusivity is "hard to define," the reasons that the strategy is superior are more concrete—it avoids a specific danger run by the alternative.

(D) Ah, but the strategy *does* rely on "buyers' estimates of value." Buyers presumably value exclusive items quite highly precisely *because* of their exclusivity, and the strategy is intended to preserve that perception of exclusivity and hence the value of such items in the minds of buyers.

(E) is a little tricky, but assume that setting the price of an exclusive item too high is what the test makers mean by "the error associated with this strategy." The point is not that no one will *notice* if the price is too high, but rather that an exorbitant price, while possibly unattainable, will not damage the item's key attribute—the perception of its exclusivity. So the author doesn't advocate the strategy for the reason cited in (E), but because the potential error associated with the strategy is much less damaging than erring on the other side.

- Don't bend over backward for an answer choice. If you have to make up a story to support a choice, or engage in extensive interpretation, you've found a wrong choice.

18. D

The biologist, in response to the problem of deer overpopulation, has proposed injecting female deer in breeding season with 10 milligrams of a fertility-suppressing hormone. Critics say that the biologist's idea would pose health risks to people who might eat the deer meat, and consume unsafe amounts of the hormone. The last sentence begins with "The biologist has responded..." and that should perk up your ears since the stem asks for the assumption underlying the biologist's response to the critics.

The biologist says that people can eat up to 10 milligrams of the hormone a day without any problems, and since no one would eat a whole deer a day, the plan is safe. What's the assumption? Well, if the deer are injected with 10 milligrams, and people can safely eat up to 10 milligrams a day, the assumption must be that there's no way that people would get *more* than 10 milligrams of the hormone from eating deer—that there's no way that there could be more of the hormone in a given deer.

This seems reasonable as long as the deer lack this hormone naturally; but if they don't, then adding another 10 milligrams may push the amount above the danger level for humans. Then, it would be conceivable that a consumable portion of deer *could* contain dangerous amounts of the hormone. (D) hits on this issue; the biologist assumes that the deer don't naturally have this hormone in them. If they did, then the deer would have more than 10 milligrams of the hormone after the injection, and the biologist's argument would be thrown into question.

(A) and (C) According to his plan, deer-eaters are safe anyway, so they needn't be warned, (A), and it wouldn't matter when the deer were killed, (C).

(B) is off the subject. "Chemically similar to human contraceptives?" That tells you nothing about whether it's harmful in the doses in question, so nothing about this need be assumed.

(E) The biologist needn't assume that most people don't eat deer often; in fact, it's made clear that even frequent deer-eaters will be safe.

- Not every statement that strengthens an argument is an assumption. Here, some wrong choices do something to allay fears about the deer meat, but that doesn't make them assumptions. The assumption will be not just something that helps the argument, but something the author relies on in drawing his conclusion.

19. D

This time you need to find the choice that would *least* contribute to an explanation of the paradox, or discrepancy, at hand. What's the problem?

The author begins by saying that a survey revealed that people are concerned about problems facing teenagers. The survey indicates that 70 percent of adult respondents said they would pay higher taxes for drug treatment programs and 60 percent said they would pay more taxes for better schools. Yet, the author says (and that's a paradox keyword), a proposition voted on in the same city, one that would fund schools by raising taxes, failed to get majority approval. Four of the choices will solve this mystery, while the correct choice will leave the mystery intact.

(A) would help resolve the puzzle by suggesting that the sample wasn't drawn in a representative, and therefore predictive, way: Maybe there were more parents or teachers or people concerned about education in the survey population than in the general voting population.

(B) readily explains the paradox, if true: If people lied on the survey, then it's no wonder that the attitudes expressed in the survey weren't reflected in the voting booth. A simple case of people not willing to "put their money where their mouth is."

(C) is pretty helpful too, since if the education plan were part of a bigger package, and people didn't like other parts of the package or thought it was too expensive, then they probably would have voted against the entire package, even though they favored one portion of it.

(D) is the answer. Just because funds for a drug treatment center weren't approved either, that doesn't help explain why the school proposition was voted down. The two are unrelated. (D) is no help, so it's correct here.

(E) is another good helper, introducing as it does the possibility that people may not have voted for the proposition simply because they didn't understand it.

- Whenever you see a survey on the LSAT, consider whether the survey is representative of the larger group. Here, the evidence concerned survey respondents, but the conclusion concerned voters. Those groups are different, even though they might overlap, and so it shouldn't be surprising that views expressed by one aren't reflected in the actions of the other.

20. B

It's another two-question stimulus for questions 20 and 21; you need to find the author's questionable Method of Argument and the main Assumption that would make the argument work.

The author begins with an attitude—these "so-called" environmentalists are messing things up by claiming that a proposed development would interfere with bird migration. She goes on to explain that this concern is just a mask for their anti-progress agenda and that the claim should be dismissed. What's the evidence? That these people have raised similar environmental objections to just about every development proposal in recent years. Sound fishy? It sure does: Who's to say that all of these claims weren't perfectly valid? Choice (B) says this: The author questions the environmentalists' motives, believing that they're just antiprogress, and she uses this prejudice to reject their argument.

(A) is kind of wordy, but all it says is that the conclusion is false because the argument doesn't prove it to be true. That's not what's happening here, since the author doesn't dispute the probability of the bird-migration problems on the basis of a lack of proof, but on the basis of her lack of confidence in those who support the position—the environmentalists.

(C) Are there any "exceptional cases" described here? No, the objections are described as the environmentalists' *standard* response, so (C) is out. If you can't match a piece of the description to something specific in the argument, it can't be the right answer in a method of argument question.

(D) The environmentalists don't provide any evidence, as far as you're told, for the assertion that the development will interfere with the migration patterns, so there's nothing for the author to "misrepresent."

(E) distinguishes between a group and a smaller segment of that group, but there's no flaw of this kind in the argument. The author refers to the same people throughout, so whether you view the environmentalists as individuals or as members of a unified group, there's nothing wrong with assuming consistency in their position.

- When an author argues against the motives of a group, check to see if there's any logical evidence supplied to support the author's opposition. Simply saying "these people have an agenda" isn't enough to damage their position.

21. A

Your work with question 20 should make this one quite manageable. For all the verbiage of the question stem, all you really need to do is to find the assumption that will make the author's argument valid, and you've already seen from the previous question what's missing from the argument: The author questions the environmentalists' argument against the development because they've objected to just about every other development plan in the past, but you don't know if these were *valid* objections or not because you don't know the circumstances of the objections.

The author believes these objections were based not on the facts but on the environmentalists' agenda. If, in fact, some or all of these objections are shown to be invalid, then she may have a legitimate point, and it would be more reasonable to believe that they really aren't all that concerned with the migration patterns. (A) works in this vein: It tells you that, indeed, not every proposal was challenged because it posed a threat to the environment. If you add the sentiment in (A) to the mix, then the author has good reason to doubt the validity of their claim.

(B) The assumption that development-blockers always disguise their motives is neither reasonable nor helpful in this context. It's not necessary to say that all development-blockers disguise their motives in order to argue that these people may be doing that.

(C) goes too far—you don't know anything about people who oppose "unrestricted development," so any assumptions about them won't help the author's argument.

(D) is out as well since *other* reasons for objecting to the development are beyond the scope. They won't help the author at all. In fact, if anything, (D) suggests that the environmentalists' professed concern for the birds is genuine.

(E) is too vague, since it talks about people who oppose development on environmental grounds in general, while you're concerned with this specific group. Furthermore, the explanation that their concern *almost always* lies elsewhere is too vague to pin this rap on the environmentalists in question.

- Notice that this is the last of five—count em', five!—double-question stimuli on this section. That's fairly high for an LSAT Logical Reasoning section. But remember that every double-question stimulus presents an opportunity to get two points for the price of one, so you should welcome these and look to use your work on the first question to help you work through the second.

22. D

Another "principle" question is up next, and a long stimulus to tackle. It's not very dense, though. Psychologists now understand that childhood is different from adulthood, and they wonder why it took people so long to figure out how silly they were to see children as little, imperfectly socialized grownups. However, the author claims, most psychologists still see people between the ages of 70 and 90 as adults with the same needs as people 35 years of age—no distinction is made in their minds. Old age, according to the author, is as different from young- and middle-adulthood as childhood is. This is attested to, she claims, by the organization of social and economic life.

So the distinctions are social and economic; remember that. It's time, she concludes, for psychological research into old age, and you need a principle that will back up this assertion. A good way to support this argument would be to shore up the author's main points—namely that old age is different from middle age because of social and economic circumstances, and thus, it has a unique psychology. This is enough of a prephrase to take with you into the choices.

(A) brings up a conflict between current psychological practice and traditional attitudes, but you don't have that conflict here. Basically, both current practice and traditional attitudes seem to think that old age isn't so different from adulthood—it's only the author who's in conflict, and she's arguing *against* current psychological practice.

(B) is a little confusing, so try to fit the circumstances of the stimulus into the mold here. Two groups of people related to each other—okay, middle-age adults and people of advanced age. And any member of the second must have been a member of the first—well, that works, since older people must have been middle-age adults.

But wait, the last clause confuses things. People in the first group, middle-age adults, shouldn't be regarded as deviant members of the second group, older people. That's not the problem—the problem is that older people are being viewed as part of the same group as middle-age adults. So (B) doesn't hit the target.

(C) says that when most practitioners do one thing, then all similar problems should be approached the same way. But if this principle were adopted, then everyone should see old age as an extension of middle-adulthood, and that would contradict, not support, the author's argument.

(D) brings up economic life, which sounds good, if you think back to the stimulus. When a society's economics are organized so that two different times of life are treated very differently—and according to the author that's true about middle adulthood and old age—then each time can only be understood in terms of a unique psychology. Yup, that's what the author wants. If this principle were adopted, her argument would be greatly enhanced, making (D) correct here. For the record:

(E) Most psychologists *don't* believe that one psychology is inadequate for these two age groups, so (E) is shot down right off the bat.

- A Section Management tip: If you're running low on time at the end of an LR section, and you turn the page to the final four or five questions, eyeball them to see if you can tell which may be time-consuming and therefore good candidates to skip. Notice how much longer question 22 is than the remaining questions—and the fact that it's a Principle question isn't too inviting either, as these often tend to be abstract and difficult. When you make decisions about what questions to do *when*, you're taking control of the test as you should.

23. E

Next up is a Point at Issue question, asking you to find the crux of Emile and Sabina's argument. Sabina begins by explaining that words are not an important part of an argument: they don't affect the facts, evidence, or conclusion. In fact, she says, if the words are used clearly and consistently, with the same definitions throughout, the words have no influence on an argument's validity. So, she concludes, the expression of an argument can have no bearing on whether it's good or not. Emile has the opposite viewpoint: Poorly chosen words can make even the most valid argument into a poor argument, since many words have connotations that influence people's response to claims that utilize those words. According to Emile, since whether people will acknowledge a fact is influenced by the way in which it is expressed, the conclusions that listeners or readers draw are affected by the words used.

So what's the point at issue? They disagree about whether words can influence the validity of an argument: Sabina says no, Emile says yes. But they're not arguing about the actual facts contained in an argument, or the logical form thereof. It's all about the influence of language and expression, right? (E) says precisely this, that the two are arguing about whether a factor (in this case language or expression) that doesn't affect the truth of an argument's evidence or the logic of the premises' relationship can have an effect on an argument's validity. Yes, it's wordy, but it's correct.

(A) raises the issue of defining words in different ways. Both people bring up the definition of words, and Sabina stresses that if words are consistently defined, there's no problem. Emile doesn't dispute this—he just claims that people will respond to the connotations of words no matter how they're defined. How words are *defined* isn't the crux of the argument.

(B) is somewhat similar, since it brings up definitions again, and, again, the two don't dispute that words can be defined without connotation: the definition isn't the point. The question is whether or not factors besides the definitions matter.

(C) No one doubts that a sound argument is better than an unsound one—they're talking about whether language can cause an argument to be sound or unsound.

(D) talks about avoiding the use of misleading words, but no one is disputing the validity of this suggestion.

- While answering a Point at Issue question, if you notice that the speakers agree on some issues, remember them. They'll probably show up as wrong answer choices.

24. C

This is a straightforward weakener—you need to undermine the author's conclusion. You learn that most plastic containers are labeled with code numbers that indicate what kind of plastic they are made of. The lowest-numbered plastics are the easiest to recycle, and the highest numbered are rarely recycled, and probably wind up in landfill. The author concludes that consumers can make significant waste reductions by refusing to buy products packed in higher-numbered plastics.

The best way to weaken this is to weaken the main evidence that higher-numbered plastics are the worst for the environment. Choice (C) does so perfectly, by explaining that high-numbered plastics have almost always already been recycled. This choice points out that these plastics aren't as unfriendly as the author believes—they are the fruits of the recycling efforts that he's supporting. Refusing to use these containers would thwart the recycling effort.

(A) concerns the cost of recycling as opposed to the cost of manufacturing new plastics, but it's not this kind of cost that's the issue—it's the cost to the *environment*. This choice is beyond the scope, and therefore it's no weakener.

(B) There's an implied "if" in the author's argument: Consumers can make a long-term reduction *if* they refuse to buy the higher-numbered items. That's the argument. The fact that many consumers aren't *aware* of the codes doesn't affect this line of reasoning, because the author is arguing about what would happen if they *were* and if they acted as he suggests.

(D) may weaken the idea that consumers will go along with the plan, since the products he wants them to buy will be more expensive, but it doesn't affect the gist of the argument—that a reduction will occur *if* they boycott those higher-numbered containers.

(E) is a vague strengthener, shoring up the idea that higher-numbered plastics are difficult to recycle.

- Any time you can translate a conclusion into if/then format, do so—it will make the argument easier to understand. Speaking of which . . .
- In an argument that takes the form "if X, then Y," choices that deal with the *likelihood* or *feasibility* of X usually have no effect on the argument. Here, wrong choices (B) and (D) play off the idea that consumers may not be willing or able to follow the author's prescription—but that's irrelevant because the argument is about what will happen *if* they *do*.

25. B

According to the author, the share of the population that reads a daily paper has gone down appreciably in the last 20 years, even though the average number of hours that people work per week has also gone down. However, the percentage of people that watch TV every day has gone up about the same amount over the same period. From this, the author concludes that increased TV viewing has caused the decline in newspaper reading.

What's the best way to weaken this conclusion? Well, you could show that even among people who *don't* watch TV, the percentage that also don't read the paper has shown an appreciable decrease. That would strongly suggest that increased TV viewing isn't the cause of decreased paper reading for these people, which would call the author's conclusion into question. That's (B).

(A) can't help you at all, since it talks about the *primary source* of current events: beyond the scope.

(C), (D) and (E) You don't know anything about the *amount of time* people spend reading—you're concerned with *whether* they read the paper every day or not. (C) is outside the scope, as are (D) and (E): (D) talks about the effect of TV on people's mental abilities, and (E) about the number of hours people have their TVs on. Scope violators every which way you turn.

- With a strong grasp of the scope of an argument, you can zero in on the correct answer and quickly eliminate many wrong answer choices.

Practice Test 3

LSAT PRACTICE TEST 3 ANSWER SHEET

Remove (or photocopy) the answer sheet and use it to complete the practice test.

How to Take the Practice Tests

Before taking each test, find a quiet place where you can work uninterrupted for about two and a half hours. Make sure you have a comfortable desk and several No. 2 pencils.

Each Practice Test includes four scored multiple-choice sections. Keep in mind that on the actual LSAT, there will be an additional multiple-choice section—the experimental section—that will not contribute to your score, plus an unscored Writing Sample.

Once you start a Practice Test, don't stop (except for a 5- to 10-minute break after the second section) until you've gone through all four sections. Remember, you can review any questions within a section, but you may not go back or forward a section.

Good luck!

Start with number 1 for each section. If a section has fewer questions than answer spaces, leave the extra spaces blank.

Section I

1. A B C D E	9. A B C D E	17. A B C D E	25. A B C D E	
2. A B C D E	10. A B C D E	18. A B C D E	26. A B C D E	
3. A B C D E	11. A B C D E	19. A B C D E	27. A B C D E	# right in Section I
4. A B C D E	12. A B C D E	20. A B C D E	28. A B C D E	
5. A B C D E	13. A B C D E	21. A B C D E	29. A B C D E	
6. A B C D E	14. A B C D E	22. A B C D E	30. A B C D E	
7. A B C D E	15. A B C D E	23. A B C D E		# wrong in Section I
8. A B C D E	16. A B C D E	24. A B C D E		

Section II

1. A B C D E	9. A B C D E	17. A B C D E	25. A B C D E	
2. A B C D E	10. A B C D E	18. A B C D E	26. A B C D E	
3. A B C D E	11. A B C D E	19. A B C D E	27. A B C D E	# right in Section II
4. A B C D E	12. A B C D E	20. A B C D E	28. A B C D E	
5. A B C D E	13. A B C D E	21. A B C D E	29. A B C D E	
6. A B C D E	14. A B C D E	22. A B C D E	30. A B C D E	
7. A B C D E	15. A B C D E	23. A B C D E		# wrong in Section II
8. A B C D E	16. A B C D E	24. A B C D E		

Section III

1. A B C D E	9. A B C D E	17. A B C D E	25. A B C D E	
2. A B C D E	10. A B C D E	18. A B C D E	26. A B C D E	
3. A B C D E	11. A B C D E	19. A B C D E	27. A B C D E	# right in Section III
4. A B C D E	12. A B C D E	20. A B C D E	28. A B C D E	
5. A B C D E	13. A B C D E	21. A B C D E	29. A B C D E	
6. A B C D E	14. A B C D E	22. A B C D E	30. A B C D E	
7. A B C D E	15. A B C D E	23. A B C D E		# wrong in Section III
8. A B C D E	16. A B C D E	24. A B C D E		

Section IV

1. Ⓐ Ⓑ Ⓒ Ⓓ Ⓔ	9. Ⓐ Ⓑ Ⓒ Ⓓ Ⓔ	17. Ⓐ Ⓑ Ⓒ Ⓓ Ⓔ	25. Ⓐ Ⓑ Ⓒ Ⓓ Ⓔ
2. Ⓐ Ⓑ Ⓒ Ⓓ Ⓔ	10. Ⓐ Ⓑ Ⓒ Ⓓ Ⓔ	18. Ⓐ Ⓑ Ⓒ Ⓓ Ⓔ	26. Ⓐ Ⓑ Ⓒ Ⓓ Ⓔ
3. Ⓐ Ⓑ Ⓒ Ⓓ Ⓔ	11. Ⓐ Ⓑ Ⓒ Ⓓ Ⓔ	19. Ⓐ Ⓑ Ⓒ Ⓓ Ⓔ	27. Ⓐ Ⓑ Ⓒ Ⓓ Ⓔ
4. Ⓐ Ⓑ Ⓒ Ⓓ Ⓔ	12. Ⓐ Ⓑ Ⓒ Ⓓ Ⓔ	20. Ⓐ Ⓑ Ⓒ Ⓓ Ⓔ	28. Ⓐ Ⓑ Ⓒ Ⓓ Ⓔ
5. Ⓐ Ⓑ Ⓒ Ⓓ Ⓔ	13. Ⓐ Ⓑ Ⓒ Ⓓ Ⓔ	21. Ⓐ Ⓑ Ⓒ Ⓓ Ⓔ	29. Ⓐ Ⓑ Ⓒ Ⓓ Ⓔ
6. Ⓐ Ⓑ Ⓒ Ⓓ Ⓔ	14. Ⓐ Ⓑ Ⓒ Ⓓ Ⓔ	22. Ⓐ Ⓑ Ⓒ Ⓓ Ⓔ	30. Ⓐ Ⓑ Ⓒ Ⓓ Ⓔ
7. Ⓐ Ⓑ Ⓒ Ⓓ Ⓔ	15. Ⓐ Ⓑ Ⓒ Ⓓ Ⓔ	23. Ⓐ Ⓑ Ⓒ Ⓓ Ⓔ	
8. Ⓐ Ⓑ Ⓒ Ⓓ Ⓔ	16. Ⓐ Ⓑ Ⓒ Ⓓ Ⓔ	24. Ⓐ Ⓑ Ⓒ Ⓓ Ⓔ	

☐ # right in Section IV

☐ # wrong in Section IV

GO ONLINE

Be sure to add your scores to your syllabus.

Practice Test 3

Section I: Analytical Reasoning

Time—35 minutes
24 questions

Directions: Each group of questions in this section is based on a set of conditions. In answering some of the questions, it may be useful to draw a rough diagram. Choose the response that most accurately and completely answers each question and blacken the corresponding space on your answer sheet.

Questions 1–6

Exactly eight consumers—F, G, H, J, K, L, M, and N—will be interviewed by market researchers. The eight will be divided into exactly two 4-person groups—group 1 and group 2—before interviews begin. Each person is assigned to exactly one of the two groups according to the following conditions:

F must be in the same group as J.
G must be in a different group from M.
If H is in group 1, then L must be in group 1.
If N is in group 2, then G must be in group 1.

1. Group 1 could consist of
   (A) F, G, H, and J
   (B) F, H, L, and M
   (C) F, J, K, and L
   (D) G, H, L, and N
   (E) G, K, M, and N

2. If K is in the same group as N, which one of the following must be true?
   (A) G is in group 1.
   (B) H is in group 2.
   (C) J is in group 1.
   (D) K is in group 2.
   (E) M is in group 1.

3. If F is in the same group as H, which one of the following must be true?
   (A) G is in group 2.
   (B) J is in group 1.
   (C) K is in group 1.
   (D) L is in group 2.
   (E) M is in group 2.

4. If L and M are in group 2, then a person who could be assigned either to group 1 or, alternatively, to group 2 is
   (A) F
   (B) G
   (C) H
   (D) J
   (E) K

5. Each of the following is a pair of people who could be in group 1 together EXCEPT
   (A) F and G
   (B) F and H
   (C) F and L
   (D) H and G
   (E) H and N

6. If L is in group 2, then each of the following is a pair of people who could be in group 1 together EXCEPT
   (A) F and M
   (B) G and N
   (C) J and N
   (D) K and M
   (E) M and N

GO ON TO THE NEXT PAGE.

Questions 7–11

Five people—Harry, Iris, Kate, Nancy, and Victor—are to be scheduled as contestants on a television show, one contestant per day, for five consecutive days from Monday through Friday. The following restrictions governing the scheduling of contestants must be observed:

Nancy is not scheduled for Monday.
If Harry is scheduled for Monday, Nancy is scheduled for Friday.
If Nancy is scheduled for Tuesday, Iris is scheduled for Monday.
Kate is scheduled for the next day after the day for which Victor is scheduled.

7. Victor can be scheduled for any day EXCEPT
   (A) Monday
   (B) Tuesday
   (C) Wednesday
   (D) Thursday
   (E) Friday

8. If Iris is scheduled for the next day after Harry, which one of the following lists all those days any one of which could be the day for which Harry is scheduled?
   (A) Monday, Tuesday
   (B) Monday, Wednesday
   (C) Monday, Thursday
   (D) Monday, Tuesday, Wednesday
   (E) Monday, Wednesday, Thursday

9. If Kate is scheduled for Wednesday, which one of the following could be true?
   (A) Iris is scheduled for Friday.
   (B) Nancy is scheduled for Tuesday.
   (C) Nancy is scheduled for an earlier day than the day for which Harry is scheduled.
   (D) Nancy is scheduled for an earlier day than the day for which Iris is scheduled.
   (E) Nancy is scheduled for an earlier day than the day for which Kate is scheduled.

10. If Kate is scheduled for Friday, which one of the following must be true?
   (A) Harry is scheduled for Tuesday.
   (B) Harry is scheduled for Wednesday.
   (C) Iris is scheduled for Monday.
   (D) Iris is scheduled for Wednesday.
   (E) Nancy is scheduled for Wednesday.

11. If Iris is scheduled for Wednesday, which one of the following must be true?
   (A) Harry is scheduled for an earlier day than the day for which Nancy is scheduled.
   (B) Harry is scheduled for an earlier day than the day for which Kate is scheduled.
   (C) Kate is scheduled for an earlier day than the day for which Harry is scheduled.
   (D) Nancy is scheduled for an earlier day than the day for which Kate is scheduled.
   (E) Nancy is scheduled for an earlier day than the day for which Iris is scheduled.

GO ON TO THE NEXT PAGE.

Questions 12–17

An art teacher will schedule exactly six of eight lectures—fresco, history, lithography, naturalism, oils, pastels, sculpture, and watercolors—for three days—1, 2, and 3. There will be exactly two lectures each day—morning and afternoon. Scheduling is governed by the following conditions:

Day 2 is the only day for which oils can be scheduled.

Neither sculpture nor watercolors can be scheduled for the afternoon.

Neither oils nor pastels can be scheduled for the same day as lithography.

If pastels is scheduled for day 1 or day 2, then the lectures scheduled for the day immediately following pastels must be fresco and history, not necessarily in that order.

12. Which one of the following is an acceptable schedule of lectures for days 1, 2, and 3, respectively?
    (A) Morning: lithography, history, sculpture Afternoon: pastels, fresco, naturalism
    (B) Morning: naturalism, oils, fresco Afternoon: lithography, pastels, history
    (C) Morning: oils, history, naturalism Afternoon: pastels, fresco, lithography
    (D) Morning: sculpture, lithography, naturalism Afternoon: watercolors, fresco, pastels
    (E) Morning: sculpture, pastels, fresco Afternoon: lithography, history, naturalism

13. If lithography and fresco are scheduled for the afternoons of day 2 and day 3, respectively, which one of the following is a lecture that could be scheduled for the afternoon of day 1?
    (A) history
    (B) oils
    (C) pastels
    (D) sculpture
    (E) watercolors

14. If lithography and history are scheduled for the mornings of day 2 and day 3, respectively, which one of the following lectures could be scheduled for the morning of day 1?
    (A) fresco
    (B) naturalism
    (C) oils
    (D) pastels
    (E) sculpture

15. If oils and lithography are scheduled for the mornings of day 2 and day 3, respectively, which one of the following CANNOT be scheduled for any day?
    (A) fresco
    (B) history
    (C) naturalism
    (D) pastels
    (E) sculpture

16. If neither fresco nor naturalism is scheduled for any day, which one of the following must be scheduled for day 1?
    (A) history
    (B) lithography
    (C) oils
    (D) pastels
    (E) sculpture

17. If the lectures scheduled for the mornings are fresco, history, and lithography, not necessarily in that order, which one of the following could be true?
    (A) Lithography is scheduled for day 3.
    (B) Naturalism is scheduled for day 2.
    (C) Fresco is scheduled for the same day as naturalism.
    (D) History is scheduled for the same day as naturalism.
    (E) History is scheduled for the same day as oils.

GO ON TO THE NEXT PAGE.

Questions 18–24

The population of a small country is organized into five clans—N, O, P, S, and T. Each year exactly three of the five clans participate in the annual harvest ceremonies. The rules specifying the order of participation of the clans in the ceremonies are as follows:

Each clan must participate at least once in any two consecutive years.

No clan participates for three consecutive years.

Participation takes place in cycles, with each cycle ending when each of the five clans has participated three times. Only then does a new cycle begin.

No clan participates more than three times within any cycle.

18. If the clans participating in the first year of a given cycle are N, O, and P, which one of the following could be the clans participating in the second year of that cycle?
    - (A) N, O, S
    - (B) N, O, T
    - (C) N, P, S
    - (D) O, P, T
    - (E) O, S, T

19. Which one of the following can be true about the clans' participation in the ceremonies?
    - (A) N participates in the first, second, and third years.
    - (B) N participates in the second, third, and fourth years.
    - (C) Both O and S participate in the first and third years.
    - (D) Both N and S participate in the first, third, and fifth years.
    - (E) Both S and T participate in the second, third, and fifth years.

20. Any cycle for the clans' participation in the ceremonies must be completed at the end of exactly how many years?
    - (A) five
    - (B) six
    - (C) seven
    - (D) eight
    - (E) nine

21. Which one of the following must be true about the three clans that participate in the ceremonies in the first year?
    - (A) At most two of them participate together in the third year.
    - (B) At least two of them participate together in the second year.
    - (C) All three of them participate together in the fourth year.
    - (D) All three of them participate together in the fifth year.
    - (E) None of them participates in the third year.

22. If, in a particular cycle, N, O, and S participate in the ceremonies in the first year, which one of the following must be true?
    - (A) N participates in the second and third years.
    - (B) O participates in the third and fourth years.
    - (C) N and O both participate in the third year
    - (D) P and T both participate in the fifth year.
    - (E) S and T both participate in the fifth year.

23. If, in a particular cycle, N, O, and T participate in the first year and if O and P participate in the fourth year, any of the following could be a clan that participates in the third year EXCEPT
    - (A) N
    - (B) O
    - (C) P
    - (D) S
    - (E) T

24. If, in a particular cycle, N, O, and S participate in the ceremonies in the first year and O, S, and T participate in the third year, then which one of the following could be the clans that participate in the fifth year?
    - (A) N, O, P
    - (B) N, O, S
    - (C) N, P, S
    - (D) O, P, S
    - (E) P, S, T

STOP

IF YOU FINISH BEFORE TIME IS CALLED, YOU MAY CHECK YOUR WORK ON THIS SECTION ONLY. DO NOT WORK ON ANY OTHER SECTION IN THE TEST.

Practice Test 3

Section II: **Logical Reasoning**

Time—35 minutes
26 questions

Directions: The questions in this section are based on the reasoning contained in brief statements or passages. For some questions, more than one of the choices could conceivably answer the question. However, you are to choose the best answer; that is, the response that most accurately and completely answers the question. You should not make assumptions that are by commonsense standards implausible, superfluous, or incompatible with the passage. After you have chosen the best answer, blacken the corresponding space on your answer sheet.

1. Paperback books wear out more quickly than hardcover books do, but paperback books cost much less. Therefore, users of public libraries would be better served if public libraries bought only paperback books, since by so doing these libraries could increase the number of new book titles added to their collections without increasing their budgets.

   Which one of the following, if true, most seriously weakens the argument?

   (A) If a public library's overall budget is cut, the budget for new acquisitions is usually cut back more than is that for day-to-day operations.
   (B) Paperback books can very inexpensively have their covers reinforced in order to make them last longer.
   (C) Many paperback books are never published in hardcover.
   (D) Library users as a group depend on their public library for access to a wide variety of up-to-date reference books that are published in hardcover only.
   (E) People are more likely to buy for themselves a copy of a book they had previously borrowed from the public library if that book is available in paperback.

2. Garbage in this neighborhood probably will not be collected until Thursday this week. Garbage is usually collected here on Wednesdays, and the garbage collectors in this city are extremely reliable. However, Monday was a public holiday, and after a public holiday that falls on a Monday, garbage throughout the city is supposed to be collected one day later than usual.

   The argument proceeds by

   (A) treating several pieces of irrelevant evidence as though they provide support for the conclusion
   (B) indirectly establishing that one thing is likely to occur by directly ruling out all of the alternative possibilities
   (C) providing information that allows application of a general rule to a specific case
   (D) generalizing about all actions of a certain kind on the basis of a description of one such action
   (E) treating something that is probable as though it were inevitable

3. When compact discs first entered the market, they were priced significantly higher than vinyl records. Manufacturers attributed the difference in price to the difference in production costs, saying that compact disc production was expensive because the technology was new and unfamiliar. As the technology became more efficient, the price of the discs did indeed come down. But vinyl records, whose production technology has long been established, then went up in price to approach that of compact discs.

   Which one of the following most helps to explain why the price of vinyl records went up?

   (A) Consumers were so enthusiastic about the improved sound quality offered by compact disc technology that they were willing to pay a higher price to obtain it.
   (B) Some consumers who continued to buy vinyl records instead of compact discs did so because they were unwilling to pay a higher price for compact discs.
   (C) As consumers bought compact discs instead of vinyl records, the number of vinyl records produced decreased, making their production less cost-efficient.
   (D) Compact disc player technology continued to change and develop even after compact discs first entered the market.
   (E) When compact discs first entered the market, many consumers continued to buy vinyl records rather than buying the equipment necessary to play compact discs.

GO ON TO THE NEXT PAGE.

4. Conservationists have established land reserves to preserve the last remaining habitat for certain species whose survival depends on the existence of such habitat. A grove of trees in Mexico that provide habitat for North American monarch butterflies in winter is a typical example of such a land reserve. If global warming occurs as predicted, however, the temperature bands within which various types of vegetation can grow will shift into regions that are currently cooler.

   If the statements above are true, they provide the most support for which one of the following?

   (A) If global warming occurs as predicted, the conservation land reserves will cease to serve their purpose.
   (B) Monarch butterflies will succeed in adapting to climatic change by shortening their migration.
   (C) If global warming occurs, it will melt polar ice and so will cause the sea level to rise so high that many coastal plants and animals will become extinct.
   (D) The natural world has adapted many times in the past to drastic global warming and cooling.
   (E) If global warming occurs rapidly, species of plants and animals now protected in conservation land reserves will move to inhabit areas that are currently used for agriculture.

5. Financial success does not guarantee happiness. This claim is not mere proverbial wisdom but a fact verified by statistics. In a recently concluded survey, only one-third of the respondents who claimed to have achieved financial success reported that they were happy.

   Which one of the following, if true, most strongly supports the conclusion drawn from the survey results?

   (A) The respondents who reported financial success were, for the most part, financially successful.
   (B) Financial success was once thought to be necessary for happiness but is no longer considered a prerequisite for happiness.
   (C) Many of the respondents who claimed not to have achieved financial success reported that they were happy five years ago.
   (D) Many of the respondents who failed to report financial success were in fact financially successful.
   (E) Most of the respondents who reported they were unhappy were in fact happy.

6. The distance that animals travel each day and the size of the groups in which they live are highly correlated with their diets. And diet itself depends in large part on the sizes and shapes of animals' teeth and faces.

   The statements above provide the most support for which one of the following?

   (A) Animals that eat meat travel in relatively small groups and across relatively small ranges compared to animals that eat plants.
   (B) Animals that have varied diets can be expected to be larger and more robust than animals that eat only one or two kinds of food.
   (C) When individual herd animals lose their teeth through age or injury, those animals are likely to travel at the rear of their herd.
   (D) Information about the size and shape of an animal's face is all that is needed to identify the species to which that animal belongs.
   (E) Information about the size and shape of an extinct animal's teeth and face can establish whether that animal is likely to have been a herd animal.

7. It is not correct that the people of the United States, relative to comparable countries, are the most lightly taxed. True, the United States has the lowest tax, as percent of gross domestic product, of the Western industrialized countries, but tax rates alone do not tell the whole story. People in the United States pay out of pocket for many goods and services provided from tax revenues elsewhere. Consider universal health care, which is an entitlement supported by tax revenues in every other Western industrialized country. United States government health-care expenditures are equivalent to about 5 percent of the gross domestic product, but private health-care expenditures represent another 7 percent. This 7 percent, then, amounts to a tax.

   The argument concerning whether the people of the United States are the most lightly taxed is most vulnerable to which one of the following criticisms?

   (A) It bases a comparison on percentages rather than on absolute numbers.
   (B) It unreasonably extends the application of a key term.
   (C) It uses negatively charged language instead of attempting to give a reason.
   (D) It generalizes from only a few instances.
   (E) It sets up a dichotomy between alternatives that are not exclusive.

GO ON TO THE NEXT PAGE.

8. Various mid-fourteenth-century European writers show an interest in games, but no writer of this period mentions the playing of cards. Nor do any of the mid-fourteenth-century statutes that proscribe or limit the play of games mention cards, though they do mention dice, chess, and other games. It is therefore likely that, contrary to what is sometimes claimed, at that time playing cards was not yet common in Europe.

The pattern of reasoning in which one of the following is most similar to that in the argument above?

(A) Neither today's newspapers nor this evening's television news mentioned a huge fire that was rumored to have happened in the port last night. Therefore, there probably was no such firc.

(B) This evening's television news reported that the cruise ship was only damaged in the fire last night, whereas the newspaper reported that it was destroyed. The television news is based on more recent information, so probably the ship was not destroyed.

(C) Among the buildings that are near the port is the newspaper's printing plant. Early editions of this morning's paper were very late. Therefore, the fire at the port probably affected areas beyond the port itself.

(D) The newspaper does not explicitly say that the port reopened after the fire, but in its listing of newly arrived ships it mentions some arrival times after the fire. Therefore, the port was probably not closed for long.

(E) The newspaper is generally more reliable than the television news, and the newspaper reported that the damage from last night's fire in the port was not severe. Therefore, the damage probably was not severe.

9. In a mature tourist market such as Bellaria there are only two ways hotel owners can increase profits: by building more rooms or by improving what is already there. Rigid land-use laws in Bellaria rule out construction of new hotels or, indeed, any expansion of hotel capacity. It follows that hotel owners cannot increase their profits in Bellaria since Bellarian hotels ______________.

Which one of the following logically completes the argument?

(A) are already operating at an occupancy rate approaching 100 percent year-round

(B) could not have been sited any more attractively than they are even in the absence of land-use laws

(C) have to contend with upward pressures on the cost of labor which stem from an incipient shortage of trained personnel

(D) already provide a level of luxury that is at the limits of what even wealthy patrons are prepared to pay for

(E) have shifted from serving mainly Bellarian tourists to serving foreign tourists traveling in organized tour groups

10. Every political philosopher of the early twentieth century who was either a socialist or a communist was influenced by Rosa Luxemburg. No one who was influenced by Rosa Luxemburg advocated a totalitarian state.

If the statements above are true, which one of the following must on the basis of them also be true?

(A) No early-twentieth-century socialist political philosopher advocated a totalitarian state.

(B) Every early-twentieth-century political philosopher who did not advocate a totalitarian state was influenced by Rosa Luxemburg.

(C) Rosa Luxemburg was the only person to influence every early-twentieth-century political philosopher who was either socialist or communist.

(D) Every early-twentieth-century political philosopher who was influenced by Rosa Luxemburg and was not a socialist was a communist.

(E) Every early-twentieth-century political philosopher who did not advocate a totalitarian state was either socialist or communist.

GO ON TO THE NEXT PAGE.

Questions 11–12

Harris: Currently, hybrid animals are not protected by international endangered-species regulations. But new techniques in genetic research suggest that the red wolf, long thought to be an independent species, is a hybrid of the coyote and the gray wolf. Hence, since the red wolf clearly deserves protection, these regulations should be changed to admit the protection of hybrids.

Vogel: Yet hybrids do not need protection. Since a breeding population that arises through hybridization descends from independent species, if any such population were to die out, it could easily be revived by interbreeding members of the species from which the hybrid is descended.

11. Which one of the following is a point at issue between Harris and Vogel?
    (A) whether the red wolf descends from the gray wolf and the coyote
    (B) whether there are some species that are currently considered endangered that are not in fact in any danger
    (C) whether the packs of red wolves that currently exist are in danger of dying out
    (D) whether there are some hybrids that ought to be protected by endangered-species regulations
    (E) whether new techniques in genetic research should be used to determine which groups of animals constitute species and which constitute hybrids

12. Which one of the following is an assumption on which Vogel's argument relies?
    (A) The techniques currently being used to determine whether a population of animals is a hybrid of other species have proven to be reliable.
    (B) The international regulations that protect endangered species and subspecies are being enforced successfully.
    (C) The gray wolf has been successfully bred in captivity.
    (D) All hybrids are the descendants of species that are currently extant.
    (E) The coyote and the red wolf are not related genetically.

13. From an analysis of broken pottery and statuary, archaeologists have estimated that an ancient settlement in southwestern Arabia was established around 1000 B.C. However, new evidence suggests that the settlement is considerably older: tests show that a piece of building timber recently uncovered at the site is substantially older than the pottery and statuary.

    Which one of the following, if true, most seriously undermines the conclusion drawn from the new evidence?
    (A) The building timber bore marks suggesting that it had been salvaged from an earlier settlement.
    (B) The pieces of pottery and fragments of statues that were analyzed come from several parts of the site.
    (C) The tests used to determine the age of the pottery and statuary had been devised more recently than those used to determine the age of the building timber.
    (D) The site has yielded many more samples of pottery and statuary than of building timber.
    (E) The type of pottery found at the site is similar to a type of pottery associated with civilizations that existed before 1000 B.C.

14. The book *To Save the Earth* is so persuasive that no one who reads it can fail to heed its environmentalist message. Members of the Earth Association have given away 2,000 copies in the last month. Thus the Earth Association can justly claim credit for at least 2,000 people in one month converted to the environmentalist cause.

    Which one of the following is an assumption on which the argument depends?
    (A) No other environmental organization gave away copies of *To Save the Earth* during the month in which the Earth Association gave away its 2,000 copies.
    (B) The people to whom the Earth Association gave copies of *To Save the Earth* would not have been willing to pay to receive it from the Earth Association.
    (C) The copies of *To Save the Earth* given away by members of the Earth Association were printed on recycled paper.
    (D) None of those who received *To Save the Earth* from a member of the Earth Association were already committed to the environmentalist cause when they received this book.
    (E) Every recipient of *To Save the Earth* will embrace the environmental program advocated by the Earth Association.

GO ON TO THE NEXT PAGE.

15. Smokers of pipes or cigars run a distinctly lower risk to their health than do cigarette smokers. However, whereas cigarette smokers who quit smoking altogether sharply reduce their risk of smoking related health problems, those who give up cigarettes and take up pipes or cigars remain in as much danger as before.

    Which one of the following, if true, offers the best prospects for an explanation of why the two changes in smoking habits do not both result in reduced health risks?

    (A) Smokers of pipes or cigars who quit smoking thereby reduce their risk of smoking-related health problems.

    (B) Cigarette smokers who quit smoking for a time and who then resume cigarette smoking do not necessarily reduce their risk of smoking-related health problems.

    (C) The kinds of illnesses that smokers run an increased risk of contracting develop no earlier in cigarette smokers than they do in smokers of pipes or cigars.

    (D) At any given period in their lives, virtually all smokers smoke either cigarettes exclusively or cigars exclusively or pipes exclusively, rather than alternating freely among various ways of smoking.

    (E) People who switch from cigarette smoking to smoking pipes or cigars inhale smoke in a way that those who have never smoked cigarettes do not.

<u>Questions 16–17</u>

Production manager: The building materials that we produce meet industry safety codes but pose some safety risk. Since we have recently developed the technology to make a safer version of our product, we should stop producing our current product and sell only the safer version in order to protect public safety.

Sales manager: If we stop selling our current product, we will have no money to develop and promote the safer product. We need to continue to sell the less-safe product in order to be in a position to market the safer product successfully.

16. Which one of the following principles, if established, most helps to justify the production manager's conclusion?

    (A) Companies should be required to develop safer products if such development can be funded from sales of existing products.

    (B) That a product does not meet industry safety codes should be taken as sufficient indication that the product poses some safety risks.

    (C) Companies should not sell a product that poses safety risks if they are technologically capable of producing a safer version of that product.

    (D) Product safety codes should be reviewed whenever an industry replaces one version of a product with a technologically more advanced version of that product.

    (E) In order to make building materials safer, companies should continually research new technologies whether or not they are required to do so in order to comply with safety codes.

17. The sales manager counters the production manager's argument by

    (A) pointing out that one part of the production manager's proposal would have consequences that would prevent successful execution of another part

    (B) challenging the production manager's authority to dictate company policy

    (C) questioning the product manager's assumption that a product is necessarily safe just because it is safer than another product

    (D) proposing a change in the standards by which product safety is judged

    (E) presenting evidence to show that the production manager has overestimated the potential impact of the new technology

GO ON TO THE NEXT PAGE.

Questions 18–19

Each year, an official estimate of the stock of cod in the Grand Banks is announced. This estimate is obtained by averaging two separate estimates of how many cod are available, one based on the number of cod caught by research vessels during a once-yearly sampling of the area and the other on the average number of tons of cod caught by various commercial vessels per unit of fishing effort expended there in the past year—a unit of fishing effort being one kilometer of net set out in the water for one hour. In previous decades, the two estimates usually agreed closely. However, for the last decade the estimate based on commercial tonnage has been increasing markedly, by about the same amount as the sampling-based estimate has been decreasing.

18. If the statements in the passage are true, which one of the following is most strongly supported by them?
    (A) Last year's official estimate was probably not much different from the official estimate ten years ago.
    (B) The number of commercial vessels fishing for cod in the Grand Banks has increased substantially over the past decade.
    (C) The sampling-based estimate is more accurate than the estimate based on commercial tonnage in that the data on which it relies is less likely to be inaccurate.
    (D) The once-yearly sampling by research vessels should be used as the sole basis for arriving at the official estimate of the stock of cod.
    (E) Twenty years ago, the overall stock of cod in the Grand Banks was officially estimated to be much larger than it is estimated to be today.

19. Which one of the following, if true, most helps to account for the growing discrepancy between the estimate based on commercial tonnage and the research-based estimate?
    (A) Fishing vessels often exceed their fishing quotas for cod and therefore often underreport the number of tons of cod that they catch.
    (B) More survey vessels are now involved in the yearly sampling effort than were involved 10 years ago.
    (C) Improvements in technology over the last 10 years have allowed commercial fishing vessels to locate and catch large schools of cod more easily.
    (D) Survey vessels count only those cod caught during a 30-day survey period, whereas commercial fishing vessels report all cod caught during the course of a year.
    (E) Because of past overfishing of cod, fewer fishing vessels now catch the maximum tonnage of cod each vessel is allowed by law to catch.

20. Pretzels can cause cavities. Interestingly, the longer that a pretzel remains in contact with the teeth when it is being eaten, the greater the likelihood that a cavity will result. What is true of pretzels in this regard is also true of caramels. Therefore, since caramels dissolve more quickly in the mouth than pretzels do, eating a caramel is less likely to result in a cavity than eating a pretzel is.

    The reasoning in the argument is vulnerable to criticism on the grounds that the argument
    (A) treats a correlation that holds within individual categories as thereby holding across categories
    (B) as well relies on the ambiguous use of a key term
    (C) makes a general claim based on particular examples that do not adequately represent the respective classes that they are each intended to represent
    (D) mistakes the cause of a particular phenomenon for the effect of that phenomenon
    (E) is based on premises that cannot all be true

Questions 21–22

Mark: Plastic-foam cups, which contain environmentally harmful chlorofluorocarbons, should no longer be used; paper cups are preferable. Styrene, a carcinogenic by-product, is generated in foam production, and foam cups, once used, persist indefinitely in the environment.

Tina: You overlook the environmental effects of paper cups. A study done 5 years ago showed that making paper for their production burned more petroleum than was used for foam cups and used 12 times as much steam, 36 times as much electricity, and twice as much cooling water. Because paper cups weigh more, their transportation takes more energy. Paper mills produce water pollution, and when the cups decay they produce methane, a gas that contributes to harmful global warming. So they are a worse choice.

21. Which one of the following, if true, could Mark cite to counter evidence offered by Tina?

(A) The use of energy for chain saws that cut down trees and for trucks that haul logs is part of the environmental cost of manufacturing paper.

(B) Foam cups are somewhat more acceptable to consumers than paper cups because of their better insulating qualities.

(C) The production and transportation of petroleum occasions serious environmental pollution, but the energy that runs paper mills now comes from burning waste wood rather than petroleum.

(D) The amount of styrene escaping into the environment or remaining in foam cups after their manufacture is negligible.

(E) Acre for acre, tree farms for the production of wood for paper have fewer beneficial effects on the environment than do natural forests that remain uncut.

22. To decide the issue between Mark and Tina, it would first be most important to decide

(A) how soon each of the kinds of harm cited by Mark and Tina would be likely to be at its maximum level

(B) whether members of some societies use, on average, more disposable goods than do members of other societies

(C) whether it is necessary to seek a third alternative that has none of the negative consequences cited with respect to the two products

(D) how much of the chains of causation involved in the production, marketing, and disposal of the products should be considered in analyzing their environmental impact

(E) whether paper and foam cups, in their most popular sizes, hold the same quantities of liquid

23. When people experience throbbing in their teeth or gums, they have serious dental problems, and if a dental problem is serious, it will be a problem either of tooth decay or of gum disease. Therefore, since throbbing in the teeth or gums is a sign of serious dental problems, and neither Sabina's teeth nor her gums are throbbing, Sabina can be suffering from neither tooth decay nor gum disease.

Which one of the following contains an error of reasoning most similar to that made in the argument above?

(A) People who drink a lot of coffee are said to have jittery nerves. Therefore, medical students who drink a lot of coffee should not become neonatologists or surgeons since neither neonatology nor surgery should be practiced by people with jittery nerves.

(B) A legally practicing psychiatrist must have both a medical degree and psychiatric training. Thus, since Emmett has not undergone psychiatric training, if he is practicing as a psychiatrist, he is not doing so legally.

(C) Someone with severe nasal congestion has a sinus infection or else is suffering from an allergy. Therefore, if Barton does not have a sinus infection, Barton probably does not have severe nasal congestion.

(D) If a person is interested in either physics or chemistry, then that person would be wise to consider a career in medicine. Yolanda, however, is interested in neither physics nor chemistry, so it would not be wise for her to consider a career in medicine.

(E) Someone who is neither an ophthalmologist nor an optometrist lacks specialized training for diagnosing defects of the eye. Therefore, Kim must have been trained in ophthalmology or optometry, given that she accurately diagnosed John's eye defect.

24. A certain airport security scanner designed to detect explosives in luggage will alert the scanner's operator whenever the piece of luggage passing under the scanner contains an explosive. The scanner will erroneously alert the operator for only one percent of the pieces of luggage that contain no explosives. Thus in ninety-nine out of a hundred alerts explosives will actually be present.

The reasoning in the argument is flawed because the argument

(A) ignores the possibility of the scanner's failing to signal an alert when the luggage does contain an explosive

(B) draws a general conclusion about reliability on the basis of a sample that is likely to be biased

(C) ignores the possibility of human error on the part of the scanner's operator once the scanner has alerted him or her

(D) fails to acknowledge the possibility that the scanner will not be equally sensitive to all kinds of explosives

(E) substitutes one group for a different group in the statement of a percentage

25. Unless negotiations begin soon, the cease-fire will be violated by one of the two sides to the dispute. Negotiations will be held only if other countries have pressured the two sides to negotiate; an agreement will emerge only if other countries continue such pressure throughout the negotiations. But no negotiations will be held until international troops enforcing the cease-fire have demonstrated their ability to counter any aggression from either side, thus suppressing a major incentive for the two sides to resume fighting.

If the statements above are true, and if negotiations between the two sides do begin soon, at the time those negotiations begin each of the following must also be true EXCEPT:

(A) The cease-fire has not been violated by either of the two sides.

(B) International troops enforcing the cease-fire have demonstrated that they can counter aggression from either of the two sides.

(C) A major incentive for the two sides to resume hostilities has been suppressed.

(D) Other countries have exerted pressure on the two sides to the dispute.

(E) The negotiations' reaching an agreement depends in part on the actions of other countries.

26. If Blankenship Enterprises has to switch suppliers in the middle of a large production run, the company will not show a profit for the year. Therefore, if Blankenship Enterprises in fact turns out to show no profit for the year, it will also turn out to be true that the company had to switch suppliers during a large production run.

The reasoning in the argument is most vulnerable to criticism on which one of the following grounds?

(A) The argument is a circular argument made up of an opening claim followed by a conclusion that merely paraphrases that claim.

(B) The argument fails to establish that a condition under which a phenomenon is said to occur is the only condition under which that phenomenon occurs.

(C) The argument involves an equivocation, in that the word "profit" is allowed to shift its meaning during the course of the argument.

(D) The argument erroneously uses an exceptional, isolated case to support a universal conclusion.

(E) The argument explains one event as being caused by another event, even though both events must actually have been caused by some third, unidentified event.

STOP

IF YOU FINISH BEFORE TIME IS CALLED, YOU MAY CHECK YOUR WORK ON THIS SECTION ONLY. DO NOT WORK ON ANY OTHER SECTION IN THE TEST.

Practice Test 3

Section III: Reading Comprehension

Time—35 minutes
27 questions

Directions: Each passage in this section is followed by a group of questions to be answered on the basis of what is stated or implied in the passage. For some of the questions, more than one of the choices could conceivably answer the question. However, you are to choose the best answer; that is, the response that most accurately and completely answers the question, and blacken the corresponding space on your answer sheet.

A major tenet of the neurosciences has been that all neurons (nerve cells) in the brains of vertebrate animals are formed early in development. An adult vertebrate, it was believed, must make do with a fixed number of neurons: those lost through disease or injury are not replaced, and adult learning takes place not through generation of new cells but through modification of connections among existing ones.

However, new evidence for neurogenesis (the birth of new neurons) has come from the study of canary song. Young canaries and other songbirds learn to sing much as humans learn to speak, by imitating models provided by their elders. Several weeks after birth, a young bird produces its first rudimentary attempts at singing; over the next few months the song becomes more structured and stable, reaching a fully developed state by the time the bird approaches its first breeding season. But this repertoire of song is not permanently learned. After each breeding season, during late summer and fall, the bird loses mastery of its developed "vocabulary," and its song becomes as unstable as that of a juvenile bird. During the following winter and spring, however, the canary acquires new songs, and by the next breeding season it has developed an entirely new repertoire.

Recent neurological research into this learning and relearning process has shown that the two most important regions of the canary's brain related to the learning of songs actually vary in size at different times of the year. In the spring, when the bird's song is highly developed and uniform, the regions are roughly twice as large as they are in the fall. Further experiments tracing individual nerve cells within these regions have shown that the number of neurons drops by about 38 percent after the breeding season, but by the following breeding season, new ones have been generated to replace them. A possible explanation for this continual replacement of nerve cells may have to do with the canary's relatively long life span and the requirements of flight. Its brain would have to be substantially larger and heavier than might be feasible for flying if it had to carry all the brain cells needed to process and retain all the information gathered over a lifetime.

Although the idea of neurogenesis in the adult mammalian brain is still not generally accepted, these findings might help uncover a mechanism that would enable the human brain to repair itself through neurogenesis. Whether such replacement of neurons would disrupt complex learning processes or long-term memory is not known, but songbird research challenges scientists to identify the genes or hormones that orchestrate neurogenesis in the young human brain and to learn how to activate them in the adult brain.

1. Which one of the following best expresses the main idea of the passage?

(A) New evidence of neurogenesis in canaries challenges an established neurological theory concerning brain cells in vertebrates and suggests the possibility that human brains may repair themselves.

(B) The brains of canaries differ from the brains of other vertebrate animals in that the brains of adult canaries are able to generate neurons.

(C) Recent studies of neurogenesis in canaries, building on established theories of vertebrate neurology, provide important clues as to why researchers are not likely to discover neurogenesis in adult humans.

(D) Recent research into neurogenesis in canaries refutes a long-held belief about the limited supply of brain cells and provides new information about neurogenesis in the adult human brain.

(E) New information about neurogenesis in canaries challenges older hypotheses and clarifies the importance of the yearly cycle in learning processes and neurological replacement among vertebrates.

GO ON TO THE NEXT PAGE.

2. According to the passage, which one of the following is true of the typical adult canary during the late summer and fall?
   (A) The canary's song repertoire takes on a fully structured and stable quality.
   (B) A process of neurogenesis replaces the song-learning neurons that were lost during the preceding months.
   (C) The canary begins to learn an entirely new repertoire of songs based on the models of other canaries.
   (D) The regions in the canary's brain that are central to the learning of song decrease in size.
   (E) The canary performs slightly modified versions of the songs it learned during the preceding breeding season.

3. Information in the passage suggests that the author would most likely regard which one of the following as LEAST important in future research on neurogenesis in humans?
   (A) research on possible similarities between the neurological structures of humans and canaries
   (B) studies that compare the ratio of brain weight to body weight in canaries to that in humans
   (C) neurological research on the genes or hormones that activate neurogenesis in the brain of human infants
   (D) studies about the ways in which long-term memory functions in the human brain
   (E) research concerning the processes by which humans learn complicated tasks

4. Which one of the following, if true, would most seriously undermine the explanation proposed by the author in the third paragraph?
   (A) A number of songbird species related to the canary have a shorter life span than the canary and do not experience neurogenesis.
   (B) The brain size of several types of airborne birds with life spans similar to those of canaries has been shown to vary according to a two-year cycle of neurogenesis.
   (C) Several species of airborne birds similar to canaries in size are known to have brains that are substantially heavier than the canary's brain.
   (D) Individual canaries that have larger-than-average repertoires of songs tend to have better developed muscles for flying.
   (E) Individual canaries with smaller and lighter brains than the average tend to retain a smaller-than-average repertoire of songs.

5. The use of the word "vocabulary" (line 23) serves primarily to
   (A) demonstrate the presence of a rudimentary grammatical structure in canary song
   (B) point out a similarity between the patterned groupings of sounds in a canary's song and the syllabic structures of words
   (C) stress the stability and uniformity of the canary's song throughout its lifetime
   (D) suggest a similarity between the possession of a repertoire of words among humans and a repertoire of songs among canaries
   (E) imply that the complexity of the canary's song repertoire is equal to that of human language

6. According to the passage, which one of the following factors may help account for the occurrence of neurogenesis in canaries?
   (A) the life span of the average canary
   (B) the process by which canaries learn songs
   (C) the frequency of canary breeding seasons
   (D) the number of regions in the canary brain related to song learning
   (E) the amount of time an average canary needs to learn a repertoire of songs

7. Which one of the following best describes the organization of the third paragraph?
   (A) A theory is presented, analyzed, and modified, and a justification for the modification is offered.
   (B) Research results are advanced and reconciled with results from other studies, and a shared principle is described.
   (C) Research results are presented, further details are provided, and a hypothesis is offered to explain the results.
   (D) Research findings are described, their implications are explained, and an application to a related field is proposed.
   (E) Research results are reported, their significance is clarified, and they are reconciled with previously established neurological tenets.

8. It can be inferred from the passage that the author would most likely describe the current understanding of neurogenesis as
   (A) exhaustive
   (B) progressive
   (C) incomplete
   (D) antiquated
   (E) incorrect

GO ON TO THE NEXT PAGE.

For too many years scholars of African American history focused on the harm done by slaveholders and by the institution of slavery, rather than on what Africans in the United States were able to accomplish despite the effects of that institution. *In Myne Owne Ground*, T. H. Breen and Stephen Innes contribute significantly to a recent, welcome shift from a white-centered to a black-centered inquiry into the role of African Americans in the American colonial period. Breen and Innes focus not on slaves, but on a small group of freed indentured servants in Northampton County (in the Chesapeake Bay region of Virginia) who, according to the authors, maintained their freedom, secured property, and interacted with persons of different races and economic standing from 1620 through the 1670s. African Americans living on the Chesapeake were to some extent disadvantaged, say Breen and Innes, but this did not preclude the attainment of status roughly equal to that of certain white planters of the area. Continuously acting within black social networks, and forming economic relationships with white planters, local Native Americans, indentured servants, and white settlers outside the gentry class, the free African Americans of Northampton County held their own in the rough-hewn world of Chesapeake Bay.

The authors emphasize that in this early period, when the percentage of African Americans in any given Chesapeake county was still no more than 10 percent of the population, very little was predetermined so far as racial status or race relations were concerned. By schooling themselves in the local legal process and by working prodigiously on the land, African Americans acquired property, established families, and warded off contentious white neighbors. Breen and Innes do acknowledge that political power on the Chesapeake was asymmetrically distributed among black and white residents. However, they underemphasize much evidence that customary law, only gradually embodied in statutory law, was closing in on free African Americans well before the 1670s: during the 1660s, when the proportion of African Americans in Virginia increased dramatically, Virginia tightened a law regulating interracial relations (1662) and enacted a statute prohibiting baptism from altering slave status (1667). Anthony Johnson, a leader in the community of free African Americans in the Chesapeake Bay region, sold the land he had cultivated for more than twenty years and moved north with his family around 1665, an action that the authors attribute to a search for "fresh, more productive land." But the answer to why the Johnsons left that area where they had labored so long may lie in their realization that their white neighbors were already beginning the transition from a largely white indentured labor force to reliance on a largely black slave labor force, and that the institution of slavery was threatening their descendants' chances for freedom and success in Virginia.

9. The author of the passage objects to many scholarly studies of African American history for which one of the following reasons?

   (A) Their emphases have been on statutory law rather than on customary law.

   (B) They have ignored specific historical situations and personages in favor of broad interpretations.

   (C) They have focused on the least eventful periods in African American history.

   (D) They have underemphasized the economic system that was the basis of the institution of slavery.

   (E) They have failed to focus to a sufficient extent on the achievements of African Americans.

10. Which one of the following can be inferred from the passage concerning the relationship between the African American population and the law in the Chesapeake Bay region of Virginia between 1650 and 1670?

   (A) The laws affecting black citizens were embodied in statutes much more gradually than were laws affecting white citizens.

   (B) As the percentage of black citizens in the population grew, the legal restrictions placed on them also increased.

   (C) Because of discriminatory laws, black farmers suffered more economic setbacks than did white farmers.

   (D) Because of legal constraints on hiring indentured servants, black farmers faced a chronic labor shortage on their farms.

   (E) The adherence to customary law was more rigid in regions with relatively large numbers of free black citizens.

GO ON TO THE NEXT PAGE.

11. The author of the passage most probably refers to Anthony Johnson and his family in order to
    (A) provide a specific example of the potential shortcomings of Breen and Innes's interpretation of historical events
    (B) provide a specific example of relevant data overlooked by Breen and Innes in their discussion of historical events
    (C) provide a specific example of data that Breen and Innes might profitably have used in proving their thesis
    (D) argue that the standard interpretation of historical events is superior to Breen and Innes's revisionist interpretation
    (E) argue that a new historiographical method is needed to provide a full and coherent reading of historical events

12. The attitude of the author of the passage toward Breen and Innes's study can best be described as one of
    (A) condescending dismissal
    (B) wholehearted acceptance
    (C) contentious challenge
    (D) qualified approval
    (E) sincere puzzlement

13. The primary purpose of the passage is to
    (A) summarize previous interpretations
    (B) advocate a new approach
    (C) propose and then illustrate a thesis
    (D) present and evaluate an interpretation
    (E) describe a historical event

GO ON TO THE NEXT PAGE.

Late-nineteenth-century books about the French artist Watteau (1684–1721) betray a curious blind spot: more than any single artist before or since, Watteau provided his age with an influential image of itself, and nineteenth-century writers accepted this image as genuine. This was largely due to the enterprise of Watteau's friends who, soon after his death, organized the printing of engraved reproductions of the great bulk of his work—both his paintings and his drawings—so that Watteau's total artistic output became and continued to be more accessible than that of any other artist until the twentieth-century advent of art monographs illustrated with photographs. These engravings presented aristocratic (and would-be aristocratic) eighteenth-century French society with an image of itself that was highly acceptable and widely imitated by other artists, however little relationship that image bore to reality. By 1884, the bicentenary of Watteau's birth, it was standard practice for biographers to refer to him as "the personification of the witty and amiable eighteenth century."

In fact, Watteau saw little enough of that "witty and amiable" century for which so much nostalgia was generally felt between about 1870 and 1920, a period during which enthusiasm for the artist reached its peak. The eighteenth century's first decades, the period of his artistic activity, were fairly calamitous ones. During his short life, France was almost continually at war: his native region was overrun with foreign troops, and Paris was threatened by siege and by a rampaging army rabble. The dreadful winter of 1709, the year of Watteau's first Paris successes, was marked by military defeat and a disastrous famine.

Most of Watteau's nineteenth-century admirers simply ignored the grim background of the works they found so lyrical and charming. Those who took the inconvenient historical facts into consideration did so only in order to refute the widely held deterministic view that the content and style of an artist's work were absolutely dictated by heredity and environment. (For Watteau admirers, such determinism was unthinkable: the artist was born in a Flemish town only six years after it first became part of France, yet Watteau was quintessentially French. As one patriotic French biographer put it, "In Dresden, Potsdam, and Berlin I have never come across a Watteau without feeling refreshed by a breath of native air.") Even such writers, however, persisted in according Watteau's canvases a privileged status as representative "personifications" of the eighteenth century. The discrepancy between historical fact and artistic vision, useful in refuting the extreme deterministic position, merely forced these writers to seek a new formula that allowed them to preserve the desired identity between image and reality, this time a rather suspiciously psychic one: Watteau did not record the society he knew, but rather "foresaw" a society that developed shortly after his death.

14. Which one of the following best describes the overall organization of the passage?
    - (A) A particular phenomenon is discussed, the reasons that it is atypical are put forward, and these reasons are evaluated and refined.
    - (B) An assumption is made, results deriving from it are compared with what is known to be true, and the assumption is finally rejected as counterfactual.
    - (C) A point of view is described, one hypothesis accounting for it is introduced and rejected, and a better hypothesis is offered for consideration.
    - (D) A general characterization is offered, examples supporting it are introduced, and its special applicability to a particular group is asserted.
    - (E) A particular viewpoint is explained, its shortcomings are discussed, and its persistence in the face of these is noted.

15. The passage suggests that late-nineteenth-century biographers of Watteau considered the eighteenth century to be "witty and amiable" in large part because of
    - (A) what they saw as Watteau's typical eighteenth-century talent for transcending reality through art
    - (B) their opposition to the determinism that dominated late-nineteenth-century French thought
    - (C) a lack of access to historical source material concerning the early eighteenth century in France
    - (D) the nature of the image conveyed by the works of Watteau and his many imitators
    - (E) their political bias in favor of aristocratic regimes and societies

GO ON TO THE NEXT PAGE.

16. According to the passage, explanations of artistic production based on determinism were unthinkable to Watteau admirers for which one of the following reasons?
    - (A) If such explanations were widely accepted, too many people who would otherwise have admired Watteau would cease to appreciate Watteau's works.
    - (B) If such explanations were adopted, they would make it difficult for Watteau admirers to explain why Watteau's works were purchased and admired by foreigners.
    - (C) If such explanations were correct, many artists who, like Watteau, considered themselves French would have to be excluded from histories of French art.
    - (D) If such simple explanations were offered, other more complex arguments concerning what made Watteau's works especially charming would go unexplored.
    - (E) If such explanations were true, Watteau's works would reflect a "Flemish" sensibility rather than the especially "French" one these admirers saw in them.

17. The phrase "curious blind spot" (lines 2–3) can best be interpreted as referring to which one of the following?
    - (A) some biographers' persistent inability to appreciate what the author considers a particularly admirable quality
    - (B) certain writers' surprising lack of awareness of what the author considers an obvious discrepancy
    - (C) some writers' willful refusal to evaluate properly what the author considers a valuable source of information about the past
    - (D) an inexplicable tendency on the part of some writers to undervalue an artist whom the author considers extremely influential
    - (E) a marked bias in favor of a certain painter and a concomitant prejudice against contemporaries the author considers equally talented

18. It can be inferred from the passage that the author's view of Watteau's works differs most significantly from that of most late-nineteenth-century Watteau admirers in which one of the following ways?
    - (A) Unlike most late-nineteenth-century Watteau admirers, the author appreciates the importance of Watteau's artistic accomplishment.
    - (B) The author finds Watteau's works to be much less lyrical and charming than did most late-nineteenth-century admirers of the works.
    - (C) In contrast to most late-nineteenth-century Watteau admirers, the author finds it misleading to see Watteau's works as accurately reflecting social reality.
    - (D) The author is much more willing to entertain deterministic explanations of the origins of Watteau's works than were most late-nineteenth-century Watteau admirers.
    - (E) Unlike most late-nineteenth-century admirers of Watteau, the author considers it impossible for any work of art to personify or represent a particular historical period.

19. The author asserts that during the period of Watteau's artistic activity French society was experiencing which one of the following?
    - (A) widespread social upheaval caused by war
    - (B) a pervasive sense of nostalgia for an idealized past
    - (C) increased domination of public affairs by a powerful aristocracy
    - (D) rapid adoption by the middle classes of aristocratic manners and life-styles
    - (E) a need to reconcile the French self-image with French social realities

20. The information given in the passage suggests that which one of the following principles accurately characterizes the relationship between an artist's work and the impact it is likely to have on a society?
    - (A) An artist's recognition by a society is most directly determined by the degree to which his or her works are perceived as lyrical and charming.
    - (B) An artist will have the greatest influence on a society that values art particularly highly.
    - (C) The works of an artist who captures the true and essential nature of a given society will probably have a great impact on that society.
    - (D) The degree of influence an artist's vision will have on a society is conditional on the visibility of the artist's work.
    - (E) An artist who is much imitated by contemporaries will usually fail to have an impact on a society unless the imitators are talented.

GO ON TO THE NEXT PAGE.

Faced with the problems of insufficient evidence, of conflicting evidence, and of evidence relayed through the flawed perceptual, retentive, and narrative abilities of witnesses, a jury is forced to draw inferences in its attempt to ascertain the truth. By applying the same cognitive tools they have developed and used over a lifetime, jurors engage in the inferential exercise that lawyers call fact-finding. In certain decision-making contexts that are relevant to the trial of lawsuits, however, these normally reliable cognitive tools may cause jurors to commit inferential errors that distort rather than reveal the truth.

Although juries can make a variety of inferential errors, most of these mistakes in judgment involve the drawing of an unwarranted conclusion from the evidence, that is, deciding that the evidence proves something that, in reality, it does not prove. For example, evidence that the defendant in a criminal prosecution has a prior conviction may encourage jurors to presume the defendant's guilt, because of their preconception that a person previously convicted of a crime must be inclined toward repeated criminal behavior. That commonly held belief is at least a partial distortion of reality; not all former convicts engage in repeated criminal behavior. Also, a jury may give more probative weight than objective analysis would allow to vivid photographic evidence depicting a shooting victim's wounds, or may underestimate the weight of defense testimony that is not delivered in a sufficiently forceful or persuasive manner. Finally, complex or voluminous evidence might be so confusing to a jury that its members would draw totally unwarranted conclusions or even ignore the evidence entirely.

Recent empirical research in cognitive psychology suggests that people tend to commit inferential errors like these under certain predictable circumstances. By examining the available information, the situation, and the type of decision being made, cognitive psychologists can describe the kinds of inferential errors a person or group is likely to make. These patterns of human decision-making may provide the courts with a guide to evaluating the effect of evidence on the reliability of the jury's inferential processes in certain situations.

The notion that juries can commit inferential errors that jeopardize the accuracy of the fact-finding process is not unknown to the courts. In fact, one of a presiding judge's duties is to minimize jury inferential error through explanation and clarification. Nonetheless, most judges now employ only a limited and primitive concept of jury inferential error: limited because it fails to recognize the potential for error outside certain traditional situations, primitive because it ignores the research and conclusions of psychologists in favor of notions about human cognition held by lawyers.

21. Which one of the following best expresses the main idea of the passage?

(A) When making decisions in certain predictable situations, juries may commit inferential errors that obscure rather than reveal the truth.
(B) The views of human cognition taken by cognitive psychologists on the one hand and by the legal profession on the other are demonstrably dissimilar.
(C) When confronting powerful preconceptions, particularly shocking evidence, or complex situations, jurors make errors in judgment.
(D) The problem of inferential error by juries is typical of the difficulties with cognitive processes that people face in their everyday lives.
(E) Juries would probably make more reliable decisions if cognitive psychologists, rather than judges, instructed them about the problems inherent in drawing unwarranted conclusions.

22. Of the following hypothetical reforms in trial procedure, which one would the author be most likely to support as the best way to address the problem of jury inferential error?

(A) a move away from jury trials
(B) the institution of minimum formal educational requirements for jurors
(C) the development of strict guidelines for defense testimony
(D) specific training for judges in the area of jury instruction
(E) restrictions on lawyers' use of psychological research

23. In the second paragraph, the author's primary purpose is to

(A) refute the idea that the fact-finding process is a complicated exercise
(B) emphasize how carefully evidence must be presented in order to avoid jury inferential error
(C) explain how commonly held beliefs affect the Jury's ability to ascertain the truth
(D) provide examples of situations that may precipitate jury errors
(E) recommend a method for minimizing mistakes by juries

GO ON TO THE NEXT PAGE.

24. Which one of the following best describes the author's attitude toward the majority of judges today?
    (A) apprehensive about whether they are consistent in their instruction of juries
    (B) doubtful of their ability to draw consistently correct conclusions based on the evidence
    (C) critical of their failure to take into account potentially helpful research
    (D) pessimistic about their willingness to make significant changes in trial procedure
    (E) concerned about their allowing the presentation of complex and voluminous evidence in the courtroom

25. Which one of the following statements, if true, would most seriously undermine the author's suggestion about the use of current psychological research in the courtroom?
    (A) All guidelines about human behavior must take account of variations in the patterns of human decision-making.
    (B) Current models of how humans make decisions apply reliably to individuals but do not hold for decisions made by groups.
    (C) The current conception of jury inferential error employed by judges has been in use for nearly a century.
    (D) Inferential errors can be more easily predicted in controlled situations such as the trial of lawsuits than in other kinds of decision-making processes.
    (E) In certain predictable circumstances, juries are less susceptible to inferential errors than they are in other circumstances.

26. It can be inferred from the passage that the author would be most likely to agree with which one of the following generalizations about lawyers?
    (A) They have a less sophisticated understanding of human cognition than do psychologists.
    (B) They often present complex or voluminous information merely in order to confuse a jury.
    (C) They are no better at making logical inferences from the testimony at a trial than are most judges.
    (D) They have worked to help judges minimize jury inferential error.
    (E) They are unrealistic about the ability of jurors to ascertain the truth.

27. The author would be most likely to agree with which one of the following generalizations about a jury's decision-making process?
    (A) The more evidence that a jury has, the more likely it is that the jury will reach a reliable verdict.
    (B) Juries usually overestimate the value of visual evidence such as photographs.
    (C) Jurors have preconceptions about the behavior of defendants that prevent them from making an objective analysis of the evidence in a criminal trial.
    (D) Most of the jurors who make inferential errors during a trial do so because they are unaccustomed to having to make difficult decisions based on inferences.
    (E) The manner in which evidence is presented to a jury may influence the jury either to overestimate or to underestimate the value of that evidence.

STOP

IF YOU FINISH BEFORE TIME IS CALLED, YOU MAY CHECK YOUR WORK ON THIS SECTION ONLY.
DO NOT WORK ON ANY OTHER SECTION IN THE TEST.

Practice Test 3

Section IV: Logical Reasoning

Time—35 minutes
24 questions

Directions: The questions in this section are based on the reasoning contained in brief statements or passages. For some questions, more than one of the choices could conceivably answer the question. However, you are to choose the best answer; that is, the response that most accurately and completely answers the question. You should not make assumptions that are by commonsense standards implausible, superfluous, or incompatible with the passage. After you have chosen the best answer, blacken the corresponding space on your answer sheet.

1. James: In my own house, I do what I want. In banning smoking on passenger airlines during domestic flights, the government has ignored the airlines' right to set smoking policies on their own property.

   Eileen: Your house is for your own use. Because a passenger airline offers a service to the public, the passengers' health must come first.

   The basic step in Eileen's method of attacking James' argument is to

   (A) draw a distinction
   (B) offer a definition
   (C) establish an analogy
   (D) derive a contradiction from it
   (E) question its motivation

2. The company that produces XYZ, a computer spreadsheet program, estimates that millions of illegally reproduced copies of XYZ are being used. If legally purchased, this number of copies would have generated millions of dollars in sales for the company, yet despite a company-wide effort to boost sales, the company has not taken available legal measures to prosecute those who have copied the program illegally.

   Which one of the following, if true, most helps to explain why the company has not taken available legal measures?

   (A) XYZ is very difficult to copy illegally, because a sophisticated anticopying mechanism in the program must first be disabled.
   (B) The legal measures that the company that produces XYZ could take against those who have copied its product became available several years before XYZ came on the market.
   (C) Many people who purchase a software program like XYZ are willing to purchase that program only after they have already used it.
   (D) The number of illegally reproduced copies of XYZ currently in use exceeds the number of legally reproduced copies currently in use.
   (E) The company that produces ABC, the spreadsheet program that is XYZ's main rival in the marketplace, is well known for taking legal action against people who have copied ABC illegally.

Questions 3–4

Kim: Some people claim that the battery-powered electric car represents a potential solution to the problem of air pollution. But they forget that it takes electricity to recharge batteries and that most of our electricity is generated by burning polluting fossil fuels. Increasing the number of electric cars on the road would require building more generating facilities since current facilities are operating at maximum capacity. So even if all of the gasoline-powered cars on the roads today were replaced by electric cars, it would at best be an exchange of one source of fossil-fuel pollution for another.

3. The main point made in Kim's argument is that

   (A) replacing gasoline-powered cars with battery-powered electric cars will require building more generating facilities
   (B) a significant reduction in air pollution cannot be achieved unless people drive less
   (C) all forms of automobile transportation are equally harmful to the environment in terms of the air pollution they produce
   (D) battery-powered electric cars are not a viable solution to the air-pollution problem
   (E) gasoline-powered cars will probably remain a common means of transportation for the foreseeable future

4. Which one of the following is an assumption on which Kim's argument depends?

   (A) Replacing gasoline-powered cars with battery-powered electric cars will not lead to a net increase in the total number of cars on the road.
   (B) Gasoline-powered cars are currently not the most significant source of fossil-fuel pollution.
   (C) Replacing gasoline-powered cars with battery-powered electric cars is justified only if electric cars produce less air pollution.
   (D) While it is being operated, a battery-powered electric car does not cause any significant air pollution.
   (E) At least some of the generating facilities built to meet the demand for electricity for battery-powered electric cars would be of a type that burns fossil fuel.

GO ON TO THE NEXT PAGE.

5. Planetary bodies differ from one another in their composition, but most of those in the Solar System have solid surfaces. Unless the core of such a planetary body generates enough heat to cause volcanic action, the surface of the body will not be renewed for millions of years. Any planetary body with a solid surface whose surface is not renewed for millions of years becomes heavily pockmarked by meteorite craters, just like the Earth's Moon. Some old planetary bodies in the Solar System, such as Europa, a very cold moon belonging to Jupiter, have solid icy surfaces with very few meteorite craters.

   If the claims above are true, which one of the following must, on the basis of them, be true?

   (A) The Earth's Moon does not have an icy surface.
   (B) If a planetary body does not have a heavily pockmarked surface, its core does not generate enough heat to cause volcanic action.
   (C) Some planetary bodies whose cores generate enough heat to cause volcanic action do not have solid icy surfaces.
   (D) Some of Jupiter's moons are heavily pockmarked by meteorite craters.
   (E) Some very cold planetary bodies have cores that generate enough heat to cause volcanic action.

6. Patient: Pharmacists maintain that doctors should not be permitted to sell the medicine that they prescribe because doctors would then be tempted to prescribe unnecessary medicines in order to earn extra income. But pharmacists have a financial interest in having a monopoly on the sale of prescription medicines, so their objection to the sale of medicines by doctors cannot be taken seriously.

   The patient's argument proceeds by

   (A) pointing out an unstated assumption on which the pharmacists' argument relies and then refuting it
   (B) attempting to discredit a position by questioning the motives of the proponents of that position
   (C) undermining the pharmacists' conclusion by demonstrating that one of the statements used to support the conclusion is false
   (D) rejecting a questionable position on the grounds that the general public does not support that position
   (E) asserting that pharmacists lack the appropriate knowledge to have informed opinions on the subject under discussion

7. Murray: You claim Senator Brandon has accepted gifts from lobbyists. You are wrong to make this criticism. That it is motivated by personal dislike is shown by the fact that you deliberately avoid criticizing other politicians who have done what you accuse Senator Brandon of doing.

   Jane: You are right that I dislike Senator Brandon, but just because I have not criticized the same failing in others doesn't mean you can excuse the senator's offense.

   If Murray and Jane are both sincere in what they say, then it can properly be concluded that they agree that

   (A) Senator Brandon has accepted gifts from lobbyists
   (B) it is wrong for politicians to accept gifts from lobbyists
   (C) Jane's criticism of Senator Brandon is motivated only by personal dislike
   (D) Senator Brandon should be criticized for accepting gifts from lobbyists
   (E) one or more politicians have accepted gifts from lobbyists

Questions 8–9

Oscar: Emerging information technologies will soon make speed of information processing the single most important factor in the creation of individual, corporate, and national wealth. Consequently, the division of the world into northern countries—in general rich—and southern countries—in general poor—will soon be obsolete. Instead, there simply will be fast countries and slow countries, and thus a country's economic well-being will not be a function of its geographical position but just a matter of its relative success in incorporating those new technologies.

Sylvia: But the poor countries of the south lack the economic resources to acquire those technologies and will therefore remain poor. The technologies will thus only widen the existing economic gap between north and south.

8. Sylvia's reasoning depends on the assumption that
   (A) the prosperity of the rich countries of the north depends, at least in part, on the natural resources of the poor countries of the south
   (B) the emergence of new information technologies will not result in a significant net increase in the total amount of global wealth
   (C) there are technologies other than information technologies whose development could help narrow the existing economic gap between north and south
   (D) at least some of the rich countries of the north will be effective in incorporating new information technologies into their economies
   (E) the speed at which information processing takes place will continue to increase indefinitely

9. The reasoning that Oscar uses in supporting his prediction is vulnerable to criticism on the ground that it
   (A) overlooks the possibility that the ability of countries to acquire new technologies at some time in the future will depend on factors other than those countries' present economic status
   (B) fails to establish that the division of the world into rich countries and poor countries is the single most important problem that will confront the world economy in the future
   (C) ignores the possibility that, in determining a country's future wealth, the country's incorporation of information-processing technologies might be outweighed by a combination of other factors
   (D) provides no reason to believe that faster information processing will have only beneficial effects on counties that successfully incorporate new information technologies into their economies
   (E) makes no distinction between those of the world's rich countries that are the wealthiest and those that are less wealthy

10. At the beginning of each month, companies report to the federal government their net loss or gain in jobs over the past month. These reports are then consolidated by the government and reported as the total gain or loss for the past month. Despite accurate reporting by companies and correct tallying by the government, the number of jobs lost was significantly underestimated in the recent recession.

    Which one of the following, if true, contributes most to a resolution of the apparent discrepancy described?
    (A) More jobs are lost in a recession than in a period of growth.
    (B) The expenses of collecting and reporting employment data have steadily increased.
    (C) More people who lose their jobs start up their own businesses.
    (D) In the recent recession a large number of failing companies abruptly ceased all operations.
    (E) The recent recession contributed to the growing preponderance of service jobs over manufacturing jobs.

GO ON TO THE NEXT PAGE.

Questions 11–12

Beverage company representative: The plastic rings that hold six-packs of beverage cans together pose a threat to wild animals, which often become entangled in the discarded rings and suffocate as a result. Following our lead, all beverage companies will soon use only those rings consisting of a new plastic that disintegrates after only three days' exposure to sunlight. Once we all complete the switchover from the old to the new plastic rings, therefore, the threat of suffocation that plastic rings pose to wild animals will be eliminated.

11. The argument depends on which one of the following assumptions?
    (A) None of the new plastic rings can disintegrate after only two days' exposure to sunlight.
    (B) The switchover to the new plastic rings can be completed without causing significant financial hardship to the beverage companies.
    (C) Wild animals will not become entangled in the new plastic rings before the rings have had sufficient exposure to sunlight to disintegrate.
    (D) Use of the old plastic rings poses no substantial threat to wild animals other than that of suffocation.
    (E) Any wild animal that becomes entangled in the old plastic rings will suffocate as a result.

12. Which one of the following, if true, most seriously weakens the representative's argument?
    (A) The switchover to the new plastic rings will take at least two more years to complete.
    (B) After the beverage companies have switched over to the new plastic rings, a substantial number of the old plastic rings will persist in most aquatic and woodland environments.
    (C) The new plastic rings are slightly less expensive than the old rings.
    (D) The new plastic rings rarely disintegrate during shipping of beverage six-packs because most trucks that transport canned beverages protect their cargo from sunlight.
    (E) The new plastic rings disintegrate into substances that are harmful to aquatic animals when ingested in substantial quantities by them.

13. Alcohol consumption has been clearly linked to high blood pressure, which increases the likelihood of developing heart disease. Yet in a study of the effects of alcohol consumption, the incidence of heart disease was lower among participants who drank moderate quantities of alcohol every day than it was among participants identified as nondrinkers.

    Which one of the following, if true, most helps to resolve the apparent discrepancy in the information above?
    (A) Because many people who do not drink alcohol are conscious of their health habits, they are likely to engage in regular exercise and to eat nutritionally well-balanced meals.
    (B) Many of the participants identified as nondrinkers were people who had been heavy drinkers but had stopped drinking alcohol prior to participating in the study.
    (C) Some of the participants who drank moderate quantities of alcohol every day said that they occasionally drank large quantities of alcohol.
    (D) Some of the participants who drank moderate quantities of alcohol every day had high blood pressure.
    (E) The two groups of participants were similar to each other with respect to the participants' age, sex, geographical origin, and economic background.

14. Some of the world's most beautiful cats are Persian cats. However, it must be acknowledged that all Persian cats are pompous, and pompous cats are invariably irritating.

    If the statements above are true, each of the following must also be true on the basis of them EXCEPT:
    (A) Some of the world's most beautiful cats are irritating.
    (B) Some irritating cats are among the world's most beautiful cats.
    (C) Any cat that is not irritating is not a Persian cat.
    (D) Some pompous cats are among the world's most beautiful cats.
    (E) Some irritating and beautiful cats are not Persian cats.

GO ON TO THE NEXT PAGE.

15. At Flordyce University any student who wants to participate in a certain archaeological dig is eligible to do so but only if the student has taken at least one archaeology course and has shown an interest in the field. Many students who have shown an interest in archaeology never take even one archaeology course. Therefore, many students who want to participate in the dig will be ineligible to do so.

The flawed reasoning of which one of the following arguments is most similar to that of the argument above?

(A) Theoretically, any jar is worth saving regardless of its size, but only if it has a lid. Therefore, since some jars are sure not to have lids, there are certain sizes of jar that are actually not worth saving.

(B) For a horse that is well schooled to be ideal for beginning riders that horse must also be surefooted and gentle. Many horses that are surefooted are not gentle. Therefore many well-schooled horses are not ideal for beginning riders.

(C) If an author's first novel has a romantic setting and a suspenseful plot, it will become a best-seller. Since many authors' first novels have neither, not many first novels become best-sellers.

(D) Any automobile that is more than a few years old is eventually sure to need repairs if it is not regularly maintained. Many automobiles are more than a few years old, but still do not need repairs. Therefore, many automobiles are regularly maintained.

(E) An expensive new building will prove to be a good investment only if it is aesthetically pleasing or provides lots of office space. However, since many expensive new buildings are not aesthetically pleasing, few expensive new buildings will prove to be good investments.

16. From the observation that each member of a group could possess a characteristic, it is fallacious to conclude immediately that it is possible for all the group's members to possess the characteristic. An example in which the fallacy is obvious: arguing that because each of the players entering a tennis tournament has a possibility of winning it, there is therefore a possibility that all will win the tournament.

Which one of the following commits the fallacy described above?

(A) You can fool some of the people all of the time and all of the people some of the time, but you cannot fool all of the people all of the time.

(B) Each of the candidates for mayor appears at first glance to possess the necessary qualifications. It would therefore be a mistake to rule out any of them without more careful examination.

(C) Each of the many nominees could be appointed to any one of the three openings on the committee. Therefore it is possible for all of the nominees to be appointed to the openings on the committee.

(D) If a fair coin is tossed five times, then on each toss the chance of heads being the result is half. Therefore the chance of heads being the result on all five tosses is also half.

(E) It is estimated that ten million planets capable of supporting life exist in our galaxy. Thus to rule out the possibility of life on worlds other than Earth, ten million planetary explorations would be needed.

GO ON TO THE NEXT PAGE.

17. Recent research shows that hesitation, shifting posture, and failure to maintain eye contact are not reliable indicators in discriminating between those who are lying and those who are telling the truth. The research indicates that behavior that cannot be controlled is a much better clue, at least when the lie is important to the liar. Such behavior includes the dilation of eye pupils, which indicates emotional arousal, and small movements of facial muscles, which indicate distress, fear, or anger.

    Which one of the following provides the strongest reason for exercising caution when relying on the "better" clues mentioned above in order to discover whether someone is lying?

    (A) A person who is lying might be aware that he or she is being closely observed for indications of lying.

    (B) Someone who is telling the truth might nevertheless have a past history of lying.

    (C) A practiced liar might have achieved great control over body posture and eye contact.

    (D) A person telling the truth might be affected emotionally by being suspected of lying or by some other aspect of the situation.

    (E) Someone who is lying might exhibit hesitation and shifting posture as well as dilated pupils.

Questions 18–19

Orthodox medicine is ineffective at both ends of the spectrum of ailments. At the more trivial end, orthodox medicine is largely ineffective in treating aches, pains, and allergies, and, at the other extreme, it has yet to produce a cure for serious, life-threatening diseases such as advanced cancer and lupus. People turn to alternative medicine when orthodox medicine fails to help them and when it produces side effects that are unacceptable to them. One of the reasons alternative medicine is free of such side effects is that it does not have any effects at all.

18. If the statements above are true, which one of the following can be properly inferred from them?

    (A) Practitioners of alternative medicine are acting in bad faith.

    (B) There are some medical conditions for which no orthodox or alternative treatment is effective.

    (C) There are some trivial illnesses that can be treated effectively by the methods of alternative medicine.

    (D) There are no effective medical treatments that are free from unacceptable side effects.

    (E) Orthodox medicine will eventually produce a solution for the diseases that are currently incurable.

19. The charge made above against alternative medicine is most seriously weakened if it is true that

    (A) predictions based on orthodox medicine have sometimes failed, as when a patient has recovered despite the judgment of doctors that an illness is fatal

    (B) alternative medicine relies on concepts of the body and of the nature of healing that differ from those on which orthodox medicine is based

    (C) alternative medicine provides hope to those for whom orthodox medicine offers no cure

    (D) a patient's belief in the medical treatment the patient is receiving can release the body's own chemical painkillers, diminish allergic reactions, and promote healing

    (E) many treatments used for a time by orthodox medicine have later been found to be totally ineffective

GO ON TO THE NEXT PAGE.

20. Humans began to spread across North America around 12,000 years ago, as the climate became warmer. During the same period the large mammals that were once abundant in North America, such as the mastodon, the woolly mammoth, and the saber-toothed tiger, became extinct. Thus, contrary to the myth that humans formerly lived in harmony with the rest of nature, it is clear that even 12,000 years ago human activity was causing the extinction of animal species.

The argument is most vulnerable to the criticism that

(A) it adopts without question a view of the world in which humans are seen as not included in nature
(B) in calling the idea that humans once lived in harmony with nature a myth the argument presupposes what it attempts to prove
(C) for early inhabitants of North America the destruction of mastodons, woolly mammoths, and saber-toothed tigers might have had very different significance than the extinction of mammal species does for modern humans
(D) there might have been many other species of animals, besides mastodons, woolly mammoths, and saber-toothed tigers, that became extinct as the result of the spread of humans across North America
(E) the evidence it cites is consistent with the alternative hypothesis that the large mammals' extinction was a direct result of the same change in climate that allowed humans to spread across North America

21. The town of Greenfield recently instituted a substantial supplementary tax on all households, whereby each household is taxed in proportion to the volume of the trash that it puts out for trash collectors to pick up, as measured by the number of standard-sized garbage bags put out. In order to reduce the volume of the trash on which their tax bill is based, Greenfield households can deliver their recyclable trash to a conveniently located local commercial recycling center, where such trash is accepted free of charge.

The supplementary tax provides some financial incentive to Greenfield households to do each of the following EXCEPT

(A) sort out recyclable trash thoroughly from their other trash
(B) dump nonrecyclable trash illegally at parks and roadsides
(C) compress and nest items of nonrecyclable trash before putting them out for pickup
(D) deliver recyclable materials to the recycling center instead of passing them on to neighbors who want to reuse them
(E) buy products without packaging or with recyclable rather than nonrecyclable packaging

22. In a survey of consumers in an Eastern European nation, respondents were asked two questions about each of 400 famous Western brands: whether or not they recognized the brand name and whether or not they thought the products bearing that name were of high quality. The results of the survey were a rating and corresponding rank order for each brand based on recognition, and a second rating-plus-ranking based on approval. The brands ranked in the top 27 for recognition were those actually available in that nation. The approval ratings of these 27 brands often differed sharply from their recognition ratings. By contrast, most of the other brands had ratings, and thus rankings, that were essentially the same for recognition as for approval.

Which one of the following, if each is a principle about consumer surveys, is violated by the survey described?

(A) Never ask all respondents a question if it cannot reasonably be answered by respondents who make a particular response to another question in the same survey.
(B) Never ask a question that is likely to generate a large variety of responses that are difficult to group into a manageable number of categories.
(C) Never ask all respondents a question that respondents cannot answer without giving up their anonymity.
(D) It is better to ask the same question about ten different products than to ask ten different questions about a single product.
(E) It is best to ask questions that a respondent can answer without fear of having gotten the answer wrong.

GO ON TO THE NEXT PAGE.

23. A certain species of bird has two basic varieties: crested and noncrested. The birds, which generally live in flocks that contain only crested or only noncrested birds, tend to select mates of the same variety as themselves. However, if a bird that is raising a flock in which all other members are crested is later moved to a mixed flock, then that bird—whether crested or noncrested—is likely to select a crested mate. This fact indicates that the birds' preference for crested or noncrested mates is learned rather than genetically determined.

Which one of the following, if true, provides the most support for the argument?

(A) Birds of other species also tend to show preferences for mates that have one or another specific physical feature.

(B) In general there are few behavioral differences between the crested and noncrested birds of the species.

(C) Both the crested and noncrested birds of the species tend to select mates that are similar to themselves in size and age.

(D) If a crested bird of the species is raised in captivity apart from other birds and is later moved to a mixed flock, that bird is likely to select a crested mate.

(E) If a bird of the species is raised in a flock that contains both crested and noncrested birds, that bird shows no preference for one variety or the other in its selection of a mate.

24. Plant species differ in that renewed growth in spring can be triggered by day length or by temperature or else by a combination of both. Day length is the same, year after year, for any given date. Therefore, any plant species that starts to grow again on widely different dates in different years resumes growth at least in part in response to temperature.

Which one of the following arguments is most similar in its pattern of reasoning to the argument above?

(A) In Xandia, medical assistant trainees must either complete a formal training course or work for one year under the close supervision of a physician. Since few physicians are willing to act as supervisors, it must be true that most medical assistant trainees in Xandia take the training course.

(B) In the Crawford area, easterly winds mean rain will come and westerly winds mean dry weather will come; winds from other directions do not occur. Therefore, since it is currently raining in Crawford, there must be an easterly wind blowing there now.

(C) Some landfills charge garbage companies by volume only, some charge by weight only, and all others use a formula sensitive to both volume and weight. So if at a particular landfill the charges for two particular loads of equal volume dumped on the same day are different, weight must determine, or help determine, charges at that landfill.

(D) Depending on volume of business, either one or two or three store detectives are needed for adequate protection against shoplifting. Therefore, if on any particular day store management has decided that three detectives will be needed, it must be because business that day is expected to be heavy.

(E) A call is more likely to be heard if it is loud rather than soft, if it is high-pitched rather than low-pitched, and especially if it is both loud and high-pitched. Therefore, anyone whose call goes unheard in spite of being at maximum loudness should try to raise the pitch of the call.

STOP

IF YOU FINISH BEFORE TIME IS CALLED, YOU MAY CHECK YOUR WORK ON THIS SECTION ONLY. DO NOT WORK ON ANY OTHER SECTION IN THE TEST.

Practice Test 3

Writing Sample

SIGNATURE ______________ / ____ / ____
DATE

LSAT WRITING SAMPLE TOPIC

Sea Coast University is hiring new faculty for its science program and has narrowed its selection to Louise Parker or the team of Joe Echevarria and Jean Mydral. Assuming the cost of hiring Parker alone or the team is comparable, write an argument supporting one choice over the other based on the following considerations:

- Sea Coast University wants to develop a science program that will attract more undergraduate science majors.
- Sea Coast University wants to increase private and public support for its scientific research.

Louise Park, an internationally recognized scientist, plans to retire in three to five years. The recipient of numerous prizes for several key discoveries, Dr. Park has published extensively in scientific journals. While many of her graduate students have become influential scientists, undergraduates often find her inaccessible. Dr. Park is eager to leave her current university for Sea Coast's warmer climate, and she will bring a large, well-equipped laboratory if she comes to Sea Coast. This year, as usual, Dr. Park has secured grants from public and private sources to support her research.

Joe Echevarria and Jean Mydral number among the most promising young scientists in the country. They have begun to publish in respected scientific journals and have received research grants from major foundations. Last year, their team-teaching approach won them a national teaching award. They recently published an article detailing their groundbreaking research on commercial uses of biotechnology; this research has attracted the attention of major corporations, several of whom are eager to fund their future work.

GO ON TO THE NEXT PAGE.

STOP

IF YOU FINISH BEFORE TIME IS CALLED, YOU MAY CHECK YOUR WORK ON THIS SECTION ONLY.
DO NOT WORK ON ANY OTHER SECTION IN THE TEST.

Practice Test 3: **Answer Key**

Section I Analytical Reasoning		Section II Logical Reasoning		Section III Reading Comprehension		Section IV Logical Reasoning	
1.	D	1.	D	1.	A	1.	A
2.	B	2.	C	2.	D	2.	C
3.	C	3.	C	3.	B	3.	D
4.	E	4.	A	4.	C	4.	E
5.	B	5.	A	5.	D	5.	E
6.	D	6.	E	6.	A	6.	B
7.	E	7.	B	7.	C	7.	E
8.	E	8.	A	8.	C	8.	D
9.	C	9.	D	9.	E	9.	C
10.	C	10.	A	10.	B	10.	D
11.	C	11.	D	11.	A	11.	C
12.	B	12.	D	12.	D	12.	B
13.	A	13.	A	13.	D	13.	B
14.	E	14.	D	14.	E	14.	E
15.	D	15.	E	15.	D	15.	B
16.	B	16.	C	16.	E	16.	C
17.	E	17.	A	17.	B	17.	D
18.	E	18.	A	18.	C	18.	B
19.	C	19.	C	19.	A	19.	D
20.	A	20.	A	20.	D	20.	E
21.	A	21.	C	21.	A	21.	D
22.	D	22.	D	22.	D	22.	A
23.	C	23.	D	23.	D	23.	E
24.	E	24.	E	24.	C	24.	C
		25.	A	25.	B		
		26.	B	26.	A		
				27.	E		

Answers and Explanations

SECTION I: ANALYTICAL REASONING

GAME 1—Consumer Research

The Action

This game announces itself pretty obviously: the word "group" appears four times in the opening paragraph. Not surprisingly, you're asked to group eight people—to divide them into two groups of four people each. The key issues are predictable:

1) Who's in what group?

2) What people can or must be in the same group?

3) What people cannot be in the same group?

The Initial Setup

F G H J K L M N

1 | ___ ___ ___ ___

2 | ___ ___ ___ ___

Keep this setup simple, just as you would if you were choosing up sides in everyday life. You can keep a roster of the entities, and since there are definitely four slots in each group, picture them that way:

The Rules

1) Rules like this are a blessing in grouping games: It means that you can treat two entities as a solid block, and whenever you get information about one, the other must tag along. To remember the rule, jot down "ALWAYS FJ" nearby (although chances are, you had this rule pretty much memorized before the game was half done).

2) Remember that G and M can never be present in the same group, but remember that it's best to build rules right into the picture whenever possible. And since you have eight definite slots to fill, one slot in each group is now filled, one by G, the other by M. Even if you choose to jot down "Never GM" off to the side, build the G/M relationship into the master sketch (see below).

3) If/then rules: Not much you can do except think them through. If H is in 1, L is in 1. Remember to also think through the contrapositive. It's true that if L isn't in group 1, then neither is H, but take that further: In this game "not in 1" is equivalent to "in group 2." So you should take note of the contrapositive: If L is in 2, H is in 2. Note that this rule DOESN'T require H and L always to be in the same group—that's a common mistake and you can bet that some questions will test whether you've recognized that.

4) Same kind of deal as Rule 3. If N's in 2, G's in 1. The contrapositive: If G's in 2, N's in 1. Note that, like the preceding rule, this one has a built-in trap. It *doesn't* mean that N and G can never be together...they can in group 1.

Deductions

Despite the fact that G appears in Rules 2 and 4, the deduction that "if N is in group 2, then G is in 1 and M is in 2" is not really worth your time. If/then rules are hypothetical only: Wait for the questions to provide concrete information. Enjoy the knowledge that, thanks to your interpretation and shorthanding of the rules, the information will be there when you need it.

What *is* important, however, are the restrictions of space. You've seen that G and M take up one slot in each group. And F and J are always together (Rule 1), so you know that one of the groups will always consist of F and J; either G or M; and one other entity. And you might stop there, or go on to realize that if H and L are in group 1 (as Rule 3 says is possible), then F and J must be in group 2. Again, don't take hypothetical reasoning too far, but whenever big deductions aren't immediately accessible (as in this game), focus on space limitations and the numbers that govern the game. Often, the answers to many of the questions will be based on these.

Finally, note the play of the if/then rules and their contrapositives that you listed along with them. You can scan the "if" column only, and whenever you know that H is in group 1, or L, N, or G is in group 2, more information is provided. Recognize, however, that if you find out that H is in group *2*, or that L, N, or G is in group *1*, these rules are of no help to you. Don't commit the fallacy of affirming the consequent!

The Final Visualization

As you move on to the questions, here's what you have to work with:

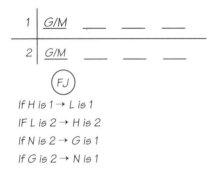

1	G/M	___	___	___
2	G/M	___	___	___

(FJ)

If H is 1 → L is 1

IF L is 2 → H is 2

If N is 2 → G is 1

If G is 2 → N is 1

The Big Picture

- Always think through and note the contrapositive of every if/then rule. It can be your best friend, especially in games that have a limited number of options.
- When a game is largely in hypothetical (if/then) form, don't take a lot of time to work out possibilities in advance. Wait for concrete info to come along.

The Questions

1. D

For this "could be true" question focusing on group 1, you need to find the single choice that violates no rules, so check each rule against each answer choice. Rule 1 eliminates (B), which separates F and J. Rule 2 eliminates (E), which mistakenly puts G and M together, and (C), which, by omitting both G and M, force this forbidden pair into group 2. Rule 3 does away with (A)—H can't be in group 1 without L. This leaves only (D), which must be an acceptable lineup for group 1.

- This "could be true" question is basically just another type of acceptability question; as in any acceptability question, test the rules against the answer choices.
- In a grouping game containing exactly two groups, remember that a complete list of entities in one group tells you more than who's in that group; it also tells you who's in the other group.

2. B

Don't just stare at it; work it out on paper. Put K and N in one group, but don't label it yet; realize that F and J have to be in the other group (if not, Rule 2 is violated). And G and M split up, so three of the four spaces in each group are set. H and L are the only ones left. Scan the 'if' conditions in your rules: Which apply? Rule 3 does. If H is in group 1, then L is too. But no matter which group above you designate as group 1 (K, N, and G or M; or F, J, and G or M), you have no room for H and L in group 1. Therefore, H must go into group 2 and L in group 1, the former of which is (B).

(A) and (E) G and M could be in either group. The only stipulation is that they not be together in the same group.

(C) and (D) Group 1: K, N, G, L and group 2: F, J, H, M shows that neither of these choices must be true.

- Whenever you're given new information in an "if" clause, remember that this information applies for that question only. Forget it when moving on to the next question.
- Sometimes you have to start linking entities up even if you don't know exactly which group to place them in. Here, just separating the F/J group from the K/N group set forth in the stem, and then separating G and M, gives you a good head start on the question.

3. C

This is question 2 revisited, this time with different entities—F and H—grouped together. Rule 1 tells you that J joins them, and Rule 2 fills out that group with either G or M. Everybody else goes into the other group: K, L, N, and either G or M. Now—which group is which? Once again you have H and L in different groups, which means that H's group has to be group 2 (remember, if H is in 1, so is L). Group 2 is therefore F, H, J, and either G or M; group 1 is N, K, L, and either G or M. The only choice that must be true under these circumstances is (C).

(A) and (E) are possible only, whereas (B) and (D) cannot be true.

- Always take an active role in pursuing the answer. Take any new information you're given, *put it down on paper,* and see where it leads you. The worst thing you can do on test day is to sit and stare at a question. If you can't think of anything to do with the new information, then skip it; but by and large, going back to the rules armed with the new information will normally lead you to, or toward, the answer.

4. E

This one promises to be easier than the previous two because it names members of a specific group—and it *is* easier. You're asked for someone who could be in either of the groups, given L and M are in group 2. Jot that down and consider the contrapositive of Rule 3: If L is in 2—which he is—then H is in 2 as well, joining L and M.

This pushes F and J into group 1, along with G (Rule 2). This much information alone allows you to cross off choices (A), (B), (C), and (D); all these entities are fixed in one group or another. You don't even have to check to make sure that K can be in both groups. When you've narrowed it down to one choice, that's our answer. Indeed, both K and N could occupy either group, but the test makers chose K as the answer.

- Don't waste time proving that an answer works when you've confidently rejected all the others. If there's only one choice left, mark it, secure in the knowledge that there are *no* questions on the LSAT without a credited answer.

5. B

Which pair of people cannot be together in group 1? See whether any pairs in the choices have appeared together in group 1 before; if so, you can cross that pair off. (D) and (E) have—both pairs appeared together in group 1 in question 1's correct answer (D). Toss those choices. And note that in question 4, F and G—(A) here—appeared together in group 1, so (A) can be eliminated too. As for (C), the group F, L, J, G can be together in 1, leaving (B) as the answer to this all EXCEPT question.

- Here's another argument for doing separate scratchwork for each question and keeping your sketches "pristine"—you can use them to help you in later questions. Why duplicate your work?

6. D

L is in group 2, and you're asked for a pair that could *not* be in group 1 together. The contrapositive of Rule 3 says that if L is in group 2, then so is H; jot that down, and recognize that from there you have to put your FJ pair in group 1. Of course, each group gets the customary G or M. N and K are left over, one per group.

Now what? If you can't figure out how to apply the rules toward the answer, use trial and error: Take each pair, combine them with the other inhabitants of group 1, and see what you're left with. You'll find that if K and M join F and J in group 1 (choice D), G and N will be forced to join group 2, which is a blatant violation of Rule 4.

- When many questions go by without a certain rule being invoked, you have to figure it'll come along sooner or later. For instance, you hadn't used Rule 4 very much until question 6—a strong indication that that rule would be useful here.

GAME 2—Game Show Contestants

The Action

A really straightforward sequencing game in which you're told to schedule five people to appear on a television show, one per day from Monday through Friday.

The Initial Setup

Since your job is to assign entities to discrete slots, you can just create those slots (labeled "M T W Th F") and list the contestants off to the side:

M T W TH F

HIKNV

___ ___ ___ ___ ___

The Rules

You get quite the cross-section of rule types here: one negative rule, two if/thens, and one concrete. Where to begin?

4) Sure: with the rule that gives you the most concrete help. Somewhere in this sequence the letters "VK" have to appear consecutively, in that order. So make a note to that effect. Just make sure you don't get it backward.

1) "No N" over your M for Monday will help you keep this rule in mind. Can't do much more than that: Only 1 of N's 5 prospects has been eliminated.

2) and 3) can be handled together because they're in the same logical form. Each gives you a hypothetical person/day assignment, and says that if that assignment occurs, then *another* person/day assignment will result. Jot them down off to the side, and just like the if/thens from the last game, be sure to think through the contrapositive of each:

NOTE: The sketch below is a graphic, but does not follow our current notation in that you've written out the names AND the days. People should be a single capital letter if days are going to be represented with three letter abbreviations.

$Harry_{Mon} \rightarrow Nan_{Fri}$ $Nan_{Tues} \rightarrow Iris_{Mon}$

$Nan_{not\ Fri} \rightarrow Harry_{not\ Mon}$ $Iris_{not\ Mon} \rightarrow Nan_{not\ Tues}$

Deductions

Given the nature of these rules, it shouldn't be too surprising that deductions are not in great supply here. However, do take special note of the "VK" pairing. They will always take up two out of the five possible spaces, and generally when a bloc of entities has to travel together, more than a couple of the questions hinge on whether or not there's adequate space for everyone. One thing you might notice—and it's not such a big deal—is that "If Nan not Fri" in the contrapositive of Rule 2 really means "If Nan is T, W, or Th" (since she's ineligible for Monday). Also, Kate can't be on Monday and Victor can't be on Friday thanks to Rule 4. Not earth-shattering stuff, but things worth noting before embarking on the questions. (Actually, this "VK" business turns question 7 into a huge "gimme.")

The Final Visualization

Here's all the info you should have heading into the questions:

NO N

M T W TH F (VK)

HIKNV

____ ____ ____ ____ ____

$Harry_{Mon} \rightarrow Nan_{Fri}$ $Nan_{Tues} \rightarrow Iris_{Mon}$

$Nan_{not\ Fri} \rightarrow Harry_{not\ Mon}$ $Iris_{not\ Mon} \rightarrow Nan_{not\ Tues}$

The Big Picture:

- Don't kill yourself looking for deductions. Some games lend themselves to big deductions and some games do not. The way to figure it out is to take rules with common elements and see whether you can combine them. Steer clear of if/then's, however, when looking for deductions; since their info is purely hypothetical, you're usually better off waiting for the question stems to give you direction.
- Always try to identify the "most significant rule" or "most significant block of entities" in a game. Target them as most likely to be helpful during the questions. Here, of course, it's the "VK" block that you need to keep in mind throughout.

The Questions

7. E

Yes, a "gimme" indeed. As you saw above, Rule 4 says that Kate is scheduled for the day *after* Victor, so Victor cannot be scheduled for the last day, Friday.

- In an "all Except" question, once you've found a choice that cannot be true, there's absolutely no reason to prove that the other choices *can* be true—you've got your answer.
- This question hinges on what one might call an "excluded ends" principle. Since V must precede K, V cannot occupy the last slot in a sequence, and for the same reason K cannot be first.

8. E

This is basically an Acceptability question, with the added information about Iris following Harry: Jot down "H I" to get started. The best way to proceed is to check each day to determine which of the days on which Harry could be scheduled. And use your pencil if you need to. (Note that there's no reason to check Monday; since it appears in every choice, it's obviously acceptable.)

If Harry is on Tuesday, Iris is on Wednesday; to slot in "V K," you need to assign Victor to Thursday and Kate to Friday. This leaves Monday for Nancy, a rule violation, so Harry can't take Tuesday after all. Cross off any choice that includes Tuesday: (A) and (D).

Now try Harry on Wednesday—no problem. Iris takes Thursday, Nancy gets Friday, and the Victor/Kate pair begin the week. Therefore, the answer must *include* Wednesday, so cross off (C).

None of the answer choices include Friday, so the last day you need check is Thursday, and again—no problem. If Harry is on Thursday, Iris takes Friday, Nancy takes Wednesday, and again the V/K pair begins the week. The answer must include Thursday, so cross off (B). The answer is therefore (E).

- Sometimes the only way to work a question is to check each choice. You can help yourself, however, by using your pencil instead of trying to work things out in your head. You can also help by looking for shortcuts (such as not bothering with Monday and Friday). These strategies can make questions like this relatively quick.

9. C

Kate is scheduled for Wednesday, so Victor takes Tuesday (Rule 4). This means that Rule 3 (Nancy on Tuesday) doesn't apply in this one. Monday is forbidden to Nancy, so she can only take Thursday or Friday. Now work with Rule 2: If H is on Monday, then N must be Friday, leaving I for Thursday—the schedule would then be "H, V, K, I, N." However, if H isn't on Monday, he must be on Thursday or Friday, with N also on Thursday or Friday, leaving I for Monday: "I, V, K, H/N, H/N" is the only other option. Checking these two options against the choices, only (C) could be true.

- Work out the implications of any new information you're given. When one entity is limited to only a few options, check them out; you may find that you can quickly cover all the bases and then simply check the choices against the schedules on your page.
- Recognize up front which rules don't apply to a given situation, and proceed to ignore them.

10. C

Don't you love how these question stems keep dealing with Kate and Victor, about whom you know so much? Kate on Friday means Victor on Thursday. Now, go back to your Rules—Rule 2 states that if Harry is on Monday, then Nancy is on Friday. Can that be? No, Kate owns Friday in this one, so Harry can't be Monday, Nancy can never be on Monday (Rule 1), which means that Iris must take Monday, (C).

Nancy and Harry end up floating between Tuesday and Wednesday, so (A), (B), and (E) are *possibly* true. But (D) is definitely false.

- In games that contain only a few entities, stay conscious of who *can't* go where; often the process of elimination will tell you who *must* go where.
- Remember the hint that the question and answer choices gave you. When the question is "what must be true" and the choices are definite statements, forge ahead boldly.

11. C

Assigning Iris to Wednesday leaves two possibilities for our V/K pair. If they take Thursday and Friday respectively, you should see (by working things out with your pencil) that things break down, because no one's available for Monday—Nancy can't take Monday ever, and putting Harry in Monday for "H N I V K" violates Rule 2. So V and K will have to take Monday and Tuesday respectively, leaving Nancy and Harry to Thursday and Friday in either order. Which must be true? Check the choices in order and stop at (C). Indeed, Kate's day precedes Harry's.

- As it turned out, working through the contrapositives of Rules 2 and 3 didn't help you too much. But that's utterly beside the point. You *must* take the time to think them through, because in 99% of games, the contrapositive *will* help. *Any* time spent thinking through rules is time well spent.

GAME 3—Art Lectures

The Action

This hybrid game combines aspects of grouping, matching *and* sequencing. You are called upon to select six of eight lectures (the grouping part); designate on which day they are scheduled (sequencing); and figure out whether they are scheduled in the morning or the afternoon of that day (matching). The issues have to do with:

1) Which lectures are scheduled on each day?

2) Which lectures are *not* scheduled on a particular day?

3) When a lecture is scheduled for a day, is it given in the morning or afternoon?

4) Which lectures can, must, or cannot be scheduled on the same day as other lectures?

5) Which lectures can, must, or cannot be scheduled immediately preceding or following other lectures?

The Initial Setup

To take care of the grouping/selection element—the choice of the 6 out of 8 lectures—list the entities in a roster, ready to circle the 6 chosen and X out the 2 rejected. As far as the scheduling goes, what did you do at the beginning of each semester when plotting out your weekly class schedule? You probably made a list of the days of the week and jotted the classes down accordingly. The process is even simpler here, because there are only three days involved, and exactly two classes per day, one in the a.m. and one in the p.m. Something like this:

	1	2	3
AM			
PM			

The Rules

Given that you have *three* separate though related tasks to attend to, it will be useful to think about which of those tasks is tied into each rule. For example:

1) On the face of it, this is a scheduling rule only: If O is chosen, it must be scheduled for day 2. But it has a selection element as well, which you might only see after thinking through the contrapositive: *If O can't be scheduled for day 2, then O isn't one of the 6 chosen.* In other words, should day 2 be occupied by two other lectures, then O will be one of the 2 lectures not scheduled that week. After you've put that all together in your head, your pencil can do the rest in the same way you've jotted down other if/then rules in this section.

2) This rule is big. Two—count 'em, two—lectures can't be in the afternoon—which means that if selected, they must be scheduled in the morning. Therefore, should all the morning slots be taken, then *sculpture and watercolors would be the 2 rejected lectures*. All the others would be automatically selected. This rule is so big and so important to remember that it may be helpful to jot it down twice: once next to the sketch, and once *within* it (see below).

3) Like most negative rules, this one can only be jotted down nearby, as a constant visual reminder never to assign oils and lithographs, or pastels and lithographs, to the same day.

4) A two-part if/then rule—complex and information-packed, and worth spending time on for those very reasons. *Should* pastels be scheduled on day 1, then fresco and history will take day 2 (sorry, oils). And should pastels be scheduled on day 2, then the same two lectures will take day 3. (You might well ask yourself, suppose pastels are chosen for day 3? In that case, all bets are off; the rule won't apply.)

What's *truly* important here is using the contrapositive to spell out the implications of this rule. If either fresco or history is unavailable for day 2 or day 3, or if another lecture is already there, then pastels will not be able to be chosen for day 1 or 2 (respectively). And you'll see all of that come up over and over in the questions. See the sketch for a common-sense way to jot down this rule, but remember: If it ain't in your head, having it on the page won't help.

Deductions

Nothing more than hypotheses. But pay special attention, once again, to the numbers game. Since sculpture and watercolors cannot be scheduled in the afternoon (Rule 2), this game is ripe for some questions in which running out of lectures that *can* be scheduled in the afternoon should lead you right to the answer.

The Final Visualization

Here's what the master sketch looks like heading into the questions:

	1	2	3	
AM				SW always here (AM)
PM				No SW here

If Ⓞ → Day 2

If not in Day 2 → No Ⓞ

If $P_{Day\ 1}$ → F, $N_{Day\ 2}$

If $P_{Day\ 2}$ → F, $N_{Day\ 3}$

The Big Picture

- A common mistake in matching games is not recognizing that when all of the other choices are ruled out, what's left must be the answer. As you proceed through this game, see whether you were hip to what *had* to be true when a bunch of possibilities were eliminated.

The Questions:

12. B

You know what to do with an Acceptability question: Check each rule against the choices. (C) puts oils on day 1 in violation of Rule 1. (D) puts watercolors in the p.m., which Rule 2 forbids. (A)'s assignment of pastels/lithography violates Rule 3, and according to Rule 4, if pastels takes day 2, then fresco and history take day 3, and that's not the case in (E).

- Acceptability questions are quick confidence builders. Save even more time by beginning with the easiest rules. And when you've eliminated a choice, cross it out completely: Doing so makes it easier to read the remaining choices.

13. A

Think about the afternoon of day 1, which is what the question is all about. Oils is impossible for day 1, period, and sculpture and watercolors are impossible in the *afternoon,* period; so (B), (D), and (E) can be rejected. And (C)'s mentioning pastels might prompt you to check Rule 4, which lo and behold would be violated if pastels were scheduled for day 1 (here, lithography in day 2 blocks you). (A) is left as the answer.

14. E

A slightly more complicated version of the previous question, with two definite assignments made. Since the question asks what could take day 1's morning slot, cross out oils (C) right away (Rule 2); and recognize that pastels (D) is also out, since you cannot have fresco and history in day 2 as Rule 4 requires.

If you sketch out the situation—with L and H in the AM slots of days 2 and 3 as specified—then a little trial and error should lead you to the right answer. If either fresco or naturalism—(A) and (B), respectively—took day 1's AM slot, fully *three* lectures would be unavailable for selection: sculpture and watercolors, which are AM only, and oils, which can only take day 2 but can't be paired up with lithography. This leaves (E), sculpture, and that would be okay—the two rejected lectures would be oils and watercolors.

- See how important the numbers game can be? Whenever you seem to be "stuck" in a Logic Games question, remember to work out the numerical possibilities.

15. D

With oils in the morning of day 2 and lithography in the morning of day 3, you should recognize that pastels are forbidden to day 1 or day 2—you can't have the fresco/history day that Rule 4 requires; and pastels is blocked from day 3, as well, since lithography's there. So pastels is out of the running altogether, (D). For the record, a schedule of sculpture, oils, lithography in the AM and fresco, history, naturalism in the PM takes care of (A), (B), (C), and (E).

- Combine a question's new information with the old rules. Ask yourself: What rule(s) can help me here?

16. B

The most helpful "if" yet: Telling you the 2 rejected lectures also tells you the 6 that are chosen, and you can proceed to think about the day assignments. Now, since fresco is out, pastels can't take day 1 or day 2; but pastels *have* to be chosen, so day 3 it is for pastels and (D) bites the dust. In the meantime, the choices continue to try to slip oils into a day other than day 2; throw out (C). But the rule that moves you to a *positive* conclusion is Rule 3: Lithography *has* to be selected, but cannot be paired up with oils (day 2) or pastels (day 3). So it's lithography that must go to day 1, (B).

17. E

The morning lectures are fresco, history, and lithography, but *not necessarily in that order.* Well, first off, with the morning lectures decided, Rule 2 demands that the two rejected lectures are sculpture and watercolors, and all of the others must be scheduled. Jot down the list of the three afternoon lectures—gotta be oils, naturalism, and pastels. And oils must be on day 2 (Rule 1), and of course that means the afternoon of day 2 here; so naturalism and pastels will take the afternoons of day 1 and 3, in either order.

Or *is* it quite so open-ended? Can you assign pastels to day 1 or 2 in line with Rule 4? No, you cannot, because you cannot follow pastels with a "fresco/history" day. So as so often in earlier questions, pastels must take day 3, leaving naturalism for the afternoon of day 1. What's the impact on the morning schedule? Lithography will have to take the day 1 slot, or else Rule 3 would be violated. So all that's uncertain is the assignment of fresco and history—they'll take day 2 and 3, in either order—so (E) is the choice that *could* be true. All the others violate the arrangement established.

- There is a ton of information to keep track of in this question. If you had success on the first five questions, this was the one to consider putting aside if it seemed unmanageable.

GAME 4—Clans & Ceremonies

The Action

This game is a variant of the "process" games that appear rarely on the LSAT, in that it requires constant reference to the rules. (It may be more amenable to scratchwork help than the average process game.) Exactly three of five clans take part in an annual harvest ceremony.

The Initial Setup

Not much to draw here. You'll want to jot down the list of the clans, and be ready to figure out what kind of behavior they undergo, and how the rules define that behavior.

The Rules

1) Don't rush to write it down. Consider what it means, in concrete terms. One year—call it year one—three clans will take part in the ceremony. Okay, so two *don't* take part. So what about them? Well, the rule means that those two clans *have to* take part in the ceremony in year two: No clan can miss two years in a row. The third clan in that second year ceremony, of course, would be one of the clans that took part in the *first* year. Now, whether you write it down or not, you need this information clear in your mind throughout. The same holds true for:

2) "No clan takes part three years in a row." So after two years in a row, a clan takes a powder. And think about what you learned in Rule 1: This rule means that the one clan that takes part in the ceremonies in years one and two cannot also take part in year three.

3) This rule introduces the new concept of a "cycle." Once each clan has taken part in exactly three ceremonies, a cycle ends.

4) Just puts a numerical limit on the business: Within any cycle, three ceremonies is the limit for each clan.

Deductions

You have to figure that Rules 3 and 4 bear consideration in tandem (because each has to do with the number of clan appearances and the composition of a cycle). Each ceremony consists of three clans; and each clan will take part in exactly three ceremonies per cycle. Okay: There are five clans—five clans that must each take part three times in a cycle. Five clans, each taking part three times, equals fifteen "appearances" in a cycle. And each ceremony allows for three participations. Fifteen divided by three equals five. Clearly, *each cycle consists of five years.*

The Final Visualization

While a customary "Final Visualization" isn't appropriate in this case—what's to draw?—it might be worth your time to do something else.

Forget the clans in the game. Think of five different clans: Call them a, b, c, d, and e. Think about and work out the five years in a possible cycle. For instance: say that a, b, and c take part in year one of a cycle. What has to happen in year two? Well, d and e, the clans that missed out in year one, will have to take part (Rule 1), as well as one of the original three: Let's say it's a, for the time being. (Jot down each list of 3 if you like, to make it more concrete.)

Year three, what happens? Well, b and c will have to be back for the ceremony—they're not allowed to miss two years in a row. And they'll be joined by either d or e; say it's d for argument's sake. So far you've got: a b c / d e a / b c d. Get the picture? Years four and five will continue, each taking the two clans that *didn't* take part the year before, as well as a third available clan. And remember: In the end, *every clan will be named exactly three times.*

Now that you've understood the process "in the abstract," using nonsense letters, you can work with the *real* clans somewhat more confidently.

The Big Picture

- Sketchwork is never a substitute for thinking. This game is a wonderful example of the importance of making abstract concepts concrete. Once you take the time to think through the behavior of entities in process games, you have a shot to rack up points quickly and accurately.

The Questions

18. E

Your "concretization," as it were, shows you how this question has to work. If N, O, and P take part in year one, the clans that missed year one—S and T—must stand and deliver in year two. The only choice that includes both of these is (E)—and remember, *any* of the three year one clans can make a reappearance in year two.

- Don't be surprised when after a complex setup, you are given a fairly straightforward opening question. The opening question will often test whether you've deduced something basic about the game. You get a reward just for hangin' in there.

19. C

Here is where your work in the Final Visualization comes through for you, abetted by your usual confidence in Acceptability questions. (A) and (B) are unacceptable because each violates Rule 2, with three consecutive appearances of a clan. Next, you can try out (C), (D), and (E), searching for the one and only one possible statement; or you can recognize from your earlier thinking that a pair of clans can only take part in, at most, two ceremonies together. No pair could be together in years 1, 3, and 5 (D), or years 2, 3, and 5 (E). Try them and see. You're left with (C), which is eminently possible.

- A process game, in the unlikely event that you see one, will almost always take more time than other games, which is why time management is so important. Save such games till last.

20. A

Already calculated.

- If you waited until now to work out that each cycle consists of five years, the first two questions may have been considerably more difficult. Actively attack each game and you'll find all of them much more manageable.

21. A

What must be true about the clans that take part in the first ceremony? You could have used the earlier thinking discussed, or how about this: You could have proceeded from, and used, question 18. Why not? There you had an acceptable set of year one clans, N, O, and P: It had to be acceptable, because the test makers provided it. Well, year two (as you saw) would have to welcome S, T, and one of the first three clans; notice that (B), the only choice mentioning year two, is false.

What about year three? Two members of the original N, O, P group will be back (whichever two skipped year two), and so you see that (A) is true. In fact, (A) could go even further: *Exactly* two members of the year one group will take part again in year three. Scan the choices. You've already worked out that "at most" and exactly two of them will be back together in year three, as (A) states. Because of that, (E) is revealed as obviously false; and you needn't stop to affirm that (C) and (D), too, are impossible, although in fact, *no* trio can take part together in any two different years.

- As you move through the questions, the rules and deductions should become more and more familiar and thus easier to use. And you will find yourself getting used to making the abstract more concrete.

22. D

If N, O, and S take part in year one, Rule 2 eliminates choice (A) right away. From there you can use our "possible" cycle to try and find a situation in which the other choices aren't necessarily true. For instance, O *could* take part in years 3 and 4, but any of the first year clans could do so instead: Cross off (B). In the same way, N and O (C) could take part together in year three, but so could N and S, and O and S, instead. Cross off (C). You're left with (D) and (E), two choices that deal with year five, and (D) turns out to be correct (which you can affirm through trial and error). There's no way to avoid a year five repairing of clans P and T—the clans not used in year one.

- Whenever you're asked for the one choice that "must" be true, remember that in order to eliminate a choice, all you have to do is find one situation in which the choice is not true.

23. C

N, O, and T are in year one's ceremony, and O and P are in year four; you're asked which clan is locked out of year three's ceremony. S and P (the two clans not used in year one) will be part of year two, and the inability of any clan to take part three years in a row makes P the clan that the question is looking for.

- Always have a game plan. Deal with any new information and then see how that new information relates to the rules.

24. E

N, O, and S are in year one's ceremony, and O, S, and T are in year three. Sneak up to year five—the topic of the question—by applying your knowledge of the rules to the concrete situation. Year two, of course, will consist of P and T and...? Not O or S, who would thereby be taking part three years in a row. Year two must be P, T, N.

Year three, you've got. Year four? Clearly, N and P will take part—remember, no clan misses two years in a row; T, however, will not take part, because that would be three T's in a row. But T has to make three appearances in the cycle, and has only taken part twice so far. Therefore, T has to be one of the clans taking part in year five. . . and if you scan the choices, only one mentions T: the correct answer, (E).

- Just because a question is the last one in a game doesn't necessarily mean that it's the most difficult. Work with each question in the same way, and you'll find that the majority of questions can be answered with the same techniques. Just be ready to move along to more fertile ground if a question gets messy.

SECTION II: LOGICAL REASONING

1. D

The argument concludes that libraries can best serve their users by purchasing only paperbacks, allowing libraries to add more new titles to their collections. The assumption being made is that adding the greatest possible number of new titles is the best way to serve library users. But if library users as a group depend on the library for access to *specific* books *only* published in hardcover, then this assumption, and the argument, falls apart.

(A) makes an irrelevant comparison. Neither issue raised here—a library's overall budget and a library's budget for day-to-day operations—gets at the paperback vs. hardcover issue.

(B) and (C) are 180 choices: (B) strengthens the argument by eliminating a possible objection to the acquisition of paperbacks, while (C) suggests another advantage of the paperback over the hardcover, thus supporting the author's recommendation for libraries to move entirely to paperback.

(E) For this to be a convincing weakener, you'd have to assume that people only use public libraries for access to books that they wouldn't buy themselves.

- For Weaken questions, look for the choice that contradicts the passage's central assumption.
- Another way to weaken an argument is to look for the choice that would directly negate the conclusion. In this case, ask yourself: "Which choice makes me believe that users would *not* be better served if the library bought only paperbacks?" (D) should then jump out.
- Be wary of choices like (E), which require additional assumptions in order to complete the logic.

2. C

The evidence is a couple of general rules about when garbage is usually collected and what happens with garbage pickup after a Monday public holiday. This evidence is then applied to the specific case of garbage collection in *this* neighborhood *this* week, which leads to the conclusion in the first sentence. So as far as the author's method of argument is concerned, the author reasons from the general to the specific, which is (C).

(A) The pieces of evidence given aren't irrelevant; they're *directly* relevant to the issue of garbage pickup and thus do support the conclusion.

(B) fails because the argument establishes its conclusion *directly*, by discussing the rules about garbage pickup, not indirectly by ruling out alternative possibilities.

(D) Reasoning from the specific to the general is the precise opposite of what this argument does.

(E) The conclusion is that garbage will *probably* be picked up on Thursday; there's no inevitability element at work here at all.

- Reading the question stem first is especially handy for Method of Argument questions, since it allows you to begin to *abstract* the reasoning in the argument as you read. In other words, you know right off the bat that you'll be asked "how" the author makes her point, not "what" specific point is being made.
- Stay familiar with the common argumentative structure featured here. Arguing from a general case to a specific example (or vice versa) appears every now and then on the LSAT—in Method questions, Flaw questions, and even Parallel Reasoning.

3. C

Why did vinyl record prices go up after CD prices, which were higher to begin with, came down? The latter were higher at first because of "different production costs"—CD technology was initially more expensive to use because it was unfamiliar. But vinyl technology's not unfamiliar, so what's the deal?

(C) provides an explanation: As CDs became more affordable and more people bought them, they bought fewer vinyl records, making it less cost-effective to produce vinyl records and therefore more expensive. Notice that this doesn't contradict the explanation for initially higher CD prices: Vinyl records ended up with "different production costs," just as CDs had at first.

(A) and (D) both entirely miss the point; in fact, neither one even *mentions* vinyl. Therefore, why some people bought CDs even though they were more expensive (A) and changes in CD technology (D) are both irrelevant issues that don't help explain the paradoxical situation.

(B) is irrelevant, too. Who cares whether people kept buying vinyl records as long as they were cheaper? You want to know why vinyl records didn't *stay* cheaper.

(E) gives a reason for people to continue buying vinyl, but ignores the issue of the increase in the cost of vinyl, so it's irrelevant.

- Although there's no reference to a "paradox" or "discrepancy" in the question stem, there's one to be solved here. Whether they use these words or not, a paradox exists if a surprising result occurs that seems counter to that which should happen.
- This is a good question for using the strategy of elimination; none of the wrong choices even remotely deals with the situation you're asked to explain.

4. A

None of the statements here is a conclusion stemming from the others—it's your job to find that conclusion among the choices. Land reserves are supposed to preserve habitats that don't exist elsewhere and that are necessary for certain species' survival. What will happen to the typical land reserve if global warming occurs as predicted? A bunch of plants now there will grow elsewhere, and you can infer a bunch of plants elsewhere will start to grow *there*. In other words, the *habitat* provided by the land reserve will change, which means that the reserve will no longer serve its purpose as the only appropriate habitat for its intended species.

(B) is unsupported; first, you can't be so sure that the butterflies will adapt; second, you know nothing about the function of migration in their survival, either now or in the future.

(C) is outside the scope, first introducing melting polar ice (remember, the stimulus only spoke of the effect of warming on vegetation), then predicting a completely unsupported consequence of the melting ice.

(D) is a distortion: Just because global warming is predicted for the future doesn't mean that you can infer that the world has adapted to drastic global warming and cooling *in the past*.

(E) The *speed* of global warming is irrelevant and therefore outside the scope, as is the idea of "agricultural areas."

- Working on inference questions, watch out for choices that introduce new vocabulary; here (E) introduces the new concepts of *rapid* global warming and *agricultural* areas.

5. A

Did you catch the scope shift in this one? The conclusion is that "Financial success does not guarantee happiness." But the evidence is based on the responses of people who "*claimed* to have achieved financial success." If most of these people were lying, then the argument falls apart for lack of evidence; (A) therefore supports the conclusion by supplying information (the people who claim financial success *are* actually financially successful) that tightens up the argument's apparent shift in scope.

(B) distorts the argument by confusing the ideas of necessity and sufficiency. The conclusion states that financial success is insufficient for happiness. Whether financial success is necessary to be happy is irrelevant.

(C) The conclusion is based on evidence concerning respondents who claimed to have achieved financial success, so the minute you see a choice beginning "many ... who claimed *not* to have achieved financial success," you should recognize it as outside the scope and immediately cross it off. (C) also introduces a time element with no bearing on the argument.

(D) suffers from the same scope problem as (C), and therefore amounts to nothing more than useless background info: The conclusion is based on the evidence provided by the respondents who reported financial success; data about respondents who falsely claimed to be financially unsuccessful can't help strengthen the link between the author's evidence and conclusion.

(E) 180. The conclusion is based on the fact that most of the people who reported financial success also reported unhappiness. If these people were, in fact, happy, the argument would be severely weakened.

- An argument that involves a scope shift necessarily depends on the assumption that the scope shift is a valid one. To strengthen the argument, select the choice that reinforces this assumption. To weaken it, pick a choice that shows the scope shift to be invalid.
- As you practice, take note of the precise way in which the LSAT uses language. For example, if a survey shows that 25 percent of the people in a group "are happy," then you must take this evidence to mean that they actually *are* happy. But if 25 percent "*report* that they are happy," you *cannot* assume their actual happiness.

6. E

This is formal logic disguised in casual argument: Two characteristics (distance traveled by animal daily and size of group) correlate well with a third (diet); and diet correlates well with yet another characteristic, size and shape of teeth and face. (E) simply applies this to a specific case, working backward: Knowing the size and shape of an extinct animal's teeth and face should be a good clue as to what its diet was, which in turn should provide some indication as to whether or not it lived in large groups.

(A), (B), and (C) all make the same mistake of manufacturing some *specific* correlation, where the stimulus only mentioned the existence of some general connection between teeth, diet, and behavior.

(A) contains an irrelevant distinction between meat eaters and plant eaters, which is nice and all but something you can't infer.

(B) involves the effects of a special kind of diet (the results are qualities never mentioned in the stimulus).

(C) deals with the effects of the *loss* of teeth. Each of these choices goes away from the correlations outlined in the stimulus, and therefore each is unsupported.

(D) is closer than the others; at least it plays off the correlation aspect of the passage. However, it goes too far; it's a distortion. An animal's teeth and face can help determine an animal's diet, which in turn can help you figure out the distance traveled each day and the size of the group in which it lives. This in no way helps you identify the animal's *species*.

- Pay careful attention to the language of the stimulus in an inference question. If the stimulus makes qualified assertions of a general nature (e.g., diet depends in large part...) you can reject any supposed inference that speaks too confidently or specifically. Learn to quickly recognize the qualified nature of an answer choice (size and shape . . . *can* establish whether . . .) that must match the tone of a qualified stimulus.

7. B

In order to show that U.S. taxes aren't as light as they seem, the author states that U.S. tax revenues provide fewer goods and services. She goes on to say that people in the U.S. have to pay out of their own pockets for additional things such as health services, and that that's the same thing as paying a tax.

But why is it the same? The author simply extends the meaning of the word "tax" in order to make her point—which is exactly what (B) says. Essentially, her argument is that if you count *voluntary private expenditures* as taxes (although she offers no reason to believe they should be), then U.S. citizens indeed pay high taxes.

(A) A comparison of percentages is appropriate here, since the question concerns tax *rates*, not total amount of money paid in taxes.

(C) The argument is not based on "negatively charged" language; the problem isn't an appeal to emotion. And she certainly does give a reason for her view—it's just a logically flawed reason.

(D) The author doesn't generalize from her example. Instead, she uses the example to *illustrate* what she means by saying "tax rates don't tell the whole story."

(E) The only obvious alternatives the author sets up—between the U.S. being the most lightly taxed of comparable countries and the U.S. *not* being so—are indeed exclusive.

- In flaw questions, if you have difficulty in seeing how an answer choice applies to the argument—like (E) perhaps—it probably doesn't describe the argument's flaw. In Logical Reasoning questions in general, if you find yourself having to go out of your way to justify an answer choice, then that choice is probably wrong.

8. A

The conclusion of the stimulus, signaled by "therefore," tells you that something probably did *not* occur. There are two important terms here that have to be recognized in your characterization: Probably (versus a definite conclusion), and the *not.*

(A) and (B) both have the right form of conclusion, so hold on to them for now and see what else you can eliminate using the conclusions. If you're left with more than one option and have to characterize the evidence as well, you'll discover that (B) deviates from the original by pointing to opposing evidence—TV said damage, the paper said full destruction—and basing the conclusion on which evidence is more recent.

(C) You've got the probably, but this conclusion is positive—the fire probably *did* affect areas beyond the port. Eliminate.

(D) is tricky. It's got "probably" and "not," but this argument doesn't conclude that something probably didn't *occur.* It introduces the new element of duration.

(E) This conclusion is parallel enough to the stimulus—"damage wasn't severe" matches up acceptably to "cards weren't common"—but its conclusion is based on the *reliability* of the source of its evidence, and that knocks (E) firmly out of the running.

- Don't neglect the preliminary step, in Parallel Reasoning, of a quick scan and comparison of the six conclusions presented, in order to reduce the number of possible choices. Once you see that the stimulus conclusion is that "phenomenon X probably didn't happen [or wasn't the case]," only (A), (B), and (E) can remain in the running.

9. D

There are only two ways to increase profits: build more rooms or improve the current rooms. The second sentence says that they can't build more rooms. So if they want to increase profits, they must improve the rooms they already have. The last sentence says they *cannot* increase profits, and then asks you to provide a reason. So there's your prephrase—the correct choice must have something to do with the fact that "their rooms can't be improved." (D) is a fancy way of saying just that.

(A), (B), and (C) all offer other limits to increasing profits; that is, other reasons that Bellarian hotel owners can't make more money. However, while plausible, these reasons have nothing to do with the alternatives given in the stimulus. Even faced with 100% occupancy rates (A), the fixed maximum attractiveness of the site (B), and the upward pressure of labor costs (C), the hotel owners could theoretically still increase profits: by making other improvements to "what's already there." Only (D) argues otherwise.

(E) introduces a completely irrelevant distinction (Bellarian vs. foreign tourists). Who these hotels serve has no impact on the two stated alternatives for increasing profits.

- Look for clues that establish the limit of the argument's scope. Here the very first sentence tells you that there are *only* two ways to do X; once you grasp that the whole argument is built around those two alternatives, it becomes easy to reject irrelevant choices.
- On fill-in questions, take note of important keywords that lead up to the blank; this signals what *type* of statement the answer must be. For example, in this case, the word "since" tells you that the answer will be a piece of evidence that supports the conclusion in the first part of the last sentence (hotel owners cannot increase their profits).

10. A

Another formal logic stimulus, this one containing two premises: 1) All early-twentieth-century socialist and communist political philosophers were influenced by Rosa Luxemburg. 2) No one influenced by Rosa Luxemburg (which obviously includes the philosophers mentioned above) advocated a totalitarian state. Put them together and you get (A): no early-twentieth-century socialist political philosopher advocated a totalitarian state. (No early-twentieth-century *communist* either, but the choices don't mention them.)

(B) Though no early-twentieth-century political philosopher influenced by Rosa Luxemburg advocated a totalitarian state, that doesn't mean that *only* those philosophers influenced by her failed to advocate a totalitarian state. Many others may have done so.

(C) is an unwarranted distortion. Rosa Luxemburg was certainly one person who did influence all the people in (C)'s group. However, there may have been many people besides her who influenced all early-twentieth-century communists or socialists—G.B. Shaw, Karl Marx, Aristotle, who knows?

(D) boils down to saying that among early-twentieth-century political philosophers, *only* socialists and communists were influenced by Rosa Luxemburg. But this does not follow from what you've been told; she may also have influenced early-twentieth century capitalists, distributists, anarchists, or anything else.

(E) Though you *can* infer that not every early-twentieth-century socialist and communist political philosopher advocated totalitarianism, you can't turn that around and say that every early-twentieth-century philosopher who didn't advocate totalitarianism was a socialist or communist.

- Many of the wrong answer choices in formal logic questions will make the mistake of reversing the legitimate inference. "Every socialist is against totalitarianism" doesn't mean "everyone against totalitarianism is a socialist." Learn to expect such traps when you scan the choices.

11. D

This one looks confusing, but actually boils down to something fairly straightforward: Harris argues that the endangered-species regulations should be expanded to admit the protection of hybrids. Vogel counters that hybrids do not need protection.

(A) and (C) can be ruled out immediately because Vogel never discusses the example of red wolves.

(B) neither Vogel nor Harris takes issue with the definition of the term "endangered." There may also be a very subtle scope shift at work here: The issue, as stated in (D), hinges more on what species should be protected, not necessarily which ones are "currently considered endangered."

(E) Vogel's argument is totally devoid of a "genetic research" component, so this certainly can't be the crux of the disagreement.

- The correct answer to a Point at Issue question must satisfy two criteria: 1) it must be a point that both characters address in their arguments; and 2) it must be a point about which the two characters disagree. Any choice that fails to meet either one of these criteria should be crossed off immediately.
- In essence, Point at Issue questions are testing little more than whether you've identified the topic and scope that two speakers have in common.

12. D

This one is ripe for prephrasing an answer: Hybrid species, argues Vogel, don't need protection because they can be easily revived by interbreeding the species from which they are descended. In order for this argument to fly, all the species from which hybrids are descended must still be around (extant).

(A) and (B) distort the issue by confusing what endangered-species regulations *can* do with what they *should* do. Vogel's argument is that hybrid species *should* not be protected. Whether those species can be identified (A), and whether the regulations can be enforced (B), are irrelevant.

(C) makes a useless distinction. What does captivity have to do with anything? Also, remember that Vogel's argument is very general; he doesn't get into the specifics of the red wolf and its descendants, so it's doubtful that his argument would rely on an unstated premise concerning the gray wolf.

(E) Same problem as (C): Vogel doesn't address the example of coyotes and red wolves, let alone speculate on the genetic relationship between them. Whether such a relationship exists has no bearing on his argument.

- When an argument contains a policy recommendation, watch out for choices that confuse what *can* be done with what *should* be done. For example, you may never be able to stamp out world hunger, but that doesn't mean you shouldn't want to.
- In dialogue stimuli, watch out for choices like (E) that deal with issues raised in the wrong character's statement. This question is about Vogel's argument, so an example used only by Harris isn't likely to help.

13. A

The conclusion: The ancient settlement dates back to significantly before 1000 B.C. The evidence: A piece of building timber found at the site is substantially older than other artifacts found there which date back to 1000 B.C. Underlying this reasoning is the assumption that the piece of timber comes from, and was once a part of, the ancient settlement in question (which would, inferably, make it a valid indicator of the settlement's age). However, if the piece of timber appears to have been salvaged from an *earlier* settlement, then its usefulness as a guide to the age of the particular settlement in this stimulus becomes doubtful.

(B) provides useless background information. Nothing in the reasoning hinges on how wide an area the site occupies.

(C) makes an irrelevant comparison. The history of the tests used to determine the age of the artifacts says nothing about their relative reliability.

(D) So what? From the very beginning, the conclusion was based on only one piece of timber as evidence. The relative paucity of lumber samples is irrelevant.

(E) A strengthener: This provides additional evidence to support the conclusion that the settlement predates 1000 B.C. Always be on the lookout for 180 answer choices in Strengthen and Weaken questions—they can be tempting because the scope is right on target.

- In a weaken the argument question, it's not necessary to completely disprove the argument's conclusion. All you have to do is select the choice that makes the conclusion *significantly less likely* to be true.
- An argument is not faulty simply because it's based on limited evidence. The key is whether the conclusion logically follows from that evidence.

14. D

The keyword in this stimulus is "converted." The author concludes that at least 2,000 people were converted because 2,000 people got the book, and it's impossible to read the book and ignore the issue...but not ignoring the issue doesn't necessarily mean "conversion." If some of the people who received copies of *To Save the Earth* were already committed to the environmentalist cause, then the number "converted" by the Earth Association would be less than 2,000.

(A) The argument deals only with the "converted" of whom Earth Association can justly take credit. Other groups giving away copies of *To Save the Earth* are outside the scope of the argument.

(B) makes an irrelevant distinction. Whether or not they were willing to pay for it, 2,000 people got a copy of *To Save the Earth* from the Earth Association.

(C) The argument states that *To Save the Earth* is so persuasive that anyone who reads it will heed its environmentalist message. Presumably this is because of the *words* in the book, not the composition of the paper on which those words are printed. So this irrelevant and distorted choice is just silly.

(E) Two problems: First, there's a scope shift. The "environmentalist cause" in the conclusion is not necessarily the same as "the environmental program advocated by the Earth Association" in this choice. Secondly, even if these things were synonymous, (E) is closer to a restatement of the evidence in the first sentence than a necessary assumption.

- You may have noticed a fairly significant scope shift in this stimulus. The argument states that "no one who reads" *To Save the Earth* can fail to heed its message. But you have no evidence that the 2,000 people who received copies of the book from the Earth Association *actually read it.* This wasn't the key to getting the correct answer here, but being able to recognize this kind of scope shift will stand you in good stead on future LSAT questions.
- In Assumption questions, beware of choices that simply restate the evidence—some students gravitate to these because of the familiarity factor ("yeah, I recognize this idea"). But just because a choice reflects or is consistent with ideas in the argument doesn't mean that it necessarily answers the question that was asked.

15. E

A paradox: Pipe and cigar smoking is less dangerous than cigarette smoking, yet cigarette smokers who switch to pipes or cigars remain at the same level of risk as they did before they switched. A possible resolution: Former cigarette smokers inhale smoke in a different, and presumably more harmful way, than those who never smoked cigarettes.

(A), (B), (C), and (D) all provide useless background information. These choices furnish data on the effects of various types of smoking—(A), (B), and (C)—or on the habits of smokers (D), but none helps to explain why cigarette smokers remain in as much danger as before despite switching to the supposedly lower risk pipes or cigars.

- Don't let the unfamiliar wording throw you. If you're asked to resolve or explain why two pieces of evidence in the passage seem at odds, or seem to lead to a surprising conclusion or result, then it's a Paradox question.
- Sometimes a very simple, general prephrase can still lead you to the correct choice. Here, for example, you may have latched onto the notion that "there has to be a difference between the way former cigarette smokers and non-cigarette smokers smoke pipes or cigars." You wouldn't necessarily come up with the specifics, but it's enough to recognize correct answer choice (E).

16. C

The production manager's second sentence states that since the company has the technology to make a safer version of the materials, they should *only* sell the safer version. (C)'s principle is a direct restatement of that sentence.

(A) is no good because it's the *sales* manager who raises the issue of funding, not the production manager, who never mentions how the improvements will be paid for.

(B) is irrelevant because the materials in question *do* meet safety codes, as the production manager states right in his first sentence.

(D) is way off. The production manager never mentions reviewing the safety codes at all, so this principle doesn't fit. Also, (D) introduces a scope shift; it involves "technologically *more advanced*" products, but you can't be sure these are the same as the *safer* products produced with the aid of new technology.

(E) is out because while the production manager does argue for making the materials safer, he doesn't claim the company should keep researching new technologies—rather, his point is that since the company happens to already have the technology, it should use it.

- The answer to a Principle question is usually the choice that expresses the key concepts and terms left out by the other choices. In this case, (C) is the only choice that directly deals with the issue of replacing the current product with a safer one.
- In dialogues, be sure to isolate the argument each person is making. Often wrong choices, like (A), will play off the *other* person's argument.
- Like lawyers, the LSAT test makers use language very precisely, and in this way often slip scope shifts into the argument or choices. As you saw in (D), *using technology* to make safer products isn't the same thing as making *technologically more advanced products.*

17. A

The sales manager argues that stopping the sale of the current, less safe product will render the company unable to develop and promote the safer product. In other words, carrying out one part of the production manager's proposal would make the company unable to carry out the other part.

(B) The sales manager never mentions authority at all, and certainly doesn't challenge the production manager's authority.

(C) The production manager doesn't assume that the new product is safe *because* it's safer than the current one; he argues that the current product *is* relatively safe (it's met the safety standards), but the new one is even *safer*.

Besides, since the sales manager uses the terms "safer" and "less safe" in the same way as the production manager, she doesn't quibble with his conclusions about safety.

(D) As you saw in (C), the sales manager *agrees* with the production manager's conclusions about safety, so she certainly doesn't propose any new standards for judging safety.

(E) Once again, it seems as if the sales manager agrees with the product manager's conclusions about safety, so nothing indicates that she's overestimated the new technology. The only thing that she possibly overestimates is the company's ability to *sell* the new technology, but that's a different issue altogether from the one in (E).

- Avoid skipping stimuli that come with two questions. Once you've taken the time to answer one of the questions, the other one usually isn't difficult.
- In dialogues, isolate the argument each person is making and read the second argument with respect to its relation to the first.

18. A

The Grand Banks cod estimate is arrived at by averaging two other estimates: a sampling-based estimate and a commercial estimate. During the last decade, the commercial estimate increased *by about the same amount* that the sampling-based estimate decreased. Based on that, it's pretty safe to infer that the average of those two numbers—that is, the official estimate—has stayed about the same for the past ten years.

(B) The old number vs. percent trap: The commercial estimate is based on the *rate* at which cod are caught: the number of fish caught per kilometer of net, per hour. The fact that this *rate* has increased is no reason to infer that the *number* of commercial vessels has also increased.

(C) makes an unsupported comparison between the two estimates, with no basis whatsoever in the stimulus.

(D) is even worse than (C), throwing out the commercial estimate entirely. There's absolutely no support given in the stimulus for this recommendation.

(E) is too precise to be drawn from the info in the passage. You can't infer anything about estimates that go back twenty years, because you simply don't have information regarding estimates at that time.

- Don't get caught up in details before you get a handle on the overall situation. Here, it was imperative that you first understood that there was one estimate, arrived at by averaging two other estimates. Then, when you find out that one of the base estimates increased as much as the other decreased, the correct inference should suggest itself.
- The stimulus simply *describes* a phenomenon; the likelihood that you can infer a recommendation (D) from a qualified descriptive neutral-sounding passage like this one is minimal.

19. C

The correct choice has to account for the difference between the trend in the commercial estimate and that in the research-based estimate. You may have been able to prephrase an answer here, something along the lines of: "The commercial vessels somehow got better at catching cod than the research vessels."

Even if you didn't prephrase, the improvement in fishing technology described by (C) should have cleared up the mystery for you. Bagging more large schools of cod explains an increase in the rate of fish caught per hour, and hence an increase in the commercial estimate. This may even help to explain the decrease in the research-based estimate; there may simply be fewer cod around for the research vessels to collect, given the new technology employed by the commercial vessel.

(A) Makes things worse, not better, since it would mean that the commercial vessels might be catching even more cod than you think—and you were already surprised by their numbers. In addition, if underreporting impacts the estimates, it may have impacted them all along, so this doesn't explain the *change*.

(B) Once again, the number of vessels involved is irrelevant, since you need to explain a discrepancy in averages.

(D) Useless background information. This simply elaborates on the stimulus' description of the two estimates, without connecting that information to the opposite changes they experience.

(E) suggests that there may be fewer cod around to catch, which could explain the decrease in the research-based estimate, but not how the commercial estimate could increase at the same time.

- For Paradox questions, make sure you understand precisely the paradox you're supposed to explain. Here the problem is the opposite *changes* in the estimates. Any choice not accounting for this kind of change is out.

20. A

The longer a pretzel remains in contact with your teeth, the more likely it is to cause a cavity. Likewise, a caramel that remains in contact with your teeth for a long time is more likely to cause a cavity than a caramel that remains in contact with your teeth for a short time. But that doesn't mean that a *pretzel* is more likely to cause a cavity than a *caramel*. You have no basis for comparing caramels to pretzels, only caramels to caramels and pretzels to pretzels. As (A) wordily puts it, you can't apply the correlation between time-in-the-mouth and likelihood-of-producing-cavities across categories (e.g. pretzels and caramels).

(B) There's no ambiguity in any of the terms used. The problem isn't in language, but in logic.

(C) The argument isn't based on examples that represent classes, but rather on general information about classes (pretzels and caramels). The problem is that the argument uses information that is valid only *within* classes to draw a conclusion *across* classes.

(D) There *is* cause-and-effect here: Eating pretzels and caramels can cause cavities (the rest of the stimulus deals with a correlation: longer tooth contact to greater cavity likelihood). Does the author confuse cause with effect? If so, then the proper cause-and-effect should be "Getting cavities causes one to eat pretzels and caramels." Uh...no.

(E) The premises don't contradict each other, and there's no reason they can't all be true. On the contrary, they seem quite plausible. It's the conclusion drawn from them that's bogus.

- In some questions, it's difficult to prephrase an answer. Don't hesitate to jump right into the answer choices when nothing occurs to you immediately.
- The chief difficulty here lies in the phrasing of the choices. When you find the choices confusing, try to zero in on key words. (A), for instance, focuses on the issue of "within categories" vs. "across categories," which should ring a bell. In (C), the crux is "general" vs. "particular," and "examples representing classes," neither of which fits the argument.

21. C

The key here is "to counter evidence offered by Tina." If a choice doesn't relate to Tina's evidence, eliminate it. Only (C) deals with an aspect of Tina's argument, the information on the heavy need for petroleum to make paper: (C), which explains that petroleum isn't used to run the paper mills anymore, is an effective counter to this.

(A), (B), (D), and (E) all fail on the same count; they're not specifically related to Tina's evidence. On top of that major flaw, there are other problems with these choices.

(A) and (E), if anything, provide additional evidence to support Tina's claim that paper cups are even more harmful to the environment than foam.

(B) is outside the scope: Consumer preference has no bearing on this discussion, since the consumers are incapable of altering the effects of cup production on the environment.

(D), which is all about styrene, a Mark issue, not only has nothing to do with Tina's evidence, but also hurts Mark's argument to boot.

- Decode the question stem carefully. Here, you're specifically asked to attack Tina's *evidence*, not simply to find something to weaken her argument. The right answer has to address a specific part of Tina's evidence, which allowed you to identify all of the wrong choices.
- Elimination works well as a strategy here. The correct choice wasn't easy to prephrase, but careful evaluation of the choices shows that (A), (B), (D), and (E) clearly don't satisfy the requirement of the question stem.

22. D

Mark argues for paper over plastic-foam cups; Tina argues for the opposite. Both base their respective viewpoints on the environmental damage caused by the production, transportation and disposal of foam and paper cups. So to evaluate their recommendations, you must first decide how much weight should be given to each part of the available evidence.

(A) doesn't help you decide the issue. Even if you knew how soon each of the kinds of harm cited by Mark and Tina would reach its maximum level, you would still have to evaluate which maximum level would be most harmful to the environment.

(B) conjures up an irrelevant distinction. Whether some societies use more disposable goods than others has no bearing on the relative ills of the two types of disposable goods under discussion.

(C) It may well be necessary to seek a new, alternative form of disposable cup, but even if you knew that, it wouldn't help you decide the issue in question—whether paper or foam is more harmful to the environment.

(E) is an irrelevant distinction. How much liquid each type of cup can hold has nothing to do with how much damage it does to the environment.

- To test an answer choice in a "relevant information" question, ask "If I knew the answer to this question, would I have a better understanding of the argument?" If the answer is no, eliminate it. Here, even if you weren't sure about correct choice (D), using this test would have helped you to eliminate the other four choices.
- If you encounter a question stem that seems unfamiliar and you're not sure how to approach it, don't get bogged down. Circle the question in your test booklet and move on. Come back to it after you've answered the rest and then let your common sense and your critical thinking skills guide you to the correct choice.

23. D

Begin by characterizing the Flaw. Because Sabina possesses neither of two symptoms of tooth decay and gum disease, says the stimulus, she must not have either ailment—ignoring the possibility that those ailments may come with *other* symptoms that Sabina may have. The same structure is present, even more clearly, in (D): Because Yolanda is interested in neither of two branches of science that are associated with a medical career, she shouldn't study medicine—ignoring the possibility that one's interest in *other* fields might make it wise for one to go into medicine.

(A) The only real "flaw" here is that the first sentence doesn't exactly provide the evidence needed to make the argument work. If you were told that people who drink a lot of coffee *do* get the jitters (as opposed to "are said to have" the jitters), then the argument would be logically valid: In that case, coffee-addicted med students should indeed not go into either specialty, because neither specialty can be handled when one has the jitters. So (A) isn't 100% sound as written, but unlike the original stimulus and (D), in no sense does it commit the "fallacy of denying the antecedent."

(B) Besides its extraneous if-clause, (B) errs by dropping a key term (medical degree) from its conclusion, something the stimulus doesn't do.

(C) Besides its extraneous "probably," (C) also drops a key term (suffering from an allergy).

(E) Besides its positive conclusion, (E) errs in its scope shift ("specialized training" vs. "accurate diagnosis") not present in the stimulus.

24. E

The first sentence merely gives you set-up information. The second sentence gives you the crux of the evidence, so paraphrase what it says to make it more concrete: If you run one hundred clean pieces of luggage past the scanner, it will wrongly sound an alert only once. The author concludes from this that in ninety-nine out of a hundred actual alerts, explosives will be present.

Did you see the scope shift? The evidence and conclusion deal with percentages based on two different groups: The evidence involves the percentage of *clean pieces* of luggage that trigger false alerts, while the conclusion deals with the percentage of *alerts* that are accurate (meaning that the luggage does contain explosives).

(A) The argument is only interested in cases when the alert actually sounds—cases when the alert fails to do so are outside the scope.

(B) The argument doesn't base a general conclusion on a sample, it bases a conclusion about one percentage on evidence about another percentage. Also, there's no reason to suspect bias.

(C) is outside the scope, since the argument only concerns the functioning of the scanner and has nothing to do with The Actions of the operator.

(D) introduces a false distinction. The argument is interested in the scanner's performance testing explosives *in general*, so it doesn't matter if some explosives are easier to detect than others.

- In questions involving percentages, keep track of what groups the percentages are based on. In a case like this, even if you can't get past the confusing statistical data, just noticing the scope shift—that is, recognizing that the groups the percentages are based on change from evidence to conclusion—should be enough to help you get to the credited answer.

25. A

When you were growing up, the phrase you used to yell when you fooled somebody was "Fake out! Fake out!" You can almost hear the test writers yelling it with regard to this question.

Each of the formal statements defines a condition necessary for a result (phrases like "unless" and "only if" signal the necessity). But just because a necessary condition has been met doesn't mean that the result must occur.

In the first sentence, cease-fire violations will occur *unless* negotiations begin soon. And negotiations *do* begin soon—the stem says so. But it's still possible that the cease-fire violations will occur, because a quick start to negotiations is only *necessary* for avoiding violations, not necessarily sufficient for doing so.

Therefore, when asked for a statement that need not be true, you have to choose (A)—it's *possible* that violations don't occur, but it's just as possible that they do. And as for all the additional conditions and clauses in the stimulus? Fake out!

(B) No negotiations can occur until the international troops have demonstrated that they can control aggression; if negotiations do begin, the international troops must have fulfilled this condition.

(C) is essentially the same inference as (B); as the last sentence says, when the international troops show they can counter aggression, they thereby suppress a major incentive for the sides to resume fighting.

(D) follows from the second sentence; negotiations can begin *only if* other countries have exerted pressure on the two sides.

(E) follows from the second part of the second sentence; an agreement will emerge *only if* other countries pressure the two sides throughout the negotiations.

- When a question stem says that all of the following EXCEPT one choice is an inference, don't bother to try to prephrase. There are infinite possibilities for non-inferences.
- If a question asks for a choice that *isn't* an inference, see if you can treat the stimulus statements in isolation and avoid getting caught up in a lengthy chain of reasoning. Look at each choice and compare it to the relevant statement or statements.

26. B

The evidence says that if Blankenship Enterprises switches suppliers, then it will not show a profit. The conclusion reverses this, and says that if Blankenship Enterprises failed to show a profit, then it must have switched suppliers.

You've come to know this as "the fallacy of affirming the consequent": you're not allowed to simply flip the "if" and "then" terms of a conditional statement. Although you know that switching suppliers would account for a failure to make a profit, it's not necessarily the only possible cause of such a failure. And that's all that (B) says, in so many words.

(A) is far from the truth: The conclusion doesn't even follow from the evidence, so it can hardly be a *restatement* of same (which is what "circular" means).

(C) There's no change in the meaning of the word "profit"—it's a constant throughout the argument.

(D) There's no universal conclusion; the author never looks beyond Blankenship Enterprises.

(E) misses the point. The issue isn't whether one event causes the other, but whether the occurrence of one event is absolutely necessary for the occurrence of a second event. Whether or not there's some basic underlying cause for the occurrence of both events is irrelevant.

- The mistake made here is one of the most common in LSAT Logical Reasoning. There are many ways to describe it—it's basically a matter of taking "if A occurs then B will also occur" to mean "B can never occur unless A does too" (or vice-versa). Keep your eye open for this flaw as you do Logical Reasoning; become an expert in spotting it. It occurs in many guises and it's always wrong.

SECTION III: READING COMPREHENSION

PASSAGE 1—Neurogenesis

Topic and Scope

Neurogenesis (the birth of new neurons)—specifically, whether traditional thinking about vertebrate neurogenesis needs modification in light of research into how the process seems to work in canary brains

Purpose and Main Idea

To suggest that current thinking about vertebrate (especially human) neurogenesis needs to be modified in light of research into canary brains. The author's main idea is that the results of this research both defy the existing theory about vertebrate neurogenesis and open up the possibility that human brains may have the capability to regenerate themselves.

Paragraph Structure

Paragraph one outlines the traditional theory that vertebrate neurogenesis basically doesn't exist—that an adult vertebrate's brain cannot create new nerve cells. The Contrast keyword "However" in line 10 signals that the passage is about to provide some evidence to the contrary and, predictably, paragraphs two and three go on to discuss in detail the behavioral and neurological evidence (from canaries) that throws the accuracy of the traditional theory into question.

In paragraph four, the author addresses the implications of these research findings for humans. The Contrast keyword "Although" in line 48 serves to distinguish the general scientific community's skeptical response from the author's much more optimistic stance that human brains may be able to regenerate themselves.

The Big Picture

- A good grasp of a passage doesn't mean assimilating all of its details (you can look them up if you have to). It means understanding what the author's doing in the text—in this case, understanding that the author's taking issue with the traditional theory of vertebrate neurogenesis (and its implications for the human brain) by providing evidence that contradicts it.
- While the author's specific main idea isn't entirely clear until you've read through the whole passage, topic, scope, and purpose are all revealed early. That makes this passage an ideal place to begin working in the Reading Comprehension section, even if you're a science-phobe. Topic, scope, and purpose, after all, are the three things you need to grab onto as quickly as possible in order to get a passage under control.
- If you suffer from "science anxiety," this passage should have come as a pleasant surprise to you. In practice, even the most jargon-filled and complex science passage won't prove very difficult if you apply the Kaplan techniques for critical reading.

The Questions

1. A

It's a Global question, so you've already done the work; (A) is a match for your prediction.

(B) focuses on a detail. Moreover, the author suggests that there's no difference between canary brains and the brains of other vertebrates in this respect—if he believed otherwise, why would he suggest that research findings about canary brains have implications for vertebrate neurogenesis in general?

(C) The author asserts precisely the opposite. Canary research breaks with the traditional theory of vertebrate neurogenesis, and supplies clues as to how researchers may discover neurogenesis in the human brain.

(D) and (E) have scope problems. Both choices have other problems as well.

(D) should have limited itself to "supply of vertebrate brain cells," not the overly broad "supply of brain cells," while (E) should have confined itself to "older hypotheses about vertebrate neurogenesis," not the more encompassing "older hypotheses."

(D) is too categorical; the author's more cautious in his conclusions. As for (E), the author never states that vertebrates other than canaries are subject to a "yearly cycle."

- Incorrect choices in global questions often include inviting familiar language. Knowing what you're looking for before you attack the choices will help protect you from being drawn in by that familiarity.

2. D

Lines 21–24 say that the canary's singing ability decreases during the late summer and fall. Lines 35–38 attribute this seasonal decrease to a 38% drop in the number of neurons in those parts of the brain that control singing. This is simply another way of saying that those regions of the brain decrease in size during the late summer and fall.

(A) 180: Lines 24–27 and 32–33 indicate that the canary's song repertoire matures in the *spring*.

(B) And 180 again: The new song-learning neurons are generated during the winter and spring months.

(C) distorts the text: Canaries do learn a new repertoire of songs (during the winter and spring), but there's no indication that these songs are based on the songs of fellow canaries.

(E) Canaries largely lose their ability to sing during the late summer and fall, after which they learn "entirely new" songs for the next breeding season.

- Never try to answer an explicit text question on a hunch or a vague remembrance of the text. Use the information or line reference in the question stem to find the relevant piece(s) of text and reread, reread, reread.

3. B

The ratio of brain weight to body weight is mentioned as a possible explanation for neurogenesis in canaries only. This ratio has no direct connection *per se* to the larger issue of general vertebrate neurogenesis, and certainly not to human neurogenesis in particular.

(A) The author's entire argument rests on the supposition that humans, like canaries, may have the capability to generate new nerve cells; thus, it's safe to infer that he'd consider research on neurological similarities to be important.

(C) The author alludes to the importance of studying infant neurogenesis in lines 54–58.

(D) The importance of understanding how long-term memory works in order to determine the possible effects of neurogenesis on long-term memory is suggested in lines 52–54.

(E) Similarly, the author suggests in lines 52–54 that it's important to understand how complex learning takes place in order to figure out the possible effects neurogenesis might have on complex learning.

- In Inference questions, beware of choices—like (B) here—that are outside the author's scope.

4. C

If it were true that birds similar to the canary have bigger brains, the author's explanation for canary neurogenesis would be placed in jeopardy. In paragraph three, after all, he argues that canary neurogenesis occurs because the canary needs to possess a lot of information in order to sing, yet has a small brain adapted for flight. Hence its brain, with its limited storage capacity, has to generate new nerve cells every year in order for it to relearn how to sing.

(A) is consistent with the author's explanation. He suggests that canary neurogenesis is spurred in part by the canary's long lifetime.

(B) The author's basic explanation, which rests on the link between limited brain capacity and neurogenesis cycles, isn't fundamentally threatened by cyclic differences from species to species.

(D) has no impact on the author's explanation, as he draws no link between the ability to sing and the ability to fly.

(E) is consistent with the author's explanation, which suggests that singing ability is directly related to brain size.

- Don't nitpick over incorrect choices. Worrying about their precise meaning will tie you up if you're not careful. Only one choice will be categorically correct. Once you've found it, quickly discard the other choices.

5. D

Lines 12–13 draw a comparison between the way canaries learn to sing and the way humans learn to speak. Thus, the word "vocabulary" is meant to evoke a sense of this similarity by applying a concept taken from human speech to canary song.

(A) echoes the substance of the detail rather than addressing *why* the author included it in the text.

(B) and (E) go too far. Indeed, the author never even discusses "patterned groupings of sounds" in canary songs or "the syllabic structures of words" (B). Nor does the text compare the level of complexity of canary song and human speech (E).

(C) goes against the text, which reveals that canary songs are anything but stable and uniform over the course of the bird's lifetime. Lines 19–27, in fact, stress just the opposite of what (C) says.

- Questions often ask about the *why* of a detail or paragraph—that's why you've got to be most interested in "paragraph sense," not in content.

6. A

Lines 40–42 explicitly state that a long life span may help to account for canary neurogenesis.

(B) through (E) mention subjects that are connected in some way to canary neurogenesis, but none of them is ever described as a possible *cause* of same.

- If you didn't go back to the text and reread, all of the choices may have looked good to you. Rereading, contrary to what you may think, will actually *save* time, by allowing you to throw out incorrect choices in short order.

7. C

Lines 28–32 present research results. Lines 32–40 provide additional details bearing on these results. And lines 40–47 furnish a possible explanation for the results.

(A) is off target. No theory is presented, let alone "analyzed" or "modified." Moreover, this choice makes no reference to the research results and facts provided in paragraph three.

(B), (D), and (E) are outside the scope of paragraph three. Only one set of research results is "advanced," and there's no talk of "a shared principle" among different studies, eliminating (B). And the research results aren't applied to "a related field" (D). Both of these choices try to tempt you into seeing a connection between research on canary and human neurogenesis that just isn't in paragraph three.

Similarly, (E) tries to tempt you by making reference to the traditional view of neurogenesis, which is brought up in paragraph one.

- Be careful not to get hooked by choices that refer to the wrong part of the passage. Don't stray too far from the detail or paragraph in question.

8. C

Beginning in line 10, the author discusses "new evidence for neurogenesis." Furthermore, this new evidence "might help uncover a mechanism" (line 50) to promote human neurogenesis, despite the fact that "neurogenesis in the adult mammalian brain is still not generally accepted" (lines 48–49). Based on these sentiments, it's clear that the author believes that the "current understanding of neurogenesis" is "incomplete."

(A) and (B) express sentiments that are the opposite of the author's. According to him, the traditional view of neurogenesis is neither comprehensive (A), nor forward-thinking (B).

(D) and (E), on the other hand, take the author's view to an unwarranted extreme. "Incomplete" is not the same thing as "antiquated" (D) or "incorrect" (E).

- Always take the passage's "temperature." Know whether the author's got an opinion on the topic, and, if he or she does, watch for words or phrases that'll give you some insight into just how committed the author is to that opinion.

PASSAGE 2—Free African Americans in Colonial Virginia

Topic and Scope

The African American experience in colonial Virginia in the 1600s—specifically, the merits and drawbacks of Breen and Innes' book *Myne Owne Ground*

Purpose and Main Idea

The author wants to argue that while Breen and Innes "contribute significantly" to a more positive and "welcome" historical view of the lives of freed African Americans, they stumble by underemphasizing "much evidence" that, as slavery became more entrenched in the 1660s, living conditions for free blacks in colonial Virginia grew tougher.

Paragraph Structure

Paragraph one cites the book's strengths, associating it with "a recent, welcome shift [in historical studies]" from those centering on slaveholder-caused misery to those centering on African American-created accomplishment.

The rest of paragraph one and the opening of paragraph two specify ways in which free African Americans exercised control over their lives. Paragraph two moves from praise to qualified criticism: Breen and Innes overlook the fact that increasing restrictions (both "customary" and "statutory" laws) in the 1660s made Virginia inhospitable for free blacks like Anthony Johnson.

The Big Picture

This passage fits some familiar and oft-repeated LSAT patterns:

- It's a book review in which the author gives a balanced evaluation, with both praise and pointed criticism. You can bet that questions will hinge on these points.
- The opening 10–20 lines—always key—offer a classic contrast: between an outdated viewpoint and a newer, hipper perspective. This kind of contrast occurs over and over in LSAT passages. (The author's Purpose, after all, is to discuss B's and I's contribution to the new perspective.)
- Note the shift between the paragraphs: paragraph one praises the book; paragraph two moves steadily into criticism. The distinct separation of focus eases your job—*finding the answers!*

The Questions

9. E

It's a detail question, so go back to the passage. (E) paraphrases a point made in the first sentence: For years, scholars tended to ignore "what Africans in the United States were able to accomplish despite the effects of [slavery]."

(A) refers to irrelevant material from paragraph two. Customary and statutory law are discussed only in relation to Breen's and Innes's book.

(B), (C), and (D) are outside the passage's scope. The author never implies that most scholars have tended to deal only in "broad interpretations" (B); and note how off-the-wall (C) and (D) sound. Historians have focused in on "the least eventful periods"? And downplayed discussion of the economic side of slavery? Oh come now. Both sound pretty unlikely, don't you think?

- If you're careful with the opening lines, the paraphrase in (E) should snap into place. The only hassle is getting past the first four choices. Luckily, though, . . .
- Three choices—(B), (C) and (D)—have nothing whatever to do with this author's ideas. Choices like these should be skimmed and dismissed, with no further thought.

10. B

The author emphasizes the major issue of growing legal restrictions in paragraph two, in the middle of which he states that customary and statutory law "was closing in on free African Americans well before the 1670s." During the previous decade, after a "dramatic" increase in the proportion of African Americans, Virginia began passing legal restrictions. (B) paraphrases the idea.

(A) contradicts the essential point: The pace of legal restrictions on black people was picking up during the period.

(C) sounds plausible but is never implied. Answers must jibe with evidence in the passage.

(D) is never implied and also picks up on irrelevant information (indentured servants) in paragraph one. Paragraph two says nothing about them. A tempting choice only if the reference to dates in lines 16–17 make you think the answer is to be found nearby.

(E) mentions growing numbers of blacks, but the notion that some regions adhered more rigidly to customary law is never implied.

- Long, wordy stems and choices can make questions look tougher than they really are. You can save such questions for last if you like, but note the clear similarity between (B) and the bigger point of paragraph two: Growing legal restrictions made life increasingly hard for free African Americans. Keep thinking, and reading, for "gist."

11. A

Details are usually mentioned to support bigger points. According to the passage, the Johnsons moved to escape worsening conditions in Virginia. The bigger point is that Breen and Innes underestimated those conditions. The Johnsons' situation, then, is mentioned to illustrate a shortcoming of Breen and Innes's thesis (A).

(B) is tempting, but the point is not that Breen and Innes failed to note the specific case of the Johnsons. To "underemphasize" (line 41) is not to "overlook."

(C) Distortion: The Johnsons' story is cited to criticize, not add support to, Breen and Innes's thesis.

(D) 180: According to the opening lines, the author is critical of the standard interpretation.

(E) Another distortion. The author cites a new historiographical approach (and praises Breen's and Innes's book for applying it) in the opening lines.

- Read the stem carefully, then check the relevant text in the passage and come up with a rough prephrase of the answer. Finally, scan the choices aggressively for a rough equivalent of your idea.
- With a good, solid prephrase in mind as you skim the five choices, the correct one is more likely to snap into place, and wrong ones can be quickly dismissed.

12. D

(D) corresponds to the shift that occurs between the paragraphs: paragraph one praises Breen and Innes's book, and paragraph two then focuses on criticism. Only (D)—"qualified approval"—corresponds to the mixed review.

(A) Far too negative.

(B) Far too positive.

(C) Too negative.

(E) There's no evidence anywhere for "puzzlement."

- If you recall the outlines of the argument (the gist of each paragraph) and roughly prephrase the likely answer (the author's attitude is "mixed"), you can sidestep distracting choices like "contentious challenge" and "sincere puzzlement" and zero straight in on (D).

13. D

You've already done the groundwork here—the author's purpose was to "argue" certain things about Breen and Innes's book. The answer choices here are very general, so you have to abstract that a bit. Only (D) jibes with the fact that this is a review of somebody's book—it's as simple as that.

(A) is far too narrow; only in the opening sentence does the author "summarize previous interpretations." The focus then changes.

(B) Also too narrow. The author praises a new historiographical approach in the passage's second sentence, but then zeroes in on Breen and Innes's book, which he isn't advocating, but evaluating.

(C) The verb "propose" is wrong: The author isn't *proposing* a thesis (of his own); he's describing somebody else's.

(E) The author's discussing a book, not a "historical event."

- In Global questions, abstract-sounding choices like these needn't pose a problem. As always, add up the gists of the paragraphs and look for the corresponding choice, which should fit like a well-tailored shirt. Accept nothing less.

PASSAGE 3—Watteau's World

Topic and Scope

Eighteenth-century artist Watteau—specifically, the relationship between Watteau's work, historical events during his lifetime, and perceptions of him by nineteenth-century writers

Purpose and Main Idea

The author's purpose is to prove that there was a "blind spot" in 19th-century books that regard Watteau as *the* guy—*the* representative of that "witty and amiable 18th century." Part one of this argument is to show that war-torn 18th-century France was anything but "witty and amiable." Part two is to offer some explanations as to why 19th-century writers so blatantly ignored the historical facts. All things considered, this passage has the air of a Logical Reasoning Paradox problem.

Paragraph Structure

Paragraph one describes Watteau's increasing popularity in the 18th and 19th centuries as an artist who captured the "witty and amiable" character of 18th-century life.

Paragraph two provides a reality check, pointing out that the early 18th century was in fact a pretty miserable period for France, notable more for its years of military defeat and disastrous famine than for its lyricism.

Paragraph three attempts to explain the "blind spot" in 19th-century books about Watteau: Some writers just ignored the facts, while others simply argued that artists aren't necessarily influenced by their environment. Note the final twist on this position—some writers were so pro-Watteau that they even argued that he was *predicting* the society that evolved after his death.

The Big Picture

- The purpose of this passage is typical LSAT: Some academic takes issue with a traditional, accepted interpretation of a historical period or an artist's work (in this case, it's both) and tries to set the record straight.

- The key thing in such passages is to keep the author's opinions separate from the views of those deluded scholars he or she is attempting to refute.
- Whether you tend to be comfortable with humanities passages or not, this one practically screamed "Attack me early in the section!" That's because of that keyword emphasis signal "curious blind spot." From those three little words virtually the entire structure is revealed to you, because you know that three questions will inevitably be raised and answered: What was the blind spot? What was the real story? And *why* were the people in question deluded? And note that all by themselves, these three questions come very close to paraphrasing the contents of correct choice (E) for question 14.

The Questions

14. E

The trick here is to be clear about the paragraph topics, and that's work you should have done up front. Once again, paragraph one outlines the viewpoint of Watteau's 19th-century biographers, paragraph two pokes it full of holes by presenting the historical facts, and paragraph three explains why those biographers persisted in their beliefs *in spite* of the evidence. (E) fits the way this argument develops.

(A) gets the link between paragraphs two and three wrong: the author doesn't *evaluate* or *refine* the evidence presented in paragraph two.

(B) The *author* doesn't use the passage to test an assumption. The passage does deal with 19th-century assumptions about Watteau, but it goes far beyond simply rejecting them as counterfactual.

(C) doesn't account for paragraph two; also, the author doesn't advance two separate theories about the historians' "blind spot."

(D) The author provides evidence that proves the *inaccuracy* of Watteau's 19th-century image. Beware of 180 answer choices—they can be tempting because they're directly on point.

- Summing up the gist of the paragraph topics really helps when the answer choice language is abstract. If you can approach the answer choices with a *fairly* clear idea of what each paragraph is about, you'll be less inclined to try to make the wrong answers fit the passage—a common misstep that students take in abstract questions like this one.

15. D

The end of paragraph one explains the most basic reason for Watteau's reputation: Writers, aristocrats, and would-be aristocrats ignored the historical facts because Watteau presented such a flattering picture of 18th-century French life.

(A) is tricky: According to paragraph three, it was only the *minority* of writers who developed the sophisticated argument that Watteau was transcending reality.

(B) also refers to this minority of writers (paragraph three) who opposed the determinist stance.

(C) is well outside the scope; no lack of historical source material is discussed.

(E) distorts the passage. Nothing as radical as a political bias towards aristocrats is mentioned.

- The keywords "Most," "those," and "Even some..." indicate that the passage is dealing with three different groups of Watteau admirers in paragraph three. Take note whenever contrasting viewpoints are mentioned, because questions that hinge on them are sure to follow.

16. E

This Detail question can be answered quickly with reference to paragraph three, which explains that the determinist viewpoint was "unthinkable" to these particular Watteau fanatics because Watteau was quintessentially French, even though born in a Flemish town. (E) captures the logic of this faction—if artists *were* primarily influenced by their environment, Watteau would have produced "quintessentially Flemish" works.

(A) 180: Watteau was widely admired precisely *because* people believed in the determinist philosophy.

(B) is geographically outside the scope—the passage never discusses Watteau's popularity outside of France.

(C) can be quickly rejected because the passage never considers Watteau's *view of himself*. Watteau is of course long dead and buried during the events and viewpoints of the passage (happy 200th birthday, Pierre—see line 20).

(D) Abstruse phrasing should flag this choice as outside the scope. There's no debate about "simple" versus "complex" explanations offered, nor is the author concerned with why Watteau's works were charming.

- Don't get sucked in by wordy choices. Go from the stem to the passage, prephrase the answer, and then scan the choices *with the author's ideas in mind*. You'll find that a lot of choices, like (B), (C) and (D) here, just don't click. The only one that's worth your time and thought is the correct one.

17. B

True to its pole position at the head of paragraph one, the "blind spot" is the problem in 19th-century scholarship that the author attacks throughout the passage. It's the "obvious discrepancy" between 19th-century writers' acceptance that Watteau portrayed his age realistically, and the historical facts mentioned in paragraph two.

(A) and (D) misrepresent the author's position: She doesn't single out anything "admirable" about Watteau's work or accuse others of not appreciating Watteau enough.

(C) presents an even wilder distortion: No willful disregard of available evidence is cited.

(E) goes beyond the scope, since no neglected contemporaries are discussed.

18. C

The correct choice nicely paraphrases the argument in paragraph two.

(A) 180: 19th-century admirers thought Watteau's accomplishments were extremely important.

(B), (D), and (E) all distort the passage. The author never endorses the deterministic standpoint (D) or indicates whether she finds Watteau's work lyrical and charming or otherwise (B). The extreme language in (E) ("*impossible* for any work of art to personify or represent a particular historical period") helps tag this wrong answer choice.

- Questions that ask about the author's attitude or viewpoint are *not* going to relate to minor issues or passing details. Sure, choices (A), (B) and (D) all remind you of issues raised in the passage. But they don't capture the overall thrust of the passage the way (C) does.

19. A

Paragraph two describes conditions in France during Watteau's lifetime: Social upheaval caused by war summarizes the "calamitous" events.

(B) describes 19th-century nostalgia for the witty and amiable past—not what actually occurred during Watteau's life.

(C) distorts paragraph one's brief mention of the aristocracy.

(D) also relates to paragraph one, but Watteau's popularity with the aristos (and aristo wannabes) occurred *after* his death.

(E) is outside the scope—no sweeping generalizations about French society in this passage.

- If the wording of the question is specific, you can bet you're looking for a specific answer. The passage discusses several different periods of French history (during Watteau's lifetime, the late 18th century, and 19th century), so the trick here was knowing which period to look at and zeroing in on the right piece of the passage.

20. D

A tricky question that depends on your picking up on the implied reasons for Watteau's success. Paragraph one explains why Watteau's work had such a powerful impact on French society: Engravings of his work were made available in such numbers that his work became "more accessible than any other artist until the 20th century." No word on whether he painted dogs playing poker or clowns on velvet.

(A) focuses on a detail. Sure, Watteau was successful partly because he produced "lyrical and charming" images. But you cannot subscribe to (A)'s inference that only "lyrical and charming" works of art will achieve wide recognition.

(B) is outside the scope. Nowhere does the author suggest that French society had an exceptional regard for art.

(C) is very tricky. The passage certainly links Watteau's long-standing appeal to the perception that he had captured the essential France of his time. But paragraph one indicates that Watteau only became France's favorite artist because his work was so widely available, so you can't infer that capturing the true nature of your society guarantees artistic success. After all, Watteau's "lyrical and charming" engravings wouldn't have had an impact if they hadn't been resurrected and sold like hot cakes. Another problem: As you know, Watteau didn't *really encapsulate* the true nature of his time; (C) makes it sound as if he did.

(E) distorts paragraph one's brief mention of Watteau's imitators.

- Always watch out for choices that aren't true to the spirit of the passage. In question 20, for example, the tricky choice (C) *sounds* somewhat plausible until you remember that it represents the viewpoint that the author spends most of the passage attacking.

PASSAGE 4—Trial By (Misguided) Jury

Topic and Scope

Inferential errors made by juries—specifically, how these errors come about and what should be done to prevent them

Purpose and Main Idea

The author's purpose is primarily to explain the kind of inferential errors that juries can make in certain specific trial situations. Paragraph two provides the real meat of the passage by listing some specific examples. The final two paragraphs only briefly suggest some measures to alleviate the problem: using cognitive psychology to assess the reliability of juries in certain situations, and making judges more aware of the issue.

Paragraph Structure

Paragraph one introduces the topic, explaining that juries sometimes make inferential errors in their search for the truth.

Paragraph two provides some specific examples of the most common errors juries make (note how clearly the keywords "For example," "also," and "finally" map out the author's presentation of evidence). You also learn that most jury errors involve unwarranted conclusions. Could the judicial system benefit from a Kaplan course in Logical Reasoning?

Paragraph three suggests one possible solution to the problem, using cognitive psychology to assess the reliability of juries in certain situations.

Paragraph four calls for greater awareness of potential jury error on the part of judges.

The Big Picture:

- A very straightforward passage rounds off the set. Once again, it's a familiar passage format for the LSAT, describing a problem and offering a couple of solutions to remedy it. The only real substance to the passage is paragraph two's detailed discussion of jury errors, but not for a moment should you get bogged down in specifics there: Skim through the paragraph, note that you're mostly getting examples of unwarranted conclusions, and expect that you're gong to be returning later to this paragraph to score some points.

The Questions

21. A

Don't let the convoluted wording of the answer choices distract you. The author's overall point is basically very simple: Juries make inferential errors in certain specific situations.

(B) is too broad—the passage is about jury error, not *human cognition*.

(C) focuses on a detail, one particular cause of jury error mentioned in paragraph three.

(D) focuses narrowly on paragraph one's passing mention of everyday inferential thinking.

(E) exaggerates paragraphs three and four. The passage isn't advocating replacing judges with cognitive psychologists. Come on.

- When confronting Global questions, high on your list of choices to watch for and shoot down should be: choices that focus on details, choices that are way too broad, and choices that go beyond the scope of the relevant discussion.

22. D

Paragraphs three and four address possible reforms. (D) fits well with paragraph four's point that judges—with their "limited and primitive" understanding of the problem—aren't always fulfilling their obligation to minimize jury error through explanation and clarification.

(A) is too extreme. An LSAT passage advocating an end to jury trials? Puhleeze.

(B) Outside the scope: Formal educational requirements is an issue often discussed in relation to juries, but isn't discussed here.

(C) Defense testimony is mentioned earlier in paragraph two, a sure sign that it's not relevant to the reform discussion (paragraphs three and four). In any case, misleading defense testimony is only one of several causes of jury error mentioned, so you can infer that monitoring defense testimony wouldn't provide a broadly effective remedy.

(E) should sound distinctly *au contraire;* the passage *advocates* wider understanding of psychological research.

- Question 22 underlines the importance of knowing and referring to the gist of each paragraph. Just knowing that paragraphs three and four discuss reforms (and therefore contain the answer) enables you to eliminate (A), (B), and (C) as beyond the scope.

23. D

This answer choice deftly summarizes paragraph two, which lists three situations in which inferential error is likely to occur.

(A) has 180 stamped all over it. If anything, paragraph two's litany of jury errors underscores the complexity of the fact-finding process.

(B) is a bit tricky, but the author doesn't specifically argue for a more careful presentation of evidence, or indeed any change in the trial process whatsoever. The gist of the passage is that judges have to be more aware that errors *are* going to occur in these specific situations.

(C) focuses narrowly on a detail. The influence of commonly held beliefs on juries (e.g., that defendants with prior conviction must be guilty) is only one cited cause of jury error.

(E) Wrong paragraph—possible reforms aren't discussed until paragraphs 3 and 4.

- Note that the keywords "For example," "also," and "finally" provide a major assist in showing that paragraph two is basically a list of specific examples.

24. C

(C) Captures both the tone and thrust of paragraph four. Judges have been guilty of having only a "limited and primitive concept of jury error" and failing to acknowledge psychologists' research into the problem.

(A) has the wrong verb; LSAT authors are rarely if ever going to sound "apprehensive." You can't recall a single instance.

(B) distorts the passage; it's the juries, not the judges, who are drawing unwarranted conclusions.

(D) is also a distortion. There's nothing in paragraph four that actually suggests opposition from judges, nor, as you noted in question 23 choice (B), is the passage advocating "significant changes in trial procedure."

(E) should scream "wrong paragraph." Paragraph two mentions excessively complex evidence, but it doesn't seem to be the judges' fault.

- A sharp take-charge attitude usually pays off with Reading Comprehension answer choices. If the verb is wrong, trash it. If the issue is beyond the scope, toss it out the window. Only the correct answer is going to satisfy your critical judgment.

25. B

Definitely a tricky question. The author's argument for using psychological research in the courtroom is based on the notion that researchers can predict the situations in which inferential error will occur (see the examples in paragraph two). (B) would present a major challenge to that argument. If researchers cannot predict how groups will act in decision-making situations, then inferential errors by juries cannot be addressed.

(A) strengthens the author's case, since he argues that human decision making conforms to patterns whereby people react in predictable ways according to the situation.

(C) isn't an effective weakener, since the author is criticizing the existing system based on the results of recent psychological research.

(D) basically strengthens the argument by asserting or implying that human decision making is predictable in controlled situations such as trials.

(E) also fits the passage in its claim that inferential error is predictable in certain situations.

- In strengthening/weakening questions like this one, the wrong answers will often stay true to the spirit of the passage. Here, in (A), (D), and (E), the phrases "patterns in human decision making," "controlled situations," and "predictable circumstances" should help you rule these choices out because they remind you of the author's basic argument.

26. A

The right choice is consistent with the overall idea that those involved in the judicial process could benefit from the insights of cognitive psychologists.

(B) is too extreme; the passage does say that "complex and voluminous" evidence is often confusing for juries, but it doesn't accuse lawyers of attempting to confuse juries.

(C) Outside the scope—the inferential abilities of judges and lawyers are never compared.

(D) is also outside the scope. The passage suggests no conscientious pursuit of the truth on the part of lawyers. (Ahem.)

(E) distorts paragraph one; the author says that lawyers call the inferential process "fact-finding," but this is far short of saying that they are unrealistic about the abilities of juries.

- Many wrong answer choices in the Reading Comprehension section are wrong because they fall outside the scope of the passage or of the relevant paragraph. That's one reason that getting a clear handle on topic and scope up front and creating tight paragraph summaries is so critical.

27. E

The right choice summarizes the cause and effect of jury error described in paragraph two: Basically, the manner in which evidence is presented leads the jury to make various types of unwarranted conclusions.

(A) 180: "complex and voluminous evidence" most often obscures the truth.

(B) distorts the passage: The author says that the jury "may" give more weight to photographic evidence, not that the jury "usually" overestimates its value.

(C) is tricky, but it's not a generalization that the author would agree with. Remember, the passage says that preconceptions about defendants with prior convictions influence juries, not that preconceptions about defendants *in general* are problematic.

(D) contradicts the passage: Juries use inferential skills "developed and used over a lifetime" (paragraph one).

- Be ready and eager to apply your Logical Reasoning skills to the Reading Comprehension section. If an answer choice makes a strong argument such as "the more evidence juries have, the better decisions they make," or "juries usually overvalue visual evidence," make sure it jibes with the passage.

SECTION IV: LOGICAL REASONING

1. A

James' argument consists of an analogy between his house and an airplane: Just as he can do as he pleases inside his own home, so too the airlines have the right to decide smoking policies on their own property—the planes—without government interference.

Eileen responds, essentially, by breaking this analogy. She points out that whereas James' house is for his own use, airlines serve the public and must therefore consider the public's health their priority. In other words, she draws a distinction between a house, which is primarily occupied by those who own it, and an airplane, which is primarily occupied by those who *don't* own it: the public.

(B) is dead wrong; Eileen doesn't offer anything resembling a definition.

(C) describes *James'* method of argument; as you saw, he establishes an analogy between his house and an airplane. But you want *Eileen's* method, not his.

(D) might have tripped you up if you thought Eileen's contradicting James is the same as "deriving a contradiction" from his argument. No. Although Eileen disagrees with James, she does so by attacking his analogy, not by showing that his argument contains a contradiction.

(E) Eileen doesn't address James' motivation at all; she merely points out that his analogy is poor.

- In dialogue questions, make sure you keep track of who's making which argument. Wrong choices often play off the *other* person's argument, as (C) does here.
- This kind of question illustrates the importance of reading the question stem first—it allows you to focus on structure as you read the argument.

2. C

The company that makes XYZ is aware that millions of illegal copies are in use, yet they take no legal action. Why? The key here is recognizing the current "company-wide effort to boost sales." That, as (C) says, many consumers prefer to use a spreadsheet program before plunking down hard cash, provides a solid, sales-boosting reason why the company might be willing to turn a blind eye to the illegalities.

(A) is useless background. The issue is not whether XYZ *can* be copied; obviously it can. The issue is why the company has taken a particular tack with regard to the illegal copies that have been made.

(B) is also fairly useless. If anything, that such legal measures have been available for so long just compounds the paradox of why the company hasn't taken those measures.

(D) This is an irrelevant distinction, emphasizing the degree of the company's illegal copying problem but doing nothing to explain why the company tolerates the copying.

(E) Some students attempt to make a case for (E) as the rationale for the non-prosecutions, figuring that the XYZ makers don't want to be perceived as corporate bad guys like their competitors. However, this kind of analysis requires too much work, and too many unwarranted assumptions about the motives of the XYZ company, to be correct. Specifically, you have to work too hard to establish a connection between (E)'s implied motive and its effect on XYZ sales. (C)'s connection, by contrast, is manifest.

- We mentioned this earlier in the first Logical Reasoning section, but it bears repeating: Paradox questions have many faces. Here, the question stem doesn't characterize the stimulus for you with a word like "paradox" or "discrepancy." Don't be thrown: the logical skills you needed here were the same as those needed for a more traditional Paradox question.
- Remember, there is no "second-best" answer on the LSAT. If a choice requires you to make a lot of assumptions to complete the logic, then it's just plain wrong. Eliminate it.

3. D

Kim's conclusion or main point is nicely highlighted in the last sentence by the keyword "So." Replacing gas-powered cars with electric cars would be, at best, an even trade in terms of air pollution. And remember, the argument is framed around the claim that the battery-powered electric car *would* solve the air pollution problem. Based on the last sentence, then, you can rest assured that the author disagrees with that claim and that (D) is the main point.

(A) simply restates part of Kim's evidence. It isn't the conclusion.

(B) Kim doesn't call for a reduction in driving, for one thing; for another, maybe there are ways of reducing air pollution besides "cleaner" cars; e.g. switching from coal to hydroelectric power plants. So (B) is way off in scope and point of view.

(C) is too extreme. Kim deals only with gasoline-powered cars and electric cars, concluding that the latter isn't better for air pollution than the former. To go one step further and say that Kim's point is that *all* cars create an *equal* amount of air pollution involves a major distortion.

(E) Maybe Kim believes that gasoline-powered cars are here to stay, maybe not. You just don't know; in any case, there's no way that this can be the point she set out to prove in her argument.

- Use the one-sentence test to identify an author's conclusion. Ask yourself, "What's the one thing that the author wants me to take away from this passage?"
- Keep in mind the scope of the author's argument. All Kim says about battery-powered cars is that they aren't an improvement over gasoline-powered cars in terms of air pollution. The argument remains silent on other issues such as noise or fuel economy.

4. E

Isolate and paraphrase the components of the argument. The evidence: 1) electric cars require (surprise!) electricity, which means building new generating facilities. 2) *Most* of our generating facilities burn fossil fuels.

Conclusion: Electric cars would cause as much fossil-fuel pollution as gasoline-powered cars. Not if the new generating facilities don't burn fossil fuels, they wouldn't—so the author must be assuming that some of the new generating facilities would, in fact, burn fossil fuels.

(A) and (D) Both of these statements can be negated without damaging Kim's logic. In fact, if the number of electric cars went through the roof (A), or if electric cars *did* cause air pollution while they're running (D), either fact would reinforce Kim's point that switching to battery-powered cars wouldn't reduce air pollution.

(B) is an irrelevant comparison. Identifying the greatest producer of fossil-fuel pollution (cars, boats, airplanes, factories) is irrelevant to this argument about whether electric cars would help solve the air pollution problem.

(C) is a distortion. One last time, Kim's argument isn't about whether to replace gasoline-powered cars with electric cars; it's about whether doing so would reduce air pollution.

- Test takers often get bogged down in fancy language and big words on the LSAT, but often it's the *smallest* words that have the greatest impact on the logical validity of an author's points. The word "most" in the second sentence will fly by many readers, but the critical reader spots it and realizes that it means that not *all* electricity is *necessarily* generated by burning fossil fuels. This realization leads directly to the author's assumption.
- An assumption fills in an essential missing piece of the argument—a gap that must be filled in order for the argument to be logically sound.
- Be wary of choices, like (B), that implicitly question the importance of the entire argument. An argument's logic is independent from its relevance to the rest of the world. This argument is very self-contained—pointing out that there are greater sources of fossil-fuel pollution in the world than gasoline-powered cars has no relevance whatsoever.

5. E

Any planetary body with a solid surface becomes heavily pockmarked if its surface isn't renewed for millions of years. Although Europa has a solid surface, it isn't heavily pockmarked. Therefore, you can conclude, its surface has been renewed.

You're told that a planetary body's surface can't be renewed unless its core generates enough heat to cause volcanic action. So Europa's core must generate enough heat to cause volcanic action. But Europa was described as "very cold"; therefore, the cores of some very cold planetary bodies—at least Europa's—have to generate enough heat to cause volcanic action.

(A) All you're told about the surface of the Earth's moon is that it's heavily pockmarked, which doesn't mean that it can't be icy.

(B) is a 180 choice. If a planetary body has a solid surface that's not heavily pockmarked, then its surface has been renewed and its core *must* generate enough heat to cause volcanic action. (You are told nothing about surfaces that aren't solid.)

(C) sounds vaguely plausible, but there's no evidence of the existence of such planetary bodies in the stimulus.

(D) The only moon of Jupiter that is described, Europa, isn't heavily pockmarked; you can't conclude anything about Jupiter's other moons.

- Long stimuli can sometimes be broken up into sections, making it easier to follow the flow of the logic. Here, the first section introduces the setting: planetary bodies and solid surfaces. The second section explains the idea of "renewal": what it means for a surface to be renewed, and what effect renewal has. The final section gives a specific case to which to apply the principle discussed in the second section.

6. B

As the patient asserts in the last sentence of the stimulus, "pharmacists have a financial interest" in having a monopoly on selling prescription drugs; therefore, their objections to letting doctors sell prescription drugs can't be taken seriously.

So rather than directly addressing the pharmacists' argument—which is that letting doctors sell prescription drugs would tempt them to prescribe unnecessary drugs in order to make extra money—the patient impugns the pharmacists' motives for making their argument. As you know, this is bogus reasoning; regardless of the pharmacists' motives, their argument may be sound and must be addressed on its own merits.

(A) and (C) Since the patient doesn't deal with the pharmacists' argument, but rather their motives, he can't be denying any assumptions they make (A), or undermining their evidence (C). (A) and (C) describe eminently *reasonable* ways of weakening arguments, but the patient just sidesteps the pharmacists' reasoning entirely.

(D) describes an appeal to popular opinion, but while this is another poor form of reasoning, it isn't what the patient does.

(E) bears no resemblance to what the patient does. Nowhere does he claim that the pharmacists don't know what they're talking about—rather, he attacks their motives, pure and simple.

- Read critically and put arguments into real-world situations. If a friend of yours made this argument, would you swallow it, or would you wonder, "What do the pharmacists' motives have to do with whether or not they're right?"
- The LSAT test makers want to know whether you can distinguish good reasoning from bad. Although the question stem here is that of a Method of Argument question, in order to answer the question correctly you need to recognize that it's a *bad* method of argument.

7. E

Murray tries to deflect Jane's criticism of Senator Brandon by saying that other politicians have done what Senator Brandon is accused of doing; therefore, he must believe that at least one other politician has accepted gifts from lobbyists.

Jane retorts that her failure to attack other politicians doesn't excuse Senator Brandon's offense; she stands by her claim that the Senator Brandon is guilty of accepting gifts from lobbyists.

Therefore, both Murray and Jane would agree that there is at least one politician (Senator Brandon in Jane's case; "other politicians" in Murray's case) who accepts gifts from lobbyists.

(A) Murray doesn't actually admit that Senator Brandon has accepted gifts from lobbyists; his point is Jane's hypocrisy in failing to criticize other politicians for doing likewise.

(B) Murray doesn't admit that there's anything wrong with accepting gifts from lobbyists; again, his argument focuses on the motivation Jane has for singling Senator Brandon out among all the others who have done the same thing.

(C) Jane admits that she dislikes Senator Brandon, but not that her dislike is her only motivation for criticizing him.

(D) There's no evidence that Murray considers this a valid reason for criticizing Senator Brandon; in fact, he explicitly says that Jane is wrong to make this criticism.

- Just as you are careful not to read anything into the stimulus argument, be careful not to read anything into the answer choices. Here, (E) doesn't require that Murray and Jane agree about *which* particular politician accepts gifts from lobbyists (Murray hasn't admitted Senator Brandon accepts gifts, and Jane hasn't committed herself to agreeing that any other politicians accept gifts).

8. D

Sylvia concludes that the gap between the rich north and the poor south will widen because the poor southern countries can't afford to acquire the new technologies. But if the economic gap is going to "widen," then she has to be assuming that some of the rich northern countries *can* acquire the new technologies.

(A) is useless background information. All that matters for Sylvia's argument is that the southern nations be poor and the northern nations be rich.

(B) The north could incorporate the new technologies and therefore increase its wealth and the total amount of global wealth, while the south remained poor, thus widening the gap. So, it's not necessary that the technology not affect an increase overall.

(C) Outside the scope: You might think this is a 180 choice; after all, Sylvia's whole point is that the existing economic gap will *widen* with the coming of the new technologies. But she's referring specifically to information technologies; consideration of other types of technologies has no bearing on the argument.

(E) The speed of information processing is irrelevant as long has some countries have access to the new technologies and some don't.

- The correct choice here seemed so reasonable you might not have recognized it as an assumption. But assumptions as a group are neither reasonable nor unreasonable—they merely represent things that the author is taking for granted as true on their face, that fill the gap between the evidence and the conclusion.
- Let the question stem guide your reading. Often, one character's argument can be evaluated independently from the other character's.

9. C

Oscar's argument includes a slight scope shift. He says that speed of information processing will soon be "the single most important factor" in the creation of wealth. But he concludes that national wealth will be "just a matter of... relative success in incorporating the new technologies"—i.e., the new technologies will be the *only* factor.

Choice (C) points out this scope shift by noting that Oscar's conclusion ignores a possible combination of other factors.

(A) is a flaw in Sylvia's argument, not Oscar's. Read the question stem carefully.

(B), (D), and (E) are all true, but none of them signify a flaw in Oscar's reasoning.

(B) isn't a flaw because it's not necessary for Oscar to establish the importance of the rich-poor division in order to draw a conclusion about it.

(D) Oscar doesn't need to show that *only* countries that successfully incorporate the new information technologies will benefit; all his argument requires is that those countries benefit *more* than countries that don't succeed in incorporating the new tech.

(E) faults Oscar for failing to make a distinction between things he has no logical obligation to distinguish. His whole point is that the old distinctions of rich and poor nations will soon be eliminated; there's no need for him to bother distinguishing the wealthy from the *really really* wealthy.

- The correct answer to a Flaw question must be an actual flaw. Statements about the argument that are true but that don't indicate a hole in the author's reasoning should be eliminated.
- An author isn't obligated to throw the whole kitchen sink into her argument. The fact that an author "fails to mention this . . ." or "ignores the possibility of that . . ." only constitutes a flaw in the argument *if* that failure damages or severs the link between her evidence and conclusion.
- Read critically, using Keywords to help you thread your way through wordy passages. Here, both characters' conclusions were clearly signaled by the same Keyword: "thus."

10. D

You seek a reason why the number of jobs lost was underestimated in the recent recession, despite the fact that companies accurately reported their net job gains and losses to the government and the government accurately calculated those figures.

One possibility that might have occurred to you is that not all companies reported their figures to the government. This is essentially what you get in (D): Due to the recession, many companies suddenly went out of business, and it's reasonable to infer that they didn't bother to report all these job losses before shutting down, thereby leaving the government's calculations drastically underestimated.

(A) This information is not only self-evident but irrelevant. You're not interested in comparing job loss in recessions vs. growth periods, but in why job losses in *this* recession were underestimated.

(B) claims that it's gotten more costly to report employment data. Fine, but since (B) *doesn't* tell you that this increased cost caused many companies not to report their job losses, it can't help you resolve the discrepancy at hand.

(C) is irrelevant. Who cares what people do once they've lost their jobs? Remember, the discrepancy involves the number of jobs *lost*, not the overall unemployment rate, so the fact that many people who lost their jobs found something else to do is irrelevant.

(E) is also irrelevant. You're not interested in changes from manufacturing to service, but in why the number of jobs lost was underestimated. And if you thought (E) meant that, say, people who lost their jobs at the auto plant found new ones at a fast-food chain, again, the discrepancy's not about the unemployment rate, so this doesn't matter.

- In Paradox questions, the correct choice will always answer the question, "How can that be?"

11. C

There will be no danger of wild animals suffocating from entanglement in the new plastic rings, says the representative, because the new rings disintegrate after only three days of exposure to sunlight. So if you know any wild animals, you should probably say "Hey, Fido—don't go near those nasty rings for three days, okay?"

Obviously, the assumption the representative makes, and one that you probably could have prephrased on your own, is that no wild animals will become entangled in the rings during that three-day window before they (the rings, not the animals) disintegrate.

(A) and (B) both raise side issues that have no effect on the risk of animals suffocating in the rings. You can negate both choices without affecting the conclusion one bit.

(D) The old rings are being eliminated anyway, so it doesn't matter what threats besides suffocation they pose to wild animals.

(E) has two problems; it's a distortion, and it's irrelevant to boot. It's not necessary to assume that *all* wild animals that become entangled in plastic rings will suffocate in order to say that the threat of suffocation is real. That's the distortion part. It's irrelevant because the representative isn't trying to prove that the threat is real; he's trying to show that the switch to the new plastic rings will totally eliminate the threat of suffocation to wild animals.

- Conceiving the argument's conclusion in specific terms will help you stay focused and avoid outside-the-scope answer choices. Here, the representative simply says that the old rings often caused wild animals to suffocate, and that the new rings will not. Immediately eliminate choices that deal with issues other than the relationship between the plastic rings and animal entanglement/suffocation.
- Beware of very strictly worded conclusions, such as the one here: ". . . the threat *will be* eliminated." That doesn't say "probably be," or "most likely be," or "could be," or even "will largely be"; it's a definite. Strictly unqualified conclusions like this are often based on assumptions that usually (there's an example of a nice qualifying word) involve alternative possibilities or exceptions that the author overlooks.

12. B

Once all beverage companies switch to the new plastic rings, says the representative, "the threat of suffocation that plastic rings pose to wild animals will be eliminated." As mentioned above, that's pretty strong language. What if there were still a significant number of the old rings lying around where wild animals could get at them? Then, even if the new rings were 100% safe, the threat would not be "eliminated." Choice (B) raises this possibility, weakening the argument considerably.

(A) Since the representative's conclusion is contingent on completion of the switchover, how long the switchover will take is irrelevant.

(C) makes a useless distinction. It's hard to see how the price of the rings affects the likelihood of animal suffocation.

(D) answers a question that is of great importance to the beverage companies (and possibly beer drinkers), but of no importance to the animals, and is therefore outside the scope of the argument.

(E) contains a scope shift. The representative doesn't claim that the new plastic rings are more eco-friendly than the old ones. All it says is that the new rings won't make animals *suffocate*.

- Arguments that make extreme-sounding claims can be weakened simply by showing that "actual results may vary." Remember, you don't have to completely disprove an argument to weaken it. You just have to pick a choice that suggests that the conclusion is less likely to be true.
- Know the test: There's lots of synergy between assumption questions and weaken the argument questions. That's because contradicting an author's assumption is a weakener.

  Question 11: What assumption does the author of the argument make?
  Answer—question 12 choice (B): *After the beverage companies have switched over to the new plastic rings, a substantial number of old plastic rings will not remain where wild animals could come in contact with them.*

Question 12: What, if true, would weaken the argument?
Answer—question 11 choice (C): *Wild animals can become entangled in the new plastic rings before the rings have had sufficient exposure to sunlight to disintegrate.*

13. B

Alcohol consumption, you're told, has been linked to high blood pressure and consequently to heart disease. But a study showed that heart disease was lower among those who drank a moderate amount daily than among people identified as nondrinkers. From what you were told you'd expect the results to be just the opposite, so what's the deal?

(B) asserts that many of the people identified as nondrinkers were heavy drinkers who'd quit, which raises the possibility that they had a higher rate of high blood pressure and heart disease left over from their drinking days. Notice that (B) doesn't contradict the stimulus; the stimulus referred only to people "identified as nondrinkers," which needn't mean they've been teetotalers their whole lives.

(A) says people who don't drink are healthier, but since the nondrinkers were the ones who *weren't* healthier, this is no help at all.

(C) and (D) might explain why the moderate drinkers had even higher rates of heart disease than one might expect—(C) because some of them overdo it sometimes and (D) because some have high blood pressure—but since you want to explain the *nondrinkers'* higher rate of heart disease, (C) and (D) are irrelevant.

(E) stresses the groups' similarity to one another, essentially ruling out a possible alternative explanation: that there was some *other* difference between the two groups studied that could account for the unexpectedly higher rate of heart disease.

- In Paradox questions, the correct choice will be one that resolves the discrepancy without contradicting the information in the stimulus.
- Since the key to a Paradox question is finding a reasonable explanation, any choice that contradicts a possible explanation, such as (E), should be discarded immediately.

14. E

You're told that all Persian cats are pompous and therefore irritating, but you cannot conclude that any *other* kind of cat is either pompous or irritating. For all you know, the only irritating cats in the world are Persian cats. In other words, there may be no irritating cats that are not Persian cats (and therefore, of course, no irritating and beautiful cats that aren't Persian cats). (E) is not necessarily true. On the other hand:

(A) and (B) are identical inferable statements. Since some of the world's most beautiful cats are Persian, and all Persian cats are irritating, some of the world's most beautiful cats (the Persians) must be irritating (A). Another way of putting this is that there *are* some irritating cats (the Persians) among the world's most beautiful cats (B).

(C) Since all Persian cats are irritating, it's impossible for a Persian to be non-irritating; any cat that isn't irritating isn't a Persian.

(D) works in the same way as (A) and (B). All Persian cats are pompous (that's why they're irritating), and some Persian cats are among the world's most beautiful cats, so some pompous cats (the Persians) are among the world's most beautiful.

15. B

It's a parallel Flaw question, so your first task is to characterize the flaw in the stimulus. The author in the stimulus erroneously assumes that all students who have shown an interest in archaeology want to go on the dig. Likewise, the author in (B) makes the unwarranted assumption that all of the sure-footed, non-gentle horses are also well schooled.

(A) The "theoretically" should've given you pause—where does *that* shine in?—and (A) contains only three terms (worth saving; having a life; size) where the stimulus contains four.

(C) does commit the fallacy of denying the antecedent, but that's not the flaw in the original.

(D) Isn't flawed at all, so it's automatically out of the running.

(E) This one is flawed, but in a different way…the evidence tells you that one of two things is required for a certain result, then the conclusion tells you that since you don't have one of those things, the result must not occur.

- Interrogate the stimulus; don't read passively. Why, you must ask, will many students who want to go on the dig be ineligible to do so?
- Use all information given in the stem. When the test makers tell you that a flaw is present, read the argument critically and *find that flaw.*

16. C

A Parallel Logic question with a twist: The stimulus saves you the trouble of analyzing the argument by characterizing the flaw for you. You're told exactly what kind of flaw you're looking for, and only have to recognize the answer choice that matches the description. And it's (C) that commits the flaw described.

The initial observation is that each member of a group (each nominee) could possess a characteristic (being appointed to one of three openings on a committee). The conclusion is that all of the group's members could possess that characteristic (all the nominees could be appointed to the committee). As with the example of the tennis tournament in the stimulus, it's actually only possible for a comparatively few members of the group to possess the characteristic.

(A) is off in many ways; it doesn't move from "each" to "all" members of a group, it doesn't describe a characteristic that "could" be possessed, and it doesn't conclude that all members of the group possess the characteristic described.

(B) This conclusion is qualified, unlike that of the stimulus fallacy; (B) doesn't conclude that all the candidates possess the necessary qualifications. Moreover, unlike the example of the tennis tournament, it *would* be possible for all candidates to possess the characteristic of being fully qualified.

(D) is tricky. The problem is the nature of the "characteristic" described: the *probability* of a head being tossed. This makes the flaw a mathematical fallacy (the real probability of all five tosses being heads is one divided by two to the fifth power, or one in thirty-two), which doesn't match the stimulus fallacy.

(E) doesn't jump to an "immediate conclusion" based on the original observation, but instead offers a way of testing the observation's accuracy.

- Don't be thrown by the fact that a question looks peculiar. Here the oddness, the fact that the stimulus described the fallacy in abstract terms, made it much easier—half the work of a typical parallel flaw question was done for you.

17. D

Make the question stem work for you by actively decoding it. In a roundabout way, you're asked to weaken the argument; that is, find something that suggests that the "better clues" may not be so great. You need only concern yourself with the last two sentences, since that's where the "better" clues are described.

These clues don't specifically indicate lying; they indicate emotional arousal or distress. So a person under stress might well exhibit these clues even if he were telling the truth.

(A) and (C) can be eliminated because they don't relate to the "better" clues described in the last sentence.

(B) A person's past history has nothing to do with the argument, which is all about physical manifestations of lying.

(E) Just because hesitation and shifting posture prove to be reliable indicators of lying in some cases doesn't mean that the better clues (uncontrolled behavior such as pupil dilation) aren't reliable indicators.

- Read actively. Decoding question stems that are very specifically worded can often save you time when it comes to selecting the correct answer choice.

18. B

Orthodox medicine is not effective in treating certain medical conditions. And alternative medicine, says the author, is *never* effective. So it has to be true that there are some medical conditions for which neither type of treatment is effective.

(A) You cannot infer that practitioners of alternative medicine are acting in bad faith, because you don't know whether they believe their treatments to be effective. Their personal beliefs, in fact, are way outside the author's scope.

(C) 180: you're told that alternative medicine doesn't have any effects at all.

(D) is a distortion. You can infer that *some* effective treatments produce unacceptable side affects; that's one of the reasons people turn to alternative medicine. But saying that *all* effective treatments have unacceptable side effects is too extreme.

(E) It would be nice to believe that orthodox medicine will eventually produce cures for incurable diseases, but the author offers no such ray of hope.

- On inference questions, think about what you know. Then think about what you don't know. The things you don't know will often show up in wrong answer choices.
- Steer clear of choices like (A) that ascribe venal or otherwise bad motives to a person or group. Such choices are usually wrong.

19. D

The charge against alternative medicine is that it has no effects. You might have expected that the way to weaken that charge would be to find positive effects in such treatments. And (D), by suggesting that the patient's belief in the treatment can help promote healing, opens up the possibility that alternative medicine *can* assist in the healing process, thus having an effect.

(A) and (E) Showing that orthodox medicine is sometimes ineffective doesn't imply that alternative medicine is therefore effective. It doesn't even damage the author's credibility, since the argument clearly *states* that orthodox treatment is sometimes ineffective.

(B) Alternative medicine may be based on different concepts than orthodox medicine, but that doesn't necessarily mean that it works.

(C) Alternative medicine may provide patients with hope, but hope is not a medical effect. To select this choice, you have to assume that hope somehow aids the healing process, and that's too big a leap—there's no evidence for it. At the same time, when you select (C) you have to find a reason why (D) must be wrong, and that's well-nigh impossible.

- Weakening an argument doesn't always mean blowing it apart completely. In fact, extreme-sounding statements (like the author's final sentence in the stimulus) can often be weakened simply by showing that other possibilities exist.
- There's a big difference between criticizing one side of an argument and supporting the other side. The old adage "the enemy of my enemy is my friend" has no logical value. In this example, you can't shore up the case for alternative medicine by breaking down the case for orthodox medicine.

20. E

The author mentions two important developments that took place in North America during the period that saw the extinction of large mammals like the mastodon, wooly mammoth, and saber-toothed tiger: the spread of human beings and climactic warming. She concludes that human activity caused the mammals' extinction. But she's ignoring an alternate possibility suggested by her own evidence—that the change in the climate caused the mammals' extinction. From what she's told you, there's no reason to choose one cause over the other.

(A) The author doesn't adopt without question the view that humans aren't *included* in nature; she attempts to disprove the view that humans lived in *harmony* with nature.

(B) The author doesn't presuppose that humans' one-time harmonious existence with nature is a myth; she draws a conclusion that she believes *demonstrates* that this idea is a myth.

(C) is irrelevant. The author's conclusion was that human activity 12,000 years ago caused the extinction of animal species; her conclusion is unrelated to the significance of that extinction to the humans of the time.

(D) would only strengthen the contention that 12,000 years ago human activity was causing species to become extinct.

- It's fairly common on LSAT Logical Reasoning for an author to err by failing to consider some alternative possibility; noticing this error can make prephrasing very easy.
- Always read actively. Treat the stimulus as a real description of a real situation. When you read that way, you're less likely to miss the importance of details like "as the climate became warmer" above.

21. D

When Greenfield households deliver recyclable trash to commercial recycling centers, that trash is accepted *for free*. That means that homeowners don't lose money, as they would if they put out the trash for collectors to add to their trash tax, but it also means they don't *gain* any money by bringing the trash to the centers. They would do just as well financially giving their recyclable trash to their neighbors; in both cases, they avoid the tax. So there's no financial incentive for The Action described in (D).

(A) Since households pay a tax for putting out nonrecyclable trash, and can dispose of their recyclable trash for free, there *is* a financial incentive to make sure they find all their recyclable trash.

(B) provides a method for avoiding the tax levied on trash put out for collection, so there's a definite financial incentive to follow this course.

(C) The trash tax is calculated based on the volume of trash put out. (C) would reduce the volume of the trash put out and therefore would reduce the tax paid.

(E) Since nonrecyclable packaging goes into the trash, using products without packaging, or with packaging that could be brought to recycling centers, would reduce the volume of trash put out and so would reduce the trash tax paid.

- This is essentially an Inference question (like question 14); given the conditions described in the stimulus, each of the choices but one describes a course of action that can be inferred to be financially advantageous.

22. A

In rather an odd survey, consumers living in an Eastern European nation are asked to rank 400 Western products according to brand name recognition and quality. But it turns out that only 27 of the products are even available in that nation. Not surprisingly, the survey results for the 27 products that are available (in terms of how name recognition correlates with perceived quality) were unlike the results for the products that aren't available.

What's the point of asking people about the quality of products they've never used? The survey violates (A): Although all the respondents can answer the question about whether they recognize the brand names, they cannot reasonably answer the question about the quality of products that are unavailable.

(B) There's no difficulty in categorizing the responses to questions; on the contrary, the survey results can be organized neatly into two rankings.

(C) It's never stated that the survey requires respondents to give up their anonymity, so there's no evidence that (C)'s principle is violated.

(D) The survey doesn't ask many questions about a single product, but two questions about 400 products.

(E) The survey abides by (E); the respondents are asked about their personal opinions of the products in question, so how could they get the answer wrong?

- If you don't recognize the principle directly, use the process of elimination. Concentrate on the violation the survey is supposed to have committed: an unmanageable number of categories (B), violating anonymity (C), asking ten questions about one product (D), respondents' fear of being wrong (E). Even if you had trouble following the stimulus, all of these are pretty clearly inapplicable.

23. E

Both crested and noncrested birds of this species tend to select mates of their own variety. Is this preference genetically determined or is it learned behavior (based on the fact that the birds generally live only with birds of their own variety)? The author concludes that the preference is learned, because when a noncrested bird is raised in a crested flock and later moved to a mixed flock, it's likely to pick a crested mate. Its mate selection seems to have been influenced by the environment it was raised in.

(E) supports this with similar evidence: When a bird is raised in a mixed flock, it shows *no* preference for one variety over the other when choosing a mate. Again, its choice of mate seems determined by its environment.

(A) is outside the scope—it speaks of other species instead of the species you're interested in, and it ignores the learned vs. genetic question which is the focus of the argument.

(B) Whether or not there are many other behavioral differences between crested and noncrested birds doesn't tell you whether their preference in mates is learned or genetic.

(C) is irrelevant; since you're only interested in why the birds choose crested or noncrested mates, their mates' other characteristics don't matter.

(D) is a 180 choice, since the bird described chooses a mate of its own variety without any environmental reason for learning such behavior.

- In order to understand an argument, you have to understand the function that each piece of evidence serves. When a section of the argument begins with "however," take the time to understand how it functions as counterevidence or as a counterbalance to what went before; above, the "however" introduces evidence showing a bird behaving in an uncharacteristic manner, apparently because of how it was raised.

24. C

The key to getting into and out of this question with a quick right answer is the nature of the conclusion, signaled by "therefore": It boils down to "A particular phenomenon occurs *at least in part because of* a particular factor." If you scan the five choices, the only one whose conclusion even comes close is (C)'s "weight must determine, *or help determine*, charges."

That's all you needed to see. Analyzing things further, the gist of both (C) and the stimulus is that two causes (day length and temperature/volume and weight), separately or together, bring about an effect (renewed plant growth/landfill charges); therefore, if one cause (day length/volume) is identical for all and thus taken out of the equation, then the other cause (temperature/weight) must have some influence on the effect.

(A) This conclusion hinges on "most" and "few," which aren't in the stimulus, and lacks an explicit parallel to the stimulus' "day length or temperature or both."

(B) The certainty of (B)'s conclusion (an easterly wind *must* now be blowing) is missing from the stimulus, and the "east means rain, west means dry" opposition has no parallel in the stimulus either.

(D) This "1 or 2 or 3" might seem like a clever parallel to "X or Y or both," but only mathematically. To be parallel, (D) would have to draw a conclusion about the number of store detectives needed, but instead its conclusion explains *why* a particular number is needed.

(E) This conclusion, first of all, is a recommendation ("X should try to do Y"), and that alone renders it impossible. (E) also deviates by bringing in four terms (loud, soft, low-pitched, and high-pitched) and its reference to "especially," none of which appears in the stimulus.

- Keep characterizing the choices and stimulus. Here, only if the stimulus' conclusion were a recommendation could (E) be correct. And here, since the stimulus' conclusion is an assertion of partial cause, only (C) need be considered.

| PART FOUR |

Getting Into Law School

Chapter 8: **Law School Admissions**

- **Where to apply**
- **When to apply**
- **How to apply**

INTRODUCTION

I can still remember the day I received my LSAT score report in the mail. I was jubilant about my score, which put me in the top two percent of all test takers. This kind of LSAT performance, I thought—combined with my high college GPA—would surely get me into any law school I desired; all I had to do was decide which one I would deign to attend. I proceeded to apply to ten top law schools, fully confident that I would be accepted by all ten.

Well, it didn't turn out quite that way. By the following April, I had received a meager two acceptance letters, one wait-list letter, and an appalling seven rejection letters, including ones from Harvard and Stanford. As the rejection letters rolled in, one after the other, my original hubris slowly and painfully gave way to humility.

Two weeks after the last rejection, still reeling from the shock, I had the good fortune to bump into an admissions officer from a local law school at a party. I cornered her and began peppering her with questions about what could possibly have gone wrong. She mentioned several potential problems and suggested that I call a friend of hers at one of the law schools I had applied to and ask her to critique my application. What I found out was eye-opening: my application could not have been more inept. In fact, just about everything I'd done had contributed to preventing my admission to law school, including carelessly misspelling my name on the application (fortunately, the University of Michigan Law School saw fit to let me attend despite these blunders).

KAPLAN EXCLUSIVE

You have to show the admissions officers how strong and well-qualified you are—by conducting an effective, meticulously organized campaign for admission.

Today, after years of conversations with other lawyers, law students, and my Kaplan LSAT classmates, I realize that my experience was hardly unique. An astonishing number of people apply to law school without a clue about the admissions process. That's why I've made something of a career out of ensuring that others don't make the same mistakes I did. In the last several years, I've spoken to admissions officers at more than 65 schools in all regions of the country, gleaning as much information from them as I could.

One cautionary note—admission officers are human beings; they don't all think alike. Attitudes and priorities vary from law school to law school. However, the suggestions that follow are the ones I've heard over and over again, straight from the most important source—the admissions officers themselves. Stick closely to these suggestions and you'll increase your chances of getting in the law school you want to attend.

WHERE TO APPLY

The question of where you should apply has two-parts. What schools should you consider, regardless of your chances, and which of these schools can you actually get into? Let's begin with the first question.

What Schools Should You Consider?

A recent article about law school education published a remarkable statistic. Upon graduation, according to one study, 58 percent of all law students end up living and working within a one-hour drive of where they went to law school. That's nearly six out of every ten students!

There are many reasons for this surprising statistic. Obviously, a lot of people attend the local law school in the town where they have always lived and want to continue living. Also, since employers tend to interview and hire from nearby law schools, many recent grads stay put. Some students find that they just like the area and don't want to leave. Still others meet and marry a local person during their three years. Whatever the explanation, a majority of all law students end up spending more than just the required three years in the city or region where they attend law school.

Despite the importance of law school selection, however, it's frightening how lightly many applicants treat the whole process, even students who spend a great deal of time studying for the LSAT or working on their applications. Horror stories abound—of distant relatives convincing someone to attend State University Law School just because they themselves did 40 years ago or of a student who decides not to apply to a school because his girlfriend's cousin heard that the social life was not so hot.

This point cannot be stressed enough. *Choosing a law school is a major decision in your life and should be treated as such.* There are several factors to consider when choosing where to apply, including reputation, location, and cost.

Reputation

How much does a law school's reputation matter? The short answer is that it matters very much in your first few years out of law school, when you're looking for your first job or two. Most employers evaluating you at this time will have little else to go on and so will tend to place a lot of weight on school reputation. After a few years, when you've established a reputation and a record of your own, the importance of your alma mater's rep will diminish.

The long answer to the question of academic reputation, however, is a little more complex. Each applicant must look at his or her situation and ask several questions:

- **Am I looking to work for a law firm or to do public service work?**
  Law firms tend to put more emphasis on the reputation of the school.
- **Do I want to stay in the area or have more mobility nationwide?**
  Some schools enjoy strong local reputations as well as strong alumni bases, whereas other schools have a nationwide appeal.
- **How competitive do I want my law school experience to be?**
  Although there are exceptions, as a general rule the schools with better reputations tend to be very competitive.
- **Do I want to consider teaching as an option?**
  Virtually all law school professors come from a handful of top-notch law schools. The same also applies for the most prestigious judicial clerkships.
- **To what extent am I willing to go into debt?**
  The schools with the biggest reputations also tend to have the biggest price tags.

What's the best way to research reputation? Many publications rank law schools. How accurate these rankings are is anybody's guess, but they tend to become self-fulfilling. Once published, they're discussed over and over by students, lawyers, and faculty until they become fact. Although the methodology behind these rankings is often suspect, the results are frequently heeded by employers. Studies rank the top fifty schools, the top fifteen schools, or categorize all schools into four or five levels. (Most of these books can be found in the reference section of your local bookstore.) Many law firms rely heavily on such rankings in making their hiring decisions.

But there are other methods to determine a school's reputation. Speak to friends who are lawyers or law students. Lawyers have a habit of noting who their most formidable opponents are and where they went to law school. Look through law school catalogs and see what schools the professors attended. Finally, ask the placement offices how many firms interview on campus each year, and compare the numbers. Their answers can give you a strong indication of what the law-firm community thinks of a school.

Location

Location is of prime importance because of the distinct possibility that you'll end up spending a significant part of your life near your law school—three years at the very least. Even under the best of conditions, law school will be a difficult period in your life. You owe it to yourself to find a place where you'll be comfortable. Pick cities or areas you already know you like or would like to live. Pay particular attention to climate problems. Think about rural areas as opposed to urban centers.

KAPLAN EXCLUSIVE

Statistics show that you'll probably end up spending at least part of your working life in the area where you went to law school. So pick one in a location you can live with (and in).

Visit as many law schools as possible, your top two or three choices at the very least. You may be surprised at what you find. For example, a recent student related that his dream was to get into the law school of one particular university because he'd visited its campus several years ago and loved it. But his dream was quickly crushed when told that the university's law school is not on the campus, but rather thirty minutes away in an area closer to downtown. Spend some time researching location by visiting *when school is in session*, which is when you'll get the most accurate picture. You should also:

- Buy a local newspaper and scan the real estate ads for prices near campus; check out campus housing to determine whether it's livable.
- Check out transportation options at the law school.
- Take the school's tour so you can hear about the area's good points.
- Look at bulletin boards for evidence of activities.

Finally, don't be afraid to wander into the student lounge and just ask several law students what they think. Most are more than willing to provide an honest appraisal, but be sure to get more than one opinion.

Costs

Cost ranks at the bottom of many law students' list of criteria to consider, because law school financial aid works in much the same manner as a credit card—you get it now and pay for it later. Each year a number of students enter law school with the goal of doing some type of public service work, but then are forced to take higher-paying firm jobs in order to meet their loan payments. This is certainly understandable when you realize that many law students rack up debts of over $100,000 over the course of three years.

Among the cost issues to consider are:

- **Low-Cost State Schools**
  State schools tend to have lower tuition, particularly for in-state residents.
- **Urban Versus Rural Living Costs**
  Schools in large urban areas will almost invariably have higher living costs than those in rural areas (although the larger cities also tend to have more part-time jobs for second- and third-year students, which can offset the extra cost).
- **Special Loan Programs**
  Many schools now offer special loan repayment or loan forgiveness programs for students who take low-paying public service jobs.
- **Special Scholarship Programs**
  Many law schools offer special scholarship programs that range from small grants to full three-year rides.

KAPLAN EXCLUSIVE

Cost should be a factor in your choice of law school. Loans have to be paid back, and a high burden of debt might force you to make a less-than-desirable career choice.

The law school application will tell you what the annual tuition was for the previous year. Many applications will even give you an estimate of living expenses. If you want to dig deeper, call the financial aid office and ask them to send you the breakdown of living expenses of the average law student. Also ask them to send information about any loan forgiveness programs and about scholarships offered by the law school.

Job Placement

With the legal job market shrinking, the proficiency of a law school's placement office is now a major factor to be considered. If interviews with law students can be believed, the competency of placement officers varies widely. Some see their job as simply setting up on-campus interviews and making sure they run smoothly. Others call and write letters on behalf of students and are constantly selling the school to employers. Some schools direct almost all of their efforts into placing students into private law firms. Other schools provide information on an entire range of opportunities. At some schools students are lucky if the placement office even provides them with a list of alumni in cities in which they'd like to live. At other schools the office calls alumni to hunt for leads.

Ask the placement office for the percentage of graduates in the most recent class who had jobs upon graduation. Don't be fooled by statistics that show 98 percent of all graduates employed. Almost all law students are eventually employed, even if they drive taxis. The key is to determine how many are placed in law jobs *before* they leave law school.

Second, stop by the placement office on your visit and look around. Ask to see the placement library and check whether it's well organized and up-to-date. Note whether it carries materials on public interest or teaching jobs and how large this section is. Also ask whether a newsletter is published to keep alumni informed of any recent job openings.

Again, talk with law students. Most have very strong opinions about the performance of their placement office. Most students recognize and appreciate when the placement office is making an extra effort.

Course Selection

One of the nicest things about law schools today is their growing number of course selections and the new areas of law that are opening up. International trade, employment discrimination, sports and entertainment, and environmental law are all areas in which schools are providing more offerings. Many law students nowadays are becoming specialists, because of both personal preference and better marketability. If you're one of the many students who enter law school without a clue about what kind of law they want to practice, look for schools that offer a lot of different areas of study.

As a rule, schools with larger student populations offer not only more classes but also a greater variety. They need more professors to handle the standard course load, and most professors also like to teach and explore new areas of law as well.

Schools list the courses most recently taught in their recruiting brochure, which they will gladly send you. One note of caution: just because a class has been taught in the past and is listed in the brochure doesn't mean that it's taught every year or will be taught in the future. If you're interested in a particular class, call the registrar's department and find out how often the class has been taught in the past and whether it will be offered again in the future. Ask to speak with the professor who has taught the course in the past.

Social Life

Although it's an important part of the law school experience, social life should rank near the bottom of the list of factors to consider when choosing a law school. Why? Because your social life at any law school is what you make of it. Almost all law schools have monthly parties or weekly Thursday night get-togethers at local bars. And if you choose to expand that schedule, you can always find a willing accomplice. Furthermore, most schools now have a comparably full range of social organizations that cover race, religion, political affiliation, and sex.

Examine the area surrounding the law school. During your first year, locale probably won't matter much. But as you get into your second and third years, you'll likely find that you do have some free time, particularly on weekends. Think about whether you want a quiet rural area where canoeing or skiing are readily available or whether you'd prefer a larger city with a vibrant restaurant and nightlife scene.

Additional Considerations

There are a few other factors that you may want to toss into the equation when deciding which law school is right for you.

Class Size: This factor is not as important as it is when choosing a college because, despite what you may read in a catalogue, virtually all first-year classes will be large. Nevertheless, there are some differences between a school such as Georgetown, with more than 2,000 students, and a school such as Stanford, with fewer than 800. In the second and third years, the larger schools tend to have more course offerings, whereas the smaller schools focus on smaller class size and more contact between professors and students. Smaller schools also tend to encourage a greater sense of camaraderie and less competition. Larger schools, on the other hand, produce more alumni and thus more contacts when it comes time for your job search.

Attrition Rates: Law schools generally try to keep their attrition rate below 10 percent. There are exceptions, however, and if the school you're interested in has an attrition rate above 10 percent, you should ask an admissions officer why. There may be a reasonable explanation, but you should probably approach the school with some caution.

KAPLAN EXCLUSIVE

At many colleges, you can create your own joint-degree program, combining a law degree with just about anything imaginable. If that kind of flexibility is important to you, make sure you choose schools that are willing to accommodate you.

Joint-Degree Programs: are designed to help students pursue two degrees jointly in less time than it would take to earn them separately. Some common examples are the Master of Public Policy (M.P.P.) or the Master of Business Administration (M.B.A.) combined with the law degree. These programs generally take four to five years to complete. Most schools are becoming more daring in this field—indeed, some are now encouraging students to create their own joint-degree program in any area that they choose, as long as it meets both departments' approval. It's not uncommon now to see joint degrees in law and foreign languages, music, or sociology. Check with the schools to see what joint-degree programs are routinely offered, but don't be limited by them. If you have a specialized program in mind, call the registrar's office and see how flexible they are.

Clinical Programs: Every law school in the country now offers one or more clinical programs. A clinic is a unique, hands-on opportunity that allows law students to see how the legal system works by handling actual civil cases for people who can't afford an attorney (and getting credit for it at the same time). Not only are these clinics a tremendous learning tool, but they are also the highlight of many law students' three years of study.

Usually the workload is heavy on landlord/tenant disputes or other debt-collection cases. However, many schools are branching out and offering specialized clinics in such areas as child abuse, domestic violence, and immigration. One word of caution: Clinics tend to be popular with students. In many cases, it's very difficult to get a spot in the class, and admission usually depends on the luck of the draw. As a general rule, the schools in large cities have bigger and more clinics because they tend to have more clients.

Internships: Like clinical programs, internships are becoming more popular and varied. Internship programs vary widely from school to school, and may include anything from working for an international trade organization in Europe for an entire year to getting three hours credit for part-time work at the local prosecutor's office. Internships are often overlooked by students who are afraid to veer from the traditional path. Yet they can be a welcome break from regular law studies and may also help in the later job search.

Computer Facilities and Law Library: Legal research is a big part of your three years in law school. Nothing will frustrate you more than to have a brief due the next day only to find that your library lacks essential volumes on the subject or that the few computers they have are either occupied or not working. If you make a visit to the law schools, check out their facilities. Again, don't be afraid to ask students for their opinions.

Where Can You Get In?

Let's turn to the second major question in the selection process: "Where do you have a chance of being accepted?"

Anyone who tells you that he can predict where you'll be accepted is fooling himself and, worse, fooling you. Stories of students accepted by a Harvard, Stanford, or Michigan only to be turned down by schools with far less glamorous reputations are common. Yet what is often overlooked is how well the process does work, considering the volume of applications and the amount of discretion exercised by admissions officers.

One reason the admissions process runs smoothly is that all law schools use the combined LSAT score and GPA as the most important determinant in making the decision. This provides a degree of consistency to the admissions process and gives the applicants some direction in deciding where to apply.

Those Legendary Law School Grids

Each year, LSAC publishes the *Official Guide to ABA-Approved Law Schools* (the LSAT application booklet tells you how to order it). This guide includes a wealth of information on all the accredited law schools in the United States. The schools themselves provide most of the information for the book, including the LSAT scores and GPAs of the most recently admitted class. These are generally presented in grid form and are the single most valuable tool in determining your chances of being accepted at any particular law school. The grid shown here is a hypothetical grid, similar to the ones found in the *Guide.*

State University Law School

	LSAT Percentile Rank						
GPA	< 40%	41–50%	51–60%	61–70%	71–80%	81–90%	91–99%
4–3.75	11/1	21/3	29/5	41/12	62/33	68/55	48/47
3.74–3.5	16/0	14/0	8/2	38/16	84/38	115/64	102/81
3.49–3.25	18/0	9/1	12/0	24/8	73/28	96/38	76/48
3.24–3.0	13/0	13/0	22/2	25/6	55/15	71/28	53/27
2.99–2.75	3/0	5/0	8/0	19/2	38/6	49/10	31/9
2.74–2.5	1/0	0/0	3/1	18/3	41/2	32/4	11/5
<2.5	1/0	1/0	3/0	9/1	9/0	6/2	3/1

Take a close look at the hypothetical grid above. Note that GPAs are divided into categories that drop .25 every line. Also note that LSAT scores are listed by percentile rank rather than by score. This is done because the scoring system for the LSAT was changed in 1991, and law schools still receive applications from students with scores under the old system. In order to use the grid, first find the line where your GPA fits in. Then read across until you find the percentage category of your existing or anticipated LSAT score. There you'll find two numbers, divided by a slash. The first number indicates the number of people in that range of LSAT scores and GPAs who applied to that school. The second number is the number accepted.

Most students apply to too few schools. According to LSAC, the average applicant applies to only about five schools. Admittedly, the cost of applications is rising, and sending out ten or more applications can result in an outlay of $500 or more. But keep in mind that if the cost of application presents a real hardship, most schools will waive the application fee—provided you give them a good, credible reason.

Assembling a List of Schools

Using the grid numbers as a guide for determining your chances of acceptance, you should create a list of schools to apply to, dividing the list into three categories: preferred schools, competitive, and safe schools.

Preferred Schools: These are schools you'd *love* to attend, but your numbers indicate a less than 40 percent chance of admission. Apply to two or three schools in this group. Long-shots rarely pay off, but daydreaming about them is always nice.

Competitive Schools: Competitive (or "good fit") schools are those where your grid numbers are in the ballpark and where, depending on the rest of your application, you have a decent chance of getting admitted. These are schools where your numbers give you a 40–80 percent chance of admission. These are the schools on which you should focus most of your attention. Applying to four to seven schools in this group is reasonable and increases your odds of getting into at least one school where you are competitive.

"Safe" Schools: These schools are not high on your preference list, but your odds of admission are excellent there. Look at the grids and determine two or three schools where your chances of getting in appear to be 80 percent or better. One suggestion for this list would be to pick schools in locations that you particularly like.

Note: Students with low numbers may need to be a little more flexible and work a little harder. Be willing to travel a little farther to go to school. Also, look at schools in areas that aren't quite as popular or that tend to draw mostly local students. Sometimes the more expensive schools are applied to by fewer applicants and can be easier to get into.

Drawbacks to Using the Law School Grids

Although the grid system is very helpful, it does have its problems. Remember that the law schools provide the grids. Some schools take the opportunity to enhance their reputation by making their numbers seem higher than they really are. This is not done by lying, but rather by the schools' selectively using pertinent information to artificially enhance the numbers. If a school's numbers don't jibe with its reputation, be skeptical.

Second, because each category in a grid covers a fairly wide range of numbers (i.e., 10 LSAT percentile points or .25 GPA points), don't be fooled into thinking that your 3.51 and 71 percent put you on the same level as the student with the 3.74 and 79 percent, even though you fall in the same place on the grids. There are wide gaps in every category.

Third, many law schools—including some of the very best—do not provide LSAC with grids. However, these schools generally will tell you the average GPA and LSAT score for the previous year's entering class. If you want to get a picture of your chances at these schools, try determining which schools are similar in reputation. You can do so using the published ranking lists discussed earlier. Then determine which one of these schools comes closest in number of applications and size of the entering class to the school in question and use that grid.

Use the application list on the following page to plot out your law school application campaign.

WHEN TO APPLY

Prior to the 1980s, the typical law school application season began in October or November with the mailing of the brochures and application forms. The schools would begin accepting applications in December or January and set a deadline for all applications to be completed by around March. Once all applications were received, the schools would begin the decision-making process, usually sending out acceptances or rejections in April, May, or June.

Schools send out application forms in August and September, begin accepting applications in October, and start sending out acceptance letters by November. (As proof that they have a heart, most law schools will not begin sending out rejection letters until after the holiday season.) Application deadlines may be in February or March, but because the schools have begun filling their classes in the fall, it is not unusual for more than 75 percent of the anticipated acceptance letters to have been sent by the spring deadline date. This is what's known as rolling admissions, which creates the scenario of unaware applicants who proudly deliver their applications on the deadline date only to find that they have put themselves at a distinct disadvantage.

KAPLAN EXCLUSIVE

Does it really pay to go to a lot of trouble to apply early? Yes, particularly in this era of rolling admissions. Start your campaign 18 months before you intend to step into your first law class.

The Advantages of Early Application

Does applying early really provide you with an advantage? Yes! Here are the major reasons why.

Rising Index Numbers

The first reason has to do with index numbers. Your index number is based on the combination of your LSAT score and your GPA. At the beginning of the application process, most schools set an automatic admittance index number. Applicants whose index numbers surpass that figure are admitted quickly with only a cursory look at their application to confirm that they are not serial killers. At the beginning of the process, law schools are always afraid that they'll have too few applicants accepting their offers, which would mean less tuition money and almost certainly some complaints from the school's administrative office. Thus, they usually begin the application process by setting the automatic admittance index number on the low side. Then they gradually increase it as the admission season wears on and they discover that, their fears are unfounded.

Fewer Available Places

Because schools have a tendency to be a little more lenient early in the process, they begin reaching their admission goals fairly quickly. By February, the school may well have sent out more than 75 percent or more of all the acceptance letters it plans to send. Yet, at this point, all of the earlier applicants haven't been rejected. Instead many people are left hanging, just in case better applicants don't start coming through the system. This means that if you apply in March, you're now shooting for fewer possible positions, yet you're still competing against a fairly substantial pool of applicants.

Application Worksheet

YOU SHOULD APPLY TO AT LEAST EIGHT SCHOOLS.

Preferred Schools

Chances of admission 40 percent or less. Choose two or three.

1. ____

2. ____

3. ____

Competitive Schools

Chances of admission 40–80 percent. Choose four to seven.

1. ____

2. ____

3. ____

4. ____

5. ____

6. ____

7. ____

"Safe" Schools

Chances of admission 80 percent or greater. Choose two or three.

1. ____

2. ____

3. ____

The "Jading" Effect

If they are candid, admissions officers will admit that by the time they get to the two thousandth essay on "Why I want to go to law school," they're burned out, and more than a little jaded. Essays or applications that might have seemed noteworthy in the beginning now strike the reader as routine.

The Nay-Sayers

A handful of prelaw advisors and admissions officers dispute the importance of early applications, and at a few schools, there may indeed be no special advantage. Law schools are almost always open to exceptional applicants, and will sometimes admit someone well after the deadline if the student can give a good reason for the late application. Furthermore, a few schools routinely accept applications up until a week or two before classes start.

But these are exceptions. We became convinced of the importance of early applications while working with a student a few years ago. She hadn't taken the LSAT until December and was running late on her applications, barely making the deadline at the eight law schools to which she applied. Eventually she was rejected by seven of the schools and accepted by one. She decided to sit out a year and try again. The next time, she applied in November to the same eight schools, changed almost nothing on her application, and was accepted at five of the schools and wait-listed at two others. The only logical explanation was the timing of the application.

When to Start

For the most part, a pre-Halloween application is overdoing it. When schools are just gearing up, you run the risk of documents being misplaced. Pre-Thanksgiving is the preferable choice and assures that you'll be among the early entries. Shortly before Christmas is not as desirable, but should still hold you in good stead. After Christmas and the holidays, however, you're on the downside and may well find yourself among the last 30 percent of all applications received. And if you go with a post-Valentine's Day application—well, you'd better have strong numbers.

Remember that this discussion applies to the date on which your application is *complete*, not just the date on which the school receives your application forms. Applications are not considered complete until the LSAT score, LSDAS (Law School Data Assembly Service) reports, transcripts, and all recommendations have been received. Even though other people are sending these pieces, it's your responsibility to see that they arrive at the law school promptly. This does *not* mean calling the law school three times a week to see if they've arrived. It means prodding your recommenders or your college to send in the necessary documentation. Explain to them the importance of early applications.

If you want to have a complete application at the law schools by, say, late November, you can't start planning just a few weeks in advance. Your campaign for admission should begin five or six months before that deadline—i.e., eighteen months before your first day as a law student. We've included, at the end of this section, a schedule that you can use to organize your campaign. As you'll see, you should plan to devote plenty of time to your applications the summer before they're due.

Here are some of the important things to do each season. For convenience, let's assume that you want to go to law school the fall after you graduate from college.

Spring of Junior Year

Your first step should be to register for the June LSAT. You won't need your LSAT score for a while yet, but if you take the June test and bomb out, you'll be able to retake the test in October. Get a copy of the *LSAT/LSDAS Registration and Information Book* at any local college or law school admissions office or at any Kaplan Center. The registration booklet will tell you not only about the LSAT but also about the LSDAS. The LSDAS is the organization that will be sending your LSAT scores and transcripts to the law schools you apply to. You'll want LSDAS to open a file on you as early as possible. The book will explain exactly how to do this and how much it will cost (yes, they charge for their mandatory services).

You can buy the *Official Guide to ABA-Approved Law Schools*, which contains those grids we talked about, as well as other information about American law schools. If you can't find it in your local bookstore, you can order it from LSDAS.

The Summer Before Senior Year

Start thinking about a "theme" for your application, which can serve as a way to stand out from the crowd and as an organizing principle for personal statements, recommendations, and everything else in your file. Think about how you'd like to be identified. As the environmentalist who plays oboe recitals for the local recycling center? Of course, you don't *have* to have a theme, but any kind of "high concept" will help your application stick in the minds of admissions officers. You should also be assembling your list of schools at this point. Visit as many of them as you can. Send for their catalogues and applications.

Early Fall of Senior Year

This is when the action really starts. Applications will start arriving. (In filling them out, follow the procedures outlined in the "How to Apply" section.) Line up your recommenders. Make sure they have everything they need to write you a great letter. (More on how to do so in the "How to Apply" section.) Take the October LSAT, if you've decided to do so. Revise your personal statement. Revise it again. And again.

Late Fall of Senior Year

Complete and submit your applications. Prod recommenders so that your applications are complete before Thanksgiving.

Applying to law school is a time-consuming process that tests your organizational skills and your attention to detail. Students who believe that they can simply plot out four hours on a weekend to complete this ordeal are kidding themselves. Plan to set aside some big blocks of time well in advance to work intensively on this important step in achieving your admission goals.

An Ideal Law School Application Schedule

Your campaign for law school admission should start up to eighteen months before you step into your first law classroom. Here's a schedule of what you should be doing when:

SPRING OF JUNIOR YEAR

- ❑ Get the *Official Guide to U.S. Law Schools*.
- ❑ Register for the June LSAT (you can retake it in October if you blow it).
- ❑ Prepare for the LSAT.
- ❑ Subscribe to LSDAS (they take care of sending your transcript and LSAT scores to each school you apply to).

SUMMER BEFORE SENIOR YEAR

- ❑ Take the June LSAT.
- ❑ Start drafting your personal statement.
- ❑ Think about whom you'll be asking for recommendations.
- ❑ Make a list of schools you'll be applying to, using the grids from the *Official Guide* as an aid.
- ❑ Send away for applications, and start visiting as many schools as you can.
- ❑ Register for the October LSAT if you're not satisfied with your June score.

EARLY FALL OF SENIOR YEAR

- ❑ Familiarize yourself with the applications as they roll in.
- ❑ Make a checklist and schedule for each application, and photocopy all forms.
- ❑ Send transcript request forms to all undergraduate and graduate schools you've attended.
- ❑ Line up your recommendation writers. Give them the specific info they need to write an outstanding recommendation of you.
- ❑ Revise your personal statement. Tailor it to specific essay topics, if any, on individual applications.

MIDFALL OF SENIOR YEAR

- ❑ Finalize your personal statements.
- ❑ Transfer application information from the photocopies to the actual application forms.
- ❑ Make sure your recommendation writers are on board.
- ❑ Take the October LSAT (if necessary).
- ❑ Send in your applications. (Make sure you don't mix up the mailings!)

LATE FALL OF SENIOR YEAR

- ❑ Remind your recommendation writers to send in recommendations ASAP.
- ❑ Get Master Law School Report from LSDAS, summarizing transcripts, etcetera.

Winter and Spring/Summer after Senior Year

- ❑ Receive monthly updates from LSDAS, telling you which schools your records have been sent to.
- ❑ Cross your fingers while you wait for the acceptances to roll in.
- ❑ Decide which offer to accept.
- ❑ Send in acceptance.
- ❑ Apply for financial aid.

Fall after Graduation

- ❑ Start your first semester at the law school of your choice.

LSDAS Checklist

☐ Get the LSAT/LSDAS Registration and Information Book.

To order a free copy, call LSAC at (215) 968-1001, or email your request to lsacinfo@lsac.org.

The book is also available at law school admission offices and prelaw adviser offices.

☐ Subscribe to LSDAS by completing the registration form in the Registration and Information Booklet.

You can subscribe to LSDAS on the same form you use to register for the LSAT.

☐ Use transcript request forms (they're in the Information Book) to request transcripts from all undergraduate and graduate institutions you've attended.

They will send transcripts directly to LSDAS.

☐ Receive LSDAS Subscription Confirmation.

☐ Receive Master Law School Report—summarizing your academic information.

They get sent shortly after LSDAS receives your transcripts.

Check it carefully; report any inaccuracies to LSAC.

☐ If you've decided to apply to more schools than you originally planned to, order extra reports from LSDAS and pay an additional fee.

☐ Receive monthly reports from LSDAS.

Check them for accuracy or discrepancies.

☐ If necessary, renew your LSDAS subscription after twelve months.

HOW TO APPLY

After you've made the decision to apply to law school and have decided where and when to apply, you need to order the application forms from the various schools you've chosen. This can be done by mail, but the quickest way is just to call the admissions offices around July and get put on their mailing lists. Once the applications begin arriving (usually around Labor Day) you'll notice one thing quickly: no two applications are exactly alike. Some require one recommendation, others two or three. Some ask you to write one essay or personal statement, while others may ask for two or even three. Some have very detailed forms requiring extensive background information; others are satisfied with your name and address and very little else.

Despite these differences, most applications follow a general pattern with variations on the same kinds of questions. So although not all of this section is relevant to all parts of every application, these guidelines will be valuable for just about any law school application you'll encounter.

KAPLAN EXCLUSIVE

You won't be writing ten different applications so much as ten variations on a single application.

The most important thing to keep in mind about your law school application is that it is, above all else, a sales pitch. The application is your single best opportunity to sell yourself. Remember, every person who applies will have strengths and weaknesses. It's how you *present* those strengths and weaknesses that counts. *You* are in control of what that admissions committee sees on your application and how they see it.

So what's the best way to sell yourself? We all know that some people are natural-born sellers in person, but the application process is written, not spoken. The key here is not natural talent but rather organization—carefully planning a coherent presentation from beginning to end and paying attention to every detail in between. But be careful not to focus so much on the overall theme that you neglect the details. That can be disastrous.

Getting Organized

You must first put together a checklist of the forms that each of your chosen schools requires, double-checking to make sure you don't overlook anything. Some schools may require you to fill out residency forms or financial aid forms in addition to the regular application forms. Don't ignore these and put them off until last. Schools may require proof of residency or income verifications that you might not have readily available.

Next, make photocopies of all forms before you complete them. Changes and corrections will have to be made no matter how careful you are. These changes should not be made on the original form, which will go to the school. Almost every admissions officer we have spoken with explicitly prizes neatness. The feeling is that if the application is sloppily prepared, the student is not very serious about attending that law school. Work on your photocopied rough draft until you are sure you are ready to transfer to the original application.

The Application Form

For the most part, filling out the application form requires simply putting down factual information. But even in something so apparently mindless, you can still make sure you present yourself as a thorough, organized person who can follow directions.

KAPLAN EXCLUSIVE

You control how you are perceived by the admissions committee—through your application. You can't afford to miss a single opportunity to make yourself seem desirable as a law student. And the first step is *getting organized*.

The key to filling out the application form can be summed up in a single sentence: *Don't make the admissions officers do more work than they have to.* Make sure that they have all of the information they need at their fingertips. If they have to hunt down your statistics, if your application is full of unexplained blanks, if they can't read what you've written—all of these things will just serve to annoy the very people you want to impress.

One key to not annoying the admissions people is to make sure you answer *all* of the questions asked on the application form. If some questions don't seem to apply to you, type in "not applicable"; leave nothing blank. If the admissions officers see blank spaces, they don't know whether you found the question not applicable, just didn't want to answer it, or overlooked it. Many schools will return the application if even a single question is left blank. This can be a real problem, because it may be a month or more before the application is looked at and returned and then filled in and looked at again. That kind of delay can easily turn an early application into a late one.

Along these same lines, don't answer questions by saying *see above* or *see line 22.* Most applications will ask you for things like your address or phone number more than once. Go ahead and fill them in again. Remember that law schools are flooded with documentation and may separate parts of the application. They don't appreciate having to find what you wrote back on line 22 if they've asked you for that information again on line 55.

As long as we're talking about practices that annoy the decision makers, another is the failure to follow directions on the forms. If the form says, "Don't write below this line," then don't write below the line. You are not an exception to this rule. If they ask for an explanation in 150 words or less, then don't give them 300 words. One admissions officer remarked that the comment, "He couldn't even follow directions," is heard several times a year in committee meetings.

Addendums

An important part of the application form will not be in the package sent from the law school. These are your addendums. Addendums (or *addenda*, if you want to be fancy) are the additional page or pages that you staple onto the forms when the space they give you to answer a question is too small.

This is where an addendum comes in. Simply write "continued on addendum" on the application form after you've used their space up, and then clearly mark what you are listing at the top of the addendum. Staple this addendum at the back, and you've solved a tricky problem. Law schools appreciate addendums because they're much neater than attempts to cram things into a limited space—*and* they show careful organization. But don't overdo it. One or two addendums should be sufficient for any application.

Addendums can be used to preserve neatness when the application blanks are of insufficient length. But they can also be helpful if an answer requires further explanation. For example, if you won the Grant R. Humphrey Science award, it's not enough just to list it. You need to explain what it is, what it's given for, and possibly how many others were competing for it or how prestigious it is.

Honesty

One final topic about the application form that needs to be discussed is honesty. If you think you can get by with a lie or two on your application—well, you may be right. Law schools as a rule don't have the resources to verify all aspects of every application. But before you go overboard and decide to put down that you were once the Prince of Wales, you should realize that you're taking a big chance.

KAPLAN EXCLUSIVE

Admissions officers are human beings. Many of them will be looking for any little excuse to reject yours and get on to the next one. Don't give them that excuse. Make sure that nothing about your application is annoying to them.

First of all, many schools are beginning to devote more time to checking up on applicants' claims. Recently, the president of an undergraduate prelaw society told us that she regularly gets calls from law schools verifying membership of applicants. Secondly, there's always the chance that, if you lie, some other part of your application will contradict the lie and get you booted.

Finally, even if you fool the law school, get in, and graduate with honors, you'll find that any state in which you apply to take the bar exam will do a much more extensive background check than that done by the law school. This check very well might include looking for contradictions in your law school application. Lying on your law school application, in fact, is considered grounds for refusing admittance to a state bar.

Additional Points

Here are a few more things to take note of when filling out the application form:

Be sure to type the application from start to finish. A surprising number of applicants still handwrite the application—something that, according to admissions officers, costs you dearly.

Don't use application forms from previous years. Most applications change from year to year, often substantially. Also, don't use other school's forms because you lost the form of the school you're applying to (yes, people have done that, believe it or not).

Staple extra sheets to the forms. Don't use paper clips unless told to do so. Paper clips—and the pages they attach—tend to get lost.

Always double- and triple-check your application for spelling errors. You lose a certain amount of credibility if you write that you were a "Roads Scholar."

Check for accidental contradictions. Make sure that your application doesn't say you worked for a law firm in 1997 when your financial aid forms say you were driving a cab that year.

Prioritize all lists. When a question asks you to list your honors or awards, don't begin with fraternity social chairman and end with Phi Beta Kappa. Let the admissions committee know that you realize what's important—that is, always list significant scholastic accomplishments first.

Craft your list of extracurricular activities. Don't list every event or every activity you ever participated in. Select the most significant and, if necessary, explain them.

Don't mention high school activities or honors. Unless there's something very unusual or spectacular about your high school background, don't mention it, even if it means you don't take note of the fact that you were senior class president.

Clear up any ambiguities. On questions concerning employment, for instance, make sure to specify whether you held a job during the school year or only during the summer. Many applications ask about this, and it may be an important point to the admissions officer.

The Personal Statement

KAPLAN EXCLUSIVE

Next to your numbers, your personal statement is probably the most important part of your application, particularly at the top schools (where so many applicants have great numbers).

There are about as many theories on what constitutes a winning personal statement as there are theories on the Kennedy assassination—and, unfortunately, many of them have about the same validity. To begin with, how can you tell 85,000 annual applicants with 85,000 different personalities and backgrounds that there is one correct way to write a personal statement? Furthermore, if even a small percentage of those applicants read and come to believe that a certain way is the correct way, it automatically becomes incorrect, because law schools despise getting personal statements that are familiar—that are, in other words, *im*personal.

For that reason, this section on personal statements has been broken down into two parts. First, we'll look at the procedure of putting together a personal statement. Then we'll look at a list of DOs and DON'Ts that admission officers most frequently mention.

Putting Together an Outstanding Personal Statement

Next to your LSAT score and GPA, the personal statement is probably the most important part of your application. If your numbers are excellent or very poor, the essay may get only a cursory glance. But if your numbers place you on the borderline at a school, then it may very well make the difference between acceptance and rejection.

What Kind of Essay to Write: The personal statement is exactly what its name implies—a statement by you that is meant to show something about your personality and character. But that doesn't mean you are to create a lengthy essay detailing every aspect of your life since birth. Nor is the personal statement intended to be a psychological profile describing all of your character attributes and flaws. Several admissions officers have said that the best essays are often only remotely related to the applicant. The point is that you need not write an in-depth personality profile baring your innermost soul. Admissions officers are adept at learning what they want to know about you from your essay, even if it doesn't contain the words *me, myself,* and *I* in every sentence.

One exception, however, should be noted. Although most schools still provide wide latitude in their directions about what the personal statement should be about, some schools are becoming more specific. The problem with specific requirements like these is that you may well have to write a separate essay for that school alone. Be sure to check the instructions carefully and follow them closely. If a law school asks for a specific type of essay and you provide them with a more general one, they'll likely feel that you're not very interested in attending that particular school.

But take heart. Most schools provide few restrictions on what you can write about, so unless you're very unlucky, you should be able to limit the number of essays you must write to two or three.

How Long an Essay to Write: How long should the personal statement be? Some schools place a word limit on the essay; others specify one or two typed pages. Always follow the specific directions, but you should be in good shape with virtually all schools if your essay is one and a half to two pages in length.

Writing the Essay: The personal statement shouldn't be done overnight. A strong personal statement may take shape over the course of months and require several different drafts. One practice that many have found particularly effective is to write a draft and then let it sit for four to six weeks. If you leave it alone for a significant period of time, you may find that your first instincts were good ones. On the other hand, you may shudder at how you could ever have considered submitting such a piece of garbage. Either way, time lends a valuable perspective.

KAPLAN EXCLUSIVE

Start drafting your personal statement now, so that you'll be able to put it aside for a while. You'll be amazed at how different it will look when you go back to it.

Try to start the essay sometime during the summer before you apply. Allow at least three months to write it, and don't be afraid to take it through numerous drafts or overhaul it completely if you're not satisfied. Get several different perspectives. Ask close friends or relatives to scrutinize it to see if it really captures what you want to convey. Be sure to ask them about their initial reaction as well as their feelings after studying it more carefully. Once you've achieved a draft that you feel comfortable with, try to have it read by some people who barely know you or who don't know you at all. If certain criticisms are consistently made, then they're probably legitimate. But don't be carried away by every suggestion every reader makes. Stick to your basic instincts because, after all, this is *your* personal statement, no one else's.

Proofreading is of critical importance. Again, don't be afraid to enlist the aid of others. If possible, let an English teacher review the essay solely for spelling and grammar mistakes.

Essay Content: As stated earlier, there's no one correct way to write an essay, but admissions officers do provide some helpful tips about what they like and don't like to see in a personal statement. Let's begin with a list of the things that officers most often mentioned they disliked seeing.

Personal Statement DON'Ts

Don't turn your personal statement into a résumé. This is the personal statement that begins at birth and simply recites every major (and sometimes minor) event of the person's life. Most of this information is repetitive since it's included on other parts of the application. But worse than that, it's just a boring format.

Avoid the "why I want to go to law school" essay. Although this can be a *part* of any law school essay, too many people make it the entire focus of their statement. The problem is that there are not many new variations on this theme, and the admissions officers have likely heard them all before, probably many times.

Avoid talking about your negatives. The personal statement is not the place to call attention to your flaws. Don't forget that you're selling yourself, and the personal statement is your most prominent sales tool.

Don't be too personal. Stories of abuse or trauma are often very moving and can be particularly effective if tied into a person's reason for wanting to practice law. Several admissions officers, however, have noted a trend towards describing such problems in graphic detail in personal statements. This kind of confessional essay can easily cross the line and become too personal.

Don't discuss legal concepts. Along those same lines, don't try to impress the reader with how much you already know about the law. The school assumes that they can teach you what you need to know, regardless of the level at which you start. By discussing a legal concept, you also run the risk of showing a certain amount of ignorance about the subject while at the same time appearing arrogant enough to have tried to discuss it.

Don't put down lawyers or the legal profession. Although it may seem that spewing cynicism about the legal profession is a clever device, trust us when we tell you that it isn't. Once you become a member of the legal profession, you can make as many lawyer jokes as you want. Until then, watch your step.

Don't try to cover too many subjects. Focus on one or two areas you really want to talk about. One of the worst mistakes applicants make is writing essays that ramble from one subject to another and back again. Fight the desire to talk about every highlight of your life.

Now that you've got a sense of what not to do in your personal statement, let's turn to a list of suggestions for things that you *should* do.

Personal Statement DOs

Tell stories. Readers respond much better to a concrete story or illustrative anecdote than to an abstract list of your attributes. Instead of just writing how determined you are, for instance, tell a story that demonstrates it. Stories stick in people's memories. The same holds true when you're trying to make sure the admissions officers remember you.

Be funny—if you can pull it off. Humor, particularly self-deprecating humor, is a very effective device. Admissions officers appreciate occasional flashes of irony. However, be careful in your use of humor. Don't overdo it—a couple of funny lines or a funny story can be great, but include too many jokes and you start to sound flippant. Finally, think about using *self-deprecating* humor. Law schools often complain about the lack of humility among students and appreciate those who show some.

Be unique. The term *unique* has been overused. Even some applications now ask you to describe what is unique about you. Applicants rack their brains trying to figure out how they're different from the other 5,000 people applying to that law school. Or worse, some interpret *unique* to mean disadvantaged and rack their brains trying to think how they have suffered more than others. But what the admissions officers want to know is what qualities or experiences in your life would make you a particularly valuable member of a law school class.

Start strong. In private moments, admissions officers will often admit that they don't read every essay carefully. They may just glance at an essay to get a general impression. That's why it's important to grab them from the beginning. Tell the ending of a story first and make them want to read on, to see how it all started, for example.

The above points are as much general advice as one can responsibly give about the personal statement in a book such as this. We hope that they'll provide you with some ideas or keep you from making some costly mistakes. In the end, however, it *is* a personal statement, and it must come from you.

KAPLAN EXCLUSIVE

Admissions officers try to assemble a law school class that includes a rich variety of perspectives. Let them know what you could contribute to the diverse intellectual atmosphere they're trying to achieve.

Recommendations

During the last ten years, as law school applications have increased dramatically and the odds against being accepted at any particular school have increased, applicants have taken various approaches to stand out from the crowd. Too often overlooked in this mad pursuit, however, is one of the very best ways for an applicant to stand out—that is, by getting terrific, vividly written recommendations.

Because so many recommendations tend to be blasé, an outstanding recommendation that goes beyond the standard language can really make an applicant stand out. Not only does such a recommendation serve the purpose of pointing out an applicant's strengths, it also shows that the recommender thought enough of the person to put time and effort into carefully writing it.

What Makes a Recommendation Outstanding?

Outstanding recommendations can vary in format, but there are several qualities they all tend to have in common.

An Outstanding Recommendation Must Be Personal: By far the most common mistake made by applicants is believing that the prestige or position of the recommender is more important than what that person writes. Admissions officers tend to treat recommendations from senators, governors, and chief executive officers of major corporations with a great deal of skepticism, because very few applicants have a truly personal relationship with such people. To make matters worse, these officials tend to respond with very standard recommendations that rarely offer any real insight into the applicant's character; in a worst-case scenario, they may even be computer-generated.

Find people who truly know you and are able to make an honest assessment of your capabilities. This means that it may be better to have the teaching assistant with whom you had daily contact write the recommendation, rather than the prestigious professor you spoke to once during the year.

KAPLAN EXCLUSIVE

Discrepancies between your personal statement and a recommendation can undermine the credibility of your entire application. Make sure your recommendation writers know who you are and what you're about.

An outstanding recommendation compares you to others: When an admissions officer reads a recommendation, he or she often has to put into perspective the meaning of overused phrases—such as *hard-working* and *quick mind*—as they relate to the applicant. A much better format, and one that admissions officers appreciate, is the comparison recommendation, one that compares the applicant to other people that the recommendation writer previously knew in the same position, or (in a best-case scenario) to people he or she has known who are alumnae of that particular law school.

An outstanding recommendation tells stories: A concrete and specific recommendation stands out. Rather than merely listing attributes, a good recommendation engages the reader by telling an insightful story about the applicant. Recently, a professor of political science chose not to submit the standard phrase about what a quick study a student was. Instead, he related a story about the student in class. It seems the professor introduced a new and difficult concept in class that the student discussed intelligently and actually took further than the professor was prepared to do. That kind of story sticks in a reader's mind.

An outstanding recommendation focuses on scholastic abilities: Although recommendations often cover a lot of ground, from the applicant's attitudes about school to his or her personality traits, admissions officers focus on comments about a person's scholastic ability. Obviously, this means that a strong recommendation from a professor carries a great deal of weight. However, a lot of people are in a position to observe a person's intellectual aptitude. Employers, friends, clergy, and workers at volunteer agencies are all usually able to discuss an applicant's scholastic abilities—and should.

An outstanding recommendation will contain some negative comments: In many ways, this is the trickiest area of writing a recommendation, yet it can also prove to be a vital component. A recommendation that is only laudatory, failing to mention a single negative thing about an applicant, may lose credibility. By pointing out a small character flaw or a potential weakness, the recommender gains credibility with the admissions officers and tends to make them less skeptical about the preceding positive comments.

One word of caution, though: Admissions officers universally hate "fake" negatives—for example, "If Suzy has one fault, it is that she works just too darn hard." Much more appreciated are such comments as, "Joe can afford to improve his attention to detail." Combined with effusive praise for the applicant's strong points, this sort of comment impresses admissions officers as being straightforward and helpful.

How to Ensure You Receive Outstanding Recommendations

Now that you know what makes for an outstanding recommendation, all you have to do is ensure that each of your recommenders produces one. While you can't actually write the recommendations yourself, you *can* have a great deal of influence over how accurate and persuasive they are.

Choose the right people to recommend you: What are the qualities of a good recommender? Obviously, you should choose someone who likes you and who thinks you're good at what you do. This doesn't mean that you have to be intimate pals, but sworn enemies don't often write good recommendations. It helps if the person is a good writer so that he or she can clearly express an opinion about you.

Most, if not all, of your recommendations for academic programs should come from professors or other academic faculty. If you've been out of school for a few years and haven't kept in touch with your professors, call or write the admissions offices of the schools to which you're applying. Don't assume that it's okay to send fewer letters than required or to substitute other kinds of information for recommendation letters. Most likely, schools will allow you to submit recommendations from employers or from other nonacademic people with knowledge about your background, skills, and goals.

KAPLAN EXCLUSIVE

When asked whether you want to see what your recommendation writers have written about you, say no! If admissions officers know that you'll be seeing your recommendations, they'll discount much of what is said in them.

Balance your list of recommendation writers: Three professors from your undergrad major department probably will have similar things to say about you, so why not include someone from another field who can speak to your thinking and writing skills?

Be considerate of your recommendation writers: As soon as you decide to go to law school, you should start sizing up potential recommenders and letting them know that you may ask them for a letter. This will give each plenty of time to get to know you better and to think about what to say in the letter. Once they've agreed, let them know about deadlines with plenty of lead time to avoid potential scheduling conflicts. The more time they have, the better the job they'll do recommending you.

Make sure your recommendation writers know what they need to know: Once someone has agreed to consider writing a letter for you, you should arrange an appointment to discuss your background and goals for your future. If you live thousands of miles away from your recommender, arrange a telephone appointment.

Bring to the appointment copies of appropriate documentation such as your transcript, papers you've written, your résumé or curriculum vitae, your personal statement, and a sheet of bullet points that you plan to feature in your application and essay. Supply the appropriate form or forms, as well as stamped, addressed envelopes and a copy of your home address and phone number.

Keep the appointment relatively brief—you're already taking up enough of their time. Give your recommenders a good idea of why you want to go to law school. Play up your good points, of course, but be reasonably humble. If you have a very specific "marketing" image that you're trying to project, let your recommenders in on it—they may want to focus on some of the same points you're trying to stress. But don't tell your recommenders what to write—don't even give them the impression that you're doing so! Recommenders tend to resent any attempts at manipulation, and may, as a consequence, refuse to write your letter. What recommenders *do* appreciate, however, is some direction as to what you'd like to see.

Keep your recommendation writers on schedule: Finally, make sure your recommenders know how important it is to complete the letters as early as possible. If they procrastinate, gently remind them that their deadline is approaching and be sure to remind them of the importance of early applications.

Common Questions About Recommendations

Here are other points about recommendations that should be considered.

How Long Should a Recommendation Be? Like the personal statement, the recommendation should be short and concise. A one-page recommendation is usually sufficient. In any case, it should be no longer than two to two and a half pages.

Should I Request to Look at the Recommendation? Easy answer—NO! Almost all schools have a box you check to indicate whether or not you would like to be able to see the recommendation once it's provided to the school. Just say no! If the school believes that the recommender cannot be completely honest for fear of offending the applicant, the school will heavily discount what is written, no matter how laudatory.

Can I Send More Recommendations Than the School Requests? Be careful. Law schools may request anywhere from one to four recommendations from an applicant (the recent trend is towards fewer recommendations). Invariably, the situation arises in which a student has three good recommendations, but the school only asks for two. Some schools are very specific in their instructions that they will not accept more than the exact number requested. If the application doesn't spell out how the school handles it, call the school and ask to make sure.

Should I Use the Letter of Recommendation Service? The Letter of Recommendation Service is set up by LSAC as a convenience. Basically, the service allows your recommenders to send letters to LSAC, who then forwards them to the law schools. Note that the same letter is sent to each school, and so school-specific letters should not be sent through this service. For more information, check out the latest *LSAT/LSDAS Information Book*, or contact your target schools to see if they prefer that you use the service.

A Final Check

After you've completed everything and are getting ready to place it in a manila envelope and mail it, make sure you go through one more time and check each document. Law schools frequently receive documents that were intended to go to another law school. With all of this paperwork, it's easy to see how that can happen, and the law schools expect a certain amount of it. However, it can be embarrassing if you've written in your personal statement that ABC Law School is the one and only place for you—and then you accidentally send it to XYZ Law School instead.

Application Checklist

The three major parts of your law school application:

1. The application form
2. The personal statement
3. Recommendations

THE APPLICATION FORM

- ☐ Working photocopies of applications made
- ☐ Information/addresses/other data gathered
- ☐ Addendums (if any) written
- ☐ Information transferred to actual application
- ☐ Application proofread
- ☐ Final check done

THE PERSONAL STATEMENT

- ☐ Theme finalized
- ☐ Readers selected and notified
- ☐ First draft written
- ☐ Self-evaluation made
- ☐ Second draft written
- ☐ Comments from readers received
- ☐ Final draft written
- ☐ Final statement proofread

RECOMMENDATIONS

- ☐ Recommendation writers chosen
- ☐ Recommendation writers on board
- ☐ Informational meeting with recommendation writers conducted
- ☐ Reminders to all recommendation writers sent
- ☐ Notice of complete application received

Chapter 9: **Special Note for International Students**

In recent years, U.S. law schools have experienced an increase in inquiries from non-U.S. citizens, some of whom are already practicing lawyers in their own countries. This surge of interest in the U.S. legal system has been attributed to the spread of the global economy. When business people from outside the United States do business with Americans, they often find themselves doing business under the American legal system. Gaining insight into how the American legal system works is of great interest around the world.

This new international interest in the U.S. legal system is having an effect on law schools. Many schools have developed special programs to accommodate the needs of this special population of lawyers and students from around the globe. If you are an international student or lawyer interested in learning more about the American legal system, or if you are considering attending law school in the United States, Kaplan can help you explore your options.

Getting into a U.S. law school can be especially challenging for students from other countries. If you are not from the United States, but are considering attending law school in the United States, here is what you'll need to get started.

- If English is not your first language, you'll probably need to take the TOEFL® (Test of English as a Foreign Language), or provide some other evidence that you are proficient in English. Most law schools require a minimum computer TOEFL score of 250 (600 on the paper-based TOEFL) or better.
- Depending on the program to which you are applying, you may also need to take the LSAT® (Law School Admissions Test). All law schools in the United States require the LSAT for their J.D. programs. LL.M. programs usually do not require the LSAT. Kaplan will help you determine if you need to take the LSAT. If you must take the LSAT, Kaplan can help you prepare for it.
- Since admission to law school is quite competitive, you may want to select three or four programs and complete applications for each school.
- You should begin the process of applying to law schools or special legal studies programs at least eighteen months before the fall of the year you plan to start your studies. Most programs will have only September start dates.

In addition, you will need to obtain an I-20 Certificate of Eligibility from the school you plan to attend if you intend to apply for an F-1 Student Visa to study in the United States.

Kaplan English Programs*

If you need more help with the complex process of law school admissions, assistance preparing for the LSAT or TOEFL, or help building your English language skills in general, you may be interested in Kaplan's programs for international students.

Kaplan English Programs were designed to help students and professionals from outside the United States meet their educational and career goals. At locations throughout the United States, international students take advantage of Kaplan's programs to help them improve their academic and conversational English skills, raise their scores on the TOEFL, LSAT, and other standardized exams, and gain admission to the schools of their choice. Our staff and instructors give international students the individualized attention they need to succeed. Here is a brief description of some of Kaplan's programs for international students:

General English Self-Study

For students needing a flexible schedule, this course helps improve general fluency skills. Kaplan's General English Self-Study course employs the communicative approach and focuses on vocabulary building, reading, and writing. You will receive books, audio, and video materials as well as three hours of instructor contact per week.

TOEFL and Academic English

Kaplan has updated its world-famous TOEFL course to prepare students for the new TOEFL iBT. Designed for high-intermediate to advanced-level English speakers, our new course focuses on the academic English skills you will need to succeed on the new test. The course includes TOEFL-focused reading, writing, listening, and speaking instruction, and hundreds of practice items similar to those on the exam. Kaplan's expert instructors help you prepare for the four sections of the TOEFL iBT, including the new Speaking Section. Our new simulated online TOEFL tests help you monitor your progress and provide you with feedback on areas where you require improvement. We will teach you how to get a higher score!

LSAT Test-Preparation Course

The LSAT is a crucial admission criterion for law schools in the United States. A high score can help you stand out from other applicants. This course includes the skills you need to succeed on each section of the LSAT, as well as access to Kaplan's exclusive practice materials.

Other Kaplan Programs

Since 1938, more than 3 million students have come to Kaplan to advance their studies, prepare for entry to American universities, and further their careers. In addition to the above programs, Kaplan offers courses to prepare for the SAT®, GMAT®, GRE®, MCAT®, DAT®, USMLE®, NCLEX®, and other standardized exams at locations throughout the United States.

Applying to Kaplan English Programs

To get more information, or to apply for admission to any of Kaplan's programs for international students and professionals, contact us at:

Kaplan English Programs
700 South Flower Street, Suite 2900
Los Angeles, CA 90017
Phone (if calling from within the United States): 800-818-9128
Phone (if calling from outside the United States): 213-452-5800
Fax: 213-892-1364
Email: world@kaplan.com
Web: www.kaplanenglish.com

*Kaplan is authorized under federal law to enroll nonimmigrant alien students. Kaplan is accredited by ACCET (Accrediting Council for Continuing Education and Training) and is a member of FIYTO and ALTO.

NOTES

NOTES